RAIL GUIDE 2021

Pip Dunn

Crécy

Crécy Publishing Ltd
www.crecy.co.uk

First published 2010
Reprinted 2010
Revised editions 2011, 2012, 2013, 2014, 2015,
2016, 2017, 2018, 2019, 2020

This Twelth Edition published 2020
by Crécy Publishing Ltd

ISBN 9781800350205

Printed in Malta by Gutenberg

Crécy Publishing Ltd
1a Ringway Trading Estate
Shadowmoss Road
Manchester
M22 5LH
Tel +44 (0) 161 499 0024

www.crecy.co.uk

Front cover top: LNER Azuma 800106 passes Upper Denton, near Haltwhistle on the Tyne Valley route, with a diverted King's Cross-Edinburgh train on 21 September 2019. *Rob France*

Front cover bottom: GBRf 50049 *Defiance* and 50007 *Hercules* move GWR HST power car 43091 and a Mk 3 coach from Long Marston to Laira on 23 March 2020, passing Norton Junction, near Worcester. *Jack Boskett*

Back cover top: DB Cargo 66019 works the 0534 Margam-Corby steel coil train past Ashwell on 19 September 2019. *Bill Atkinson*

Back cover bottom: Northern 195004 passes Trowell Junction on 17 February 2020. *Paul Robertson*

Maps are based on the official National Rail Network maps

Rail Guide information is correct to 9 November 2020

Introduction

Welcome to the 2021 edition of the Crécy Rail Guide. This is the first edition with a new editor. We have implemented a few changes and I hope you like them. If you have any comments, input or corrections then please do get in touch via the publisher.

This has been an exceptionally challenging book to put together because of the Covid-19 pandemic that has brought large parts of the country to standstill. But the effect it has had one me as writer is nothing compared with the effect the pandemic has had on the railways.

Overnight, passenger numbers fell off a cliff. Most people simply could not travel as they were in lockdown, with many people working from home or furloughed. And when restrictions were eased, travelling by train was initially actively discouraged except for essential reasons. Patronage dropped by as much as 95%.

While patronage has slowly increased, it is still a fraction of pre-pandemic levels. This has had a major impact on the railway, which has relied on private companies to run the majority of train operations. In September the Government announced it was ending the franchising system, and what shape the UK's railway will take once the pandemic has passed or been contained is open to conjecture, but it is unlikely to be the same structure as it was before March 2020.

It is likely the operation of the railways will essentially be renationalised 'by stealth', so to speak. It is most likely operations will still be contracted out, but the risk will be carried by the taxpayer. Hopefully, we can see some better standardisation on train types, fares, connectivity and other issues. The perfect scenario would be the adoption of the best features of a nationalised railway using the best practices of a private operation, but how and if that can be delivered is open to debate.

Indeed, as I write this, and as the book goes through the stages from delivery to laying out to printing, all manner of factors could change. The information, therefore, is what is known when the book went to press in early September.

Before the pandemic the UK's railway was already undergoing massive changes with a mass of new fleets being introduced to provide extra capacity, replace older stock and also allow elimination of old ex-BR vehicles that do not meet modern-day standards.

There are also major infrastructure projects under way, such as Crossrail – which is heavily delayed – electrification of routes such as to Corby and, of course, HS2 is looming on the horizon, a massive project that will provide much needed capacity on the network, but also runs the risk of costing an astronomical amount. HS2 desperately needs to come in under budget, and at the very least, be delivered on time (and ideally, delivered early), if similar investment is ever likely to be authorised in the future. That said, part of the high figures for HS2 are a worst-case scenario with lots of contingency to allow the project to be delivered for a lot less than the headline figures being repeated – and inflated – in the mainstream press.

The aim of this rail guide is to provide a handy reference resource for the current UK railway. That includes Northern Ireland, but we have decided that covering the Republic of Ireland is not of relevance as this is not a European rail guide.

It is split into passenger train operating companies (TOCs), Open Access operators, Channel Tunnel operators, private train operating companies, Northern Ireland, light rail – London Underground and trams, rolling stock providers, freight operating companies (FOCs) and maintenance and spot-hire companies.

It also deals with off lease vehicles still in the UK, Network Rail, those ex-UK locos now in use (or stored) abroad, main-line preservation groups and other key industry bodies. It's not aimed as a 'mark them off' spotters' book.

Of course, there is some overlap – especially with loco hire where vehicles are owned by FOCs but used by TOCs. In these instances, the vehicles are listed under the owner, the FOC, but mention is made of them in the relevant TOC chapter.

Official Guidelines

Train Operators and Network Rail welcome rail enthusiasts and photographers, but in today's safety-led railway and with the continued concerns about possible transport terrorism, guidelines are very important and we encourage all to follow these published guidelines as much as possible. They are available to view and download from the National Rail and ROG websites, but are reproduced in full below to assist you with this information. However, in the current Covid-19 pandemic, visiting stations for photography is not recommended.

The Official Railway Enthusiasts Guidelines

- Network Rail welcomes rail enthusiasts to our stations.
- The following guidelines are designed to help you to have a safe and enjoyable experience. Please keep them with you when you are at Network Rail-managed stations.
- You may also wish to take a copy of the Railway by-laws which are available from the Office of Public Sector Information website.

Before you enter the platform

- When you arrive at a station, please let the staff at the Network Rail Reception Desk know that you are on the station. This will help keep station staff informed so that they can go about their duties without concern as to your reasons for being there.
- You may require a platform ticket to allow access to platforms.

While you are on the platform

- You need to act safely and sensibly at all times.
  - Stay clear of the platform edge and stay behind the yellow lines where they are provided.
  - Be aware of your surroundings.

Please DO NOT:

  - Trespass on to the tracks or any other part of the railway that is not available to passengers.
  - Use flash photography because it can distract train drivers and train despatch staff and so is potentially very dangerous.
  - Climb on any structure or interfere with platform equipment.
  - Obstruct any signalling equipment or signs which are vital to the safe running of the railway.
  - Wear anything which is similar in colour to safety clothing, such as high-visibility jackets, as this could cause confusion to drivers and other railway employees.
  - Gather together in groups at busy areas of the platform (e.g. customer information points, departure screens, waiting areas, seating etc.) or where this may interfere with the duties of station staff.
- If possible, please try to avoid peak hours which are Monday – Friday 6:00am (06.00) – 10:30am (10.30) and 3:30pm (15.30) – 7:30pm (19.30).

Extra eyes and ears

- If you see anything suspicious or notice any unusual behaviour or activities, please tell a member of staff immediately.
- For emergencies and serious incidents, either call: The British Transport Police on 0800 40 50 40. Or text a message to 61016. The Police on 999, or 101.
- Your presence at a station can be very helpful to us as extra 'eyes and ears' and can have a positive security benefit.

Photography

- You can take photographs at stations provided you do not sell them. However, you are not allowed to take photographs of security-related equipment, such as CCTV cameras.
- Flash photography on platforms is not allowed at any time. It can distract train drivers and train despatch staff and so is potentially very dangerous.
- Tripod legs must be kept away from platform edges and behind the yellow lines. On busy stations, you may not be allowed to use a tripod because it could be a dangerous obstruction to passengers.

Railway by-laws

For safety and ease of travel on the railway system (which includes passengers, staff, property and equipment), the by-laws must be observed by everyone. A copy of the by-laws can be obtained at stations or downloaded from the Office of Public Sector Information website.

General

Train operators must put the safety of their passengers and staff first. You may very occasionally be asked by station staff to move to another part of the station or to leave the station altogether. Station staff should be happy to explain why this is necessary. If you are travelling by train, they may ask you to remain in the normal waiting areas with other passengers. If this occurs, please follow their instructions with goodwill as staff have many things to consider, including the safety and security of all passengers, and are authorised to use judgement in this regard.

West Coast Railways' 47245 passes Staveley on June 30 2018 with the 1440 Oxenholme-Windermere. *Rob France*

Contents

About This Book

This book is aimed at providing a guide to the ever-changing modern UK railway system with key facts and fleet details. The railway is hugely complex and relies on hundreds of companies, and it's easy to get confused and bogged down with ownership, users and operators!

As regards the Franchised Train Operating Companies, and indeed most of the Open Access operators, trains are owned by Rolling Stock Leasing companies (ROSCOs) and when a franchise changes company, the rolling stock changes with them.

On the freight side, there is more of a mix, with locos owned by the FOCs – although leasing, especially of new locos, is far more prevalent these days. Some vehicles may be on long-term hire, as opposed to leases. Other vehicles may simply be spot-hired to meet fluctuating and seasonal demand.

This book is split into several chapters, or sections, but the main premise is an operator-by-operator breakdown. It includes all UK operators, including those in Northern Ireland. Southern Ireland Railways, nor any other EU country, are not included.

Vehicles are listed by their current number, old number (if relevant), pool code if relevant, livery, owner and place of allocation. There are, as is to be expected, a number of grey areas. Those TOCs that hire in – as opposed to lease – locomotives do not have these locos listed as such in their section, although, of course, reference is made to them.

The locos themselves are listed under their owning FOC or supplier. The exception are those vehicles that are owned by private individuals or preservation groups are but on longer-term use by a particular FOC. The same applies to the Class 66s owned by DB Cargo but now used by DRS.

Those locos such as Class DRS Class 68s that are used by Transpennine or Chiltern Railways are listed under DRS. This is because DRS only needs to supply a set number of locos a day to these TOCs and any locos in these pools not being used by the TOCs are therefore free to be used by DRS for its own traffic.

Vehicles listed as (Q) are under test, be it static, driver training or mileage accumulation. Those listed (Z) are being rebuilt. (U) means the vehicle is stored unserviceable ad (S) means it is stored serviceable. Main-line locos listed as (I) are in industrial use only and not passed to work on the national network.

Southeastern's 375616 works the 0940 Charing Cross-Dover Priory past Shakespeare Cliff on July 12 2019.
Anthony Hicks

Franchise Overview

As has been well documented, when the railways were privatised, the passenger operations were let as twenty-five franchises of predefined periods. The freight operations were sold off in their entirety and the infrastructure was sold via a public flotation – Railtrack – later renationalised as Network Rail.

Franchising was meant to be a simple way to allow the private sector into the railway – operate the trains, take the risk, show innovation and provide a better and theoretically cheaper service to passengers. Over the years, franchises have been amalgamated, split, redrawn and generally reduced so much so now that there are twenty different operations.

Sadly, after twenty-five years those original aims are far from being realised in some cases, although in other criteria the new regime has indeed proved better than the old BR. Pretty much all routes have benefited from either brand new trains or at least refurbished and much-improved ones. There are many routes that now have a much better service with many more trains operating than in the old nationalised days; generally – not always – there are earlier and later timetabled trains and Sunday services on many routes that simply did not have them. Stations have reopened and in some cases – especially in Wales and Scotland – new lines have been built or freight lines upgraded to passenger use. There have been many success stories along the way.

That said, the level of subsidy that is provided to the private railway has been in the region of three times more than BR received, which does always beg the question 'what if' BR had had that level of funding. We will never know!

But there have been many horror stories as well and all too easily private TOCs have simply 'thrown in the towel' when 'the going got tough'. And in such cases there is no alternative other than for the government to step in and start running the trains so there is no change to the timetable for passengers.

The ECML franchise, for example, has been defaulted on three times – by GNER, then National Express and more recently Stagecoach. Sometimes bids for franchises are wildly optimistic and reliant on sustained passenger growth, and it only takes an economic crash like in 2008 to make those growth plans fall flat.

And while no one could have foreseen the carnage to the rail industry brought about by the Covid-19 pandemic, it has focused people's minds on the issues of a privatised railway. What form the railway takes in 2021 onwards… well that is anyone's guess, but nationalisation seems highly probable, possibly with operations contracted out to private firms on pre-defined criteria. What happens, however, if the contractors fail to deliver on that remains to be seen.

What is the best franchise option has always been one for debate. When the initial deals were agreed in the mid-1990s there were a mix of short seven-year deals and longer 15-year deals. Many TOCs argued longer franchised allowed them to invest more and better improve their operations, but the counterargument was that long deals could make them complacent.

In the intervening 25 years there has been to-ing and fro-ing in this belief, and while Chiltern was given a 20-year deal in 2002, no franchise of this length has been awarded since. The recent trend has been for shorter seven-year deals with options to extend, sometimes automatically triggered when certain criteria are met.

Current make-up

Two franchises are currently being operated by the Department for Transport Operator of Last Resort (OLR); they are the East Coast Main Line, now branded as London North Eastern Railway, and Northern, which runs local and commuter trains across the north of England.

Under normal circumstances, the DfT would have most probably been looking to let these franchises again, possibly on a management contract agreement, but the aforementioned pandemic situation means there is little immediate likelihood of this happening anytime soon.

First Group operates two franchises in its own right – Great Western Railway and Transpennine Express, both due to expire in 2022 and 2023 respectively but both with two-year extension options.

First is also involved on joint ventures on two other franchises – with MTR for South Western Railway and with Trenitalia on the Avanti West Coast franchise. In both ventures First is the majority stakeholder, with 70% in each case. The West Coast is a recent award, ousting incumbent Virgin Trains (and so ending its association with UK train operation for the foreseeable future) in December 2019 for an 11-year period. SWR was awarded two years earlier, in August 2017, for only seven years but both have extension options; a year for SWR and three for AWC.

While Trenitalia has a 30% stake in the AWC operation, it is the outright operator of the c2c system, formerly a National Express franchise. NatEx, once one of the 'giants' of UK rail franchises, is, like Virgin Trains, now no longer involved. This franchise runs until late 2029 with a six-month extension an option.

With three franchises in its portfolio, Arriva Trains – owned by Germany's Deutsche Bahn – is still a big player. And until recently, it had a fourth franchise, the troubled Northern operation. It was stripped of this franchise from 1 March 2020. That has still left it with the Chiltern Railways, CrossCountry Trains and London Overground operation to run, plus its Open Access Grand Central business. In September the XCT franchise was extended by three years to run until October 2023.

Likewise, Chiltern only runs until December 2021, albeit with an eight-month extension option. This franchise is interesting, as it was let way back in March 2002 as a long franchise of nearly 20 years and has invested heavily in new trains, new routes, infrastructure upgrades and additional services. The final Arriva franchise is London Overground, a complex franchise of heavy rail trains in the capital. This runs until May 2024,

MTR – Mass Transit Railway Corporation – is a Hong Kong-based company that has the franchise to run Crossrail, a major infrastructure project that is running way behind schedule. Crossrail currently runs some trains out of Paddington to Reading and Liverpool Street to Shenfield but is still some way off connecting the two with the new tunnelled rail section in London. It has a mass fleet of Class 345s, many of which are in store in sidings at Old Oak Common. MTR also has a 30% stake in South Western Railway, but has also made a number of unsuccessful bids to run other franchises in the UK.

Abellio, the new trading name for NedRail, which is the Dutch state railways Nederlandse Spoorwegen, operates outright two franchises and has a share in three others. It has total control of East Midlands Railway and ScotRail, which run to August 2027 and March 2022 respectively, while it is the 60% majority shareholder in Greater Anglia, the other 40% owned by Japanese company Mitsui, and this runs until October 2025 – with a year extension option. Finally, Abellio along with Mitsui and JR East – East Japan Railway company – will operate the West Midlands Trains franchise until March 2026, with an option to March 2029. The two Far East companies only have 15% stake each, with the Dutch owning 70%. Finally, the Merseyrail franchise is a 50/50 split between Abellio and Serco, a deal that should run until July 2028.

Serco's other involvement in the UK rail operations is currently the Caledonian Sleeper franchise. This was a 15-year deal let in 2015 and runs until March 2030. The firm has completely overhauled the old ScotRail operation it inherited. It uses GB Railfreight to provide traction and traincrew, with Serco leasing the coaches and providing the on-board crew

French company Keolis has an interest in operating three franchises, Transport for Wales is a 60/40 split between Keolis and Amey, while it owns 35% of Govia, which operates the Southeastern and Thameslink franchises.

With 11 different companies, 12 if you include OLR, running 20 franchises, for varying time periods, then it's easy to see why the franchising system is still far from simple.

TOC trading name	Operator(s)	Franchise start date	Franchise end date	Extension option
Avanti West Coast	First Group/Trenitalia	8/12/19	31/3/31	31/3/34
Caledonian Sleeper	Serco	31/3/15	31/3/30	
c2c	Trenitalia	10/2/17	10/11/29	10/5/30
Chiltern Railways	Arriva	3/3/02	11/12/21	11/7/22
Cross Country Trains	Arriva	11/11/07	17/10/23	
Crossrail	MTR	31/5/15	27/5/23	27/5/25
East Midlands Railway	Abellio	18/8/19	21/8/27	21/8/29
Govia Thameslink	Go-Ahead/Keolis	14/9/14	18/9/21	18/9/23
Greater Anglia	Abellio/Mitsui	16/10/16	11/10/25	11/10/26
Great Western Railway	First Group	20/9/15	31/3/22	31/3/24
London North Eastern Railway	DfT (was Stagecoach/Virgin)	24/6/18	n/a	
London Overground	Arriva	14/11/16	25/5/24	
Merseyrail	Serco/Abellio	20/7/03	22/7/28	
Northern Rail	DfT (was Arriva)	1/4/16	n/a	
ScotRail	Abellio	1/4/15	31/3/22	
Southeastern	Go-Ahead/Keolis	1/4/06	16/10/21	31/3/22
South Western Railway	First Group/MTR	20/8/17	17/8/24	17/7/25
Transpennine Express	First Group	1/4/16	31/3/23	31/3/25
Transport for Wales	KeolisAmey	14/10/18	15/10/33	
West Midlands Trains	Abellio/JR East/Mitsui	10/12/17	31/3/26	31/3/28

Royal 67006 *Royal Sovereign* passes Upton Noble with UK Rail Tours' "Torbay Flyer" trip on 15 September 2018. *Glen Batten*

Avanti West Coast

Contact details

Website: www.avantiwestcoast.co.uk
Twitter: @AvantiWestCoast

Key personnel

Managing Director: Phil Whittingham
Executive Director Operations: Jonathan Dunster

Glasgow Central
Edinburgh Waverley
Motherwell
Lockerbie
Carlisle
Penrith North Lakes
Oxenholme Lake District
Kirkham & Wesham
Lancaster
Blackpool North
Poulton-le-Fylde
Preston
Wigan North Western
Warrington Bank Quay
Manchester Piccadilly
Liverpool Lime Street
Runcorn
Stockport
Holyhead
Chester
Wilmslow
Bangor
Llandudno Junction
Colwyn Bay
Rhyl
Prestatyn
Flint
Macclesfield
Crewe
Wrexham General
Stoke-on-Trent
Stafford
Telford Central
Shrewsbury
Wellington
Wolverhampton
Sandwell & Dudley
Birmingham New Street
Birmingham International
Coventry
Lichfield Trent Valley
Tamworth
Nuneaton
Rugby
Northampton
Milton Keynes Central
Watford Junction
London Euston

Overview

AWC operates the inter-city trains along the West Coast Main Line from London Euston to Birmingham New Street, Shrewsbury, Liverpool Lime Street, Manchester Piccadilly, Blackpool North, Holyhead, Glasgow Central and Edinburgh.

The fleet is reliant on two main train types – five-car Bombardier Class 221 DEMUs – and a mix of nine and 11-car Alstom Class 390 tilting Pendolino units.

Both fleets were inherited from Virgin Trains, which ran the InterCity West Coast franchise from 1997 until 2019 until transfer to a joint venture between First Group and Trenitalia from 8 December.

The fleet is progressively being reliveried in Avanti graphene dark green livery with trains in plain white or Virgin's red/white livery. During the life of Virgin, new services to Shrewsbury, Wrexham and Blackpool were introduced.

AWC is looking to introduce new services, to Walsall and Llandudno from 2021 and Gobowen from 2022, as well as additional trains to Liverpool from 2022. To meet these additional services, AWC has ordered 13 Class 805 five-car bi-mode Hitachi AT300 units, and ten Class 807 seven-car 25kV AC EMUs from the same platform.

The company has a contract with Direct Rail Services to provide four Class 57/3s to act as rescue 'Thunderbird' locos; 57304/307/308/309 and these are strategically stabled at key points along the WCML.

The West Coast Partnership Development (WCPD) will also be responsible for operating the first trains on the new HS2 line from Euston to Birmingham Curzon Street from 2026, and new trains for this will be necessary.

Nos 221116 and 221114 approach Carstairs on the 1200 Glasgow Central-Euston on 8 February 2020.
Robin Ralston

Class 221

Bombardier-built tilting Voyager DEMUs ordered by Virgin CrossCountry. Twenty sets were transferred to Virgin West Coast in December 2017 when some CrossCountry routes were added to the West Coast Franchise with the rest of the fleet – 221119-141/144 transferring to Arriva's CrossCountry Trains franchise. All are in the HFHQ pool.

				DMS	MS	MS	MSRMB	DMF	
221101	WHI	BEA	CZ	60351	60951	60851	60751	60451	*101 Squadron*
221102	VTS	BEA	CZ	60352	60952	60852	60752	60452	
221103	VTS	BEA	CZ	60353	60953	60853	60753	60453	
221104	VTS	BEA	CZ	60354	60954	60854	60754	60454	
221105	WHI	BEA	CZ	60355	60955	60855	60755	60455	
221106	WHI	BEA	CZ	60356	60956	60856	60756	60456	
221107	VTS	BEA	CZ	60357	60957	60857	60757	60457	
221108	WHI	BEA	CZ	60358	60958	60858	60758	60458	
221109	WHI	BEA	CZ	60359	60959	60859	60759	60459	
221110	VTS	BEA	CZ	60360	60960	60860	60760	60460	
221111	WHI	BEA	CZ	60361	60961	60861	60761	60461	
221112	VTS	BEA	CZ	60362	60962	60862	60762	60462	
221113	WHI	BEA	CZ	60363	60963	60863	60763	60463	
221114	VTS	BEA	CZ	60364	60964	60864	60764	60464	*Royal Air Force Centenary 1918-2018*
221115	WHI	BEA	CZ	60365	60965	60865	60765	60465	
221116	VTS	BEA	CZ	60366	60966	60866	60766	60466	*City of Bangor Dinas Bangor*
221117	VTS	BEA	CZ	60367	60967	60867	60767	60467	
221118	VTS	BEA	CZ	60368	60968	60868	60768	60468	
221142	VTS	BEA	CZ	60392	60992	60892	60792	60492	
221143	VTS	BEA	CZ	60393	60993	60893	60793	60493	

Class 390

Alstom-built tilting 25kV AC EMUs. 53 sets were ordered by Virgin West Coast as nine-car sets and entered traffic from 2002 – some as eight-car sets – followed by an additional order for four 11-car sets delivered in 2010.

31 of the original sets were then extended by two cars in 2010/11 to make them eleven-cars and renumbered from 3900xx to 3901xx. Unit 390033 was written off in the Grayrigg derailment in February 2007.

Only 390155/156 carry full AWC livery on all vehicles, others listed as in this livery currently only have the wrap on the driving cars with the remaining vehicles still in plain white. No. 390119 was unveiled in a Pride wrap in late August. All are in the HFHQ pool.

Class 390/0

Original nine-car sets, some delivered as eight-car sets.

				DMRF	MF	PTF	MS	TS	MS	PTSRMB	MS	DMS	
390001	WHI	ANG	MA	69101	69401	69501	69601	68801	69701	69801	69901	69201	*Bee Together*
390002	WHI	ANG	MA	69102	69402	69502	69602	68802	69702	69802	69902	69202	*Stephen Sutton*
390005	WHI	ANG	MA	69105	69405	69505	69605	68805	69705	69805	69905	69205	*City of Wolverhampton*
390006	AWC	ANG	MA	69106	69406	69506	69606	68806	69706	69806	69906	69206	*Rethink Mental Illness*
390008	AWC	ANG	MA	69108	69408	69508	69608	68808	69708	69808	69908	69208	*Charles Rennie Mackintosh*
390009	AWC	ANG	MA	69109	69409	69509	69609	68809	69709	69809	69909	69209	*Treaty of the Union*
390010	WHI	ANG	MA	69110	69410	69510	69610	68810	69710	69810	69910	69210	*Cumbrian Spirit*
390011	AWC	ANG	MA	69111	69411	69511	69611	68811	69711	69811	69911	69211	*City of Lichfield*
390013	AWC	ANG	MA	69113	69413	69513	69613	68813	69713	69813	69913	69213	*Blackpool Belle*
390016	WHI	ANG	MA	69116	69416	69516	69616	68816	69716	69816	69916	69216	
390020	WHI	ANG	MA	69120	69420	69520	69620	68820	69720	69820	69920	69220	
390039	WHI	ANG	MA	69139	69439	69539	69639	68839	69739	69839	69939	69239	*Lady Godiva*
390040	AWC	ANG	MA	69140	69440	69540	69640	68840	69740	69840	69940	69240	
390042	WHI	ANG	MA	69142	69442	69542	69642	68842	69742	69842	69942	69242	
390043	AWC	ANG	MA	69143	69443	69543	69643	68843	69743	69843	69943	69243	
390044	AWC	ANG	MA	69144	69444	69544	69644	68844	69744	69844	69944	69244	
390045	AWC	ANG	MA	69145	69445	69545	69645	68845	69745	69845	69945	69245	
390046	WHI	ANG	MA	69146	69446	69546	69646	68846	69746	69846	69946	69246	
390047	AWC	ANG	MA	69147	69447	69547	69647	68847	69747	69847	69947	69247	
390049	AWC	ANG	MA	69149	69449	69549	69649	68849	69749	69849	69949	69249	
390050	WHI	ANG	MA	69150	69450	69550	69650	68850	69750	69850	69950	69250	

Class 390/1

Original nine-car sets increased to 11-car sets; 390154-157 were additional sets delivered in 2010-12 as 11-cars.

	Old No.				DMRF	MF	PTF	MS	TS	MS	TS	MS	PTSRMB	MS	DMS	
390103	390003	AWC	ANG	MA	69103	69403	69503	69603	65303	68903	68803	69703	69803	69903	69203	
390104	390004	AWC	ANG	MA	69104	69404	69504	69604	65304	68904	68804	69704	69804	69904	69204	*Alstom Pendolino*
390107	390007	WHI	ANG	MA	69107	69407	69507	69607	65307	68907	68807	69707	69807	69907	69207	
390112	390012	WHI	ANG	MA	69112	69412	69512	69612	65312	68912	68812	69712	69812	69912	69212	
390114	390014	WHI	ANG	MA	69114	69414	69514	69614	65314	68914	68814	69714	69814	69914	69214	*City of Manchester*
390115	390015	WHI	ANG	MA	69115	69415	69515	69615	65315	68915	68815	69715	69815	69915	69215	*Crewe – All Change*
390117	390017	AWC	ANG	MA	69117	69417	69517	69617	65317	68917	68817	69717	69817	69917	69217	*Blue Peter*
390118	390018	WHI	ANG	MA	69118	69418	69518	69618	65318	68918	68818	69718	69818	69918	69218	
390119	390019	PRI	ANG	MA	69119	69419	69519	69619	65319	68919	68819	69719	69819	69919	69219	*Progress*
390121	390021	AWC	ANG	MA	69121	69421	69521	69621	65321	68921	68821	69721	69821	69921	69221	
390122	390022	WHI	ANG	MA	69122	69422	69522	69622	65322	68922	68822	69722	69822	69922	69222	*Penny the Pendolino*
390123	390023	AWC	ANG	MA	69123	69423	69523	69623	65323	68923	68823	69723	69823	69923	69223	
390124	390024	AWC	ANG	MA	69124	69424	69524	69624	65324	68924	68824	69724	69824	69924	69224	
390125	390025	WHI	ANG	MA	69125	69425	69525	69625	65325	68925	68825	69725	69825	69925	69225	*Virgin Stagecoach*
390126	390026	WHI	ANG	MA	69126	69426	69526	69626	65326	68926	68826	69726	69826	69926	69226	
390127	390027	WHI	ANG	MA	69127	69427	69527	69627	65327	68927	68827	69727	69827	69927	69227	
390128	390028	AWC	ANG	MA	69128	69428	69528	69628	65328	68928	68828	69728	69828	69928	69228	*City of Preston*
390129	390029	WHI	ANG	MA	69129	69429	69529	69629	65329	68929	68829	69729	69829	69929	69229	*City of Stoke-on-Trent*
390130	390030	AWC	ANG	MA	69130	69430	69530	69630	65330	68930	68830	69730	69830	69930	69230	*City of Edinburgh*
390131	390031	WHI	ANG	MA	69131	69431	69531	69631	65331	68931	68831	69731	69831	69931	69231	*City of Liverpool*
390132	390032	AWC	ANG	MA	69132	69432	69532	69632	65332	68932	68832	69732	69832	69932	69232	*City of Birmingham*
390134	390034	AWC	ANG	MA	69134	69434	69534	69634	65334	68934	68834	69734	69834	69934	69234	*City of Carlisle*
390135	390035	AWC	ANG	MA	69135	69435	69535	69635	65335	68935	68835	69735	69835	69935	69235	*City of Lancaster*
390136	390036	AWC	ANG	MA	69136	69436	69536	69636	65336	68936	68836	69736	69836	69936	69236	*City of Coventry*
390137	390037	AWC	ANG	MA	69137	69437	69537	69637	65337	68937	68837	69737	69837	69937	69237	
390138	390038	AWC	ANG	MA	69138	69438	69538	69638	65338	68938	68838	69738	69838	69938	69238	*City of London*

390141	390041	AWC	ANG	MA	69141	69441	69541	69641	65341	68941	68841	69741	69841	69941	69241	
390148	390048	AWC	ANG	MA	69148	69448	69548	69648	65348	68948	68848	69748	69848	69948	69248	*Flying Scouseman*
390151	390051	AWC	ANG	MA	69151	69451	69551	69651	65351	68951	68851	69751	69851	69951	69251	
390152	390052	AWC	ANG	MA	69152	69452	69552	69652	65352	68952	68852	69752	69852	69952	69252	
390153	390053	AWC	ANG	MA	69153	69453	69553	69653	65353	68953	68853	69753	69853	69953	69253	
390154		WHI	ANG	MA	69154	69454	69554	69654	65354	68954	68854	69754	69854	69954	69254	
390155		AWC	ANG	MA	69155	69455	69555	69655	65355	68955	68855	69755	69855	69955	69255	
390156		AWC	ANG	MA	69156	69456	69556	69656	65356	68956	68856	69756	69856	69956	69256	*Pride and Prosperity*
390157		AWC	ANG	MA	69157	69457	69557	69657	65357	68957	68857	69757	69857	69957	69257	*Chad Varah*

No. 390104 passes Symington on the 1839 Glasgow Central-Euston on 23 July 2020. *Robin Ralston*

Trains on order

Avanti West Coast has placed orders with Hitachi for 13 five-car Class 805 EMUs and ten seven-car Class 807 bi-mode EMUs to replace the Class 221 DEMUs. They will be financed through Rock Rail and should be delivered in 2022.

Plain white 221101 calls at Crewe with a northbound train. *Avanti West Coast*

No. 390119 in its new Pride wrap on 23 August 2020. *Avanti West Coast*

Caledonian Sleeper

Contact details

Website: www.sleeper.scot
Twitter: @CalSleeper

Key personnel

Managing Director: Kathryn Darbandi
Engineering Director: Graham Eastwood
Operations Director: Fraser Hood

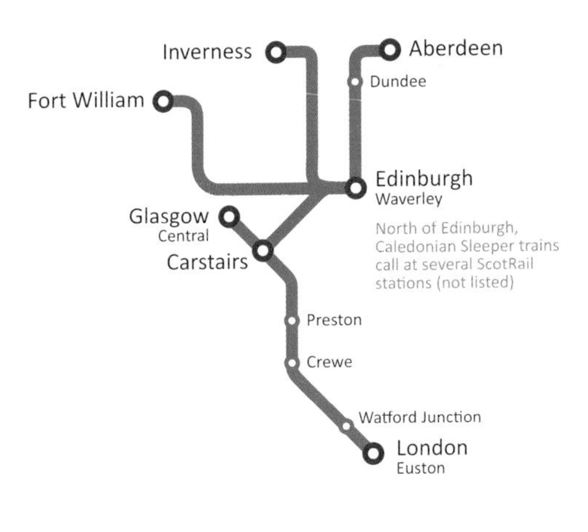

Overview

The company, part of the Serco group, does not own or lease its own locomotives; instead it hires traction and drivers from GB Railfreight to work its trains (see page 295) from Euston to Glasgow Central/Edinburgh and to Inverness/Aberdeen/Fort William. It uses Class 92s south of Edinburgh or Glasgow Central and Class 73/9s north of Edinburgh.

Since its creation in 2014, CS has completely overhauled its fleet. Out have gone the Mk 2/3 coaches hauled by DB Cargo Class 67s and 90s and they have been replaced by a brand-new fleet of purpose-built Mk 5 coaches from CAF. These were seriously delayed into traffic and also suffered many teething problems.

Most of these have been overcome but the company has then been badly affected by the Covid-19 pandemic, which saw many of its trains suspended.

The new Spanish-built Mk 5s were introduced in 2019. They have Dellner couplers so can only be hauled by locos fitted with similar couplers, which means just Class 73/9 and 92s. GBRf's 47s with Dellners cannot haul the Mk 5s.

There are four sets in use every night from Sundays to Fridays; two trains leaving from Euston northbound and one leaving Glasgow Central and another leaving Inverness. The former has a portion from Edinburgh added to it at Carstairs, while the latter has portions from Aberdeen and Fort William added to it at Edinburgh. The northbound trains have corresponding portions detached at Carstairs and Edinburgh.

Each train from London works as 16 coaches, with each portion comprising a half-brake/half-seated accommodation, a lounge car, a fully accessible sleeping car and varying numbers of sleeping cars.

The fleet is maintained at Polmadie by Alstom. The traction supplied by GB Railfreight are six Class 73/9s, 73966-971, all in CS livery. Typically a pair work the Inverness train and single locos are booked for the Fort William and Aberdeen portions.

South of Edinburgh, the trains are worked by Class 92s, with 92006/010/014/018/023/033/038 in CS colours and 92020/028/043 in GBRf livery.

No changes are expected to the operation in the next year and most of the company's attention will be focused on rebuilding the business in the wake of the pandemic.

Mk 5 brake/seated coaches

15001	CAL	LOM	PO
15002	CAL	LOM	PO
15003	CAL	LOM	PO
15004	CAL	LOM	PO
15005	CAL	LOM	PO
15006	CAL	LOM	PO
15007	CAL	LOM	PO
15008	CAL	LOM	PO
15009	CAL	LOM	PO
15010	CAL	LOM	PO
15011	CAL	LOM	PO

Mk 5 lounge cars

15101	CAL	LOM	PO
15102	CAL	LOM	PO
15103	CAL	LOM	PO
15104	CAL	LOM	PO
15105	CAL	LOM	PO
15106	CAL	LOM	PO
15107	CAL	LOM	PO
15108	CAL	LOM	PO
15109	CAL	LOM	PO
15110	CAL	LOM	PO

Mk 5 accessible sleeping cars

15201	CAL	LOM	PO
15202	CAL	LOM	PO
15203	CAL	LOM	PO
15204	CAL	LOM	PO
15205	CAL	LOM	PO
15206	CAL	LOM	PO
15207	CAL	LOM	PO
15208	CAL	LOM	PO
15209	CAL	LOM	PO
15210	CAL	LOM	PO
15211	CAL	LOM	PO
15212	CAL	LOM	PO
15213	CAL	LOM	PO
15214	CAL	LOM	PO

Mk 5 sleeping cars

15301	CAL	LOM	PO
15302	CAL	LOM	PO
15303	CAL	LOM	PO
15304	CAL	LOM	PO
15305	CAL	LOM	PO
15306	CAL	LOM	PO
15307	CAL	LOM	PO
15308	CAL	LOM	PO
15309	CAL	LOM	PO
15310	CAL	LOM	PO
15311	CAL	LOM	PO
15312	CAL	LOM	PO
15313	CAL	LOM	PO
15314	CAL	LOM	PO
15315	CAL	LOM	PO
15316	CAL	LOM	PO
15317	CAL	LOM	PO
15318	CAL	LOM	PO
15319	CAL	LOM	PO
15320	CAL	LOM	PO
15321	CAL	LOM	PO
15322	CAL	LOM	PO
15323	CAL	LOM	PO
15324	CAL	LOM	PO
15325	CAL	LOM	PO
15326	CAL	LOM	PO
15327	CAL	LOM	PO
15328	CAL	LOM	PO
15329	CAL	LOM	PO
15330	CAL	LOM	PO
15331	CAL	LOM	PO
15332	CAL	LOM	PO
15333	CAL	LOM	PO
15334	CAL	LOM	PO
15335	CAL	LOM	PO
15336	CAL	LOM	PO
15337	CAL	LOM	PO
15338	CAL	LOM	PO
15339	CAL	LOM	PO
15340	CAL	LOM	PO

Service vehicles

6392	81588, 92183	CAL	Mk 1	Brake force runner
6397	81600, 92190	CAL	Mk 1	Brake force runner
96604	86337, 96156	CAL	GUV	Brake force runner
96606	86324, 96213	CAL	GUV	Brake force runner
96608	86385, 96216	CAL	GUV	Brake force runner
96609	86327, 96217	CAL	GUV	Brake force runner

GBRf's 92043 passes Auchengray, between Midcalder Junction and Carstairs, with the 0818 Edinburgh-Polmadie ECS on 4 May 2019. *Robin Ralston*

No. 73968 waits to leave Oban with the 1030 ECS to Polmadie on 25 March 2017. *Anthony Hicks*

Sleeping car 15322 at Craigenhill on 27 February 2020. *Robin Ralston*

Lounge car 15105 at Leggatfoot, between Abington and Carstairs, on 28 June 2019. *Robin Ralston*

Brake coach 15011 Craigenhill on 27 February 2020. *Robin Ralston*

c2c

Contact details

Website: www.c2c-online.co.uk
Twitter: @c2c_Rail

Key personnel

Managing Director: Julian Drury
Engineering Director: Jeff Baker

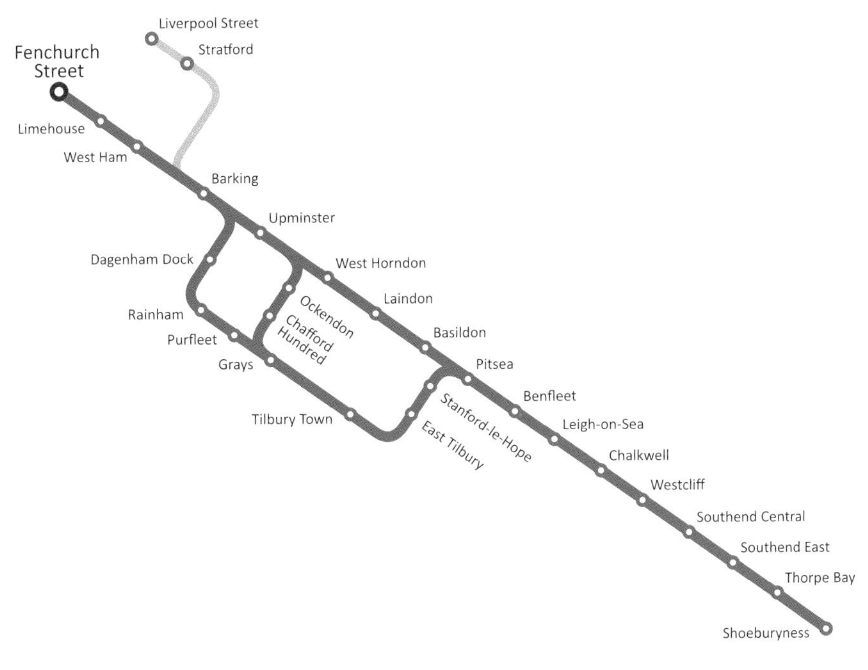

Overview

Until recently, c2c fleet was formed solely of four-car Class 357 Bombardier Electrostars delivered in 1999-2002 to operate from Fenchurch St-Southend / Shoeburyness, via Tilbury. They were ordered by the original franchise holder in the late 1990s to replace the London Tilbury Southend line's collection of old slam-door Class 302 and 310 / 312 units and sliding-door Class 317s. The sub-classes differentiate the owning ROSCO, while the renumbered 357 / 3s are those units with fewer seats for high-density commuter operations. The original order of 357 / 0s was for 44 units but two additional units were added to the production run as 'compensation' for late delivery.

In 2016, six four-car Class 387 / 3s joined the fleet to allow extra seats. They were only a short-term stopgap to meet increased demand for c2c and will be returned to Porterbrook when the TOC's new Class 720 / 6s are delivered. They are expected to then move to GWR.

The franchise is pretty self-contained, being a mass people mover for commuters in the week yet offering leisure travel to the likes of Southend and Leigh-on-sea.

The company has ten six-car Class 720 Bombardier Aventra units on order, which are expected to be delivered in 2021.

Class 357

All are in the HTHQ pool.

Class 357/0

Porterbrook units.

				DMS	MS	PTS	DMS	Name
357001	C2C	POR	EM	67651	74151	74051	67751	*Barry Flaxman*
357002	C2C	POR	EM	67652	74152	74052	67752	*Arthur Lewis Stride 1841-1922*
357003	C2C	POR	EM	67653	74153	74053	67753	*Southend city on sea*
357004	C2C	POR	EM	67654	74154	74054	67754	*Tony Amos*
357005	C2C	POR	EM	67655	74155	74055	67755	*Southend 2017 Alternative City of Culture*
357006	C2C	POR	EM	67656	74156	74056	67756	*Diamond Jubilee 1952-2012*
357007	C2C	POR	EM	67657	74157	74057	67757	*Sir Andrew Foster*
357008	C2C	POR	EM	67658	74158	74058	67758	
357009	C2C	POR	EM	67659	74159	74059	67759	
357010	C2C	POR	EM	67660	74160	74060	67760	
357011	C2C	POR	EM	67661	74161	74061	67761	*John Lowing*
357012	C2C	POR	EM	67662	74162	74062	67762	
357013	C2C	POR	EM	67663	74163	74063	67763	
357014	C2C	POR	EM	67664	74164	74064	67764	
357015	C2C	POR	EM	67665	74165	74065	67765	
357016	C2C	POR	EM	67666	74166	74066	67766	
357017	C2C	POR	EM	67667	74167	74067	67767	
357018	C2C	POR	EM	67668	74168	74068	67768	*Remembering our Fallen*
357019	C2C	POR	EM	67669	74169	74069	67769	
357020	C2C	POR	EM	67670	74170	74070	67770	
357021	C2C	POR	EM	67671	74171	74071	67771	
357022	C2C	POR	EM	67672	74172	74072	67772	
357023	C2C	POR	EM	67673	74173	74073	67773	
357024	C2C	POR	EM	67674	74174	74074	67774	
357025	C2C	POR	EM	67675	74175	74075	67775	
357026	C2C	POR	EM	67676	74176	74076	67776	
357027	C2C	POR	EM	67677	74177	74077	67777	
357028	C2C	POR	EM	67678	74178	74078	67778	*London Tilbury & Southend Railway 1854-2004*
357029	C2C	POR	EM	67679	74179	74079	67779	*Thomas Whitelegg 1840-1922*
357030	C2C	POR	EM	67680	74180	74080	67780	*Robert Harben Whitelegg 1871-1957*
357031	C2C	POR	EM	67681	74181	74081	67781	
357032	C2C	POR	EM	67682	74182	74082	67782	
357033	C2C	POR	EM	67683	74183	74083	67783	
357034	C2C	POR	EM	67684	74184	74084	67784	
357035	C2C	POR	EM	67685	74185	74085	67785	
357036	C2C	POR	EM	67686	74186	74086	67786	

No. 357026 passes Leigh-on-Sea on 15 July 2019. *Paul Bigland*

357037	C2C	POR	EM	67687	74187	74087	67787
357038	C2C	POR	EM	67688	74188	74088	67788
357039	C2C	POR	EM	67689	74189	74089	67789
357040	C2C	POR	EM	67690	74190	74090	67790
357041	C2C	POR	EM	67691	74191	74091	67791
357042	C2C	POR	EM	67692	74192	74092	67792
357043	C2C	POR	EM	67693	74193	74093	67793
357044	C2C	POR	EM	67694	74194	74094	67794
357045	C2C	POR	EM	67695	74195	74095	67795
357046	C2C	POR	EM	67696	74196	74096	67796

Class 357/2

The same as 357/0s just financed Angel Trains. Those renumbered in the 357/3 series have high-density interiors with fewer seats.

No. 387306 leads 387304 and 387302 past Leigh-on-Sea on 15 July 2019. *Paul Bigland*

	Old No.				DMS	MS	PS	DMS	Name
357201		C2C	ANG	EM	68601	74701	74601	68701	*Ken Bird*
357202		C2C	ANG	EM	68602	74702	74602	68702	*Kenny Mitchell*
357203		C2C	ANG	EM	68603	74703	74603	68703	*Henry Pumfrett*
357204		C2C	ANG	EM	68604	74704	74604	68704	*Derek Fowers*
357205		C2C	ANG	EM	68605	74705	74605	68705	*John D'Silva*
357206		C2C	ANG	EM	68606	74706	74606	68706	*Martin Aungier*
357207		C2C	ANG	EM	68607	74707	74607	68707	*John Page*
357208		C2C	ANG	EM	68608	74708	74608	68708	*Dave Davis*
357209		C2C	ANG	EM	68609	74709	74609	68709	*James Snelling*
357210		C2C	ANG	EM	68610	74710	74610	68710	
357211		C2C	ANG	EM	68611	74711	74611	68711	
357312	357212	C2C	ANG	EM	68612	74712	74612	68712	
357313	357213	C2C	ANG	EM	68613	74713	74613	68713	*Upminster IECC*
357314	357214	C2C	ANG	EM	68614	74714	74614	68714	
357315	357215	C2C	ANG	EM	68615	74715	74615	68715	
357316	357216	C2C	ANG	EM	68616	74716	74616	68716	
357317	357217	C2C	ANG	EM	68617	74717	74617	68717	*Allan Burnell*
357318	357218	C2C	ANG	EM	68618	74718	74618	68718	
357319	357219	C2C	ANG	EM	68619	74719	74619	68719	
357320	357220	C2C	ANG	EM	68620	74720	74620	68720	
357321	357221	C2C	ANG	EM	68621	74721	74621	68721	
357322	357222	C2C	ANG	EM	68622	74722	74622	68722	
357323	357223	C2C	ANG	EM	68623	74723	74623	68723	
357324	357224	C2C	ANG	EM	68624	74724	74624	68724	
357325	357225	C2C	ANG	EM	68625	74725	74625	68725	
357326	357226	C2C	ANG	EM	68626	74726	74626	68726	
357327	357227	C2C	ANG	EM	68627	74727	74627	68727	*Southend United*
357328	357228	C2C	ANG	EM	68628	74728	74628	68728	

Class 387/3

Similar to the Class 357s from the same Electrostar platform, these units differ by having corridor connections allowing them to run in eight- and 12-car formations with through connections between units for staff and passengers alike. All are in the HTHQ pool.

				DMS	MS	PTS	DMS
387301	C2C	POR	EM	421301	422301	423301	424301
387302	C2C	POR	EM	421302	422302	423302	424302
387303	C2C	POR	EM	421303	422303	423303	424303
387304	C2C	POR	EM	421304	422304	423304	424304
387305	C2C	POR	EM	421305	422305	423305	424305
387306	C2C	POR	EM	421306	422306	423306	424306

Future trains

Class 720/6

Another variant of the Bombardier Aventra platform, these ten six-car units, 720601-610, are high-density commuter trains funded through Porterbrook. They will replace the Class 387s as well as allowing extra seats. Individual vehicle numbers yet to be confirmed. These units may take different numbers as the Class 720/5 order has been increased. All will be in the HTHQ pool.

Chiltern Railways

Contact details

Website: www.chilternrailways.co.uk
Twitter: @chilternrailway

Key personnel

Managing Director: Richard Allan
Engineering and Safety Director: Ian Hyde

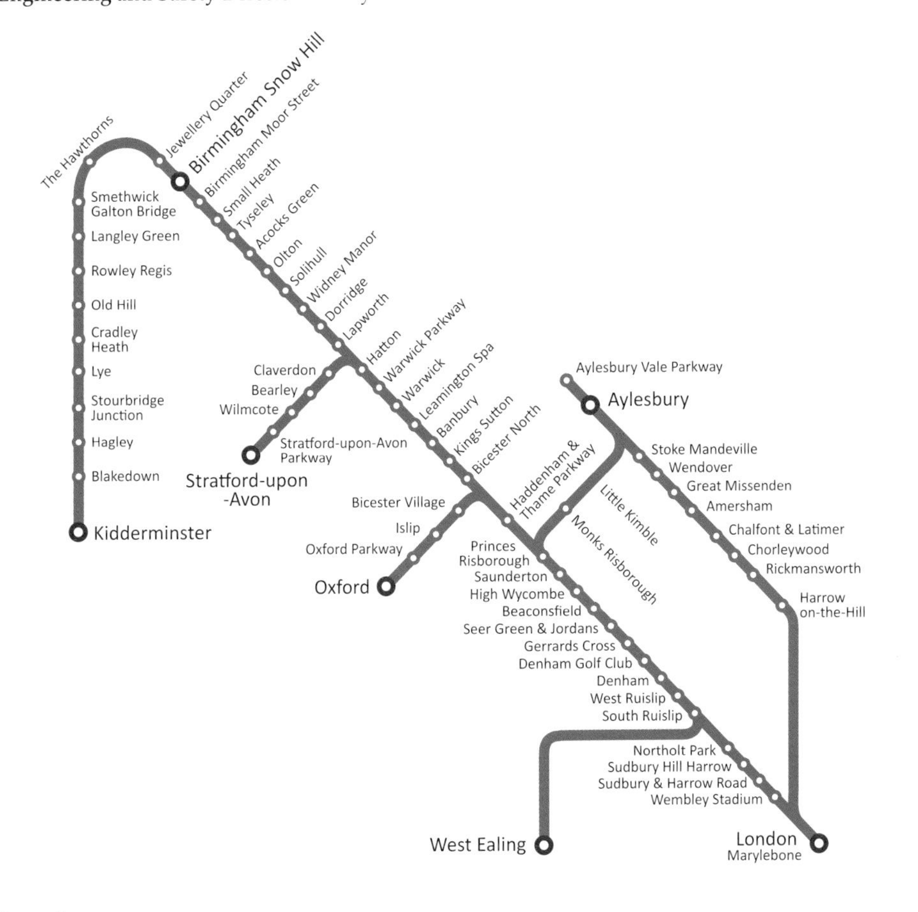

Overview

Owned by Arriva, Chiltern Railways runs from London Marylebone to Birmingham Moor Street and Kidderminster, Marylebone to Aylesbury/Oxford and Aylesbury to Princes Risborough.

It has been a pretty static fleet since it was privatised, inheriting 39 ex-BR Class 165s of two- and three-car types before ordering Bombardier Class 168s.

Chiltern has frequently ordered small batches of new trains, and grown to a fleet of 32 new trains of two-, three- and four-car types. The four most recent acquisitions are four two-car Class 172/1s, which differed in being diesel mechanical as opposed to diesel hydraulics units.

The firm also operates loco-hauled trains between Marylebone and Birmingham Moor St/Kidderminster. These comprise six modified Mk 3 coaches – with sliding doors – plus a Driving Van Trailer, sets powered by a pool of eight dedicated Stadler Class 68s hired from Direct Rail Services; 68008-015, of which 68010-015 are in Chiltern livery (see page 285). The locos are on the country end of the trains. They are maintained by DRS at Crewe with routine running exams undertaken at Wembley. Three sets stable at Stourbridge Junction each evening. Class 68s replaced Class 67s from DB Cargo in 2015. The coaches were previously used by Open Access operator Wrexham, Shropshire and Marylebone Railway with Class 67s. The DMU fleet is all based at Aylesbury. Chiltern also has a Ruston 0-6-0 shunter based at Aylesbury but this is not passed to run on Network Rail infrastructure.

There has not been too much to report on the TOC since the swap to Class 68s in late 2014 through to early 2015, and the opening of the Bicester chord in 2015 to allow Chiltern to operate into Oxford directly from Marylebone.

There are no changes to the TOC's operations as the franchise only runs until December 2021.

Class 165

BREL York Networker Turbo units built in 1991/92 and used two- or three-car sets. All are in the HOHQ pool.

				DMSL	MS	DMS
165001	CRO	ANG	AL	58801		58834
165002	CRW	ANG	AL	58802		58835
165003	CRW	ANG	AL	58803		58836
165004	CRW	ANG	AL	58804		58837
165005	CRW	ANG	AL	58805		58838
165006	CRW	ANG	AL	58806		58839
165007	CRW	ANG	AL	58807		58840
165008	CRW	ANG	AL	58808		58841
165009	CRW	ANG	AL	58809		58842
165010	CRO	ANG	AL	58810		58843
165011	CRO	ANG	AL	58811		58844
165012	CRW	ANG	AL	58812		58845
165013	CRW	ANG	AL	58813		58846
165014	CRW	ANG	AL	58814		58847
165015	CRO	ANG	AL	58815		58848
165016	CRW	ANG	AL	58816		58849
165017	CRW	ANG	AL	58817		58850
165018	CRW	ANG	AL	58818		58851
165019	CRW	ANG	AL	58819		58852
165020	CRO	ANG	AL	58820		58853
165021	CRW	ANG	AL	58821		58854
165022	CRO	ANG	AL	58822		58855
165023	CRW	ANG	AL	58873		58867
165024	CRO	ANG	AL	58874		58868
165025	CRO	ANG	AL	58875		58869
165026	CRO	ANG	AL	58876		58870
165027	CRW	ANG	AL	58877		58871
165028	CRO	ANG	AL	58878		58872
165029	CRW	ANG	AL	58823	55404	58856
165030	CRO	ANG	AL	58824	55405	58857
165031	CRW	ANG	AL	58825	55406	58858

165032	CRO	ANG	AL	58826	55407	58859
165033	CRO	ANG	AL	58827	55408	58860
165034	CRO	ANG	AL	58828	55409	58861
165035	CRW	ANG	AL	58829	55410	58862
165036	CRO	ANG	AL	58830	55411	58863
165037	CRW	ANG	AL	58831	55412	58864
165038	CRO	ANG	AL	58832	55413	58865
165039	CRW	ANG	AL	58833	55414	58866

Class 168

Branded as Clubman units, despite being from the same platform as the Turbostar units, the different sub-classes are mainly determined on within which batch of units they were ordered rather than their configuration or owner. The first five units differed in cab design, but on units delivered from 168106 the cab has been the same as the standard Turbostar family. All are in the HOHQ pool.

Class 168/0

Original four-car Clubman units with old-style cabs.

				DMSL	MS/MSL	MSL/MS	DMSL
168001	CRS	POR	AL	58151	58651	58451	58251
168002	CRS	POR	AL	58152	58652	58452	58252
168003	CRS	POR	AL	58153	58453	58653	58253
168004	CRS	POR	AL	58154	58654	58454	58254
168005	CRS	POR	AL	58155	58655	58455	58255

Class 168/1

Later build units featuring Class 170 Turbostar cabs.

				DMSL	MSL	MS	DMSL
168106	CRS	POR	AL	58156	58756	58456	58256
168107	CRS	POR	AL	58157	58757	58457	58257
168108	CRS	POR	AL	58158		58458	58258
168109	CRS	POR	AL	58159		58459	58259
168110	CRS	POR	AL	58160		58460	58260
168111	CRS	EVS	AL	58161		58461	58261
168112	CRS	EVS	AL	58162		58462	58262
168113	CRS	EVS	AL	58163		58463	58263

Class 168/2

Later build units featuring Class 170 Turbostar cabs.

				DMSL	MSL	MS	DMSL
168214	CRS	POR	AL	58164		58464	58264
168215	CRS	POR	AL	58165	58365	58465	58265
168216	CRS	POR	AL	58166	58366	58466	58266
168217	CRS	POR	AL	58167	58367	58467	58267
168218	CRS	POR	AL	58168		58468	58268
168219	CRS	POR	AL	58169		58469	58269

No. 68010 *Oxford Flyer* passes Kings Sutton hauling the 1615 Marylebone-Kidderminster on 26 June 2018. *Robin Ralston*

Class 168/3

Former South West Trains Class 170/3 two-car units.

					DMSL	DMSL
168321	170301	CRS	POR	AL	50301	79301
168322	170302	CRS	POR	AL	50302	79302
168323	170303	CRS	POR	AL	50303	79303
168324	170304	CRS	POR	AL	50304	79304
168325	170305	CRS	POR	AL	50305	79305
168326	170306	CRS	POR	AL	50306	79306
168327	170307	CRS	POR	AL	50307	79307
168328	170308	CRS	POR	AL	50308	79308
168329	170399, 170309	CRS	POR	AL	50399	79399

Class 172/1

These two-car Turbostar units date from 2009/10. They are not allowed to run on the Amersham to Marylebone line on the Metropolitan lines. All are in the HOHQ pool.

				DMSL	DMS
172101	CRO	ANG	AL	59111	59211
172102	CRO	ANG	AL	59112	59212
172103	CRO	ANG	AL	59113	59213
172104	CRO	ANG	AL	59114	59214

Loco-hauled coaches

Chiltern has a fleet of six Driving Van Trailers and Mk 3 coaches for Marylebone to Birmingham services. Five sets are in use daily, and three trains a day start or end at Kidderminster and these sets are stabled overnight at Stourbridge Junction.

Nos 68010-015 are the preferred locos, as they are painted in Chiltern livery. However, 68008/009 are also modified to work with the coaches yet remain in DRS livery.

Driving Van Trailers

82301	CRS	ARV	AL
82302	CRS	ARV	AL
82303	CRS	ARV	AL
82304	CRS	ARV	AL
82305	CRS	ARV	AL
82309	CRS	ARV	AL

Mk 3 coaches

RFO kitchen buffet first Mk 3.

10271	CRS	ARV	AL
10272	CRS	ARV	AL
10273	CRS	ARV	AL
10273	CRS	ARV	AL

FO – First Open Mk 3

11029	CRS	ARV	AL
11031	CRS	ARV	AL

SO – Standard Open

12017	CRS	ARV	AL
12036	CRS	ARV	AL
12054	CRS	ARV	AL
12094	CRS	ARV	AL
12119	CRS	ARV	AL

SO – Standard Open

12602	CRS	ARV	AL
12603	CRS	ARV	AL
12604	CRS	ARV	AL
12605	CRS	ARV	AL
12606	CRS	ARV	AL
12607	CRS	ARV	AL
12608	CRS	ARV	AL
12609	CRS	ARV	AL
12610	CRS	ARV	AL
12613	CRS	ARV	AL
12614	CRS	ARV	AL
12615	CRS	ARV	AL
12616	CRS	ARV	AL
12617	CRS	ARV	AL
12618	CRS	ARV	AL
12619	CRS	ARV	AL
12620	CRS	ARV	AL
12621	CRS	ARV	AL
12623	CRS	ARV	AL
12625	CRS	ARV	AL
12627	CRS	ARV	AL

Mk 3 10271 at Birmingham Moor Street on 21 May 2019. *Antony Christie*

DVT 82304 leads the 1255 Birmingham Moor Street-Marylebone, approaching Kings Sutton on 20 August 2020. *Bill Atkinson*

No. 168106/8107 approach Banbury on 27 August 2017 working the 1055 Birmingham Moor Street-Marylebone. *Bill Atkinson*

Below: No. 172101 passes the now-demolished signal box at Banbury in 2015. *Mark Pike*

CrossCountry Trains

Contact details

Website: www.crosscountrytrains.co.uk
Twitter: @CrossCountryUK

Key personnel

Managing Director: Tom Joyner
Service Delivery Director: Richard Morris

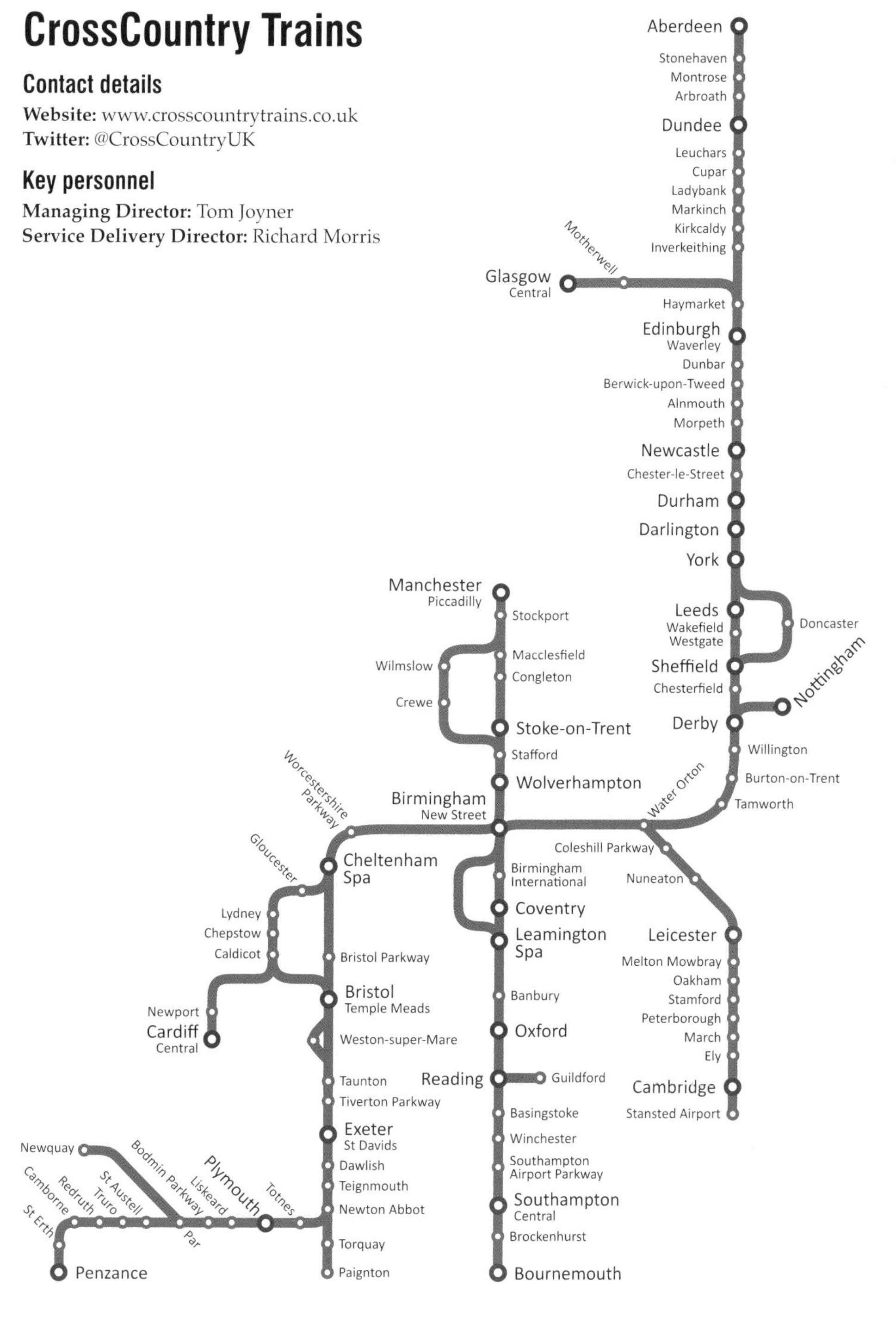

Overview

CrossCountry Trains is a nationwide operator of inter-city trains from Penzance to Aberdeen, although its operation is much changed from the days when the franchise was first let to Virgin in 1996 with it no longer serving the WCML north of Manchester, nor to Brighton. However it does also now include the Birmingham to Stansted and Nottingham to Cardiff routes that were previously part of Central Trains.

The routes it currently operates are Penzance to Aberdeen via Birmingham New Street and Newcastle, Birmingham-Bournemouth, Birmingham-Manchester, Birmingham-Stansted and Cardiff-Nottingham.

The XCT fleet relies on three main traction types; Class 220/221 Bombardier Voyager DEMUs, which work most of the long-distance routes, supplemented by five HST sets on the Edinburgh-Plymouth route. Class 170 Turbostars work the Cardiff-Nottingham and Birmingham-Stansted corridors.

There have been no major developments to the fleet or operations in the past 12 months other than taking two additional Angel Trains HST power cars, ex-LNER 43208/239. These were yet to enter traffic by early September.

Six centre cars from ex-West Midlands Trains Class 170/6s are to be inserted in XCT's remaining six Class 170/5s, which will make all but seven of its 29 Class 170s three-car sets, just 170111-117 remaining as two cars.

Class 43/2

MTU-powered Class 43 HST sets. The Class 43s are now allocated to Laira with their maintenance undertaken under contract by First Great Western. All are in the EHPC pool.

43207	43007	XCT	ANG	LA
43208	43008	XCT	ANG	LA
43239	43039	XCT	ANG	LA
43285	43085	XCT	POR	LA
43301	43101	XCT	POR	LA
43303	43103	XCT	POR	LA
43304	43104	XCT	ANG	LA
43321	43121	XCT	POR	LA
43357	43157	XCT	POR	LA
43366	43166	XCT	ANG	LA
43378	43178	XCT	ANG	LA
43384	43184	XCT	ANG	LA

HST Trailers

XCT's HST sets run as five seven-vehicle sets with a TF, TCK, four TSs and a TGS with six spare trailers.

TF – Trailer First

41026	XCT	ANG	LA
41035	XCT	ANG	LA
41193	XCT	POR	LA
41194	XCT	POR	LA
41195	XCT	POR	LA

TS – Trailer Standard

42036	XCT	ANG	LA
42037	XCT	ANG	LA
42038	XCT	ANG	LA
42051	XCT	ANG	LA
42052	XCT	ANG	LA
42053	XCT	ANG	LA
42097	XCT	ANG	LA
42234	XCT	POR	LA
42290	XCT	POR	LA
42342	XCT	ANG	LA
42366	XCT	POR	LA
42367	XCT	POR	LA
42368	XCT	POR	LA
42369	XCT	POR	LA
42370	XCT	POR	LA
42371	XCT	POR	LA
42372	XCT	POR	LA
42373	XCT	POR	LA
42374	XCT	POR	LA
42375	XCT	POR	LA
42376	XCT	POR	LA
42377	XCT	POR	LA
42378	XCT	POR	LA
42379	XCT	ANG	LA
42380	XCT	ANG	LA

TGS – Trailer Guard's Standard

44012	XCT	ANG	LA
44017	XCT	ANG	LA
44021	XCT	POR	LA
44052	XCT	POR	LA
44072	XCT	POR	LA

TCK – Trailer Composite Kitchen			
45001	XCT	POR	LA
45002	XCT	POR	LA
45003	XCT	POR	LA
45004	XCT	POR	LA
45005	XCT	POR	LA

CrossCountry Trains HST formations

XC01	41193	45001	42342	42097	42377	42374	44021
XC02	41194	45002	42324	42037	42367	42371	44072
XC03	41195	45003	42370	42378	42036	42376	44052
XC04	41026	45004	42375	42369	42051	42366	44012
XC05	41035	45005	42052	42038	42053	42379	44017
Spare	42290	42368	42372	42373	42380		

Class 170/1

Former Midland Mainline two- or three-car sets, delivered in 1998 as two-car sets, with ten units strengthened to three-cars. All are in the EHXC pool.

				DMSL	MS	DMCL
170101	XCT	POR	TS	50101	55101	79101
170102	XCT	POR	TS	50102	55102	79102
170103	XCT	POR	TS	50103	55103	79103
170104	XCT	POR	TS	50104	55104	79104
170105	XCT	POR	TS	50105	55105	79105
170106	XCT	POR	TS	50106	55106	79106
170107	XCT	POR	TS	50107	55107	79107
170108	XCT	POR	TS	50108	55108	79108
170109	XCT	POR	TS	50109	55109	79109
170110	XCT	POR	TS	50110	55110	79110
170111	XCT	POR	TS	50111		79111
170112	XCT	POR	TS	50112		79112
170113	XCT	POR	TS	50113		79113
170114	XCT	POR	TS	50114		79114
170115	XCT	POR	TS	50115		79115
170116	XCT	POR	TS	50116		79116
170117	XCT	POR	TS	50117		79117

Class 170/3

Former Central Trains three-car sets. All are in the EHXC pool.

				DMSL	MS	DMCL
170397	XCT	POR	TS	50397	55397	79397
170398	XCT	POR	TS	50398	55398	79398

No. 170116 heads north past Vigo Bridge on the Lickey incline with a Cardiff-Nottingham train on 21 May 2019.
Antony Christie

Class 170/5

Former Central Trains two-car sets that are being strengthened using the six centre cars, 56630-635, from units 170630-635, following their release from West Midlands Trains after the arrival of Class 196s. All are in the EHXC pool.

				DMSL	MS	DMCL
170518	XCT	POR	TS	50518		79518
170519	XCT	POR	TS	50519		79519
170520	XCT	POR	TS	50520	56632	79520
170521	XCT	POR	TS	50521		79521
170522	XCT	POR	TS	50522		79522
170523	XCT	POR	TS	50523	56635	79523

Class 170/6

Former Central Trains three-car sets. All are in the EHXC pool.

				DMSL	MS	DMCL
170636	XCT	POR	TS	50636	56636	79636
170637	XCT	POR	TS	50637	56637	79637
170638	XCT	POR	TS	50638	56638	79638
170639	XCT	POR	TS	50639	56639	79639

No. 220021 passes Teignmouth on 16 July 2020. *Antony Christie*

Class 220

Former Virgin CrossCountry four-car Voyager DEMUs, maintained by Bombardier at Central Rivers depot. All are in the EHXC pool.

				DMS	MS	MS	DMF
220001	XCT	BEA	CZ	60301	60701	60201	60401
220002	XCT	BEA	CZ	60302	60702	60202	60402
220003	XCT	BEA	CZ	60303	60703	60203	60403
220004	XCT	BEA	CZ	60304	60704	60204	60404
220005	XCT	BEA	CZ	60305	60705	60205	60405
220006	XCT	BEA	CZ	60306	60706	60206	60406
220007	XCT	BEA	CZ	60307	60707	60207	60407
220008	XCT	BEA	CZ	60308	60708	60208	60408
220009	XCT	BEA	CZ	60309	60709	60209	60409
220010	XCT	BEA	CZ	60310	60710	60210	60410
220011	XCT	BEA	CZ	60311	60711	60211	60411
220012	XCT	BEA	CZ	60312	60712	60212	60412
220013	XCT	BEA	CZ	60313	60713	60213	60413
220014	XCT	BEA	CZ	60314	60714	60214	60414
220015	XCT	BEA	CZ	60315	60715	60215	60415
220016	XCT	BEA	CZ	60316	60716	60216	60416
220017	XCT	BEA	CZ	60317	60717	60217	60417
220018	XCT	BEA	CZ	60318	60718	60218	60418

220019	XCT	BEA	CZ	60319	60719	60219	60419
220020	XCT	BEA	CZ	60320	60720	60220	60420
220021	XCT	BEA	CZ	60321	60721	60221	60421
220022	XCT	BEA	CZ	60322	60722	60222	60422
220023	XCT	BEA	CZ	60323	60723	60223	60423
220024	XCT	BEA	CZ	60324	60724	60224	60424
220025	XCT	BEA	CZ	60325	60725	60225	60425
220026	XCT	BEA	CZ	60326	60726	60226	60426
220027	XCT	BEA	CZ	60327	60727	60227	60427
220028	XCT	BEA	CZ	60328	60728	60228	60428
220029	XCT	BEA	CZ	60329	60729	60229	60429
220030	XCT	BEA	CZ	60330	60730	60230	60430
220031	XCT	BEA	CZ	60331	60731	60231	60431
220032	XCT	BEA	CZ	60332	60732	60232	60432
220033	XCT	BEA	CZ	60333	60733	60233	60433
220034	XCT	BEA	CZ	60334	60734	60234	60434

Class 221

Former Virgin CrossCountry four- or five-car tilting Super Voyager DEMUs. The tilting function is now isolated. All are in the EHXC pool.

No. 43357 heads south near Parson Street, Bristol, leading the 0606 Edinburgh-Plymouth on 11 April 2019. No. 43366 is on the rear. *Glen Batten*

				DMS	MS	MS	MS	DMF
221119	XCT	BEA	CZ	60369	60769	60969	60869	60469
221120	XCT	BEA	CZ	60370	60770	60970	60870	60470
221121	XCT	BEA	CZ	60371	60771	60971	60871	60471
221122	XCT	BEA	CZ	60372	60772	60972	60872	60472
221123	XCT	BEA	CZ	60373	60773	60973	60873	60473
221124	XCT	BEA	CZ	60374	60774	60974	60874	60474
221125	XCT	BEA	CZ	60375	60775	60975	60875	60475
221126	XCT	BEA	CZ	60376	60776	60976	60876	60476
221127	XCT	BEA	CZ	60377	60777	60977	60877	60477
221128	XCT	BEA	CZ	60378	60778	60978	60878	60478
221129	XCT	BEA	CZ	60379	60779	60979	60879	60479
221130	XCT	BEA	CZ	60380	60780	60980	60880	60480
221131	XCT	BEA	CZ	60381	60781	60981	60881	60481
221132	XCT	BEA	CZ	60382	60782	60982	60882	60482
221133	XCT	BEA	CZ	60383	60783	60983	60883	60483
221134	XCT	BEA	CZ	60384	60784	60984	60884	60484
221135	XCT	BEA	CZ	60385	60785	60985	60885	60485
221136	XCT	BEA	CZ	60386	60786		60886	60486
221137	XCT	BEA	CZ	60387	60787	60987	60887	60487
221138	XCT	BEA	CZ	60388	60788	60988	60888	60488
221139	XCT	BEA	CZ	60389	60789	60989	60889	60489
221140	XCT	BEA	CZ	60390	60790		60890	60490
221141	XCT	BEA	CZ	60391	60791	60991		60491
221144	XCT	BEA	CZ	60394	60794	60990		60494

Trailer Standard coach 42376 near Drem on 5 September 2018. *Robin Ralston*

Crossrail (Elizabeth Line)

Contact details

Website: crossrail.co.uk
Twitter: @Crossrail

Key personnel

Chief Executive: Mark Wild
Technical Director: Colin Brown

Overview

Currently, Crossrail just operates between Reading-Paddington (since May 2018) and Liverpool St-Shenfield (since June 2017) using some of its brand-new fleet of 70 nine-car Class 345 EMUs. However, the main section of Crossrail – which will be marketed as the Elizabeth line, under the city of London, is still to open and latest forecasts suggest it won't until 2022, some four years later than initially planned.

All the Bombardier Aventra units have now been delivered but with the main part of the route still not open, many are in store at Old Oak Common. Those that are now used are running as seven-cars. Presently, several elderly Class 315s are still used by Crossrail for local services but these will be replaced by 345s in time.

The main change to this franchise will come with that opening of the much-delayed main section, which will finally allow through services from Reading to Shenfield to operate.

Crossrail will also serve Heathrow Airport terminals 1-4 in the west and a branch in the east via Canary Wharf and under the Thames to north-east London at Abbey Wood, which uses much of the old National Rail line trackbed of the old North Woolwich branch. The first Class 345 to work to Heathrow Airport was in late July 2020.

When the Elizabeth line opens in its entirety, operations will pass to Transport for London.

Class 315

Ex-BR four-car 25kV AC units dating from 1980/81, these units are progressively being withdrawn as more Class 345s enter traffic. All are in the EXHQ pool.

				DMS	TS	PTS	DMS	
315818	TFL	EVS	IL	64495	71298	71406	64496	
315819	TFL	EVS	IL	64497	71299	71407	64498	
315820	TFL	EVS	IL	64499	71300	71408	64500	
315826	TFL	EVS	IL	64511	71306	71414	64512	
315829	TFL	EVS	IL	64517	71309	71417	64518	*London Borough of Havering Celebrating 40 Years*
315837	TFL	EVS	IL	64533	71317	71425	64534	
315838	TFL	EVS	IL	64535	71318	71426	64536	
315839	TFL	EVS	IL	64537	71319	71427	64538	
315843	TFL	EVS	IL	64545	71323	71431	64546	
315844	TFL	EVS	IL	64547	71324	71432	64548	
315847	TFL	EVS	IL	64553	71327	71435	64554	
315848	TFL	EVS	IL	64540	71328	71436	64556	
315849	TFL	EVS	IL	64557	71329	71437	64558	
315851	TFL	EVS	IL	64561	71331	71439	64562	
315853	TFL	EVS	IL	64565	71333	71441	64566	
315854	TFL	EVS	IL	64567	71334	71442	64568	
315856	TFL	EVS	IL	64571	71336	71444	64572	
315857	TFL	EVS	IL	64573	71337	71445	64574	

Being phased out, ex-BR 315847 calls at Chadwell Heath on 14 November 2018. *Paul Bigland*

Class 345

Brand-new 25kV AC Bombardier Aventra units, some of which were delivered as seven-car sets, these nine-car sets will be the only trains used on the Elizabeth line when it is fully opened. There is an option for 14 extra units if required. They are owned by Crossrail.

Some sets are already in use as seven- and nine-car units. Many units are in store, mostly at Old Oak Common. Although all allocated to Old Oak Common, some units may be in store at Old Dalby or Worksop and the situation changes weekly. All units are listed as nine-car but may currently be formed of just seven cars. All are in the EXHQ pool.

				DMS	PMS	MS	MS	TS	MS	MS	PMS	DMS
345001	XRL	XRL	OC	340101	340201	340301	340401	340501	340601	340701	340801	340901
345002	XRL	XRL	OC	340102	340202	340302	340402	340502	340602	340702	340802	340902
345003	XRL	XRL	OC	340103	340203	340303	340403	340503	340603	340703	340803	340903
345004	XRL	XRL	OC	340104	340204	340304	340404	340504	340604	340704	340804	340904
345005	XRL	XRL	OC	340105	340205	340305	340405	340505	340605	340705	340805	340905
345006	XRL	XRL	OC	340106	340206	340306	340406	340506	340606	340706	340806	340906
345007	XRL	XRL	OC	340107	340207	340307	340407	340507	340607	340707	340807	340907
345008	XRL	XRL	OC	340108	340208	340308	340408	340508	340608	340708	340808	340908
345009	XRL	XRL	OC	340109	340209	340309	340409	340509	340609	340709	340809	340909
345010	XRL	XRL	OC	340110	340210	340310	340410	340510	340610	340710	340810	340910
345011	XRL	XRL	OC	340111	340211	340311	340411	340511	340611	340711	340811	340911
345012	XRL	XRL	OC	340112	340212	340312	340412	340512	340612	340712	340812	340912
345013	XRL	XRL	OC	340113	340213	340313	340413	340513	340613	340713	340813	340913
345014	XRL	XRL	OC	340114	340214	340314	340414	340514	340614	340714	340814	340914
345015	XRL	XRL	OC	340115	340215	340315	340415	340515	340615	340715	340815	340915
345016	XRL	XRL	OC	340116	340216	340316	340416	340516	340616	340716	340816	340916
345017	XRL	XRL	OC	340117	340217	340317	340417	340517	340617	340717	340817	340917
345018	XRL	XRL	OC	340118	340218	340318	340418	340518	340618	340718	340818	340918
345019	XRL	XRL	OD(S)	340119	340219	340319	340419	340519	340619	340719	340819	340919
345020	XRL	XRL	OC	340120	340220	340320	340420	340520	340620	340720	340820	340920
345021	XRL	XRL	OC	340121	340221	340321	340421	340521	340621	340721	340821	340921
345022	XRL	XRL	OC	340122	340222	340322	340422	340522	340622	340722	340822	340922
345023	XRL	XRL	OC	340123	340223	340323	340423	340523	340623	340723	340823	340923
345024	XRL	XRL	OC	340124	340224	340324	340424	340524	340624	340724	340824	340924
345025	XRL	XRL	OC	340125	340225	340325	340425	340525	340625	340725	340825	340925
345026	XRL	XRL	OC	340126	340226	340326	340426	340526	340626	340726	340826	340926
345027	XRL	XRL	OC	340127	340227	340327	340427	340527	340627	340727	340827	340927
345028	XRL	XRL	OC	340128	340228	340328	340428	340528	340628	340728	340828	340928
345029	XRL	XRL	OC	340129	340229	340329	340429	340529	340629	340729	340829	340929
345030	XRL	XRL	OC	340130	340230	340330	340430	340530	340630	340730	340830	340930
345031	XRL	XRL	OC	340131	340231	340331	340431	340531	340631	340731	340831	340931
345032	XRL	XRL	OC	340132	340232	340332	340432	340532	340632	340732	340832	340932
345033	XRL	XRL	OC	340133	340233	340333	340433	340533	340633	340733	340833	340933
345034	XRL	XRL	OC	340134	340234	340334	340434	340534	340634	340734	340834	340934
345035	XRL	XRL	OC	340135	340235	340335	340435	340535	340635	340735	340835	340935
345036	XRL	XRL	OC	340136	340236	340336	340436	340536	340636	340736	340836	340936
345037	XRL	XRL	OC	340137	340237	340337	340437	340537	340637	340737	340837	340937
345038	XRL	XRL	OC	340138	340238	340338	340438	340538	340638	340738	340838	340938
345039	XRL	XRL	OC	340139	340239	340339	340439	340539	340639	340739	340839	340939

345040	XRL	XRL	OC	340140	340240	340340	340440	340540	340640	340740	340840	340940
345041	XRL	XRL	OC	340141	340241	340341	340441	340541	340641	340741	340841	340941
345042	XRL	XRL	OC	340142	340242	340342	340442	340542	340642	340742	340842	340942
345043	XRL	XRL	OC	340143	340243	340343	340443	340543	340643	340743	340843	340943
345044	XRL	XRL	OC	340144	340244	340344	340444	340544	340644	340744	340844	340944
345045	XRL	XRL	OD(S)	340145	340245	340345	340445	340545	340645	340745	340845	340945
345046	XRL	XRL	OD(S)	340146	340246	340346	340446	340546	340646	340746	340846	340946
345047	XRL	XRL	OC	340147	340247	340347	340447	340547	340647	340747	340847	340947
345048	XRL	XRL	WK(S)	340148	340248	340348	340448	340548	340648	340748	340848	340948
345049	XRL	XRL	OC	340149	340249	340349	340449	340549	340649	340749	340849	340949
345050	XRL	XRL	OC	340150	340250	340350	340450	340550	340650	340750	340850	340950
345051	XRL	XRL	OC	340151	340251	340351	340451	340551	340651	340751	340851	340951
345052	XRL	XRL	OC	340152	340252	340352	340452	340552	340652	340752	340852	340952
345053	XRL	XRL	OC	340153	340253	340353	340453	340553	340653	340753	340853	340953
345054	XRL	XRL	OC	340154	340254	340354	340454	340554	340654	340754	340854	340954
345055	XRL	XRL	OC	340155	340255	340355	340455	340555	340655	340755	340855	340955
345056	XRL	XRL	OC	340156	340256	340356	340456	340556	340656	340756	340856	340956
345057	XRL	XRL	OC	340157	340257	340357	340457	340557	340657	340757	340857	340957
345058	XRL	XRL	OC	340158	340258	340358	340458	340558	340658	340758	340858	340958
345059	XRL	XRL	OC	340159	340259	340359	340459	340559	340659	340759	340859	340959
345060	XRL	XRL	OC	340160	340260	340360	340460	340560	340660	340760	340860	340960
345061	XRL	XRL	OC	340161	340261	340361	340461	340561	340661	340761	340861	340961
345062	XRL	XRL	OC	340162	340262	340362	340462	340562	340662	340762	340862	340962
345063	XRL	XRL	OC	340163	340263	340363	340463	340563	340663	340763	340863	340963
345064	XRL	XRL	OC	340164	340264	340364	340464	340564	340664	340764	340864	340964
345065	XRL	XRL	OC	340165	340265	340365	340465	340565	340665	340765	340865	340965
345066	XRL	XRL	OC	340166	340266	340366	340466	340566	340666	340766	340866	340966
345067	XRL	XRL	OC	340167	340267	340367	340467	340567	340667	340767	340867	340967
345068	XRL	XRL	OC	340168	340268	340368	340468	340568	340668	340768	340868	340968
345069	XRL	XRL	OC	340169	340269	340369	340469	340569	340669	340769	340869	340969
345070	XRL	XRL	OC	340170	340270	340370	340470	340570	340670	340770	340870	340970

On 5 July 2018, running as a seven-car set, 345017, approaches West Ealing with a train for Paddington. *Mark Pike*

East Midlands Railway

Contact details

Website: eastmidlandsrailways.co.uk
Twitter: @EastMidRailway

Key personnel

Managing Director: Will Rogers
Engineering Director: Tony Wrighton

Overview

The routes operated by EMR are the inter-city services from St Pancras to Nottingham, Derby and Sheffield, semi-fast trains from St Pancras to Corby, long-distance regional trains from Liverpool to Norwich and local regional trains from Peterborough-Lincoln/Doncaster, Derby-Skegness, Derby-Matlock, Derby-Crewe, Nottingham-Worksop and Nottingham-Grimsby.

For so long a diesel-only fleet, East Midlands Railway – the new name for the former Stagecoach East Midlands Railway franchise – will soon start operating ex-Greater Anglia Class 360 EMUs on the St Pancras-Corby service following the extension of the electrification of the Midland Main Line north of Bedford.

The company has also recently overhauled its HST fleet, taking many MTU-engined Class 43/2 HST power cars released by the end of their use with LNER on the ECML. These have been acquired to replace VP185-engine 43/0s, which are being returned to their ROSCOs for redeployment or disposal. The move also saw LNER trailer vehicles move to EMR as they had compliant toilets for new legislation.

On the DMU fleet, the single-car Class 153 units are being relinquished. This is made possible by Class 156s arriving from Greater Anglia and Class 170s from both ScotRail and – eventually – West Midlands Trains coming on stream. The latter are dependent on deliveries of Class 196s.

Four ex-Hull Trains Class 180s are also planned to be added to the fleet for bolstering Midland Main Line operations, and this will lead to three different fleets – 180, 222 and HST – on one route. By early September, the 180s had yet to enter service.

The fleet is being reliveried into a new aubergine livery, although some 222s are just having this new colour on their cab ends, while white and purple is the new livery for 156/158s.

Looking ahead, 33 five-car Class 810 Hitachi AT300 bi-mode Aurora multiple units are on order to replace all trains – Class 180s, 222s and HSTs – used on the MML route.

Class 08

Five ex-BR Class 08 shunters, four at Neville Hill and one at Derby Etches Park, were inherited by EMR, although the Leeds-based locos do not see any use presently and have been replaced by hired-in locos. All are in the EMSL pool.

08525	EMT	EMB	NL (S)	*Duncan Bedford*
08690	EMT	EMB	NL (S)	*David Thirkill*
08899	EMT	MID	DY	*Midland Counties Railway 175 Years 1839-2014*
08908	EMT	EMB	NL (S)	*Ivan Stephenson*
08950	EMT	EMB	NL (S)	*David Lightfoot*

Class 43/0

The VP185 Class 43/0 HST power cars are rapidly being returned to their leasing companies and replaced by ex-LNER MTU-powered Class 43/2s. All are in the EMPC pool.

43047	EMB	POR	NL	
43049	EMB	POR	NL	*Neville Hill*
43073	EMB	POR	NL	

Class 43/2

These are MTU-engined HST power cars that were formerly with LNER. All are in the EMPC pool.

43238	43038	LEM	ANG	NL
43251	43051	VEM	POR	NL
43257	43057	VEM	POR	NL
43272	43072	VEM	POR	NL
43274	43074	VEM	POR	NL
43290	43090	VEM	POR	NL
43295	43095	VEM	ANG	NL
43296	43096	VEM	ANG	NL
43299	43099	VEM	POR	NL
43302	43102	VEM	POR	NL
43305	43105	VEM	ANG	NL
43306	43106	VEM	ANG	NL (U)
43307	43107	VEM	ANG	NL
43308	43108	VEM	ANG	NL (U)
43309	43109	VEM	ANG	NL
43310	43110	VEM	ANG	NL
43314	43114	VEM	ANG	NL
43316	43116	VEM	ANG	NL
43317	43117	VEM	ANG	NL
43318	43118	VEM	ANG	NL
43319	43119	VEM	ANG	NL
43320	43120	VEM	ANG	NL

Class 43/4

These are MTU-engined HST power cars which were formerly with Grand Central. All are in the EMPC pool.

43423	43123	EMU	ANG	NL	*VALENTA 1972-2010*
43465	43065	EMU	ANG	NL	
43467	43067	EMU	ANG	NL	*British Transport Police Nottingham / Nottinghamshire Fire and Rescue Service*
43468	43068	EMU	ANG	NL	
43480	43080	EMU	ANG	NL	*West Hampstead PB*
43484	43084	EMU	ANG	NL	

Mk 3 HST trailers

The EMR fleet of HST trailers is a mix of ex-LNER vehicles (in LNE livery) and ex-East Midlands Trains vehicles (in EMW livery). The latter have dispensation to run until 31 December 2020.

Trailer First Buffet TFB			
40204	EMW	ANG	DY
40205	EMW	ANG	DY
40221	EMW	ANG	DY
Trailer Kitchen Buffet First TFKB			
40700	EMW	POR	NL
40701	VEM	POR	NL
40702	VEM	POR	NL
40705	VEM	ANG	NL
40711	VEM	ANG	NL
40730	EMW	POR	NL
40735	VEM	ANG	NL
40737	VEM	ANG	NL
40741	EMW	POR	NL
40746	EMW	POR	NL
40748	VEM	ANG	NL
40749	EMW	POR	NL
40750	VEM	ANG	NL
40753	EMW	POR	NL
40754	EMW	POR	NL
40756	EMW	POR	NL

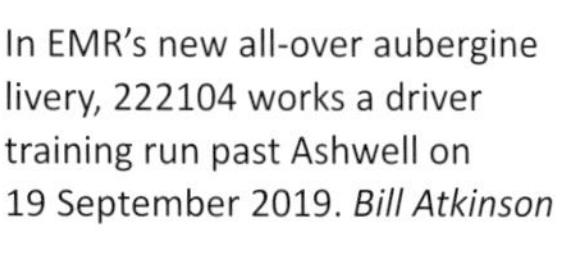

In EMR's new all-over aubergine livery, 222104 works a driver training run past Ashwell on 19 September 2019. *Bill Atkinson*

Trailer First – TF

41039	VEM	ANG	NL
41040	VEM	ANG	NL
41041	EMW	POR	NL
41044	VEM	ANG	NL
41046	EMW	POR	NL
41057	EMW	POR	NL
41061	EMW	POR	NL
41066	VEM	ANG	NL
41067	EMW	POR	NL
41069	EMW	POR	NL
41070	EMW	POR	NL
41071	EMW	POR	NL
41072	EMW	POR	NL
41075	EMW	POR	NL
41076	EMW	POR	NL
41077	EMW	POR	NL
41079	EMW	POR	NL
41084	EMW	POR	NL
41090	VEM	ANG	NL
41095	VEM	POR	NL
41097	VEM	ANG	NL
41098	VEM	ANG	NL
41099	VEM	ANG	NL
41100	VEM	ANG	NL
41111	EMW	POR	NL
41113	EMW	POR	NL
41115	VEM	POR	NL
41117	EMW	POR	NL
41120	VEM	ANG	NL
41150	VEM	ANG	NL
41151	VEM	ANG	NL
41152	VEM	ANG	NL
41156	EMW	POR	NL
41159	VEM	POR	NL
41165	VEM	POR	NL
41185	VEM	POR	NL
41190	VEM	POR	NL
41204	EMW	ANG	DY
41205	EMW	ANG	DY
41206	EMW	ANG	DY
41207	EMW	ANG	DY
41208	EMW	ANG	DY
41209	EMW	ANG	DY

Trailer Standard – TS

42057	VEM	ANG	NL
42058	VEM	ANG	NL
42059	VEM	ANG	NL
42063	VEM	ANG	NL
42064	VEM	ANG	NL
42065	VEM	ANG	NL
42091	VEM	ANG	NL
42100	EMW	POR	NL
42109	VEM	POR	NL
42110	VEM	POR	NL
42111	EMW	POR	NL
42112	EMW	POR	NL
42113	EMW	POR	NL
42116	VEM	ANG	NL
42119	EMW	POR	NL
42120	EMW	POR	NL
42121	EMW	POR	NL
42124	EMW	POR	NL
42127	VEM	ANG	NL
42128	VEM	ANG	NL
42131	EMW	POR	NL
42132	EMW	POR	NL
42133	EMW	POR	NL
42135	EMW	POR	NL
42136	EMW	POR	NL
42137	EMW	POR	NL
42139	EMW	POR	NL
42140	EMW	POR	NL
42141	EMW	POR	NL
42146	VEM	ANG	NL
42148	EMW	POR	NL
42149	EMW	POR	NL
42150	VEM	ANG	NL
42151	EMW	POR	NL
42152	EMW	POR	NL
42153	EMW	POR	NL
42154	VEM	ANG	NL
42155	EMW	POR	NL
42156	EMW	POR	NL
42157	EMW	POR	NL
42159	VEM	POR	NL
42160	VEM	POR	NL
42164	EMW	POR	NL
42165	EMW	POR	NL
42182	VEM	ANG	NL
42186	VEM	ANG	NL
42189	VEM	ANG	NL
42190	VEM	ANG	NL
42191	VEM	ANG	NL
42192	VEM	ANG	NL
42193	VEM	ANG	NL
42198	VEM	ANG	NL
42199	VEM	ANG	NL
42220	EMW	POR	NL
42230	EMW	POR	NL
42238	VEM	ANG	NL
42239	VEM	ANG	NL
42240	VEM	ANG	NL
42307	VEM	POR	NL
42322	VEM	POR	NL
42326	VEM	POR	NL
42327	EMW	POR	NL
42328	EMW	POR	NL
42329	EMW	POR	NL
42330	VEM	POR	NL
42331	EMW	POR	NL
42337	EMW	POR	NL
42339	EMW	POR	NL
42341	EMW	POR	NL
42354	VEM	ANG	NL
42384	EMW	POR	NL
42401	EMW	ANG	DY
42402	EMW	ANG	DY
42404	EMW	ANG	DY
42405	EMW	ANG	DY
42407	EMW	ANG	DY
42408	EMW	ANG	DY
42584	EMW	ANG	DY
42585	EMW	ANG	DY
42586	EMW	ANG	DY

Trailer Guard's standard – TGS

44019	VEM	ANG	NL
44041	EMW	POR	NL
44044	EMW	POR	NL
44045	VEM	ANG	NL
44046	EMW	POR	NL
44047	EMW	POR	NL
44048	EMW	POR	NL
44051	EMW	POR	NL
44054	EMW	POR	NL
44057	VEM	POR	NL
44061	VEM	ANG	NL
44063	VEM	ANG	NL
44070	EMW	POR	NL
44071	EMW	POR	NL
44075	VEM	POR	NL
44077	VEM	ANG	NL
44080	VEM	ANG	NL
44085	EMW	POR	NL
44094	VEM	ANG	NL

EMR HST set formations

NL01-12 are the former EMT sets that are being phased out. DY21-23 are the former Grand Central sets and generally work with the Class 43/4s, while EC51-63 are former LNER sets and usually work with Class 43/2s, although the power cars are interchangeable.

NL01	41057	41084	40730	42327	42111	42112	42113	44041
NL03	41061	41067	40741	42337	42119	42120	42121	44054
NL04	41077	41064	40749	42151	42164	42165	42153	44047
NL06	41156	41041	40746	42132	42131	42331	42133	44046
NL07	41111	41070	40754	42339	42135	42136	42137	44044
NL08	41071	41072	40753	42329	42139	42140	42141	44048
NL10	41075	41076	40756	42328	42341	42148	42149	44051
NL11	41117	41046	40728	42220	42100	42230	42124	44085
NL12	41079	41069	40700	42155	42156	42157	42152	44070
DY21	41207	40205	41206	42408	42584	42585		
DY22	41208	40221	41205	42401	42405	42404		
DY23	41209	40204	41204	42402	42586	42407		
EC51	41120	41150	40748	42091	42146	42150	42154	44094
EC52	41039	41040	40735	42189	42057	42058	42059	44019
EC53	41090	41044	40737	42127	42063	42064	42065	44045
EC57	41151	41152	40740	42128	42182	42186	42190	44080
EC58	41097	41098	40750	42238	42191	42192	42193	44061
EC59	41099	41100	40711	42239	42240	42198	42199	44063
EC61	41115	41165	40702	42159	42160	42109	42110	44057
EC62	41185	41095	40701	42326	42330	42237	42307	44075
Spares	40705	41066	41190	42116	42354	44077		

HST barrier vehicles

6398	81471, 92126	EMR	Mk 1
6399	81367, 92994	EMR	Mk 1

In the old East Midland Trains livery, 158799 passes Attenborough on 31 July 2020. *Paul Robertson*

The new EMT Regional white and aubergine livery, 158773 works the 1554 Norwich-Sheffield past Highdyke on 31 May 2020. *Bill Atkinson*

Class 153

The single-car Class 153s are being replaced by other units. They are currently used on local trains on the EMR network plus on Northern's Barton-on-Humber branch. All are in the EMHQ pool.

				DMSL	
153308	EMT	ANG	NM	52308	
153311	EMT	POR	NM	52311	
153319	EMT	ANG	NM	52319	
153355	EMT	ANG	NM	57355	
153357	EMT	ANG	NM	57357	
153376	EMT	ANG	NM	57376	*X24-Expiditious*
153379	EMT	POR	NM	57379	
153381	EMT	POR	NM	57381	
153383	EMT	POR	NM	57383	*Ecclesbourne Valley Railway 150 Years*
153384	EMT	POR	NM	57384	
153385	EMT	POR	NM	57385	

Class 156

The two-car Class 156 fleet has been strengthened with the addition of nine units cascaded from Greater Anglia. These are renumbered as 156/9s due to modified toilets. All are in the EMHQ pool.

						DMSL	DMS
156401		EMT	POR	EMR	DY	52401	57401
156403		EMT	POR	EMR	DY	52403	57403
156404		EMT	POR	EMR	DY	52404	57404
156405		EMR	POR	EMR	DY	52405	57405
156406		EMR	POR	EMR	DY	52406	57406
156408		EMT	POR	EMR	DY	52408	57408
156410		EMT	POR	EMR	DY	52410	57410
156411		EMB	POR	EMR	DY	52411	57411
156413		EMB	POR	EMR	DY	52413	57413
156414		EMB	POR	EMR	DY	52414	57414
156415		EMT	POR	EMR	DY	52415	57415
156470		EMT	POR	EMR	DY	52470	57470
156473		EMT	POR	EMR	DY	52473	57473
156497		EMT	POR	EMR	DY	52497	57497
156498		EMT	POR	EMR	DY	52498	57498
156902	156402	WHI	POR	EMR	DY	52402	57402
156907	156407	EMR	POR	EMR	DY	52407	57407
156909	156409	EMR	POR	EMR	DY	52409	57409
156912	156412	EMR	POR	EMR	DY	52412	57412
156916	156416	EMR	POR	EMR	DY	52416	57416
156917	156417	EMR	POR	EMR	DY	52417	57417
156918	156418	EMR	POR	EMR	DY	52418	57418
156919	156419	EMR	POR	EMR	DY	52419	57419
156922	156422	EMR	POR	EMR	DY	52422	57422

Class 158

Currently used for Liverpool to Norwich services, plus other EMR secondary workings as required. All are in the EMHQ pool.

				DMSL	DMSL	
158770	EMW	POR	NM	52770	57770	
158773	EMR	POR	NM	52773	57773	
158774	WHI	POR	NM	52774	57774	
158777	EMW	POR	NM	52777	57777	
158780	EMW	ANG	NM	52783	57783	
158783	EMW	ANG	NM	52783	57783	
158785	EMW	ANG	NM	52785	57785	
158788	EMW	ANG	NM	52788	57788	
158799	EMW	POR	NM	52799	57799	
158806	EMW	POR	NM	52806	57806	
158810	EMW	POR	NM	52810	57810	
158812	EMW	POR	NM	52812	57812	
158813	EMW	POR	NM	52813	57813	
158846	EMW	ANG	NM	52846	57846	
158847	EMW	ANG	NM	52847	57847	*Lincoln Castle Explorer*
158852	EMW	ANG	NM	52852	57852	
158854	EMW	ANG	NM	52854	57854	*The Station Volunteer*
158856	EMW	ANG	NM	52856	57856	
158857	EMW	ANG	NM	52857	57857	
158858	EMW	ANG	NM	52858	57858	
158862	EMW	ANG	NM	52862	57862	
158863	EMW	ANG	NM	52863	57863	
158864	EMW	ANG	NM	52864	57864	
158865	EMW	ANG	NM	52865	57865	
158866	EMW	ANG	NM	52866	57866	
158889	EMW	POR	NM	52808	57808	

Class 170

Several Turbostar units are due to move from ScotRail and West Midlands Trains. The former – Class 170/4s – are spare from enhanced electrification north of the border and the latter – Class 170/5 and 170/6s – are displaced by new CAF Class 196 DMUs. The 170/6s were three-car units but the centre cars will be removed and redeployed with Cross Country Trains. All are in the EDHQ pool.

Unit	Livery	Owner	Depot	DMCL	MS	DMCL
170416	EMP	EVS	DY	50416	56416	79416
170417	EMP	EVS	DY	50417	56417	79417
170418	EMP	EVS	DY	50418	56418	79418
170419	EMP	EVS	BH (S)	50419	56419	79419
170420	EMP	EVS	DY	50420	56420	79420

Opposite top: No. 222023 passes Sawley on 21 July 2020. The unit is in the old EMT livery. *Paul Robertson*

Bottom: Ex-Grand Central 43467 passes Attenborough on 6 August 2020. *Paul Robertson*

Class 180

The fours 'spare' Adelante units are due to be added to the EMR operational fleet. All are in the EDHQ pool.

				DMSL	MFL	MSL	MSLRB	DMSL
180109	EMR	ANG	DY	50909	54909	55909	56909	59909
180110	EMR	ANG	DY	50910	54910	55910	56910	59910
180111	EMR	ANG	DY	50911	54911	55911	56911	59911
180113	FIR	ANG	DY	50913	54913	55913	56913	59913

Class 222

Based on the Bombardier Class 220 Voyager units, the Meridians were ordered by Midland Mainline and delivered in 2003-05. Initially there were seven nine-cars and 16 four-car sets but all have been re-formed now so the fleet is a mix of five- and seven-cars as well as the four-car ex-Hull Trains Class 222/1s. All are in the EMHQ pool.

Class 222/0

These were delivered as nine-car sets 222001-007 and four-car sets 222008-023 but re-formation of the vehicles has created six seven-car sets and 17 five-car sets.

				DMF	MF/MC	MF	MSRMB	MS	MS	DMS	
222001	EMW	EVS	DY	60241	60445	60341	60621	60561	60551	60161	*The Entrepreneur Express*
222002	EMW	EVS	DY	60242	60346	60342	60622	60562	60544	60162	*The Cutlers' Company*
222003	EMW	EVS	DY	60243	60446	60343	60623	60563	60553	60163	*Tornado*
222004	EMR	EVS	DY	60244	60345	60344	60624	60564	60554	60164	*Children's Hospital Sheffield*
222005	EMW	EVS	DY	60245	60347	60443	60625	60555	60565	60165	
222006	EMR	EVS	DY	60246	60447	60441	60626	60566	60556	60166	*The Carbon Cutter*
222007	EMW	EVS	DY	60247	60442		60627		60567	60167	
222008	EMW	EVS	DY	60248	60918		60628		60545	60168	*Derby Etches Park*
222009	EMR	EVS	DY	60249	60919		60629		60557	60169	
222010	EMR	EVS	DY	60250	60920		60630		60546	60170	
222011	EMR	EVS	DY	60251	60921		60631		60531	60171	
222012	EMR	EVS	DY	60252	60922		60632		60532	60172	
222013	EMW	EVS	DY	60253	60923		60633		60533	60173	
222014	EMR	EVS	DY	60254	60924		60634		60534	60174	
222015	EMW	EVS	DY	60255	60925		60635		60535	60175	*175 years of Derby's Railways 1839-2014*
222016	EMW	EVS	DY	60256	60926		60636		60536	60176	
222017	EMW	EVS	DY	60257	60927		60637		60537	60177	*Lions Club International Centenary 1917-2017*
222018	EMR	EVS	DY	60258	60928		60638		60444	60178	
222019	EMW	EVS	DY	60259	60929		60639		60547	60179	
222020	EMW	EVS	DY	60260	60930		60640		60543	60180	
222021	EMW	EVS	DY	60261	60931		60641		60552	60181	
222022	EMR	EVS	DY	60262	60932		60642		60542	60182	*Invest in Nottingham*
222023	EMW	EVS	DY	60263	60933		60643		60541	60167	

Ex-LNER 43318 and 43257 work the 1C43 1053 Leeds-St Pancras past Wing on 5 July 2020. *Anthony Hicks*

Class 222/1

Former Hull Trains four-car sets.

222101	EMR	EVS	DY	60271	60571	60681	60191
222102	EMW	EVS	DY	60272	60572	60682	60192
222103	EMW	EVS	DY	60273	60573	60683	60193
222104	EMP	EVS	DY	60274	60574	60684	60194

Future stock

The fleet of 21 four-car Class 360s are due to join EMR. The company also has 33 five-car bi-mode Class 810 Hitachi AT300 Aurora units on order for delivery in 2023, financed through Rock Rail.

EMR Regional unbranded blue 156414 works the 1245 Nottingham-Skegness past Elton & Orston on 24 June 2020. *Bill Atkinson*

Govia Thameslink Railway

Contact details

Websites: www.thameslinkrailway.com; www.southernrailway.com; www.greatnorthernrail.com; www.gatwickexpress.com
Twitter: @GNRailUK, @SouthernRailUK, @TLRailUK, @GatwickExpress

Key personnel

Chief Executive Officer: Patrick Verwer
Chief Operating Officer: Steve White
Managing Directors:
Southern & Gatwick Express – Angie Doll; Thameslink & Great Northern – Tom Moran
Engineering Director: Steve Lammin

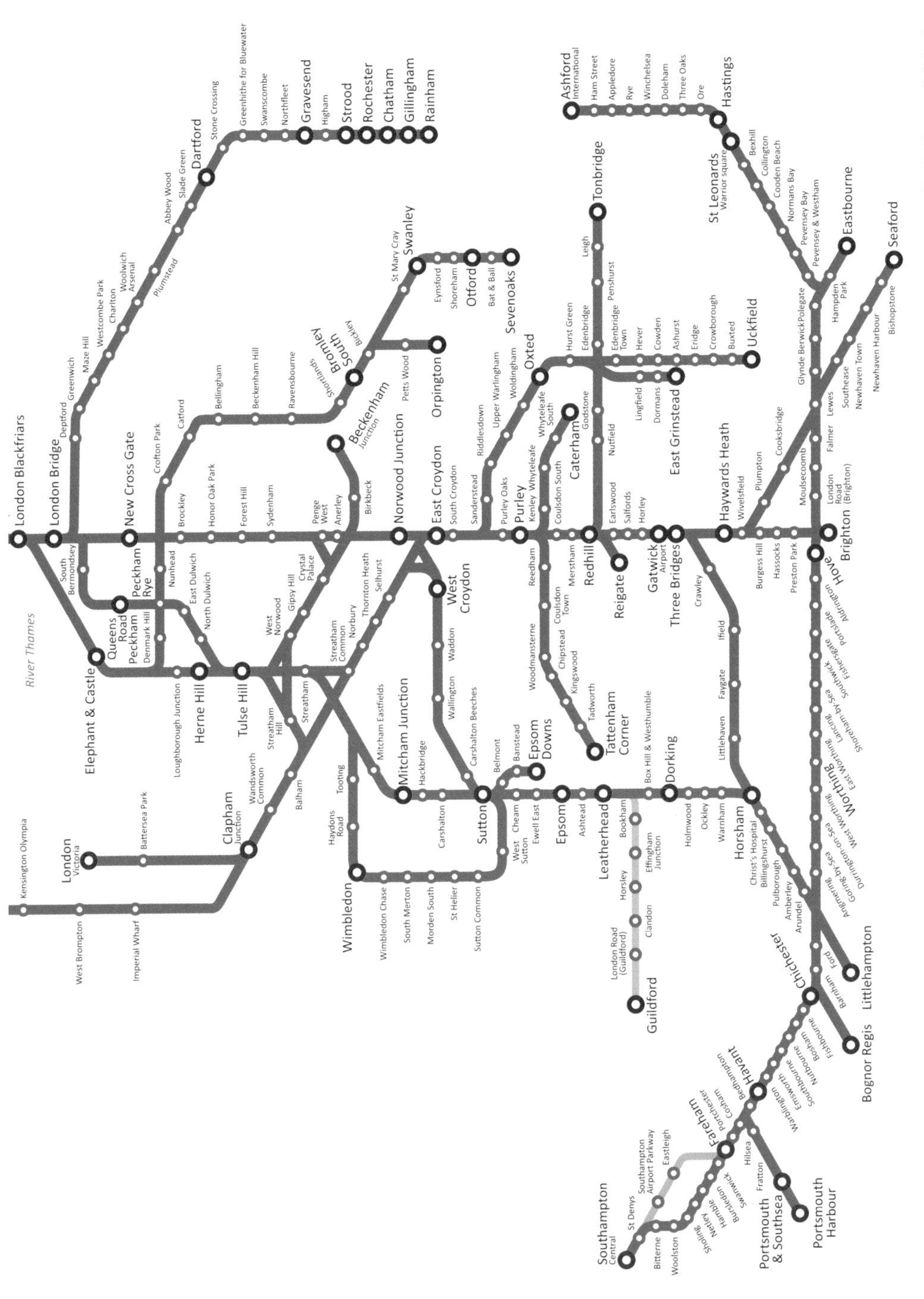
Govia Thameslink Railway
River Thames
London Blackfriars
London Bridge
New Cross Gate
Elephant & Castle
Queens Road Peckham
Peckham Rye
South Bermondsey
Denmark Hill
Nunhead
East Dulwich
North Dulwich
Loughborough Junction
Herne Hill
Tulse Hill
Brockley
Honor Oak Park
Forest Hill
Sydenham
Penge West
Anerley
Birkbeck
Beckenham Junction
Norwood Junction
East Croydon
South Croydon
West Croydon
Crystal Palace
Gipsy Hill
West Norwood
Streatham Hill
Streatham
Streatham Common
Norbury
Thornton Heath
Selhurst
London Victoria
Battersea Park
Clapham Junction
Wandsworth Common
Balham
Kensington Olympia
West Brompton
Imperial Wharf
Wimbledon
Haydons Road
Tooting
Mitcham Eastfields
Mitcham Junction
Hackbridge
Wimbledon Chase
South Merton
Morden South
St Helier
Sutton Common
West Sutton
Sutton
Carshalton
Carshalton Beeches
Wallington
Waddon
Cheam
Ewell East
Belmont
Banstead
Epsom Downs
Epsom
Ashtead
Leatherhead
Bookham
Effingham Junction
Horsley
Clandon
London Road (Guildford)
Guildford
Box Hill & Westhumble
Dorking
Holmwood
Ockley
Warnham
Horsham
Littlehaven
Faygate
Ifield
Crawley
Three Bridges
Gatwick Airport
Horley
Salfords
Earlswood
Redhill
Reigate
Merstham
Coulsdon South
Coulsdon Town
Reedham
Woodmansterne
Chipstead
Kingswood
Tadworth
Tattenham Corner
Purley
Purley Oaks
Kenley
Whyteleafe
Whyteleafe South
Caterham
Sanderstead
Riddlesdown
Upper Warlingham
Woldingham
Oxted
Hurst Green
Edenbridge
Edenbridge Town
Hever
Cowden
Ashurst
Eridge
Crowborough
Buxted
Uckfield
Lingfield
Dormans
East Grinstead
Nutfield
Godstone
Penshurst
Leigh
Tonbridge
Deptford
Greenwich
Maze Hill
Westcombe Park
Charlton
Woolwich Arsenal
Plumstead
Abbey Wood
Slade Green
Dartford
Stone Crossing
Greenhithe for Bluewater
Swanscombe
Northfleet
Gravesend
Higham
Strood
Rochester
Chatham
Gillingham
Rainham
Crofton Park
Catford
Bellingham
Beckenham Hill
Ravensbourne
Shortlands
Bromley South
Bickley
Petts Wood
Orpington
St Mary Cray
Swanley
Eynsford
Shoreham
Otford
Bat & Ball
Sevenoaks
Ashford International
Ham Street
Appledore
Rye
Winchelsea
Doleham
Three Oaks
Ore
Hastings
St Leonards Warrior square
Bexhill
Collington
Cooden Beach
Normans Bay
Pevensey Bay
Pevensey & Westham
Eastbourne
Hampden Park
Polegate
Glynde
Berwick
Lewes
Southease
Newhaven Town
Newhaven Harbour
Bishopstone
Seaford
Falmer
Moulsecoomb
London Road (Brighton)
Brighton
Cooksbridge
Plumpton
Wivelsfield
Haywards Heath
Burgess Hill
Hassocks
Preston Park
Hove
Aldrington
Portslade
Fishersgate
Southwick
Shoreham-by-Sea
Lancing
East Worthing
Worthing
West Worthing
Durrington-on-Sea
Goring-by-Sea
Angmering
Littlehampton
Ford
Arundel
Amberley
Pulborough
Billingshurst
Christ's Hospital
Barnham
Bognor Regis
Chichester
Fishbourne
Bosham
Nutbourne
Southbourne
Emsworth
Warblington
Havant
Bedhampton
Cosham
Portchester
Fareham
Hilsea
Fratton
Portsmouth & Southsea
Portsmouth Harbour
Swanwick
Bursledon
Hamble
Netley
Sholing
Woolston
Bitterne
St Denys
Southampton Central
Southampton Airport Parkway
Eastleigh

Overview

This 'super franchise' is the amalgamation of the Southern, Great Northern, Gatwick Express and Thameslink operations, which has led to a huge TOC. The 'separate' operations do keep their former identities to a degree – such as websites and Twitter.

On the Great Northern lines the franchise runs from Peterborough and King's Lynn to King's Cross and also local commuter trains out of Moorgate to Hitchin. The former Southern operations are Victoria or London Bridge to Portsmouth Harbour and Southampton Central, Littlehampton, Horsham via Epsom or Gatwick Airport, Epsom Downs, Tattenham Corner, Reigate, Brighton, Seaford, Eastbourne, East Grinstead, Uckfield and Caterham, plus Redhill-Tonbridge, Ashford International-Eastbourne, and Milton Keynes-Clapham Junction, the latter route requiring dual-voltage EMUs

The Thameslink network links Bedford, Cambridge and Peterborough in the north to Sutton, Rainham (Kent), Brighton, Orpington, Sevenoaks, East Grinstead, Horsham and Littlehampton.

Finally, the franchise incorporates the former InterCity Gatwick Express operation, but instead of just being a Victoria to Gatwick shuttle, this is now a Victoria to Brighton service and uses Class 387/2s.

It has a fleet that mostly comprises of EMUs – with Class 700s on the Thameslink and Great Northern trains and Class 377s on the former Southern duties – but there are diesel units – Class 171 Turbostars – used on the non-electrified lines to Uckfield and Ashford to Hastings.

Other fleets are Class 313/2s, which work local services out of Brighton, while a handful of Class 365s, some of the last trains built for BR, BREL York-built four-car Networker units, remain in traffic owned by the DfT and used on the Great Northern line from King's Cross to Peterborough. Some 365s were briefly moved to Scotland to act as cover for delayed new train, but they have all been taken off lease now. They work alongside Class 387/1s, on the King's Cross-Peterborough/King's Lynn services. Class 717s – a metro version of the Class 700s – have replaced the ageing Class 313/0s in recent times. Some 455s area also retained for local trains in London.

Class 73

Southern has one ex Gatwick Express Class 73/2 loco that sees occasional use as a Thunderbird or route-learning loco. It is in the MBED pool.

73202	SOU	POR	SL	*Graham Stenning*

Class 171

These Bombardier Turbostars, which differ from Class 170s by having a different coupling system (Dellner). The fleet has been bolstered by the recent acquisition of four units from ScotRail. All are in the ETHQ pool.

Class 171/2

Ex-ScotRail units re-formed from three- to two-car sets.

	Old No				DMOCL(W)	DMOSL
171201	170421	SOU	EVS	SU	50421	79421
171202	170423	SOU	EVS	SU	50423	79423

Class 171/4

Ex-ScotRail units re-formed from three- to four-car sets.

	Old No				DMOCL(W)	MOS	MOS	DMOCL
171401	170422	SOU	EVS	SU	50422	56421	56422	79422
171402	170424	SOU	EVS	SU	50424	56423	56424	79424

Class 171/7

Two-car sets. Delivered as 170/7s and renumbered to 171/7s when fitted with Dellner couplers.

	Old No				DMOCL(W)	DMOSL
171721	170721	SOU	POR	SU	50721	79721
171722	170722	SOU	POR	SU	50722	79722
171723	170723	SOU	POR	SU	50723	79723
171724	170724	SOU	POR	SU	50724	79724
171725	170725	SOU	POR	SU	50725	79725
171726	170726	SOU	POR	SU	50726	79726
171727		SOU	POR	SU	50727	79727
171728		SOU	POR	SU	50728	79728
171729		SOU	POR	SU	50729	79729
171730	170392	SOU	POR	SU	50392	79392

Class 171/8

Four-car sets.

				DMOCL(W)	MOS	MOS	DMOCL
171801	SOU	POR	SU	50801	54801	56801	79801
171802	SOU	POR	SU	50802	54802	56802	79802
171803	SOU	POR	SU	50803	54803	56803	79803
171804	SOU	POR	SU	50804	54804	56804	79804
171805	SOU	POR	SU	50805	54805	56805	79805
171806	SOU	POR	SU	50806	54806	56806	79806

Class 313

These ex-BR three-car 750V DC units. All are in the ETHQ pool.

	Old No.				DMS	TS	BDMS
313201	313101	BRG	BEA	BI	62529	71213	62593
313202	313102	SOU	BEA	BI	62530	71214	62594
313203	313103	SOU	BEA	BI	62531	71215	62595
313204	313104	SOU	BEA	BI	62532	71216	62596
313205	313105	SOU	BEA	BI	62533	71217	62597
313206	313106	SOU	BEA	BI	62534	71218	62598
313207	313107	SOU	BEA	BI	62535	71219	62599
313208	313108	SOU	BEA	BI	62536	71220	62600
313209	313109	SOU	BEA	BI	62537	71221	62601
313210	313110	SOU	BEA	BI	62538	71222	62602
313211	313111	SOU	BEA	BI	62539	71223	62603
313212	313112	SOU	BEA	BI	62540	71224	62604
313213	313113	SOU	BEA	BI	62541	71225	62605
313214	313114	SOU	BEA	BI	62542	71226	62606
313215	313115	SOU	BEA	BI	62543	71227	62607
313216	313116	SOU	BEA	BI	62544	71228	62608
313217	313117	SOU	BEA	BI	62545	71229	62609
313219	313119	SOU	BEA	BI	62547	71231	62611
313220	313120	SOU	BEA	BI	62548	71232	62612

Class 365

Other units remain in warm store, also owned by the DfT and are available for reuse if required. No. 365526 was written off in 2002. All are in the ETHQ pool.

				DMC	TS	PTS	DMC
365502	TLK	DFT	HE	65895	72243	72242	65936
365504	TLK	DFT	HE	65897	72247	72246	65938
365506	TLK	DFT	HE	65899	72251	72250	65940
365508	TLK	DFT	HE	65901	72255	72254	65942
365510	TLK	DFT	HE	65903	72259	72258	65944
365511	TLK	DFT	HE	65904	72261	72260	65945
365512	TLK	DFT	HE	65905	72263	72262	65946
365514	TLK	DFT	HE	65907	72267	72266	65948
365516	TLK	DFT	HE	65909	72271	72270	65950
365518	TLK	DFT	HE	65911	72275	72274	65952
365520	TLK	DFT	HE	65913	72279	72278	65954
365522	TLK	DFT	HE	65915	72283	72282	65956
365524	TLK	DFT	HE	65917	72287	72286	65958
365528	TLK	DFT	HE	65921	72295	72294	65962
365530	TLK	DFT	HE	65923	72299	72298	65964
365532	TLK	DFT	HE	65925	72303	72302	65966
365534	TLK	DFT	HE	65927	72307	72306	65968
365536	TLK	DFT	HE	65929	72311	72310	65970
365538	TLK	DFT	HE	65931	72315	72314	65972
365539	TLK	DFT	HE	65932	72317	72316	65973
365540	TLK	DFT	HE	65933	72319	72318	65974

Class 377

Bombardier Electrostar units work on the former Southern routes on commuter trains across the south of England. They are a mix of three-, four- and five-car units and some have dual-voltage capability for working to Milton Keynes. All are in the ETHQ pool.

Class 377/1

750V DC units

				DMOS	MOS	PTOSL	DMOS
377101	SOU	POR	SU	78501	77101	78901	78701
377102	SOU	POR	SU	78502	77102	78902	78702
377103	SOU	POR	SU	78503	77103	78903	78703
377104	SOU	POR	SU	78504	77104	78904	78704
377105	SOU	POR	SU	78505	77105	78905	78705
377106	SOU	POR	SU	78506	77106	78906	78706
377107	SOU	POR	SU	78507	77107	78907	78707
377108	SOU	POR	SU	78508	77108	78908	78708
377109	SOU	POR	SU	78509	77109	78909	78709
377110	SOU	POR	SU	78510	77110	78910	78710
377111	SOU	POR	SU	78511	77111	78911	78711
377112	SOU	POR	SU	78512	77112	78912	78712

377113	SOU	POR	SU	78513	77113	78913	78713
377114	SOU	POR	SU	78514	77114	78914	78714
377115	SOU	POR	SU	78515	77115	78915	78715
377116	SOU	POR	SU	78516	77116	78916	78716
377117	SOU	POR	SU	78517	77117	78917	78717
377118	SOU	POR	SU	78518	77118	78918	78718
377119	SOU	POR	SU	78519	77119	78919	78719
377120	SOU	POR	SU	78520	77120	78920	78720
377121	SOU	POR	SU	78521	77121	78921	78721
377122	SOU	POR	SU	78522	77122	78922	78722
377123	SOU	POR	SU	78523	77123	78923	78723
377124	SOU	POR	SU	78524	77124	78924	78724
377125	SOU	POR	SU	78525	77125	78925	78725
377126	SOU	POR	SU	78526	77126	78926	78726
377127	SOU	POR	SU	78527	77127	78927	78727
377128	SOU	POR	SU	78528	77128	78928	78728
377129	SOU	POR	SU	78529	77129	78929	78729
377130	SOU	POR	SU	78530	77130	78930	78730
377131	SOU	POR	SU	78531	77131	78931	78731
377132	SOU	POR	SU	78532	77132	78932	78732
377133	SOU	POR	SU	78533	77133	78933	78733
377134	SOU	POR	SU	78534	77134	78934	78734
377135	SOU	POR	SU	78535	77135	78935	78735
377136	SOU	POR	SU	78536	77136	78936	78736
377137	SOU	POR	SU	78537	77137	78937	78737
377138	SOU	POR	SU	78538	77138	78938	78738
377139	SOU	POR	SU	78539	77139	78939	78739
377140	SOU	POR	SU	78540	77140	78940	78740
377141	SOU	POR	SU	78541	77141	78941	78741
377142	SOU	POR	SU	78542	77142	78942	78742
377143	SOU	POR	SU	78543	77143	78943	78743
377144	SOU	POR	SU	78544	77144	78944	78744
377145	SOU	POR	SU	78545	77145	78945	78745
377146	SOU	POR	SU	78546	77146	78946	78746
377147	SOU	POR	SU	78547	77147	78947	78747
377148	SOU	POR	SU	78548	77148	78948	78748
377149	SOU	POR	SU	78549	77149	78949	78749
377150	SOU	POR	SU	78550	77150	78950	78750
377151	SOU	POR	SU	78551	77151	78951	78751
377152	SOU	POR	SU	78552	77152	78952	78752
377153	SOU	POR	SU	78553	77153	78953	78753
377154	SOU	POR	SU	78554	77154	78954	78754
377155	SOU	POR	SU	78555	77155	78955	78755
377156	SOU	POR	SU	78556	77156	78956	78756
377157	SOU	POR	SU	78557	77157	78957	78757
377158	SOU	POR	SU	78558	77158	78958	78758
377159	SOU	POR	SU	78559	77159	78959	78759
377160	SOU	POR	SU	78560	77160	78960	78760
377161	SOU	POR	SU	78561	77161	78961	78761
377162	SOU	POR	SU	78562	77162	78962	78762

Class 377/2

Dual-voltage units.

			DMOS	MOSL	PTOSL	DMOS	
377201	SOU	POR	SU	78571	77171	78971	78771
377202	SOU	POR	SU	78572	77172	78972	78772
377203	SOU	POR	SU	78573	77173	78973	78773
377204	SOU	POR	SU	78574	77174	78974	78774
377205	SOU	POR	SU	78575	77175	78975	78775
377206	SOU	POR	SU	78576	77176	78976	78776
377207	SOU	POR	SU	78577	77177	78977	78777
377208	SOU	POR	SU	78578	77178	78978	78778
377209	SOU	POR	SU	78579	77179	78979	78779
377210	SOU	POR	SU	78580	77180	78980	78780
377211	SOU	POR	SU	78581	77181	78981	78781
377212	SOU	POR	SU	78582	77182	78982	78782
377213	SOU	POR	SU	78583	77183	78983	78783
377214	SOU	POR	SU	78584	77184	78984	78784
377215	SOU	POR	SU	78585	77185	78985	78785

Turbostar DMU 171723 works the 1733 Ashford International-Brighton past Rye on 9 May 2018. *Anthony Hicks*

Class 377/3

750V DC units.

					DMOS	PTOSL	DMOC
377301	375301	SOU	POR	SU	68201	74801	68401
377302	375302	SOU	POR	SU	68202	74802	68402
377303	375303	SOU	POR	SU	68203	74803	68403
377304	375304	SOU	POR	SU	68204	74804	68404
377305	375305	SOU	POR	SU	68205	74805	68405
377306	375306	SOU	POR	SU	68206	74806	68406
377307	375307	SOU	POR	SU	68207	74807	68407
377308	375308	SOU	POR	SU	68208	74808	68408
377309	375309	SOU	POR	SU	68209	74809	68409
377310	375310	SOU	POR	SU	68210	74810	68410
377311	375311	SOU	POR	SU	68211	74811	68411
377312	375312	SOU	POR	SU	68212	74812	68412
377313	375313	SOU	POR	SU	68213	74813	68413
377314	375314	SOU	POR	SU	68214	74814	68414
377315	375315	SOU	POR	SU	68215	74815	68415
377316	375316	SOU	POR	SU	68216	74816	68416
377317	375317	SOU	POR	SU	68217	74817	68417
377318	375318	SOU	POR	SU	68218	74818	68418
377319	375319	SOU	POR	SU	68219	74819	68419
377320	375320	SOU	POR	SU	68220	74820	68420
377321	375321	SOU	POR	SU	68221	74821	68421
377322	375322	SOU	POR	SU	68222	74822	68422
377323	375323	SOU	POR	SU	68223	74823	68423
377324	375324	SOU	POR	SU	68224	74824	68424
377325	375325	SOU	POR	SU	68225	74825	68425
377326	375326	SOU	POR	SU	68226	74826	68426
377327	375327	SOU	POR	SU	68227	74827	68427
377328	375328	SOU	POR	SU	68228	74828	68428
377342	377442	SOU	POR	SU	73442	78642	73842

Note: No. 377342 is 377442 with MOSL 78842 removed following fire damage. This unit is expected to be re-formed as 377442 at the end of 2020.

Inner suburban ex-BREL unit 455802 passes Hackbridge on 25 August 2017.
Paul Winter

Class 377/4

750V DC units. Vehicle 78842 was removed from 377442 following fire damage. The unit was re-formed as three-car 377342 while repairs were undertaken.

				DMOS	MSOL	PTOSL	DMS
377401	SOU	POR	SU	73401	78801	78601	73801
377402	SOU	POR	SU	73402	78802	78602	73802
377403	SOU	POR	SU	73403	78803	78603	73803
377404	SOU	POR	SU	73404	78804	78604	73804
377405	SOU	POR	SU	73405	78805	78605	73805
377406	SOU	POR	SU	73406	78806	78606	73806
377407	SOU	POR	SU	73407	78807	78607	73807
377408	SOU	POR	SU	73408	78808	78608	73808
377409	SOU	POR	SU	73409	78809	78609	73809
377410	SOU	POR	SU	73410	78810	78610	73810
377411	SOU	POR	SU	73411	78811	78611	73811
377412	SOU	POR	SU	73412	78812	78612	73812
377413	SOU	POR	SU	73413	78813	78613	73813
377414	SOU	POR	SU	73414	78814	78614	73814
377415	SOU	POR	SU	73415	78815	78615	73815
377416	SOU	POR	SU	73416	78816	78616	73816
377417	SOU	POR	SU	73417	78817	78617	73817
377418	SOU	POR	SU	73418	78818	78618	73818
377419	SOU	POR	SU	73419	78819	78619	73819
377420	SOU	POR	SU	73420	78820	78620	73820
377421	SOU	POR	SU	73421	78821	78621	73821
377422	SOU	POR	SU	73422	78822	78622	73822
377423	SOU	POR	SU	73423	78823	78623	73823
377424	SOU	POR	SU	73424	78824	78624	73824
377425	SOU	POR	SU	73425	78825	78625	73825
377426	SOU	POR	SU	73426	78826	78626	73826
377427	SOU	POR	SU	73427	78827	78627	73827
377428	SOU	POR	SU	73428	78828	78628	73828
377429	SOU	POR	SU	73429	78829	78629	73829
377430	SOU	POR	SU	73430	78830	78630	73830
377431	SOU	POR	SU	73431	78831	78631	73831
377432	SOU	POR	SU	73432	78832	78632	73832
377433	SOU	POR	SU	73433	78833	78633	73833
377434	SOU	POR	SU	73434	78834	78634	73834
377435	SOU	POR	SU	73435	78835	78635	73835
377436	SOU	POR	SU	73436	78836	78636	73836
377437	SOU	POR	SU	73437	78837	78637	73837
377438	SOU	POR	SU	73438	78838	78638	73838
377439	SOU	POR	SU	73439	78839	78639	73839
377440	SOU	POR	SU	73440	78840	78640	73840
377441	SOU	POR	SU	73441	78841	78641	73841
377443	SOU	POR	SU	73443	78843	78643	73843
377444	SOU	POR	SU	73444	78844	78644	73844
377445	SOU	POR	SU	73445	78845	78645	73845

377446	SOU	POR	SU	73446	78846	78646	73846
377447	SOU	POR	SU	73447	78847	78647	73847
377448	SOU	POR	SU	73448	78848	78648	73848
377449	SOU	POR	SU	73449	78849	78649	73849
377450	SOU	POR	SU	73450	78850	78650	73850
377451	SOU	POR	SU	73451	78851	78651	73851
377452	SOU	POR	SU	73452	78852	78652	73852
377453	SOU	POR	SU	73453	78853	78653	73853
377454	SOU	POR	SU	73454	78854	78654	73854
377455	SOU	POR	SU	73455	78855	78655	73855
377456	SOU	POR	SU	73456	78856	78656	73856
377457	SOU	POR	SU	73457	78857	78657	73857
377458	SOU	POR	SU	73458	78858	78658	73858
377459	SOU	POR	SU	73459	78859	78659	73859
377460	SOU	POR	SU	73460	78860	78660	73860
377461	SOU	POR	SU	73461	78861	78661	73861
377462	SOU	POR	SU	73462	78862	78662	73862
377463	SOU	POR	SU	73463	78863	78663	73863
377464	SOU	POR	SU	73464	78864	78664	73864
377465	SOU	POR	SU	73465	78865	78665	73865
377466	SOU	POR	SU	73466	78866	78666	73866
377467	SOU	POR	SU	73467	78867	78667	73867
377468	SOU	POR	SU	73468	78868	78668	73868
377469	SOU	POR	SU	73469	78869	78669	73869
377470	SOU	POR	SU	73470	78870	78670	73870
377471	SOU	POR	SU	73471	78871	78671	73871
377472	SOU	POR	SU	73472	78872	78672	73872
377473	SOU	POR	SU	73473	78873	78673	73873
377474	SOU	POR	SU	73474	78874	78674	73874
377475	SOU	POR	SU	73475	78875	78675	73875
Spare	SOU	POR	SU		78842		

On 24 March 2018, Electrostar 377451 stands at Bognor Regis. *Pip Dunn*

Class 377/6

750V DC units.

				DMOS	MOSL	PTOSL	MOS	DMOS
377601	SOU	POR	SU	70101	70201	70301	70401	70501
377602	SOU	POR	SU	70102	70202	70302	70402	70502
377603	SOU	POR	SU	70103	70203	70303	70403	70503
377604	SOU	POR	SU	70104	70204	70304	70404	70504
377605	SOU	POR	SU	70105	70205	70305	70405	70505
377606	SOU	POR	SU	70106	70206	70306	70406	70506
377607	SOU	POR	SU	70107	70207	70307	70407	70507
377608	SOU	POR	SU	70108	70208	70308	70408	70508
377609	SOU	POR	SU	70109	70209	70309	70409	70509
377610	SOU	POR	SU	70110	70210	70310	70410	70510
377611	SOU	POR	SU	70111	70211	70311	70411	70511
377612	SOU	POR	SU	70112	70212	70312	70412	70512
377613	SOU	POR	SU	70113	70213	70313	70413	70513
377614	SOU	POR	SU	70114	70214	70314	70414	70514
377615	SOU	POR	SU	70115	70215	70315	70415	70515
377616	SOU	POR	SU	70116	70216	70316	70416	70516
377617	SOU	POR	SU	70117	70217	70317	70417	70517
377618	SOU	POR	SU	70118	70218	70318	70418	70518
377619	SOU	POR	SU	70119	70219	70319	70419	70519
377620	SOU	POR	SU	70120	70220	70320	70420	70520
377621	SOU	POR	SU	70121	70221	70321	70421	70521
377622	SOU	POR	SU	70122	70222	70322	70422	70522
377623	SOU	POR	SU	70123	70223	70323	70423	70523
377624	SOU	POR	SU	70124	70224	70324	70424	70524
377625	SOU	POR	SU	70125	70225	70325	70425	70525
377626	SOU	POR	SU	70126	70226	70326	70426	70526

Class 377/7

Dual-voltage units.

				DMOS	MOSL	PTOSL	MOS	DMOS
377701	SOU	POR	SU	65201	70601	65601	70701	65401
377702	SOU	POR	SU	65202	70602	65602	70702	65402
377703	SOU	POR	SU	65203	70603	65603	70703	65403
377704	SOU	POR	SU	65204	70604	65604	70704	65404
377705	SOU	POR	SU	65205	70605	65605	70705	65405
377706	SOU	POR	SU	65206	70606	65606	70706	65406
377707	SOU	POR	SU	65207	70607	65607	70707	65407
377708	SOU	POR	SU	65208	70608	65608	70708	65408

Class 387

Later version of the Bombardier Electrostar platform, but capable of 110mph. All are in the ETHQ pool.

Class 387/1

Dual voltage four car units used on the King's Cross to King's Lynn and Peterborough routes.

				DMOS	MOSL	PTOSL	MOS	
387101	TLK	POR	HE	421101	422101	423101	424101	
387102	TLK	POR	HE	421102	422102	423102	424102	
387103	TLK	POR	HE	421103	422103	423103	424103	
387104	TLK	POR	HE	421104	422104	423104	424104	
387105	TLK	POR	HE	421105	422105	423105	424105	
387106	TLK	POR	HE	421106	422106	423106	424106	
387107	TLK	POR	HE	421107	422107	423107	424107	
387108	TLK	POR	HE	421108	422108	423108	424108	
387109	TLK	POR	HE	421109	422109	423109	424109	
387110	TLK	POR	HE	421110	422110	423110	424110	
387111	TLK	POR	HE	421111	422111	423111	424111	
387112	TLK	POR	HE	421112	422112	423112	424112	
387113	TLK	POR	HE	421113	422113	423113	424113	
387114	TLK	POR	HE	421114	422114	423114	424114	
387115	TLK	POR	HE	421115	422115	423115	424115	
387116	TLK	POR	HE	421116	422116	423116	424116	
387117	TLK	POR	HE	421117	422117	423117	424117	
387118	TLK	POR	HE	421118	422118	423118	424118	
387119	TLK	POR	HE	421119	422119	423119	424119	
387120	TLK	POR	HE	421120	422120	423120	424120	
387121	TLK	POR	HE	421121	422121	423121	424121	
387122	TLK	POR	HE	421122	422122	423122	424122	
387123	TLK	POR	HE	421123	422123	423123	424123	
387124	TLK	POR	HE	421124	422124	423124	424124	*Paul McCann*
387125	TLK	POR	HE	421125	422125	423125	424125	
387126	TLK	POR	HE	421126	422126	423126	424126	
387127	TLK	POR	HE	421127	422127	423127	424127	
387128	TLK	POR	HE	421128	422128	423128	424128	
387129	TLK	POR	HE	421129	422129	423129	424129	

Class 387/2

Used on the Victoria-Gatwick-Brighton route.

				DMOS	MOSL	PTOSL	MOS
387201	GEX	POR	SL	421201	422201	423201	424201
387202	GEX	POR	SL	421202	422202	423202	424202
387203	GEX	POR	SL	421203	422203	423203	424203
387204	GEX	POR	SL	421204	422204	423204	424204
387205	GEX	POR	SL	421205	422205	423205	424205
387206	GEX	POR	SL	421206	422206	423206	424206
387207	GEX	POR	SL	421207	422207	423207	424207
387208	GEX	POR	SL	421208	422208	423208	424208
387209	GEX	POR	SL	421209	422209	423209	424209
387210	GEX	POR	SL	421210	422210	423210	424210

387211	GEX	POR	SL	421211	422211	423211	424211
387212	GEX	POR	SL	421212	422212	423212	424212
387213	GEX	POR	SL	421213	422213	423213	424213
387214	GEX	POR	SL	421214	422214	423214	424214
387215	GEX	POR	SL	421215	422215	423215	424215
387216	GEX	POR	SL	421216	422216	423216	424216
387217	GEX	POR	SL	421217	422217	423217	424217
387218	GEX	POR	SL	421218	422218	423218	424218
387219	GEX	POR	SL	421219	422219	423219	424219
387220	GEX	POR	SL	421220	422220	423220	424220
387221	GEX	POR	SL	421221	422221	423221	424221
387222	GEX	POR	SL	421222	422222	423222	424222
387223	GEX	POR	SL	421223	422223	423223	424223
387224	GEX	POR	SL	421224	422224	423224	424224
387225	GEX	POR	SL	421225	422225	423225	424225
387226	GEX	POR	SL	421226	422226	423226	424226
387227	GEX	POR	SL	421227	422227	423227	424227

Class 455/8

Ex-BR four-car inner suburban commuter EMUs dating from 1982-84, they usually operate as eight-car sets in the peak. All are in the ETHQ pool.

				DTS	MS	TS	DTS
455801	SOU	EVS	SL	77627	62709	71657	77580
455802	SOU	EVS	SL	77581	62710	71664	77582
455803	SOU	EVS	SL	77583	62711	71639	77584
455804	SOU	EVS	SL	77585	62712	71640	77586
455805	SOU	EVS	SL	77587	62713	71641	77588
455806	SOU	EVS	SL	77589	62714	71642	77590
455807	SOU	EVS	SL	77591	62715	71643	77592
455808	SOU	EVS	SL	77637	62716	71644	77594
455809	SOU	EVS	SL	77623	62717	71648	77602
455810	SOU	EVS	SL	77597	62718	71646	77598
455811	SOU	EVS	SL	77599	62719	71647	77600
455812	SOU	EVS	SL	77595	62720	71645	77626
455813	SOU	EVS	SL	77603	62721	71649	77604
455814	SOU	EVS	SL	77605	62722	71650	77606
455815	SOU	EVS	SL	77607	62723	71651	77608
455816	SOU	EVS	SL	77609	62724	71652	77633
455817	SOU	EVS	SL	77611	62725	71653	77612
455818	SOU	EVS	SL	77613	62726	71654	77632
455819	SOU	EVS	SL	77615	62727	71637	77616
455820	SOU	EVS	SL	77617	62728	71656	77618
455821	SOU	EVS	SL	77619	62729	71655	77620
455822	SOU	EVS	SL	77621	62730	71658	77622
455823	SOU	EVS	SL	77601	62731	71659	77596
455824	SOU	EVS	SL	77593	62732	71660	77624
455825	SOU	EVS	SL	77579	62733	71661	77628
455826	SOU	EVS	SL	77630	62734	71662	77629

Gatwick Express unit 387210 at Kensington Olympic on 29 January 2016. *Paul Winter*

455827	SOU	EVS	SL	77610	62735	71663	77614
455828	SOU	EVS	SL	77631	62736	71638	77634
455829	SOU	EVS	SL	77635	62737	71665	77636
455830	SOU	EVS	SL	77625	62738	71666	77638
455831	SOU	EVS	SL	77639	62739	71667	77640
455832	SOU	EVS	SL	77641	62740	71668	77642
455833	SOU	EVS	SL	77643	62741	71669	77644
455834	SOU	EVS	SL	77645	62742	71670	77646
455835	SOU	EVS	SL	77647	62743	71671	77648
455836	SOU	EVS	SL	77649	62744	71672	77650
455837	SOU	EVS	SL	77651	62745	71673	77652
455838	SOU	EVS	SL	77653	62746	71674	77654
455839	SOU	EVS	SL	77655	62747	71675	77656
455840	SOU	EVS	SL	77657	62748	71676	77658
455841	SOU	EVS	SL	77659	62749	71677	77660
455842	SOU	EVS	SL	77661	62750	71678	77662
455843	SOU	EVS	SL	77663	62751	71679	77664
455844	SOU	EVS	SL	77665	62752	71680	77666
455845	SOU	EVS	SL	77667	62753	71681	77668
455846	SOU	EVS	SL	77669	62754	71682	77670

Class 700

The Class 700 is dual-voltage Siemens Desiro City train aimed at moving large numbers of commuters into the capital, although they do work long-distance trains such as Peterborough to Horsham and so do not have a metro-style seat arrangement. They are a mix of eight- (RLU – reduced-length unit) and 12-car (FLU – full-length unit) sets. All are in the ETHQ pool.

Class 700/0

Eight-car sets.

				DMC	PTS	MS	TS	TS	MS	PTS	DMC
700001	TLK	CLT	TB	401001	402001	403001	406001	407001	410001	411001	412001
700002	TLK	CLT	TB	401002	402002	403002	406002	407002	410002	411002	412002
700003	TLK	CLT	TB	401003	402003	403003	406003	407003	410003	411003	412003
700004	TLK	CLT	TB	401004	402004	403004	406004	407004	410004	411004	412004
700005	TLK	CLT	TB	401005	402005	403005	406005	407005	410005	411005	412005
700006	TLK	CLT	TB	401006	402006	403006	406006	407006	410006	411006	412006
700007	TLK	CLT	TB	401007	402007	403007	406007	407007	410007	411007	412007
700008	TLK	CLT	TB	401008	402008	403008	406008	407008	410008	411008	412008
700009	TLK	CLT	TB	401009	402009	403009	406009	407009	410009	411009	412009
700010	TLK	CLT	TB	401010	402010	403010	406010	407010	410010	411010	412010
700011	TLK	CLT	TB	401011	402011	403011	406011	407011	410011	411011	412011
700012	TLK	CLT	TB	401012	402012	403012	406012	407012	410012	411012	412012
700013	TLK	CLT	TB	401013	402013	403013	406013	407013	410013	411013	412013
700014	TLK	CLT	TB	401014	402014	403014	406014	407014	410014	411014	412014
700015	TLK	CLT	TB	401015	402015	403015	406015	407015	410015	411015	412015
700016	TLK	CLT	TB	401016	402016	403016	406016	407016	410016	411016	412016
700017	TLK	CLT	TB	401017	402017	403017	406017	407017	410017	411017	412017
700018	TLK	CLT	TB	401018	402018	403018	406018	407018	410018	411018	412018
700019	TLK	CLT	TB	401019	402019	403019	406019	407019	410019	411019	412019
700020	TLK	CLT	TB	401020	402020	403020	406020	407020	410020	411020	412020
700021	TLK	CLT	TB	401021	402021	403021	406021	407021	410021	411021	412021
700022	TLK	CLT	TB	401022	402022	403022	406022	407022	410022	411022	412022
700023	TLK	CLT	TB	401023	402023	403023	406023	407023	410023	411023	412023
700024	TLK	CLT	TB	401024	402024	403024	406024	407024	410024	411024	412024
700025	TLK	CLT	TB	401025	402025	403025	406025	407025	410025	411025	412025
700026	TLK	CLT	TB	401026	402026	403026	406026	407026	410026	411026	412026
700027	TLK	CLT	TB	401027	402027	403027	406027	407027	410027	411027	412027
700028	TLK	CLT	TB	401028	402028	403028	406028	407028	410028	411028	412028
700029	TLK	CLT	TB	401029	402029	403029	406029	407029	410029	411029	412029
700030	TLK	CLT	TB	401030	402030	403030	406030	407030	410030	411030	412030
700031	TLK	CLT	TB	401031	402031	403031	406031	407031	410031	411031	412031
700032	TLK	CLT	TB	401032	402032	403032	406032	407032	410032	411032	412032
700033	TLK	CLT	TB	401033	402033	403033	406033	407033	410033	411033	412033
700034	TLK	CLT	TB	401034	402034	403034	406034	407034	410034	411034	412034
700035	TLK	CLT	TB	401035	402035	403035	406035	407035	410035	411035	412035
700036	TLK	CLT	TB	401036	402036	403036	406036	407036	410036	411036	412036
700037	TLK	CLT	TB	401037	402037	403037	406037	407037	410037	411037	412037
700038	TLK	CLT	TB	401038	402038	403038	406038	407038	410038	411038	412038
700039	TLK	CLT	TB	401039	402039	403039	406039	407039	410039	411039	412039
700040	TLK	CLT	TB	401040	402040	403040	406040	407040	410040	411040	412040
700041	TLK	CLT	TB	401041	402041	403041	406041	407041	410041	411041	412041
700042	TLK	CLT	TB	401042	402042	403042	406042	407042	410042	411042	412042
700043	TLK	CLT	TB	401043	402043	403043	406043	407043	410043	411043	412043
700044	TLK	CLT	TB	401044	402044	403044	406044	407044	410044	411044	412044
700045	TLK	CLT	TB	401045	402045	403045	406045	407045	410045	411045	412045

700046	TLK	CLT	TB	401046	402046	403046	406046	407046	410046	411046	412046
700047	TLK	CLT	TB	401047	402047	403047	406047	407047	410047	411047	412047
700048	TLK	CLT	TB	401048	402048	403048	406048	407048	410048	411048	412048
700049	TLK	CLT	TB	401049	402049	403049	406049	407049	410049	411049	412049
700050	TLK	CLT	TB	401050	402050	403050	406050	407050	410050	411050	412050
700051	TLK	CLT	TB	401051	402051	403051	406051	407051	410051	411051	412051
700052	TLK	CLT	TB	401052	402052	403052	406052	407052	410052	411052	412052
700053	TLK	CLT	TB	401053	402053	403053	406053	407053	410053	411053	412053
700054	TLK	CLT	TB	401054	402054	403054	406054	407054	410054	411054	412054
700055	TLK	CLT	TB	401055	402055	403055	406055	407055	410055	411055	412055
700056	TLK	CLT	TB	401056	402056	403056	406056	407056	410056	411056	412056
700057	TLK	CLT	TB	401057	402057	403057	406057	407057	410057	411057	412057
700058	TLK	CLT	TB	401058	402058	403058	406058	407058	410058	411058	412058
700059	TLK	CLT	TB	401059	402059	403059	406059	407059	410059	411059	412059
700060	TLK	CLT	TB	401060	402060	403060	406060	407060	410060	411060	412060

Returned to its original British Rail blue and grey livery, 313201 stands at Bognor on 24 March 2018. *Pip Dunn*

Class 700/1

Twelve-car sets.

				DMC	PTS	MS	MS	TS	TS	TS	TS	MS	MS	PTS	DMC
700101	TLK	CLT	TB	401101	402101	403101	404101	405101	406101	407101	408101	409101	410101	411101	412101
700102	TLK	CLT	TB	401102	402102	403102	404102	405102	406102	407102	408102	409102	410102	411102	412102
700103	TLK	CLT	TB	401103	402103	403103	404103	405103	406103	407103	408103	409103	410103	411103	412103
700104	TLK	CLT	TB	401104	402104	403104	404104	405104	406104	407104	408104	409104	410104	411104	412104
700105	TLK	CLT	TB	401105	402105	403105	404105	405105	406105	407105	408105	409105	410105	411105	412105
700106	TLK	CLT	TB	401106	402106	403106	404106	405106	406106	407106	408106	409106	410106	411106	412106
700107	TLK	CLT	TB	401107	402107	403107	404107	405107	406107	407107	408107	409107	410107	411107	412107
700108	TLK	CLT	TB	401108	402108	403108	404108	405108	406108	407108	408108	409108	410108	411108	412108
700109	TLK	CLT	TB	401109	402109	403109	404109	405109	406109	407109	408109	409109	410109	411109	412109
700110	TLK	CLT	TB	401110	402110	403110	404110	405110	406110	407110	408110	409110	410110	411110	412110
700111	TLK	CLT	TB	401111	402111	403111	404111	405111	406111	407111	408111	409111	410111	411111	412111
700112	TLK	CLT	TB	401112	402112	403112	404112	405112	406112	407112	408112	409112	410112	411112	412112
700113	TLK	CLT	TB	401113	402113	403113	404113	405113	406113	407113	408113	409113	410113	411113	412113
700114	TLK	CLT	TB	401114	402114	403114	404114	405114	406114	407114	408114	409114	410114	411114	412114
700115	TLK	CLT	TB	401115	402115	403115	404115	405115	406115	407115	408115	409115	410115	411115	412115
700116	TLK	CLT	TB	401116	402116	403116	404116	405116	406116	407116	408116	409116	410116	411116	412116
700117	TLK	CLT	TB	401117	402117	403117	404117	405117	406117	407117	408117	409117	410117	411117	412117
700118	TLK	CLT	TB	401118	402118	403118	404118	405118	406118	407118	408118	409118	410118	411118	412118
700119	TLK	CLT	TB	401119	402119	403119	404119	405119	406119	407119	408119	409119	410119	411119	412119
700120	TLK	CLT	TB	401120	402120	403120	404120	405120	406120	407120	408120	409120	410120	411120	412120
700121	TLK	CLT	TB	401121	402121	403121	404121	405121	406121	407121	408121	409121	410121	411121	412121
700122	TLK	CLT	TB	401122	402122	403122	404122	405122	406122	407122	408122	409122	410122	411122	412122
700123	TLK	CLT	TB	401123	402123	403123	404123	405123	406123	407123	408123	409123	410123	411123	412123
700124	TLK	CLT	TB	401124	402124	403124	404124	405124	406124	407124	408124	409124	410124	411124	412124
700125	TLK	CLT	TB	401125	402125	403125	404125	405125	406125	407125	408125	409125	410125	411125	412125
700126	TLK	CLT	TB	401126	402126	403126	404126	405126	406126	407126	408126	409126	410126	411126	412126
700127	TLK	CLT	TB	401127	402127	403127	404127	405127	406127	407127	408127	409127	410127	411127	412127
700128	TLK	CLT	TB	401128	402128	403128	404128	405128	406128	407128	408128	409128	410128	411128	412128
700129	TLK	CLT	TB	401129	402129	403129	404129	405129	406129	407129	408129	409129	410129	411129	412129

700130	TLK	CLT	TB	401130	402130	403130	404130	405130	406130	407130	408130	409130	410130	411130	412130
700131	TLK	CLT	TB	401131	402131	403131	404131	405131	406131	407131	408131	409131	410131	411131	412131
700132	TLK	CLT	TB	401132	402132	403132	404132	405132	406132	407132	408132	409132	410132	411132	412132
700133	TLK	CLT	TB	401133	402133	403133	404133	405133	406133	407133	408133	409133	410133	411133	412133
700134	TLK	CLT	TB	401134	402134	403134	404134	405134	406134	407134	408134	409134	410134	411134	412134
700135	TLK	CLT	TB	401135	402135	403135	404135	405135	406135	407135	408135	409135	410135	411135	412135
700136	TLK	CLT	TB	401136	402136	403136	404136	405136	406136	407136	408136	409136	410136	411136	412136
700137	TLK	CLT	TB	401137	402137	403137	404137	405137	406137	407137	408137	409137	410137	411137	412137
700138	TLK	CLT	TB	401138	402138	403138	404138	405138	406138	407138	408138	409138	410138	411138	412138
700139	TLK	CLT	TB	401139	402139	403139	404139	405139	406139	407139	408139	409139	410139	411139	412139
700140	TLK	CLT	TB	401140	402140	403140	404140	405140	406140	407140	408140	409140	410140	411140	412140
700141	TLK	CLT	TB	401141	402141	403141	404141	405141	406141	407141	408141	409141	410141	411141	412141
700142	TLK	CLT	TB	401142	402142	403142	404142	405142	406142	407142	408142	409142	410142	411142	412142
700143	TLK	CLT	TB	401143	402143	403143	404143	405143	406143	407143	408143	409143	410143	411143	412143
700144	TLK	CLT	TB	401144	402144	403144	404144	405144	406144	407144	408144	409144	410144	411144	412144
700145	TLK	CLT	TB	401145	402145	403145	404145	405145	406145	407145	408145	409145	410145	411145	412145
700146	TLK	CLT	TB	401146	402146	403146	404146	405146	406146	407146	408146	409146	410146	411146	412146
700147	TLK	CLT	TB	401147	402147	403147	404147	405147	406147	407147	408147	409147	410147	411147	412147
700148	TLK	CLT	TB	401148	402148	403148	404148	405148	406148	407148	408148	409148	410148	411148	412148
700149	TLK	CLT	TB	401149	402149	403149	404149	405149	406149	407149	408149	409149	410149	411149	412149
700150	TLK	CLT	TB	401150	402150	403150	404150	405150	406150	407150	408150	409150	410150	411150	412150
700151	TLK	CLT	TB	401151	402151	403151	404151	405151	406151	407151	408151	409151	410151	411151	412151
700152	TLK	CLT	TB	401152	402152	403152	404152	405152	406152	407152	408152	409152	410152	411152	412152
700153	TLK	CLT	TB	401153	402153	403153	404153	405153	406153	407153	408153	409153	410153	411153	412153
700154	TLK	CLT	TB	401154	402154	403154	404154	405154	406154	407154	408154	409154	410154	411154	412154
700155	TLK	CLT	TB	401155	402155	403155	404155	405155	406155	407155	408155	409155	410155	411155	412155

Class 717

Similar to the Class 700, these dual-voltage EMUs are a metro-style version of the Siemens Desiro City. They are used on commuter trains from Moorgate and, unlike the Class 700s, do not have toilets. All are in the ETHQ pool.

				DMS	TS	TS	MS	PTS	DMS
717001	TLK	ROC	HE	451101	452101	453101	454101	455001	456001
717002	TLK	ROC	HE	451102	452102	453102	454102	455002	456002
717003	TLK	ROC	HE	451103	452103	453103	454103	455003	456003
717004	TLK	ROC	HE	451104	452104	453104	454104	455004	456004
717005	TLK	ROC	HE	451105	452105	453105	454105	455005	456005
717006	TLK	ROC	HE	451106	452106	453106	454106	455006	456006
717007	TLK	ROC	HE	451107	452107	453107	454107	455007	456007
717008	TLK	ROC	HE	451108	452108	453108	454108	455008	456008
717009	TLK	ROC	HE	451109	452109	453109	454109	455009	456009
717010	TLK	ROC	HE	451110	452110	453110	454110	455010	456010
717011	TLK	ROC	HE	451111	452111	453111	454111	455011	456011
717012	TLK	ROC	HE	451112	452112	453112	454112	455012	456012
717013	TLK	ROC	HE	451113	452113	453113	454113	455013	456013
717014	TLK	ROC	HE	451114	452114	453114	454114	455014	456014
717015	TLK	ROC	HE	451115	452115	453115	454115	455015	456015
717016	TLK	ROC	HE	451116	452116	453116	454116	455016	456016
717017	TLK	ROC	HE	451117	452117	453117	454117	455017	456017
717018	TLK	ROC	HE	451118	452118	453118	454118	455018	456018
717019	TLK	ROC	HE	451119	452119	453119	454119	455019	456019
717020	TLK	ROC	HE	451120	452120	453120	454120	455020	456020
717021	TLK	ROC	HE	451121	452121	453121	454121	455021	456021
717022	TLK	ROC	HE	451122	452122	453122	454122	455022	456022
717023	TLK	ROC	HE	451123	452123	453123	454123	455023	456023
717024	TLK	ROC	HE	451124	452124	453124	454124	455024	456024
717025	TLK	ROC	HE	451125	452125	453125	454125	455025	456025

Nos 365502/540 wait to set off with the 0735 Peterborough-King's Cross on 13 August 2020. *Pip Dunn*

No. 700018 works the 0724 Peterborough-King's Cross past Abbots Ripton on 25 August 2018. *Bill Atkinson*

Nos 387101/107 work the 1229 Cambridge-King's Cross past Shepreth on 6 November 2017. *Bill Atkinson*

Siemens Desiro City unit 717008 at Alexandra Palace on a test run on 13 November 2018. *Mark Pike*

Greater Anglia

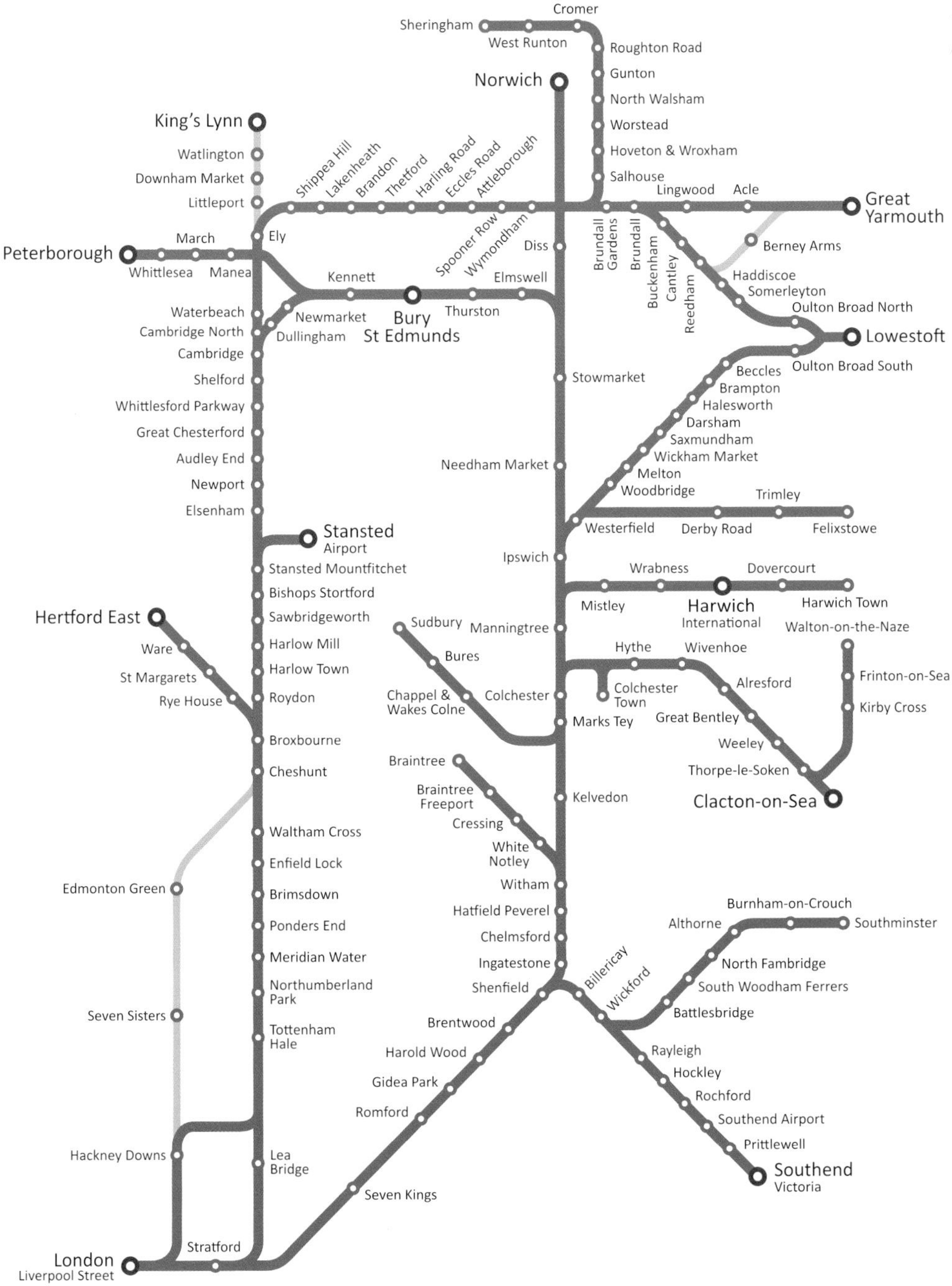

Contact details

Website: greateranglia.co.uk
Twitter: @greateranglia
Key personnel
Managing Director: Jamie Burles
Fleet Director: Martin Beable

Overview

Greater Anglia operates the inter-city route from Liverpool St to Norwich but also commuter trains from Liverpool St to Hertford East, Stansted, Southend Victoria, Southminster, Clacton, Walton-on-the-Naze and Harwich Town. It also operates local trains to Braintree, Ipswich-Felixstowe, Marks Tey-Sudbury and in Suffolk and Norfolk from Norwich-Cambridge, Norwich-Sheringham, Great Yarmouth and Lowestoft, Ipswich-Peterborough and Ipswich-Lowestoft.

Greater Anglia has been undergoing a sweeping fleet change in recent years with brand-new trains from Stadler and Bombardier now being delivered and introduced. This has allowed the company to dispense with its older ex-BR Class 153/156 DMUs and its ex-Anglia Railways Class 170/2, which have moved to East Midlands Railway (156s) and Transport for Wales (153s and 170/2s). September 2019 saw the TOC dispense with its hired-in DRS Class 37 'short set' for Wherry lines operations.

Since 1 February 2020, all the GA rural routes have been operated by a mix of 14 three-car and 24 four-car Class 755 bi-mode multiple units.

The existing Norwich to Cambridge service has been extended to Stansted using Class 745s (from December 2019), while the Ipswich to Peterborough service is due to be doubled in frequency to hourly using 745s, but timing depends on some infrastructure upgrades with the tracks from Soham to Ely being doubled.

The last loco-hauled Class 90 and Mk 3 set operated on 24 March 2020 and the 15 locos were redeployed with two, 90001/002, going to Locomotive Services and the other 13, 90003-015, moving to Freightliner.

In their place have come ten 12-car Class 745/0s for use on the Liverpool Street-Norwich route, with ten 12-car Class 745/1s now starting to be phased in on the Stansted Express route.

Class 317

The four-car ex-BR units, which date from 1981-86, are based at Ilford and used out of Liverpool Street on commuter trains in West Anglia to Hertford East, Bishops Stortford, as well as Meridian Water-Stratford and most trains between Liverpool Street and Cambridge. They will be returned to their ROSCO after the Class 720 fleet is all in traffic. All are in the EBHQ pool.

No. 360121 at Colchester on 1138 Liverpool Street-Colchester Town on 22 October 2018. *Robin Ralston*

Class 317/3

Outer suburban units. Units 317345/346 have derogation to run until May 2021 only. 317337-344/347/348 have been modified to meet current PPM standards.

				DTC	MS	TC	DTS	
317337	AGA	ANG	IL	77036	62671	71613	77084	
317338	AGA	ANG	IL	77037	62698	71614	77085	
317339	AGA	ANG	IL	77038	62699	71615	77086	
317340	AGA	ANG	IL	77039	62700	71616	77087	
317341	AGA	ANG	IL	77040	62701	71617	77088	
317342	AGA	ANG	IL	77041	62702	71618	77089	
317343	AGA	ANG	IL	77042	62703	71619	77090	*Driver John Webb*
317344	AGA	ANG	IL	77043	62704	71620	77091	
317345	AGA	ANG	IL	77044	62705	71621	77092	
317346	AGA	ANG	IL	77045	62706	71622	77093	
317347	AGA	ANG	IL	77046	62707	71623	77094	
317348	AGA	ANG	IL	77047	62708	71624	77095	*Richard A Jenner*

Class 317/5

Outer suburban units.

Units 317503/505/509/514 have derogation to run until May 2021 only. 317501/502/504/506-508/510-514/515 have been modified to meet current PPM standards.

				DTC	MS	TC	DTS	
317501	AGA	ANG	IL	77024	62661	71577	77048	
317502	AGA	ANG	IL	77001	62662	71578	77049	
317503	AGA	ANG	IL	77002	62663	71579	77050	
317504	AGA	ANG	IL	77003	62664	71580	77051	
317505	AGA	ANG	IL	77004	62665	71581	77052	
317506	AGA	ANG	IL	77005	62666	71582	77053	
317507	AGA	ANG	IL	77006	62667	71583	77054	*University of Cambridge 800 Years 1209-2009*
317508	AGA	ANG	IL	77010	62697	71587	77058	
317509	AGA	ANG	IL	77011	62672	71588	77059	
317510	AGA	ANG	IL	77012	62673	71589	77060	
317511	AGA	ANG	IL	77014	62675	71591	77062	
317512	AGA	ANG	IL	77015	62676	71592	77063	
317513	AGA	ANG	IL	77016	62677	71593	77064	
317514	AGA	ANG	IL	77017	62678	71594	77065	
317515	AGA	ANG	IL	77019	62680	71596	77067	

Class 317/6

Outer suburban units. Units 317649-658/661/664-667/670/672 have derogation to run until May 2021 only.

				DTC	MS	TC	DTS	
317649	AGA	ANG	IL	77200	62846	71734	77220	
317650	AGA	ANG	IL	77201	62847	71735	77221	
317651	AGA	ANG	IL	77202	62848	71736	77222	
317652	AGA	ANG	IL	77203	62849	71737	77223	
317653	AGA	ANG	IL	77204	62850	71738	77224	
317654	AGA	ANG	IL	77205	62851	71739	77225	*Richard Wells*
317658	AGA	ANG	IL	77209	62855	71743	77229	
317666	AGA	ANG	IL	77217	62863	71751	77237	
317670	AGA	ANG	IL	77281	62887	71763	77285	

Class 317/7

These former London Overground units are due to be taken on by Greater Anglia as short term cover until May 2021.

				DTS	MS	TS/TC	DTS
317708	LOR	ANG	NN (S)	77007	62668	71584	77055
317709	LOR	ANG	NN (S)	77008	62668	71585	77056
317710	LOR	ANG	NN (S)	77009	62670	71586	77057
317714	LOR	ANG	IL	77013	62674	71590	77061
317719	LOR	ANG	NN (S)	77018	62679	71595	77066
317723	LOR	ANG	IL	77022	62683	71599	77070
317729	LOR	ANG	IL	77028	62689	71605	77076
317732	LOR	ANG	IL	77031	62692	71608	77079

Class 317/8

Outer suburban units. These units have been modified to meet current PPM standards.

				DTC	MS	TC	DTS
317881	AGA	ANG	IL	77020	62681	71597	77068
317882	AGA	ANG	IL	77023	62684	71600	77071
317883	AGA	ANG	IL	77000	62685	71601	77073
317884	AGA	ANG	IL	77025	62686	71602	77073
317885	AGA	ANG	IL	77026	62687	71603	77074
317886	AGA	ANG	IL	77027	62688	71604	77075

Class 321/322

A slightly newer ex-BR EMU design, nevertheless they are still over 30 years old, having been built by BREL York in 1988-90. These units are also based at Ilford for working commuter and local trains from Liverpool Street to Southend Victoria, the majority of trains to Chelmsford, Braintree, Clacton, Colchester, Harwich and Walton-on-the-Naze and some trains to Ipswich.

Pending deliveries of new Class 745s for inter-city duties on the Norwich to Liverpool St line, some 321s have been used as cover following the withdrawal of Class 90-hauled Mk 3 sets. All will be returned to their ROSCOs when all the Class 720 fleet is all accepted into traffic. All are in the EBHQ pool.

Class 321/3

Outer suburban units.

				DTS	MS	TS	DTC
321301	GAW	EVS	IL	78049	62975	71880	77853
321302	GAW	EVS	IL	78050	62976	71881	77854
321303	GAW	EVS	IL	78051	62977	71882	77855
321304	GAW	EVS	IL	78052	62978	71883	77856
321305	GAW	EVS	IL	78053	62979	71884	77857
321306	GAW	EVS	IL	78054	62980	71885	77858
321307	GAW	EVS	IL	78055	62981	71886	77859
321308	GAW	EVS	IL	78056	62982	71887	77860
321309	GAW	EVS	IL	78057	62983	71888	77861
321310	GAW	EVS	IL	78058	62984	71889	77862
321311	GAW	EVS	IL	78059	62985	71890	77863
321312	GAW	EVS	IL	78060	62986	71891	77864
321313	GAW	EVS	IL	78061	62987	71892	77865

321314	GAW	EVS	IL	78062	62988	71893	77866	
321315	GAW	EVS	IL	78063	62989	71894	77867	
321316	GAW	EVS	IL	78064	62990	71895	77868	
321317	GAW	EVS	IL	78065	62991	71896	77869	
321318	GAW	EVS	IL	78066	62992	71897	77870	
321319	GAW	EVS	IL	78067	62993	71898	77871	
321320	GAW	EVS	IL	78068	62994	71899	77872	
321321	GAW	EVS	IL	78069	62995	71900	77873	
321322	GAW	EVS	IL	78070	62996	71901	77874	
321323	GAW	EVS	IL	78071	62997	71902	77875	
321324	GAW	EVS	IL	78072	62998	71903	77876	
321325	GAW	EVS	IL	78073	62999	71904	77877	
321326	GAW	EVS	IL	78074	63001	71905	77878	
321327	GAW	EVS	IL	78075	63001	71906	77879	
321328	GAW	EVS	IL	78076	63002	71907	77880	
321329	GAW	EVS	IL	78077	63003	71908	77881	
321330	GAW	EVS	IL	78078	63004	71909	77882	
321331	GAW	EVS	IL	78079	63005	71910	77883	
321332	GAW	EVS	IL	78080	63006	71911	77884	
321333	GAW	EVS	IL	78081	63007	71912	77885	
321334	GAW	EVS	IL	78082	63008	71913	77886	*Amsterdam*
321335	GAW	EVS	IL	78083	63009	71914	77887	
321336	GAW	EVS	IL	78084	63010	71915	77888	*Geoffrey Freeman Allen*
321337	GAW	EVS	IL	78085	63011	71916	77889	
321338	GAW	EVS	IL	78086	63012	71917	77890	
321339	GAW	EVS	IL	78087	63013	71918	77891	
321340	GAW	EVS	IL	78088	63014	71919	77892	
321341	GAW	EVS	IL	78089	63015	71920	77893	
321342	GAW	EVS	IL	78090	63016	71921	77894	*R Barnes*
321343	GAW	EVS	IL	78091	63017	71922	77895	*RSA Railway Study Association*
321344	GAW	EVS	IL	78092	63018	71923	77896	
321345	GAW	EVS	IL	78093	63019	71924	77897	
321346	GAW	EVS	IL	78094	63020	71925	77898	
321347	GAW	EVS	IL	78131	63105	71991	78280	
321348	GAW	EVS	IL	78132	63106	71992	78281	
321349	GAW	EVS	IL	78133	63107	71993	78282	
321350	GAW	EVS	IL	78134	63108	71994	78283	
321351	GAW	EVS	IL	78135	63109	71995	78284	*London Stansted Airport*
321352	GAW	EVS	IL	78136	63110	71996	78285	
321353	GAW	EVS	IL	78137	63111	71997	78286	
321354	GAW	EVS	IL	78138	63112	71998	78287	
321355	GAW	EVS	IL	78139	63113	71999	78288	
321356	GAW	EVS	IL	78140	63114	72000	78289	
321357	GAW	EVS	IL	78141	63115	72001	78290	
321358	GAW	EVS	IL	78142	63116	72002	78291	
321359	GAW	EVS	IL	78143	63117	72003	78292	
321360	GAW	EVS	IL	78144	63118	72004	78293	
321361	GAW	EVS	IL	78145	63119	72005	78294	*Phoenix*
321362	GAW	EVS	IL	78146	63120	72006	78295	
321363	GAW	EVS	IL	78147	63121	72007	78296	
321364	GAW	EVS	IL	78148	63122	72008	78297	
321365	GAW	EVS	IL	78149	63123	72009	78298	
321366	GAW	EVS	IL	78150	63124	72010	78299	

Class 321/4

Outer suburban units.

				DTS	MS	TS	DTC	
321402	GAW	EVS	IL	78096	63064	71950	77944	
321405	GAW	EVS	IL	78099	63067	71953	77947	
321406	GAW	EVS	IL	78100	63068	71954	77948	
321407	GAW	EVS	IL	78101	63069	71955	77949	
321408	GAW	EVS	IL	78102	63070	71956	77950	*Dame Alice Owen's School 400 Years of Learning*
321409	GAW	EVS	IL	78103	63071	71957	77951	
321410	GAW	EVS	IL	78104	63072	71958	77952	
321419	GAW	EVS	IL	78113	63081	71967	77961	
321421	GAW	EVS	IL	78115	63083	71969	77963	
321422	GAW	EVS	IL	78116	63084	71970	77964	
321423	GAW	EVS	IL	78117	63085	71971	77965	
321424	GAW	EVS	IL	78118	63086	71972	77966	
321425	GAW	EVS	IL	78119	63087	71973	77967	
321426	GAW	EVS	IL	78120	63088	71974	77968	
321427	GAW	EVS	IL	78121	63089	71975	77969	
321428	GAW	EVS	IL	78122	63090	71976	77970	*The Essex Commuter*
321429	GAW	EVS	IL	78123	63091	71977	77971	
321430	GAW	EVS	IL	78124	63092	71978	77972	
321431	GAW	EVS	IL	78151	63125	72011	78300	
321432	GAW	EVS	IL	78152	63126	72012	78301	
321433	GAW	EVS	IL	78153	63127	72013	78302	
321434	GAW	EVS	IL	78154	63128	72014	78303	
321435	GAW	EVS	IL	78155	63129	72015	78304	
321436	GAW	EVS	IL	78156	63130	72016	78305	
321437	GAW	EVS	IL	78157	63131	72017	78306	
321438	GAW	EVS	IL	78158	63132	72018	78307	
321439	GAW	EVS	IL	78159	63133	72019	78308	
321440	GAW	EVS	IL	78160	63134	72020	78309	
321441	GAW	EVS	IL	78161	63135	72021	78310	
321442	GAW	EVS	IL	78162	63136	72022	78311	*Crouch Valley 1889-2014*
321443	GAW	EVS	IL	78125	63099	71985	78274	
321444	GAW	EVS	IL	78126	63100	71986	78275	*Essex Lifeboats*
321445	GAW	EVS	IL	78127	63101	71987	78276	
321446	GAW	EVS	IL	78128	63102	71988	78277	*George Mullings*
321447	GAW	EVS	IL	78129	63103	71989	78278	
321448	REN	EVS	IL	78130	63104	71990	78279	

Class 321/9

Redundant Northern units replaced by Class 331s, these units have been moved to Greater Anglia to provide additional capacity following the withdrawal of Class 90-hauled Mk 3 sets.

				DTS	MS	TS	DTC
321901	NBL	EVS	IL	77990	63153	72128	77993
321902	NBL	EVS	IL	77991	63154	72129	77994
321903	NBL	EVS	CC (S)	77992	63155	72130	77995

Class 322

Like the 321/9s, the units were spare after use with Northern and have also transferred to AGA use.

				DTS	MS	TS	DTC
322481	NBL	EVS	IL	78163	63137	72023	77985
322482	NBL	EVS	IL	78164	63138	72024	77986
322483	NBL	EVS	IL	78165	63139	72025	77987
322484	NBL	EVS	CC (S)	78166	63140	72026	77988
322485	NBL	EVS	IL	78167	63141	72027	77989

Class 360

This fleet of 21 four-car Siemens Desiro Units was ordered by First Great Eastern and delivered in 2002/03. They work mostly from Liverpool Street to Clacton, and also some trains to Ipswich.

Their time with GA is coming to a close as they are all due to move to East Midlands Railway to operate its new St Pancras-Corby service. Currently one unit a week is being stopped for modifications to allow them to run at 110mph for these duties. They will also be refurbished prior to their switch. EMR is due to have all 360s by the end of 2020 but this is now unlikely to happen until 2021. All are in the EBHQ pool.

				DMC	PTS	TS	DMC
360101	FIR	ANG	IL	65551	72551	74551	68551
360102	FIR	ANG	IL	65552	72552	74552	68552
360103	FIR	ANG	IL	65553	72553	74553	68553
360104	FIR	ANG	IL	65554	72554	74554	68554
360105	FIR	ANG	IL	65555	72555	74555	68555
360106	FIR	ANG	IL	65556	72556	74556	68556
360107	FIR	ANG	IL	65557	72557	74557	68557
360108	FIR	ANG	IL	65558	72558	74558	68558
360109	FIR	ANG	IL	65559	72559	74559	68559
360110	FIR	ANG	IL	65560	72560	74560	68560
360111	FIR	ANG	IL	65561	72561	74561	68561
360112	FIR	ANG	IL	65562	72562	74562	68562
360113	FIR	ANG	IL	65563	72563	74563	68563
360114	FIR	ANG	IL	65564	72564	74564	68564
360115	FIR	ANG	IL	65565	72565	74565	68565
360116	FIR	ANG	IL	65566	72566	74566	68566
360117	FIR	ANG	IL	65567	72567	74567	68567
360118	FIR	ANG	IL	65568	72568	74568	68568
360119	FIR	ANG	IL	65569	72569	74569	68569
360120	FIR	ANG	IL	65570	72570	74570	68570
360121	FIR	ANG	IL	65571	72571	74571	68571

Class 379

These Bombardier Electrostar Units were ordered by Greater Anglia and delivered in 2010/11 for use on the Liverpool St-Stansted and Cambridge routes.

Presently they work from Liverpool Street to Stansted and peak trains to Cambridge, although Class 745s are starting to enter service on the Stansted Express route. Those 379s released will be cascaded to replace Class 317s to allow their withdrawal to be hastened. Eventually when all the 720s are in traffic, the 379s will too be returned to their ROSCO, expected to be circa 2022/23. All are in the EBHQ pool.

				DMS	MS	PTS	DMC	
379001	NEX	MAQ	IL	61201	61701	61901	62101	
379002	NEX	MAQ	IL	61202	61702	61902	62102	
379003	NEX	MAQ	IL	61203	61703	61903	62103	
379004	NEX	MAQ	IL	61204	61704	61904	62104	
379005	NEX	MAQ	IL	61205	61705	61905	62105	*Stansted Express*
379006	NEX	MAQ	IL	61206	61706	61906	62106	
379007	NEX	MAQ	IL	61207	61707	61907	62107	
379008	NEX	MAQ	IL	61208	61708	61908	62108	
379009	NEX	MAQ	IL	61209	61709	61909	62109	
379010	NEX	MAQ	IL	61210	61710	61910	62110	
379011	NEX	MAQ	IL	61211	61711	61911	62111	*Ely Cathedral*
379012	NEX	MAQ	IL	61212	61712	61912	62112	*The West Anglian*
379013	NEX	MAQ	IL	61213	61713	61913	62113	
379014	NEX	MAQ	IL	61214	61714	61914	62114	
379015	NEX	MAQ	IL	61215	61715	61915	62115	*City of Cambridge*
379016	NEX	MAQ	IL	61216	61716	61916	62116	
379017	NEX	MAQ	IL	61217	61717	61917	62117	
379018	NEX	MAQ	IL	61218	61718	61918	62118	
379019	NEX	MAQ	IL	61219	61719	61919	62119	
379020	NEX	MAQ	IL	61220	61720	61920	62120	
379021	NEX	MAQ	IL	61221	61721	61921	62121	
379022	NEX	MAQ	IL	61222	61722	61922	62122	
379023	NEX	MAQ	IL	61223	61723	61923	62123	
379024	NEX	MAQ	IL	61224	61724	61924	62124	
379025	NEX	MAQ	IL	61225	61725	61925	62125	*Go Discover*
379026	NEX	MAQ	IL	61226	61726	61926	62126	
379027	NEX	MAQ	IL	61227	61727	61927	62127	
379028	NEX	MAQ	IL	61228	61728	61928	62128	
379029	NEX	MAQ	IL	61229	61729	61929	62129	
379030	NEX	MAQ	IL	61230	61730	61930	62130	

Class 720

The new Bombardier EMUs are now being delivered and will be used for commuter trains from Liverpool St to allow 317/321s to be withdrawn and the 360 – and ultimately the 379s – to be redeployed with other franchises.

The original order was for 89 five-car 720/5 sets and 22 ten-car 720/1s. However, the latter have now been changed to 44 more five-car sets instead. Are the time of going to press, rather than running all 133 five-car sets as 720501-633, because 720601-610 are earmarked for c2c's units, it means the numbering would be 720101-144 and 720501-589. That could be subject to change.

The vehicles are slightly longer so each five-car set is the equivalent of a six-car formation. Some infrastructure work needed will be needed across the GA network with some stations needing their platforms to be extended and some signal repositioned to improve sighting. These enhancements should be done by 2022 when the full fleet is expected to have been delivered and commissioned.

All are in the EBHQ pool.

Class 720/1

Originally planned as 22 ten-car sets, the order has been changed to 44 five-car sets, and so the numbers may change. None of these units are built yet.

			DMS	PMS	MS	MS	DTS
720101	AGG	ANG	450101	451101	452101	453101	459101
720102	AGG	ANG	450102	451102	452102	453102	459102
720103	AGG	ANG	450103	451103	452103	453103	459103
720104	AGG	ANG	450104	451104	452104	453104	459104
720105	AGG	ANG	450105	451105	452105	453105	459105
720106	AGG	ANG	450106	451106	452106	453106	459106
720107	AGG	ANG	450107	451107	452107	453107	459107
720108	AGG	ANG	450108	451108	452108	453108	459108
720109	AGG	ANG	450109	451109	452109	453109	459109
720110	AGG	ANG	450110	451110	452110	453110	459110
720111	AGG	ANG	450111	451111	452111	453111	459111
720112	AGG	ANG	450112	451112	452112	453112	459112
720113	AGG	ANG	450113	451113	452113	453113	459113
720114	AGG	ANG	450114	451114	452114	453114	459114
720115	AGG	ANG	450115	451115	452115	453115	459115
720116	AGG	ANG	450116	451116	452116	453116	459116
720117	AGG	ANG	450117	451117	452117	453117	459117
720118	AGG	ANG	450118	451118	452118	453118	459118
720119	AGG	ANG	450119	451119	452119	453119	459119
720120	AGG	ANG	450120	451120	452120	453120	459120
720121	AGG	ANG	450121	451121	452121	453121	459121
720122	AGG	ANG	450122	451122	452122	453122	459122
720123	AGG	ANG	450123	451123	452123	453123	459123
720124	AGG	ANG	450124	451124	452124	453124	459124
720125	AGG	ANG	450125	451125	452125	453125	459125
720126	AGG	ANG	450126	451126	452126	453126	459126
720127	AGG	ANG	450127	451127	452127	453127	459127
720128	AGG	ANG	450128	451128	452128	453128	459128
720129	AGG	ANG	450129	451129	452129	453129	459129
720130	AGG	ANG	450130	451130	452130	453130	459130
720131	AGG	ANG	450131	451131	452131	453131	459131
720132	AGG	ANG	450132	451132	452132	453132	459132
720133	AGG	ANG	450133	451133	452133	453133	459133
720134	AGG	ANG	450134	451134	452134	453134	459134
720135	AGG	ANG	450135	451135	452135	453135	459135
720136	AGG	ANG	450136	451136	452136	453136	459136
720137	AGG	ANG	450137	451137	452137	453137	459137
720138	AGG	ANG	450138	451138	452138	453138	459138
720139	AGG	ANG	450139	451139	452139	453139	459139
720140	AGG	ANG	450140	451140	452140	453140	459140
720141	AGG	ANG	450141	451141	452141	453141	459141
720142	AGG	ANG	450142	451142	452142	453142	459142
720143	AGG	ANG	450143	451143	452143	453143	459143
720144	AGG	ANG	450144	451144	452144	453144	459144

Class 720/5

These units are now being delivered and undergoing testing. Many units are in store at Old Dalby or Worksop. The first six have been accepted, though were not in passenger service as of early November 2020.

				DMS	PMS	MS	MS	DTS
720501	AGG	ANG	WK (S)	450501	451501	452501	453501	459501
720502	AGG	ANG	ZD (S)	450502	451502	452502	453502	459502
720503	AGG	ANG	WK (S)	450503	451503	452503	453503	459503
720504	AGG	ANG	ZD (S)	450504	451504	452504	453504	459504
720505	AGG	ANG	WK (S)	450505	451505	452505	453505	459505
720506	AGG	ANG	ZD (S)	450506	451506	452506	453506	459506
720507	AGG	ANG	WK (S)	450507	451507	452507	453507	459507
720508	AGG	ANG	ZD (S)	450508	451508	452508	453508	459508
720509	AGG	ANG	IL (Q)	450509	451509	452509	453509	459509
720510	AGG	ANG	WK (S)	450510	451510	452510	453510	459510
720511	AGG	ANG	IL	450511	451511	452511	453511	459511
720512	AGG	ANG	ZD (S)	450512	451512	452512	453512	459512
720513	AGG	ANG	OD (S)	450513	451513	452513	453513	459513
720514	AGG	ANG	ZD (S)	450514	451514	452514	453514	459514
720515	AGG	ANG	IL	450515	451515	452515	453515	459515
720516	AGG	ANG	ZD (S)	450516	451516	452516	453516	459516
720517	AGG	ANG	IL	450517	451517	452517	453517	459517
720518	AGG	ANG	ZD (S)	450518	451518	452518	453518	459518
720519	AGG	ANG	WK (S)	450519	451519	452519	453519	459519
720520	AGG	ANG	WK (S)	450520	451520	452520	453520	459520
720521	AGG	ANG	ZD (S)	450521	451521	452521	453521	459521
720522	AGG	ANG	WK (S)	450522	451522	452522	453522	459522
720523	AGG	ANG	IL (S)	450523	451523	452523	453523	459523
720524	AGG	ANG	WK (S)	450524	451524	452524	453524	459524
720525	AGG	ANG	ZD (S)	450525	451525	452525	453525	459525
720526	AGG	ANG	ZD (S)	450526	451526	452526	453526	459526
720527	AGG	ANG	ZD (S)	450527	451527	452527	453527	459527
720528	AGG	ANG	WK (S)	450528	451528	452528	453528	459528
720529	AGG	ANG	ZD (S)	450529	451529	452529	453529	459529
720530	AGG	ANG	WK (S)	450530	451530	452530	453530	459530
720531	AGG	ANG	ZD (S)	450531	451531	452531	453531	459531
720532	AGG	ANG	WK (S)	450532	451532	452532	453532	459532
720533	AGG	ANG	ZD (S)	450533	451533	452533	453533	459533
720534	AGG	ANG	ZD (S)	450534	451534	452534	453534	459534
720535	AGG	ANG	ZD (S)	450535	451535	452535	453535	459535
720536	AGG	ANG	IL	450536	451536	452536	453536	459536
720537	AGG	ANG	IL	450537	451537	452537	453537	459537
720538	AGG	ANG	IL	450538	451538	452538	453538	459538
720539	AGG	ANG	ZD (Q)	450539	451539	452539	453539	459539
720540	AGG	ANG	ZD (Q)	450540	451540	452540	453540	459540
720541	AGG	ANG	ZD (S)	450541	451541	452541	453541	459541
720542	AGG	ANG	ZD (Q)	450542	451542	452542	453542	459542
720543	AGG	ANG	ZD (S)	450543	451543	452543	453543	459543

720544	AGG	ANG	ZD (S)	450544	451544	452544	453544	459544
720545	AGG	ANG	ZD (S)	450545	451545	452545	453545	459545
720546	AGG	ANG	ZD (S)	450546	451546	452546	453546	459546
720547	AGG	ANG	ZD (S)	450547	451547	452547	453547	459547
720548	AGG	ANG	ZD (S)	450548	451548	452548	453548	459548
720549	AGG	ANG	ZD (S)	450549	451549	452549	453549	459549
720550	AGG	ANG	ZD (S)	450550	451550	452550	453550	459550
720551	AGG	ANG		450551	451551	452551	453551	459551
720552	AGG	ANG		450552	451552	452552	453552	459552
720553	AGG	ANG		450553	451553	452553	453553	459553
720554	AGG	ANG		450554	451554	452554	453554	459554
720555	AGG	ANG		450555	451555	452555	453555	459555
720556	AGG	ANG		450556	451556	452556	453556	459556
720557	AGG	ANG		450557	451557	452557	453557	459557
720558	AGG	ANG		450558	451558	452558	453558	459558
720559	AGG	ANG		450559	451559	452559	453559	459559
720560	AGG	ANG		450560	451560	452560	453560	459560
720561	AGG	ANG		450561	451561	452561	453561	459561
720562	AGG	ANG		450562	451562	452562	453562	459562
720563	AGG	ANG		450563	451563	452563	453563	459563
720564	AGG	ANG		450564	451564	452564	453564	459564
720565	AGG	ANG		450565	451565	452565	453565	459565
720566	AGG	ANG		450566	451566	452566	453566	459566
720567	AGG	ANG		450567	451567	452567	453567	459567
720568	AGG	ANG		450568	451568	452568	453568	459568
720569	AGG	ANG		450569	451569	452569	453569	459569
720570	AGG	ANG		450570	451570	452570	453570	459570
720571	AGG	ANG		450571	451571	452571	453571	459571
720572	AGG	ANG		450572	451572	452572	453572	459572
720573	AGG	ANG		450573	451573	452573	453573	459573
720574	AGG	ANG		450574	451574	452574	453574	459574
720575	AGG	ANG		450575	451575	452575	453575	459575
720576	AGG	ANG		450576	451576	452576	453576	459576
720577	AGG	ANG		450577	451577	452577	453577	459577
720578	AGG	ANG		450578	451578	452578	453578	459578
720579	AGG	ANG		450579	451579	452579	453579	459579
720580	AGG	ANG		450580	451580	452580	453580	459580
720581	AGG	ANG		450581	451581	452581	453581	459581
720582	AGG	ANG		450582	451582	452582	453582	459582
720583	AGG	ANG		450583	451583	452583	453583	459583
720584	AGG	ANG		450584	451584	452584	453584	459584
720585	AGG	ANG		450585	451585	452585	453585	459585
720586	AGG	ANG		450586	451586	452586	453586	459586
720587	AGG	ANG		450587	451587	452587	453587	459587
720588	AGG	ANG		450588	451588	452588	453588	459588
720589	AGG	ANG		450589	451589	452589	453589	459589

Two of the new Bombardier Class 720s Aventra units, 720537/538, pass Slindon on the WCML on a Rugby to Wolverton, via Crewe, test run on 17 July 2020. *Brad Joyce*

No. 755402 works the 1201 Ipswich-Peterborough past Turves on 18 January 2020. *Bill Atkinson*

Class 745

There are two sub-classes of these 25kV AC EMUs Stadler units; the twelve-car sets 745/0s are used for Liverpool Street to Norwich inter-city services and have replaced Class 90-hauled Mk 3 sets, while the 745/1s are destined for use on the Liverpool Street-Stansted Airport shuttles.

Class 745/0

Twelve-car sets for Liverpool St-Norwich services with first- and standard-class seats. All are in the EBHQ pool.

				DMF	PTF	TS	TS	TS	MS	MS	TS	TS	TS	PTS	DMS
745001	AGG	ROC	NC	413001	426001	332001	343001	341001	301001	302001	342001	344001	346001	322001	312001
745002	AGG	ROC	NC	413002	426002	332002	343002	341002	301002	302002	342002	344002	346002	322002	312002
745003	AGG	ROC	NC	413003	426003	332003	343003	341003	301003	302003	342003	344003	346003	322003	312003
745004	AGG	ROC	NC	413004	426004	332004	343004	341004	301004	302004	342004	344004	346004	322004	312004
745005	AGG	ROC	NC	413005	426005	332005	343005	341005	301005	302005	342005	344005	346005	322005	312005
745006	AGG	ROC	NC	413006	426006	332006	343006	341006	301006	302006	342006	344006	346006	322006	312006
745007	AGG	ROC	NC	413007	426007	332007	343007	341007	301007	302007	342007	344007	346007	322007	312007
745008	AGG	ROC	NC	413008	426008	332008	343008	341008	301008	302008	342008	344008	346008	322008	312008
745009	AGG	ROC	NC	413009	426009	332009	343009	341009	301009	302009	342009	344009	346009	322009	312009
745010	AGG	ROC	NC	413010	426010	332010	343010	341010	301010	302010	342010	344010	346010	322010	312010

Class 745/1

Twelve-car sets for Liverpool St-Stansted Airport services with standard-class seats. only. All are in the ENHQ pool.

				DMF	PTF	TS	TS	TS	MS	MS	TS	TS	TS	PTS	DMS
745101	AGG	ROC	NC	313101	326101	332101	343101	341101	301101	302101	342101	344101	346101	322101	312101
745102	AGG	ROC	NC	313102	326102	332102	343102	341102	301102	302102	342102	344102	346102	322102	312102
745103	AGG	ROC	NC	313103	326103	332103	343103	341103	301103	302103	342103	344103	346103	322103	312103
745104	AGG	ROC	NC	313104	326104	332104	343104	341104	301104	302104	342104	344104	346104	322104	312104
745105	AGG	ROC	NC	313105	326105	332105	343105	341105	301105	302105	342105	344105	346105	322105	312105
745106	AGG	ROC	NC	313106	326106	332106	343106	341106	301106	302106	342106	344106	346106	322106	312106
745107	AGG	ROC	NC	313107	326107	332107	343107	341107	301107	302107	342107	344107	346107	322107	312107
745108	AGG	ROC	NC	313108	326108	332108	343108	341108	301108	302108	342108	344108	346108	322108	312108
745109	AGG	ROC	NC	313109	326109	332109	343109	341109	301109	302109	342109	344109	346109	322109	312109
745110	AGG	ROC	NC	313110	326110	332110	343110	341110	301110	302110	342110	344110	346110	322110	312110

Greater Anglia

Class 755

These bi-mode Stadler multiple units are all now in traffic and used on local services on the AGA operation. They have replaced Class 153/156/170 and Class 37-hauled trains in the area, including the local lines from Norwich and the Sudbury to Marks Tey branch.

Although numbered as four- and five-car, the PP vehicle is non-passenger carrying and contains each unit's Deutz engines, of which there are four in the five-car sets and two in the four-car sets. All are in the EBHQ pool.

Class 755/3

				DMS	PP	PTS	DMS
755325	AGG	ROC	NC	911325	971325	981325	912325
755326	AGG	ROC	NC	911326	971326	981326	912326
755327	AGG	ROC	NC	911327	971327	981327	912327
755328	AGG	ROC	NC	911328	971328	981328	912328
755329	AGG	ROC	NC	911329	971329	981329	912329
755330	AGG	ROC	NC	911330	971330	981330	912330
755331	AGG	ROC	NC	911331	971331	981331	912331
755332	AGG	ROC	NC	911332	971332	981332	912332
755333	AGG	ROC	NC	911333	971333	981333	912333
755334	AGG	ROC	NC	911334	971334	981334	912334
755335	AGG	ROC	NC	911335	971335	981335	912335
755336	AGG	ROC	NC	911336	971336	981336	912336
755337	AGG	ROC	NC	911337	971337	981337	912337
755338	AGG	ROC	NC	911338	971338	981338	912338

No. 321433 waits its next duty at Liverpool Street on 18 May 2019. *Pip Dunn*

Class 755/4

				DMS	PTS	PP	PTS	DMS
755401	AGG	ROC	NC	911401	961401	971401	981401	912401
755402	AGG	ROC	NC	911402	961402	971402	981402	912402
755403	AGG	ROC	NC	911403	961403	971403	981403	912403
755404	AGG	ROC	NC	911404	961404	971404	981404	912404
755405	AGG	ROC	NC	911405	961405	971405	981405	912405
755406	AGG	ROC	NC	911406	961406	971406	981406	912406
755407	AGG	ROC	NC	911407	961407	971407	981407	912407
755408	AGG	ROC	NC	911408	961408	971408	981408	912408
755409	AGG	ROC	NC	911409	961409	971409	981409	912409
755410	AGG	ROC	NC	911410	961410	971410	981410	912410
755411	AGG	ROC	NC	911411	961411	971411	981411	912411
755412	AGG	ROC	NC	911412	961412	971412	981412	912412
755413	AGG	ROC	NC	911413	961413	971413	981413	912413
755414	AGG	ROC	NC	911414	961414	971414	981414	912414
755415	AGG	ROC	NC	911415	961415	971415	981415	912415
755416	AGG	ROC	NC	911416	961416	971416	981416	912416
755417	AGG	ROC	NC	911417	961417	971417	981417	912417
755418	AGG	ROC	NC	911418	961418	971418	981418	912418
755419	AGG	ROC	NC	911419	961419	971419	981419	912419
755420	AGG	ROC	NC	911420	961420	971420	981420	912420
755421	AGG	ROC	NC	911421	961421	971421	981421	912421
755422	AGG	ROC	NC	911422	961422	971422	981422	912422
755423	AGG	ROC	NC	911423	961423	971423	981423	912423
755424	AGG	ROC	NC	911424	961424	971424	981424	912424

The first day of passenger service of new Class 745s on the Stansted Airport service, 28 July 2020, sees 745103 at the terminus. *Greater Anglia*

Great Western Railway

Contact details

Website: www.gwr.com
Twitter: @GWRHelp

Key personnel

Managing Director: Matthew Golton
Engineering Director: Simon Green

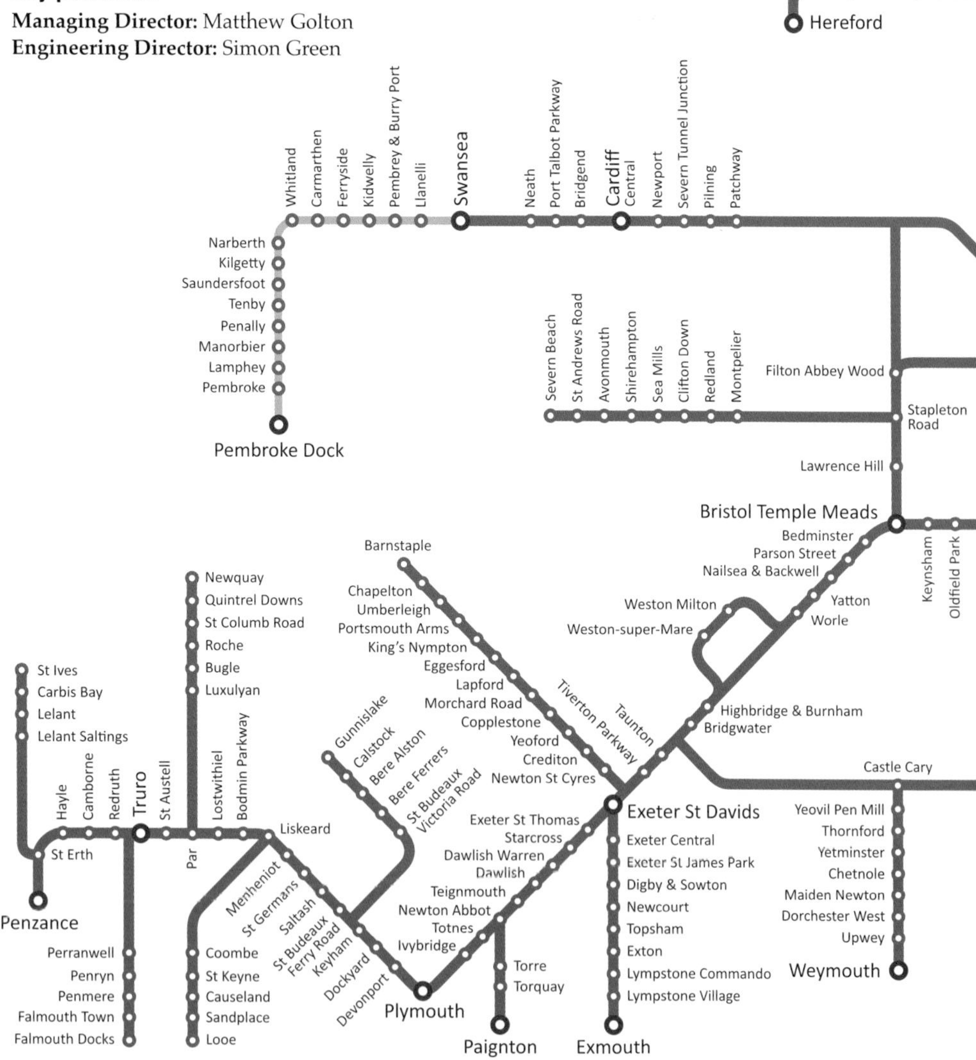

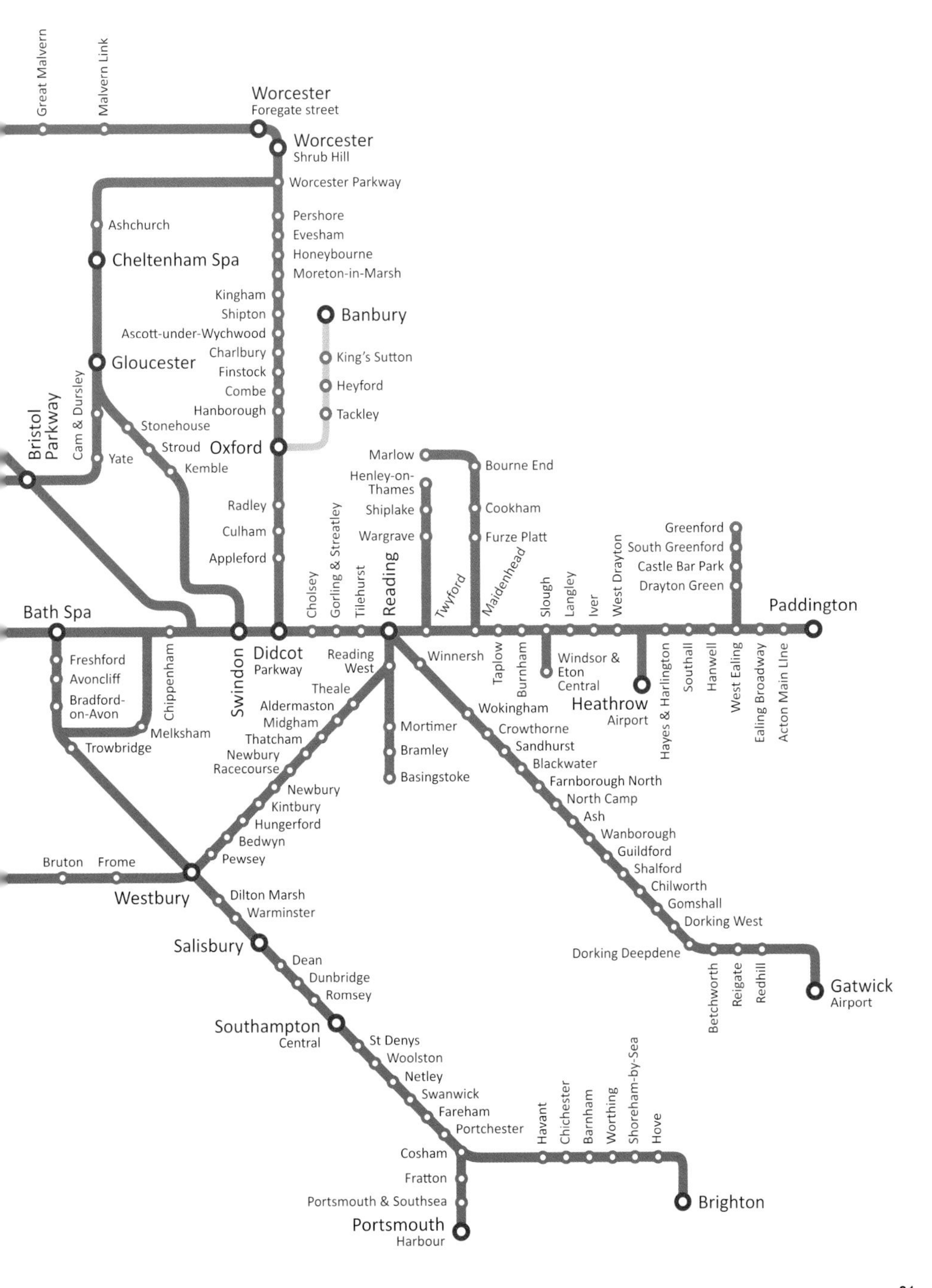
Great Malvern
Malvern Link
Worcester
Foregate street
Worcester
Shrub Hill
Worcester Parkway
Pershore
Evesham
Honeybourne
Moreton-in-Marsh
Kingham
Shipton
Ascott-under-Wychwood
Charlbury
Finstock
Combe
Hanborough
Oxford
Radley
Culham
Appleford
Banbury
King's Sutton
Heyford
Tackley
Ashchurch
Cheltenham Spa
Gloucester
Cam & Dursley
Yate
Bristol Parkway
Stonehouse
Stroud
Kemble
Bath Spa
Freshford
Avoncliff
Bradford-on-Avon
Melksham
Trowbridge
Chippenham
Swindon
Didcot Parkway
Cholsey
Gorling & Streatley
Tilehurst
Reading
Reading West
Theale
Aldermaston
Midgham
Thatcham
Newbury Racecourse
Newbury
Kintbury
Hungerford
Bedwyn
Pewsey
Bruton
Frome
Westbury
Dilton Marsh
Warminster
Salisbury
Dean
Dunbridge
Romsey
Southampton
Central
St Denys
Woolston
Netley
Swanwick
Fareham
Portchester
Cosham
Fratton
Portsmouth & Southsea
Portsmouth
Harbour
Havant
Chichester
Barnham
Worthing
Shoreham-by-Sea
Hove
Brighton
Mortimer
Bramley
Basingstoke
Marlow
Henley-on-Thames
Shiplake
Wargrave
Bourne End
Cookham
Furze Platt
Twyford
Maidenhead
Winnersh
Wokingham
Crowthorne
Sandhurst
Blackwater
Farnborough North
North Camp
Ash
Wanborough
Guildford
Shalford
Chilworth
Gomshall
Dorking West
Dorking Deepdene
Betchworth
Reigate
Redhill
Gatwick
Airport
Taplow
Burnham
Slough
Windsor &
Eton
Central
Langley
Iver
West Drayton
Heathrow
Airport
Hayes & Harlington
Southall
Hanwell
West Ealing
Ealing Broadway
Acton Main LIne
Greenford
South Greenford
Castle Bar Park
Drayton Green
Paddington

Overview

GWR runs all the inter-city trains from Paddington to Hereford, Cheltenham, Bristol TM, Cardiff, Swansea and Carmarthen and to Exeter, Paignton, Plymouth, Truro and Penzance.

It also runs local trains on the Exmouth to Barnstaple route, the Cornish branches, Reading to Gatwick Airport, Bristol TM to Weymouth, Portsmouth and Brighton, Bristol to Severn Beach, Cardiff, Worcester.

The GWR fleet is incredibly mixed. New Hitachi bi-mode Class 800 IETs now work all inter-city operations out of Paddington, while a fleet of short-formed HSTs has been retained and upgraded to work local trains in Devon and Cornwall and also in the Avon and Cardiff area. GWR has just agreed to take seven more power cars and eight more trailers to allow it to create two further Castle Class mini-HST sets.

A fleet of ex-BR DMUs of Classes 150/158/165/166s work local services across the entire GWR network while new Class 387 EMUs are now used on Paddington-Heathrow Airport/Reading/Swindon local commuter trains following extensive electrification of the region.

Class 57s and Mk 3 coaches work the nightly Penzance-Paddington 'Night Riviera' 'sleeper' service. GWR has four 57/6s and hires 57/3s from DRS if required.

As more parts of the GWML from Paddington to Bristol TM and Cardiff have been energised, the use of electric trains has increased.

Class 08

GWR retain five Class 08s, based at Laira, Penzance and Bristol St Philip's Marsh. It has recently sold 08410/483/663. All are in the EFSH pool.

08641	GWR	BRW	LA	*Pride of Laira*
08644	GWR	BRW	LA	*Laira Diesel Depot 50 Years 1962-2012*
08645	GWR	KER	PZ	*St Piran*
08822	GWR	ICS	PM	*Dave Mills*
08836	GWR	GWR	LA	

No. 158766 arrives at Newton Abbot on the 1551 Exeter St David's-Plymouth on 22 August 2019. *Robin Ralston*

Class 43

Once the mainstay of the GWR inter-city operation, the popular HST sets have been replaced from top-link duties by Class 800 Hitachi units.

However, several power cars and Mk 3 trailers – the latter modified to have sliding doors – are retained as 'Castle class' 2+4 sets.

Initially 11 sets and 24 power cars were to be kept, many of the vehicles owned by First Group, others leased from Angel. However, additional HST Power Cars 43009/010/022/027/029/171/172 are to be added to the fleet and will be repainted into GWR green.

No. 43195 has collision damage and is kept at Laira as a source of spares but other power cars listed as stored serviceable or unserviceable may be reinstated if required.

Several Angel HST power cars remain in the GWR active pool even though they are not in use with the TOC. All are in the EFPC pool.

43004	GWR	ANG	LA	*Caerphilly Castle*
43005	GWR	ANG	LA	*St. Michael's Mount*
43009	GWR	ANG	LA	
43010	FGB	ANG	LA	
43016	GWR	ANG	LA	*Powderham Castle*
43022	FGB	ANG	LA	
43027	GWR	ANG	LA	
43029	FGB	ANG	LA	
43040	GWR	ANG	LA	*Berry Pomeroy Castle*
43041	GWR	ANG	LA	*St Catherine's Castle*
43042	GWR	ANG	LA	*Tregenna Castle*
43088	GWR	FIR	LA	
43092	GWR	FIR	LA	*Cromwell's Castle*
43093	GWA	FIR	LA	*Castle-an-Dinas*
43094	GWR	FIR	LA	*St. Mawes Castle*
43097	GWR	FIR	LA	*Castle Drogo*
43098	GWR	FIR	LA	*Walton Castle*
43122	GWR	FIR	LA	*Dunster Castle*
43153	GWR	FIR	LA	*Chûn Castle*
43154	GWR	FIR	LA	*Compton Castle*
43155	GWR	FIR	LA	*Rougemont Castle*
43156	FGB	FIR	LA (S)	
43158	GWR	FIR	LA	*Kingswear Castle*
43160	GWR	FIR	LA	
43162	GWR	FIR	LA	
43170	GWR	ANG	LA	*Chepstow Castle*
43171	GWR	ANG	LA	
43172	GWR	ANG	LA	
43186	GWR	ANG	LA	*Taunton Castle*
43187	GWR	ANG	LA	*Cardiff Castle*
43188	GWR	ANG	LA	*Newport Castle*
43189	GWR	ANG	LA	*Launceston Castle*
43192	GWR	ANG	LA	*Trematon Castle*
43194	GWR	FIR	LA	*Okehampton Castle*
43195	FGB	FIR	LA (U)	
43198	GWR	FIR	LA	*Driver Stan Martin/Driver Brian Cooper*

HST trailers

The 'Castle' HST sets rely on fixed formation four-car sets comprising three Trailer Standards and one TGS. There are two spare of each type. Authorisation for more 'Castle' HSTs will require more Mk 3 coaches to be recovered from store and overhauls and modified.

48101	GWR	FIR	LA	48125	GWR	ANG	LA
48102	GWR	FIR	LA	48126	GWR	ANG	LA
48103	GWR	FIR	LA	48127	GWR	ANG	LA
48104	GWR	FIR	LA	48128	GWR	ANG	LA
48105	GWR	FIR	LA	48129	GWR	ANG	LA
48106	GWR	FIR	LA	48130	GWR	ANG	LA
48107	GWR	FIR	LA	48131	GWR	FIR	LA
48108	GWR	FIR	LA	48132	GWR	ANG	LA
48109	GWR	FIR	LA	48133	GWR	ANG	LA
48110	GWR	FIR	LA	48134	GWR	ANG	LA
48111	GWR	FIR	LA	48135	GWR	ANG	LA
48112	GWR	FIR	LA	49101	GWR	FIR	LA
48113	GWR	FIR	LA	49102	GWR	FIR	LA
48114	GWR	FIR	LA	49103	GWR	FIR	LA
48115	GWR	ANG	LA	49104	GWR	FIR	LA
48116	GWR	ANG	LA	49105	GWR	FIR	LA
48118	GWR	ANG	LA	49106	GWR	ANG	LA
48117	GWR	ANG	LA	49107	GWR	ANG	LA
48119	GWR	ANG	LA	49108	GWR	ANG	LA
48120	GWR	ANG	LA	49109	GWR	ANG	LA
48121	GWR	ANG	LA	49110	GWR	ANG	LA
48122	GWR	ANG	LA	49111	GWR	ANG	LA
48123	GWR	ANG	LA	49112	GWR	ANG	LA
48124	GWR	ANG	LA	49113	GWR	ANG	LA

One of the new 'Castle class' mini-HSTs, 43042 and 43153, pass Powderham with the 1550 Penzance-Exeter on 23 June 2020. *Antony Christie*

GW Castle Class HST formations

As a rule the GWR HST vehicle trailers stay in fixed formations, but the four spare vehicles may replace vehicles as required for heavy maintenance or because of faults or damage. Power cars will be swapped around as required and are not assigned to any particular set.

	TGS	TS	TS	TS
GW01	49101	48101	48102	48103
GW02	49102	48104	48105	48106
GW03	49103	48107	48108	48109
GW04	49104	48110	48111	48112
GW05	49105	48113	48114	48115
GW06	49106	48116	48117	48118
GW07	49107	48119	48120	48121
GW08	49108	48122	48123	48124
GW09	49109	48125	48126	48127
GW10	49110	48128	48129	48130
GW11	49111	48131	48132	48133

Spare vehicles

These vehicles, are spare vehicles for use in Castle HSTs

TGS	
49112	FIR
49113	FIR
TS	
48134	FIR
48135	FIR

Vehicles undergoing conversion

The following HST Mk 3 trailers are currently undergoing conversions to additional Castle class vehicles and will be renumbered

42005	ANG	42066	ANG	42173	POR	42580	POR
42015	ANG	42071	ANG	42195	POR	44002	ANG
42016	ANG	42074	ANG	42217	POR	44005	ANG
42048	ANG	42081	ANG	42310	POR	44016	ANG
42050	ANG	42087	POR	42353	POR	44042	POR

Class 57s

Four Class 57/6s, Class 47s rebuilt with General Motors engines, work the Paddington-Penzance 'Night Riviera' 'sleeper' service. The fleet is sometimes supplemented by a DRS Class 57/3, usually 57306. All are in the EFOO pool.

57602	47337	GWR	POR	PZ	*Restormel Castle*
57603	47349	GWR	POR	PZ	*Tintagel Castle*
57604	47209	GWE	POR	PZ	*Pendennis Castle*
57605	47206	GWR	POR	PZ	*Totnes Castle*

Sprinter 150244 departs Lapford on 1 April 2019. *Antony Christie*

Loco-hauled coaches

A small fleet of loco-hauled coaches are retained for the 'Night Riviera'. They are three Kitchen Buffet Firsts, 11 SLEPs, three TSO and three BSOs. All are based at Penzance Long Rock. They do not remain in fixed sets.

Kitchen Buffet First			
10217	GWR	POR	PZ
10219	GWR	POR	PZ
10225	GWR	POR	PZ
Sleeper car with pantry			
10532	GWR	POR	PZ
10534	GWR	POR	PZ
10563	GWR	POR	PZ
10584	GWR	POR	PZ
10589	GWR	POR	PZ
10590	GWR	POR	PZ
10594	GWR	POR	PZ
10596	GWR	POR	PZ
10601	GWR	POR	PZ
10612	GWR	POR	PZ
10616	GWR	POR	PZ

Open Standard			
12100	GWR	POR	PZ
12142	GWR	POR	PZ
12161	GWR	POR	PZ
Open Brake			
17173	GWR	POR	PZ
17174	GWR	POR	PZ
17175	GWR	POR	PZ

Class 143

These two-car railbuses are due for withdrawal. All are in the EFHQ pool.

				DMS	DMSL
143603	GWR	POR	EX	55658	55669
143611	GWR	POR	EX	55652	55677
143612	GWR	POR	EX	55653	55678
143617	GWR	GWR	EX	55644	55683
143618	GWR	GWR	EX	55659	55684
143619	GWR	GWR	EX	55660	55685
143620	GWR	POR	EX	55661	55686
143621	GWR	POR	EX	55662	55687

Class 150

The two-car Sprinter DMUs built by BREL in 1986/87 are based at Exeter for use on Devon and Cornish branch line workings such as Exeter to Exmouth and Barnstaple, Plymouth-Gunnislake, Liskeard-Looe, Par-Newquay, Truro-Falmouth and St Erth-St Ives. All are in the EFHQ pool.

Class 150/2

Second production series built of the Class 150 Sprinters, these two-car units have corridor connections.

				DMSL	DMS
150202	GWR	ANG	EX	52202	57202
150207	GWR	ANG	EX	52207	57207
150216	GWR	ANG	EX	52216	57216
150219	FIR	ANG	EX	52219	57219
150221	GWR	ANG	EX	52221	57221
150232	GWR	ANG	EX	52232	57232
150233	GWR	ANG	EX	52233	57233
150234	GWR	ANG	EX	52234	57234
150238	FIR	ANG	EX	52238	57238
150239	GWR	ANG	EX	52239	57239
150243	GWR	ANG	EX	52243	57243
150244	GWR	ANG	EX	52244	57244
150246	GWR	ANG	EX	52246	57246
150247	GWR	ANG	EX	52247	57247
150248	GWR	ANG	EX	52248	57248
150249	GWR	ANG	EX	52249	57249
150261	GWR	ANG	EX	52261	57261
150263	GWR	ANG	EX	52263	57263
150265	GWR	ANG	EX	52265	57265
150266	GWR	ANG	EX	52266	57266

Class 158

The two- and three-car sets, built in 1990 by BREL, are used between Exeter and Penzance on those trains not worked by HSTs and from Exeter to Bristol TM. The three-car sets tend to be used on the Bristol to Weymouth, Portsmouth and Brighton routes. Although numbered in the 15895x series, these are just re-formed three-car Class 158/0s. All are in the EFHQ pool.

				DMSL	DMSL	DMSL
158745	GWR	POR	EX	52745		57745
158747	GWR	POR	EX	52747		57747
158749	GWR	POR	EX	52749		57749
158750	GWR	POR	EX	52750		57750
158760	GWR	POR	EX	52760		57760
158762	GWR	POR	EX	52762		57762
158763	GWR	POR	EX	52763		57763
158765	GWR	POR	EX	52765		57765
158766	GWR	POR	EX	52766		57766
158767	GWR	POR	EX	52767		57767
158769	GWR	POR	EX	52769		57769
158798	GWR	POR	PM	52798	58715	57798
158950	GWR	POR	PM	57751	52761	57761
158951	GWR	POR	PM	52751	52764	57764
158956	GWR	POR	PM	52748	52768	57768
158957	GWR	POR	PM	57748	52771	57771
158958	GWR	POR	PM	57746	52776	57776
158959	GWR	POR	PM	52746	52778	57778

Note: 58715 is an MSL.

Class 165

Once the mainstay of local commuter duties from Paddington, many of the Network Turbo units built by BREL at York in 1991-93 have been displaced by EMUs. Nevertheless, they still work the branch lines in the Thames Valley such as to Windsor & Eton Riverside, Marlow and Henley-on-Thames and also some Paddington-Oxford trains.

Spare units displaced from the Thames Valley have been reallocated to Bristol for working to Severn Beach, Portsmouth, Taunton and other local services in the Avon and Somerset areas. All are in the EFHQ pool.

Class 165/1

				DMSL	MS	DMS
165101	GWR	ANG	RG	58953	55415	58916
165102	GWR	ANG	RG	58954	55416	58917
165103	GWR	ANG	RG	58955	55417	58918
165104	GWR	ANG	RG	58956	55418	58919
165105	GWR	ANG	RG	58957	55419	58920
165106	GWR	ANG	RG	58958	55420	58921
165107	GWR	ANG	RG	58959	55421	58922
165108	GWR	ANG	RG	58960	55422	58923
165109	GWR	ANG	RG	58961	55423	58924
165110	GWR	ANG	RG	58962	55424	58925
165111	GWR	ANG	RG	58963	55425	58926
165112	GWR	ANG	RG	58964	55426	58927
165113	GWR	ANG	RG	58965	55427	58928
165114	GWR	ANG	RG	58966	55428	58929
165116	GWR	ANG	RG	58968	55430	58931
165117	GWR	ANG	RG	58969	55431	58932
165118	GWR	ANG	RG	58879		58933
165119	GWR	ANG	RG	58880		58934
165120	GWR	ANG	RG	58881		58935
165121	GWR	ANG	RG	58882		58936
165122	GWR	ANG	RG	58883		58937
165123	GWR	ANG	RG	58884		58938
165124	GWR	ANG	RG	58885		58939
165125	GWR	ANG	RG	58886		58940
165126	GWR	ANG	RG	58887		58941
165127	GWR	ANG	RG	58888		58942
165128	GWR	ANG	PM	58889		58943
165129	GWR	ANG	PM	58890		58944
165130	GWR	ANG	PM	58891		58945
165131	GWR	ANG	PM	58892		58946
165132	GWR	ANG	PM	58893		58947
165133	GWR	ANG	PM	58894		58948
165134	GWR	ANG	PM	58895		58949
165135	GWR	ANG	PM	58896		58950
165136	GWR	ANG	PM	58897		58951
165137	GWR	ANG	PM	58898		58952

Class 166

These ex-Thames units are all now based at Bristol St Philip's Marsh for local Avon and Somerset duties. They have recently been passed to work to Barnstaple, and are expected to start working through to Brighton soon. All are in the EFHQ pool.

				DMCL	MS	DMSL	
166201	FIR	ANG	PM	58101	58601	58122	
166202	FIR	ANG	PM	58102	58602	58123	
166203	FIR	ANG	PM	58103	58603	58124	
166204	GWR	ANG	PM	58104	58604	58125	*Norman Topsham MBE*
166205	GWR	ANG	PM	58105	58605	58126	
166206	GWR	ANG	PM	58106	58606	58127	
166207	FIR	ANG	PM	58107	58607	58128	
166208	GWR	ANG	PM	58108	58608	58129	
166209	FIR	ANG	PM	58109	58609	58130	
166210	GWR	ANG	PM	58110	58610	58131	
166211	FIR	ANG	PM	58111	58611	58132	
166212	GWR	ANG	PM	58112	58612	58133	
166213	GWR	ANG	PM	58113	58613	58134	
166214	GWR	ANG	PM	58114	58614	58135	
166215	FIR	ANG	PM	58115	58615	58136	
166216	GWR	ANG	PM	58116	58616	58137	
166217	GWR	ANG	PM	58117	58617	58138	
166218	GWR	ANG	PM	58118	58618	58139	
166219	GWR	ANG	PM	58119	58619	58140	
166220	GWR	ANG	PM	58120	58620	58141	*Roger Watkins – the GWR Master Train Planner*
166221	FIR	ANG	PM	58121	58621	58142	*Reading Train Care Depot*

Class 387

These Bombardier Electrostar 25kV AC EMUs work out of Paddington along the Thames corridor to Reading, Didcot and Swindon. They also work the Paddington-Heathrow Airport shuttles (387130-141) alongside Class 332s and 360/2s. All are in the EFHQ pool.

				DMC	MS	PTS	DMS
387130	HEX	POR	RG	421130	422130	423130	424130
387131	HEX	POR	RG	421131	422131	423131	424131
387132	HEX	POR	RG	421132	422132	423132	424132
387133	HEX	POR	RG	421133	422133	423133	424133
387134	HEX	POR	RG	421134	422134	423134	424134
387135	HEX	POR	RG	421135	422135	423135	424135
387136	HEX	POR	RG	421136	422136	423136	424136
387137	HEX	POR	RG	421137	422137	423137	424137
387138	HEX	POR	RG	421138	422138	423138	424138
387139	HEX	POR	RG	421139	422139	423139	424139
387140	HEX	POR	RG	421140	422140	423140	424140
387141	GWR	POR	RG	421141	422141	423141	424141
387142	GWR	POR	RG	421142	422142	423142	424142
387143	GWR	POR	RG	421143	422143	423143	424143

387144	GWR	POR	RG	421144	422144	423144	424144
387145	GWR	POR	RG	421145	422145	423145	424145
387146	GWR	POR	RG	421146	422146	423146	424146
387147	GWR	POR	RG	421147	422147	423147	424147
387148	GWR	POR	RG	421148	422148	423148	424148
387149	GWR	POR	RG	421149	422149	423149	424149
387150	GWR	POR	RG	421150	422150	423150	424150
387151	GWR	POR	RG	421151	422151	423151	424151
387152	GWR	POR	RG	421152	422152	423152	424152
387153	GWR	POR	RG	421153	422153	423153	424153
387154	GWR	POR	RG	421154	422154	423154	424154
387155	GWR	POR	RG	421155	422155	423155	424155
387156	GWR	POR	RG	421156	422156	423156	424156
387157	GWR	POR	RG	421157	422157	423157	424157
387158	GWR	POR	RG	421158	422158	423158	424158
387159	GWR	POR	RG	421159	422159	423159	424159
387160	GWR	POR	RG	421160	422160	423160	424160
387161	GWR	POR	RG	421161	422161	423161	424161
387162	GWR	POR	RG	421162	422162	423162	424162
387163	GWR	POR	RG	421163	422163	423163	424163
387164	GWR	POR	RG	421164	422164	423164	424164
387165	GWR	POR	RG	421165	422165	423165	424165
387166	GWR	POR	RG	421166	422166	423166	424166
387167	GWR	POR	RG	421167	422167	423167	424167
387168	GWR	POR	RG	421168	422168	423168	424168
387169	GWR	POR	RG	421169	422169	423169	424169
387170	GWR	POR	RG	421170	422170	423170	424170
387171	GWR	POR	RG	421171	422171	423171	424171
387172	GWR	POR	RG	421172	422172	423172	424172
387173	GWR	POR	RG	421173	422173	423173	424173
387174	GWR	POR	RG	421174	422174	423174	424174

Shunter 08836 on display at Old Oak Common on 20 April 2017. *Jack Boskett*

Class 769

Nineteen Class 769 FLEX units are being converted from redundant Thameslink Class 319s by Brush Traction are destined for the GWR franchise. They will retain their dual-voltage 25kV AC and 750V DC capabilities but also have diesel engines to work 'off the wires'. They will be used for Oxford-Gatwick Airport services.

The first units have now been delivered for driver training. All are in the EFHQ pool.

					DMC	MS	TS	DMC
769922	319422	GWR	POR	RG	77333	62912	71793	77332
769923	319423	GWR	POR	RG	77335	62913	71794	77334
769925	319425	GWR	POR	RG	77339	62915	71796	77338
769927	319427	GWR	POR	RG	77343	62917	71798	77342
769928	319428	GWR	POR	RG	77345	62918	71799	77344
769930	319430	GWR	POR	RG	77349	62920	71801	77348
769932	319432	GWR	POR	RG	77353	62922	71803	77352
769935	319435	GWR	POR	RG	77359	62925	71806	77358
769936	319436	GWR	POR	RG	77361	62926	71807	77360
769937	319437	GWR	POR	RG	77363	62927	71808	77362
769938	319438	GWR	POR	RG	77365	62928	71809	77364
769939	319439	GWR	POR	RG	77367	62929	71810	77366
769940	319440	GWR	POR	RG	77369	62930	71811	77368
769943	319443	GWR	POR	RG	77375	62933	71814	77374
769944	319444	GWR	POR	RG	77377	62934	71815	77376
769946	319446	GWR	POR	RG	77381	62936	71817	77380
769947	319447	GWR	POR	RG	77431	62961	71866	77430
769949	319449	GWR	POR	RG	77435	62963	71868	77434
769959	319459	GWR	POR	RG	77455	62973	71878	77454

Class 800

GWR was the first TOC to put the new Hitachi InterCity Express Trains (IET) units into traffic and the full fleet is now in use and has allowed the elimination of HST workings to Paddington. All are in the EFHQ pool.

Electrostar unit 387152 at Maidenhead Sidings on 30 June 2017.
Jack Boskett

Class 800/0

Bi-mode 25kV AC and diesel five-car units

				PDTS	MS	MS	MS	PDTRBF	
800001	GWR	AGI	NP	811001	812001	813001	814001	815001	
800002	GWR	AGI	NP	811002	812002	813002	814002	815002	
800003	GWR	AGI	NP	811003	812003	813003	814003	815003	
800004	GWR	AGI	NP	811004	812004	813004	814004	815004	
800005	GWR	AGI	NP	811005	812005	813005	814005	815005	
800006	GWR	AGI	NP	811006	812006	813006	814006	815006	
800007	GWR	AGI	NP	811007	812007	813007	814007	815007	
800008	GWR	AGI	NP	811008	812008	813008	814008	815008	
800009	GWR	AGI	NP	811009	812009	813009	814009	815009	*Sir Gareth Edwards/ John Charles*
800010	GWR	AGI	NP	811010	812010	813010	814010	815010	*Michael Bond/ Paddington Bear*
800011	GWR	AGI	NP	811011	812011	813011	814011	815011	
800012	GWR	AGI	NP	811012	812012	813012	814012	815012	
800013	GWR	AGI	NP	811013	812013	813013	814013	815013	
800014	GWR	AGI	NP	811014	812014	813014	814014	815014	*Megan Lloyd George CH/Edith New*
800015	GWR	AGI	NP	811015	812015	813015	814015	815015	
800016	GWR	AGI	NP	811016	812016	813016	814016	815016	
800017	GWR	AGI	NP	811017	812017	813017	814017	815017	
800018	GWR	AGI	NP	811018	812018	813018	814018	815018	
800019	GWR	AGI	NP	811019	812019	813019	814019	815019	*Joy Lofthouse/Johnny Johnson MBE DFM*
800020	GWR	AGI	NP	811020	812020	813020	814020	815020	*Bob Woodward/ Elizabeth Ralph*
800021	GWR	AGI	NP	811021	812021	813021	814021	815021	
800022	GWR	AGI	NP	811022	812022	813022	814022	815022	
800023	GWR	AGI	NP	811023	812023	813023	814023	815023	*Firefighter Fleur Lombard QGM/ Kathryn Osmond*
800024	GWR	AGI	NP	811024	812024	813024	814024	815024	
800025	GWR	AGI	NP	811025	812025	813025	814025	815025	
800026	GWR	AGI	NP	811026	812026	813026	814026	815026	*Don Cameron*
800027	GWR	AGI	NP	811027	812027	813027	814027	815027	
800028	GWR	AGI	NP	811028	812028	813028	814028	815028	
800029	GWR	AGI	NP	811029	812029	813029	814029	815029	
800030	GWR	AGI	NP	811030	812030	813030	814030	815030	
800031	GWR	AGI	NP	811031	812031	813031	814031	815031	
800032	GWR	AGI	NP	811032	812032	813032	814032	815032	
800033	GWR	AGI	NP	811033	812033	813033	814033	815033	
800034	GWR	AGI	NP	811034	812034	813034	814034	815034	
800035	GWR	AGI	NP	811035	812035	813035	814035	815035	
800036	GWR	AGI	NP	811036	812036	813036	814036	815036	*Dr Paul Stephenson OBE*

Class 800/3

Bi-mode 25kV AC and diesel nine-car units. All are in the EFHQ pool.

				PDTS	MS	MS	TS	MS	TS	MS	MF	PDTRBF
800301	GWR	AGI	NP	821001	822001	823001	824001	825001	826001	827001	828001	829001
800302	GWR	AGI	NP	821002	822002	823002	824002	825002	826002	827002	828002	829002
800303	GWR	AGI	NP	821003	822003	823003	824003	825003	826003	827003	828003	829003
800304	GWR	AGI	NP	821004	822004	823004	824004	825004	826004	827004	828004	829004
800305	GWR	AGI	NP	821005	822005	823005	824005	825005	826005	827005	828005	829005
800306	GWR	AGI	NP	821006	822006	823006	824006	825006	826006	827006	828006	829006
800307	GWR	AGI	NP	821007	822007	823007	824007	825007	826007	827007	828007	829007
800308	GWR	AGI	NP	821008	822008	823008	824008	825008	826008	827008	828008	829008
800309	GWR	AGI	NP	821009	822009	823009	824009	825009	826009	827009	828009	829009
800310	GWR	AGI	NP	821010	822010	823010	824010	825010	826010	827010	828010	829010
800311	GWR	AGI	NP	821011	822011	823011	824011	825011	826011	827011	828210	829011
800312	GWR	AGI	NP	821012	822012	823012	824012	825012	826012	827012	828012	829012
800313	GWR	AGI	NP	821013	822013	823013	824013	825013	826013	827013	828013	829013
800314	GWR	AGI	NP	821014	822014	823014	824014	825014	826014	827014	828014	829014
800315	GWR	AGI	NP	821015	822015	823015	824015	825015	826015	827015	828015	829015
800316	GWR	AGI	NP	821016	822016	823016	824016	825016	826016	827016	828016	829016
800317	GWR	AGI	NP	821017	822017	823017	824017	825017	826017	827017	828017	829017
800318	GWR	AGI	NP	821018	822018	823018	824018	825018	826018	827018	828018	829018
800319	GWR	AGI	NP	821019	822019	823019	824019	825019	826019	827019	828019	829019
800320	GWR	AGI	NP	821020	822020	823020	824020	825020	826020	827020	828020	829020
800321	GWR	AGI	NP	821021	822021	823021	824021	825021	826021	827021	828021	829021

800306 is named *Allan Leonard Lewis VC/Harold Day DSC*
800314 is named *Odette Hallowes*

GWR Turbo unit 165104 passes Hungerford on 11 April 2019. *Paul Robertson*

Class 802

The same as Class 800s but with modifications to work along the Dawlish sea wall.

Class 802/0

Bi-mode 25kV AC and diesel five-car units. All are in the EFHQ pool.

				PDTS	MS	MS	MS	PDTRBF	
802001	GWR	EVS	NP	831001	832001	833001	834001	835001	
802002	GWR	EVS	NP	831002	832002	833002	834002	835002	
802003	GWR	EVS	NP	831003	832003	833003	834003	835003	
802004	GWR	EVS	NP	831004	832004	833004	834004	835004	
802005	GWR	EVS	NP	831005	832005	833005	834005	835005	
802006	GWR	EVS	NP	831006	832006	833006	834006	835006	*Harry Billinge MBE*
802007	GWR	EVS	NP	831007	832007	833007	834007	835007	
802008	GWR	EVS	NP	831008	832008	833008	834008	835008	*Rick Rescorla/RNLB Solomon Browne*
802009	GWR	EVS	NP	831009	832009	833009	834009	835009	
802010	GWR	EVS	NP	831010	832010	833010	834010	835010	*Corporal George Sheard*
802011	GWR	EVS	NP	831011	832011	833011	834011	835011	*Sir Joshua Reynolds PRA/Capt. Robert Falcon Scott RN CVO*
802012	GWR	EVS	NP	831012	832012	833012	834012	835012	
802013	GWR	EVS	NP	831013	832013	833013	834013	835013	*Michael Eavis CBE*
802014	GWR	EVS	NP	831014	832014	833014	834014	835014	
802015	GWR	EVS	NP	831015	832015	833015	834015	835015	
802016	GWR	EVS	NP	831016	832016	833016	834016	835016	
802017	GWR	EVS	NP	831017	832017	833017	834017	835017	
802018	GWR	EVS	NP	831018	832018	833018	834018	835018	
802019	GWR	EVS	NP	831019	832019	833019	834019	835019	
802020	GWA	EVS	NP	831020	832020	833020	834020	835020	
802021	GWR	EVS	NP	831021	832021	833021	834021	835021	
802022	GWR	EVS	NP	831022	832022	833022	834022	835022	

Nine-car bi-mode 800302 passes Hungerford on 11 April 2019. *Paul Robertson*

Class 802/1

Bi-mode 25kV AC and diesel nine-car units. All are in the WFHQ pool.

				PDTS	MS	MS	TS	MS	TS	MS	MF	PDTRBF	
802101	GWR	EVS	NP	831101	832101	833101	834101	835101	836101	837101	838101	839101	*Nancy Astor CH*
802102	GWR	EVS	NP	831102	832102	833102	834102	835102	836102	837102	838102	839102	
802103	GWR	EVS	NP	831103	832103	833103	834103	835103	836103	837103	838103	839103	
802104	GWR	EVS	NP	831104	832104	833104	834104	835104	836104	837104	838104	839104	
802105	GWR	EVS	NP	831105	832105	833105	834105	835105	836105	837105	838105	839105	
802106	GWR	EVS	NP	831106	832106	833106	834106	835106	836106	837106	838106	839106	
802107	GWR	EVS	NP	831107	832107	833107	834107	835107	836107	837107	838107	839107	
802108	GWR	EVS	NP	831108	832108	833108	834108	835108	836108	837108	838108	839108	
802109	GWR	EVS	NP	831109	832109	833109	834109	835109	836109	837109	838109	839109	
802110	GWR	EVS	NP	831110	832110	833110	834110	835110	836110	837110	838110	839110	
802111	GWR	EVS	NP	831111	832111	833111	834111	835111	836111	837111	838311	839111	
802112	GWR	EVS	NP	831112	832112	833112	834112	835112	836112	837112	838112	839112	
802113	GWR	EVS	NP	831113	832113	833113	834113	835113	836113	837113	838113	839113	
802114	GWR	EVS	NP	831114	832114	833114	834114	835114	836114	837114	838114	839114	

Five-car bi-mode 802008 works the 1203 Paddington-Penzance past Hungerford Common on 29 October 2018. *Bill Atkinson*

London North Eastern Railway

Contact details

Website: lner.co.uk
Twitter: @LNER
Key personnel
Managing Director: David Horne
Engineering Director: John Doughty

Overview

The main East Coast Main Line operator, which runs from King's Cross to Leeds and Edinburgh, but also some trains to Lincoln, Hull and Aberdeen and a limited number of services to Inverness, Glasgow Central and soon Huddersfield and Middlesbrough.

The operation of passenger services on the ECML has been a something of a nightmare for the government ever since it was privatised, with GNER, National Express and more recently Stagecoach all overbidding for this perceived 'jewel in the crown' of franchises.

All have failed miserably, resulting in the state stepping in each time to run the trains. Before COVID, it was still the government's intention to re-let the franchise yet again, but there seems to be no immediate likelihood of that happening.

Under LNER, there has been some stability. The new Hitachi AT300 trains, while in no way perfect, have finally been put into traffic and allowed most of the older trains to be laid up. However, ten Class 91s are to be retained longer than expected into 2023.

The LNER fleet has undergone a full overhaul, a process started when it was still operated by Stagecoach/Virgin. Out have gone the HST diesel sets and their Mk 3 trailers, while over two-thirds of the Class 91-hauled Mk 4 sets have also been retired.

In their place has come a fleet of Class 800/801 Hitachi AT300 high-speed multiple units. All the new trains are technically bi-mode, but the reality is the Class 801s are effectively straight electric units and only have one engine for emergency use to clear the running line if there is an issue with the electric power. The Class 800s are bi-mode for those services that run to destinations away from the core King's Cross-Leeds/Edinburgh electrified route.

The new bi-mode trains have allowed LNER to not only replace HSTs on operations to Inverness, Harrogate, Hull and Aberdeen, but will also allow some new – albeit limited – services such as Huddersfield and Middlesbrough into its timetable.

Most of the transition for LNER is complete, however Covid-19 has badly affected the profitability of the franchise which will now remain in state ownership until further notice.

Class 91

The fleet of 31 locos has already been cut by to 12, with 91119/124 also due to depart the fleet to leave ten locos – 91101/105-107/109-111/114/127/130. Other locos are now in store and could move to other operators, while some could be exported. All are in the IECA pool.

91101	91001	VFS	EVS	BN	*FLYING SCOTSMAN*
91105	91005	VEC	EVS	BN	
91106	91006	VEA	EVS	BN	
91107	91007	VEC	EVS	BN	*SKYFALL*
91109	91009	VEC	EVS	BN	*Sir Bobby Robson*
91110	91010	BBM	EVS	BN	*BATTLE OF BRITAIN MEMORIAL FLIGHT*
91111	91011	FTF	EVS	BN	*For the Fallen*
91114	91014	VEA	EVS	BN	*Durham Cathedral*
91119	91019	ICS	EVS	BN	*Bounds Green INTERCITY Depot 1977-2017*
91124	91024	VEC	EVS	BN	
91127	91027	VEC	EVS	BN	
91130	91030	VEC	EVS	BN	*Lord Mayor of Newcastle*

Class 800

These are bi-mode Azuma units of nine- and five-car sets. The latter can run as ten-car sets if required, including for some services where the trains splits. All are in the HBHQ pool.

Class 800/1

Bi-mode 25kV AC and diesel nine-car units. No. 800109 was damaged in a collision at Leeds in November 2019 and is being repaired.

				PTDS	MS	MS	TSRB	MS	TS	MC	MF	PDTRBF
800101	LNE	AGI	DN	811101	812101	813101	814101	815101	816101	817101	818101	819101
800102	LNE	AGI	DN	811102	812102	813102	814102	815102	816102	817102	818102	819102
800103	LNE	AGI	DN	811103	812103	813103	814103	815103	816103	817103	818103	819103
800104	LNE	AGI	DN	811104	812104	813104	814104	815104	816104	817104	818104	819104
800105	LNE	AGI	DN	811105	812105	813105	814105	815105	816105	817105	818105	819105
800106	LNE	AGI	DN	811106	812106	813106	814106	815106	816106	817106	818106	819106
800107	LNE	AGI	DN	811107	812107	813107	814107	815107	816107	817107	818107	819107
800108	LNE	AGI	DN	811108	812108	813108	814108	815108	816108	817108	818108	819108
800109	LNE	AGI	ZN (U)	811109	812109	813109	814109	815109	816109	817109	818109	819109
800110	LNE	AGI	DN	811110	812110	813110	814110	815110	816110	817110	818110	819110
800111	LNE	AGI	DN	811111	812111	813111	814111	815111	816111	817111	818111	819111
800112	LNE	AGI	DN	811112	812112	813112	814112	815112	816112	817112	818112	819112
800113	LNE	AGI	DN	811113	812113	813113	814113	815113	816113	817113	818113	819113

A handful of Class 91s are being retained by LNER until 2023. No. 91110 *Battle of Britain Memorial Flight* passes Ryther on 31 May 2020. *Anthony Hicks*

The new order for ECML trains are bi-mode Class 800 IET units. No. 800106 works the diverted 1128 King's Cross-Edinburgh past Turves on 18 January 2020. *Bill Atkinson*

Class 800/2

Bi-mode 25kV AC and diesel five-car units.

				PTDS	MRSB	MS	MC	PDTRBF
800201	LNE	AGI	DN	811201	812201	813201	814201	815201
800202	LNE	AGI	DN	811202	812202	813202	814202	815202
800203	LNE	AGI	DN	811203	812203	813203	814203	815203
800204	LNE	AGI	DN	811204	812204	813204	814204	815204
800205	LNE	AGI	DN	811205	812205	813205	814205	815205
800206	LNE	AGI	DN	811206	812206	813206	814206	815206
800207	LNE	AGI	DN	811207	812207	813207	814207	815207
800208	LNE	AGI	DN	811208	812208	813208	814208	815208
800209	LNE	AGI	DN	811209	812209	813209	814209	815209
800210	LNE	AGI	DN	811210	812210	813210	814210	815210

Class 801

These units are essentially electric only (they do have a single diesel engine for emergency use only) and so restricted to the King's Cross-Leeds / Edinburgh / Stirling route only. All are in the HBHQ pool.

Class 801/1

Bi-mode 25kV AC and single-engine diesel five-car units.

				PTDS	MRSB	MS	MC	PDTRBF
801101	LNE	AGI	DN	821101	822101	823101	824101	825101
801102	LNE	AGI	DN	821102	822102	823102	824102	825102
801103	LNE	AGI	DN	821103	822103	823103	824103	825103
801104	LNE	AGI	DN	821104	822104	823104	824104	825104
801105	LNE	AGI	DN	821105	822105	823105	824105	825105
801106	LNE	AGI	DN	821106	822106	823106	824106	825106
801107	LNE	AGI	DN	821107	822107	823107	824107	825107
801108	LNE	AGI	DN	821108	822108	823108	824108	825108
801109	LNE	AGI	DN	821109	822109	823109	824109	825109
801110	LNE	AGI	DN	821110	822110	823110	824110	825110
801111	LNE	AGI	DN	821111	822111	823111	824111	825111
801112	LNE	AGI	DN	821112	822112	823112	824112	825112

LNER had 91119 returned to its original InterCity livery for the last couple of years of its working life with the TOC. It works the 1633 King's Cross to Leeds past Highdyke on 2 June 2020. *Bill Atkinson*

LNER

Class 801/2

Bi-mode 25kV AC and single-engine diesel nine-car units.

				PDTS	MS	MS	TRSB	MS	TS	MC	MF	PDTRBF
801201	LNE	AGI	DN	821201	822201	823201	824201	825201	826201	827201	828201	829201
801202	LNE	AGI	DN	821202	822202	823202	824202	825202	826202	827202	828202	829202
801203	LNE	AGI	DN	821203	822203	823203	824203	825203	826203	827203	828203	829203
801204	LNE	AGI	DN	821204	822204	823204	824204	825204	826204	827204	828204	829204
801205	LNE	AGI	DN	821205	822205	823205	824205	825205	826205	827205	828205	829205
801206	LNE	AGI	DN	821206	822206	823206	824206	825206	826206	827206	828206	829206
801207	LNE	AGI	DN	821207	822207	823207	824207	825207	826207	827207	828207	829207
801208	LNE	AGI	DN	821208	822208	823208	824208	825208	826208	827208	828208	829208
801209	LNE	AGI	DN	821209	822209	823209	824209	825209	826209	827209	828209	829209
801210	LNE	AGI	DN	821210	822210	823210	824210	825210	826210	827210	828210	829210
801211	LNE	AGI	DN	821211	822211	823211	824211	825211	826211	827211	828211	829211
801212	LNE	AGI	DN	821212	822212	823212	824212	825212	826212	827212	828212	829212
801213	LNE	AGI	DN	821213	822213	823213	824213	825213	826213	827213	828213	829213
801214	LNE	AGI	DN	821214	822214	823214	824214	825214	826214	827214	828214	829214
801215	LNE	AGI	DN	821215	822215	823215	824215	825215	826215	827215	828215	829215
801216	LNE	AGI	DN	821216	822216	823216	824216	825216	826216	827216	828216	829216
801217	LNE	AGI	DN	821217	822217	823217	824217	825217	826217	827217	828217	829217
801218	LNE	AGI	DN	821218	822218	823218	824218	825218	826218	827218	828218	829218
801219	LNE	AGI	DN	821219	822219	823219	824219	825219	826219	827219	828219	829219
801220	LNE	AGI	DN	821220	822220	823220	824220	825220	826220	827220	828220	829220
801221	LNE	AGI	DN	821221	822221	823221	824221	825221	826221	827221	828221	829221
801222	LNE	AGI	DN	821222	822222	823222	824222	825222	826222	827222	828222	829222
801223	LNE	AGI	DN	821223	822223	823223	824223	825223	826223	827223	828223	829223
801224	LNE	AGI	DN	821224	822224	823224	824224	825224	826224	827224	828224	829224
801225	LNE	AGI	DN	821225	822225	823225	824225	825225	826225	827225	828225	829225
801226	LNE	AGI	DN	821226	822226	823226	824226	825226	826226	827226	828226	829226
801227	LNE	AGI	DN	821227	822227	823227	824227	825227	826227	827227	828227	829227
801228	LNE	AGI	DN	821228	822228	823228	824228	825228	826228	827228	828228	829228
801229	LNE	AGI	DN	821229	822229	823229	824229	825229	826229	827229	828229	829229
801230	LNE	AGI	DN	821230	822230	823230	824230	825230	826230	827230	828230	829230

Mk 4 Open First coach 11405 at Doncaster on 31 August 2018. This vehicle is no longer in use with LNER. *Robin Ralston*

Mk 4 trailers

These former BR coaches are being retained to work with Class 91s until 2023. They run in fixed formations of nine coaches plus a DVT.

Kitchen Buffet Standard			
10300	VEM	EVS	BN
10306	VEM	EVS	BN
10309	VEM	EVS	BN
10313	VEM	EVS	BN
10333	VEM	EVS	BN

Open First			
11229	VEM	EVS	BN
11279	VEM	EVS	BN
11284	VEM	EVS	BN
11285	VEM	EVS	BN
11286	VEM	EVS	BN
11288	VEM	EVS	BN
11295	VEM	EVS	BN
11306	VEM	EVS	BN
11308	VEM	EVS	BN
11312	VEM	EVS	BN
11313	VEM	EVS	BN
11315	VEM	EVS	BN
11317	VEM	EVS	BN
11326	VEM	EVS	BN
11406	VEM	EVS	BN
11408	VEM	EVS	BN
11412	VEM	EVS	BN
11413	VEM	EVS	BN
11415	VEM	EVS	BN
11417	VEM	EVS	BN
11426	VEM	EVS	BN

Open Standard (end)			
12205	VEM	EVS	BN
12208	VEM	EVS	BN
12212	VEM	EVS	BN
12220	VEM	EVS	BN
12223	VEM	EVS	BN
12226	VEM	EVS	BN
12228	VEM	EVS	BN

Open Standard (disabled)			
12303	VEM	EVS	BN
12309	VEM	EVS	BN
12311	VEM	EVS	BN
12313	VEM	EVS	BN
12325	VEM	EVS	BN
12328	VEM	EVS	BN
12330	VEM	EVS	BN

Open Standard			
12404	VEM	EVS	BN
12406	VEM	EVS	BN
12407	VEM	EVS	BN
12409	VEM	EVS	BN
12422	VEM	EVS	BN
12424	VEM	EVS	BN
12426	VEM	EVS	BN
12427	VEM	EVS	BN
12429	VEM	EVS	BN
12430	VEM	EVS	BN
12431	VEM	EVS	BN
12432	VEM	EVS	BN
12442	VEM	EVS	BN
12444	VEM	EVS	BN
12465	VEM	EVS	BN
12469	VEM	EVS	BN
12474	VEM	EVS	BN
12481	VEM	EVS	BN
12485	VEM	EVS	BN
12515	VEM	EVS	BN

Mk 4 DVTs

82208	VEM	EVS	BN
82211	VEM	EVS	BN
82212	VEM	EVS	BN
82213	VEM	EVS	BN
82214	VEM	EVS	BN
82223	VEM	EVS	BN
82225	VEM	EVS	BN

LNER Mk 4 formations

BN06	12208	12406	12420	12422	12313	10309	11279	11306	11406	82208
BN08	12205	12481	12485	12407	12328	10300	11229	11308	11408	82211
BN12	12212	12431	12404	12426	12330	10333	11284	11312	11412	82212
BN13	12228	12469	12430	12424	12311	10313	11285	11313	11413	82213
BN15	12226	12442	12409	12515	12309	10306	11286	11315	11415	82214
BN17	12223	12444	12427	12432	12303	10324	11288	11317	11417	82225
BN26	12220	12474	12465	12429	12325	10311	11295	11326	11426	82223

London Overground

Contact details

Website: www.arrivaraillondon.co.uk
Twitter: LDNOverground

Key personnel

Managing Director: Paul Hutchings
Engineering Director: Kate Marjoribanks

Overview

Arriva Rail London is the train operating company responsible for running the London Overground network under a Concession Agreement with Transport for London (TfL). The seven-and-a-half-year concession commenced on 13 November 2016 and expires on 24 May 2024.

Working in partnership with TfL, Arriva Rail London plans to deliver further improvements on London Overground through more frequent services, new trains and improved interchanges as well as developing stations and lines to meet increasing passenger demand and to support new homes and jobs.

London Overground operates local commuter trains within the Greater London. Much of the fleet is new Bombardier Class 378 and Class 710 EMUs – the latter have replaced the TOC's only remaining diesel trains following recent electrification of the Gospel Oka to Barking line.

Class 09

The only diesel traction left on the LOROL fleet is an ex-BR Class 09 shunter, based at Willesden depot.

09007	GRW	LOR	WN

Diesel shunter 09007 rests at its home depot, Willesden TMD in London, on 20 June 2018. *Paul Bigland*

Class 378

These new Bombardier Electrostars are metro-style trains similar in internal layout to a tube train. There were delivered as three-car sets but strengthened firstly to four-cars and now five-car sets. They work out of Euston to Watford and also on the Stratford to Clapham Junction and West Croydon to Highbury. All are in the EKHQ pool.

Class 378/1

750V DC five-car units.

				DMS	MS	TS	MS	DMS
378135	LOR	QWL	NG	38035	38235	38335	38435	38135
378136	LOR	QWL	NG	38036	38236	38336	38436	38136
378137	LOR	QWL	NG	38037	38237	38337	38437	38137
378138	LOR	QWL	NG	38038	38238	38338	38438	38138
378139	LOR	QWL	NG	38039	38239	38339	38439	38139
378140	LOR	QWL	NG	38040	38240	38340	38440	38140
378141	LOR	QWL	NG	38041	38241	38341	38441	38141
378142	LOR	QWL	NG	38042	38242	38342	38442	38142
378143	LOR	QWL	NG	38043	38243	38343	38443	38143
378144	LOR	QWL	NG	38044	38244	38344	38444	38144
378145	LOR	QWL	NG	38045	38245	38345	38445	38145
378146	LOR	QWL	NG	38046	38246	38346	38446	38146
378147	LOR	QWL	NG	38047	38247	38347	38447	38147
378148	LOR	QWL	NG	38048	38248	38348	38448	38148
378149	LOR	QWL	NG	38049	38249	38349	38449	38149
378150	LOR	QWL	NG	38050	38250	38350	38450	38150
378151	LOR	QWL	NG	38051	38251	38351	38451	38151
378152	LOR	QWL	NG	38052	38252	38352	38452	38152
378153	LOR	QWL	NG	38053	38253	38353	38453	38153
378154	LOR	QWL	NG	38054	38254	38354	38454	38154

One of the new Bombardier Aventra units new in traffic with London Overground, 710264 calls at Blackhorse Road on 28 August 2019. *Paul Bigland*

Class 378/2

25kV AC and 750V DC dual-voltage five-car units. The first 24 units were originally three-car Class 378/0s.

					DMS	MS	PTS	MS	DMS
378201	378001	LOR	QWL	NG	38001	38201	38301	38401	38101
378202	378002	LOR	QWL	NG	38002	38202	38302	38402	38102
378203	378003	LOR	QWL	NG	38003	38203	38303	38403	38103
378204	378004	LOR	QWL	NG	38004	38204	38304	38404	38104
378205	378005	LOR	QWL	NG	38005	38205	38305	38405	38105
378206	378006	LOR	QWL	NG	38006	38206	38306	38406	38106
378207	378007	LOR	QWL	NG	38007	38207	38307	38407	38107
378208	378008	LOR	QWL	NG	38008	38208	38308	38408	38108
378209	378009	LOR	QWL	NG	38009	38209	38309	38409	38109
378210	378010	LOR	QWL	NG	38010	38210	38310	38410	38110
378211	378011	LOR	QWL	NG	38011	38211	38311	38411	38111
378212	378012	LOR	QWL	NG	38012	38212	38312	38412	38112
378213	378013	LOR	QWL	NG	38013	38213	38313	38413	38113
378214	378014	LOR	QWL	NG	38014	38214	38314	38414	38114
378215	378015	LOR	QWL	NG	38015	38215	38315	38415	38115
378216	378016	LOR	QWL	NG	38016	38216	38316	38416	38116
378217	378017	LOR	QWL	NG	38017	38217	38317	38417	38117
378218	378018	LOR	QWL	NG	38018	38218	38318	38418	38118
378219	378019	LOR	QWL	NG	38019	38219	38319	38419	38119
378220	378020	LOR	QWL	NG	38020	38220	38320	38420	38120
378221	378021	LOR	QWL	NG	38021	38221	38321	38421	38121
378222	378022	LOR	QWL	NG	38022	38222	38322	38422	38122
378223	378023	LOR	QWL	NG	38023	38223	38323	38423	38123
378224	378024	LOR	QWL	NG	38024	38224	38324	38424	38124
378225		LOR	QWL	NG	38025	38225	38325	38425	38125
378226		LOR	QWL	NG	38026	38226	38326	38426	38126
378227		LOR	QWL	NG	38027	38227	38327	38427	38127
378228		LOR	QWL	NG	38028	38228	38328	38428	38128
378229		LOR	QWL	NG	38029	38229	38329	38429	38129
378230		LOR	QWL	NG	38030	38230	38330	38430	38130
378231		LOR	QWL	NG	38031	38231	38331	38431	38131
378232		LOR	QWL	NG	38032	38232	38332	38432	38132
378233		LOR	QWL	NG	38033	38233	38333	38433	38133
378234		LOR	QWL	NG	38034	38234	38334	38434	38134
378255		LOR	QWL	NG	38055	38255	38355	38455	38155
378256		LOR	QWL	NG	38056	38256	38356	38456	38156
378257		LOR	QWL	NG	38057	38257	38357	38457	38157

378232 is named *Jeff Langston*

Class 710

New Bombardier Aventra units for Gospel Oak-Barking, Liverpool Street to Enfield and Watford Junction to Euston routes. This fleet is still being delivered. The Class 710/1 units are 25kV AC and the 710/2s are dual voltage. All are in the EKHQ pool.

Class 710/1

25kV AC four-car sets.

				DMS	MS	PMS	DMS
710101	LOR	RFL	WN	431101	431201	431301	431501
710102	LOR	RFL	WN	431102	431202	431302	431502
710103	LOR	RFL	WN	431103	431203	431303	431503
710104	LOR	RFL	WN	431104	431204	431304	431504
710105	LOR	RFL	WN	431105	431205	431305	431505
710106	LOR	RFL	WN	431106	431206	431306	431506
710107	LOR	RFL	WN	431107	431207	431307	431507
710108	LOR	RFL	WN	431108	431208	431308	431508
710109	LOR	RFL	WN	431109	431209	431309	431509
710110	LOR	RFL	WN	431110	431210	431310	431510
710111	LOR	RFL	WN	431111	431211	431311	431511
710112	LOR	RFL	WN	431112	431212	431312	431512
710113	LOR	RFL	WN	431113	431213	431313	431513
710114	LOR	RFL	WN	431114	431214	431314	431514
710115	LOR	RFL	WN	431115	431215	431315	431515
710116	LOR	RFL	WN	431116	431216	431316	431516
710117	LOR	RFL	WN	431117	431217	431317	431517
710118	LOR	RFL	WN	431118	431218	431318	431518
710119	LOR	RFL	WN	431119	431219	431319	431519
710120	LOR	RFL	WN	431120	431220	431320	431520
710121	LOR	RFL	WN	431121	431221	431321	431521
710122	LOR	RFL	WN	431122	431222	431322	431522
710123	LOR	RFL	WN	431123	431223	431323	431523
710124	LOR	RFL	WN	431124	431224	431324	431524
710125	LOR	RFL	WN	431125	431225	431325	431525
710126	LOR	RFL	WN	431126	431226	431326	431526
710127	LOR	RFL	WN	431127	431227	431327	431527
710128	LOR	RFL	WN	431128	431228	431328	431528
710129	LOR	RFL	WN	431129	431229	431329	431529
710130	LOR	RFL	WN	431130	431230	431330	431530

Class 710/2

Dual-voltage 750V DC and 25kV AC four-car sets.

				DMS	MS	PMS	DMS
710256	LOR	RFL	WN	432156	432256	432356	432556
710257	LOR	RFL	WN	432157	432257	432357	432557
710258	LOR	RFL	WN	432158	432258	432358	432558
710259	LOR	RFL	WN	432159	432259	432359	432559
710260	LOR	RFL	WN	432160	432260	432360	432560
710261	LOR	RFL	WN	432161	432261	432361	432561
710262	LOR	RFL	WN	432162	432262	432362	432562
710263	LOR	RFL	WN	432163	432263	432363	432563
710264	LOR	RFL	WN	432164	432264	432364	432564
710265	LOR	RFL	WN	432165	432265	432365	432565
710266	LOR	RFL	WN	432166	432266	432366	432566
710267	LOR	RFL	WN	432167	432267	432367	432567
710268	LOR	RFL	WN	432168	432268	432368	432568
710269	LOR	RFL	WN	432169	432269	432369	432569
710270	LOR	RFL	WN	432170	432270	432370	432570
710271	LOR	RFL	WN	432171	432271	432371	432571
710272	LOR	RFL	WN	432172	432272	432372	432572
710273	LOR	RFL	WK (Q)	432173	432273	432373	432573

Class 710/2

Dual-voltage 750V DC and 25kV AC five-car sets.

				DMS	MS	PMS	MS	DMS
710274	LOR	RFL	OD (Q)	432174	432274	432374	432474	432574
710275	LOR	RFL	OD (Q)	432175	432275	432375	432475	432575
710276	LOR	RFL	WN	432176	432276	432376	432476	432576
710277	LOR	RFL	OD (Q)	432177	432277	432377	432477	432577
710278	LOR	RFL	WN	432178	432278	432378	432478	432578
710279	LOR	RFL	WN	432179	432279	432379	432479	432579

Bombardier Capitalstars EMU 378215 passes Hoxton on 26 February 2020.
Paul Bigland

Merseyrail

Contact details

Website: www.merseyrail.org
Twitter: @merseyrail

Key personnel

Managing Director: Andy Heath
Engineering Director: Mike Roe

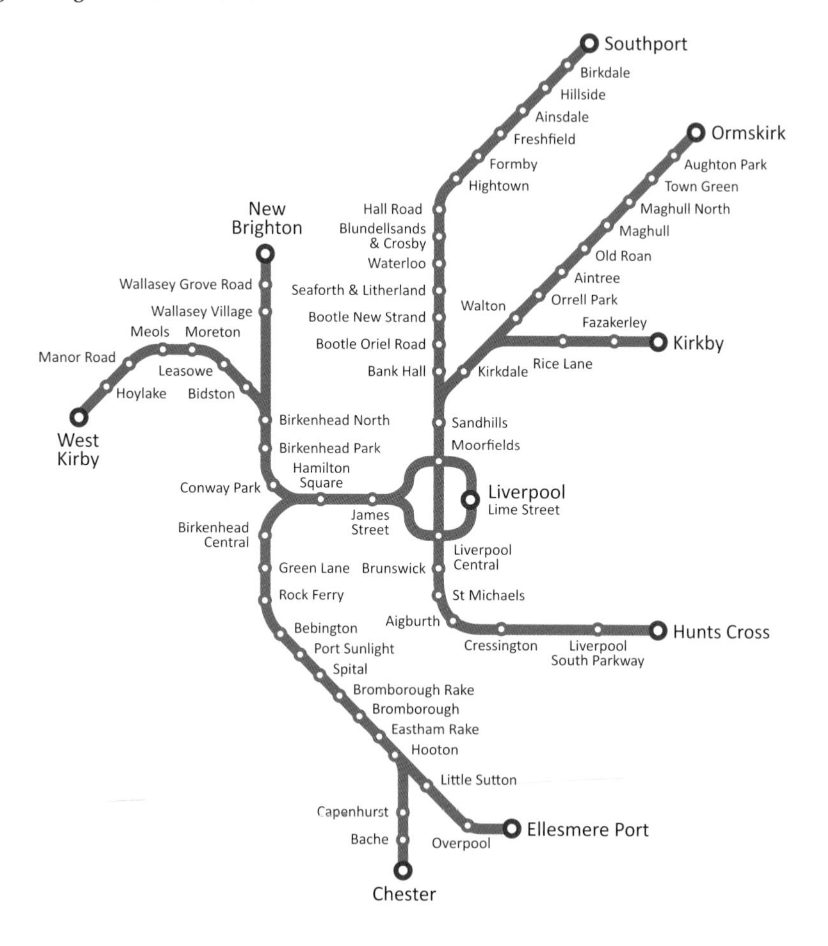

Overview

Merseyrail is a successful operation serving Liverpool and the Wirral and up to Southport. Its elderly fleet of Class 507/508 ex-BR EMUs are now on borrowed time following the delivery of the first Class 777 EMUs from Stadler.

It covers routes from Liverpool to New Brighton, West Kirby, Chester, Ellesmere Port, Hunts Cross, Ormskirk, Kirkby and Southport.

Class 507

Ex-BR units dating from 1978-80, they are due for replacement by Class 777s. All are in the HEHQ pool.

				BDMS	TS	DMS	
507001	MER	ANG	BD	64367	71342	64405	
507002	ADV	ANG	BD	64368	71343	64406	
507003	MER	ANG	BD	64369	71344	64407	
507004	MER	ANG	BD	64370	71345	64408	*Bob Paisley*
507005	MER	ANG	BD	64371	71346	64409	
507006	MER	ANG	BD	64372	71347	64410	
507007	MER	ANG	BD	64373	71348	64411	
507008	MER	ANG	BD	64374	71349	64412	*Harold Wilson*
507009	MER	ANG	BD	64375	71350	64413	*Dixie Dean*
507010	MER	ANG	BD	64376	71351	64414	
507011	MER	ANG	BD	64377	71352	64415	
507012	MER	ANG	BD	64378	71353	64416	
507013	MER	ANG	BD	64379	71354	64417	
507014	MER	ANG	BD	64380	71355	64418	
507015	MER	ANG	BD	64381	71356	64419	
507016	MER	ANG	BD	64382	71357	64420	*Merseyrail*
507017	MER	ANG	BD	64383	71358	64421	
507018	MER	ANG	BD	64384	71359	64422	
507019	MER	ANG	BD	64385	71360	64423	
507020	MER	ANG	BD	64386	71361	64424	*John Peel*
507021	MER	ANG	BD	64387	71362	64425	*Red Rum*
507023	MER	ANG	BD	64389	71364	64427	*Operations Inspector Stuart Mason*
507024	MER	ANG	BD	64390	71365	64428	
507025	MER	ANG	BD	64391	71366	64429	
507026	MER	ANG	BD	64392	71367	64430	*Councillor George Howard*
507027	MER	ANG	BD	64393	71368	64431	
507028	MER	ANG	BD	64394	71369	64432	
507029	MER	ANG	BD	64395	71370	64433	
507030	MER	ANG	BD	64396	71371	64434	
507031	MER	ANG	BD	64397	71372	64435	
507032	MER	ANG	BD	64398	71373	64436	
507033	MER	ANG	BD	64399	71374	64437	*Councillor Jack Spriggs*

No. 508110 calls at Hall Road on 10 August 2017 with the 1813 Southport-Hunts Cross. *Paul Robertson*

Class 508

Ex-BR units dating from 1978-80, originally used on the Southern Region, they are due for replacement by Class 777s. Some units have now been moved for scrap. All are in the HEHQ pool.

				DMS	TS	BDMS	
508103	MER	ANG	BD	64651	71485	64694	
508104	MER	ANG	BD	64652	71486	64695	
508108	MER	ANG	BD	64656	71490	64699	
508111	ADV	ANG	BD	64659	71493	64702	*The Beatles*
508112	MER	ANG	BD	64660	71494	64703	
508114	MER	ANG	BD	64662	71496	64705	
508115	MER	ANG	BD	64663	71497	64706	
508117	MER	ANG	BD	64665	71499	64708	
508120	MER	ANG	BD	64668	71502	64711	
508122	ADV	ANG	BD	64670	71504	64713	
508123	MER	ANG	BD	64671	71505	64714	*William Roscoe*
508124	MER	ANG	BD	64672	71506	64715	
508125	MER	ANG	BD	64673	71507	64716	
508126	MER	ANG	BD	64674	71508	64717	
508127	MER	ANG	BD	64675	71509	64718	
508128	MER	ANG	BD	64676	71510	64719	
508130	MER	ANG	BD	64678	71512	64721	
508131	MER	ANG	BD	64679	71513	64722	
508136	MER	ANG	BD	64684	71518	64727	*Wilfred Owen MC*
508137	MER	ANG	BD	64685	71519	64728	
508138	MER	ANG	BD	64686	71520	64729	
508139	MER	ANG	BD	64687	71521	64730	
508140	MER	ANG	BD	64688	71522	64731	
508141	MER	ANG	BD	64689	71523	64732	
508143	MER	ANG	BD	64691	71525	64734	

Class 777

New Stadler-built four-car EMUs, being assembled in Poland and Switzerland, to replace the Class 507/508 fleets. They are now being delivered and the first units are undergoing testing in Merseyside. They are owned by Merseytravel and leased to Merseyrail. All are expected to be in the HEHQ pool.

				DMS	MS	MS	DMS
777001	MER	MET		427001	428001	429001	430001
777002	MER	MET		427002	428002	429002	430002
777003	MER	MET	BD (Q)	427003	428003	429003	430003
777004	MER	MET	BD (Q)	427004	428004	429004	430004
777005	MER	MET	BD (Q)	427005	428005	429005	430005
777006	MER	MET	BD (Q)	427006	428006	429006	430006
777007	MER	MET	BD (Q)	427007	428007	429007	430007
777008	MER	MET	BD (Q)	427008	428008	429008	430008
777009	MER	MET	BD (Q)	427009	428009	429009	430009
777010	MER	MET	BD (Q)	427010	428010	429010	430010
777011	MER	MET		427011	428011	429011	430011

777012	MER	MET	427012	428012	429012	430012
777013	MER	MET	427013	428013	429013	430013
777014	MER	MET	427014	428014	429014	430014
777015	MER	MET	427015	428015	429015	430015
777016	MER	MET	427016	428016	429016	430016
777017	MER	MET	427017	428017	429017	430017
777018	MER	MET	427018	428018	429018	430018
777019	MER	MET	427019	428019	429019	430019
777020	MER	MET	427020	428020	429020	430020
777021	MER	MET	427021	428021	429021	430021
777022	MER	MET	427022	428022	429022	430022
777023	MER	MET	427023	428023	429023	430023
777024	MER	MET	427024	428024	429024	430024
777025	MER	MET	427025	428025	429025	430025
777026	MER	MET	427026	428026	429026	430026
777027	MER	MET	427027	428027	429027	430027
777028	MER	MET	427028	428028	429028	430028
777029	MER	MET	427029	428029	429029	430029
777030	MER	MET	427030	428030	429030	430030
777031	MER	MET	427031	428031	429031	430031
777032	MER	MET	427032	428032	429032	430032
777033	MER	MET	427033	428033	429033	430033
777034	MER	MET	427034	428034	429034	430034
777035	MER	MET	427035	428035	429035	430035
777036	MER	MET	427036	428036	429036	430036
777037	MER	MET	427037	428037	429037	430037
777038	MER	MET	427038	428038	429038	430038
777039	MER	MET	427039	428039	429039	430039
777040	MER	MET	427040	428040	429040	430040
777041	MER	MET	427041	428041	429041	430041
777042	MER	MET	427042	428042	429042	430042
777043	MER	MET	427043	428043	429043	430043
777044	MER	MET	427044	428044	429044	430044
777045	MER	MET	427045	428045	429045	430045
777046	MER	MET	427046	428046	429046	430046
777047	MER	MET	427047	428047	429047	430047
777048	MER	MET	427048	428048	429048	430048
777049	MER	MET	427049	428049	429049	430049
777050	MER	MET	427050	428050	429050	430050
777051	MER	MET	427051	428051	429051	430051
777052	MER	MET	427052	428052	429052	430052

No. 507002 pauses at Liverpool Moorfields on 14 April 2017.
Rob France

In a promotional livery, 508122 stops at Fazakerley on 27 September 2018. These units are now being withdrawn. *Paul Bigland*

The Class 507s date from the late 1970s and are due to be replaced by Class 777s in the next year. No. 507017 leaves Bidston on 24 March 2019. *Anthony Hicks*

Northern Rail

Contact details

Website: www.northernrail.org
Twitter: @northernassist

Key personnel

Managing Director: Nick Donovan
Engineering Director: Ben Ackroyd

Overview

Currently operated by the DfT via its Operator of Last Resort, Northern runs local services across Yorkshire, Merseyside, Lancashire, Cheshire and Cumbria and also into Nottinghamshire and Lincolnshire.

Northern was operated by Arriva until the spring of 2020 when due to poor performance, it was stripped of its franchise and is now operate by the DfT. This happened just before the Covid pandemic and what happens to this TOC post-pandemic is undecided.

The operation is currently undergoing a massive overhaul of its train fleet. New CAF-built Class 195 DMUs – in two- and three-car formations – are now in traffic, as is a fleet of 43 Class 331 EMUs – 31 three-cars and 12 four-cars, also built by CAF and sharing the same bodyshells as the 195s.

The new DMUs are replacing the Class 142/144 railbuses, although a few lingered on in traffic when this book closed for press. The rest of the DMU fleet now comprises Class 150, 153, 155, 156, 158 and a handful of Class 170 Turbostars – relatively new arrivals from ScotRail.

The EMU fleet, as well as the new CAF trains, has a fleet of 16 four-car Siemens/CAF Class 333 EMUs, a few ex-Thameslink Class 319s and 17 Class 323 three-car sets. Some bi-mode Class 769s are also due to enter traffic.

Class 142

Although due to be withdrawn, dispensation has been granted for Northern to keep a handful of Class 142s in traffic. All are in the EDHQ pool.

				DMS	DMSL
142004	NOR	ANG	NH	55545	55595
142018	NOR	ANG	NH	55559	55609
142058	NOR	ANG	NH	55708	55754
142065	NOR	ANG	NH	55715	55761
142068	NOR	ANG	NH	55718	55764
142070	NOR	ANG	NH	55720	55766
142071	NOR	ANG	NH	55721	55767
142078	NOR	ANG	NH	55728	55774
142087	NOR	ANG	NH	55737	55783
142090	NOR	ANG	NH	55740	55786
142094	NOR	ANG	NH	55744	55790

Northern Rail

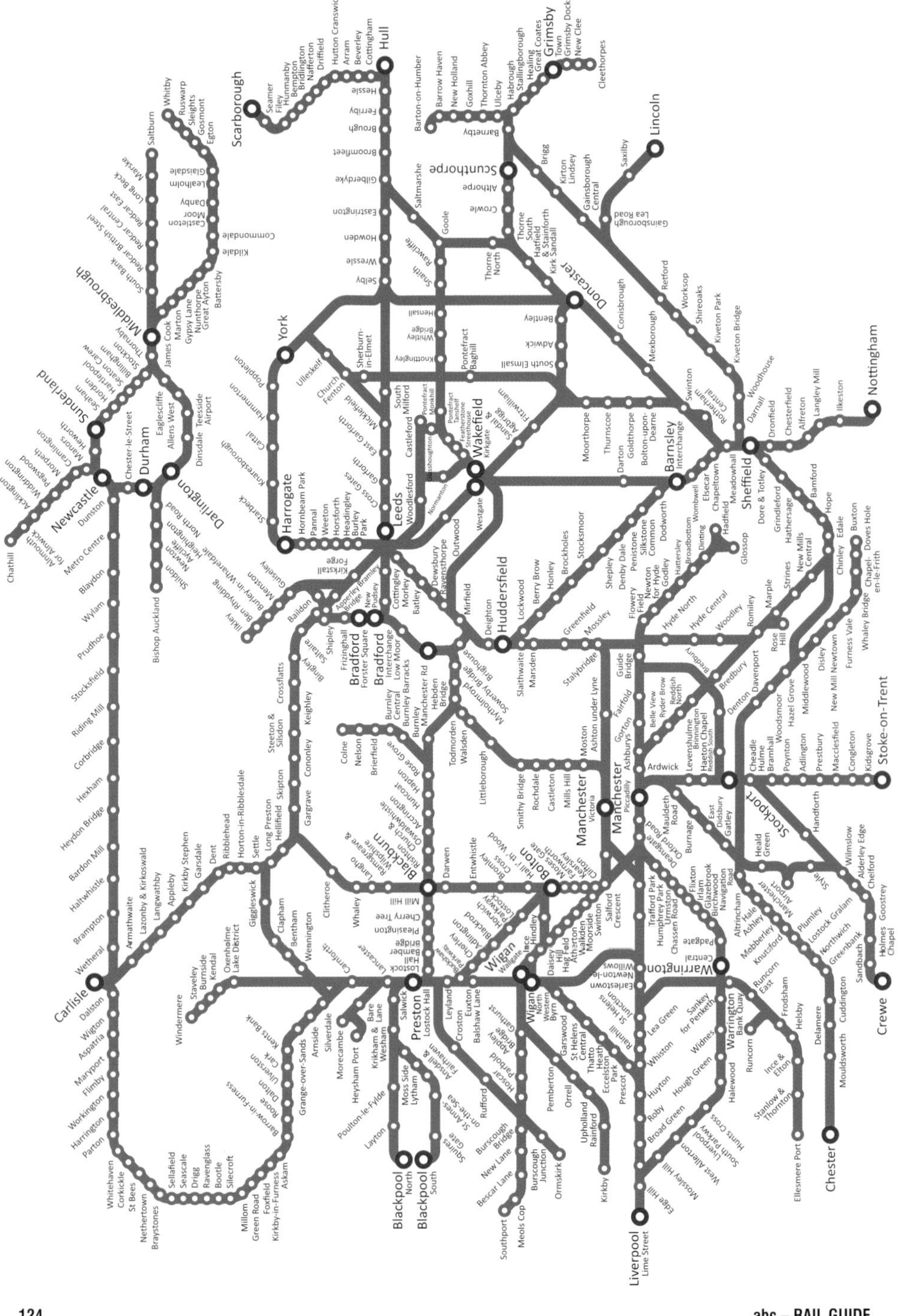

Class 150

These DMUs date from 1984-87. The Class 150/1s have no corridor connections, a feature added to the later batch of 150/2s at construction. Northern has recently taken both three-car 150/0s from GWR.

All are based at Newton Heath in Manchester and are used mostly for local trains emanating from the Manchester area, although they do work into West Yorkshire. All are in the EDHQ pool.

Class 150/0

Original three-car trial units. No. 150002 was numbered 154001 from March 1987, then 154002 in March 1988 before becoming 150002 in February 1992.

				DMSL	MS	DMS
150001	NOR	ANG	NH	55200	55400	55300
150002	NOR	ANG	NH	55201	55401	55301

The Northern Class 142s are in the final few months of use. On 13 August 2019, 142071 leaves Melling Tunnel near Wennington as it heads to Leeds. *Rob France*

Class 150/1

				DMSL	DMS
150101	NOR	ANG	NH	52101	57101
150102	NOR	ANG	NH	52102	57102
150103	NOR	ANG	NH	52103	57103
150104	NOR	ANG	NH	52104	57104
150105	LMR	ANG	NH	52105	57105
150106	NOR	ANG	NH	52106	57106
150107	LMR	ANG	NH	52107	57107
150108	NOR	ANG	NH	52108	57108
150109	LMR	ANG	NH	52109	57109
150110	NOR	ANG	NH	52110	57110
150111	NOR	ANG	NH	52111	57111
150112	NOR	ANG	NH	52112	57112
150113	NOR	ANG	NH	52113	57113
150114	NOR	ANG	NH	52114	57114
150115	NOR	ANG	NH	52115	57115
150116	NOR	ANG	NH	52116	57116
150117	NOR	ANG	NH	52117	57117
150118	NOR	ANG	NH	52118	57118
150119	NOR	ANG	NH	52119	57119
150120	NOR	ANG	NH	52120	57120
150121	NOR	ANG	NH	52121	57121
150122	NOR	ANG	NH	52122	57122
150123	NOR	ANG	NH	52123	57123
150124	NOR	ANG	NH	52124	57124
150125	NOR	ANG	NH	52125	57125
150126	NOR	ANG	NH	52126	57126
150127	NOR	ANG	NH	52127	57127
150128	NOR	ANG	NH	52128	57128
150129	NOR	ANG	NH	52129	57129
150130	NOR	ANG	NH	52130	57130
150131	NOR	ANG	NH	52131	57131
150132	NOR	ANG	NH	52132	57132
150133	NOR	ANG	NH	52133	57133
150134	NOR	ANG	NH	52134	57134
150135	NOR	ANG	NH	52135	57135
150136	NOR	ANG	NH	52136	57136
150137	NOR	ANG	NH	52137	57137
150138	NOR	ANG	NH	52138	57138
150139	NOR	ANG	NH	52139	57139
150140	NOR	ANG	NH	52140	57140
150141	NOR	ANG	NH	52141	57141
150142	NOR	ANG	NH	52142	57142
150143	NOR	ANG	NH	52143	57143
150144	NOR	ANG	NH	52144	57144
150145	NOR	ANG	NH	52145	57145
150146	NOR	ANG	NH	52146	57146
150147	NOR	ANG	NH	52147	57147
150148	NOR	ANG	NH	52148	57148
150149	NOR	ANG	NH	52149	57149
150150	NOR	ANG	NH	52150	57150

No. 150111 calls at Ilkeston with a Leeds to Nottingham train on 27 January 2020. *Paul Robertson*

Class 150/2

150201	NOR	ANG	NL	52201	57201	
150203	NOR	ANG	NL	52203	57203	
150204	NOR	ANG	NL	52204	57204	
150205	NOR	ANG	NL	52205	57205	
150206	NOR	ANG	NL	52206	57206	
150209	NOR	ANG	NH	57212	57209	
150210	NOR	ANG	NL	52210	57210	
150211	NOR	ANG	NL	52211	57211	
150214	NOR	ANG	NL	52214	57214	*The Bentham Line A Dementia-Friendly Railway*
150215	NOR	ANG	NL	52215	57215	
150218	NOR	ANG	NL	52218	57218	
150220	NOR	ANG	NL	52220	57220	
150222	NOR	ANG	NL	52222	57222	
150223	NOR	ANG	NL	52223	57223	
150224	NOR	ANG	NH	52224	57224	
150225	NOR	ANG	NL	52225	57225	
150226	NOR	ANG	NH	52226	57226	
150228	NOR	POR	NL	52228	57228	
150268	NOR	POR	NH	52268	57268	
150269	NOR	POR	NL	52269	57269	
150270	NOR	POR	NL	52270	57270	
150271	NOR	POR	NL	52271	57271	
150272	NOR	POR	NL	52272	57272	
150273	NOR	POR	NL	52273	57273	
150274	NOR	POR	NL	52274	57274	
150275	NOR	POR	NL	52275	57275	*The Yorkshire Regiment Yorkshire Warrior*
150276	NOR	POR	NL	52276	57276	
150277	NOR	POR	NL	52277	57277	

No. 153352 leads 156490 at Nethertown on the 1533 Barrow-in-Furness-Carlisle on 21 April 2018. *Robin Ralston*

Class 153

These single-car units were converted from two-car Class 155s in 1991/92 and are often used to strengthen two-car trains. All are in the EDHQ pool.

				DMSL	
153301	NOR	ANG	NH	52301	
153304	NOR	ANG	NH	52304	
153307	NOR	ANG	NH	52307	
153315	NOR	ANG	NH	52315	
153316	NOR	POR	NH	52316	*John 'Longitude' Harrison Inventor of the Marine Chronometer*
153317	NOR	ANG	NH	52317	
153324	NOR	POR	NH	52324	
153328	NOR	ANG	NH	52328	
153330	NOR	POR	NH	52330	
153331	NOR	ANG	NH	52331	
153332	NOR	POR	NH	52332	
153351	NOR	ANG	NH	57351	
153352	NOR	ANG	NH	57352	
153358	NOR	POR	NH	57358	
153359	NOR	POR	NH	57359	
153360	NOR	POR	NH	57360	
153363	NOR	POR	NH	57363	
153373	NOR	ANG	NH	57373	
153378	NOR	ANG	NH	57378	
153380	NOR	ANG	NH	57380	

Class 155

Seven Class 155s were retained and not covered into pairs of Class 153s. They are all based at Neville Hill and work in the West and North Yorkshire area. All are in the EDHQ pool.

				DMSL	DMS
155341	NOR	POR	NL	52341	57341
155342	NOR	POR	NL	52342	57342
155343	NOR	POR	NL	52343	57343
155344	NOR	POR	NL	52344	57344
155345	NOR	POR	NL	52345	57345
155346	NOR	POR	NL	52346	57346
155347	NOR	POR	NL	52347	57347

No. 155342 departs East Garforth with a local train from Leeds to York on 16 March 2020. *Anthony Hicks*

Class 156

Metro Cammell units that are based at Heaton and Newton Heath and work across the majority of the Northern network, but especially in the North-East and North-West. All are in the EDHQ pool.

				DMSL	DMS	
156420	NOR	POR	NH	52420	57420	
156421	NOR	POR	NH	52421	57421	
156423	NOR	POR	NH	52423	57423	
156424	NOR	POR	NH	52424	57424	
156425	NOR	POR	NH	52425	57425	
156426	NOR	POR	NH	52426	57426	
156427	NOR	POR	NH	52427	57427	
156428	NOR	POR	HT	52428	57428	
156429	NOR	POR	HT	52429	57429	
156438	NOR	ANG	HT	52438	57438	
156440	NOR	POR	HT	52440	57440	
156441	NOR	POR	HT	52441	57441	
156443	NOR	ANG	HT	52443	57443	
156444	NOR	ANG	HT	52444	57444	
156447	FIR	ANG	HT	52447	57447	
156448	NOR	ANG	HT	52448	57448	
156449	FIR	ANG	HT	52449	57449	
156451	NOR	ANG	HT	52451	57451	
156452	NOR	POR	NH	52452	57452	
156454	NOR	ANG	HT	52454	57454	
156455	NOR	POR	NH	52455	57455	
156459	NOR	POR	NH	52459	57459	
156460	NOR	POR	NH	52460	57460	
156461	NOR	POR	NH	52461	57461	
156463	NOR	ANG	HT	52463	57463	
156464	NOR	POR	NH	52464	57464	*Lancashire Dalesrail*
156465	NOR	ANG	HT	52465	57465	
156466	NOR	POR	NH	52466	57466	
156468	NOR	ANG	HT	52468	57468	
156469	NOR	ANG	HT	52469	57469	*The Royal Northumberland Fusiliers (The Fighting Fifth)*
156471	NOR	ANG	HT	52471	57471	
156472	NOR	ANG	HT	52472	57472	
156475	NOR	ANG	HT	52475	57475	
156479	NOR	ANG	HT	52479	57479	
156480	NOR	ANG	HT	52480	57480	*Spirit of The Royal Air Force*
156481	NOR	ANG	HT	52481	57481	
156482	NOR	ANG	HT	52482	57482	
156483	NOR	ANG	HT	52483	57483	*William George 'Billy' Hardy*
156484	NOR	ANG	HT	52484	57484	
156485	FIR	ANG	HT	52485	57485	
156486	NOR	ANG	HT	52486	57486	
156487	NOR	ANG	HT	52487	57487	
156488	NOR	ANG	HT	52488	57488	
156489	NOR	ANG	HT	52489	57489	
156490	NOR	ANG	HT	52490	57490	
156491	NOR	ANG	HT	52491	57491	
156496	NOR	ANG	HT	52496	57496	

Class 158

These units work across the Northern network but especially in the North-East from Newcastle, and from Carlisle and Leeds. All are in the EDHQ pool.

				DMSL	MSL	DMSL	
158752	NOR	POR	NL	52752	58716	57752	
158753	NOR	POR	NL	52753	58710	57753	
158754	NOR	POR	NL	52754	58708	57754	
158755	NOR	POR	NL	52755	58702	57755	
158756	NOR	POR	NL	52756	58712	57756	
158757	NOR	POR	NL	52757	58706	57757	
158758	NOR	POR	NL	52758	58714	57758	
158759	NOR	POR	NL	52759	58713	57759	
158782	NOR	ANG	NL	52782		57782	
158784	NOR	ANG	NL	52784		57784	*Barbara Castle*
158786	NOR	ANG	NL	52786		57786	
158787	NOR	ANG	NL	52787		57787	
158789	NOR	ANG	NL	52789		57789	
158790	NOR	ANG	NL	52790		57790	
158791	NOR	ANG	NL	52791		57791	*County of Nottinghamshire*
158792	NOR	ANG	HT	52792		57792	
158793	NOR	ANG	HT	52793		57793	
158794	NOR	ANG	NL	52794		57794	
158795	NOR	ANG	NL	52795		57795	
158796	NOR	ANG	NL	52796		57796	
158797	NOR	ANG	NL	52797		57797	*Jane Tomlinson*
158815	NOR	ANG	HT	52815		57815	
158816	NOR	ANG	HT	52816		57816	
158817	NOR	ANG	HT	52817		57817	
158842	NOR	ANG	HT	52842		57842	
158843	NOR	ANG	HT	52843		57843	
158844	NOR	ANG	HT	52844		57844	
158845	NOR	ANG	HT	52845		57845	
158848	NOR	ANG	HT	52848		57848	
158849	NOR	ANG	HT	52849		57849	
158850	NOR	ANG	HT	52850		57850	
158851	NOR	ANG	HT	52851		57851	
158853	NOR	ANG	HT	52853		57853	
158855	NOR	ANG	HT	52855		57855	
158859	NOR	ANG	HT	52859		57859	
158860	NOR	ANG	HT	52860		57860	*Ian Dewhurst*
158861	NOR	ANG	HT	52861		57861	*Magna Carta 800 Lincoln 2015*
158867	NOR	ANG	NL	52867		57867	
158868	NOR	ANG	NL	52868		57868	
158869	NOR	ANG	NL	52869		57869	
158870	NOR	ANG	NL	52870		57870	
158871	NOR	ANG	NL	52871		57871	
158872	NOR	ANG	NL	52872		57872	

Class 158/9

Former West Yorkshire PTE Metro units.

				DMSL	MSL	DMSL
158901	NOR	EVS	NL	52901		57901
158902	NOR	EVS	NL	52902		57902
158903	NOR	EVS	NL	52903		57903
158904	NOR	EVS	NL	52904		57904
158905	NOR	EVS	NL	52905		57905
158906	NOR	EVS	NL	52906		57906
158907	NOR	EVS	NL	52907		57907
158908	NOR	EVS	NL	52908		57908
158909	NOR	EVS	NL	52909		57909
158910	NOR	EVS	NL	52910		57910

Class 170

These Turbostar units released from ScotRail work mostly in Yorkshire on services such as the Harrogate Circle. All are in the EDHQ pool.

				DMSL	MS	DMSL
170453	NOR	POR	NL	50453	56453	79453
170454	NOR	POR	NL	50454	56454	79454
170455	NOR	POR	NL	50455	56455	79455
170456	NOR	POR	NL	50456	56456	79456
170457	NOR	POR	NL	50457	56457	79457
170458	NOR	POR	NL	50458	56458	79458
170459	NOR	POR	NL	50459	56459	79459
170460	NOR	POR	NL	50460	56460	79460
170461	NOR	POR	NL	50461	56461	79461
170472	NOR	POR	NL	50472	56472	79472
170473	NOR	POR	NL	50473	56473	79473
170474	NOR	POR	NL	50474	56474	79474
170475	NOR	POR	NL	50475	56475	79475
170476	NOR	POR	NL	50476	56476	79476
170477	NOR	POR	NL	50477	56477	79477
170478	NOR	POR	NL	50478	56478	79478

Nos 170453-457 have a DMCL instead of a DMSL.

Metro-Cammell 156484 arrives at its destination with the 1319 Newcastle-Hexham on 29 September 2018. *Anthony Hicks*

Class 195

These new CAF diesel units are all now in traffic and work many local and regional services especially in the North-West and Yorkshire. All are in the EDHQ pool.

Class 195/0

Two-car sets.

				DMS	DMS
195001	NOR	EVS	NH	101001	103001
195002	NOR	EVS	NH	101002	103002
195003	NOR	EVS	NH	101003	103003
195004	NOR	EVS	NH	101004	103004
195005	NOR	EVS	NH	101005	103005
195006	NOR	EVS	NH	101006	103006
195007	NOR	EVS	NH	101007	103007
195008	NOR	EVS	NH	101008	103008
195009	NOR	EVS	NH	101009	103009
195010	NOR	EVS	NH	101010	103010
195011	NOR	EVS	NH	101011	103011
195012	NOR	EVS	NH	101012	103012
195013	NOR	EVS	NH	101013	103013
195014	NOR	EVS	NH	101014	103014
195015	NOR	EVS	NH	101015	103015
195016	NOR	EVS	NH	101016	103016
195017	NOR	EVS	NH	101017	103017
195018	NOR	EVS	NH	101018	103018
195019	NOR	EVS	NH	101019	103019
195020	NOR	EVS	NH	101020	103020
195021	NOR	EVS	NH	101021	103021
195022	NOR	EVS	NH	101022	103022
195023	NOR	EVS	NH	101023	103023
195024	NOR	EVS	NH	101024	103024
195025	NOR	EVS	NH	101025	103025

No. 158849 leaves Doncaster with the 0835 Bridlington-Sheffield on 31 August 2018. *Robin Ralston*

Class 195/1

Three-car sets.

				DMS	MS	DMS	
195101	NOR	EVS	NH	101101	102101	103101	
195102	NOR	EVS	NH	101102	102102	103102	
195103	NOR	EVS	NH	101103	102103	103103	
195104	NOR	EVS	NH	101104	102104	103104	*Deva Victrix*
195105	NOR	EVS	NH	101105	102105	103105	
195106	NOR	EVS	NH	101106	102106	103106	
195107	NOR	EVS	NH	101107	102107	103107	
195108	NOR	EVS	NH	101108	102108	103108	
195109	NOR	EVS	NH	101109	102109	103109	
195110	NOR	EVS	NH	101110	102110	103110	
195111	NOR	EVS	NH	101111	102111	103111	
195112	NOR	EVS	NH	101112	102112	103112	
195113	NOR	EVS	NH	101113	102113	103113	
195114	NOR	EVS	NH	101114	102114	103114	
195115	NOR	EVS	NH	101115	102115	103115	
195116	NOR	EVS	NH	101116	102116	103116	
195117	NOR	EVS	NH	101117	102117	103117	
195118	NOR	EVS	NH	101118	102118	103118	
195119	NOR	EVS	NH	101119	102119	103119	
195120	NOR	EVS	NH	101120	102120	103120	
195121	NOR	EVS	NH	101121	102121	103121	
195122	NOR	EVS	NH	101122	102122	103122	
195123	NOR	EVS	NH	101123	102123	103123	
195124	NOR	EVS	NH	101124	102124	103124	
195125	NOR	EVS	NH	101125	102125	103125	
195126	NOR	EVS	NH	101126	102126	103126	
195127	NOR	EVS	NH	101127	102127	103127	
195128	NOR	EVS	NH	101128	102128	103128	*Calder Champion*
195129	NOR	EVS	NH	101129	102129	103129	
195130	NOR	EVS	NH	101130	102130	103130	
195131	NOR	EVS	NH	101131	102131	103131	
195132	NOR	EVS	NH	101132	102132	103132	
195133	NOR	EVS	NH	101133	102133	103133	

Ex-ScotRail Turbostar, now with Northern, 170478 works the 1029 Leeds-York into Poppleton on 18 January 2020. *Anthony Hicks*

Class 319

These ex-Thameslink dual-voltage EMUs, displaced by Class 700s, work Liverpool to Wigan, Blackpool and Manchester Airport. All are in the EDHQ pool.

				DTS	MS	TS	DTS
319361	NOR	POR	AN	77459	63043	71929	77458
319366	NOR	POR	AN	77469	63048	71934	77468
319367	NOR	POR	AN	77471	63049	71935	77470
319368	NOR	POR	AN	77473	63050	71936	77472
319369	NOR	POR	AN	77475	63051	71937	77474
319370	NOR	POR	AN	77477	63052	71938	77476
319372	NOR	POR	AN	77481	63054	71940	77480
319375	NOR	POR	AN	77487	63057	71943	77486
319378	NOR	POR	AN	77493	63060	71946	77492
319379	NOR	POR	AN	77495	63061	71947	77494
319381	NOR	POR	AN	77973	63093	71979	77974
319383	NOR	POR	AN	77977	63095	71981	77978
319384	NOR	POR	AN	77979	63096	71982	77980
319385	NOR	POR	AN	77981	63097	71983	77982
319386	NOR	POR	AN	77983	63098	71984	77984

Class 323

These ex-BR units, built in 1992/93 by Hunslet, are used out of Manchester to Glossop/Hadfield, Manchester Airport, Crewe and Stoke. Some of the West Midlands Trains Class 323 fleet are expected to join the fleet when displaced by Class 730s. All are in the EDHQ pool.

				DMS	TS	DMS
323223	NOR	POR	AN	64023	75323	65023
323224	NOR	POR	AN	64024	75324	65024
323225	NOR	POR	AN	64025	75325	65025
323226	NOR	POR	AN	64026	75326	65026
323227	NOR	POR	AN	64027	75327	65027
323228	NOR	POR	AN	64028	75328	65028
323229	NOR	POR	AN	64029	75329	65029
323230	NOR	POR	AN	64030	75330	65030
323231	NOR	POR	AN	64031	75331	65031
323232	NOR	POR	AN	64032	75332	65032
323233	NOR	POR	AN	64033	75333	65033
323234	NOR	POR	AN	64034	75334	65034
323235	NOR	POR	AN	64035	75335	65035
323236	NOR	POR	AN	64036	75336	65036
323237	NOR	POR	AN	64037	75337	65037
323238	NOR	POR	AN	64038	75338	65038
323239	NOR	POR	AN	64039	75339	65039

Class 331

These new CAF units are now at work out of Leeds, Manchester and Liverpool on the electrified routes on the Northern Network. All are in the EDHQ pool.

Class 331/0

Three-car sets.

				DMS	PTS	DTS
331001	NOR	EVS	AN	463001	464001	466001
331002	NOR	EVS	AN	463002	464002	466002
331003	NOR	EVS	AN	463003	464003	466003
331004	NOR	EVS	AN	463004	464004	466004
331005	NOR	EVS	AN	463005	464005	466005
331006	NOR	EVS	AN	463006	464006	466006
331007	NOR	EVS	AN	463007	464007	466007
331008	NOR	EVS	AN	463008	464008	466008
331009	NOR	EVS	AN	463009	464009	466009
331010	NOR	EVS	AN	463010	464010	466010
331011	NOR	EVS	AN	463011	464011	466011
331012	NOR	EVS	AN	463012	464012	466012
331013	NOR	EVS	AN	463013	464013	466013
331014	NOR	EVS	AN	463014	464014	466014
331015	NOR	EVS	AN	463015	464015	466015
331016	NOR	EVS	AN	463016	464016	466016
331017	NOR	EVS	AN	463017	464017	466017
331018	NOR	EVS	AN	463018	464018	466018
331019	NOR	EVS	AN	463019	464019	466019
331020	NOR	EVS	AN	463020	464020	466020
331021	NOR	EVS	AN	463021	464021	466021
331022	NOR	EVS	AN	463022	464022	466022
331023	NOR	EVS	AN	463023	464023	466023
331024	NOR	EVS	AN	463024	464024	466024
331025	NOR	EVS	AN	463025	464025	466025
331026	NOR	EVS	AN	463026	464026	466026
331027	NOR	EVS	AN	463027	464027	466027
331028	NOR	EVS	AN	463028	464028	466028
331029	NOR	EVS	AN	463029	464029	466029
331030	NOR	EVS	AN	463030	464030	466030
331031	NOR	EVS	AN	463031	464031	466031

One of the new CAF Class 195 DMUs, 195008 works 1L53, the 1138 Leeds-Lincoln Central past Stow Park on 6 March 2020. *Bill Atkinson*

Class 331/1

Four-car units.

				DMS	PTS	MS	DTS
331101	NOR	EVS	NL	463101	464101	465101	466101
331102	NOR	EVS	AN	463102	464102	465102	466102
331103	NOR	EVS	AN	463103	464103	465103	466103
331104	NOR	EVS	NL	463104	464104	465104	466104
331105	NOR	EVS	AN	463105	464105	465105	466105
331106	NOR	EVS	NL	463106	464106	465106	466106
331107	NOR	EVS	AN	463107	464107	465107	466107
331108	NOR	EVS	NL	463108	464108	465108	466108
331109	NOR	EVS	NL	463109	464109	465109	466109
331110	NOR	EVS	NL	463110	464110	465110	466110
331111	NOR	EVS	AN	463111	464111	465111	466111
331112	NOR	EVS	AN	463112	464112	465112	466112

Class 333

These Siemens / CAF units were similar in design to the Heathrow Express Class 332s. They work Aire Valley line trains from Leeds to Skipton, Bradford and Ilkley. All are in the EDHQ pool.

				DMS	PTS	MS	DMS
333001	NOR	ANG	NL	78451	74461	74477	78452
333002	NOR	ANG	NL	78453	74462	74478	78454
333003	NOR	ANG	NL	78455	74463	74479	78456
333004	NOR	ANG	NL	78457	74464	74480	78458
333005	NOR	ANG	NL	78459	74465	74481	78460
333006	NOR	ANG	NL	78461	74466	74482	78462
333007	NOR	ANG	NL	78463	74467	74483	78464
333008	NOR	ANG	NL	78465	74468	74484	78466
333009	NOR	ANG	NL	78467	74469	74485	78468
333010	NOR	ANG	NL	78469	74470	74486	78470
333011	NOR	ANG	NL	78471	74471	74487	78472
333012	NOR	ANG	NL	78473	74472	74488	78474
333013	NOR	ANG	NL	78475	74473	74489	78476
333014	NOR	ANG	NL	78477	74474	74490	78478
333015	NOR	ANG	NL	78479	74475	74491	78480
333016	NOR	ANG	NL	78481	74476	74492	78482

Class 769

Northern has eight bi-mode FLEX units converted from redundant Class 319s on order for working Liverpool to Stalybridge. However, none have yet to enter traffic and are still undergoing testing. All are in the EDHQ pool.

					DMC	MS	TS	DMS
769424	319424	NOR	POR	AN	77337	62914	71795	77336
769431	319431	NOR	POR	AN	77351	62921	71802	77350
769434	319434	NOR	POR	AN	77357	62924	71805	77356
769442	319442	NOR	POR	AN	77373	62932	71813	77372
769448	319448	NOR	POR	AN	77433	62962	71867	77432
769450	319450	NOR	POR	AN	77437	62964	71869	77436
769456	319456	NOR	POR	AN	77449	62970	71875	77448
769458	319458	NOR	POR	AN	77453	62972	71877	77452

The CAF 331 EMUs share the same body design as their Class 195 cousins. No. 331109 passes Burley-in-Wharfedale as it heads towards Leeds on 14 May 2020. *Anthony Hicks*

ScotRail

Contact details

Website: www.scotrail.co.uk
Twitter: @Scotrail

Key personnel

Managing Director: Alex Hynes
Engineering Director: Angus Thom

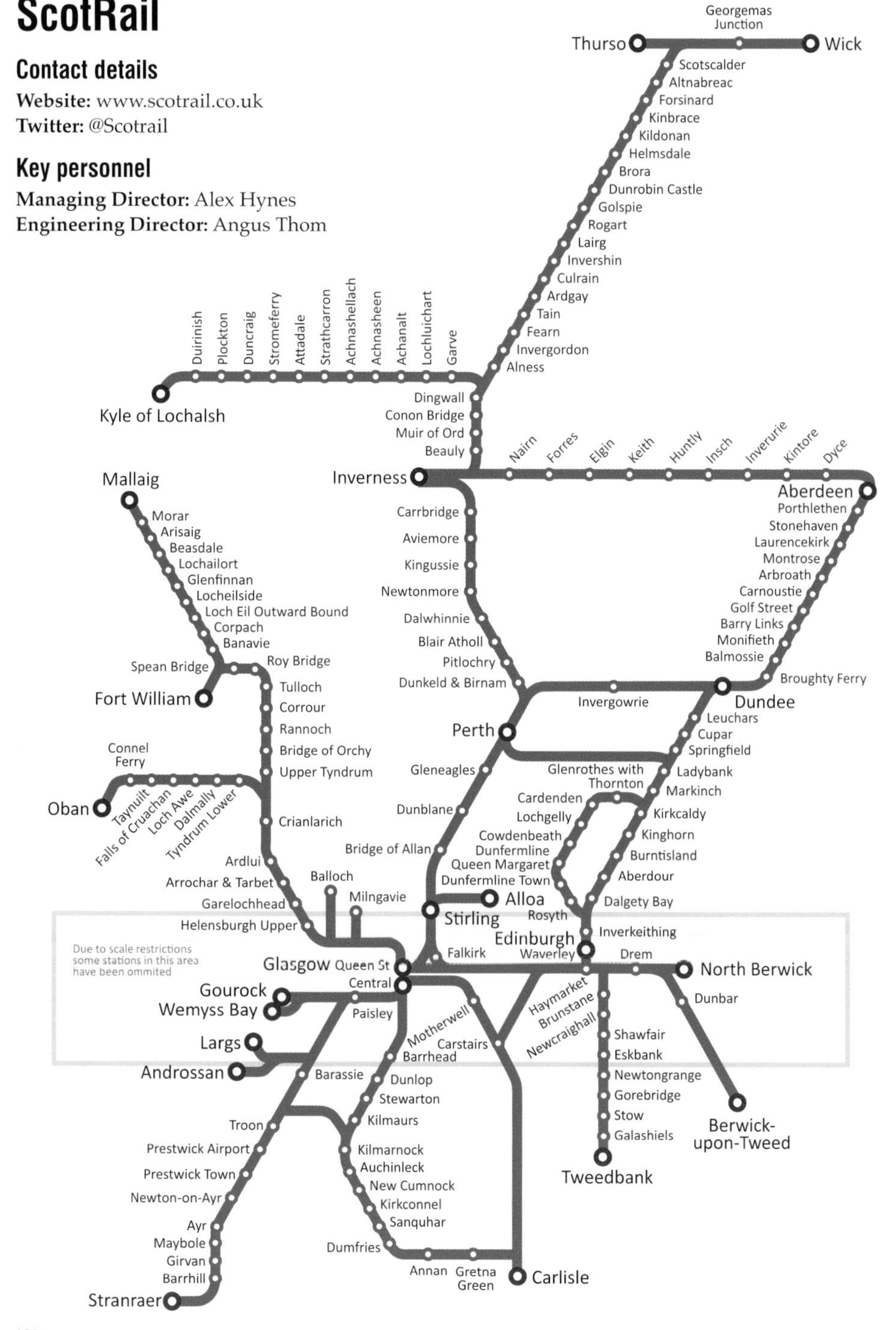

Overview

ScotRail operates all regional and commuter routes in Scotland, plus some trains on the Carlisle to Newcastle line.

Recent electrification of many central belt routes has led to an increased demand for electric multiple units and this has been met by delivery of 46 three-car and 24 four-car Class 385 Hitachi AT200 EMUs in 2016-18, with all now in traffic.

It means the EMU fleet north of the border is now a mix of Class 318s from 1985/86, Class 320s from 1990 (recently bolstered by 12 ex-London Midland units), Alstom Class 334s from 1999-2001 and Siemens Class 380s from 2009/10. The new fleets allowed the elderly Class 314s to be withdrawn and some DMUs to be moved to other TOCs.

The EMUs work most services in North Ayrshire, Inverclyde, to Balloch/Helensburgh, Edinburgh-Glasgow via Falkirk, Bathgate, Shotts and Carstairs and from Edinburgh to North Berwick, Dunblane and Dunbar.

Class 156s remain in use on the West Highland and Glasgow South Western routes, while the Class 158s and 170s work to Tweedbank, the Highland Main Line, Aberdeen to Inverness, the Fife Circle and other commuter routes. The lines north of Inverness are worked by Class 158s.

The other development has been in the acquisition of 54 ex-FGW HST power cars to run with 121 trailers in four-car sets on Glasgow QS/Edinburgh-Inverness/Aberdeen routes.

The TOC has finally been able to dispense with its hired-in Class 68-hauled Fife Circle operations. Five redundant Class 153 single car DMUs are being modified to run as luggage- and bike-carrying vehicles for the West Highland line.

Most of the investment and enhancement in Scotland has already been completed, but looking ahead there are plans to reinstate the Levan branch in Fife, and Alloa to Kincardine for passenger use. A longer-term aspiration is reopening of the remaining part of the Waverley route, the 63 miles from Tweedbank to Carlisle. Other station reopenings are planned across the network.

Nos 318262 and 320301 approach Lanark with the 1650 from Glasgow Central on 24 May 2019. *Robin Ralston*

Class 43

A fleet of ex-FGW HSTs were taken on by ScotRail for fast inter-city operations between seven cities – Glasgow, Edinburgh, Stirling, Perth, Inverness, Dundee and Aberdeen. They run on Glasgow QS-Inverness, Glasgow QS-Aberdeen, Edinburgh-Aberdeen, Edinburgh-Inverness and Inverness-Aberdeen routes.

Fifty-four power cars, are leased from Angel Trains and all are in the HAPC pool.

Following the fatal accident near Stonehaven on 12 August 2020, 43140 was seriously damaged and will be written off, with a replacement expected from the Angel pool of off-lease vehicles.

43003	HAPC	SCT	ANG	HA	43137	HAPC	SCT	ANG	HA
43012	HAPC	SCT	ANG	HA	43138	HAPC	SCT	ANG	HA
43015	HAPC	SCT	ANG	HA	43139	HAPC	SCT	ANG	HA
43021	HAPC	SCT	ANG	HA	43140	HAPC	SCT	ANG	HA (U)
43026	HAPC	SCT	ANG	HA	43141	HAPC	SCT	ANG	HA
43028	HAPC	SCT	ANG	HA	43142	HAPC	SCT	ANG	HA
43030	HAPC	SCT	ANG	HA (U)	43143	HAPC	SCT	ANG	HA
43031	HAPC	SCT	ANG	HA	43144	HAPC	SCT	ANG	HA
43032	HAPC	SCT	ANG	HA	43145	HAPC	SCT	ANG	HA
43033	HAPC	SCT	ANG	HA	43146	HAPC	SCT	ANG	HA
43034	HAPC	SCT	ANG	HA	43147	HAPC	SCT	ANG	HA
43035	HAPC	SCT	ANG	HA	43148	HAPC	SCT	ANG	HA
43036	HAPC	SCT	ANG	HA	43149	HAPC	SCT	ANG	HA
43037	HAPC	SCT	ANG	HA	43150	HAPC	SCT	ANG	HA
43124	HAPC	SCT	ANG	HA	43151	HAPC	SCT	ANG	HA
43125	HAPC	SCT	ANG	HA	43152	HAPC	SCT	ANG	HA
43126	HAPC	SCT	ANG	HA	43163	HAPC	SCT	ANG	HA
43127	HAPC	SCT	ANG	HA	43164	HAPC	SCT	ANG	HA
43128	HAPC	SCT	ANG	HA	43168	HAPC	SCT	ANG	HA
43129	HAPC	SCT	ANG	HA	43169	HAPC	SCT	ANG	HA
43130	HAPC	SCT	ANG	HA	43175	HAPC	SCT	ANG	HA
43131	HAPC	SCT	ANG	HA	43176	HAPC	SCT	ANG	HA
43132	HAPC	SCT	ANG	HA	43177	HAPC	SCT	ANG	HA
43133	HAPC	SCT	ANG	HA	43179	HAPC	SCT	ANG	HA
43134	HAPC	SCT	ANG	HA	43181	HAPC	SCT	ANG	HA
43135	HAPC	SCT	ANG	HA	43182	HAPC	SCT	ANG	HA
43136	HAPC	SCT	ANG	HA	43183	HAPC	SCT	ANG	HA

Mk 3 trailers

All are in HAHQ pool.

TGFB – First-Class Trailer Guard with buffet counter

40600	SCT	ANG	IS	40614	SCT	ANG	IS
40601	SCT	ANG	IS	40615	SCT	ANG	IS
40602	SCT	ANG	IS	40616	SCT	ANG	IS
40603	SCT	ANG	IS	40617	SCT	ANG	IS
40604	SCT	ANG	IS	40618	SCT	ANG	IS
40605	SCT	ANG	IS	40619	SCT	ANG	IS
40606	SCT	ANG	IS	40620	SCT	ANG	IS
40607	SCT	ANG	IS	40621	SCT	ANG	IS
40608	SCT	ANG	IS (U)	40622	SCT	ANG	IS
40609	SCT	ANG	IS	40623	SCT	ANG	IS
40610	SCT	ANG	IS	40624	SCT	ANG	IS
40611	SCT	ANG	IS	40625	SCT	ANG	IS
40612	SCT	ANG	IS	40626	SCT	ANG	IS
40613	SCT	ANG	IS				

TF – Trailer First

These vehicles will be replaced by refurbished TGFBs.

41022	SCT	ANG	IS	41130	SCT	ANG	IS
41104	SCT	ANG	IS	41140	SCT	ANG	IS
41124	SCT	ANG	IS	41144	SCT	ANG	IS
41126	SCT	ANG	IS	41158	SCT	ANG	IS

No. 158727 nears Dalmeny with 1716 Edinburgh-Glenrothes with Thornton on 14 July 2019. *Robin Ralston*

TS – Trailer Standard

42004	SCT	ANG	IS
42007	SCT	ANG	IS
42014	SCT	ANG	IS
42019	SCT	ANG	IS (U)
42021	SCT	ANG	IS
42034	SCT	ANG	IS
42045	SCT	ANG	IS
42046	SCT	ANG	IS
42055	SCT	ANG	IS
42069	SCT	ANG	IS
42072	SCT	ANG	IS
42075	SCT	ANG	IS
42107	SCT	ANG	IS
42118	SCT	ANG	IS
42143	SCT	ANG	IS
42145	SCT	ANG	IS
42183	SCT	ANG	IS
42184	SCT	ANG	IS
42207	SCT	ANG	IS
42252	SCT	ANG	IS
42253	SCT	ANG	IS
42257	SCT	ANG	IS
42259	SCT	ANG	IS
42261	SCT	ANG	IS
42265	SCT	ANG	IS
42268	SCT	ANG	IS
42269	SCT	ANG	IS
42275	SCT	ANG	IS (U)
42276	SCT	ANG	IS
42277	SCT	ANG	IS
42281	SCT	ANG	IS
42287	SCT	ANG	IS
42288	SCT	ANG	IS
42289	SCT	ANG	IS
42291	SCT	ANG	IS
42292	SCT	ANG	IS
42293	SCT	ANG	IS
42297	SCT	ANG	IS
42299	SCT	ANG	IS
42300	SCT	ANG	IS
42333	SCT	ANG	IS
42343	SCT	ANG	IS
42344	SCT	ANG	IS
42345	SCT	ANG	IS
42350	SCT	ANG	IS
42360	SCT	ANG	IS
42551	SCT	ANG	IS
42553	SCT	ANG	IS
42555	SCT	ANG	IS
42557	SCT	ANG	IS
42559	SCT	ANG	IS
42561	SCT	ANG	IS
42562	SCT	ANG	IS
42564	SCT	ANG	IS
42567	SCT	ANG	IS
42571	SCT	ANG	IS (U)
42574	SCT	ANG	IS
42576	SCT	ANG	IS
42577	SCT	ANG	IS
42578	SCT	ANG	IS

TGS – Trailer Guard's Standard

Unrefurbished ex-FGW vehicles.

44023	SCT	ANG	IS
44030	SCT	ANG	IS
44037	SCT	ANG	IS

TC – Trailer Composite

Unrefurbished ex-FGW vehicle.

46010	SCT	ANG	IS

ScotRail HST formations

As a rule the ScotRail HST vehicle trailers stay in fixed formations, but the spare examples may replace others as required for heavy maintenance or because of faults or damage. Power cars will be swapped around as required and are not assigned to any particular set.

Sets HA01-26 are refurbished sets but set HA22 was written off in August 2020.

Set	TGFB	TSD	TS	TSL
HA01	40601	42004	42561	42046
HA02	40602	42292	42562	42045
HA03	40603	42021	42557	42143
HA04	40604	42183	42559	42343
HA05	40605	42345	42034	42184
HA06	40606	42206	42581	42208
HA07	40607	42207	42574	42288
HA08	40608	42055	42571	42019
HA09	40609	42253	42107	42257
HA10	40610	42360	42551	42252
HA11	40611	42267	42325	42301
HA12	40612	42275	42576	42276
HA13	40613	42279	42280	42296
HA14	40614	42012	42245	42013
HA15	40615	42030	42579	42010
HA16	40616	42291	42577	42075
HA17	40617	42295	42558	42250
HA18	40618	42297	42555	42014
HA19	40619	42255	42575	42256
HA20	40620	42200	42568	42129
HA21	40621	42299	42300	42277
HA22 (U)	40622	42007	42564	42145
HA23	40623	42268	42567	42269
HA24	40624	42265	42553	42293
HA25	40625	42259	42578	42333
HA26	40626	42281	42072	42350
HA31	41126	42344	42261	44030
HA32	46010	42069	42118	44023
HA33	41140	42287	42289	44037

Spare vehicles

42269
42301
42759

Class 153

These five former FGW Class 153s have been acquired for conversion to luggage/bike vehicles. Some seats are removed, but not all, and the units will have free wi-fi and at-seat power sockets fitted. A refurbished toilet with controlled emission toilet (CET) tank is also fitted. They will work with Class 156s on the West Highland lines to provide much-needed capacity for skis, rucksacks and bikes.

Each unit can carry up to 20 bikes in custom-designed racks as well as sporting equipment and large items of luggage as well as more seats for customers. All are being outshopped in an artistic wrap depicting typical Highland scenery. All are expected to be in the HAHQ pool.

				DMSL
153305	UND	ANG	ZM (R)	52305
153370	GWR	ANG	ZM (R)	57370
153373	NOR	ANG	ZM(R)	57373
153377	ADV	ANG	ZM (R)	57377
153380	NOR	ANG	ZM(R)	57380

ScotRail has taken five Class 153 single-car DMUs and is having them converted to provide extra seats and, most importantly, additional luggage space for West Highland Line trains. The first refurbished is 153377. *ScotRail*

Class 156

These two-car Metro Cammell units have been the mainstay of the West Highland and Glasgow South Western routes since 1989, plus they are used on a local commuter trains in the Glasgow area as required. They used to work Glasgow QS-Edinburgh briefly in 1989 until displaced by Class 158s.

Nos 156445/446/450/453/456-458/474/476-478/492/493/466/500 have RETB fitted for working on the West Highland Line. All are in the HAHQ pool.

				DMSL	DMS
156430	SCR	ANG	CK	52430	57430
156431	SCR	ANG	CK	52431	57431
156432	SCR	ANG	CK	52432	57432
156433	SCR	ANG	CK	52433	57433
156434	SCR	ANG	CK	52434	57434
156435	SCR	ANG	CK	52435	57435
156436	SCR	ANG	CK	52436	57436
156437	SCR	ANG	CK	52437	57437
156439	SCR	ANG	CK	52439	57439
156442	SCR	ANG	CK	52442	57442
156445	SCR	ANG	CK	52445	57445
156446	SCR	ANG	CK	52446	57446
156450	SCR	ANG	CK	52450	57450
156453	SCR	ANG	CK	52453	57453
156456	SCR	ANG	CK	52456	57456
156457	SCR	ANG	CK	52457	57457
156458	SCR	ANG	CK	52458	57458
156462	SCR	ANG	CK	52462	57462
156467	SCR	ANG	CK	52467	57467
156474	SCR	ANG	CK	52474	57474
156476	SCR	ANG	CK	52476	57476
156477	SCR	ANG	CK	52477	57477
156478	SCR	BRO	CK	52478	57478
156492	SCR	ANG	CK	52492	57492
156493	SCR	ANG	CK	52493	57493
156494	SCR	ANG	CK	52494	57494
156495	SCR	ANG	CK	52495	57495
156499	SCR	ANG	CK	52499	57499
156501	SCR	ANG	CK	52501	57501
156502	SCR	ANG	CK	52502	57502
156503	SCR	ANG	CK	52503	57503
156504	SCR	ANG	CK	52504	57504
156505	SCR	ANG	CK	52505	57505
156506	SCR	ANG	CK	52506	57506
156507	SCR	ANG	CK	52507	57507
156508	SCR	ANG	CK	52508	57508
156509	SCR	ANG	CK	52509	57509
156510	SCR	ANG	CK	52510	57510
156511	SCR	ANG	CK	52511	57511
156512	SCR	ANG	CK	52512	57512
156513	SCR	ANG	CK	52513	57513
156514	SCR	ANG	CK	52514	57514

No. 380020 passes Lanark Junction with the 1050 Ayr-Edinburgh on 7 September 2019. *Robin Ralston*

Class 158

These BREL-built two-car units work across all trains north of Inverness to Wick and Kyle of Lochalsh. They also work some trains from Inverness to Aberdeen, and on the Highland Main line, plus on the Borders Railway from Edinburgh to Tweedbank. They also work other local commuter trains as required across Scotland. Nos 158701-736/738-741 are RETB compliant. All are in the HAHQ pool.

				DMSL	DMSL
158701	SCR	POR	IS	52701	57701
158702	SCR	POR	IS	52702	57702
158703	SCR	POR	IS	52703	57703
158704	SCR	POR	IS	52704	57704
158705	SCR	POR	IS	52705	57705
158706	SCR	POR	IS	52706	57706
158707	SCR	POR	IS	52707	57707
158708	SCR	POR	IS	52708	57708
158709	SCR	POR	IS	52709	57709
158710	SCR	POR	IS	52710	57710
158711	SCR	POR	IS	52711	57711
158712	SCR	POR	IS	52712	57712
158713	SCR	POR	IS	52713	57713
158714	SCR	POR	IS	52714	57714
158715	SCR	POR	IS	52715	57715
158716	SCR	POR	IS	52716	57716
158717	SCR	POR	IS	52717	57717
158718	SCR	POR	IS	52718	57718
158719	SCR	POR	IS	52719	57719
158720	SCR	POR	IS	52720	57720
158721	SCR	POR	IS	52721	57721
158722	SCR	POR	IS	52722	57722
158723	SCR	POR	IS	52723	57723
158724	SCR	POR	IS	52724	57724
158725	SCR	POR	IS	52725	57725
158726	SCR	POR	CK	52726	57726
158727	SCR	POR	CK	52727	57727
158728	SCR	POR	CK	52728	57728
158729	SCR	POR	CK	52729	57729
158730	SCR	POR	CK	52730	57730
158731	SCR	POR	CK	52731	57731
158732	SCR	POR	CK	52732	57732
158733	SCR	POR	CK	52733	57733
158734	SCR	POR	CK	52734	57734
158735	SCR	POR	CK	52735	57735
158736	SCR	POR	CK	52736	57736
158737	SCR	POR	CK	52737	57737
158738	SCR	POR	CK	52738	57738
158739	SCR	POR	CK	52739	57739
158740	SCR	POR	CK	52740	57740
158741	SCR	POR	CK	52741	57741

No. 170406 near Greenloaning, north of Dunblane, working the 0844 Inverness-Glasgow Queen Street on 13 March 2019. *Robin Ralston*

Class 170

These three-car Turbostar units were delivered from Bombardier in 1999-2005. Initially the ScotRail fleet comprised 170401-434 / 450-461 / 470-478 but units have redeployed over the years to Southern, Northern and more recently East Midland Railway. The remaining Scottish units are used on the Borders Railway, and on other commuter and inter-city routes across Scotland. Their use on the Highland Main Line and to Aberdeen had reduced following the introduction of HSTs. All are in the HAHQ pool.

				DMCL	MS	DMCL
170393	SCR	POR	HA	50393	56393	79393
170394	SCR	POR	HA	50394	56394	79394
170395	SCR	POR	HA	50395	56395	79394
170396	SCR	POR	HA	50396	56396	79396
170401	SCR	POR	HA	50401	56401	79401
170402	SCR	POR	HA	50402	56402	79402
170403	SCR	POR	HA	50403	56403	79403
170404	SCR	POR	HA	50404	56404	79404
170405	SCR	POR	HA	50405	56405	79405
170406	SCR	POR	HA	50406	56406	79406
170407	ADV	POR	HA	50407	56407	79407
170408	SCR	POR	HA	50408	56408	79408
170409	SCR	POR	HA	50409	56409	79409
170410	SCR	POR	HA	50410	56410	79410
170411	SCR	POR	HA	50411	56411	79411
170412	SCR	POR	HA	50412	56412	79412
170413	SCR	POR	HA	50413	56413	79413
170414	SCR	POR	HA	50414	56414	79414
170415	SCR	POR	HA	50415	56415	79415
170425	SCR	POR	HA	50425	56425	79425
170426	SCR	POR	HA	50426	56426	79426
170427	SCR	POR	HA	50427	56427	79427
170428	SCR	POR	HA	50428	56428	79428
170429	SCR	POR	HA	50429	56429	79429
170430	SCR	POR	HA	50430	56430	79430
170431	SCR	POR	HA	50431	56431	79431
170432	SCR	POR	HA	50432	56432	79432
170433	SCR	POR	HA	50433	56433	79433
170434	SCR	POR	HA	50434	56434	79434
170450	SCR	POR	HA	50450	56450	79450
170451	SCR	POR	HA	50451	56451	79451
170452	SCR	POR	HA	50452	56452	79452
170470	SCR	POR	HA	50470	56470	79470
170471	SCR	POR	HA	50471	56471	79471

Class 318

These BREL units that date from 1985-87 are used on local trains south of the River Clyde to the likes of Lanark, Neilston and in Ayrshire. All are in the HAHQ pool.

				DTS	MS	DTS
318250	SCR	EVS	GW	77240	62866	77260
318251	SCR	EVS	GW	77241	62867	77261
318252	SCR	EVS	GW	77242	62868	77262
318253	SCR	EVS	GW	77243	62869	77263
318254	SCR	EVS	GW	77244	62870	77264
318255	SCR	EVS	GW	77245	62871	77265
318256	SCR	EVS	GW	77246	62872	77266
318257	SCR	EVS	GW	77247	62873	77267
318258	SCR	EVS	GW	77248	62874	77268
318259	SCR	EVS	GW	77249	62875	77269
318260	SCR	EVS	GW	77250	62876	77270
318261	SCR	EVS	GW	77251	62877	77271
318262	SCR	EVS	GW	77252	62878	77272
318263	SCR	EVS	GW	77253	62879	77273
318264	SCR	EVS	GW	77254	62880	77274
318265	SCR	EVS	GW	77255	62881	77275
318266	SCR	EVS	GW	77256	62882	77276
318267	SCR	EVS	GW	77257	62883	77277
318268	SCR	EVS	GW	77258	62884	77278
318269	SCR	EVS	GW	77259	62885	77279
318270	SCR	EVS	GW	77288	62890	77289

Class 320

These BREL-built units were delivered to ScotRail in 1990, initially in Strathclyde PTE orange. They work mostly north of the Clyde on local commuter trains. More recently they have been joined by 12 Class 320/4s. These were former London Midland Region Class 321s that were delivered as four-car sets. They were shortened to three-car sets and renumbered from Class 321 to 320 to create a unified fleet. All are in the HAHQ pool.

No. 385022 stands at Lanark on 1520 from Glasgow Central on 26 July 2020.
Robin Ralston

Class 320/3

Original three-car Class 320s built for ScotRail.

				DMS	PTS	DMS
320301	SCR	EVS	GW	77899	63021	77921
320302	SCR	EVS	GW	77900	63022	77922
320303	SCR	EVS	GW	77901	63023	77923
320304	SCR	EVS	GW	77902	63024	77924
320305	SCR	EVS	GW	77903	63025	77925
320306	SCR	EVS	GW	77904	63026	77926
320307	SCR	EVS	GW	77905	63027	77927
320308	SCR	EVS	GW	77906	63028	77928
320309	SCR	EVS	GW	77907	63029	77929
320310	SCR	EVS	GW	77908	63030	77930
320311	SCR	EVS	GW	77909	63031	77931
320312	SCR	EVS	GW	77910	63032	77932
320313	SCR	EVS	GW	77911	63033	77933
320314	SCR	EVS	GW	77912	63034	77934
320315	SCR	EVS	GW	77913	63035	77935
320316	SCR	EVS	GW	77914	63036	77936
320317	SCR	EVS	GW	77915	63037	77937
320318	SCR	EVS	GW	77916	63038	77938
320319	SCR	EVS	GW	77917	63039	77939
320320	SCR	EVS	GW	77918	63040	77940
320321	SCR	EVS	GW	77919	63041	77941
320322	SCR	EVS	GW	77920	63042	77942

Class 320/4

Converted from ex-London Midland Class 321/4s reduced from four- to three-car sets.

					DTS	MS	DTS
320401	321401	SCR	EVS	GW	78095	63063	77943
320403	321403	SCR	EVS	GW	78097	63065	77945
320404	321404	SCR	EVS	GW	78098	63066	77946
320411	321411	SCR	EVS	GW	78105	63073	77953
320412	321412	SCR	EVS	GW	78106	63074	77954
320413	321413	SCR	EVS	GW	78107	63075	77955
320414	321414	SCR	EVS	GW	78108	63076	77956
320415	321415	SCR	EVS	GW	78109	63077	77957
320416	321416	SCR	EVS	GW	78110	63078	77958
320417	321417	SCR	EVS	GW	78111	63079	77959
320418	321418	SCR	EVS	GW	78112	63080	77962
320420	321420	SCR	EVS	GW	78114	63082	77960

Class 334

These Alstom Juniper 25kV AC three-car units were built at Washwood Heath in 1999-2001 and were the first new EMUs for Scotland after privatisation. They are used on many local services, mostly in the Glasgow area but also do work to Edinburgh. All are in the HAHQ pool.

				DMS	PTS	DMS
334001	SCR	EVS	GW	64101	74301	65101
334002	SCR	EVS	GW	64102	74302	65102
334003	SCR	EVS	GW	64103	74303	65103
334004	SCR	EVS	GW	64104	74304	65104
334005	SCR	EVS	GW	64105	74305	65105
334006	SCR	EVS	GW	64106	74306	65106
334007	SCR	EVS	GW	64107	74307	65107
334008	SCR	EVS	GW	64108	74308	65108
334009	SCR	EVS	GW	64109	74309	65109
334010	SCR	EVS	GW	64110	74310	65110
334011	SCR	EVS	GW	64111	74311	65111
334012	SCR	EVS	GW	64112	74312	65112
334013	SCR	EVS	GW	64113	74313	65113
334014	SCR	EVS	GW	64114	74314	65114
334015	SCR	EVS	GW	64115	74315	65115
334016	SCR	EVS	GW	64116	74316	65116
334017	SCR	EVS	GW	64117	74317	65117
334018	SCR	EVS	GW	64118	74318	65118
334019	SCR	EVS	GW	64119	74319	65119
334020	SCR	EVS	GW	64120	74320	65120
334021	SCR	EVS	GW	64121	74321	65121
334022	SCR	EVS	GW	64122	74322	65122
334023	SCR	EVS	GW	64123	74323	65123
334024	SCR	EVS	GW	64124	74324	65124
334025	SCR	EVS	GW	64125	74325	65125
334026	SCR	EVS	GW	64126	74326	65126
334027	SCR	EVS	GW	64127	74327	65127
334028	SCR	EVS	GW	64128	74328	65128
334029	SCR	EVS	GW	64129	74329	65129
334030	SCR	EVS	GW	64130	74330	65130
334031	SCR	EVS	GW	64131	74331	65131
334032	SCR	EVS	GW	64132	74332	65132
334033	SCR	EVS	GW	64133	74333	65133
334034	SCR	EVS	GW	64134	74334	65134
334035	SCR	EVS	GW	64135	74335	65135
334036	SCR	EVS	GW	64136	74336	65136
334037	SCR	EVS	GW	64137	74337	65137
334038	SCR	EVS	GW	64138	74338	65138
334039	SCR	EVS	GW	64139	74339	65139
334040	SCR	EVS	GW	64140	74340	65140

Class 380

Siemens Desiro units built in Krefeld and delivered in 2009/10, they are used on many Inverclyde services and other local trains across the Central Belt. All are in the HAHQ pool.

Class 380/0

Three-car units.

				DMS	PTS	DMS
380001	SCR	EVS	GW	38501	38601	38701
380002	SCR	EVS	GW	38502	38602	38702
380003	SCR	EVS	GW	38503	38603	38703
380004	SCR	EVS	GW	38504	38604	38704
380005	SCR	EVS	GW	38505	38605	38705
380006	SCR	EVS	GW	38506	38606	38706
380007	SCR	EVS	GW	38507	38607	38707
380008	SCR	EVS	GW	38508	38608	38708
380009	SCR	EVS	GW	38509	38609	38709
380010	SCR	EVS	GW	38510	38610	38710
380011	SCR	EVS	GW	38511	38611	38711
380012	SCR	EVS	GW	38512	38612	38712
380013	SCR	EVS	GW	38513	38613	38713
380014	SCR	EVS	GW	38514	38614	38714
380015	SCR	EVS	GW	38515	38615	38715
380016	SCR	EVS	GW	38516	38616	38716
380017	SCR	EVS	GW	38517	38617	38717
380018	SCR	EVS	GW	38518	38618	38718
380019	SCR	EVS	GW	38519	38619	38719
380020	SCR	EVS	GW	38520	38620	38720
380021	SCR	EVS	GW	38521	38621	38721
380022	SCR	EVS	GW	38522	38622	38722

No. 156494 passes Enterkinfoot on the Glasgow South Western route on 22 April 2019. *Anthony Hicks*

Class 380/1

Four-car units.

				DMS	PTS	TS	DMS
380101	SCR	EVS	GW	38551	38651	38851	38751
380102	SCR	EVS	GW	38552	38652	38852	38752
380103	SCR	EVS	GW	38553	38653	38853	38753
380104	SCR	EVS	GW	38554	38654	38854	38754
380105	SCR	EVS	GW	38555	38655	38855	38755
380106	SCR	EVS	GW	38556	38656	38856	38756
380107	SCR	EVS	GW	38557	38657	38857	38757
380108	SCR	EVS	GW	38558	38658	38858	38758
380109	SCR	EVS	GW	38559	38659	38859	38759
380110	SCR	EVS	GW	38560	38660	38860	38760
380111	SCR	EVS	GW	38561	38661	38861	38761
380112	SCR	EVS	GW	38562	38662	38862	38762
380113	SCR	EVS	GW	38563	38663	38863	38763
380114	SCR	EVS	GW	38564	38664	38864	38764
380115	SCR	EVS	GW	38565	38665	38865	38765
380116	SCR	EVS	GW	38566	38666	38866	38766

Class 385

Hitachi AT200 units delivered in 2016-18, built at Newton Aycliffe and Kasado in Japan. They are used on Glasgow QS-Edinburgh, Glasgow Central-Edinburgh, Glasgow QS-Dunblane and other local commuter workings in the Scottish Central Belt. All are in the HAHQ pool.

No. 43149, with 43135 on the rear, works the 0929 Edinburgh-Inverness past Burntisland on 12 May 2019.
Anthony Hicks

Class 385/0

Hitachi AT200 three-car units.

				DMS	PTS	DMS
385001	SCR	CRL	EC	441001	442001	444001
385002	SCR	CRL	EC	441002	442002	444002
385003	SCR	CRL	EC	441003	442003	444003
385004	SCR	CRL	EC	441004	442004	444004
385005	SCR	CRL	EC	441005	442005	444005
385006	SCR	CRL	EC	441006	442006	444006
385007	SCR	CRL	EC	441007	442007	444007
385008	SCR	CRL	EC	441008	442008	444008
385009	SCR	CRL	EC	441009	442009	444009
385010	SCR	CRL	EC	441010	442010	444010
385011	SCR	CRL	EC	441011	442011	444011
385012	SCR	CRL	EC	441012	442012	444012
385013	SCR	CRL	EC	441013	442013	444013
385014	SCR	CRL	EC	441014	442014	444014
385015	SCR	CRL	EC	441015	442015	444015
385016	SCR	CRL	EC	441016	442016	444016
385017	SCR	CRL	EC	441017	442017	444017
385018	SCR	CRL	EC	441018	442018	444018
385019	SCR	CRL	EC	441019	442019	444019
385020	SCR	CRL	EC	441020	442020	444020
385021	SCR	CRL	EC	441021	442021	444021
385022	SCR	CRL	EC	441022	442022	444022
385023	SCR	CRL	EC	441023	442023	444023
385024	SCR	CRL	EC	441024	442024	444024
385025	SCR	CRL	EC	441025	442025	444025
385026	SCR	CRL	EC	441026	442026	444026
385027	SCR	CRL	EC	441027	442027	444027
385028	SCR	CRL	EC	441028	442028	444028
385029	SCR	CRL	EC	441029	442029	444029
385030	SCR	CRL	EC	441030	442030	444030
385031	SCR	CRL	EC	441031	442031	444031
385032	SCR	CRL	EC	441032	442032	444032
385033	SCR	CRL	EC	441033	442033	444033
385034	SCR	CRL	EC	441034	442034	444034
385035	SCR	CRL	EC	441035	442035	444035
385036	SCR	CRL	EC	441036	442036	444036
385037	SCR	CRL	EC	441037	442037	444037
385038	SCR	CRL	EC	441038	442038	444038
385039	SCR	CRL	EC	441039	442039	444039
385040	SCR	CRL	EC	441040	442040	444040
385041	SCR	CRL	EC	441041	442041	444041
385042	SCR	CRL	EC	441042	442042	444042
385043	SCR	CRL	EC	441043	442043	444043
385044	SCR	CRL	EC	441044	442044	444044
385045	SCR	CRL	EC	441045	442045	444045
385046	SCR	CRL	EC	441046	442046	444046

Class 385/1

Hitachi AT200 four-car units.

				DMS	PTS	TS	DMS
385101	SCR	CRL	EC	441101	442101	443101	444101
385101	SCR	CRL	EC	441101	442101	443101	444101
385102	SCR	CRL	EC	441102	442102	443102	444102
385103	SCR	CRL	EC	441103	442103	443103	444103
385104	SCR	CRL	EC	441104	442104	443104	444104
385105	SCR	CRL	EC	441105	442105	443105	444105
385106	SCR	CRL	EC	441106	442106	443106	444106
385107	SCR	CRL	EC	441107	442107	443107	444107
385108	SCR	CRL	EC	441108	442108	443108	444108
385109	SCR	CRL	EC	441109	442109	443109	444109
385110	SCR	CRL	EC	441110	442110	443110	444110
385111	SCR	CRL	EC	441111	442111	443111	444111
385112	SCR	CRL	EC	441112	442112	443112	444112
385113	SCR	CRL	EC	441113	442113	443113	444113
385114	SCR	CRL	EC	441114	442114	443114	444114
385115	SCR	CRL	EC	441115	442115	443115	444115
385116	SCR	CRL	EC	441116	442116	443116	444116
385117	SCR	CRL	EC	441117	442117	443117	444117
385118	SCR	CRL	EC	441118	442118	443118	444118
385119	SCR	CRL	EC	441119	442119	443119	444119
385120	SCR	CRL	EC	441120	442120	443120	444120
385121	SCR	CRL	EC	441121	442121	443121	444121
385122	SCR	CRL	EC	441122	442122	443122	444122
385123	SCR	CRL	EC	441123	442123	443123	444123
385124	SCR	CRL	EC	441124	442124	443124	444124

No. 320304 stands at Glasgow Central on 29 May 2019. *Pip Dunn*

Southeastern

Route map

Contact details

Website: www.southeasternrailway.co.uk
Twitter: @Se_Railway

Key personnel

Managing Director: David Statham
Engineering Director: Mark Johnson

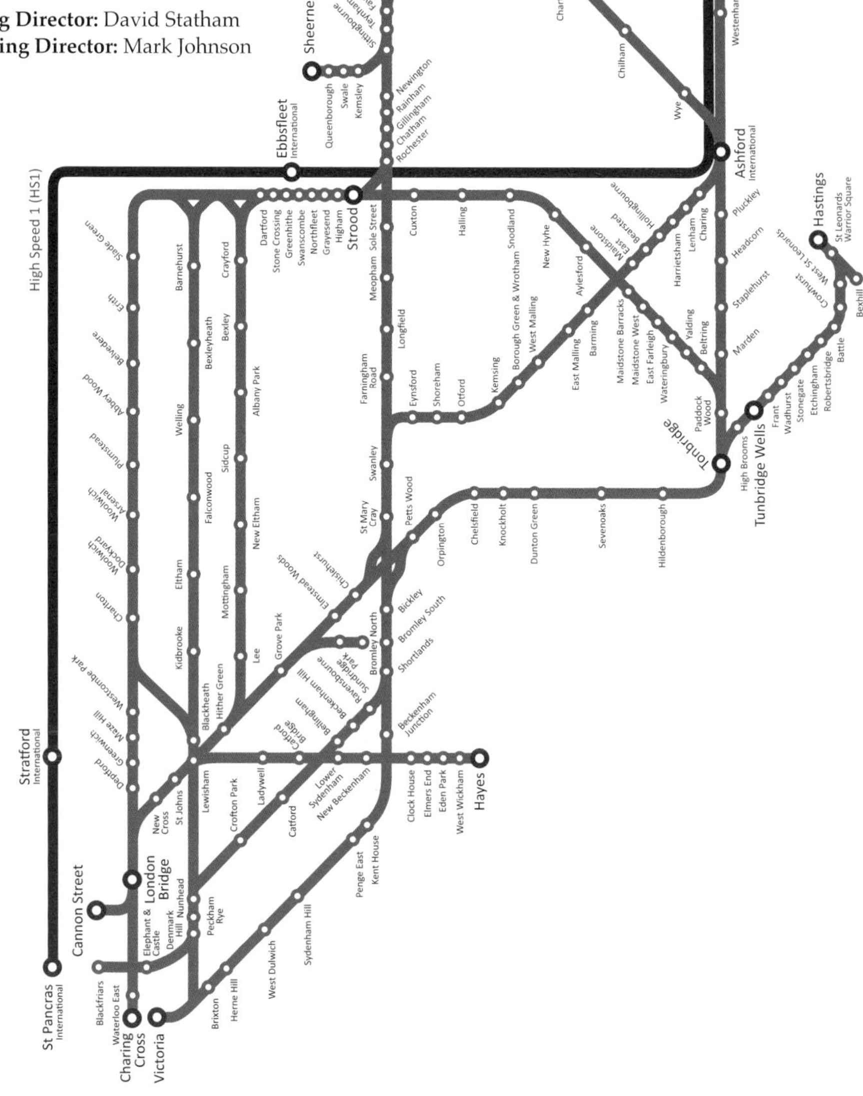

Overview

Southeastern operates commuter trains across the South-East of England in Kent and East Sussex. It replaced most of its all-electric fleet in the late 1990s and early 2000s and as well as the Class 465/466 Networker units it inherited from BR days, it now has a mostly Electrostar fleet, including the Class 376 metro-style trains.

It also operates high-speed domestic trains on HS1 using 29 six-car Class 395 Hitachi Javelin units.

It is due to receive the 30 five-car Siemens Desiro City Class 707 units from South Western Railway when they are replaced by Class 701s in 2021.

Class 375

These Bombardier Electrostar units work the majority of Southeastern's outer suburban commuter services. Most are four-car units, although the 375/3s are three-car sets. All are in the HUHQ pool.

				DMS	TS	DMC
375301	SEB	EVS	RM	67921	74351	67931
375302	SEB	EVS	RM	67922	74352	67932
375303	SEB	EVS	RM	67923	74353	67933
375304	SEB	EVS	RM	67924	74354	67934
375305	SEB	EVS	RM	67925	74355	67935
375306	SEB	EVS	RM	67926	74356	67936
375307	SEB	EVS	RM	67927	74357	67937
375308	SEB	EVS	RM	67928	74358	67938
375309	SEB	EVS	RM	67929	74359	67939
375310	SEB	EVS	RM	67930	74360	67940

Electrostar 375905 leads a six-car train past Etchingham, between Tunbridge Wells and Hastings, on 5 May 2018. *Anthony Hicks*

Class 375/6

Dual-voltage 750V DC and 25kV AC units.

				DMS	MC	PTS	DMS	
375601	SEB	EVS	RM	67801	74251	74201	67851	
375602	SEB	EVS	RM	67802	74252	74202	67852	
375603	SEB	EVS	RM	67803	74253	74203	67853	
375604	SEB	EVS	RM	67804	74254	74204	67854	
375605	SEB	EVS	RM	67805	74255	74205	67855	
375606	SEB	EVS	RM	67806	74256	74206	67856	
375607	SEB	EVS	RM	67807	74257	74207	67857	
375608	SEB	EVS	RM	67808	74258	74208	67858	
375609	SEB	EVS	RM	67809	74259	74209	67859	
375610	SEB	EVS	RM	67810	74260	74210	67860	
375611	SEB	EVS	RM	67811	74261	74211	67861	
375612	SEB	EVS	RM	67812	74262	74212	67862	
375613	SEB	EVS	RM	67813	74263	74213	67863	
375614	SEB	EVS	RM	67814	74264	74214	67864	
375615	SEB	EVS	RM	67815	74265	74215	67865	
375616	SEB	EVS	RM	67816	74266	74216	67866	
375617	SEB	EVS	RM	67817	74267	74217	67867	
375618	SEB	EVS	RM	67818	74268	74218	67868	
375619	SEB	EVS	RM	67819	74269	74219	67869	*Driver John Neve*
375620	SEB	EVS	RM	67820	74270	74220	67870	
375621	SEB	EVS	RM	67821	74271	74221	67871	
375622	SEB	EVS	RM	67822	74272	74222	67872	
375623	SEB	EVS	RM	67823	74273	74223	67873	*Hospice in the Weald*
375624	SEB	EVS	RM	67824	74274	74224	67874	
375625	SEB	EVS	RM	67825	74275	74225	67875	
375626	SEB	EVS	RM	67826	74276	74226	67876	
375627	SEB	EVS	RM	67827	74277	74227	67877	
375628	SEB	EVS	RM	67828	74278	74228	67878	
375629	SEB	EVS	RM	67829	74279	74229	67879	
375630	SEB	EVS	RM	67830	74280	74230	67880	

Class 375/7

750V DC express units with limited first-class seats.

				DMS	MC	TS	DMS	
375701	SEB	EVS	RM	67831	74281	74231	67881	*Kent Air Ambulance Explorer*
375702	SEB	EVS	RM	67832	74282	74232	67882	
375703	SEB	EVS	RM	67833	74283	74233	67883	
375704	SEB	EVS	RM	67834	74284	74234	67884	
375705	SEB	EVS	RM	67835	74285	74235	67885	
375706	SEB	EVS	RM	67836	74286	74236	67886	
375707	SEB	EVS	RM	67837	74287	74237	67887	
375708	SEB	EVS	RM	67838	74288	74238	67888	
375709	SEB	EVS	RM	67839	74289	74239	67889	

375710	SEB	EVS	RM	67840	74290	74240	67890	*Rochester Castle*
375711	SEB	EVS	RM	67841	74291	74241	67891	
375712	SEB	EVS	RM	67842	74292	74242	67892	
375713	SEB	EVS	RM	67843	74293	74243	67893	
375714	SEB	EVS	RM	67844	74294	74244	67894	*Rochester Cathedral*
375715	SEB	EVS	RM	67845	74295	74245	67895	

Class 375/8

750V DC express units with limited first-class seats.

				DMS	MC	TS	DMS	
375801	SEB	EVS	RM	73301	79001	78201	73701	
375802	SEB	EVS	RM	73302	79002	78202	73702	
375803	SEB	EVS	RM	73303	79003	78203	73703	
375804	SEB	EVS	RM	73304	79004	78204	73704	
375805	SEB	EVS	RM	73305	79005	78205	73705	
375806	SEB	EVS	RM	73306	79006	78206	73706	
375807	SEB	EVS	RM	73307	79007	78207	73707	
375808	SEB	EVS	RM	73308	79008	78208	73708	
375809	SEB	EVS	RM	73309	79009	78209	73709	
375810	SEB	EVS	RM	73310	79010	78210	73710	
375811	SEB	EVS	RM	73311	79011	78211	73711	
375812	SEB	EVS	RM	73312	79012	78212	73712	
375813	SEB	EVS	RM	73313	79013	78213	73713	
375814	SEB	EVS	RM	73314	79014	78214	73714	
375815	SEB	EVS	RM	73315	79015	78215	73715	
375816	SEB	EVS	RM	73316	79016	78216	73716	
375817	SEB	EVS	RM	73317	79017	78217	73717	
375818	SEB	EVS	RM	73318	79018	78218	73718	
375819	SEB	EVS	RM	73319	79019	78219	73719	
375820	SEB	EVS	RM	73320	79020	78220	73720	
375821	SEB	EVS	RM	73321	79021	78221	73721	
375822	SEB	EVS	RM	73322	79022	78222	73722	
375823	SEB	EVS	RM	73323	79023	78223	73723	*Ashford Proudly Served by Rail for 175 years*
375824	SEB	EVS	RM	73324	79024	78224	73724	
375825	SEB	EVS	RM	73325	79025	78225	73725	
375826	SEB	EVS	RM	73326	79026	78226	73726	
375827	SEB	EVS	RM	73327	79027	78227	73727	
375828	SEB	EVS	RM	73328	79028	78228	73728	
375829	SEB	EVS	RM	73329	79029	78229	73729	
375830	SEB	EVS	RM	73330	79030	78230	73730	

Class 375/9

750V DC outer suburban units with first class.

				DMC	MS	TS	DMC
375901	SEB	EVS	RM	73331	79031	79061	73731
375902	SEB	EVS	RM	73332	79032	79062	73732
375903	SEB	EVS	RM	73333	79033	79063	73733
375904	SEB	EVS	RM	73334	79034	79064	73734
375905	SEB	EVS	RM	73335	79035	79065	73735
375906	SEB	EVS	RM	73336	79036	79066	73736
375907	SEB	EVS	RM	73337	79037	79067	73737
375908	SEB	EVS	RM	73338	79038	79068	73738
375909	SEB	EVS	RM	73339	79039	79069	73739
375910	SEB	EVS	RM	73340	79040	79070	73740
375911	SEB	EVS	RM	73341	79041	79071	73741
375912	SEB	EVS	RM	73342	79042	79072	73742
375913	SEB	EVS	RM	73343	79043	79073	73743
375914	SEB	EVS	RM	73344	79044	79074	73744
375915	SEB	EVS	RM	73345	79045	79075	73745
375916	SEB	EVS	RM	73346	79046	79076	73746
375917	SEB	EVS	RM	73347	79047	79077	73747
375918	SEB	EVS	RM	73348	79048	79078	73748
375919	SEB	EVS	RM	73349	79049	79079	73749
375920	SEB	EVS	RM	73350	79050	79080	73750
375921	SEB	EVS	RM	73351	79051	79081	73751
375922	SEB	EVS	RM	73352	79052	79082	73752
375923	SEB	EVS	RM	73353	79053	79083	73753
375924	SEB	EVS	RM	73354	79054	79084	73754
375925	SEB	EVS	RM	73355	79055	79085	73755
375926	SEB	EVS	RM	73356	79056	79086	73756
375927	SEB	EVS	RM	73357	79057	79087	73757

The Class 376 is a metro-style Electrostar EMU. No. 376028 passes Petts Woods on 18 September 2017.
Paul Winter

Class 376

These five-car Bombardier Electrostar metro-style trains are used on inner-suburban commuter services only as they have no toilets. They also do not have corridor connections. All are in the HUHQ pool.

				DMS	MS	TS	MS	DMS
376001	SEW	EVS	SG	61101	63301	64301	63501	61601
376002	SEW	EVS	SG	61102	63302	64302	63502	61602
376003	SEW	EVS	SG	61103	63303	64303	63503	61603
376004	SEW	EVS	SG	61104	63304	64304	63504	61604
376005	SEW	EVS	SG	61105	63305	64305	63505	61605
376006	SEW	EVS	SG	61106	63306	64306	63506	61606
376007	SEW	EVS	SG	61107	63307	64307	63507	61607
376008	SEW	EVS	SG	61108	63308	64308	63508	61608
376009	SEW	EVS	SG	61109	63309	64309	63509	61609
376010	SEW	EVS	SG	61110	63310	64310	63510	61610
376011	SEW	EVS	SG	61111	63311	64311	63511	61611
376012	SEW	EVS	SG	61112	63312	64312	63512	61612
376013	SEW	EVS	SG	61113	63313	64313	63513	61613
376014	SEW	EVS	SG	61114	63314	64314	63514	61614
376015	SEW	EVS	SG	61115	63315	64315	63515	61615
376016	SEW	EVS	SG	61116	63316	64316	63516	61616
376017	SEW	EVS	SG	61117	63317	64317	63517	61617
376018	SEW	EVS	SG	61118	63318	64318	63518	61618
376019	SEW	EVS	SG	61119	63319	64319	63519	61619
376020	SEW	EVS	SG	61120	63320	64320	63520	61620
376021	SEW	EVS	SG	61121	63321	64321	63521	61621
376022	SEW	EVS	SG	61122	63322	64322	63522	61622
376023	SEW	EVS	SG	61123	63323	64323	63523	61623
376024	SEW	EVS	SG	61124	63324	64324	63524	61624
376025	SEW	EVS	SG	61125	63325	64325	63525	61625
376026	SEW	EVS	SG	61126	63326	64326	63526	61626
376027	SEW	EVS	SG	61127	63327	64327	63527	61627
376028	SEW	EVS	SG	61128	63328	64328	63528	61628
376029	SEW	EVS	SG	61129	63329	64329	63529	61629
376030	SEW	EVS	SG	61130	63330	64330	63530	61630
376031	SEW	EVS	SG	61131	63331	64331	63531	61631
376032	SEW	EVS	SG	61132	63332	64332	63532	61632
376033	SEW	EVS	SG	61133	63333	64333	63533	61633
376034	SEW	EVS	SG	61134	63334	64334	63534	61634
376035	SEW	EVS	SG	61135	63335	64335	63535	61635
376036	SEW	EVS	SG	61136	63336	64336	63536	61636

Class 377

These units are essentially the same as the Class 375s. When ordered, Southeastern classed its Electrostar as Class 375s and Southern opted for 377s. These dual-voltage units were ordered by Southern, then sub-leased to First Capital Connect before moving to Southeastern when displaced by Class 700s. All are in the HUHQ pool.

				DMC	MS	PTS	DMS
377163	SOU	POR	RM	78563	77163	78963	78763
377164	SOU	POR	RM	78564	77164	78964	78764
377501	FIR	POR	RM	73501	75901	74901	73601
377502	FIR	POR	RM	73502	75902	74902	73602
377503	FIR	POR	RM	73503	75903	74903	73603
377504	FIR	POR	RM	73504	75904	74904	73604
377505	FIR	POR	RM	73505	75905	74905	73605
377506	FIR	POR	RM	73506	75906	74906	73606
377507	FIR	POR	RM	73507	75907	74907	73607
377508	FIR	POR	RM	73508	75908	74908	73608
377509	FIR	POR	RM	73509	75909	74909	73609
377510	FIR	POR	RM	73510	75910	74910	73610
377511	FIR	POR	RM	73511	75911	74911	73611
377512	FIR	POR	RM	73512	75912	74912	73612
377513	FIR	POR	RM	73513	75913	74913	73613
377514	FIR	POR	RM	73514	75914	74914	73614
377515	FIR	POR	RM	73515	75915	74915	73615
377516	FIR	POR	RM	73516	75916	74916	73616
377517	FIR	POR	RM	73517	75917	74917	73617
377518	FIR	POR	RM	73518	75918	74918	73618
377519	FIR	POR	RM	73519	75919	74919	73619
377520	FIR	POR	RM	73520	75920	74920	73620
377521	FIR	POR	RM	73521	75921	74921	73621
377522	FIR	POR	RM	73522	75922	74922	73622
377523	FIR	POR	RM	73523	75923	74923	73623

High-speed trains from London to Kent are operated by Southeastern using Hitachi Class 395 Javelin units. Nos 395019 and 395015 wait their next turns at St Pancras International on 15 September 2017. *Paul Bigland*

Class 395

These six-car Hitachi-built trains, called Javelins, work on the HS1 route from St Pancras to Ashford and Dover. All are in the HUHQ pool.

				PDTS	MS	MS	MS	MS	PDTS	
395001	SEB	EVS	AD	39011	39012	39013	39014	39015	39016	*Dame Kelly Holmes*
395002	SEB	EVS	AD	39021	39022	39023	39024	39025	39026	*Sebastian Coe*
395003	SEB	EVS	AD	39031	39032	39033	39034	39035	39036	*Sir Steve Redgrave*
395004	SEB	EVS	AD	39041	39042	39043	39044	39045	39046	*Sir Chris Hoy*
395005	SEB	EVS	AD	39051	39052	39053	39054	39055	39056	*Dame Tanni Grey-Thompson*
395006	SEB	EVS	AD	39061	39062	39063	39064	39065	39066	*Daley Thompson*
395007	SEB	EVS	AD	39071	39072	39073	39074	39075	39076	*Steve Backley*
395008	SEB	EVS	AD	39081	39082	39083	39084	39085	39086	*Ben Ainslie*
395009	SEB	EVS	AD	39091	39092	39093	39094	39095	39096	*Rebecca Adlington*
395010	SEB	EVS	AD	39101	39102	39103	39104	39105	39106	*Duncan Goodhew*
395011	SEB	EVS	AD	39111	39112	39113	39114	39115	39116	*Katherine Grainger*
395012	SEB	EVS	AD	39121	39122	39123	39124	39125	39126	
395013	SEB	EVS	AD	39131	39132	39133	39134	39135	39136	*Hornby Visitor Centre*
395014	SEB	EVS	AD	39141	39142	39143	39144	39145	39146	*Dina Asher-Smith*
395015	SEB	EVS	AD	39151	39152	39153	39154	39155	39156	
395016	SEB	EVS	AD	39161	39162	39163	39164	39165	39166	
395017	SEB	EVS	AD	39171	39172	39173	39174	39175	39176	
395018	SEB	EVS	AD	39181	39182	39183	39184	39185	39186	*Mo Farah*
395019	SEB	EVS	AD	39191	39192	39193	39194	39195	39196	*Jessica Ennis*
395020	SEB	EVS	AD	39201	39202	39203	39204	39205	39206	*Jason Kenny*
395021	SEB	EVS	AD	39211	39212	39213	39214	39215	39216	*Ed Clancy MBE*
395022	SEB	EVS	AD	39221	39222	39223	39224	39225	39226	*Alistair Brownlee*
395023	SEB	EVS	AD	39231	39232	39233	39234	39235	39236	*Ellie Simmonds*
395024	SEB	EVS	AD	39241	39242	39243	39244	39245	39246	*Jonnie Peacock*
395025	SEB	EVS	AD	39251	39252	39253	39254	39255	39256	*Victoria Pendleton*
395026	SEB	EVS	AD	39261	39262	39263	39264	39265	39266	*Marc Woods*
395027	SEB	EVS	AD	39271	39272	39273	39274	39275	39276	*Hannah Cockroft*
395028	SEB	EVS	AD	39281	39282	39283	39284	39285	39286	*Laura Trott*
395029	SEB	EVS	AD	39291	39292	39293	39294	39295	39296	*David Weir*

Class 465

The Class 465s are four-car BREL Networker units built in the early 1990s and work many commuter trains out of London. All are in the HUHQ pool.

				DMS	TS	TS	DMS
465001	SEW	EVS	SG	64759	72028	72029	64809
465002	SEW	EVS	SG	64760	72030	72031	64810
465003	SEW	EVS	SG	64761	72032	72033	64811
465004	SEW	EVS	SG	64762	72034	72035	64812
465005	SEW	EVS	SG	64763	72036	72037	64813
465006	SEW	EVS	SG	64764	72038	72039	64814
465007	SEW	EVS	SG	64765	72040	72041	64815
465008	SEW	EVS	SG	64766	72042	72043	64816

465009	SEW	EVS	SG	64767	72044	72045	64817
465010	SEW	EVS	SG	64768	72046	72047	64818
465011	SEW	EVS	SG	64769	72048	72049	64819
465012	SEW	EVS	SG	64770	72050	72051	64820
465013	SEW	EVS	SG	64771	72052	72053	64821
465014	SEW	EVS	SG	64772	72054	72055	64822
465015	SEW	EVS	SG	64773	72056	72057	64823
465016	SEW	EVS	SG	64774	72058	72059	64824
465017	SEW	EVS	SG	64775	72060	72061	64825
465018	SEW	EVS	SG	64776	72062	72063	64826
465019	SEW	EVS	SG	64777	72064	72065	64827
465020	SEW	EVS	SG	64778	72066	72067	64828
465021	SEW	EVS	SG	64779	72068	72069	64829
465022	SEW	EVS	SG	64780	72070	72071	64830
465023	SEW	EVS	SG	64781	72072	72073	64831
465024	SEW	EVS	SG	64782	72074	72075	64832
465025	SEW	EVS	SG	64783	72076	72077	64833
465026	SEW	EVS	SG	64784	72078	72079	64834
465027	SEW	EVS	SG	64785	72080	72081	64835
465028	SEW	EVS	SG	64786	72082	72083	64836
465029	SEW	EVS	SG	64787	72084	72085	64837
465030	SEW	EVS	SG	64788	72086	72087	64838
465031	SEW	EVS	SG	64789	72088	72089	64839
465032	SEW	EVS	SG	64790	72090	72091	64840
465033	SEW	EVS	SG	64791	72092	72093	64841
465034	SEW	EVS	SG	64792	72094	72095	64842
465035	SEW	EVS	SG	64793	72096	72097	64843
465036	SEW	EVS	SG	64794	72098	72099	64844
465037	SEW	EVS	SG	64795	72100	72101	64845
465038	SEW	EVS	SG	64796	72102	72103	64846
465039	SEW	EVS	SG	64797	72104	72105	64847
465040	SEW	EVS	SG	64798	72106	72107	64848
465041	SEW	EVS	SG	64799	72108	72109	64849
465042	SEW	EVS	SG	64800	72110	72111	64850
465043	SEW	EVS	SG	64801	72112	72113	64851
465044	SEW	EVS	SG	64802	72114	72115	64852
465045	SEW	EVS	SG	64803	72116	72117	64853
465046	SEW	EVS	SG	64804	72118	72119	64854
465047	SEW	EVS	SG	64805	72120	72121	64855
465048	SEW	EVS	SG	64806	72122	72123	64856
465049	SEW	EVS	SG	64807	72124	72125	64857
465050	SEW	EVS	SG	64808	72126	72127	64858
465151	SEW	EVS	SG	65800	72900	72901	65847
465152	SEW	EVS	SG	65801	72902	72903	65848
465153	SEW	EVS	SG	65802	72904	72905	65849
465154	SEW	EVS	SG	65803	72906	72907	65850
465155	SEW	EVS	SG	65804	72908	72909	65851
465156	SEW	EVS	SG	65805	72910	72911	65852
465157	SEW	EVS	SG	65806	72912	72913	65853
465158	SEW	EVS	SG	65807	72914	72915	65854
465159	SEW	EVS	SG	65808	72916	72917	65855
465160	SEW	EVS	SG	65809	72918	72919	65856
465161	SEW	EVS	SG	65810	72920	72921	65857

465162	SEW	EVS	SG	65811	72922	72923	65858
465163	SEW	EVS	SG	65812	72924	72925	65859
465164	SEW	EVS	SG	65813	72926	72927	65860
465165	SEW	EVS	SG	65814	72928	72929	65861
465166	SEW	EVS	SG	65815	72930	72931	65862
465167	SEW	EVS	SG	65816	72932	72933	65863
465168	SEW	EVS	SG	65817	72934	72935	65864
465169	SEW	EVS	SG	65818	72936	72937	65865
465170	SEW	EVS	SG	65819	72938	72939	65866
465171	SEW	EVS	SG	65820	72940	72941	65867
465172	SEW	EVS	SG	65821	72942	72943	65868
465173	SEW	EVS	SG	65822	72944	72945	65869
465174	SEW	EVS	SG	65823	72946	72947	65870
465175	SEW	EVS	SG	65824	72948	72949	65871
465176	SEW	EVS	SG	65825	72950	72951	65872
465177	SEW	EVS	SG	65826	72952	72953	65873
465178	SEW	EVS	SG	65827	72954	72955	65874
465179	SEW	EVS	SG	65828	72956	72957	65875
465180	SEW	EVS	SG	65829	72958	72959	65876
465181	SEW	EVS	SG	65830	72960	72961	65877
465182	SEW	EVS	SG	65831	72962	72963	65878
465183	SEW	EVS	SG	65832	72964	72965	65879
465184	SEW	EVS	SG	65833	72966	72967	65880
465185	SEW	EVS	SG	65834	72968	72969	65881
465186	SEW	EVS	SG	65835	72970	72971	65882
465187	SEW	EVS	SG	65836	72972	72973	65883
465188	SEW	EVS	SG	65837	72974	72975	65884
465189	SEW	EVS	SG	65838	72976	72977	65885
465190	SEW	EVS	SG	65839	72978	72979	65886
465191	SEW	EVS	SG	65840	72980	72981	65887
465192	SEW	EVS	SG	65841	72982	72983	65888
465193	SEW	EVS	SG	65842	72984	72985	65889
465194	SEW	EVS	SG	65843	72986	72987	65890
465195	SEW	EVS	SG	65844	72988	72989	65891
465196	SEW	EVS	SG	65845	72990	72991	65892
465197	SEW	EVS	SG	65846	72992	72993	65893
465235	SEW	ANG	SG	65734	72787	72788	65784
465236	SEW	ANG	SG	65735	72789	72790	65785
465237	SEW	ANG	SG	65736	72791	72792	65786
465238	SEW	ANG	SG	65737	72793	72794	65787
465239	SEW	ANG	SG	65738	72795	72796	65788
465240	SEW	ANG	SG	65739	72797	72798	65789
465241	SEW	ANG	SG	65740	72799	72800	65790
465242	SEW	ANG	SG	65741	72801	72802	65791
465243	SEW	ANG	SG	65742	72803	72804	65792
465244	SEW	ANG	SG	65743	72805	72806	65793
465245	SEW	ANG	SG	65744	72807	72808	65794
465246	SEW	ANG	SG	65745	72809	72810	65795
465247	SEW	ANG	SG	65746	72811	72812	65796
465248	SEW	ANG	SG	65747	72813	72814	65797
465249	SEW	ANG	SG	65748	72815	72816	65798
465250	SEW	ANG	SG	65749	72817	72818	65799

Class 465/9

Refurbished units converted from Class 465/2s in 2005 and with some first-class seats added.

					DMC	TS	TS	DMC
465901	465201	SEW	ANG	SG	65700	72719	72720	65750
465902	465202	SEW	ANG	SG	65701	72721	72722	65751
465903	465203	SEW	ANG	SG	65702	72723	72724	65752
465904	465204	SEW	ANG	SG	65703	72725	72726	65753
465905	465205	SEW	ANG	SG	65704	72727	72728	65754
465906	465206	SEW	ANG	SG	65705	72729	72730	65755
465907	465207	SEW	ANG	SG	65706	72731	72732	65756
465908	465208	SEW	ANG	SG	65707	72733	72734	65757
465909	465209	SEW	ANG	SG	65708	72735	72736	65758
465910	465210	SEW	ANG	SG	65709	72737	72738	65759
465911	465211	SEW	ANG	SG	65710	72739	72740	65760
465912	465212	SEW	ANG	SG	65711	72741	72742	65761
465913	465213	SEW	ANG	SG	65712	72743	72744	65762
465914	465214	SEW	ANG	SG	65713	72745	72746	65763
465915	465215	SEW	ANG	SG	65714	72747	72748	65764
465916	465216	SEW	ANG	SG	65715	72749	72750	65765
465917	465217	SEW	ANG	SG	65716	72751	72752	65766
465918	465218	SEW	ANG	SG	65717	72753	72754	65767
465919	465219	SEW	ANG	SG	65718	72755	72756	65768
465920	465220	SEW	ANG	SG	65719	72757	72758	65769
465921	465221	SEW	ANG	SG	65720	72759	72760	65770
465922	465222	SEW	ANG	SG	65721	72761	72762	65771
465923	465223	SEW	ANG	SG	65722	72763	72764	65772
465924	465224	SEW	ANG	SG	65723	72765	72766	65773
465925	465225	SEW	ANG	SG	65724	72767	72768	65774
465926	465226	SEW	ANG	SG	65725	72769	72770	65775
465927	465227	SEW	ANG	SG	65726	72771	72772	65776
465928	465228	SEW	ANG	SG	65727	72773	72774	65777
465929	465229	SEW	ANG	SG	65728	72775	72776	65778
465930	465230	SEW	ANG	SG	65729	72777	72778	65779
465931	465231	SEW	ANG	SG	65730	72779	72780	65780
465932	465232	SEW	ANG	SG	65731	72781	72782	65781
465933	465233	SEW	ANG	SG	65732	72783	72784	65782
465934	465234	SEW	ANG	SG	65733	72785	72786	65783

Class 466

Two-car Networker units for inner-suburban commuter services, they are usually added to eight-car Class 465 sets to strengthen to ten cars. All are in the HUHQ pool.

				DMS	DTS
466001	SEW	ANG	SG	64860	78312
466002	SEW	ANG	SG	64861	78313
466003	SEW	ANG	SG	64862	78314
466004	SEW	ANG	SG	64863	78315
466005	SEW	ANG	SG	64864	78316
466006	SEW	ANG	SG	64865	78317
466007	SEW	ANG	SG	64866	78318
466008	SEW	ANG	SG	64867	78319
466009	SEW	ANG	SG	64868	78320
466010	SEW	ANG	SG	64869	78321
466011	SEW	ANG	SG	64870	78322
466012	SEW	ANG	SG	64871	78323
466013	SEW	ANG	SG	64872	78324
466014	SEW	ANG	SG	64873	78325
466015	SEW	ANG	SG	64874	78326
466016	SEW	ANG	SG	64875	78327
466017	SEW	ANG	SG	64876	78328
466018	SEW	ANG	SG	64877	78329
466019	SEW	ANG	SG	64878	78330
466020	SEW	ANG	SG	64879	78331
466021	SEW	ANG	SG	64880	78332
466022	SEW	ANG	SG	64881	78333
466023	SEW	ANG	SG	64882	78334
466024	SEW	ANG	SG	64883	78335
466025	SEW	ANG	SG	64884	78336
466026	SEW	ANG	SG	64885	78337
466027	SEW	ANG	SG	64886	78338
466028	SEW	ANG	SG	64887	78339
466029	SEW	ANG	SG	64888	78340
466030	SEW	ANG	SG	64889	78341
466031	SEW	ANG	SG	64890	78342
466032	SEW	ANG	SG	64891	78343
466033	SEW	ANG	SG	64892	78344
466034	SEW	ANG	SG	64893	78345
466035	SEW	ANG	SG	64894	78346
466036	SEW	ANG	SG	64895	78347
466037	SEW	ANG	SG	64896	78348
466038	SEW	ANG	SG	64897	78349
466039	SEW	ANG	SG	64898	78350
466040	SEW	ANG	SG	64899	78351
466041	SEW	ANG	SG	64900	78352
466042	SEW	ANG	SG	64901	78353
466043	SEW	ANG	SG	64902	78354

Southeastern still uses many ex-Network SouthEast Class 465/466s EMUs. No. 465043 calls at London Bridge on 7 March 2019. *Paul Bigland*

South Western Railway

Contact details

Website: www.southwesternrailway.com
Twitter: @SW Help

Key personnel

Managing Director: Mark Hopwood
Engineering Director: Neil Drury

Overview

South Western Railway is the newish name for what was the old South West Trains franchise. It has a mostly EMU fleet, although a fleet of DMUs are used for the Waterloo-Salisbury-Exeter line and Bristol TM-Portsmouth cross-country workings.

A massive order for Class 701 units was placed when the new franchise was let in 2017, which will allow for older EMUs of Classes 455/456 to be withdrawn. It will also allow SWR to return its Class 458 and brand-new Class 707s to their ROSCOs; the latter are already earmarked for the Southeastern operation.

Class 73

A single ex-BR Class 73 Electro diesel is retained as a Thunderbird / stock move loco.

73235	73135	POR	SWT	BM

Class 158

Ex-BR two-car units released from Transpennine Express in 2007, they are used for local services in the Wessex area. All are in the HYHQ pool.

	old no				DMCL	DMSL
158880	158737	SWW	POR	SA	52737	57737
158881	158742	SWW	POR	SA	52742	57742
158882	158743	SWW	POR	SA	52743	57743
158883	158744	SWW	POR	SA	52744	57744
158884	158772	SWW	POR	SA	52772	57772
158885	158775	SWW	POR	SA	52775	57775
158886	158779	SWW	POR	SA	52779	57779
158887	158781	SWR	POR	SA	52781	57781
158888	158802	SWR	POR	SA	52802	57802
158890	158814	SWR	POR	SA	52814	57814

Class 159

This fleet of three-car trains was built by BREL for Network SouthEast in 1992/93 to replace loco-hauled trains on the Exeter St David's-Waterloo line. They are essentially the same as a Class 158. The fleet has been expanded with additional Class 158s – some being renumbered as Class 159/1s – added to the fleet to provide additional services and extra capacity. All are in the HYHQ pool.

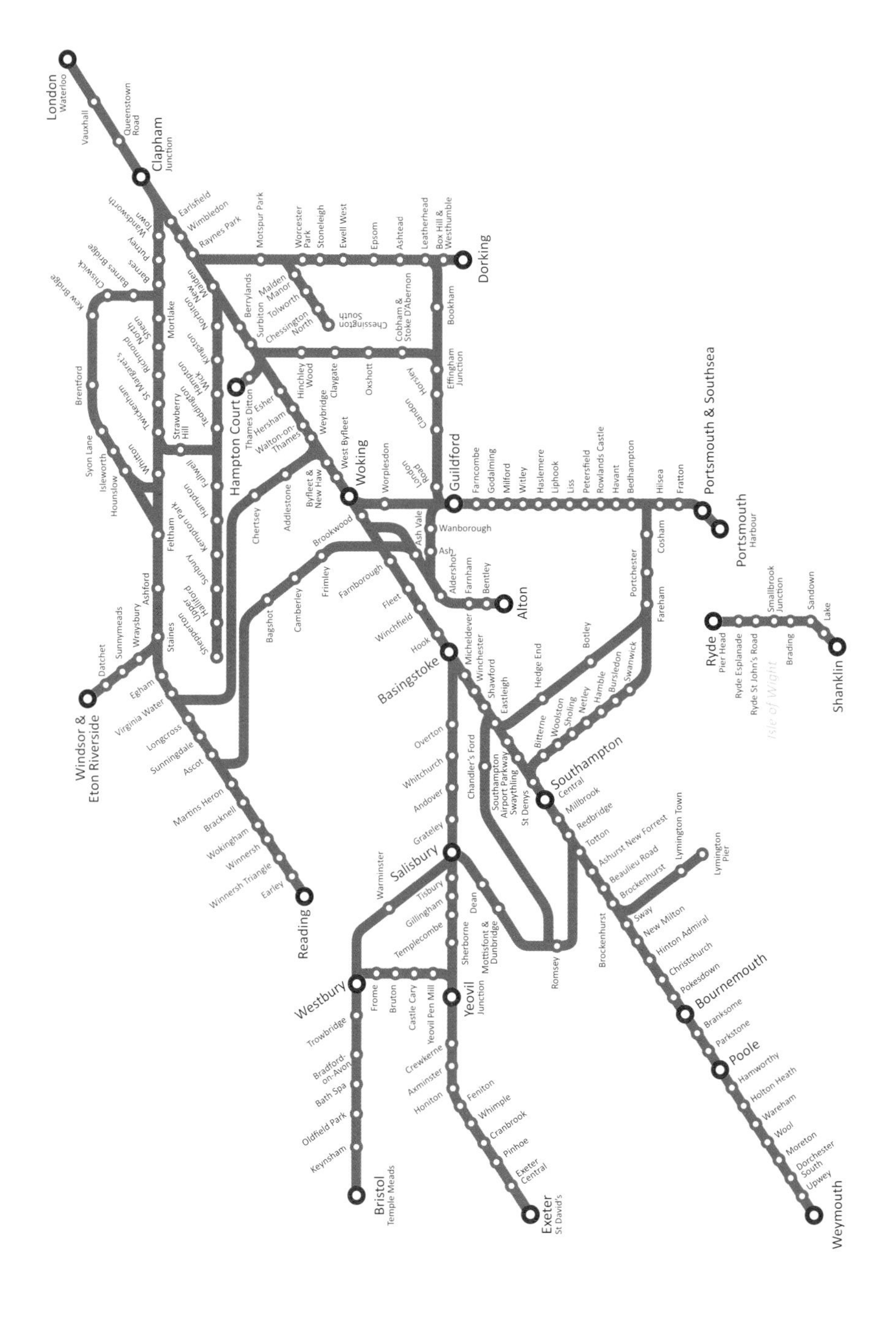
South Western Railway
London
Waterloo
Vauxhall
Queenstown Road
Clapham
Junction
Earlsfield
Wimbledon
Raynes Park
Motspur Park
Worcester Park
Stoneleigh
Ewell West
Epsom
Ashtead
Leatherhead
Box Hill & Westhumble
Dorking
Wandsworth Town
Putney
Barnes
Barnes Bridge
Chiswick
Kew Bridge
Brentford
Syon Lane
Isleworth
Hounslow
Mortlake
North Sheen
Richmond
St Margaret's
Twickenham
Whitton
Feltham
Ashford
Staines
Wraysbury
Sunnymeads
Datchet
Windsor &
Eton Riverside
Egham
Virginia Water
Longcross
Sunningdale
Ascot
Martins Heron
Bracknell
Wokingham
Winnersh
Winnersh Triangle
Earley
Reading
New Malden
Norbiton
Kingston
Hampton Wick
Teddington
Strawberry Hill
Fulwell
Hampton
Kempton Park
Sunbury
Upper Halliford
Shepperton
Berrylands
Surbiton
Malden Manor
Tolworth
Chessington North
Chessington South
Hampton Court
Thames Ditton
Esher
Hersham
Walton-on-Thames
Weybridge
Hinchley Wood
Claygate
Oxshott
Cobham & Stoke D'Abernon
Bookham
Effingham Junction
Horsley
Clandon
London Road
Guildford
Woking
West Byfleet
Byfleet & New Haw
Addlestone
Chertsey
Worplesdon
Brookwood
Bagshot
Camberley
Frimley
Farnborough
Fleet
Winchfield
Hook
Basingstoke
Ash Vale
Wanborough
Ash
Aldershot
Farnham
Bentley
Alton
Farncombe
Godalming
Milford
Witley
Haslemere
Liphook
Liss
Petersfield
Rowlands Castle
Havant
Bedhampton
Hilsea
Fratton
Portsmouth & Southsea
Portsmouth
Harbour
Cosham
Portchester
Fareham
Botley
Hedge End
Micheldever
Winchester
Shawford
Eastleigh
Swanwick
Bursledon
Hamble
Netley
Sholing
Woolston
Bitterne
Overton
Whitchurch
Andover
Grateley
Salisbury
Chandler's Ford
Southampton Airport Parkway
Swaythling
St Denys
Southampton
Central
Millbrook
Redbridge
Totton
Ashurst New Forrest
Beaulieu Road
Brockenhurst
Lymington Town
Lymington Pier
Sway
New Milton
Hinton Admiral
Christchurch
Pokesdown
Bournemouth
Branksome
Parkstone
Poole
Hamworthy
Holton Heath
Wareham
Wool
Moreton
Dorchester South
Upwey
Weymouth
Romsey
Mottisfont & Dunbridge
Dean
Warminster
Tisbury
Gillingham
Templecombe
Sherborne
Yeovil
Junction
Yeovil Pen Mill
Castle Cary
Bruton
Frome
Westbury
Trowbridge
Bradford-on-Avon
Bath Spa
Oldfield Park
Keynsham
Bristol
Temple Meads
Crewkerne
Axminster
Honiton
Feniton
Whimple
Cranbrook
Pinhoe
Exeter Central
Exeter
St David's
Ryde
Pier Head
Ryde Esplanade
Ryde St John's Road
Smallbrook Junction
Brading
Sandown
Lake
Shanklin
Isle of Wight

Class 159/0

The 22 Class 159/0s are ex-BR units from 1992/93 purposely built for the Exeter St David's-Waterloo route.

				DMCL	MSL	DMSL
159001	SWR	POR	SA	52873	58718	57873
159002	SWR	POR	SA	52874	58719	57874
159003	SWR	POR	SA	52875	58720	57875
159004	SWR	POR	SA	52876	58721	57876
159005	SWR	POR	SA	52877	58722	57877
159006	SWR	POR	SA	52878	58723	57878
159007	SWR	POR	SA	52879	58724	57879
159008	SWR	POR	SA	52880	58725	57880
159009	SWR	POR	SA	52881	58726	57881
159010	SWR	POR	SA	52882	58727	57882
159011	SWR	POR	SA	52883	58728	57883
159012	SWR	POR	SA	52884	58729	57884
159013	SWR	POR	SA	52885	58730	57885
159014	SWR	POR	SA	52886	58731	57886
159015	SWR	POR	SA	52887	58732	57887
159016	SWR	POR	SA	52888	58733	57888
159017	SWR	POR	SA	52889	58734	57889
159018	SWR	POR	SA	52890	58735	57890
159019	SWR	POR	SA	52891	58736	57891
159020	SWR	POR	SA	52892	58737	57892
159021	SWR	POR	SA	52893	58738	57893
159022	SWR	POR	SA	52894	58739	57894

Class 159/1

The SWT diesel fleet was increased with eight additional ex-Transpennine Class 158 three-car sets dating from 1990, which were refurbished and renumbered as Class 159/1s in 2006/07. They replaced Class 170/3 Turbostars and work alongside the Class 159/0s.

					DMCL	MSL	DMSL
159101	158800	SWW	POR	SA	52800	58717	57800
159102	158803	SWW	POR	SA	52803	58703	57803
159103	158804	SWW	POR	SA	52804	58704	57804
159104	158805	SWW	POR	SA	52805	58705	57805
159105	158807	SWW	POR	SA	52807	58707	57807
159106	158809	SWW	POR	SA	52809	58709	57809
159107	158811	SWW	POR	SA	52811	58711	57811
159108	158801	SWW	POR	SA	52801	58701	57801

Class 442

These units date from 1987/88 and were built for the Waterloo-Weymouth line after the final stretch from Bournemouth was energised in 1988. They used traction equipment recovered from Class 432 4-REP units.

They were redeployed on Gatwick Express duties and were due to be withdrawn in 2017, but as part of its franchise commitment, South Western Railway has taken on 18 sets, which are being refurbished and returned to traffic in 2021. The units not taken on by SWR, 442401/405/407/412/421/424 are being scrapped or sold. All are in the HYHQ pool.

				DTS	TS	MBS	TS	DTS
442402	SWR	ANG	BM	77383	71819	62938	71843	77407
442403	SWR	ANG	BM	77384	71820	62939	71844	77408
442404	SWR	ANG	BM	77385	71821	62940	71845	77409
442406	SWR	ANG	BM	77387	71823	62942	71847	77411
442408	SWR	ANG	BM	77389	71825	62944	71849	77413
442409	SWR	ANG	BM	77390	71826	62945	71850	77414
442410	SWR	ANG	BM	77391	71827	62946	71851	77415
442411	SWR	ANG	BM	77392	71828	62947	71852	77422
442413	SWR	ANG	BM	77394	71830	62949	71854	77418
442414	SWR	ANG	BM	77395	71831	62950	71855	77419
442415	SWR	ANG	BM	77396	71832	62951	71856	77420
442416	SWR	ANG	BM	77397	71833	62952	71857	77421
442417	SWR	ANG	BM	77398	71834	62953	71858	77416
442418	SWR	ANG	BM	77399	71835	62954	71859	77423
442419	SWR	ANG	BM	77400	71836	62955	71860	77424
442420	SWR	ANG	BM	77401	71837	62956	71861	77425
442422	SWR	ANG	BM	77403	71839	62958	71863	77427
442423	SWR	ANG	BM	77404	71840	62959	71864	77428

No. 158887 arrives at Eastleigh with a Salisbury-Romsey (via Southampton) train on 18 April 2018. *Mark Pike*

Class 444

Siemens Desiro five-car inter-city units ordered by SWT and delivered in 2003-04 from Krefeld / Vienna. All are in the HYHQ pool.

				DMS	TS	TS	TS	DMC	
444001	SWW	ANG	NT	63801	67101	67151	67201	63851	*Naomi House*
444002	SWW	ANG	NT	63802	67102	67152	67202	63852	
444003	SWW	ANG	NT	63803	67103	67153	67203	63853	
444004	SWW	ANG	NT	63804	67104	67154	67204	63854	
444005	SWR	ANG	NT	63805	67105	67155	67205	63855	
444006	SWR	ANG	NT	63806	67106	67156	67206	63856	
444007	SWR	ANG	NT	63807	67107	67157	67207	63857	
444008	SWW	ANG	NT	63808	67108	67158	67208	63858	
444009	SWW	ANG	NT	63809	67109	67159	67209	63859	
444010	SWW	ANG	NT	63810	67110	67160	67210	63860	
444011	SWR	ANG	NT	63811	67111	67161	67211	63861	
444012	SWR	ANG	NT	63812	67112	67162	67212	63862	*Destination Weymouth*
444013	SWW	ANG	NT	63813	67113	67163	67213	63863	
444014	SWW	ANG	NT	63814	67114	67164	67214	63864	
444015	SWR	ANG	NT	63815	67115	67165	67215	63865	
444016	SWW	ANG	NT	63816	67116	67166	67216	63866	
444017	SWR	ANG	NT	63817	67117	67167	67217	63867	
444018	SWR	ANG	NT	63818	67118	67168	67218	63868	*The Fab 444*
444019	SWP	ANG	NT	63819	67119	67169	67219	63869	
444020	SWW	ANG	NT	63820	67120	67170	67220	63870	
444021	SWR	ANG	NT	63821	67121	67171	67221	63871	
444022	SWW	ANG	NT	63822	67122	67172	67222	63872	
444023	SWW	ANG	NT	63823	67123	67173	67223	63873	
444024	SWR	ANG	NT	63824	67124	67174	67224	63874	
444025	SWW	ANG	NT	63825	67125	67175	67225	63875	
444026	SWW	ANG	NT	63826	67126	67176	67226	63876	
444027	SWW	ANG	NT	63827	67127	67177	67227	63877	
444028	SWW	ANG	NT	63828	67128	67178	67228	63878	
444029	SWR	ANG	NT	63829	67129	67179	67229	63879	
444030	SWW	ANG	NT	63830	67130	67180	67230	63880	
444031	SWW	ANG	NT	63831	67131	67181	67231	63881	
444032	SWW	ANG	NT	63832	67132	67182	67232	63882	
444033	SWW	ANG	NT	63833	67133	67183	67233	63883	
444034	SWW	ANG	NT	63834	67134	67184	67234	63884	
444035	SWW	ANG	NT	63835	67135	67185	67235	63885	
444036	SWW	ANG	NT	63836	67136	67186	67236	63886	
444037	SWR	ANG	NT	63837	67137	67187	67237	63887	
444038	SWR	ANG	NT	63838	67138	67188	67238	63888	*South Western Railway*
444039	SWW	ANG	NT	63839	67139	67189	67239	63889	
444040	SWO	ANG	NT	63840	67140	67190	67240	63890	*The D-Day Story Portsmouth*
444041	SWW	ANG	NT	63841	67141	67191	67241	63891	
444042	SWR	ANG	NT	63842	67142	67192	67242	63892	
444043	SWW	ANG	NT	63843	67143	67193	67243	63893	
444044	SWW	ANG	NT	63844	67144	67194	67244	63894	
444045	SWW	ANG	NT	63845	67145	67195	67245	63895	

Class 450

Four-car Siemens Desiro EMUs built in 2002-06, they are used on semi-fast and outer suburban workings. Those numbered in the 450/5 series had revised seat layouts but are now back with their original set numbers. All are in the HYHQ pool.

					DMC	TS	TS	DMC	
450001		SWB	ANG	NT	63201	64201	68101	63601	
450002		SWB	ANG	NT	63202	64202	68102	63602	
450003		SWB	ANG	NT	63203	64203	68103	63603	
450004		SWB	ANG	NT	63204	64204	68104	63604	
450005		SWB	ANG	NT	63205	64205	68105	63605	
450006		SWR	ANG	NT	63206	64206	68106	63606	
450007		SWB	ANG	NT	63207	64207	68107	63607	
450008		SWB	ANG	NT	63208	64208	68108	63608	
450009		SWB	ANG	NT	63209	64209	68109	63609	
450010		SWB	ANG	NT	63210	64210	68110	63610	
450011		SWB	ANG	NT	63211	64211	68111	63611	
450012		SWR	ANG	NT	63212	64212	68112	63612	
450013		SWB	ANG	NT	63213	64213	68113	63613	*Desiro*
450014		SWB	ANG	NT	63214	64214	68114	63614	
450015		SWB	ANG	NT	63215	64215	68115	63615	
450016		SWB	ANG	NT	63216	64216	68116	63616	
450017		SWB	ANG	NT	63217	64217	68117	63617	
450018		SWB	ANG	NT	63218	64218	68118	63618	
450019		SWB	ANG	NT	63219	64219	68119	63619	
450020		SWR	ANG	NT	63220	64220	68120	63620	
450021		SWR	ANG	NT	63221	64221	68121	63621	
450022		SWB	ANG	NT	63222	64222	68122	63622	
450023		SWB	ANG	NT	63223	64223	68123	63623	
450024		SWB	ANG	NT	63224	64224	68124	63624	
450025		SWB	ANG	NT	63225	64225	68125	63625	
450026		SWB	ANG	NT	63226	64226	68126	63626	
450027		SWB	ANG	NT	63227	64227	68127	63627	
450028		SWB	ANG	NT	63228	64228	68128	63628	
450029		SWB	ANG	NT	63229	64229	68129	63629	
450030		SWB	ANG	NT	63230	64230	68130	63630	
450031		SWB	ANG	NT	63231	64231	68131	63631	
450032		SWB	ANG	NT	63232	64232	68132	63632	
450033		SWB	ANG	NT	63233	64233	68133	63633	
450034		SWB	ANG	NT	63234	64234	68134	63634	
450035		SWB	ANG	NT	63235	64235	68135	63635	
450036		SWR	ANG	NT	63236	64236	68136	63636	
450037		SWB	ANG	NT	63237	64237	68137	63637	
450038		SWB	ANG	NT	63238	64238	68138	63638	
450039		SWB	ANG	NT	63239	64239	68139	63639	
450040		SWB	ANG	NT	63240	64240	68140	63640	
450041		SWB	ANG	NT	63241	64241	68141	63641	
450042		SWB	ANG	NT	63242	64242	68142	63642	*Treloar College*
450043	450543	SWR	ANG	NT	63243	64243	68143	63643	

450044	450544	SWB	ANG	NT	63244	64244	68144	63644
450045	450545	SWB	ANG	NT	63245	64245	68145	63645
450046	450546	SWB	ANG	NT	63246	64246	68146	63646
450047	450547	SWB	ANG	NT	63247	64247	68147	63647
450048	450548	SWB	ANG	NT	63248	64248	68148	63648
450049	450549	SWB	ANG	NT	63249	64249	68149	63649
450050	450550	SWB	ANG	NT	63250	64250	68150	63650
450051	450551	SWB	ANG	NT	63251	64251	68151	63651
450052	450552	SWB	ANG	NT	63252	64252	68152	63652
450053	450553	SWB	ANG	NT	63253	64253	68153	63653
450054	450554	SWB	ANG	NT	63254	64254	68154	63654
450055	450555	SWB	ANG	NT	63255	64255	68155	63655
450056	450556	SWB	ANG	NT	63256	64256	68156	63656
450057	450557	SWB	ANG	NT	63257	64257	68157	63657
450058	450558	SWB	ANG	NT	63258	64258	68158	63658
450059	450559	SWB	ANG	NT	63259	64259	68159	63659
450060	450560	SWB	ANG	NT	63260	64260	68160	63660
450061	450561	SWB	ANG	NT	63261	64261	68161	63661
450062	450562	SWB	ANG	NT	63262	64262	68162	63662
450063	450563	SWB	ANG	NT	63263	64263	68163	63663
450064	450564	SWB	ANG	NT	63264	64264	68164	63664
450065	450565	SWB	ANG	NT	63265	64265	68165	63665
450066	450566	SWB	ANG	NT	63266	64266	68166	63666
450067	450567	SWB	ANG	NT	63267	64267	68167	63667
450068	450568	SWB	ANG	NT	63268	64268	68168	63668
450069	450569	SWB	ANG	NT	63269	64269	68169	63669
450070	450570	SWB	ANG	NT	63270	64270	68170	63670
450071		SWB	ANG	NT	63271	64271	68171	63671
450072		SWB	ANG	NT	63272	64272	68172	63672
450073		SWB	ANG	NT	63273	64273	68173	63673
450074		SWB	ANG	NT	63274	64274	68174	63674
450075		SWB	ANG	NT	63275	64275	68175	63675
450076		SWB	ANG	NT	63276	64276	68176	63676
450077		SWB	ANG	NT	63277	64277	68177	63677
450078		SWB	ANG	NT	63278	64278	68178	63678
450079		SWB	ANG	NT	63279	64279	68179	63679
450080		SWB	ANG	NT	63280	64280	68180	63680
450081		SWB	ANG	NT	63281	64281	68181	63681
450082		SWB	ANG	NT	63282	64282	68182	63682
450083		SWB	ANG	NT	63283	64283	68183	63683
450084		SWB	ANG	NT	63284	64284	68184	63684
450085		SWB	ANG	NT	63285	64285	68185	63685
450086		SWB	ANG	NT	63286	64286	68186	63686
450087		SWB	ANG	NT	63287	64287	68187	63687
450088		SWB	ANG	NT	63288	64288	68188	63688
450089		SWB	ANG	NT	63289	64289	68189	63689
450090		SWB	ANG	NT	63290	64290	68190	63690
450091		SWB	ANG	NT	63291	64291	68191	63691
450092		SWB	ANG	NT	63292	64292	68192	63692

450093	SWB	ANG	NT	63293	64293	68193	63693	
450094	SWB	ANG	NT	63294	64294	68194	63694	
450095	SWB	ANG	NT	63295	64295	68195	63695	
450096	SWB	ANG	NT	63296	64296	68196	63696	
450097	SWB	ANG	NT	63297	64297	68197	63697	
450098	SWB	ANG	NT	63298	64298	68198	63698	
450099	SWB	ANG	NT	63299	64299	68199	63699	
450100	SWB	ANG	NT	63300	64300	68200	63700	
450101	SWR	ANG	NT	63701	66851	66801	63751	
450102	SWB	ANG	NT	63702	66852	66802	63752	
450103	SWB	ANG	NT	63703	66853	66803	63753	
450104	SWB	ANG	NT	63704	66854	66804	63754	
450105	SWB	ANG	NT	63705	66855	66805	63755	
450106	SWR	ANG	NT	63706	66856	66806	63756	
450107	SWR	ANG	NT	63707	66857	66807	63757	
450108	SWB	ANG	NT	63708	66858	66808	63758	
450109	SWB	ANG	NT	63709	66859	66809	63759	
450110	SWB	ANG	NT	63710	66860	66810	63760	
450111	SWO	ANG	NT	63901	66921	66901	63921	
450112	SWB	ANG	NT	63902	66922	66902	63922	
450113	SWB	ANG	NT	63903	66923	66903	63923	
450114	SWB	ANG	NT	63904	66924	66904	63924	*Fairbridge Investing in the Future*
450115	SWB	ANG	NT	63905	66925	66905	63925	
450116	SWB	ANG	NT	63906	66926	66906	63926	
450117	SWR	ANG	NT	63907	66927	66907	63927	
450118	SWB	ANG	NT	63908	66928	66908	63928	
450119	SWR	ANG	NT	63909	66929	66909	63929	
450120	SWB	ANG	NT	63910	66930	66910	63930	
450121	SWB	ANG	NT	63911	66931	66911	63931	
450122	SWB	ANG	NT	63912	66932	66912	63932	
450123	SWB	ANG	NT	63913	66933	66913	63933	
450124	SWB	ANG	NT	63914	66934	66914	63934	
450125	SWB	ANG	NT	63915	66935	66915	63935	
450126	SWB	ANG	NT	63916	66936	66916	63936	
450127	SWR	ANG	NT	63917	66937	66917	63937	*Dave Gunson*

On 24 September 2018, 159010 passes Lockington, near Long Eaton, returning to SWR after overhaul at Brush Loughborough. *Paul Robertson*

The two-car Class 456s will leave the SWR fleet soon. No. 456024 arrives at Twickenham leading two Class 455s on 4 July 2019. *Paul Bigland*

Class 455s are also on borrowed time with SWR when new Class 701s replace them in 2021. No. 5717 calls at Clapham Junction on 1 May 2019. *Paul Bigland*

No. 444008 calls at Eastleigh on 29 January 2017 with the 1359 Portsmouth Harbour to Basingstoke. The unit is in the old SWT livery. *Glen Batten*

One of the converted Alstom five-car Class 458/5s, 458509 approaches Clapham Junction with a train for Waterloo on 9 July 2016. *Mark Pike*

Class 455

These BREL units are the oldest EMUs in the SWR fleet, dating from 1982-85, and are used on many inner suburban services from Waterloo. They will be withdrawn when the new Class 701s enter traffic. The TS vehicles in 5701-50 were previously in Class 508 units and date from 1979. All are in the HYHQ pool.

				DTS	MS	TS	DTS
5701	SWM	POR	WD	77727	62783	71545	77728
5702	SWM	POR	WD	77729	62784	71547	77730
5703	SWM	POR	WD	77731	62785	71540	77732
5704	SWM	POR	WD	77733	62786	71548	77734
5705	SWM	POR	WD	77735	62787	71565	77736
5706	SWM	POR	WD	77737	62788	71534	77738
5707	SWM	POR	WD	77739	62789	71536	77740
5708	SWM	POR	WD	77741	62790	71560	77742
5709	SWM	POR	WD	77743	62791	71532	77744
5710	SWM	POR	WD	77745	62792	71566	77746
5711	SWM	POR	WD	77747	62793	71542	77748
5712	SWM	POR	WD	77749	62794	71546	77750
5713	SWM	POR	WD	77751	62795	71567	77752
5714	SWM	POR	WD	77753	62796	71539	77754
5715	SWM	POR	WD	77755	62797	71535	77756
5716	SWM	POR	WD	77757	62798	71564	77758
5717	SWM	POR	WD	77759	62799	71528	77760
5718	SWM	POR	WD	77761	62800	71557	77762
5719	SWM	POR	WD	77763	62801	71558	77764
5720	SWM	POR	WD	77765	62802	71568	77766
5721	SWM	POR	WD	77767	62803	71553	77768
5722	SWM	POR	WD	77769	62804	71533	77770
5723	SWM	POR	WD	77771	62805	71526	77772
5724	SWM	POR	WD	77773	62806	71561	77774
5725	SWM	POR	WD	77775	62807	71541	77776
5726	SWM	POR	WD	77777	62808	71556	77778
5727	SWM	POR	WD	77779	62809	71562	77780
5728	SWM	POR	WD	77781	62810	71527	77782
5729	SWM	POR	WD	77783	62811	71550	77784
5730	SWM	POR	WD	77785	62812	71551	77786
5731	SWM	POR	WD	77787	62813	71555	77788
5732	SWA	POR	WD	77789	62814	71552	77790
5733	SWM	POR	WD	77791	62815	71549	77792
5734	SWM	POR	WD	77793	62816	71531	77794
5735	SWM	POR	WD	77795	62817	71563	77796
5736	SWM	POR	WD	77797	62818	71554	77798
5737	SWM	POR	WD	77799	62819	71544	77800
5738	SWM	POR	WD	77801	62820	71529	77802
5739	SWM	POR	WD	77803	62821	71537	77804
5740	SWM	POR	WD	77805	62822	71530	77806
5741	SWM	POR	WD	77807	62823	71559	77808
5742	SWM	POR	WD	77809	62824	71543	77810
5750	SWM	POR	WD	77811	62825	71538	77812

5847	SWM	POR	WD	77671	62755	71683	77672
5848	SWM	POR	WD	77673	62756	71684	77674
5849	SWM	POR	WD	77675	62757	71685	77676
5850	SWM	POR	WD	77677	62758	71686	77678
5851	SWM	POR	WD	77679	62759	71687	77680
5852	SWM	POR	WD	77681	62760	71688	77682
5853	SWM	POR	WD	77683	62761	71689	77684
5854	SWM	POR	WD	77685	62762	71690	77686
5855	SWM	POR	WD	77687	62763	71691	77688
5856	SWM	POR	WD	77689	62764	71692	77690
5857	SWM	POR	WD	77691	62765	71693	77692
5858	SWM	POR	WD	77693	62766	71694	77694
5859	SWM	POR	WD	77695	62767	71695	77696
5860	SWM	POR	WD	77697	62768	71696	77698
5861	SWM	POR	WD	77699	62769	71697	77700
5862	SWM	POR	WD	77701	62770	71698	77702
5863	SWM	POR	WD	77703	62771	71699	77704
5864	SWM	POR	WD	77705	62772	71700	77706
5865	SWM	POR	WD	77707	62773	71701	77708
5866	SWM	POR	WD	77709	62774	71702	77710
5867	SWM	POR	WD	77711	62775	71703	77712
5868	SWM	POR	WD	77713	62776	71704	77714
5869	SWM	POR	WD	77715	62777	71705	77716
5870	SWM	POR	WD	77717	62778	71706	77718
5871	SWM	POR	WD	77719	62779	71707	77720
5872	SWM	POR	WD	77721	62780	71708	77722
5873	SWM	POR	WD	77723	62781	71709	77724
5874	SWM	POR	WD	77725	62782	71710	77726
5901	SWM	POR	WD	77813	62826	71714	77814
5902	SWM	POR	WD	77815	62827	71715	77816
5903	SWM	POR	WD	77817	62828	71716	77818
5904	SWM	POR	WD	77819	62829	71717	77820
5905	SWM	POR	WD	77821	62830	71725	77822
5906	SWM	POR	WD	77823	62831	71719	77824
5907	SWM	POR	WD	77825	62832	71720	77826
5908	SWM	POR	WD	77827	62833	71721	77828
5909	SWM	POR	WD	77829	62834	71722	77830
5910	SWM	POR	WD	77831	62835	71723	77832
5911	SWM	POR	WD	77833	62836	71724	77834
5912	SWM	POR	WD	77835	62837	67400	77836
5913	SWM	POR	WD	77837	67301	71726	77838
5914	SWM	POR	WD	77839	62839	71727	77840
5915	SWM	POR	WD	77841	62840	71728	77842
5916	SWM	POR	WD	77843	62841	71729	77844
5917	SWM	POR	WD	77845	62842	71730	77846
5918	SWM	POR	WD	77847	62843	71732	77848
5919	SWM	POR	WD	77849	62844	71718	77850
5920	SWM	POR	WD	77851	62845	71733	77852

Class 456

These two-car BREL units transferred from Southern in 2014. They work inner-suburban services in London. They are due to be returned to their ROSCO when Class 701s enter service. All are in the HYHQ pool.

				DMS	DTS
456001	SWM	POR	WD	64735	78250
456002	SWM	POR	WD	64736	78251
456003	SWM	POR	WD	64737	78252
456004	SWM	POR	WD	64738	78253
456005	SWM	POR	WD	64739	78254
456006	SWM	POR	WD	64740	78255
456007	SWM	POR	WD	64741	78256
456008	SWM	POR	WD	64742	78257
456009	SWM	POR	WD	64743	78258
456010	SWM	POR	WD	64744	78259
456011	SWM	POR	WD	64745	78260
456012	SWM	POR	WD	64746	78261
456013	SWM	POR	WD	64747	78262
456014	SWM	POR	WD	64748	78263
456015	SWM	POR	WD	64749	78264
456016	SWM	POR	WD	64750	78265
456017	SWM	POR	WD	64751	78266
456018	SWM	POR	WD	64752	78267
456019	SWM	POR	WD	64753	78268
456020	SWM	POR	WD	64754	78269
456021	SWM	POR	WD	64755	78270
456022	SWM	POR	WD	64756	78271
456023	SWM	POR	WD	64757	78272
456024	SWM	POR	WD	64758	78273

Desiro 450101 in SWR colours arrives at Basingstoke with a London-bound train on 20 July 2020. *Mark Pike*

Class 458

These Alstom Juniper units were ordered when the South West Trains franchise was first let in 1996 and were delivered from 1998-2000. They had a troubled start with reliability issues. They were initially four-cars but in 2013 the eight eight-car Class 460s units that had been built for Gatwick Express were disbanded, and six of them became five-car Class 458s – 458531-536, and each of the original 30 Class 458/5s had an additional vehicle added to make them five-cars sets. This project was completed in 2016. Four 'left over' Class 460 vehicles – all driving cars – were scrapped at the end of the project.

The 458s are due to be redundant with SWR once the Class 701 fleet is fully accepted into traffic. All are in the HYHQ pool.

				DMC	TS	TS	MS	DMC
458501	SWB	POR	WD	67601	74431	74001	74101	67701
458502	SWB	POR	WD	67602	74421	74002	74102	67702
458503	SWB	POR	WD	67603	74441	74003	74103	67703
458504	SWB	POR	WD	67604	74451	74004	74104	67704
458505	SWB	POR	WD	67605	74425	74005	74105	67705
458506	SWB	POR	WD	67606	74436	74006	74106	67706
458507	SWB	POR	WD	67607	74428	74007	74107	67707
458508	SWB	POR	WD	67608	74433	74008	74108	67708
458509	SWB	POR	WD	67609	74452	74009	74109	67709
458510	SWB	POR	WD	67610	74405	74010	74110	67710
458511	SWB	POR	WD	67611	74435	74011	74111	67711
458512	SWB	POR	WD	67612	74427	74012	74112	67712
458513	SWB	POR	WD	67613	74437	74013	74113	67713
458514	SWB	POR	WD	67614	74407	74014	74114	67714
458515	SWB	POR	WD	67615	74404	74015	74115	67715
458516	SWB	POR	WD	67616	74406	74016	74116	67716
458517	SWB	POR	WD	67617	74426	74017	74117	67717
458518	SWB	POR	WD	67618	74432	74018	74118	67718
458519	SWB	POR	WD	67619	74403	74019	74119	67719
458520	SWB	POR	WD	67620	74401	74020	74120	67720
458521	SWB	POR	WD	67621	74438	74021	74121	67721
458522	SWB	POR	WD	67622	74424	74022	74122	67722
458523	SWB	POR	WD	67623	74434	74023	74123	67723
458524	SWB	POR	WD	67624	74402	74024	74124	67724
458525	SWB	POR	WD	67625	74422	74025	74125	67725
458526	SWB	POR	WD	67626	74442	74026	74126	67726
458527	SWB	POR	WD	67627	74412	74027	74127	67727
458528	SWB	POR	WD	67628	74408	74028	74128	67728
458529	SWB	POR	WD	67629	74423	74029	74129	67729
458530	SWB	POR	WD	67630	74411	74030	74130	67730
458531	SWB	POR	WD	67913	74418	74446	74458	67912
458532	SWB	POR	WD	67904	74417	74447	74457	67905
458533	SWB	POR	WD	67917	74413	74443	74453	67916
458534	SWB	POR	WD	67914	74414	74444	74454	67918
458535	SWB	POR	WD	67915	74415	74445	74455	67911
458536	SWB	POR	WD	67906	74416	74448	74456	67902

Class 483

Elderly ex-London Underground stock dating from 1940-42, and converted for Isle of Wight use in 1989, these units are due for replacement in 2021. All are in the HYHQ pool.

				DMS	DMS
483002	ISL	SWR	RY (U)	122	225
483004	ISL	SWR	RY	124	224
483006	ISL	SWR	RY	126	226
483007	ISL	SWR	RY	127	227
483008	ISL	SWR	RY	128	228
483009	ISL	SWR	RY (U)	129	229

Class 484

VivaRail units on order for the Island Line operation on the Isle of Wight. They are being constructed using ex-London Underground D78 stock and allow replacement of the Class 483s. The first units were unveiled in August 2020.

				DMS	DMS
484001	SWR	LOM	RY (Q)	131	231
484002	SWR	LOM	RY (Q)	132	232
484003	SWR	LOM	RY (Q)	133	233
484004	SWR	LOM	RY (Q)	134	234
484005	SWR	LOM	RY (Q)	135	235

On 27 July 2019, 483004 arrives at Shanklin with a train from Ryde Pier Head. These 1938-built ex-LUL units are due for replacement in 2021. *Pip Dunn*

Class 701

New Bombardier Aventra five- and ten-car units to replace the elderly Class 455 and 456 units as well as the more recent Alstom Class 458 and brand-new Class 707, the latter of which will move to Southeastern.

SWR has the option for five additional five-car 701 / 1s, 701061-065, but as of August 2020 this order had not been taken up.

The first of the Class 701 units are now being delivered and undergoing main-line testing. They will be used on the Reading, Windsor and West London suburban routes. These units are branded as Arterio by SWR. All are expected to be in the HYHQ pool.

				DMS	MS	TS	MS	MS	MS	MS	TS	MS	DMS
701001	SWR	ROC		480001	481001	482001	483001	484001	485001	486001	487001	488001	489001
701002	SWR	ROC	WD (Q)	480002	481002	482002	483002	484002	485002	486002	487002	488002	489002
701003	SWR	ROC		480003	481003	482003	483003	484003	485003	486003	487003	488003	489003
701004	SWR	ROC	WD (Q)	480004	481004	482004	483004	484004	485004	486004	487004	488004	489004
701005	SWR	ROC	WD (Q)	480005	481005	482005	483005	484005	485005	486005	487005	488005	489005
701006	SWR	ROC		480006	481006	482006	483006	484006	485006	486006	487006	488006	489006
701007	SWR	ROC		480007	481007	482007	483007	484007	485007	486007	487007	488007	489007
701008	SWR	ROC		480008	481008	482008	483008	484008	485008	486008	487008	488008	489008
701009	SWR	ROC		480009	481009	482009	483009	484009	485009	486009	487009	488009	489009
701010	SWR	ROC		480010	481010	482010	483010	484010	485010	486010	487010	488010	489010
701011	SWR	ROC		480011	481011	482011	483011	484011	485011	486011	487011	488011	489011
701012	SWR	ROC		480012	481012	482012	483012	484012	485012	486012	487012	488012	489012
701013	SWR	ROC		480013	481013	482013	483013	484013	485013	486013	487013	488013	489013
701014	SWR	ROC		480014	481014	482014	483014	484014	485014	486014	487014	488014	489014
701015	SWR	ROC		480015	481015	482015	483015	484015	485015	486015	487015	488015	489015
701016	SWR	ROC		480016	481016	482016	483016	484016	485016	486016	487016	488016	489016
701017	SWR	ROC		480017	481017	482017	483017	484017	485017	486017	487017	488017	489017
701018	SWR	ROC		480018	481018	482018	483018	484018	485018	486018	487018	488018	489018
701019	SWR	ROC		480019	481019	482019	483019	484019	485019	486019	487019	488019	489019
701020	SWR	ROC		480020	481020	482020	483020	484020	485020	486020	487020	488020	489020
701021	SWR	ROC		480021	481021	482021	483021	484021	485021	486021	487021	488021	489021
701022	SWR	ROC		480022	481022	482022	483022	484022	485022	486022	487022	488022	489022
701023	SWR	ROC		480023	481023	482023	483023	484023	485023	486023	487023	488023	489023
701024	SWR	ROC		480024	481024	482024	483024	484024	485024	486024	487024	488024	489024
701025	SWR	ROC		480025	481025	482025	483025	484025	485025	486025	487025	488025	489025
701026	SWR	ROC		480026	481026	482026	483026	484026	485026	486026	487026	488026	489026
701027	SWR	ROC		480027	481027	482027	483027	484027	485027	486027	487027	488027	489027
701028	SWR	ROC		480028	481028	482028	483028	484028	485028	486028	487028	488028	489028
701029	SWR	ROC		480029	481029	482029	483029	484029	485029	486029	487029	488029	489029
701030	SWR	ROC		480030	481030	482030	483030	484030	485030	486030	487030	488030	489030
701031	SWR	ROC		480031	481031	482031	483031	484031	485031	486031	487031	488031	489031
701032	SWR	ROC		480032	481032	482032	483032	484032	485032	486032	487032	488032	489032
701033	SWR	ROC		480033	481033	482033	483033	484033	485033	486033	487033	488033	489033
701034	SWR	ROC		480034	481034	482034	483034	484034	485034	486034	487034	488034	489034
701035	SWR	ROC		480035	481035	482035	483035	484035	485035	486035	487035	488035	489035
701036	SWR	ROC		480036	481036	482036	483036	484036	485036	486036	487036	488036	489036
701037	SWR	ROC		480037	481037	482037	483037	484037	485037	486037	487037	488037	489037
701038	SWR	ROC		480038	481038	482038	483038	484038	485038	486038	487038	488038	489038

701039	SWR	ROC	480039	481039	482039	483039	484039	485039	486039	487039	488039	489039
701040	SWR	ROC	480040	481040	482040	483040	484040	485040	486040	487040	488040	489040
701041	SWR	ROC	480041	481041	482041	483041	484041	485041	486041	487041	488041	489041
701042	SWR	ROC	480042	481042	482042	483042	484042	485042	486042	487042	488042	489042
701043	SWR	ROC	480043	481043	482043	483043	484043	485043	486043	487043	488043	489043
701044	SWR	ROC	480044	481044	482044	483044	484044	485044	486044	487044	488044	489044
701045	SWR	ROC	480045	481045	482045	483045	484045	485045	486045	487045	488045	489045
701046	SWR	ROC	480046	481046	482046	483046	484046	485046	486046	487046	488046	489046
701047	SWR	ROC	480047	481047	482047	483047	484047	485047	486047	487047	488047	489047
701048	SWR	ROC	480048	481048	482048	483048	484048	485048	486048	487048	488048	489048
701049	SWR	ROC	480049	481049	482049	483049	484049	485049	486049	487049	488049	489049
701050	SWR	ROC	480050	481050	482050	483050	484050	485050	486050	487050	488050	489050
701051	SWR	ROC	480051	481051	482051	483051	484051	485051	486051	487051	488051	489051
701052	SWR	ROC	480052	481052	482052	483052	484052	485052	486052	487052	488052	489052
701053	SWR	ROC	480053	481053	482053	483053	484053	485053	486053	487053	488053	489053
701054	SWR	ROC	480054	481054	482054	483054	484054	485054	486054	487054	488054	489054
701055	SWR	ROC	480055	481055	482055	483055	484055	485055	486055	487055	488055	489055
701056	SWR	ROC	480056	481056	482056	483056	484056	485056	486056	487056	488056	489056
701057	SWR	ROC	480057	481057	482057	483057	484057	485057	486057	487057	488057	489057
701058	SWR	ROC	480058	481058	482058	483058	484058	485058	486058	487058	488058	489058
701059	SWR	ROC	480059	481059	482059	483059	484059	485059	486059	487059	488059	489059
701060	SWR	ROC	480060	481060	482060	483060	484060	485060	486060	487060	488060	489060

Siemens Desiro City units 707006/014 wait to work the 1452 Waterloo-Weybridge on 20 February 2020.
Pip Dunn

Class 701/5

All are expected to be in the HYHQ pool.

				DMS	MS	TS	MS	DMS
701501	SWR	ROC	Velim	480101	481101	482101	483101	484101
701502	SWR	ROC	OD (Q)	480102	481102	482102	483102	484102
701503	SWR	ROC		480103	481103	482103	483103	484103
701504	SWR	ROC		480104	481104	482104	483104	484104
701505	SWR	ROC		480105	481105	482105	483105	484105
701506	SWR	ROC		480106	481106	482106	483106	484106
701507	SWR	ROC		480107	481107	482107	483107	484107
701508	SWR	ROC		480108	481108	482108	483108	484108
701509	SWR	ROC		480109	481109	482109	483109	484109
701510	SWR	ROC		480110	481110	482110	483110	484110
701511	SWR	ROC		480111	481111	482111	483111	484111
701512	SWR	ROC		480112	481112	482112	483112	484112
701513	SWR	ROC		480113	481113	482113	483113	484113
701514	SWR	ROC		480114	481114	482114	483114	484114
701515	SWR	ROC		480115	481115	482115	483115	484115
701516	SWR	ROC		480116	481116	482116	483116	484116
701517	SWR	ROC		480117	481117	482117	483117	484117
701518	SWR	ROC		480118	481118	482118	483118	484118
701519	SWR	ROC		480119	481119	482119	483119	484119
701520	SWR	ROC		480120	481120	482120	483120	484120
701521	SWR	ROC		480121	481121	482121	483121	484121
701522	SWR	ROC		480122	481122	482122	483122	484122
701523	SWR	ROC		480123	481123	482123	483123	484123
701524	SWR	ROC		480124	481124	482124	483124	484124
701525	SWR	ROC		480125	481125	482125	483125	484125
701526	SWR	ROC		480126	481126	482126	483126	484126
701527	SWR	ROC		480127	481127	482127	483127	484127
701528	SWR	ROC		480128	481128	482128	483128	484128
701529	SWR	ROC		480129	481129	482129	483129	484129
701530	SWR	ROC		480130	481130	482130	483130	484130

Bombardier Aventra 10-car unit for SWR, 701002 leaves Basingstoke on a training run on 10 August 2020. *Mark Herriott*

Class 707

These new Siemens Desiro City inner-suburban EMUs units are to be replaced by new Class 701s and will then move to the Southeastern operation. All are in the HYHQ pool.

				DMS	TS	TS	TS	DMS
707001	SWM	ANG	WD	421001	422001	423001	424001	425001
707002	SWM	ANG	WD	421002	422002	423002	424002	425002
707003	SWM	ANG	WD	421003	422003	423003	424003	425003
707004	SWM	ANG	WD	421004	422004	423004	424004	425004
707005	SWM	ANG	WD	421005	422005	423005	424005	425005
707006	SWM	ANG	WD	421006	422006	423006	424006	425006
707007	SWM	ANG	WD	421007	422007	423007	424007	425007
707008	SWM	ANG	WD	421008	422008	423008	424008	425008
707009	SWM	ANG	WD	421009	422009	423009	424009	425009
707010	SWM	ANG	WD	421010	422010	423010	424010	425010
707011	SWM	ANG	WD	421011	422011	423011	424011	425011
707012	SWM	ANG	WD	421012	422012	423012	424012	425012
707013	SWM	ANG	WD	421013	422013	423013	424013	425013
707014	SWM	ANG	WD	421014	422014	423014	424014	425014
707015	SWM	ANG	WD	421015	422015	423015	424015	425015
707016	SWM	ANG	WD	421016	422016	423016	424016	425016
707017	SWM	ANG	WD	421017	422017	423017	424017	425017
707018	SWM	ANG	WD	421018	422018	423018	424018	425018
707019	SWM	ANG	WD	421019	422019	423019	424019	425019
707020	SWM	ANG	WD	421020	422020	423020	424020	425020
707021	SWM	ANG	WD	421021	422021	423021	424021	425021
707022	SWM	ANG	WD	421022	422022	423022	424022	425022
707023	SWM	ANG	WD	421023	422023	423023	424023	425023
707024	SWM	ANG	WD	421024	422024	423024	424024	425024
707025	SWM	ANG	WD	421025	422025	423025	424025	425025
707026	SWM	ANG	WD	421026	422026	423026	424026	425026
707027	SWM	ANG	WD	421027	422027	423027	424027	425027
707028	SWM	ANG	WD	421028	422028	423028	424028	425028
707029	SWM	ANG	WD	421029	422029	423029	424029	425029
707030	SWM	ANG	WD	421030	422030	423030	424030	425030

New VivaRail Class 484s will be introduced on the Isle of Wight to replace Class 483s. No. 484001 was unveiled in mid-August. *SWR*

Transpennine Express

Contact details

Website: www.tpexpress.co.uk
Twitter: @TPExpressTrains

Key personnel

Interim Managing Director: Liz Collins
Fleet Director: Paul Staples

Overview

The First Group-operated franchise runs from Liverpool Lime Street to Scarborough, Middlesbrough and Newcastle, from Manchester Piccadilly to Cleethorpes and Hull, via the Hope Valley and also from Manchester Airport to Edinburgh and Glasgow Central via the WCML and from Liverpool to Edinburgh via the ECML.

The TPE fleet has gone through a complete overhaul in recent times. The 51 three-car Class 185s are on lease until December 2020, with 15 sets due to return once that lease has ended. Which 15 sets will be returned had not been decided as of August 2020.

In their place have come 13 sets of Mk 5 CAF coaches hauled by Stadler Class 68s. The locos are provided by Direct Rail Services, of which 68019-032 are in TPE livery and 68033/034 are 'spare locos' that remain in DRS colours. The locos remain owned and maintained by DRS and 13 a day (with 11 in traffic) will be necessary when the full Mk 5 timetable is finally introduced. Any locos not used by TPE are free to be used by DRS if required.

A dozen brand-new, five-car Class 397 Civity units from CAF have now entered traffic replacing ten four-car Class 350/4s on the Manchester Airport to Glasgow Central and Edinburgh route, allowing more services and more seats.

The TOC has started new services via the ECML north of York using Class 802 Nova 1s, thus offering an alternative to LNER and CrossCountry Trains. It now also operates more services on the WCML to Glasgow and Edinburgh.

The fleet transition is still ongoing and the planned 11 sets a day of loco-hauled trains is still some way off being the norm, a situation not helped by the Covid-19 pandemic.

Class 185

These three-car Siemens Desiro units have been the mainstay of TPE's workings since their introduction in 2005/06. The advent of new Mk 5 coaches means the need for 185s is set to reduce with 15 units due to return to their ROSCO. They will continue to be used on the Hope Valley line and to Cleethorpes and Hull. All are in the EAHQ pool.

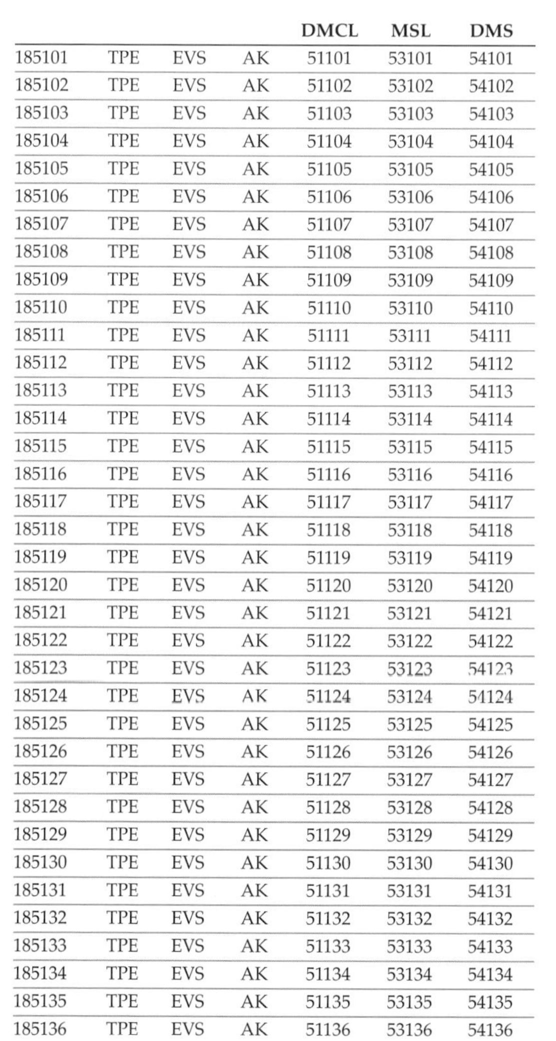

				DMCL	MSL	DMS
185101	TPE	EVS	AK	51101	53101	54101
185102	TPE	EVS	AK	51102	53102	54102
185103	TPE	EVS	AK	51103	53103	54103
185104	TPE	EVS	AK	51104	53104	54104
185105	TPE	EVS	AK	51105	53105	54105
185106	TPE	EVS	AK	51106	53106	54106
185107	TPE	EVS	AK	51107	53107	54107
185108	TPE	EVS	AK	51108	53108	54108
185109	TPE	EVS	AK	51109	53109	54109
185110	TPE	EVS	AK	51110	53110	54110
185111	TPE	EVS	AK	51111	53111	54111
185112	TPE	EVS	AK	51112	53112	54112
185113	TPE	EVS	AK	51113	53113	54113
185114	TPE	EVS	AK	51114	53114	54114
185115	TPE	EVS	AK	51115	53115	54115
185116	TPE	EVS	AK	51116	53116	54116
185117	TPE	EVS	AK	51117	53117	54117
185118	TPE	EVS	AK	51118	53118	54118
185119	TPE	EVS	AK	51119	53119	54119
185120	TPE	EVS	AK	51120	53120	54120
185121	TPE	EVS	AK	51121	53121	54121
185122	TPE	EVS	AK	51122	53122	54122
185123	TPE	EVS	AK	51123	53123	54123
185124	TPE	EVS	AK	51124	53124	54124
185125	TPE	EVS	AK	51125	53125	54125
185126	TPE	EVS	AK	51126	53126	54126
185127	TPE	EVS	AK	51127	53127	54127
185128	TPE	EVS	AK	51128	53128	54128
185129	TPE	EVS	AK	51129	53129	54129
185130	TPE	EVS	AK	51130	53130	54130
185131	TPE	EVS	AK	51131	53131	54131
185132	TPE	EVS	AK	51132	53132	54132
185133	TPE	EVS	AK	51133	53133	54133
185134	TPE	EVS	AK	51134	53134	54134
185135	TPE	EVS	AK	51135	53135	54135
185136	TPE	EVS	AK	51136	53136	54136

The Class 185 was Siemens' only DMU design for the UK and 51 three-car sets were ordered for Transpennine routes. No. 185115 passes Old Denaby, near Mexborough, on 11 July 2018. *Rob France*

185137	TPE	EVS	AK	51137	53137	54137
185138	TPE	EVS	AK	51138	53138	54138
185139	TPE	EVS	AK	51139	53139	54139
185140	TPE	EVS	AK	51140	53140	54140
185141	TPE	EVS	AK	51141	53141	54141
185142	TPE	EVS	AK	51142	53142	54142
185143	TPE	EVS	AK	51143	53143	54143
185144	TPE	EVS	AK	51144	53144	54144
185145	TPE	EVS	AK	51145	53145	54145
185146	TPE	EVS	AK	51146	53146	54146
185147	TPE	EVS	AK	51147	53147	54147
185148	TPE	EVS	AK	51148	53148	54148
185149	TPE	EVS	AK	51149	53149	54149
185150	TPE	EVS	AK	51150	53150	54150
185151	TPE	EVS	AK	51151	53151	54151

Bottom: On 15 September 2019, 68026 *Enterprise* waits at Liverpool Lime Street with the 1552 to Scarborough. *Pip Dunn*

Below: CAF Civity EMU 397010 passes Wandel with the 1708 Glasgow Central-Manchester Piccadilly on 24 June 2020. *Robin Ralston*

Class 397

These Nova 2 12 five-car CAF Civity 25kV units have replaced Class 350s. All are now in traffic and work all Manchester Airport/Liverpool to Glasgow/Edinburgh services. All are in the TPEC pool.

				DMF	PTS	MS	PTS	DMS
397001	TPE	EWS	MA	471001	472001	473001	474001	475001
397002	TPE	EWS	MA	471002	472002	473002	474002	475002
397003	TPE	EWS	MA	471003	472003	473003	474003	475003
397004	TPE	EWS	MA	471004	472004	473004	474004	475004
397005	TPE	EWS	MA	471005	472005	473005	474005	475005
397006	TPE	EWS	MA	471006	472006	473006	474006	475006
397007	TPE	EWS	MA	471007	472007	473007	474007	475007
397008	TPE	EWS	MA	471008	472008	473008	474008	475008
397009	TPE	EWS	MA	471009	472009	473009	474009	475009
397010	TPE	EWS	MA	471010	472010	473010	474010	475010
397011	TPE	EWS	MA	471011	472011	473011	474011	475011
397012	TPE	EWS	MA	471012	472012	473012	474012	475012

Class 802/2

All 19 of these new Nova 1 Hitachi bi-mode AT300 units are in traffic and used on Liverpool-Edinburgh (via York) and Manchester Airport to Newcastle routes. All are in the EAHQ pool.

				PDTS	MS	MS	MC	PDTF
802201	TPE	ANG	DN	831201	832201	833201	834201	835201
802202	TPE	ANG	DN	831202	832202	833202	834202	835202
802203	TPE	ANG	DN	831203	832203	833203	834203	835203
802204	TPE	ANG	DN	831204	832204	833204	834204	835204
802205	TPE	ANG	DN	831205	832205	833205	834205	835205
802206	TPE	ANG	DN	831206	832206	833206	834206	835206
802207	TPE	ANG	DN	831207	832207	833207	834207	835207
802208	TPE	ANG	DN	831208	832208	833208	834208	835208
802209	TPE	ANG	DN	831209	832209	833209	834209	835209
802210	TPE	ANG	DN	831210	832210	833210	834210	835210
802211	TPE	ANG	DN	831211	832211	833211	834211	835211
802212	TPE	ANG	DN	831212	832212	833212	834212	835212
802213	TPE	ANG	DN	831213	832213	833213	834213	835213
802214	TPE	ANG	DN	831214	832214	833214	834214	835214
802215	TPE	ANG	DN	831215	832215	833215	834215	835215
802216	TPE	ANG	DN	831216	832216	833216	834216	835216
802217	TPE	ANG	DN	831217	832217	833217	834217	835217
802218	TPE	ANG	DN	831218	832218	833218	834218	835218
802219	TPE	ANG	DN	831219	832219	833219	834219	835219

Opposite: Hitachi Class 802 bi-mode units 802201/202 working a Peterborough to Heaton Depot crew training and mileage accumulation run past Claypole on 6 June 2019.
Bill Atkinson

Mk 5 coaches

TPE has ordered 66 Mk 5 coaches from CAF in Spain, which is enough vehicles to form 13 full sets of five-car loco-hauled sets comprising a Driving Open Brake Standard (of which 14 have been delivered), three Open Standards and an Open First next to the loco.

These Nova 3 trains work in push-pull mode on the Liverpool-Scarborough route but will also be deployed on some Manchester Airport-Middlesbrough / Redcar trains when all sets are in traffic. All are in the EAHQ pool.

Open First			
11501	TPE	BEA	MA
11502	TPE	BEA	MA
11503	TPE	BEA	MA
11504	TPE	BEA	MA
11505	TPE	BEA	MA
11506	TPE	BEA	MA
11507	TPE	BEA	MA
11508	TPE	BEA	MA
11509	TPE	BEA	MA
11510	TPE	BEA	MA
11511	TPE	BEA	MA
11512	TPE	BEA	MA
11513	TPE	BEA	MA
Open Standard			
12701	TPE	BEA	MA
12702	TPE	BEA	MA
12703	TPE	BEA	MA
12704	TPE	BEA	MA
12705	TPE	BEA	MA
12706	TPE	BEA	MA
12707	TPE	BEA	MA
12708	TPE	BEA	MA
12709	TPE	BEA	MA
12710	TPE	BEA	MA
12711	TPE	BEA	MA
12712	TPE	BEA	MA
12713	TPE	BEA	MA
12714	TPE	BEA	MA
12715	TPE	BEA	MA
12716	TPE	BEA	MA
12717	TPE	BEA	MA
12718	TPE	BEA	MA
12719	TPE	BEA	MA
12720	TPE	BEA	MA
12721	TPE	BEA	MA
12722	TPE	BEA	MA
12723	TPE	BEA	MA
12724	TPE	BEA	MA
12725	TPE	BEA	MA
12726	TPE	BEA	MA
12727	TPE	BEA	MA
12728	TPE	BEA	MA
12729	TPE	BEA	MA
12730	TPE	BEA	MA
12731	TPE	BEA	MA
12732	TPE	BEA	MA
12733	TPE	BEA	MA
12734	TPE	BEA	MA
12735	TPE	BEA	MA
12736	TPE	BEA	MA
12737	TPE	BEA	MA
12738	TPE	BEA	MA
12739	TPE	BEA	MA
Driving Open Brake Standard			
12801	TPE	BEA	MA
12802	TPE	BEA	MA
12803	TPE	BEA	MA
12804	TPE	BEA	MA
12805	TPE	BEA	MA
12806	TPE	BEA	MA
12807	TPE	BEA	MA
12808	TPE	BEA	MA
12809	TPE	BEA	MA
12810	TPE	BEA	MA
12811	TPE	BEA	MA
12812	TPE	BEA	MA
12813	TPE	BEA	MA
12814	TPE	BEA	MA

Transport for Wales/Trafnidiaeth Cymru

Contact details

Website: www.tfwrail.wales or www.trctrenau.cymru
Twitter: @TfWrail

Key personnel

Chief Executive: Kevin Thomas
Chief Operations Office: Andy Thomas

Overview

Transport for Wales is the name given to what was the Wales & Borders franchise previously run by Arriva under the name Arriva Trains Wales. Awarded to Keolis Amey Operations, it was initially due to run until October 2033 but will now be taken under government control from early 2021.

It inherited a mix of ex-BR rolling stock, with many outdated Class 142/143 units due for replacement soon, as well as the full fleet of Alstom Class 175 Coradia units. The operation also had two loco-hauled sets of Mk 3 coaches that have been used from Holyhead to Cardiff to Manchester using DB Cargo Class 67s.

However, four dedicated Class 67s and ex-LNER Mk 4s are being introduced soon to allow more trains on the Welsh Marches route to be loco hauled. Nos 67008/014/017/025 have been prepared by DBC and painted in TfW livery (see page 276).

Also, a new fleet of Class 197, 231 and 398 units are on order, while five VivaRail Class 230 and eight FLEX Class 769s are also undergoing testing with the TOC.

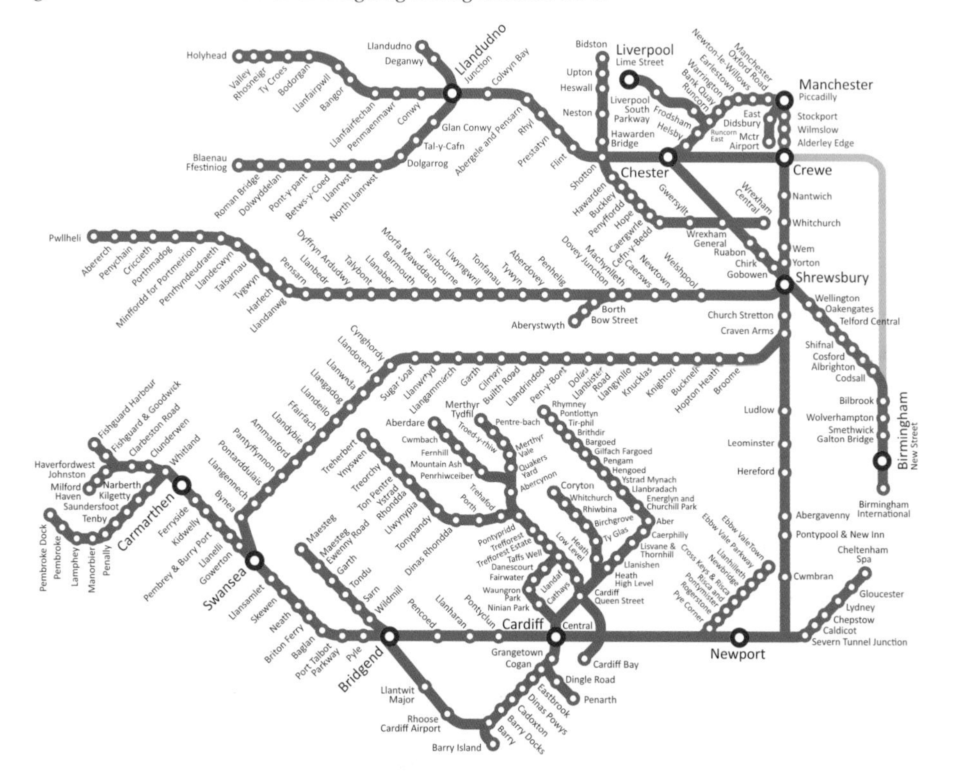

The Class 230s are planned for use on the Wrexham Central to Bidston, Conwy Valley and Crewe-Chester lines, although they are delayed in entering traffic. Also delayed is the introduction of the 769s on the Valley Lines.

Class 142

The remaining Class 142 and 143 Pacer railbuses are used on the Penarth/Cardiff to Rhymney, Bridgend/Barry Island to Aberdare/Merthyr Tydfil, Cardiff to Treherbert, Radyr to Coryton and Cardiff Bay to Cardiff Queen Street shuttle services. They work these alongside Class 150 and 153s. They have dispensation to run until 31 December 2020.

				DMS	DMSL
142002	ARV	ANG	CF	55543	55593
142006	ARV	ANG	CF	55547	55597
142010	ARV	ANG	CF	55551	55601
142069	ARV	ANG	CF	55719	55765
142072	ARV	ANG	CF	55722	55768
142073	ARV	ANG	CF	55723	55769
142074	ARV	ANG	CF	55724	55770
142075	ARV	ANG	CF	55725	55771
142076	ARV	ANG	CF	55726	55772
142077	ARV	ANG	CF	55727	55773
142080	ARV	ANG	CF	55730	55776
142081	ARV	ANG	CF	55731	55777
142082	ARV	ANG	CF	55732	55778
142083	ARV	ANG	CF	55733	55779
142085	ARV	ANG	CF	55735	55781

Class 143

These work the same duties as the 142s and are also due for withdrawal but also have dispensation to run until 31 December 2020.

				DMS	DMSL
143601	ARV	MGC	CF	55642	55667
143602	ARB	POR	CF	55651	55668
143604	ARB	POR	CF	55645	55670
143605	ARB	POR	CF	55646	55671
143606	ARB	POR	CF	55647	55672
143607	ARB	POR	CF	55648	55673
143608	ARB	POR	CF	55649	55674
143609	ARV	SGC	CF	55650	55675
143610	ARV	MGC	CF	55643	55676
143614	ARV	MGC	CF	55655	55680
143616	ARB	POR	CF	55657	55682
143622	ARB	POR	CF	55663	55688
143623	ARB	POR	CF	55664	55689
143624	ARB	POR	CF	55665	55690
143625	ARB	POR	CF	55666	55691

Alstom-built 175002 leaves Dinmore Tunnel on a Holyhead-Cardiff train on 29 August 2019. *Anthony Hicks*

Class 150

These share duties with railbuses but also work Crewe to Chester, Chester to Liverpool, Carmarthen / Swansea to Shrewsbury / Crewe, Blaenau Ffestiniog to Llandudno, Wrexham Central to Bidston (due to be replaced by Class 230s), Fishguard Harbour / Pembroke Dock to Swansea, Swansea to Cardiff Central, Maesteg to Cheltenham Spa and Fishguard Harbour to Gloucester, all duties they share with other TfW units. All are in the HLHQ pool.

				DMSL	DMS
150208	ARV	POR	CF	52208	57208
150213	ARV	POR	CF	52213	57213
150217	ARV	POR	CF	52217	57217
150227	ARV	POR	CF	52227	57227
150229	ARV	POR	CF	52229	57229
150230	ARV	POR	CF	52230	57230
150231	ARV	POR	CF	52231	57231
150235	ARV	POR	CF	52235	57235
150236	ARV	POR	CF	52236	57236
150237	ARV	POR	CF	52237	57237
150240	ARV	POR	CF	52240	57240
150241	ARV	POR	CF	52241	57241
150242	ARV	POR	CF	52242	57242
150245	ARV	POR	CF	52245	57245
150250	ARV	POR	CF	52250	57250
150251	ARV	POR	CF	52251	57251
150252	ARV	POR	CF	52252	57252
150253	ARV	POR	CF	52253	57253
150254	ARV	POR	CF	52254	57254
150255	ARV	POR	CF	52255	57255
150256	ARV	POR	CF	52256	57256
150257	ARV	POR	CF	52257	57257
150258	ARV	POR	CF	52258	57258
150259	ARV	POR	CF	52259	57259
150260	ARV	POR	CF	52260	57260
150262	ARV	POR	CF	52262	57262
150264	ARV	POR	CF	52264	57264
150267	ARV	POR	CF	52267	57267
150278	ARV	POR	CF	52278	57278
150279	ARV	POR	CF	52279	57279
150280	ARV	POR	CF	52280	57280
150281	ARV	POR	CF	52281	57281
150282	ARV	POR	CF	52282	57282
150283	ARV	POR	CF	52283	57283
150284	ARV	POR	CF	52284	57284
150285	ARV	POR	CF	52285	57285

Class 153

The fleet has recently been enlarged with surplus units released by East Midlands Railway and they work pretty much the same duties as 150s. All are in the HLHQ pool.

				DMSL
153303	ARV	ANG	CF	52303
153306	AGA	POR	CF	52306
153309	AGA	POR	CF	52309
153310	EMT	POR	CF	52310
153312	ARV	ANG	CF	52312
153313	EMT	POR	CF	52313
153314	AGA	POR	CF	52314
153320	TFW	POR	CF	52320
153321	EMT	POR	CF	52321
153322	AGA	POR	CF	52322
153323	TFW	POR	CF	52323
153325	TFW	POR	CF	52325
153326	EMT	POR	CF	52326
153327	TFW	ANG	CF	52327
153329	FIR	POR	CF	52329
153333	TFW	POR	CF	52333
153335	AGA	POR	CF	52335
153353	TFW	ANG	CF	57353
153361	FIR	POR	CF	57361
153362	ARV	ANG	CF	57362
153367	TFW	POR	CF	57367
153369	FIR	POR	CF	57369

Class 158

These units are fitted with ERTMS in-cab signalling equipment, meaning they are the only TfW trains that can work Cambrian line duties from Aberystwyth and Pwllheli to Birmingham International.

They are also used on Birmingham International to Holyhead, Manchester Airport to Llandudno, Crewe to Chester, Chester to Liverpool and sometimes on the South West wakes routes. They are currently being refurbished. All are in the HLHQ pool.

				DMSL	DMSL
158818	TFW	ANG	MN	52818	57818
158819	TFW	ANG	MN	52819	57819
158820	TFW	ANG	MN	52820	57820
158821	TFW	ANG	MN	52821	57821
158822	TFW	ANG	MN	52822	57822
158823	TFW	ANG	MN	52823	57823
158824	TFW	ANG	MN	52824	57824
158825	TFW	ANG	MN	52825	57825
158826	TFW	ANG	MN	52826	57826
158827	TFW	ANG	MN	52827	57827
158828	TFW	ANG	MN	52828	57828
158829	TFW	ANG	MN	52829	57829
158830	TFW	ANG	MN	52830	57830
158831	TFW	ANG	MN	52831	57831
158832	TFW	ANG	MN	52832	57832
158833	TFW	ANG	MN	52833	57833
158834	TFW	ANG	MN	52834	57834
158835	TFW	ANG	MN	52835	57835
158836	TFW	ANG	MN	52836	57836
158837	TFW	ANG	MN	52837	57837
158838	TFW	ANG	MN	52838	57838
158839	TFW	ANG	MN	52839	57839
158840	TFW	ANG	MN	52840	57840
158841	TFW	ANG	MN	52841	57841

Class 170/2

TfW has recently taken 12 Class 170 Turbostars displaced by Greater Anglia. The eight three-car and four two-car sets are now used on Maesteg to Cheltenham Spa and Bridgend to Ebbw Vale Town routes. All are in the HLHQ pool.

				DMCL	MSL	DMSL
170201	AGA	POR	CF	50201	56201	79201
170202	AGA	POR	CF	50202	56202	79202
170203	AGA	POR	CF	50203	56203	79203
170204	AGA	POR	CF	50204	56204	79204
170205	AGA	POR	CF	50205	56205	79205
170206	AGA	POR	CF	50206	56206	79206
170207	AGA	POR	CF	50207	56207	79207
170208	AGA	POR	CF	50208	56208	79208
170270	AGA	POR	CF	50270		79270
170271	AGA	POR	CF	50271		79271
170272	AGA	POR	CF	50272		79272
170273	AGA	POR	CF	50273		79273

VivaRail three-car 230006 passes Evesham Station on test on 20 May 2020. *Jack Boskett*

Class 175

Alstom two- and three-car units used mostly on the Welsh Marches, North Wales Coast and South West Wales routes. All are in the HLHQ pool.

Class 175/0

Original two-car sets.

				DMSL	DMSL
175001	TFW	ANG	CH	50701	79701
175002	TFW	ANG	CH	50702	79702
175003	TFW	ANG	CH	50703	79703
175004	ARV	ANG	CH	50759	79759
175005	ARV	ANG	CH	50705	79751
175006	TFW	ANG	CH	50706	79765
175007	ARV	ANG	CH	50707	79707
175008	ARV	ANG	CH	50708	79708
175009	TFW	ANG	CH	50709	79709
175010	ARV	ANG	CH	50710	79710
175011	TFW	ANG	CH	50711	79711

Class 175/1

Original three-car sets.

				DMSL	MSL	DMSL
175101	TFW	ANG	CH	50751	56751	79704
175102	ARV	ANG	CH	50702	56752	79752
175103	TFW	ANG	CH	50753	56753	79753
175104	ARV	ANG	CH	50754	56754	79754
175105	ARV	ANG	CH	50755	56755	79755
175106	ARV	ANG	CH	50756	56756	79756
175107	TFW	ANG	CH	50757	56757	79757
175108	ARV	ANG	CH	50758	56758	79758
175109	ARV	ANG	CH	50704	56759	79759
175110	ARV	ANG	CH	50760	56760	79760
175111	ARV	ANG	CH	50761	56761	79761
175112	ARV	ANG	CH	50762	56762	79762
175113	TFW	ANG	CH	50763	56763	79763
175114	ARV	ANG	CH	50764	56764	79764
175115	ARV	ANG	CH	50765	56765	79706
175116	TFW	ANG	CH	50766	56766	79766

Class 230s

VivaRail diesel-battery hybrid units converted from former London Underground D78 stock. The first units are currently undergoing testing.

				DMS	TS	DMS
230006	TFW	VIV	(Q)	300006	300206	300106
230007	TFW	VIV	(Q)	300007	300207	300107
230008	TFW	VIV	LM (Q)	300008	300208	300108
230009	TFW	VIV		300009	300209	300109
230010	TFW	VIV		300010	300210	300110

Class 769

The first of these ex-Class 319 EMUs now converted to bi-mode operation are now undergoing testing. All are expected to be in the HLHQ pool.

					DMC	MS	TS	DMS
769002	319002	TFW	POR	CF	77293	62892	71773	77292
769003	319003	TFW	POR	CF	77295	62893	71774	77294
769006	319006	TFW	POR	CF	77301	62896	71777	77300
769007	319007	TFW	POR	CF	77303	62897	71778	77302
769008	319008	TFW	POR	CF	77305	62898	71779	77304
769421	319421	TFW	POR	LM (S)	77331	62911	71792	77330
769426	319426	TFW	POR	LB (U)	77341	62916	71796	77340
769445	319445	TFW	POR	CF	77379	62935	71816	77378
769452	319452	TFW	POR	CF	77441	62966	71871	77440

Loco-hauled coaches

Three sets of ex-LNER Mk 4 coaches for push-pull operation with Class 67s are being prepared for use on the Welsh Marches route. They will replace two sets of Mk 3 coaches that have been previously used and are now off lease, albeit owned by Arriva. All are in the HLHQ pool.

Mk 4 Kitchen Buffet Standard			
10312	TFW	ARV	CF
10325	TFW	ARV	CF
10328	TFW	ARV	CF
Mk 4 Open First			
11323	TFW	ARV	CF
11324	TFW	ARV	CF
11325	TFW	ARV	CF

Mk 4 Open Standard (end)			
12217	TFW	ARV	CF
12219	TFW	ARV	CF
12225	TFW	ARV	CF
Mk 4 Open Standard (disabled)			
12318	TFW	ARV	CF
12319	TFW	ARV	CF
12322	TFW	ARV	CF

Mk 4 Open Standard			
12446	TFW	ARV	CF
12447	TFW	ARV	CF
12454	TFW	ARV	CF
Mk 4 DVT			
82216	TFW	ARV	CF
82226	TFW	ARV	CF
82229	TFW	ARV	CF

New trains on order

The following new trains are on order for TfW to replace Classes 142, 143, 150, 153, 158 and 175.

Class	Numbers	Sets (vehicles)	Make	Type	Routes
197/0	197001-051	51x2 (102)	CAF Civity	DMU	Wales & Borders
197/1	197101-126	26x3 (78)	CAF Civity	DMU	Wales & Borders
231	231001-011	11x4 (44)	Stadler Flirt	DEMU	South Wales Metro
398	398001-036	36x3 (108)	Stadler Citylink	Metro	Central Metro
756/0	756001-007	7x3 (21)	Stadler Flirt	TMMU	Central Metro
756/1	756101-117	17x4 (68)	Stadler Flirt	TMMU	Central Metro

No. 158826 heads west at Mostyn on 4 May 2019. *Antony Christie*

Cascaded from Greater Anglia, Turbostar 170272 stands at Cardiff Central on 21 February 2020. *Antony Christie*

No. 153322 is stabled on Cardiff Canton depot on 21 February 2020. *Antony Christie*

Four DB Cargo Class 67s are being prepared for Transport for Wales Holyhead-Cardiff operations with Mk 4 coaches. No. 67025 stands at Eastleigh on 11 November 2019. *Mark Pike*

West Midlands Trains

Contact details

Websites: www.westmidlandsrailway.co.uk (WMR); www.londonnorthwesternrailway.co.uk (LNWR)
Twitter: @WestMidRailway or @LNRailway

Key personnel

Managing Director: Julian Edwards
Engineering Director: Zena Dent

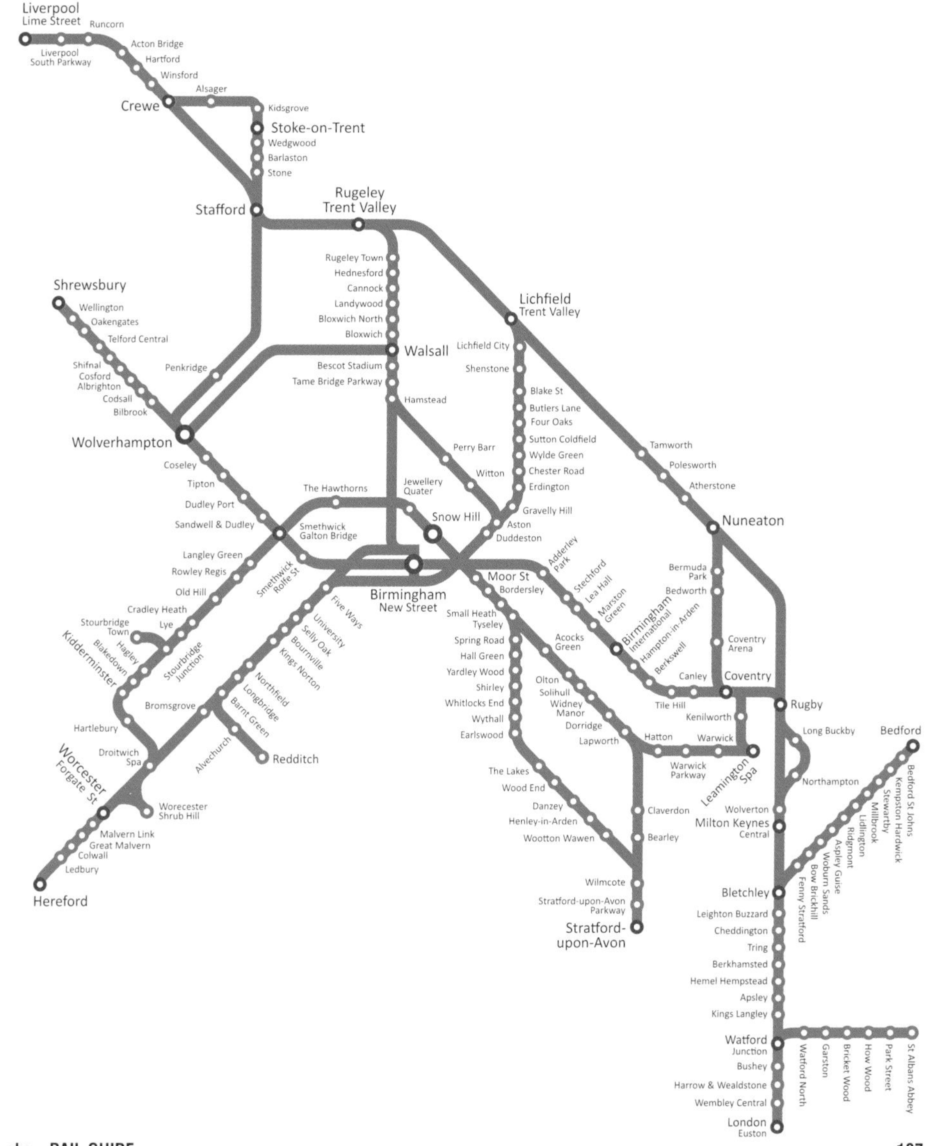

Overview

Formed out of the old London Midland Railway franchise, which was previously part of the Silverlink operations, West Midlands Trains is split in two: London North Western Railway (LNWR) and West Midlands Railway (WMR).

The former runs the Euston to Liverpool semi-fast trains (via Northampton) as well as the Bedford to Bletchley and Watford Junction to St Albans Abbey branches, while the latter covers most of the local and commuter trains in, and emanating from, the West Midlands, extending as far as Leamington Spa, Stratford-on-Avon, Worcester, Shrewsbury, Rugeley and the Cross-city line from Redditch / Bromsgrove to Lichfield.

The two operations have their own liveries, with LNWR featuring dark green and WMR using a gold and purple colour scheme.

It has a mixed fleet of ex-BR rolling stock and early post-privatisation trains but is now taking deliveries of its CAF Class 196 units and they will be followed by a fleet of Class 730s. This will allow some of its older trains to be replaced.

Class 08

The TOC has two Class 08 shunters, one based at Tyseley and one based at Soho.

Both are in the EJLO pool.

08616	LMR	LON	TS	*Tyseley 100*
08805	RSR	LON	SI	*Robin Jones 40 Years Service*

Class 139

These single-car units are part of the WMR fleet built by Parry People Mover. They work exclusively on the ¾-mile Stourbridge Junction to Stourbridge Town branch. The units are currently being tested to run on biomethane. Both are in the EJHQ pool.

				DMM
139001	WMG	POR	SJ	39001
139002	WMG	POR	SJ	39002

Class 153

These WMR single-car units are used to strengthen services formed of other DMUs. They are currently in warm store at Tyseley. All are in the EJHQ pool.

				DMSL
153334	LMR	POR	TS	52334
153354	LMR	POR	TS	57354
153356	LMR	POR	TS	57356
153364	LMR	POR	TS	57364
153365	LMR	POR	TS	57365
153366	LMR	POR	TS	57366
153371	LMR	POR	TS	57371
153375	LMR	POR	TS	57375

Class 170

All to move to East Midlands Railway or CrossCountry Trains. All are in the EJHQ pool.

Class 170/5

These two-car ex-Central Trains units are now 20 years old. They work mostly from Birmingham NS to Hereford and Shrewsbury.

				DMSL	DMSL
170501	WMG	POR	TS	50501	79501
170502	WMG	POR	TS	50502	79502
170503	WMG	POR	TS	50503	79503
170504	WMG	POR	TS	50504	79504
170505	WMG	POR	TS	50505	79505
170506	WMG	POR	TS	50506	79506
170507	WMG	POR	TS	50507	79507
170508	WMG	POR	TS	50508	79508
170509	WMG	POR	TS	50509	79509
170510	WMG	POR	TS	50510	79510
170511	WMG	POR	TS	50511	79511
170512	WMG	POR	TS	50512	79512
170513	WMG	POR	TS	50513	79513
170514	WMG	POR	TS	50514	79514
170515	WMG	POR	TS	50515	79515
170516	WMG	POR	TS	50516	79516
170517	WMG	POR	TS	50517	79517
170532	WMG	POR	TS	50632	79632
170535	WMG	POR	TS	50635	79635

Class 170/6

Also ex-Central Trains units, these are three-car versions and do not have corridor connections. They work alongside the 170/5s. The centre cars will move to CrossCountry Trains and the rest eventually to EMR as 170/5s.

				DMSL	MS	DMSL
170630	WMG	POR	TS	50630	56630	79630
170631	WMG	POR	TS	50631	56631	79631
170633	WMG	POR	TS	50633	56633	79633
170634	WMG	POR	TS	50634	56634	79634

Class 172

All are in the EJHQ pool.

One of two Parry People Movers used by West Midlands Railway, 139002 arrives at Stourbridge Junction on 25 February 2017. *Rob France*

Class 172/0

These two-car units were previously ordered and used by London Overground for the Gospel Oak-Barking line, but have now transferred to WMR and are used on the Nuneaton to Leamington Spa service, via the new station at Kenilworth. They do not have corridor connections. They are also used to strengthen other services on the WMR operation.

				DMSL	DMS
172001	WMG	ANG	TS	59311	59411
172002	WMG	ANG	TS	59312	59412
172003	WMG	ANG	TS	59313	59413
172004	WMG	ANG	TS	59314	59414
172005	WMG	ANG	TS	59315	59415
172006	WMG	ANG	TS	59316	59416
172007	WMG	ANG	TS	59317	59417
172008	WMG	ANG	TS	59318	59418

Class 172/1

These two-car units, along with the three-car Class 172/3s, were ordered by WMR. They have corridor connections. They work local trains from Leamington Spa and Stratford-upon-Avon to Stourbridge Junction and Worcester, via Birmingham Snow Hill.

				DMSL	DMS
172211	WMG	POR	TS	50211	79211
172212	WMG	POR	TS	50212	79212
172213	WMG	POR	TS	50213	79213
172214	WMG	POR	TS	50214	79214
172215	WMG	POR	TS	50215	79215
172216	WMG	POR	TS	50216	79216
172217	WMG	POR	TS	50217	79217
172218	WMG	POR	TS	50218	79218
172219	WMG	POR	TS	50219	79219
172220	WMG	POR	TS	50220	79220
172221	WMG	POR	TS	50221	79221
172222	WMG	POR	TS	50222	79222

Class 172/3

Like the 172/2s, these three-car units have corridor connections and the two fleets work side by side. Between these two fleets, WMR is able to work two-, three-, four-, five- and six-car Class 172 formations.

				DMSL	MS	DMS
172331	WMG	POR	TS	50331	56631	79331
172332	WMG	POR	TS	50332	56632	79332
172333	WMG	POR	TS	50333	56633	79333
172334	WMG	POR	TS	50334	56634	79334
172335	WMG	POR	TS	50335	56635	79335
172336	WMG	POR	TS	50336	56636	79336
172337	WMG	POR	TS	50337	56637	79337
172338	WMG	POR	TS	50338	56638	79338
172339	WMG	POR	TS	50339	56639	79339
172340	WMG	POR	TS	50340	56640	79340
172341	WMG	POR	TS	50341	56641	79341
172342	WMG	POR	TS	50342	56642	79342
172343	WMG	POR	TS	50343	56643	79343
172344	WMG	POR	TS	50344	56644	79344
172345	WMG	POR	TS	50345	56645	79345

Class 196

These new CAF Civity DMUs will work the Birmingham NS-Hereford/Shrewsbury and Snow Hill line services. The first units are now on test. All are expected to be in the EJHQ pool.

Class 196/0

These two-car units will be built after the 196/1s and should start to enter traffic in 2021.

				DMS	DMS
196001	WMG	COR	TS (Q)	121001	124001
196002	WMG	COR		121002	124002
196003	WMG	COR		121003	124003
196004	WMG	COR		121004	124004
196005	WMG	COR		121005	124005
196006	WMG	COR		121006	124006
196007	WMG	COR		121007	124007
196008	WMG	COR		121008	124008
196009	WMG	COR		121009	124009
196010	WMG	COR		121010	124010
196011	WMG	COR		121011	124011
196012	WMG	COR		121012	124012

Class 196/1

The first of these three-car CAF units are now on test.

				DMS	MS	MS	DMS
196101	WMG	COR	TS (Q)	121101	122101	123101	124101
196102	WMG	COR	(Q)	121102	122102	123102	124102
196103	WMG	COR	(Q)	121103	122103	123103	124103
196104	WMG	COR	TS (Q)	121104	122104	123104	124104
196105	WMG	COR		121105	122105	123105	124105
196106	WMG	COR		121106	122106	123106	124106
196107	WMG	COR		121107	122107	123107	124107
196108	WMG	COR		121108	122108	123108	124108
196109	WMG	COR		121109	122109	123109	124109
196110	WMG	COR		121110	122110	123110	124110
196111	WMG	COR		121111	122111	123111	124111
196112	WMG	COR		121112	122112	123112	124112
196113	WMG	COR		121113	122113	123113	124113
196114	WMG	COR		121114	122114	123114	124114

Three Class 230 VivaRail units are now in use on the Bedford-Bletchley line. No. 230003 calls at Kempston Hardwick on 19 December 2019. *Rob France*

Class 230

LNWR has three VivaRail Class 230 DMUs made using London Underground D78 Stock bodies. They run a two-car set on the Bedford-Bletchley Marston Vale line, releasing the TOC's last three Class 150s for redeployment with Northern. All are in the EJHQ pool.

				DMS	DMS
230003	LMR	VIV	BY	300003	300103
230004	LMR	VIV	BY	300004	300104
230005	LMR	VIV	BY	300005	300105

Class 319

LMR was another TOC to take some surplus Class 319s when displaced from Thameslink. It uses the sets on the Watford Junction to St Albans Abbey branch and also on additional WCML workings from Euston to Northampton. They will be replaced in the fullness of time. All are in the EJHQ pool.

				DTS	MS	TS	DTS
319005	TKB	POR	NN	77299	62895	71776	77298
319012	TKB	POR	NN	77313	62902	71783	77312
319013	LMR	POR	NN	77315	62903	71784	77314
319214	TKB	POR	NN	77317	62904	71785	77316
319215	TKB	POR	NN	77319	62905	71786	77318
319216	LMR	POR	NN	77321	62906	71787	77320
319217	TKB	POR	NN	77323	62907	71788	77322
319218	TKB	POR	NN	77325	62908	71789	77324
319219	TKB	POR	NN	77327	62909	71790	77326
319220	TKB	POR	NN	77329	62910	71791	77328
319429	LMR	POR	NN	77347	62919	71800	77346
319433	LMR	POR	NN	77355	62923	71804	77354
319441	LMR	POR	NN	77371	62931	71812	77370
319457	LMR	POR	NN	77451	62971	71876	77450
319460	LMR	POR	NN	77457	62974	71879	77456

The first of the new CAF Class 196 DMUs being built for WMR on test. The first units are now testing in the UK. *WMR*

Class 323

These WMR units are used mostly on the Cross-City line from Bromsgrove and Redditch to Lichfield via Birmingham NS and Sutton Coldfield. They also work Walsall-Wolverhampton via Aston and the Chase line from Birmingham NS to Rugeley, which was recently electrified north of Walsall. When new Class 730s arrive, many of the fleet should move to Northern. All are in the EJHQ pool.

				DMS	TS	DMS	
323201	WMG	POR	SO	64001	75301	65001	
323202	WMG	POR	SO	64002	75302	65002	
323203	WMG	POR	SO	64003	75303	65003	
323204	WMG	POR	SO	64004	75304	65004	
323205	WMG	POR	SO	64005	75305	65005	
323206	WMG	POR	SO	64006	75306	65006	
323207	WMG	POR	SO	64007	75307	65007	
323208	WMG	POR	SO	64008	75308	65008	
323209	WMG	POR	SO	64009	75309	65009	
323210	WMG	POR	SO	64010	75310	65010	
323211	WMG	POR	SO	64011	75311	65011	
323212	WMG	POR	SO	64012	75312	65012	
323213	WMG	POR	SO	64013	75313	65013	
323214	WMG	POR	SO	64014	75314	65014	
323215	WMG	POR	SO	64015	75315	65015	
323216	WMG	POR	SO	64016	75316	65016	
323217	WMG	POR	SO	64017	75317	65017	
323218	WMG	POR	SO	64018	75318	65018	
323219	WMG	POR	SO	64019	75319	65019	
323220	WMG	POR	SO	64020	75320	65020	
323221	WMG	POR	SO	64021	75321	65021	
323222	WMG	POR	SO	64022	75322	65022	
323240	WMG	POR	SO	64040	75340	65040	
323241	WMG	POR	SO	64041	75341	65041	*David Pomroy 323 Fleet Engineer 40 Years Service*
323242	WMG	POR	SO	64042	75342	65042	
323243	WMG	POR	SO	64043	75343	65043	

In the old London Midland livery, 319013 passes Old Linslade with the 0753 Bletchley-Euston on 24 May 2019.
Paul Shannon

Class 350

The mainstay of the LNWR fleet that work most trains from Euston to Birmingham NS and Birmingham NS to Liverpool plus local services in the West Midlands. They sometimes work alongside 323s on the Chase line. All are in the EJHQ pool.

Class 350/0

Units originally ordered by the Strategic Rail Authority.

				DMC	TC	PTS	DMS
350101	LNW	ANG	NN	63761	66811	66861	63711
350102	LNW	ANG	NN	63762	66812	66862	63712
350103	LNW	ANG	NN	63763	66813	66863	63713
350104	LNW	ANG	NN	63764	66814	66864	63714
350105	LMR	ANG	NN	63765	66815	66865	63715
350106	WHI	ANG	NN	63766	66816	66866	63716
350107	LMR	ANG	NN	63767	66817	66867	63717
350108	LNW	ANG	NN	63768	66818	66868	63718
350109	LMR	ANG	NN	63769	66819	66869	63719
350110	LMR	ANG	NN	63770	66820	66870	63720
350111	LMR	ANG	NN	63771	66821	66871	63721
350112	LNW	ANG	NN	63772	66822	66872	63722
350113	LMR	ANG	NN	63773	66823	66873	63723
350114	LMR	ANG	NN	63774	66824	66874	63724
350115	LNW	ANG	NN	63775	66825	66875	63725
350116	LMR	ANG	NN	63776	66826	66876	63726
350117	LMR	ANG	NN	63777	66827	66877	63727
350118	LMR	ANG	NN	63778	66828	66878	63728
350119	LMR	ANG	NN	63779	66829	66879	63729
350120	LMR	ANG	NN	63780	66830	66880	63730
350121	LMR	ANG	NN	63781	66831	66881	63731
350122	LNW	ANG	NN	63782	66832	66882	63732
350123	WHI	ANG	NN	63783	66833	66883	63733
350124	LMR	ANG	NN	63784	66834	66884	63734
350125	LNW	ANG	NN	63785	66835	66885	63735
350126	LMR	ANG	NN	63786	66836	66886	63736
350127	LMR	ANG	NN	63787	66837	66887	63737
350128	LMR	ANG	NN	63788	66838	66888	63738
350129	WHI	ANG	NN	63789	66839	66889	63739
350130	LNW	ANG	NN	63790	66840	66890	63740

Class 350/2

The units were due to return to their ROSCOs, but this may be postponed.

350231	LNW	POR	NN	61431	65231	67531	61531
350232	LNW	POR	NN	61432	65232	67532	61532
350233	LMR	POR	NN	61433	65233	67533	61533
350234	LNW	POR	NN	61434	65234	67534	61534
350235	LMR	POR	NN	61435	65235	67535	61535
350236	LMR	POR	NN	61436	65236	67536	61536
350237	LMR	POR	NN	61437	65237	67537	61537
350238	LMR	POR	NN	61438	65238	67538	61538
350239	LNW	POR	NN	61439	65239	67539	61539
350240	LNW	POR	NN	61440	65240	67540	61540
350241	LMR	POR	NN	61441	65241	67541	61541
350242	LMR	POR	NN	61442	65242	67542	61542
350243	LMR	POR	NN	61443	65243	67543	61543
350244	LNW	POR	NN	61444	65244	67544	61544
350245	LNW	POR	NN	61445	65245	67545	61545
350246	LMR	POR	NN	61446	65246	67546	61546
350247	LMR	POR	NN	61447	65247	67547	61547
350248	LMR	POR	NN	61448	65248	67548	61548
350249	LMR	POR	NN	61449	65249	67549	61549
350250	LMR	POR	NN	61450	65250	67550	61550
350251	LMR	POR	NN	61451	65251	67551	61551
350252	LNW	POR	NN	61452	65252	67552	61552
350253	LNW	POR	NN	61453	65253	67553	61553
350254	LNW	POR	NN	61454	65254	67554	61554
350255	LMR	POR	NN	61455	65255	67555	61555
350256	LMR	POR	NN	61456	65256	67556	61556
350257	LNW	POR	NN	61457	65257	67557	61557
350258	LNW	POR	NN	61458	65258	67558	61558
350259	LNW	POR	NN	61459	65259	67559	61559
350260	LMR	POR	NN	61460	65260	67560	61560
350261	LMR	POR	NN	61461	65261	67561	61561
350262	LNW	POR	NN	61462	65262	67562	61562
350263	LNW	POR	NN	61463	65263	67563	61563
350264	LMR	POR	NN	61464	65264	67564	61564
350265	LMR	POR	NN	61465	65265	67565	61565
350266	LMR	POR	NN	61466	65266	67566	61566
350267	LNW	POR	NN	61467	65267	67567	61567

Class 350/3

350368	LNW	ANG	NN	60141	60511	60651	60151
350369	LNW	ANG	NN	60142	60512	60652	60152
350370	LNW	ANG	NN	60143	60513	60653	60153
350371	LNW	ANG	NN	60144	60514	60654	60154
350372	LNW	ANG	NN	60145	60515	60655	60155
350373	LNW	ANG	NN	60146	60516	60656	60156
350374	LNW	ANG	NN	60147	60517	60657	60157
350375	LNW	ANG	NN	60148	60518	60658	60158
350376	LNW	ANG	NN	60149	60519	60659	60159
350377	LNW	ANG	NN	60150	60520	60660	60160

Class 350/4

Ex-Transpennine Express units.

350401	LNW	ANG	NN	60691	60901	60941	60671
350402	LNW	ANG	NN	60692	60902	60942	60672
350403	LNW	ANG	NN	60693	60903	60943	60673
350404	LNW	ANG	NN	60694	60904	60944	60674
350405	LNW	ANG	NN	60695	60905	60945	60675
350406	LNW	ANG	NN	60696	60906	60946	60676
350407	LNW	ANG	NN	60697	60907	60947	60677
350408	LNW	ANG	NN	60698	60908	60948	60678
350409	LNW	ANG	NN	60699	60909	60949	60679
350410	LNW	ANG	NN	60700	60910	60950	60680

Turbostar 172331 calls at Birmingham Snow Hill on 25 July 2019. *Paul Bigland*

Class 730

These Bombardier Aventra units are now being built, and the first unit has moved to Velim for testing. The three-car Class 730/0s will work on the Cross-city line and also from Wolverhampton to Birmingham NS and Walsall.

Class 730/0

Three-car units.

			DMS	PMS	DMS
730001	WMG	CO	490001	491001	492001
730002	WMG	CO	490002	491002	492002
730003	WMG	CO	490003	491003	492003
730004	WMG	CO	490004	491004	492004
730005	WMG	CO	490005	491005	492005
730006	WMG	CO	490006	491006	492006
730007	WMG	CO	490007	491007	492007
730008	WMG	CO	490008	491008	492008
730009	WMG	CO	490009	491009	492009
730010	WMG	CO	490010	491010	492010
730011	WMG	CO	490011	491011	492011
730012	WMG	CO	490012	491012	492012
730013	WMG	CO	490013	491013	492013
730014	WMG	CO	490014	491014	492014
730015	WMG	CO	490015	491015	492015
730016	WMG	CO	490016	491016	492016
730017	WMG	CO	490017	491017	492017
730018	WMG	CO	490018	491018	492018
730019	WMG	CO	490019	491019	492019
730020	WMG	CO	490020	491020	492020
730021	WMG	CO	490021	491021	492021
730022	WMG	CO	490022	491022	492022
730023	WMG	CO	490023	491023	492023
730024	WMG	CO	490024	491024	492024
730025	WMG	CO	490025	491025	492025
730026	WMG	CO	490026	491026	492026
730027	WMG	CO	490027	491027	492027
730028	WMG	CO	490028	491028	492028
730029	WMG	CO	490029	491029	492029
730030	WMG	CO	490030	491030	492030
730031	WMG	CO	490031	491031	492031
730032	WMG	CO	490032	491032	492032
730033	WMG	CO	490033	491033	492033
730034	WMG	CO	490034	491034	492034
730035	WMG	CO	490035	491035	492035
730036	WMG	CO	490036	491036	492036

Class 730/1

These five-car units will be used for the outer suburban LNWR operations from Euston to Birmingham NS.

		DMS	MS	PMS	MS	DMS
730101	CO	490101	491101	492101	493101	494101
730102	CO	490102	491102	492102	493102	494102
730103	CO	490103	491103	492103	493103	494103
730104	CO	490104	491104	492104	493104	494104
730105	CO	490105	491105	492105	493105	494105
730106	CO	490106	491106	492106	493106	494106
730107	CO	490107	491107	492107	493107	494107
730108	CO	490108	491108	492108	493108	494108
730109	CO	490109	491109	492109	493109	494109
730110	CO	490110	491110	492110	493110	494110
730111	CO	490111	491111	492111	493111	494111
730112	CO	490112	491112	492112	493112	494112
730113	CO	490113	491113	492113	493113	494113
730114	CO	490114	491114	492114	493114	494114
730115	CO	490115	491115	492115	493115	494115
730116	CO	490116	491116	492116	493116	494116
730117	CO	490117	491117	492117	493117	494117
730118	CO	490118	491118	492118	493118	494118
730119	CO	490119	491119	492119	493119	494119
730120	CO	490120	491120	492120	493120	494120
730121	CO	490121	491121	492121	493121	494121
730122	CO	490122	491122	492122	493122	494122
730123	CO	490123	491123	492123	493123	494123
730124	CO	490124	491124	492124	493124	494124
730125	CO	490125	491125	492125	493125	494125
730126	CO	490126	491126	492126	493126	494126
730127	CO	490127	491127	492127	493127	494127
730128	CO	490128	491128	492128	493128	494128
730129	CO	490129	491129	492129	493129	494129

Used on local trains across the West Midlands, 323222 calls at Smethwick Galton Bridge on 21 May 2019.
Antony Christie

Class 730/2

These five-car units will be used for the longer-distance LNWR operations from Euston to Crewe.

		DMS	MS	PMS	MS	DMS
730201	CO	490201	491201	492201	493201	494201
730202	CO	490202	491202	492202	493202	494202
730203	CO	490203	491203	492203	493203	494203
730204	CO	490204	491204	492204	493204	494204
730205	CO	490205	491205	492205	493205	494205
730206	CO	490206	491206	492206	493206	494206
730207	CO	490207	491207	492207	493207	494207
730208	CO	490208	491208	492208	493208	494208
730209	CO	490209	491209	492209	493209	494209
730210	CO	490210	491210	492210	493210	494210
730211	CO	490211	491211	492211	493211	494211
730212	CO	490212	491212	492212	493212	494212
730213	CO	490213	491213	492213	493213	494213
730214	CO	490214	491214	492214	493214	494214
730215	CO	490215	491215	492215	493215	494215
730216	CO	490216	491216	492216	493216	494216

In the new dark green LNWR livery, 350262 passes Old Linslade on 20 May 2020. *Paul Robertson*

Open Access Operators Overview

When the railways were privatised in the mid-1990s, the existing passenger operations – which had already been split into three sectors – InterCity, Regional Railways and Network SouthEast, were split into 25 – mostly regional – franchises that were then let for pre-defined periods.

One of the cornerstones of privatisation, however, was to allow entrepreneurs and free enterprise to run their own operations. This means – theoretically – anyone can have access to the railway to operate their own trains, providing they meet certain criteria.

This has led to a number of what are called Open Access operators – privately funded companies who operate their own trains, take their own risk and enjoy their own profits. It's not a simple as that, of course, but that is the theory.

For a start, OA operators are not allowed to stop at certain station if they will seriously impinge on the revenue of the established franchised TOCs but likewise, they can exploit what is known as ORCATs raiding, where they get a percentage of all fares on certain types of ticket from certain stations on certain routes regardless of whether passengers actually use their trains.

Open Access successes

The first OA operator was Heathrow Express, which started operating on the Paddington to Heathrow Airport line in 1998.

In September 2000, Hull Trains, set up by Renaissance Railways, part funded by GB Railways, started its Hull-King's Cross operation running hired in Anglia Railways Class 170 Turbostars on three trains a day. Now owned by First Group, Hull Trains has grown and, after periods using new-build Class 222/1s and then Class 180 Adelante units, now uses brand-new, five-car Class 802/3 Hitachi AT300 bi-mode units, of the same design as the Azuma sets used by LNER.

In December 2007 Grand Central started its Sunderland to King's Cross operation and expanded to start running from Bradford in 2010. It started operations using HSTs, then added Class 180 DMUs to its fleet for the Bradford trains. It has since dispensed with its HSTs, which moved to East Midlands Trains, and now has a fleet of ten Class 180s.

Open Access failures

At the same time GC was granted operating rights, Wrexham, Shropshire & Marylebone Railway started operations in April 2008 from Wrexham to Marylebone via Shrewsbury. It saw a gap in the market for Shrewsbury to London through trains, a service Virgin had ended. However, Virgin complained and the WSMR operation was not allowed to stop at Birmingham New Street or Coventry, so instead called at Tame Bridge Parkway and Birmingham International.

WSMR, which was another Renaissance Railways venture, was sold to Deutsche Bahn in 2009 and used DB Schenker Class 67s and Mk 3 stock, with DVTs. When the WSMR service ended in January 2011 having failed to meet its business case expectations, the locos and stock transferred to Chiltern Railways, which was also own by DB Regio.

New operations

Several Open Access operations have been mooted in the last 25 years, some truly fanciful, and two new operations were due to start soon but sadly one has been shelved due to the Covid pandemic.

Now not happening is Grand Central starting its Blackpool to Euston service. This would have seen DB Cargo Class 90s and ex-LNER Mk 4 coaches on five trains in each direction (four on Sundays). The first three locos, 90020/026/029, were already repainted into GC black, but the other two due to follow will now not happen.

First Group is also launching its own ECML service from Edinburgh to King's Cross, with five trains a day in each direction using five brand-new, five-car Class 803 Hitachi AT300 EMUs. The stopping pattern will be Stevenage, Newcastle and Morpeth, and 'an average' £25 fare is being touted. The trains are standard class only.

East Coast Trains

Contact details

Website: www.firstgroupplc.com

Key personnel

Managing Director: tba
Fleet Director: tba

Overview

East Coast Trains is an Open Access operation run by First Group on the Edinburgh-King's Cross ECML. Its five trains a day will call at Morpeth, Newcastle and Stevenage. ECT says the 'average' fare between Edinburgh and King's Cross will be just £25.

The ECT operation will use five brand-new, five-car Hitachi AT300 Class 803 EMUs. The units are electric only, and do not have diesel engines, but batteries will keep the train supply live in the event of a failure. They only have standard-class seating.

The units are currently being assembled at Newton Aycliffe using bodyshells shipped from Japan.

The operation is due to start in October 2021 and will compete with LNER across the whole route, plus also Transpennine Express and CrossCountry trains on the section north of Newcastle.

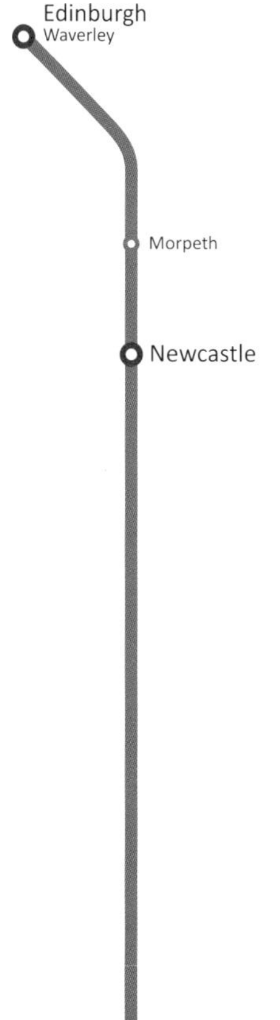

Class 803

			PDTS	MS	MS	MC	PDTF
803001	FEC	BEA	tba	tba	tba	tba	tba
803002	FEC	BEA	tba	tba	tba	tba	tba
803003	FEC	BEA	tba	tba	tba	tba	tba
803004	FEC	BEA	tba	tba	tba	tba	tba
803005	FEC	BEA	tba	tba	tba	tba	tba

Grand Central

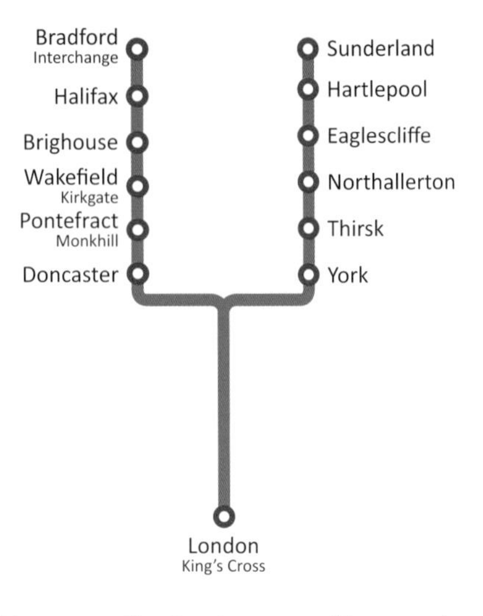

Contact details

Website: www.grandcentralrail.com
Twitter: @GC_Rail

Key personnel

Managing Director: Richard McClean
Fleet Director: Dave Hatfield

Overview

Grand Central's first route was launched in December 2007 from King's Cross to Sunderland, calling at York, Thirsk, Northallerton, Eaglescliffe and Hartlepool.

In May 2010, a new service from Bradford Interchange to King's Cross was launched, serving Halifax, Brighouse, Wakefield, Pontefract and Doncaster, with stops at Mirfield added in 2011 and Low Moor in 2017.

Despite running 'under the wires' for the majority of its routes, diesel trains are used because the section from Northallerton to Sunderland and from Bradford to Hare Park Junction are not electrified.

After starting its operations with three HSTs, expansion saw GC acquire ex-FGW Class 180s to run new services. It has since relinquished its HSTs to concentrate on a wholly Class 180 fleet. All the trains received a full interior and exterior refurbishment in 2018/19.

A new venture by GC had been the plan to start running between Blackpool and London Euston on the WCML. Initially planned to start operations in spring 2020, Grand Central's planned expansion on to the WCML was initially put on hold due to the Covid-19 pandemic and was officially scrapped in mid-September. The new service would have been five trains a day each way (four on Sundays) between Euston and Blackpool North.

The fleet was Class 90s hired from sister company DB Cargo hauling rakes of ex-LNER Mk 4 coaches with Driving Van Trailers.

Class 180

Ten five-car Class 180s DMUs, built by Alstom in 2000-01, form the GC fleet for its ECML operations. All are based at Heaton. All are in the ECGC pool.

				DMSL	MFL	MSL	MSLRB	DMSL	
180101	GCR	ANG	HT	50901	54901	55901	56901	59901	
180102	GCR	ANG	HT	50902	54902	55902	56902	59902	
180103	GCR	ANG	HT	50903	54903	55903	56903	59903	
180104	GCR	ANG	HT	50904	54904	55904	56904	59904	
180105	GCR	ANG	HT	50905	54905	55905	56905	59905	
180106	GCR	ANG	HT	50906	54906	55906	56906	59906	*The Yorkshire Artist Ashley Jackson*
180107	GCR	ANG	HT	50907	54907	55907	56907	59907	*Hart of the North*
180108	GCR	ANG	HT	50908	54908	55908	56908	59908	*William Shakespeare*
180112	GCR	ANG	HT	50912	54912	55912	56912	59912	*James Herriot Celebrating 100 years 1916-2016*
180114	GCR	ANG	HT	50914	54914	55914	56914	59914	*Kirkgate Calling*

On 7 March 2020, 180104 waits to head north with the 1627 King's Cross-Bradford Interchange. *Pip Dunn*

Class 90s and ex-LNER Mk 4 coaches were to be introduced on the Blackpool-Euston line with Grand Central but this has now been shelved. No. 90029 hauls a Widnes-Wembley test run with 90026 on the rear at Heamies Farm on 26 June 2020. *Brad Joyce*

Heathrow Express

Contact details

Website: www.heathrowexpress.com
Twitter: @HeathrowExpress

Key personnel

Managing Director: Richard Robinson
Fleet Director: Stephen Head

Southall
Hanwell
West Ealing
Ealing Broadway
Hayes & Harlington
London Paddington
London Heathrow Terminals 1, 2 & 3
Terminal 5
Terminal 4

Overview

The first Open Access operator, launched in 1998, HEx operates a regular non-stop Paddington to Heathrow Airport shuttle. It later introduced the Heathrow Connect that stopped at some intermediate station on the GWML from Airport Junction to Paddington.

It started with a fleet of 14 Class 334 four-car units, five of which were increased to five cars. It then acquired five four-car Class 360/2 Siemens Desiros units for its Connect service.

A dozen GWR Class 387/1s have now been hired and modified for use on HEx, which operationally will now be managed by GWR. The trains, 387130-141, are being reliveried in HEx colours and have been modified internally to include first-class accommodation, higher-speed Wi-Fi and have additional luggage racks as well as on-board entertainment.

Class 332

New CAF/Siemens four-car sets, five additional vehicles were delivered in 2002 and added to 332005-009. All are in the HMHQ pool.

				DMS	TS	PTS	TS	DMF
332001	ADV	HEX	OH	78400	72412	63400		78401
332002	ADV	HEX	OH	78402	72409	63406		78403
332003	ADV	HEX	OH	78404	72407	63402		78405
332004	ADV	HEX	OH	78406	72405	63403		78407
332005	ADV	HEX	OH	78408	72411	63404	72417	78409
332006	ADV	HEX	OH	78410	72410	63405	72415	78411
332007	ADV	HEX	OH	78412	72401	63401	72414	78413
332008	ADV	HEX	OH	78414	72413	63407	72418	78415
332009	ADV	HEX	OH	78416	72400	63408	72416	78417
332010	ADV	HEX	OH	78418	72402	63409		78419
332011	ADV	HEX	OH	78420	72402	63410		78421
332012	ADV	HEX	OH	78422	72404	63411		78423
332013	ADV	HEX	OH	78424	72408	63412		78425
332014	ADV	HEX	OH	78426	72406	63413		78427

Class 360/2

The first four of these Siemens Desiro units were delivered as four-cars. Additional fifth cars, plus a new five-car set, were delivered in 2007 and 2005 respectively. They are currently in warm store. All are in the EXHW pool.

				DMS	PTS	TS	TS	DMS
360201	HEC	CRO	OH	78431	63421	72431	72421	78441
360202	HEC	CRO	OH	78432	63422	72432	72422	78442
360203	HEC	CRO	OH	78433	63423	72433	72423	78443
360204	HEC	CRO	OH	78434	63424	72434	72424	78444
360205	HEC	CRO	OH	78435	63425	72435	72425	78445

No. 332013 stands at Paddington on 7 September 2019. *Antony Christie*

One of the five five-car Class 360 Siemens Desiros used on the Heathrow Connect service, 360204 calls at Acton Main Line on 1 May 2018. *Paul Shannon*

Hull Trains

Contact details

Website: www.hulltrains.co.uk
Twitter: @Hull_Trains

Key personnel

Managing Director: Louise Cheeseman
Production Director: Louise Mendham

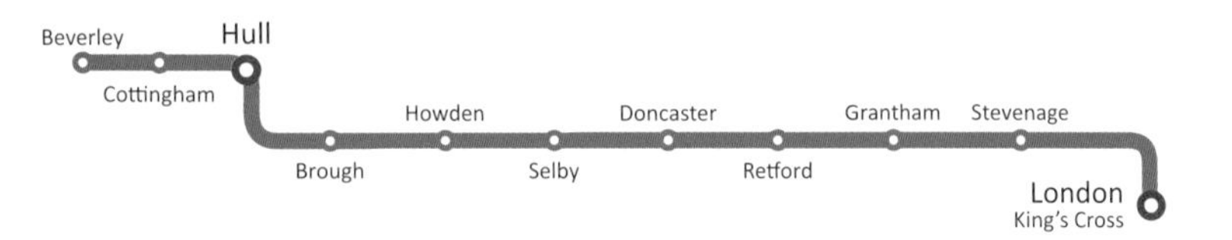

Overview

Hull Trains was the second Open Access operator and has been running trains between Hull and King's Cross since September 2000. It initially used hired Anglia Railways Class 170 Turbostars before acquiring its own four three-car Class 170/3s in 2004. These were replaced by four four-car Class 222/1s in 2005.

These were moved to East Midlands Trains in 2008/09 and replaced by four five-car Class 180 Adelante units. These have recently been replaced by five brand-new, five-car Class 802/3 bi-mode Hitachi AT300 multiple units.

HT has used a hired FGW HST as cover in previous years, and also a Class 86 and Mk 3 coaches for Doncaster to King's Cross workings when short of units. Some trains start at Beverley.

Class 802

All are in the PFHQ pool.

				PDTS	MS	MS	MC	PDTF
802301	HUL	ANG	DN	831301	832301	833301	834301	835301
802302	HUL	ANG	DN	831302	832302	833302	834302	835302
802303	HUL	ANG	DN	831303	832303	833303	834303	835303
802304	HUL	ANG	DN	831304	832304	833304	834304	835304
802305	HUL	ANG	DN	831305	832305	833305	834305	835305

Hull Trains has introduced new bi-mode Hitachi trains on its operations; 802301 works the 1233 Hull-King's Cross past Cromwell on 6 February 2020. *Bill Atkinson*

Channel Tunnel Operations Overview

The Channel Tunnel opened in 1994 linking Cheriton in the UK with Coquelles in France and is the only fixed connection between the UK and mainland Europe. It is over 31 miles long and features three tunnels, two for trains and a service tunnel in between.

It is owned and managed by Getlink – which retains the Eurotunnel trading name – and this company also operates the lorry-carrying and car-carrying shuttle trains. International passenger trains using the tunnel are operated by Eurostar.

Other operators, such as Deutsche Bahn, have expressed interest in operating through the Channel Tunnel and ran a promotional train to St Pancras in 2010, but as yet no operations are foreseen.

St Pancras International
Ebbsfleet
Ashford International
Calais
Lille
Paris
Paris Marne-la-Vallé
Avignon
Bourg-St-Maurice
Amsterdam
Rotterdam
Brussels

Siemens e320 Velaro 374031 passes Stratford International on 24 April 2019. *Mark Pike*

Eurostar

Contact details

Website: www.eurostar.com
Twitter: @EurostarUK

Key personnel

Chief Executive Officer: Mike Cooper

Overview

Eurostar is – currently – the only operator of passenger trains through the Channel Tunnel and operates out of St Pancras International in London via the HS1 High Speed line to the Tunnel and then on into France, Belgium and now the Netherlands. Trains run to Paris Gard du Nord, Bruxelles Midi and now Amsterdam Centraal.

The fleet is made up of a mix of older refurbished Class 373 units that date from the mid-1990s and new Class 374 Siemens Velaro e320 units delivered in 2012-17.

The 373s were owned by Eurostar, UK or SNCF but used indiscriminately. However, some 373.3s were used for French domestic services but have since been withdrawn and scrapped. One Class 373 is in use with SNCF majority-owned operator Thalys and used for that company's 'Izy' low-cost service between Paris and Brussels, while other sets have been sent for scrap at EMR in Kingsbury.

Each train runs with a driving power car at the head of a rake of eight vehicles all coupled via articulated bogies, and they run in pairs, essentially permanently coupled, to create a 20-coach train, a power car and then five standard-class coaches, a buffet and three first-class coaches in one half of the train, and the same in reverse in the second half so each train has two buffets, six first- and ten standard-class coaches between the two power cars. There is a spare power car, 3999, which can be used to replace any long-term defective sister vehicle.

It is expected that Eurostar and Thalys will merge in 2021, forming a new company provisionally named 'Greenspeed', both companies are majority owned by French State Railways SNCF with part shares owned by Belgium's SNCB; Eurostar also has private shareholders, whilst Dutch operator NS is a part shareholder in Thalys.

St Pancras International station on 28 January 2017 with two Class 374s and an older Class 373 set at the bufferstops. *Jack Boskett*

Class 08

Sole shunter based at Temple Mills. It is in the GPSS pool.

08948	EUK	EUK	TI

Class 373

These units only carry the last four digits of their numbers on the power car cabside; they carry the full European Vehicle Number on each vehicle. They are based at Temple Mills depot in East London. These sets have been refurbished and any original unrefurbished units have been disposed of.

3007	ESB	EUK	TI	3212	ESB	EUK	TI	3221	ESB	EUK	TI
3008	ESB	EUK	TI	3213	LZY	EUK	TI	3222	ESB	EUK	TI
3015	ESB	EUK	TI	3214	ESO	EUK	TI	3223	ESO	EUK	TI
3016	ESB	EUK	TI	3215	ESO	EUK	TI	3224	LZY	EUK	TI
3205	ESB	EUK	TI	3216	ESO	EUK	TI	3229	ESB	EUK	TI
3206	ESB	EUK	TI	3217	ESO	EUK	TI	3230	ESB	EUK	TI
3209	ESB	EUK	TI	3218	ESO	EUK	TI	9999	ESB	EUK	TI
3210	ESB	EUK	TI	3219	ESB	EUK	TI				
3211	ESB	EUK	TI	3220	ESB	EUK	TI				

Class 374

New Siemens Velaro e320 trains delivered 2012-17 to replace unrefurbished Class 373s and provide new capacity.

4001	ESB	EUK	TI	4013	ESB	EUK	TI	4025	ESB	EUK	TI
4002	ESB	EUK	TI	4014	ESB	EUK	TI	4026	ESB	EUK	TI
4003	ESB	EUK	TI	4015	ESB	EUK	TI	4027	ESB	EUK	TI
4004	ESB	EUK	TI	4016	ESB	EUK	TI	4028	ESB	EUK	TI
4005	ESB	EUK	TI	4017	ESB	EUK	TI	4029	ESB	EUK	TI
4006	ESB	EUK	TI	4018	ESB	EUK	TI	4030	ESB	EUK	TI
4007	ESB	EUK	TI	4019	ESB	EUK	TI	4031	ESB	EUK	TI
4008	ESB	EUK	TI	4020	ESB	EUK	TI	4032	ESB	EUK	TI
4009	ESB	EUK	TI	4021	ESB	EUK	TI	4033	ESB	EUK	TI
4010	ESB	EUK	TI	4022	ESB	EUK	TI	4034	ESB	EUK	TI
4011	ESB	EUK	TI	4023	ESB	EUK	TI				
4012	ESB	EUK	TI	4024	ESB	EUK	TI				

Barrier Vehicles

96380	86386, 6380	EUK	Mk 1	Eurostar barrier
96381	86187, 6381	EUK	Mk 1	Eurostar barrier
96383	86664, 6383	EUK	Mk 1	Eurostar barrier
96384	86955, 6384	EUK	Mk 1	Eurostar barrier

Eurotunnel

Contact details

Website: www.eurotunnel.com
Twitter: @LeShuttle

Key personnel

CEO: Jacques Gounon

Overview

The Channel Tunnel is marketed as Eurotunnel but is managed and operated by Getlink (Groupe Eurotunnel – link). It operates tourist shuttles – for cars, caravans, and motorhomes – and freight shuttles for trucks and large vans. The latter are naturally heavier so use dedicated freight locos.

Each freight shuttle uses a loco, a club car, two 16-wagon rakes – to give 32 wagons, a club car and a loco – and are 745m long. The first vehicle will drive on from a platform via a ramp and then drive the length of the empty train so it will be the first off at the other end. Subsequent vehicles follow it and the last one off will have to drive the length of the train to disembark, and will be the last truck off the train. The trains run at a maximum of 140kmh (87mph), whereas Eurostar trains can run at 160kmh (100mph) in the Tunnel.

Shuttle locos

The shuttle locos were built by Brush from 1993-2003.

The initial fleet was 38 7,500hp locos built in 1992-94, for both freight shuttles (trucks) and tourist shuttles (cars). Loco 9030 was written off in the 1996 Tunnel fire and 9040 was built as a replacement for it in 1998.

Nos 9101-113 were built 1998-2001 as dedicated freight locos at 7,500hp supplemented by 9701-07 in 2001/02 at 9,400hp. The 91xx locos were then uprated to 9,400hp and renumbered as 97xx locos. Between 2004 and 2012, 24 of the original locos from the 90xx series were uprated to 9,400hp power output and renumbered as 98xx, the last two digits remaining the same.

90xx locos

Original Bo-Bo-Bo locos built by Brush 1992-94, many have now been upgraded to higher power for use of freight shuttles. The remaining original locos tend to work tourist shuttles only.

No.	Livery	Owner	Depot	
9005	EUT	EUT	CO	*Jessye Norman*
9007	EUT	EUT	CO	*Dame Joan Sutherland*
9011	EUT	EUT	CO	*José Van Dam*
9013	EUT	EUT	CO	*Maria Callas*
9015	EUT	EUT	CO	*Lötschberg 1913*
9018	EUT	EUT	CO	*Wilhelmenia Fernandez*
9022	EUT	EUT	CO	*Dame Janet Baker*
9024	EUT	EUT	CO	*Gotthard 1882*
9026	EUT	EUT	CO	*Furkatunnel 1982*
9029	EUT	EUT	CO	*Thomas Allen*
9033	EUT	EUT	CO	*Monserrat Caballe*
9036	EUT	EUT	CO	*Alain Foundary*
9037	EUT	EUT	CO	

97xx locos

Dedicated freight locos, these 9,400hp locos – of which 9711-13 were originally 7,500hp – work alongside 98xx locos.

No.	Old No.	Livery	Owner	Depot
9701		EUT	EUT	CO
9702		EUT	EUT	CO
9703		EUT	EUT	CO
9704		EUT	EUT	CO
9705		EUT	EUT	CO
9706		EUT	EUT	CO
9707		EUT	EUT	CO
9708		EUT	EUT	CO
9709		EUT	EUT	CO
9710		EUT	EUT	CO
9711	9101	EUT	EUT	CO
9712	9102	EUT	EUT	CO
9713	9103	EUT	EUT	CO
9714	9104	EUT	EUT	CO
9715	9105	EUT	EUT	CO
9716	9106	EUT	EUT	CO
9717	9107	EUT	EUT	CO
9718	9108	EUT	EUT	CO
9719	9109	EUT	EUT	CO
9720	9110	EUT	EUT	CO
9721	9111	EUT	EUT	CO
9722	9112	EUT	EUT	CO
9723	9113	EUT	EUT	CO

98xx locos

These were originally 90xx locos but rebuilt with higher power for working freight shuttles.

No.	Old No.	Livery	Owner	Depot	
9801	9001	EUT	EUT	CO	*Lesley Garrett*
9802	9002	EUT	EUT	CO	*Stuart Burrows*
9803	9003	EUT	EUT	CO	*Benjamin Luxon*
9804	9004	EUT	EUT	CO	
9806	9006	EUT	EUT	CO	*Regine Crespin*
9808	9008	EUT	EUT	CO	*Elisabeth Soderstrom*
9809	9009	EUT	EUT	CO	
9810	9010	EUT	EUT	CO	
9812	9012	EUT	EUT	CO	
9814	9014	EUT	EUT	CO	*Lucia Popp*
9816	9016	EUT	EUT	CO	
9819	9019	EUT	EUT	CO	*Maria Ewing*
9820	9020	EUT	EUT	CO	*Nicolai Ghiarov*
9821	9021	EUT	EUT	CO	
9823	9023	EUT	EUT	CO	*Dame Elisabeth Legge-Schwarzkoff*
9825	9025	EUT	EUT	CO	
9827	9027	EUT	EUT	CO	*Barbara Hendricks*
9828	9028	EUT	EUT	CO	
9831	9031	EUT	EUT	CO	
9832	9032	EUT	EUT	CO	*Renata Tebaldi*
9834	9034	EUT	EUT	CO	*Mirella Freni*
9835	9035	EUT	EUT	CO	*Nicolai Gedda*
9838	9038	EUT	EUT	CO	*Hildegard Behrens*
9840	9040	EUT	EUT	CO	

Recovery and maintenance locos

Getlink has three bespoke fleets of locos used for recovering failed trains or working maintenance trains. The MaK (Maschinenbau Kiel) Bo-Bo locos can run on the HS1 route through to St Pancras, although only 0001-0005 have TVM signalling, meaning any of the 0006-0010 fleet can only be used if in multiple with one of the earlier locos.

Because of their ability to appear on HS1, these ten locos have TOPS numbers in the Class 21/9 series.

The MaK Bo-Bos, built in 1991-92, are 1,275hp locos used to operate any maintenance trains plus act as Thunderbirds to recover any stricken trains.

ET No.	TOPS No.	Livery	Owner	Depot
0001	21901	EUY	EUT	CT
0002	21902	EUY	EUT	CT
0003	21903	EUY	EUT	CT
0004	21904	EUY	EUT	CT
0005	21905	EUY	EUT	CT

MaK Bo-Bo locos built in 1990-91 for Dutch operator NS but rebuilt for Channel Tunnel use in 2011 or 2016, these 1,580hp locos are also used to operate any maintenance trains plus act as Thunderbirds to recover any stricken trains. They also act as shunters if required

ET No.	Old NS No.	TOPS No.	Livery	Owner	Depot
0006	6456	21906	EUY	EUT	CT
0007	6457	21907	EUY	EUT	CT
0008	6450	21908	EUY	EUT	CT
0009	6451	21909	EUY	EUT	CT
0010	6447	21910	EUY	EUT	CT

These small 230hp 0-4-0 locos were built by Hunslet Engine Company in Leeds in 1990 at 900mm gauge but in 1993/94 were rebuilt by Schöma in Germany to standard gauge. They are used as shunters and maintenance inspection locos.

ET No.	Livery	Owner	Depot	Name
0031	EUY	EUT	CT	*Frances*
0032	EUY	EUT	CT	*Elisabeth*
0033	EUY	EUT	CT	*Silke*
0034	EUY	EUT	CT	*Amanda*
0035	EUY	EUT	CT	*Mary*
0036	EUY	EUT	CT	*Laurence*
0037	EUY	EUT	CT	*Lydie*
0038	EUY	EUT	CT	*Jenny*
0039	EUY	EUT	CT	*Pacita*
0040	EUY	EUT	CT	*Jill*
0041	EUY	EUT	CT	*Kim*
0042	EUY	EUT	CT	*Nicole*

Channel Tunnel freight operators

Freight trains throughout the Channel Tunnel are operated by either DB Cargo or GB Railfreight. Some Class 92s owned by both companies are fitted with TVM430 signalling to allow them to also operate on HS1 and through the Channel Tunnel.

In late 2020, the DBC fleet in the WFBC pool passed for HS1 use were 92011/015/019/036/041/042 (with withdrawn 92009/016/031 also TVM430 compatible), while GBRf had 92010/018/028/038/043 in its GBST pool with 92023/032/044 also TVM430 compatible). These locos are listed in their relevant owner's sections.

Shuttle loco 9810 was originally an 90xx loco but rebuilt with higher power for working freight shuttles.
Keith Fender

Locomotive Services Limited

Contact details

Website: www.lsltoc.co.uk
Twitter: @CharterRail

Key personnel

Managing Director: Tony Bush

Overview

A relatively new train operating company, Locomotive Services Limited is owned by businessman Jeremy Hosking.

It has a nationwide train operating licence and is one of four TOCs that is capable of operating steam alongside West Coast Railways, DB Cargo and Vintage Trains. It promotes its own charters through its Saphos Trains and Rail Charter Services banners.

LSL owns several steam, diesel and electric locos as well as a Class 121 single-car DMU, a fleet of coaches and has recently acquired an HST set with the power cars, which is to be repainted into the Blue Pullman livery of the 1960s.

Included in its steam fleet – either owned or under its custody – are 46100 *Royal Scot*, 70000 *Britannia*, 6024 *King Edward I*, 60532 *Blue Peter*, 34046 *Braunton*, 35027 *Port Line* and 35022 *Holland America Line*, although not all are currently in traffic.

Class 08

08631 is at Wolsingham for contract repairs.

08483		GRW	LSL	CD	*Bungle*
08631	MBDL	BRW	LSL	WO	
08737		GWS	LSL	SO	
08780	LSLO	GRW	LSL	CD	*Zippy*

Class 20

Ex-HNRC locos acquired in 2020.

20096	LSLO	GYP	LSL	CD	
20107	LSLO	GYP	LSL	CD	*Jocelyn Feilding 1940-2020*

Class 37

No. 37688 is on long-term hire, with 37190 on long-term loan to the Severn Valley Railway.

37190	37314	MBDL	BRB	LSL	KV
37521	37117	LSLO	GYP	LSL	CD
37667	37151	LSLO	GYP	LSL	CD
37688	37205	LSLO	TLA	D05	CD

Class 40

Main-line registered loco, it is owned by Shaun Wright and on a long-term hire deal with LSL. The company has also hired preserved 40145 for six months from August 2020.

40013	LSLO	GYP	SW	CD	*Andania*

Nos 37667 and 37521, both in BR green and bearing original D numbers, pass East Garforth with the 0801 Crewe-Tyne Yard on 20 March 2020. *Anthony Hicks*

Class 40 D213 *Andania* is not owned by LSL but on long-term hire to the company and on 2 May 2016 it was on display at Bristol St Philip's Marsh Open Day. *Glen Batten*

Above: No. 47593 *Galloway Princess* arrives at Settle with the 1758 Appleby-Skipton on 20 July 2020. *Anthony Hicks*

Left: LSL has bought two Class 20s from HNRC, and repainted both into British Railways green. No. 20107 was at Appleby on 13 August 2020 with the 1438 to Skipton. *Pip Dunn*

Class 43

These ex-EMR HST Power Cars, along with a rake of Mk 3 trailers, will be repainted into Blue Pullman livery.

43046	BPU	LSL	CD
43055	BPU	LSL	CD
43058	EMB	LSL	CD
43059	EMB	LSL	CD
43083	EMB	LSL	CD

Class 45

This loco is undergoing contract repairs at Barrow Hill.

45118	LSLS	BRB	LSL	BH (U)	*Royal Artilleryman*

Class 47

The mainstay of the LSL diesel fleet, 47712/828 are on long-term hire while 47811/816 are spares donors only.

47501		LSLO	GYP	LSL	CD	*Craftsman*
47593	47272, 47673, 47790	LSLO	BLL	LSL	CD	*Galloway Princess*
47712	47505	LSLO	SCO	D05	CD	*Lady Diana Spencer*
47805	47257, 47650	LSLO	GYP	LSL	CD	*Roger Hosking MA 1925-2013*
47810	47247, 47655	LSLO	GYP	LSL	CD	*Crewe Diesel Depot*
47811	47128, 47656	DHLT	FPG	LSL	CD (U)	
47816	47066, 47661	DHLT	FPG	LSL	CD (U)	
47828	47266, 47629	AWCA	ICS	DO5	CD	
47853	47141, 47614	LSLO	BRB	LSL	CD	

Class 55

Main-line registered Deltic, the loco is undergoing repairs to return it to use.

55022		LSLS	BRB	LSL	CD (U)	*Royal Scots Grey*

Class 73

Electro diesel bought from preservation.

73001	73901	MBED	BRB	LSL	CD

Class 86

Ex-ACLG main-line registered locomotive recently repainted into InterCity Swallow livery.

86101	86201	LSLO	ICS	LSL	CD	*Sir William A Stanier FRS*

Class 87

Like 86101, also bought from the ACLG for main-line use and repainted into InterCity colours.

87002	LSLO	ICS	LSL	CD	*Royal Sovereign*

Class 90

Two ex-Greater Anglia locos bought from Porterbrook and both repainted into InterCity colours.

90001	LSLO	ICS	LSL	CD	*Royal Scot*
90002	LSLO	ICS	LSL	CD	*Wolf of Badenoch*

Class 121

Single-car DMU.

55034	121034	GYP	LSL	CD

Coaches

Not all these vehicles are currently in traffic.

No.	Old No.	Livery	Type	Name
1203	3291	CAC	Mk 2 RFO	
1211	3305	PUL	Mk 2 RFO	*Car No. 1211*
1658		BRB	Mk 1 RBR	
1659		CAC	Mk 1 RBR	
1679		Green/Cream	Mk 1 RBR	
1696		SR Green	Mk 1 RBR	
1863		Chocolate/Cream	Mk 1 RMB	
1883	80021	CAC	Mk 1 Bar	
1954		Maroon	Mk 1 RUK	
3045		Chocolate/Cream	Mk 1 FO	
3051		Chocolate/Cream	Mk 1 FO	
3060		CAC	Mk 1 FO	
3091		Chocolate/Cream	Mk 1 FO	
3100		CAC	Mk 1 FO	
3107		CAC	Mk 1 FO	
3112		CAC	Mk 1 FO	
3122		CAC	Mk 1 FO	
3125		CAC	Mk 1 FO	
3140		CAC	Mk 1 FO	
3148		CAC	Mk 1 FO	
3188		PUL	Mk 2 FO	*Cadir Idris*
3223		Blue/Cream	Mk 2 FO	*Diamond*
3229		PUL	Mk 2 FO	*Snowdon*
3231		PUL	Mk 2 FO	*Ben Cruachan*
3240		Blue/Cream	Mk 2 FO	*Sapphire*
3277		Anglia	Mk 2 FO	
3295		Anglia	Mk 2 FO	
3312		PUL	Mk 2 FO	*Helvellyn*
3330		CAC	Mk 2 FO	
3344		PUL	Mk 2 FO	*Scafell*
3348		PUL	Mk 2 FO	*Ingleborough*
3384		PUL	Mk 2 FO	*Pen-Y-Ghent*
3426		PUL	Mk 2 FO	*Ben Nevis*
3438		PUL	Mk 2 FO	*Ben Lomond*
5054		Chocolate/Cream	Mk 1 TSO	
5366		CAC	Mk 2 TSO	
5797		InterCity	Mk 2 TSO	
5912		CAC	Mk 2 TSO	
5991		CAC	Mk 2 TSO	
6311	92911	CAC	Mk 1 BG Generator Car	
6412	3168	Maroon	Mk 2 SO	
6705		Caledonian	Mk 2 RLO	
6706		Caledonian	Mk 2 RLO	
6708		PUL	Mk 2 RLO	*Mount Helicon*
9479		PUL	Mk 2 BSO	*Car No. 9479*

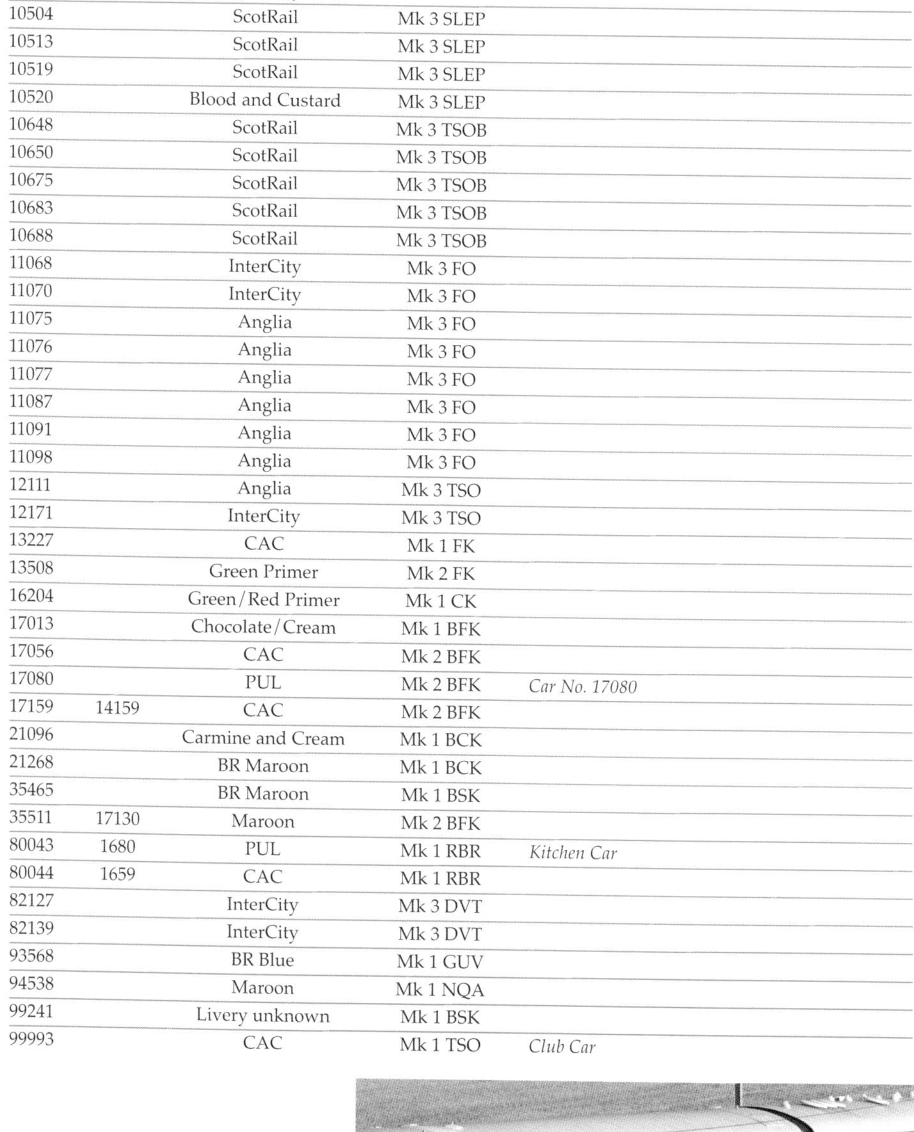

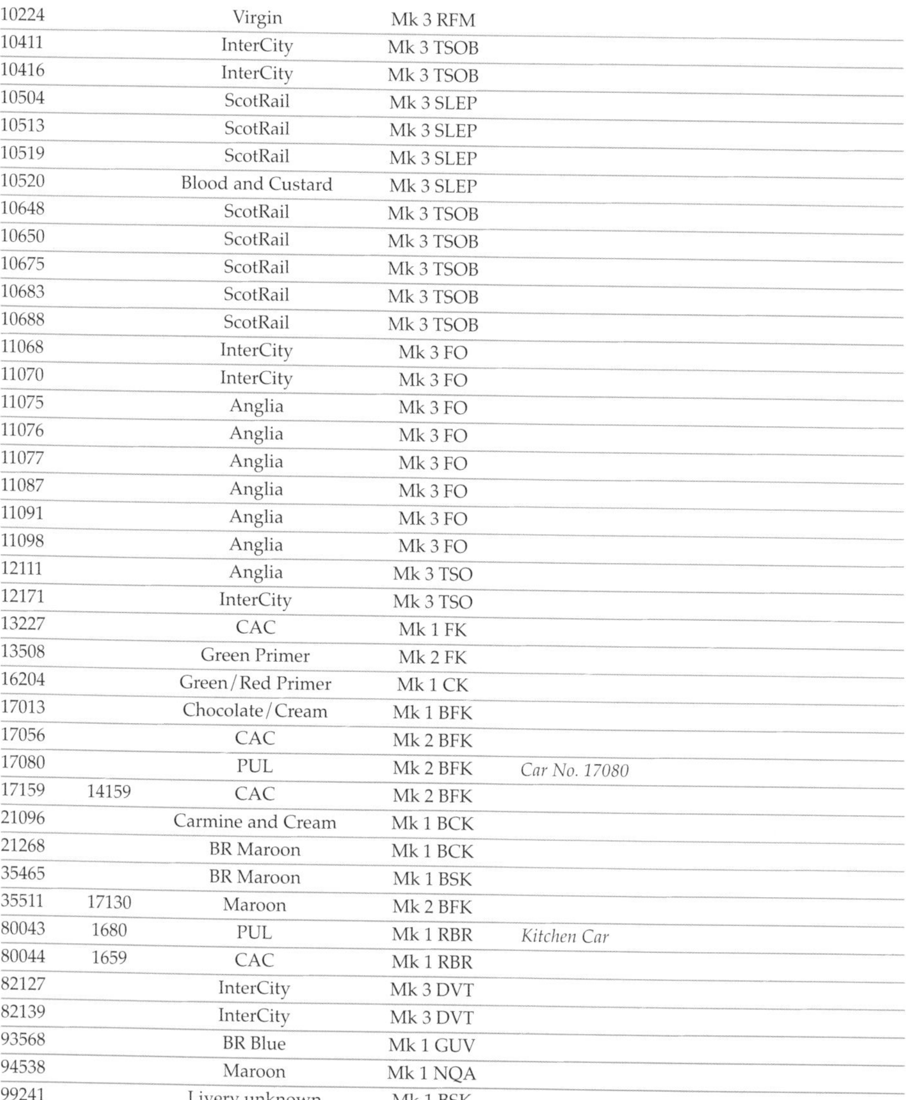

10224		Virgin	Mk 3 RFM	
10411		InterCity	Mk 3 TSOB	
10416		InterCity	Mk 3 TSOB	
10504		ScotRail	Mk 3 SLEP	
10513		ScotRail	Mk 3 SLEP	
10519		ScotRail	Mk 3 SLEP	
10520		Blood and Custard	Mk 3 SLEP	
10648		ScotRail	Mk 3 TSOB	
10650		ScotRail	Mk 3 TSOB	
10675		ScotRail	Mk 3 TSOB	
10683		ScotRail	Mk 3 TSOB	
10688		ScotRail	Mk 3 TSOB	
11068		InterCity	Mk 3 FO	
11070		InterCity	Mk 3 FO	
11075		Anglia	Mk 3 FO	
11076		Anglia	Mk 3 FO	
11077		Anglia	Mk 3 FO	
11087		Anglia	Mk 3 FO	
11091		Anglia	Mk 3 FO	
11098		Anglia	Mk 3 FO	
12111		Anglia	Mk 3 TSO	
12171		InterCity	Mk 3 TSO	
13227		CAC	Mk 1 FK	
13508		Green Primer	Mk 2 FK	
16204		Green/Red Primer	Mk 1 CK	
17013		Chocolate/Cream	Mk 1 BFK	
17056		CAC	Mk 2 BFK	
17080		PUL	Mk 2 BFK	*Car No. 17080*
17159	14159	CAC	Mk 2 BFK	
21096		Carmine and Cream	Mk 1 BCK	
21268		BR Maroon	Mk 1 BCK	
35465		BR Maroon	Mk 1 BSK	
35511	17130	Maroon	Mk 2 BFK	
80043	1680	PUL	Mk 1 RBR	*Kitchen Car*
80044	1659	CAC	Mk 1 RBR	
82127		InterCity	Mk 3 DVT	
82139		InterCity	Mk 3 DVT	
93568		BR Blue	Mk 1 GUV	
94538		Maroon	Mk 1 NQA	
99241		Livery unknown	Mk 1 BSK	
99993		CAC	Mk 1 TSO	*Club Car*

LSL's Mk 2f 3438 *Ben Lomond* passing Ravenstruther on 27 October 2017. *Robin Ralston*

Mk 3 HST vehicles

LSL has acquired several HST Mk 3 trailers formerly in use with First Great Western. Several vehicles are being repainted into Blue Pullman livery.

40801	Blue Pullman	TRFB
40802	Blue Pullman	TRFB
40804	First Group	TRFB
40808	First Group	TRFB
40106	First Group	TRSMB
41059	Blue Pullman	TF
41108	Blue Pullman	TF
41149	First Group	TF
41162	Blue Pullman	TF
41169	Blue Pullman	TF
41176	Blue Pullman	TF
41182	Blue Pullman	TF
41187	First Group	TF
42319	First Group	TS
42583	First Group	TS
44078	Blue Pullman	TGS
44081	First Group	TGS
46006	Blue Pullman	TC
46012	First Group	TC
46014	Blue Pullman	TC

Ex-Anglia Railways Mk 3 11091 now in use with LSL's Rail Charter services on 13 August 2020 at Skipton. *Pip Dunn*

Mk 1 Kitchen Car 80043 passing Ravenstruther on 27 October 2017. *Robin Ralston*

Support coaches

The following coaches are support vehicles for LSL's steam fleet and now used in the general fleet.

17013	99130	BR Chocolate/Cream	Mk 1 BFK
35317		BR Carmine/Cream	Mk 1 BSK
35333		BR Chocolate/Cream	Mk 1 BSK
35451		BR Carmine/Cream	Mk 1 BSK
35461		BR Chocolate/Cream	Mk 1 BSK
35465		BR Carmine/Cream	Mk 1 BSK
35511	17130	Maroon	Mk 1 BFK

West Coast Railways

Contact details

Website: www.westcoastrailways.co.uk
Twitter: @westcoastrail

Key personnel

Chairman: David Smith
Managing Director: Patricia Marshall

Overview

West Coast Railways is an independent train operator, best known for its steam operations including the annual summer Fort William-Mallaig 'Jacobite', which it started to run in 1998. It has its main base at Carnforth but also operates out of Southall in West London.

In 2000 it gained a nationwide operating licence and started to grow its fleet of diesel locos. It now owns Class 33s, 37s, 47s and 57s and has recently added the first 25kV AC electric loco to its fleet, 86401. However, it also operates other loco types, steam, diesel and electric, owned by other companies.

Modern traction-wise, the firm started by acquiring a 47 and then a 57 from Porterbrook and has since gone on to grow to typically about 30 locos, although all are never in traffic at the same time. It has a large fleet of Mk 1 and 2 coaches.

It owns the Northern Belle, plus the Queen of Scots Pullman, although the latter is only used very occasionally for special events.

WCR's growth seemed unstoppable until 2015 when it suffered a near fatal SPAD that led to it receiving two bans from the ORR. Since then the company has streamlined its operations and addressed its shortfalls.

Understandably, WCR suffered from the Covid-19 pandemic, but was quick to adapt its coaches to allow services – most notably the 'Jacobite' – to restart in mid-July with social distancing measures in place.

No. 37668 passes Carluke with the 0712 Fort William-Carnforth ECS on 2 October 2019. *Robin Ralston*

Above: WCR has three Class 33s in its fleet; 33029 stands at Paddington on 7 March 2020 having arrived from Lancaster with a charter train. *Pip Dunn*

Left: Class 47s are the mainstay of the WCR fleet. On 25 February 2017, 47760 pilots steam loco 45690 *Leander* at Preston on an empty stock move. *Rob France*

Below: No. 57314 leads the 1102 Sheffield-Grantham Northern Belle past Bottesford on 10 May 2019. *Bill Atkinson*

Class 03

These locos were inherited when WCR acquired Steamtown, apart from 03084, which is owned by Chris Beet.

03084	GWS	CRB	CS	
03196	GNY	WCR	CS	
D2381	GNY	WCR	CS (U)	

Class 08

08678 was inherited when WCR acquired Steamtown; the other two locos were bought from EWS.

08418	AWCA	EWS	WCR	CS
08485	AWCA	BRW	WCR	CS
08678	AWCX	WCR	WCR	CS

Class 33

Ex-DRS locos acquired in 2005, 33030 has never run for WCR and is used as a source of spares.

33025	AWCA	WCR	WCR	CS	
33029	AWCA	WCR	WCR	CS	
33030	AWCX	DRU	WCR	CS (U)	
33207	AWCA	WCR	WCR	CS	*Jim Martin*

Class 37

Locos mostly acquired directly or indirectly from EWS, 37165/517/710 have never run for WCR and are used as a source of spares along with 37712.

37165	37374		CCT	WCR	CS (U)	
37516	37086	AWCA	WCR	WCR	CS	*Loch Laidon*
37517	37018		LHO	WCR	CS (U)	
37518	37076	AWCA	WCR	WCR	CS	*Fort William/An Gearasdan*
37668	37257	AWCA	WCR	WCR	CS	
37669	37129	AWCA	WCR	WCR	CS	
37676	37126	AWCA	WCR	WCR	CS	*Loch Rannoch*
37685	37234	AWCA	WCR	WCR	CS	*Loch Arkaig*
37706	37016	AWCA	WCR	WCR	CS	
37710	37044		LHO	WCR	CS (U)	
37712	37102	AWCX	WCR	WCR	CS (U)	

Class 47

Locos acquired mostly from Porterbrook, EWS and FM Rail, 47194/368/492/526/768/776 have never run for WCR and are used as a source of spares. No 47580 is on long-term hire from a preservation group.

47194		AWCX	RFD	WCR	CS (U)	
47237		AWCA	WCR	WCR	CS	
47245		AWCA	WCR	WCR	CS	*VE Day 75th Anniversary*
47270'		AWCA	BRB	WCR	CS (S)	*SWIFT*
47355		AWCX	FRG	WCR	CS (U)	
47368			TTG	WCR	CS (U)	
47492		AWCX	RES	WCR	CS (U)	
47526			BLL	WCR	CS (U)	
47580	47167, 47732	MBDL	BRF	SFG	BU (U)	*County of Essex*
47746	47160, 47605	AWCA	WCR	WCR	CS	*Chris Fudge 29.7.70-22.6.10*
47760	47036, 47562, 47672	AWCA	WCR	WCR	BU (U)	
47768	47490	AWCX	UND	WCR	CS (U)	
47772	47537	AWCA	WCR	WCR	CS	*Carnforth TMD*
47776	47181, 47578	AWCX	RES	WCR	CS (U)	
47786	47138, 47607, 47821	AWCA	WCR	WCR	CS (U)	*Roy Castle OBE*
47787	47163, 47610, 47823	AWCX	WCR	WCR	CS (U)	
47802	47552	AWCA	WCR	WCR	CS	
47804	47265, 47591, 47792	AWCA	WCR	WCR	CS	
47826	47274, 47637	AWCA	WCR	WCR	CS	
47832	47031, 47560	AWCA	WCR	WCR	CS	
47851	47064, 47639	AWCA	WCR	WCR	CS	
47854	47271, 47604, 47674	AWCA	WCR	WCR	CS	*Diamond Jubilee*

Class 57

Locos acquired from Porterbrook and Advenza, 57005 has never run for WCR and is used as a source of spares.

57001	47356	AWCA	WCR	WCR	CS	
57005	47350	AWCX	ADZ	WCR	CS (U)	
57006	47187	AWCX	WCR	WCR	CS (S)	
57313	47371	AWCA	NOB	WCR	CS	*Scarborough Castle*
57314	47372	AWCA	WCR	WCR	CS	
57315	47234	AWCA	WCR	WCR	CS (S)	
57316	47290	AWCA	WCR	WCR	CS	
57601	47165, 47590, 47825	AWCA	NOB	WCR	CS	*Windsor Castle*

Class 86

Acquired for the ACLG, this loco is expected to move into a WCR operational pool soon. It will work alongside preserved 86259.

86401	86001	GBCH	CAL	WCR	CS	*Mons Meg*

Mk 2 BSO 9391 passes Carluke as part of an ECS move on 2 October 2019. *Robin Ralston*

WCR Mk 1 FO 99122 at Exeter on 8 March 2020. *Antony Christie*

Coaches

WCR also owns many scrap vehicles, which it retains for spare parts, and these are not currently in traffic and are not listed here.

No.	Other No.	Livery	Type	Status	Name
1221		ICS	Mk 2 RFB	CS	
1666		WCR	Mk 1 RBR	CS	
1861		WCR	Mk 1 RMB	CS	
1961		WCR	Mk 1 RBR	CS	
3058		WCR	Mk 1 FO	CS	*Florence*
3093		WCR	Mk 1 FO	CS	*Florence*
3136		WCR	Mk 1 FO	CS	*Diana*
3143		WCR	Mk 1 FO	CS	*Patricia*
3313		WCR	Mk 2 FO	CS	
3326		WCR	Mk 2 FO	CS	
3350		WCR	Mk 2 FO	CS	
3352		WCR	Mk 2 FO	CS	
3392		WCR	Mk 2 FO	CS	
3395		WCR	Mk 2 FO	CS	
3431		WCR	Mk 2 FO	CS	
4854		WCR	Mk 1 TSO	CS	
4905		WCR	Mk 1 TSO	CS	
4940		WCR	Mk 1 TSO	CS	
4951		WCR	Mk 1 TSO	CS	
4960		WCR	Mk 1 TSO	CS	
4973		WCR	Mk 1 TSO	CS	
4984		WCR	Mk 1 TSO	CS	
4994		WCR	Mk 1 TSO	CS	
5032		WCR	Mk 1 TSO	CS	
5035		WCR	Mk 1 TSO	CS	
5171		WCR	Mk 2 TSO	CS	
5200		WCR	Mk 2 TSO	CS	
5216		WCR	Mk 2 TSO	CS	
5222		WCR	Mk 2 TSO	CS	
5229		WCR	Mk 2 TSO	CS	
5236		WCR	Mk 2 TSO	CS	
5237		WCR	Mk 2 TSO	CS	
5239		WCR	Mk 2 TSO	CS	
5249		WCR	Mk 2 TSO	CS	
5278		WCR	Mk 2 TSO	CS	
5419		WCR	Mk 2 TSO	CS	
5487		WCR	Mk 2 TSO	CS	
5592		WCR	Mk 2 TSO	CS	
5903		WCR	Mk 2 TSO	CS	
6021		WCR	Mk 2 TSO	CS	
6022		WCR	Mk 2 TSO	CS	
6103		WCR	Mk 2 TSO	CS	
6115		WCR	Mk 2 TSO	CS	
6312	81023	WCR	Mk 1 BG	CS	

6528		WCR	Mk 2 TSO	CS	
9104		WCR	Mk 2 BSO	CS	
9391		WCR	Mk 2 BSO	CS	
9392		WCR	Mk 2 BSO	CS	
9401		WCR	Mk 2 BSO	CS	
9493		WCR	Mk 2 BSO	CS	
13320		WCR	Mk 1 FK	CS	*Anna*
13440		WCR	Mk 2 FK	CS	
21266		WCR	Mk 1 BCK	CS	
95402	326	PUL	Mk 1 FP	CS	*Emerald*
99025	325	PUL	Mk 1 FP	CS	*Amber*
99035	35322	WCR	Mk 1 BSK	CS	
99121	3105	WCR	Mk 1 FO	CS	*Julia*
99122	3106	WCR	Mk 1 FO	CS	*Alexandra*
99125	3113	WCR	Mk 1 FO	CS	*Jessica*
99127	3117	WCR	Mk 1 FO	CS	*Christina*
99128	3130	WCR	Mk 1 FO	CS	*Pamela*
99304	21256	WCR	Mk 1 BCK	CS	
99311	1882	WCR	Mk 1 RMB	CS	
99316	13321	WCR	Mk 1 FK	CS	
99318	4912	WCR	Mk 1 TSO	CS	
99326	4954	WCR	Mk 1 TSO	CS	
99327	5044	WCR	Mk 1 TSO	CS	
99328	5033	WCR	Mk 1 TSO	CS	
99329	4931	WCR	Mk 1 TSO	CS	
99347	347	WCR	Mk 1 SP	CS	
99348	348	PUL	Mk 1 SP	CS	*Topaz*
99350	350	PUL	Mk 1 SP	CS	*Tanzanite*
99351	351	PUL	Mk 1 SP	CS	*Sapphire*
99352	352	PUL	Mk 1 SP	CS	*Amethyst*
99354	354	PUL	Mk 1 BAR	CS	*The Hadrian Bar*
99371	3128	WCR	Mk 1 FO	CS	*Victoria*
99680	17102	WCR	Mk 2 BFK	CS	
99710	18767	WCR	Mk 1 SK	CS	
99716	25808	WCR	Mk 1 SK	CS	
999506		WCR	Inspection Saloon	CS	
99678	504	PUL	Mk 2 PFK	CS	*Ullswater*
99679	506	PUL	Mk 2 PFK	CS	*Windermere*
99670	546	PUL	Mk 2 PFP	CS	*City Of Manchester*
99671	548	PUL	Mk 2 PFP	CS	*Grasmere*
99672	549	PUL	Mk 2 PFP	CS	*Bassenthwaite*
99673	550	PUL	Mk 2 PFP	CS	*Rydal Water*
99674	551	PUL	Mk 2 PFP	CS	*Buttermere*
99675	552	PUL	Mk 2 PFP	CS	*Ennerdale Water*
99676	553	PUL	Mk 2 PFP	CS	*Crummock Water*
99677	586	PUL	Mk 2 PFB	CS	*Derwent Water*
1566		NOB	Mk 1 RKB	CS	
1953		NOB	Mk 1 RU	CS	
3174		NOB	Mk 2 FO	CS	*Glamis*

3182		NOB	Mk 2 FO	CS	*Warwick*
3232		NOB	Mk 2 FO	CS	
3247		NOB	Mk 2 FO	CS	*Chatsworth*
3267		NOB	Mk 2 FO	CS	*Belvoir*
3273		NOB	Mk 2 FO	CS	*Alnwick*
3275		NOB	Mk 2 FO	CS	*Harlech*
3362		NOB	Mk 2 FO	CS	
17167		NOB	Mk 2 BFK	CS	*Mow Cop*
10569		NOB	Mk 3 SLEP	CS	
10729		NOB	Mk 3 SLE	CS	
10734		NOB	Mk 3 SLE	CS	*Balmoral*
159		L&NWR		CS	
807		Teak		CS	
9004		NOB		CS	
99886	35407	L&NWR	Mk 1 BSK	CS	

Support coaches

These are usually used to support WCR's steam locos and as a rule are not used in its normal charter trains, although being brake vehicles would not preclude that.

17025		BR Maroon	Mk 1 BFK
35447		Maroon	Mk 1 BSK
35518	17097	BR Green	Mk 1 BFK
80204	3529	BR Maroon	Mk 1 BSK
80217	35299	BR Maroon	Mk 1 BSK
80220	35276	BR Maroon	Mk 1 BSK
99035	35322	BR Maroon	Mk 1 BSK
99312	35463	BR Maroon	Mk 1 BSK
99723	35459	BR Maroon	Mk 1 BSK

Mk 1 Kitchen Car 1566 passes Midcalder Junction on 22 March 2020. *Robin Ralston*

Vintage Trains

Contact details

Website: www.vintagetrains.co.uk
Twitter: @Vintage_Trains

Key personnel

Chairman: Michael Whitehouse

Overview

Vintage Trains is based at Tyseley Locomotives Works and recently gained its own Train Operating Licence after years of using West Coast Railways to run its charter trains.

It owns a handful of steam locos and a single Class 47, 47773, which in the summer of 2020 was undergoing bodywork repairs and a repaint at Kidderminster Diesel depot. It also owns a Class 08.

The company has also provided drivers for testing, delivery and training VivaRail Class 230 units.

Vintage Trains owns one diesel loco, 47773. It pauses at Oakengates on 9 June 2019. It was undergoing overhaul in late 2020. *Antony Christie*

Class 08

Depot shunter at Tyseley Locomotive Works.

08021 TLW BLK TM

Class 47

An ex-EWS loco, this dual-barked 47 is the main support loco for VTL's steam operations. It is in the MBDL pool.

47773 47541 GYP VIN TM

Coaches

No.	Other No.	Livery	Type	Status	Name
99349	349	PUL	Pullman SP		CAR No 349
99353	353	PUL	Pullman SP		CAR No 353
99361	311	PUL	Pullman FK	TS (U)	EAGLE
3351		Chocolate/Cream	Mk 2 FO	TS (U)	
5157		Chocolate/Cream	Mk 2 TSO		
5177		Chocolate/Cream	Mk 2 TSO		
5191		Chocolate/Cream	Mk 2 TSO		
5198		Chocolate/Cream	Mk 2 TSO		
5212		Chocolate/Cream	Mk 2 TSO		
9101		Chocolate/Cream	Mk 2 BFK		
35470		Chocolate/Cream	Mk 1 BSK		

Mk 1 BSK 35470 at Telford on 9 June 2019. *Antony Christie*

Northern Ireland Railways

Contact details

Website: www.translink.co.uk
Twitter: @nirailways

Key personnel

General Manager Rail Services Operations: Richard Knox
Head of Rail Fleet Engineering: Richard Noble

Overview

Unlike the passenger operations in England, Scotland and Wales, those in Northern Ireland were not privatised in the mid-1990s. There are not a lot of routes in the country and those that remain emanate mostly from Belfast.

The trains are operated by Northern Ireland Railways (NIR), which is a subsidiary of Translink. Unlike the British mainland, the gauge is not the standard 4ft 8½in but the same 5ft 3in gauge as used in the Republic of Ireland.

Through inter-city trains between Belfast to Dublin are operated by Iarnród Éireann using 201 Class GM diesel locos in push-pull mode. NIR owns two of these locos, 208/209, which are used on a common user basis with the rest of the fleet, 201-207/210-234, although several locos have now been stored.

The routes operated are Belfast-Londonderry/Portrush, Belfast-Newry, Belfast-Bangor and Belfast-Larne.

The majority of the NIR fleet is multiple units and there has been extensive fleet replacement in the last decade to allow elderly trains to be withdrawn.

In December 2018, 21 additional vehicles were ordered from CAF at a cost of £50m. These will be used to lengthen seven of the 20 Class 4000 units (4001-4007) to six-car sets. The extra vehicles are due for delivery in 2021 and expected to enter service in 2022.

111 Class

These three GM Co-Co locos, built in 1980-84, are the same as IÉ's 071 Class locos and are used on infrastructure trains on the NIR network.

8111	*Great Northern*
112	*Northern Counties*
8113	*Belfast & County Down*

201 Class

These two GM Co-Co locos are used alongside similar locos operated by IÉ. They work Belfast to Dublin De Detrich trainsets alongside IÉ locos, although the latter's fleet also work elsewhere across the Republic of Ireland.

8208	*River Lagan*
209	

3000 Class

These 90mph three-car DMUs were built by CAF in Spain in 2004-05, can operate at up to 90mph and are used on local trains from Belfast.

They replaced the old 80 Class DEMUs and 450 Class DMUs, although a handful of the former were retained as Sandite units until 2017.

Unit	DMSO	MSO	DMSO
3001	3301	3501	3401
3002	3302	3502	3402
3003	3303	3503	3403
3004	3304	3504	3404
3005	3305	3505	3405
3006	3306	3506	3406
3007	3307	3507	3407
3008	3308	3508	3408
3009	3309	3509	3409
3010	3310	3510	3410
3011	3311	3511	3411
3012	3312	3512	3412
3013	3313	3513	3413
3014	3314	3514	3414
3015	3315	3515	3415
3016	3316	3516	3416
3017	3317	3517	3417
3018	3318	3518	3418
3019	3319	3519	3419
3020	3320	3520	3420
3021	3321	3521	3421
3022	3322	3522	3422
3023	3323	3523	3423

4000 Class

Visually the same as the 3000 Class units, these CAF built units were delivered in 2010-11. They differ by having an alternative driveline.

These trains were ordered to replace the 450 Class DMUs and also to provide extra capacity on NIR operations.

Unit	DMSO	MSO	DMSO
4001	4301	4501	4401
4002	4302	4502	4402
4003	4303	4503	4403
4004	4304	4504	4404
4005	4305	4505	4405
4006	4306	4506	4406
4007	4307	4507	4407
4008	4308	4508	4408
4009	4309	4509	4409
4010	4310	4510	4410
4011	4311	4511	4411
4012	4312	4512	4412
4013	4313	4513	4413
4014	4314	4514	4414
4015	4315	4515	4415
4016	4316	4516	4416
4017	4317	4517	4417
4018	4318	4518	4418
4019	4319	4519	4419
4020	4320	4520	4420

London Underground

The London Underground is understandably the UK's busiest and best-known metro system, with as many as five million journeys made each day. It comprises 11 lines covering 250 miles and 270 stations. It includes a number of 'sub-surface' lines which head out into the suburbs and are far from underground on these sections.

Bakerloo Line

Map Colour: Brown
Routes: Harrow & Wealdstone to Elephant and Castle via Willesden Junction, Paddington, Marylebone, Piccadilly Circus, Waterloo
Mileage: 14.4 miles
Number of stations: 25
Trains: 36 × seven-car sets built in 1972

Central Line

Map Colour: Red
Routes: West Ruislip / Ealing Broadway to Epping via Greenford, White City, Oxford Circus, Bank, Liverpool St, Stratford and Leytonstone; loop line from Leytonstone to Woodford via Grange Hill
Mileage: 46
Number of stations: 49
Trains: 85 × eight-car sets built in 1992

Circle Line

Map Colour: Yellow
Routes: Edgware Road to Hammersmith via Paddington, Victoria, Embankment, Cannon St, Liverpool St, King's Cross St Pancras, Baker St, Edgware Road and Latimer Road
Mileage: 17
Number of stations: 36
Trains: 132 × seven-car sets built in 2008-12. These trains are shared between the District and Hammersmith & City lines

District Line

Map Colour: Green
Routes: Ealing Broadway to Upminster via Turnham Green, Earls Court, Victoria, Embankment. Tower Hill, Bow Road, West Ham, Barking and Dagenham East; Edgware Road to Wimbledon; branches from Kensington Olympia to Earls Court and Turnham Green to Richmond
Mileage: 40
Number of stations: 60
Trains: 132 × seven-car sets built in 2008-12. These trains are shared between the Central and Hammersmith & City lines

Hammersmith & City Line

Map Colour: Pink
Routes: Hammersmith to Barking, via Paddington, Euston Square, King's Cross St Pancras, Liverpool St, Bow Road and West Ham
Mileage: 15.8
Number of stations: 29
Trains: 132 × seven-car sets built in 2008-12. These trains are shared between the District and Circle lines

Jubilee Line

Map Colour: Silver
Routes: Stanmore to Stratford via Neasden, Baker St, Green Park, Waterloo, London Bridge, Canary Wharf and Canning Town
Mileage: 22.5
Number of stations: 27
Trains: 63 × seven-car sets built in 1996

Metropolitan Line

Map Colour: Maroon
Routes: Amersham to Aldgate via Rickmansworth, Harrow-on-the-Hill, Wembley Park, Baker St, King's Cross St Pancras and Liverpool Street; branches from Chalfont & Latimer to Chesham, Moor Park to Watford, Harrow-on-the-Hill to Uxbridge
Mileage: 42
Number of stations: 34
Trains: 60 × eight-car sets built in 2008-12

Northern Line

Map Colour: Black
Routes: Edgware to Morden via Brent Cross, Camden Town, Euston, Tottenham Court Road, Waterloo, Stockwell, Balham and Colliers Wood; branches from Camden Town to High Barnet via Finchley Central, Finchley Central to Mill Hill East and Camden Town to Kennington via King's Cross St Pancras, Bank and London Bridge
Mileage: 42
Number of stations: 34
Trains: 106 × six-car sets built in 1995

Piccadilly Line

Colour: Dark blue
Routes: Cockfosters to Uxbridge via Finsbury Park, King's Cross St Pancras, Leicester Square, Earls Court, Acton Town, Rayners Lane, and Ruislip; branches from Acton Town to Heathrow terminals 2/3 and 5, plus a loop from Hatton Cross to Terminals 23
Mileage: 44
Number of stations: 53
Trains: 86 × six-car sets built in 1973

Victoria Line

Colour: Light blue
Routes: Walthamstow Central to Brixton via Finsbury Park, King's Cross St Pancras, Euston, Green Park, Victoria and Vauxhall
Mileage: 13
Number of stations: 16
Trains: 47 × eight-car sets built in 2009

Waterloo & City Line

Colour: Turquoise
Routes: Bank to Waterloo
Mileage: 1.5
Number of stations: 2
Trains: 5 × four-car sets built in 1992

The London Underground is the oldest metro system and provides a vital transport network for commuters and tourists alike. On 3 July 2018, a Piccadilly line train leaves King's Cross for Heathrow. *Pip Dunn*

Blackpool & Fleetwood Tramway

Routes: Fleetwood to Starr Gate via Broadwater, Bispham, Blackpool Tower and Burlington Road West
Mileage: 11
Number of stations: 38
Trains: 18 × Bombardier Flexity five-section trams

Dating from 1885, this is one of the oldest tramway systems anywhere in the world, it comprises one main route. It is electrified using a 600V DC overhead line.

The line was recently modernised to transition from a heritage tourist attraction to a viable, modern light rail system. Part of that upgrade saw delivery of a fleet of German-built Bombardier Flexity trams dating from 2011/12. They are numbered 001-018 and are referred to as the 'A' Fleet.

The system also has nine 'balloon' double-deck single-car trams dating from the 1930s; the 'B fleet'. While these do not meet modern standards, they have exemptions for use but are typically only used in the high summer or autumn Illuminations seasons. They are numbered in the 700 series, although some are in store.

A fleet of vintage trams, some as old as 1901, are also allowed to be used on special workings and private operations such as for weddings and functions. This is the 'C fleet'.

All the new trams are maintained at a new purpose-built depot at Starr Gate at the southern end of the line, while the original Rigby Road depot is retained for the maintenance and storage of the holder heritage trams.

'A' Fleet Blackpool tram 012 passes Heathfield Road at the Fleetwood end of the system on 31 May 2014.
Rob France

London Tramlink

Routes: Wimbledon to New Addington via Mitcham, East Croydon and Sandlands; branches to Elmers End and Beckenham Junction
Mileage: 17.5
Number of stations: 39
Trains: 24 × Bombardier Flexity Swift and 12 × Stadler Variobhan

This system, which first opened in May 2000, uses many former heavy rail lines converted to tram operation including Wimbledon to West Croydon and Elmers End to Addiscombe. In addition to their conversions, there were extension into the centre of Croydon and a wholly new line from East Croydon to New Addington and also from Arena to Beckenham Junction.

The system uses 750V DC overhead lines. It has its only depot at Therapia Lane, midway on the Wimbledon branch, and this maintains the fleet of 24 Bombardier Flexity Swift three-section trams that were delivered to launch the service, and now a new fleet of 12 Stadler Variobahn five-section trams that date from 2011-16. One tram, 2551, was involved in a serious accident in 2016 when it fell on its side when the driver took a corner way too fast. It is stored and unlikely to return to service.

The London Tramlink system uses many old heavy rail lines combined with new routes and a new street network in the heart of Croydon. On 10 September 2014, 2557 is at East Croydon heading for Elmers End. In the background, one of the older trams, 2550, heads to Wimbledon. *Paul Bigland*

Edinburgh Trams

Routes: Edinburgh Airport-York Place via Edinburgh Park, Haymarket and Princes Street
Mileage: 8.5
Number of stations: 16
Trains: 27 × CAF Urbos 3

One of the newer tram systems, and a bespoke operation, it opened on 31 May 2014, running one just one route from Edinburgh Airport in the west, through the city centre and out to York Place in the east.

It uses 750V DC overheads and has a fleet of 27 seven-section CAF Urbos 3 trams, maintained at the system's one depot at Gogar.

The system is being extended from York Place to Newhaven, while there is a proposal to build a second branch from Haymarket to Granton. Longer term, a line from Ingliston to Newbridge is a possibility.

One of the newer tram systems is that in Edinburgh. On 20 March 2019, 277 passes Saughton. *Rob France*

Glasgow Underground

Routes: Buchannan St to Buchannan St via Govan (circular route)
Mileage: 6.5
Number of stations: 15
Trains: 41 vehicles running in two- and three-car sets
This 600V DC third rail underground system opened way back in 1896 and uses a non-standard 4ft track gauge. It is known as the clockwork orange as the trains – in bright orange livery ran – on the system's circular route.

The current fleet is varied. It has 33 power cars, which ran in pairs, dating from 1977-79 and entered traffic in 1980. These were supplemented by eight centre-trailer cars from 1992 to allow three-car trains to run.

However, all are on the cusp of being replaced by 17 new four-car Stadler trains, which will be able to be operated driverless.

One of the new Glasgow Subway cars at the new extension to the Govan depot on 6 August 2020. *Robin Ralston*

Manchester Metrolink

Routes: Bury to Altrincham via Manchester Victoria, Old Trafford and Timperley, Rochdale to East Didsbury, via Milnrow, Oldham, Failsworth, Manchester Victoria, Chorlton and West Didsbury; Eccles to Ashton-under-Lyne via Salford Quays, Manchester Piccadilly and Droylesden; Manchester Victoria to Manchester Airport; Trafford Centre to Cornbrook
Mileage: 63
Number of stations: 99
Trains: 120 two-car articulated Bombardier M5000 series 750V DC overhead trams
The Manchester Metrolink is a glowing example of how a good modern light rail system can flourish. The first line opened in April 1992 running from Bury to Altrincham, mostly using old BR lines. It ran into the centre of Manchester and served both of the city's main stations at Victoria and Piccadilly, but the sections from Queens Road to Bury and Old Trafford to Altrincham were ex-BR lines. The Bury line was 1,200V DC third rail, while the new tram system was 750V DC overhead.

In 2000, a new branch from Manchester to Eccles was added, followed by a spur to Media City in in 2010.

In 2013, the transformation of the Dean Lane to Rochdale, via Oldham, was converted from heavy rail to Metrolink with an extension into Rochdale town centre. At the same time, a new branch in the east to Droylsden was added and this was extended to Ashton-under-Lyne in 2014. Also, a short branch from Old Trafford to Chorlton opened in 2013 and was extended to East Didsbury the following year, as was a new line from Chorlton to Manchester Airport.

A second crossing through the city centre opened in 2017, while in 2020 a new line to the Trafford centre brought the network's total mileage up to 63.

The original fleet of trams have been replaced and now the fleet comprises 120 3000 series Flexity Swift two-section trams delivered progressively from 2009 to 2016, with additional orders made as new lines opened. The fleet is maintained at the Queens Road depot close to Victoria.

Bombardier Flexity Swift tram 3089 arrives at Manchester Piccadilly with a train for Media City on 16 May 2015. *Rob France*

Nottingham Express Transit

Routes: Hucknall to Clifton South via Bulwell, Trent University, Nottingham Station and Clifton Centre; Toton Lane to Nottingham via Beeston and University of Nottingham; branch from Phoenix Park to Highbury Vale
Mileage: 20
Number of stations: 50
Trains: 37 × five-section 750V DC overhead trams

Another of the newer, but flourishing, tram systems is that in Nottingham. Phase 1 was from Nottingham Station to Hucknall in the north, with a short spur from Highbury Vale to Phoenix Park. It opened in March 2004.

Phase two was two new branches, one to the south to Clifton via Ruddington Lane, which opened in July 2015, and another to the west to Chilwell via the university and hospital. This line was then extended to Toton Lane, a park and ride station near the M1. It opened in August 2015.

The system uses two fleets of five-section trams. The Bombardier Incentro units were delivered for opening of Phase 1 and built at nearby Derby. When additional trams were needed, NET opted for Spanish-built Alstom Citadis 302 trams. All are maintained at the Wilson Street Depot.

Bombardier Incentro tram 209 at Toton Lane with a service to Hucknall on 25 June 2018. *Paul Robertson*

South Yorkshire Supertram

Routes: Meadowhall-Halfway, Middlewood to Herdings Park
Mileage: 21.5 miles
Number of stations: 50
Trains: 32 × five-section trams

Although understandably not quite of the scale of the Manchester Metrolink, Sheffield's 750V DC overhead tram system has grown slowly since the first section opened in 1994 from Meadowhall to Fitzalan Square in the city centre and then on to Gleadless Townend in the south of the city.

The year 1995 saw this branch extended to terminate at Halfway and Herdings Park, while a new line in the north to Middlewood with a spur to Malin Bridge also opened in October that year.

A new line from Meadowhall south to Parkgate via Rotherham Central opened in October 2018 and this section involved running over some Network Rail infrastructure as a first example of a new tram-train operation. For that reason, the seven trains that run on this section are Class 399s on TOPS.

The initial trams used was a fleet of 25 three-section Siemens units built in Düsseldorf, numbered 101-125. The Class 399s are Stadler Citylink three-section trams. They are numbered 201-207 for Supertram's purposes, but 399201-207 for Network Rail. The entire fleet it maintained at Nunnery depot in the north-east of the city.

Sheffield Supertram 108 at Sheffield station on 25 July 2018. This tram cannot run to Rotherham, which uses Network Rail infrastructure. *Paul Robertson*

Tyne & Wear Metro

Routes: Newcastle-South Shield and South Hylton, St James to Whitley Bay, Newcastle-Airport
Mileage: 48
Number of stations: 60
Trains: 90 × two-car

The first example of heavy rail commuter lines being converted to light rail was the Tyne & Wear metro, the first stage of which opened in August 1980 from Haymarket to Tynemouth.

In the north the system was gradually extended and by November 1982 it ran over all of the former loop line from Newcastle to Whitley Bay via Wallsend. South of the River Tyne estuary, from March 1984 it also ran on a new line adjacent to the BR route from Felling to South Shields, with the BR line stations closing and the track becoming freight only. Some of these freight lines have since closed.

The system was extended to run from Bank Foot to Newcastle Airport in November 1991 and from March 2002 from Pelaw to South Hylton, sharing tracks with Network Rail as far as Sunderland. The former BR freight-only line from Percy Main to Northumberland Park is mooted for being added to the system.

After two prototypes were built in 1975, the system started with these and a fleet of an additional 88 two-car units built in 1978-81. These are naturally quite dated now and in January 2020 Stadler won a contract for 42 brand-new, five-car trains, the first of which should be delivered in late 2021. There is an option for five additional trains should they be needed.

Docklands Light Railway

Routes: Tower Gateway/Bank to Stratford, Beckton, Stratford-Woolwich Arsenal, Canary Wharf-Lewisham
Mileage: 24
Number of stations: 45
Trains: 94 × two-section trains

Famous for using driverless trains, the 750V DC Docklands Light Railway is another light rail system that has grown organically since it first opened in 1987.

The initial network was from Tower Gateway to Island Gardens, in the Isle of Dogs, with a branch from Poplar to Stratford. In 1991 a short spur to serve Bank station in the City of London also opened.

The first major extension came in 1994 with Poplar to Beckton opening. The next new line, built just in time for the Millennium, was from Island Gardens to Lewisham, which included a new tunnel under the Thames and the resiting and closure of the original Island Gardens station.

Canning Town to King George V opened in December 2005 and this line was extended – again under the Thames – to Woolwich Arsenal in January 2009. The last expansion was from Stratford International to Canning Town.

The initial 21 trains, numbered 01-21, were two-car units – which could run in pairs – built by BN in Belgium. These were withdrawn in 1991-95 (as they could not work to Bank) and sold for use in Germany.

They were replaced by 23 new trains, 22-44, and then supplemented by another 47 units from 1992-95. Then, as further expansion of the network dictated further new trains, another 24 units, 92-99 and 01-16 from 2002-03, built by Bombardier, were added. Finally, 55 more units were delivered from 2007-10, also built by Bombardier and numbered 101-155. These newest units were built in Germany, the rest in Belgium. The trains are maintained at depots at Poplar and Beckton.

West Midlands Metro

Routes: Centenary Square-Wolverhampton St Georges
Mileage: 13
Number of stations: 29
Trains: 21 × five-section trams
This 750V DC system only has one route, from Birmingham City centre to Wolverhampton St Georges, but goes through the heart of the Black Country, serving the likes of West Bromwich, Dudley and Wednesbury.

A short extension to meet with Wolverhampton railway station is under construction, while an extension from the City Centre to Edgbaston is also being built.

It has one depot at Wednesbury to maintain the fleet. The initial 16 three-section Ansaldo trams, 01-16, have now been retired and are in store. They have been replaced by 21 newer CAF Urbos 3 five-section units, numbered 17-37.

The West Midland Metro runs from the centre of Birmingham to Wolverhampton via the heart of the Black Country. *WMM*

Riviera Trains

Contact details

Website: www.riviera-trains.co.uk

Overview

Riviera Trains is a rolling stock provider to the charter train market and TOCs. It has a large fleet of mostly ex-BR coaches and supplies Mk 1 and Mk 2 trains to the likes of UK Railtours, Pathfinder Tours (which is owns), Nenta Traintours and others.

It has previously supplied Mk 2 coaches to various TOCs including ScotRail, Transport for Wales and DB Schenker.

Class 08

08507	RTSO	RIV	OXB	ZG

Coaches

Present No	Other Number	Livery	Type
1212	3427	BR Blue/Grey	Mk 2 RFB
1651		BR Carmine/Cream	Mk 1 RBR
1657		BR Blue/Grey	Mk 2 TSO
1671		BR Chocolate/Cream	Mk 1 RBR
1683		Blue	Mk 1 RBR
1691		BR Blue/Grey	Mk 1 RBR
1813		BR Chocolate/Cream	Mk 1 RMB
1832		BR Carmine/Cream	Mk 1 FO
3066		BR Carmine/Cream	Mk 1 FO
3068		BR Carmine/Cream	Mk 1 FO
3097		BR Chocolate/Cream	Mk 1 FO
3098		BR Chocolate/Cream	Mk 1 FO
3110		BR Chocolate/Cream	Mk 1 FO
3112		BR Chocolate/Cream	Mk 1 FO
3119		BR Chocolate/Cream	Mk 1 FO
3120		BR Chocolate/Cream	Mk 1 FO
3121		BR Chocolate/Cream	Mk 1 FO
3123		BR Carmine/Cream	Mk 1 FO
3141		BR Chocolate/Cream	Mk 1 FO
3146		BR Chocolate/Cream	Mk 1 FO
3147		BR Chocolate/Cream	Mk 1 FO
3149		BR Chocolate/Cream	Mk 1 FO
3278		BR Blue/Grey	Mk 2 FO
3304		BR Blue/Grey	Mk 2 FO
3314		BR Blue/Grey	Mk 2 FO
3333		BR Blue/Grey	Mk 2 FO
3340		BR Blue/Grey	Mk 2 FO
3345		BR Blue/Grey	Mk 2 FO
3356		BR Blue/Grey	Mk 2 FO
3364		BR Blue/Grey	Mk 2 FO
3386		BR Blue/Grey	Mk 2 FO
3390		BR Blue/Grey	Mk 2 FO
3397		BR Blue/Grey	Mk 2 FO
4927		BR Carmine/Cream	Mk 1 TSO
4946		BR Chocolate/Cream	Mk 1 TSO
4949		BR Chocolate/Cream	Mk 1 TSO
4959		BR Chocolate/Cream	Mk 1 TSO
4991		BR Chocolate/Cream	Mk 1 TSO
4998		BR Chocolate/Cream	Mk 1 TSO
5009		BR Chocolate/Cream	Mk 1 TSO
5292		BR Carmine/Cream	Mk 2 TSO
5910		BR Blue/Grey	Mk 2 TSO
5921		Anglia unbranded	Mk 2 TSO
5929		BR Blue/Grey	Mk 2 TSO
5950		Anglia unbranded	Mk 2 TSO
5952		BR Blue/Grey	Mk 2 TSO
5955		ScotRail	Mk 2 TSO
5961		BR Blue/Grey	Mk 2 TSO
5965		ScotRail	Mk 2 TSO
5976		ScotRail	Mk 2 TSO
5985		Anglia unbranded	Mk 2 TSO
5987		ScotRail	Mk 2 TSO
5998		BR Blue/Grey	Mk 2 TSO
6006		Anglia unbranded	Mk 2 TSO
6024		BR Blue/Grey	Mk 2 TSO

6027		ScotRail	Mk 2 TSO
6042		Anglia unbranded	Mk 2 TSO
6051		BR Blue/Grey	Mk 2 TSO
6054		BR Blue/Grey	Mk 2 TSO
6067		BR Blue/Grey	Mk 2 TSO
6137		ScotRail	Mk 2 TSO
6141		Virgin red	Mk 2 TSO
6158		BR Blue/Grey	Mk 2 TSO
6176		BR Blue/Grey	Mk 2 TSO
6177		ScotRail	Mk 2 TSO
6183		ScotRail	Mk 2 TSO
6310	81448	BR Chocolate/Cream	Mk 1 BIG Generator van
9504		BR Blue/Grey	Mk 2 BSO
9507		BR Blue/Grey	Mk 2 BSO

9520		Anglia unbranded	Mk 2 BSO
9509		Anglia unbranded	Mk 2 BSO
9520		Anglia unbranded	Mk 2 TSO
9526		BR Blue/Grey	Mk 2 TSO
9527		ScotRail	Mk 2 TSO
9537		Virgin Red	Mk 2 TSO
9539		ScotRail	Mk 2 TSO
17105		BR Blue/Grey	Mk 2 BFO
21245		BR Maroon	Mk 1 BCK
21269		BR Carmine/Cream	Mk 1 BCK
21272		BR Chocolate/Cream	Mk 1 BCK
35469		BR Chocolate/Cream	Mk 1 BSK
88041	1690	Maroon	Mk 1 Kitchen car
88042	1646	BR Blue/Grey	Mk 1

Right: Riviera Trains had had a rake of its Mk 2 air-conditioned coaches repainted back into BR Grey and blue livery. FO 3345 passes Nethertown on the Cumbrian Coast line on 21 April 2018. *Robin Ralston*

Below: Ex-BR Mk 1 FO 3149, now owned by Riviera Trains, passes Craigenhill on 23 September 2018. *Robin Ralston*

Eastern Rail Services

Contact details

E-mail: enquiries@easternrailservices.co.uk

Key personnel

Managing Director: James Steward

Overview

Eastern Rail Services is a new rolling stock provider that has grown rapidly over the last two years and is currently supply vehicles to customers, including Network Rail for its Infrastructure Monitoring trains.

It has acquired several redundant Mk 2/3 coaches displaced by new stock from the likes of Caledonian Sleeper and Great Anglia.

It has vehicles stored at the Mid Norfolk Railway and had recently taken on the previously redundant carriage sidings at Great Yarmouth, which it has brought back into use for storing vehicles between contracts. It has based a Class 08 shunter there; 08762. In 2020 the company also bought RMS Locotec and acquired several Class 08 shunters as a result (see page 323).

It also owns one Class 08 as an ERS asset – 08870 – and has recently acquired 31452, which it will use for train supply testing.

In March 2019 it obtained former Mk 3 Nightstar generator coach 96371, one of five high-output generator coaches for use on the proposed cross-Channel 'sleeper' trains that never happened. The coach contains two engine and generator sets, which combined have a train heat index of 140. This is currently at UKRL's Leicester depot being modified. It has more recently acquired 96374.

In October 2019 it bought the entire Caledonian Sleeper Mk 2 fleet, consisting of two Mk 2f RFO lounges, six Mk 2f RLO lounge cars, and nine Mk 2e BUO brakes. Five are in use with NR, while others are stored at the Weardale Railway.

In December 2019 ERS obtained two Mk 3 kitchen cars while in January some of the BUOs also entered service with Network Rail. More recently, ERS has acquired further 'sleeper' coaches and Greater Anglia Mk 3s.

Eastern Rail Services' ex-Caledonian Sleeper Mk 2 BUO 9806 is now used by Network Rail for its IM trains. It is seen at Exeter on 14 May 2020. *Antony Christie*

Class 08

08870 MBDL RMS ERS WO

Class 31

31452 31228 HTLX DCG ERS OK

Coaches

No.	Livery	Type
1210	ScotRail	Mk 2 RFB
1220	ScotRail	Mk 2 RFB
1254	Blue/Grey	Mk 2 RFB
1692	Chocolate/Cream	Mk 1 RBR
3133	Maroon	Mk 1 FO
3181	Oxford Blue	Mk 2 FO
3374	Blue/Grey	Mk 2 FO
3385	InterCity	Mk 2 FO
5482	Blue/Grey	Mk 2 TSO
5647	Blue/Grey	Mk 2 TSO
5866	InterCity	Mk 2 TSO
5906	InterCity	Mk 2 TSO
5960	Virgin red	Mk 2 TSO
5989	InterCity	Mk 2 TSO
6059	InterCity	Mk 2 TSO
6168	InterCity	Mk 2 TSO
6411	LUL Brown	Mk 2 TSO
6700	Caledonian Sleeper	Mk 2 RFO
6702	ScotRail	Mk 2 RFO
6703	Caledonian Sleeper	Mk 2 RFO
6704	ScotRail	Mk 2 RFO
6707	ScotRail	Mk 2 RFO
9448	West Coast Maroon	Mk 2 BSO
9497	Caledonian Sleeper	Mk 2 BSO
9500	InterCity	Mk 2 BSO
9513	InterCity	Mk 2 BSO
9800	Caledonian Sleeper	Mk 2 BUO
9801	ScotRail	Mk 2 BUO
9802	Caledonian Sleeper	Mk 2 BUO
9803	ScotRail	Mk 2 BUO
9804	ScotRail	Mk 2 BUO
9805	ScotRail	Mk 2 BUO
9806	ScotRail	Mk 2 BUO
9807	ScotRail	Mk 2 BUO
9808	ScotRail	Mk 2 BUO
9809	ScotRail	Mk 2 BUO
9810	ScotRail	Mk 2 BUO
10212	Virgin Silver	Mk 3 RFM
10229	Greater Anglia	Mk 3 RFM
10413	Greater Anglia	Mk 3 TSOB
10501	ScotRail	Mk 3 SLEP
10502	ScotRail	Mk 3 SLEP
10600	ScotRail	Mk 3 SLEP
10699	ScotRail	Mk 3 SLED
11078	Greater Anglia	Mk 3 FOD
12021	Greater Anglia	Mk 3 TSO
12098	Greater Anglia	Mk 3 TSO
92901	InterCity	Mk 1 BG
96371	Grey	Mk 3 GV
96374	Grey	Mk 3 GV

SRPS

Contact details

Website: www.srps.org.uk
Twitter: @srpsrailtours

Overview

Based at the Bo'ness & Kinneil Railway, the volunteer-led SRPS has long had its own rolling stock for its charter trains, operated first by BR and then more recently by private TOCs such as EWS, WCR and GBRf among others.

It generally has a rake of between 9-11 Mk 1s available for its own use and to hire to other promoters.

It also has 37403 *Isle of Mull*, which is fully main-line compliant (see page 359), and this has been hired to DRS and also used by GBRf.

Coaches

Present No	Livery	Type
1730	BR Maroon	Mk 1 RBR
1859	BR Maroon	Mk 1 RMB
3096	BR Maroon	Mk 1 FO
3115	BR Maroon	Mk 1 FO
3150	BR Maroon	Mk 1 FO
4215	BR Maroon	Mk 1 TSO
4831	BR Maroon	Mk 1 TSO
4832	BR Maroon	Mk 1 TSO
4836	BR Maroon	Mk 1 TSO
4856	BR Maroon	Mk 1 TSO
5028	BR Maroon	Mk 1 TSO
5157	BR Maroon	Mk 1 TSO
4856	BR Maroon	Mk 1 TSO
5412	BR Maroon	Mk 2 TSO
13229	BR Maroon	Mk 1 FK
13230	BR Maroon	Mk 1 FK
21241	BR Maroon	Mk 1 BCK
35185	BR Maroon	Mk 1 BSK

Belmond

Contact details

Website: www.belmond.com/uk
Twitter: @Belmond

Overview

Belmond is a global company but in the UK has two rail operations; the first being the British Pullman, which operates mostly from London on both repeat itinerary and ad hoc day trips. It is also available for hiring for corporate events.

It uses DB Cargo to haul this train, with two Class 67s, 67021/024, repainted to match the umber and cream coaches.

The second operation, the Royal Scotsman, operates each summer across Scotland, although it usually does an annual tour of the UK that brings it to England and Wales. This train is operated by GB Railfreight with two Class 66s, 665743/746, in matching livery.

British Pullman

These vehicles are based and maintained by Belmond at Stewarts Lane in London.

No.	Other No.	Livery	Type	Name
6313	92167	Umber/Cream	Mk 1 BG	
9502		Umber/Cream	Mk 2 BSO	
99530		Umber/Cream	Parlour First	PERSEUS
99531		Umber/Cream	Parlour First	PHOENIX
99532		Umber/Cream	Parlour First	CYGNUS
99534		Umber/Cream	Kitchen First	IBIS
99535		Umber/Cream	Parlour First	MINERVA
99536		Umber/Cream	Parlour First	ZENA
99537		Umber/Cream	Parlour First	AUDREY
99539		Umber/Cream	Kitchen First	IONE
99541		Umber/Cream	Parlour First	LUCILLE
99543		Umber/Cream	Parlour First	VERA
99545	35466	Umber/Cream	Mk 1 BSK	Baggage Car No. 11
99546		Umber/Cream	Kitchen First	GWEN

Royal Scotsman

These coaches are maintained by Assenta and housed at its Hamilton depot when not in use.

Present No.	Other Number	Livery	Type
99337		Maroon	PSK
99961		Maroon	State Car No. 1
99962		Maroon	State Car No. 2
99963		Maroon	State Car No. 3
99964		Maroon	State Car No. 4
99965		Maroon	Observation Car
99967		Maroon	Dining Car
99968	10541	Maroon	Mk 3 SLEP State Car No. 5
99969	10556	Maroon	Mk 3 SLEP Service Car

Bottom: No. 66746 leaves Aviemore on 10 May 2017 with the Royal Scotsman. *Anthony Hicks*

Right: Royal Scotsman State Car No. 1 near Carstairs on 22 May 2019. *Robin Ralston*

Below: The Royal Scotsman Observation Car near Drem on 5 September 2018. *Robin Ralston*

Main-line registered support coaches

A number of coaches are used as support vehicles mostly for steam locos. They are main-line registered and not used for carrying fare-paying passengers.

Present No	Other Number	Livery	Type	User
14007	17007	BR Maroon	Mk 1 BFK	NYMR
14060		BR Maroon	Mk 2 BFK	Bahamas Loco Society / 45596
14099	17099	BR Maroon	Mk 2 BFK	GCR (ex 45305 / 70013)
17096	14096	Umber / Cream	Mk 2 BFK	Stewarts Lane / 35028
21096		BR Maroon	Mk 1 BCK	A4 Loco Society / 60007
21249		BR Carmine / Cream	Mk 1 BCK	A1 Steam loco Trust / 60163
21268		BR Maroon	Mk 1 BCK	Peak Rail
35453		BR Chocolate / Cream	Mk 1 BSK	61306 Mayflower
35457		BR Maroon	Mk 1 BSK	NNR (ex 76084)
35479		BR Maroon	Mk 1 BSK	D Buck / 61306
35486		BR Maroon	Mk 1 BSK	J. Cameron / 60009
35508	17128	Maroon	Mk 1 BFK	I. Riley / 44871 / 45212 / 45407
35517	1708	BR Maroon	Mk 1 BFK	I. Riley / 44871 / 45212 / 45407
99041	35476	LMS Maroon	Mk 1 BSK	PRCLT MRC / 6233
99953	35468	BR Maroon	Mk 1 BSK	NRM York / 60103

Heritage railways' stock

In recent years, two heritage railways have extended their services to run on the national network on otherwise sparsely used lines. They started with the North Yorkshire Moors gaining access rights for the Battersby to Whitby section of the Esk Valley line. It typically runs just between Grosmont and Whitby using steam and heritage diesels but sometimes runs westwards to Battersby as well.

It has Class 25 D7628 (25278) (see page 358) for this role, but has also hired Class 20s and 31s from other operators, plus used preserved main-line diesels such as 40145, 50049, D1015 and 55022.

The North Norfolk Railway runs a few dining trains each year to Cromer. These are top-and-tailed by steam and diesel, and for this role 20227 is hired as it its main-line registered. Only approved coaches can be used for these two operations.

North Yorkshire Moors Railway

The following vehicles are main-line certified for use between Battersby and Whitby only.

Present No	Livery	Type	Status
3872	BR Maroon	Mk 1 TSO	
4000	BR Maroon	Mk 1 TSO	
4252	BR Carmine / Cream	Mk 1 TSO	
4290	BR Maroon	Mk 1 TSO	
4455	BR Maroon	Mk 1 TSO	
4817	BR Maroon	Mk 1 TSO	
5000	BR Maroon	Mk 1 TSO	
5029	BR Maroon	Mk 1 TSO	
9267	BR Maroon	Mk 1 TSO	(On loan to SDRT)
9274	BR Maroon	Mk 1 TSO	
16156	BR Carmine / Cream	Mk 1 TSO	

North Norfolk Railway

The following vehicles are main-line certified for use between Sheringham and Cromer only.

Present No	Livery	Type
1969	Crimson & Cream	Mk 1 RBR
3116	Crimson & Cream	Mk 1 FO
4372	Crimson & Cream	Mk 1 SO
81033	Crimson & Cream	Mk 1 BG

Royal Train

No.	Other No.	Converted	Intended use	Status
2903	11001	1977	The Queen's lounge, bedroom and bathroom	In service
2904	12001	1977	The Duke of Edinburgh's lounge, bedroom and bathroom	In service
2915	10735	1985	Royal Household sleeping car	In service
2916	40512	1986	Royal Family dining car with kitchen	In service
2917	40514	1986	Royal Household dining car with kitchen	In service
2918	40515	1986	Royal Household car	Stored
2919	40518	1986	Royal Household car	Stored
2920	14109, 17109	1986	Royal Household couchette, diesel generator & brake van	In service
2921	14107, 17107	1986	Royal Household couchette, kitchen & brake van	In service
2922		New 1987	The Prince of Wales's sleeping car	In service
2923		New 1987	The Prince of Wales's saloon	In service

Royal Household couchette, kitchen and brake van 2921 near Symington on 28 June 2019. *Robin Ralston*

The Prince of Wales's sleeping car 2922 near Symington on 28 June 2019. *Robin Ralston*

Royal Household couchette, diesel generator and brake van coach 2920 nears Symington, between Abington and Carstairs, on 28 June 2019. *Robin Ralston*

Railfreight Operators Overview

The railfreight market has changed immeasurably in recently years. The major player DB Cargo – which as EWS bought five of the six freight businesses back in 1996 – has lost much business and had to trim its fleet. It still remains the largest railfreight operator in the UK, but that may not be the case for too much longer.

Freightliner, now owned by American company Genesee & Wyoming, was that sixth business sold off in 1995, but has moved away from just being an intermodal operator and is now a big player in the bulk trainload market. Its biggest recent gain has been the operation of the stone trains from the Mendips for Aggregates Industries, which saw it take ownership of 14 Class 59s.

Possibly the biggest success story in the railfreight sector has been the birth and growth of GB Railfreight. A new company started in 1999 with just seven Class 66s and a single contract with Railtrack, it now has well over 150 locos in its fleet, 96 of them Class 66s as well as Class 47s, 60s, 73/9s and 92s. It is still actively expanding its fleet and 2021 should see its Class 69s take to the rails – rebuilt Class 56s.

Other recent new entrants are Colas Railfreight, DC Rail and Rail Operations Group and all three are growing their portfolios.

However, the railfreight market has been affected by the Covid pandemic, which has particularly affected intermodal traffic, a sector that DBC, Freightliner, GBRf and DRS all operate in.

No. 37175 passes Freshford with the 1126 Westbury-Westbury via Bristol Barton Hill IM train on 19 July 2018.
Glen Batten

Colas Rail Freight

Contact details

Website: www.colasrail.co.uk
Twitter: @ColasRailUK

Key personnel

Chief Executive Officer: Jean-Pierre Bertrand

Overview

Colas has grown steadily over the last decade and after starting UK operations with an initial fleet of just three Class 47s (all now sold to GB Railfreight), the company has a varied fleet of new Class 66s, 67s and 70s aided by several ex-BR Class 37 and 56s. It briefly had a fleet of ten Class 60s but these too are now part of the GBRf fleet.

The 37s and 67s are used mostly for Infrastructure Monitoring trains for Network Rail while the other locos are used for a mix of freight. Colas operates aggregates, fuel and metals traffic. It has recently taken two HST power cars for evaluation on IM trains.

Class 37

These locos are used mostly on IM trains but will support the business as required. Two locos, 37025/418, are on long-term hire. Nos 37418/421 have recently been on hire to Transport for Wales, but this work has now ended. All are in the COTS pool.

37025		BLL	STG	NE	*Inverness TMD*
37057		COL	COL	NE	
37099	37324	COL	COL	NE	*MERL EVANS 1947-2016*
37116		COL	COL	NE	
37175		COL	COL	NE	
37219		COL	COL	NE	*Jonty Jarvis 8-12-1998 to 18-3-2005*
37254		COL	COL	NE	*Cardiff Canton*
37418	37271	BLL	BEN	NE	*An Comunn Gaidhealach*
37421	37267	COL	COL	NE	

Class 43

Colas has taken two ex-EMT power cars to evaluate for IM train operation.

43050	COTS	EMT	POR	HQ
43060	COTS	EMT	POR	HQ

No. 66848 approaches Radley running light from Westbury to Oxford Hinksey on 10 September 2019.
Mark Pike

Class 56

These locos are used for heavy freight. No. 56051 had yet to return to traffic but was close to doing so until the Covid-19 pandemic.

56049		COFS	COL	BEA	NE	*Robin of Templecombe 1938-2013*
56051		COLS	COL	BEA	NE (U)	
56078		COFS	COL	BEA	NE	
56087		COFS	COL	BEA	NE	
56090		COFS	COL	BEA	NE	
56094		COFS	COL	BEA	NE	
56096		COFS	COL	BEA	NE	
56105		COFS	COL	BEA	NE	
56113		COFS	COL	BEA	NE	
56302	56124	COFS	COL	BEA	NE	*PECO The Railway Modeller 2016 70 years*

Class 66

These locos, formerly in use with Freightliner, are used for heavy trainload work. All are in the COLO pool.

66846	66573	COL	BEA	RU	
66847	66574	COL	BEA	RU	*Terry Baker*
66848	66575	COL	BEA	RU	
66849	66576	COL	BEA	RU	*Wylam Dilly*
66850	66577	COL	BEA	RU	*David Maidment OBE*

Class 67

These ex-DB Cargo locos are used for any IM trains that are required to operate at 100mph or faster. Both are in the COTS pool.

67023	COL	BEA	RU	*Charlotte*
67027	COL	BEA	RU	*Stella*

Class 70

Colas ordered two batches of Class 70s; the first comprised former demonstrator loco 70099 and the nine locos of the Freightliner option that was not taken up, while 70811-817 were ordered for business growth. All Colas 66, 67 and 70s are owned by Beacon Rail. All are in the COLO pool.

70801	70099	COL	BEA	CF
70802		COL	BEA	CF
70803		COL	BEA	CF
70804		COL	BEA	CF
70805		COL	BEA	CF
70806		COL	BEA	CF
70807		COL	BEA	CF
70808		COL	BEA	CF
70809		COL	BEA	CF
70810		COL	BEA	CF
70811		COL	BEA	CF
70812		COL	BEA	CF
70813		COL	BEA	CF
70814		COL	BEA	CF
70815		COL	BEA	CF
70816		COL	BEA	CF
70817		COL	BEA	CF

No. 67027 *Charlotte* and 67023 *Stella* work an 1150 Hull-Heaton Infrastructure Monitoring train past Barlby, near Selby, on 10 November 2019. *Anthony Hicks*

No. 70811 heads north along the S&C with the 0915 Mountsorrel-Carlisle, passing Selside, on 21 July 2020. *Anthony Hicks*

DC Rail

Contact details

Website: www.dcrail.com
Twitter: @DCRail2018

Key personnel

Managing Director: Garcia Hanson
Head of Engineering: Alan Lee

Overview

DC Rail has been operating for several years now but has always been a relatively small player in the railfreight market. However, it now has the backing of the Cappagh Group, which has seen it invest in four Class 60s that have been fully overhauled by DB Cargo at Toton and returned to traffic. The firm also has two Class 56s in its fleet. It has also hired 50008 on occasions from the firm's MD, Garcia Hanson.

It operates a number of bulk trainload flows and has invested in new aggregates wagons for these; flows include from Scunthorpe to London. DC Rail has also undertaken stock moves.

Class 56

Ex-EWS locos, both are in the DCRO pool.

56091	DCRO	DCN	DCR	LR	*Driver Wayne Gaskell The Godfather*
56103	DCRO	DCN	DCR	LR	

Class 60

DC Rail's parent company, Cappagh, has bought four Class 60s from DB Cargo, who then overhauled them for the company and they are all now in traffic. A fifth loco has been obtained for spares.

60028	DCRS	CAP	CAP	TO	
60029	DCRS	DCR	CAP	TO	*Ben Nevis*
60046	DCRS	DCR	CAP	TO	*William Wilberforce*
60055	DCRS	DCR	CAP	TO	*Thomas Barnardo*
60060	WQDA	TEW	CAP	TO (U)	

Of the four Class 60s recently overhauled for DC Rail, 60028 was painted in the livery of the company's owning group, Cappagh. It passes Attenborough on 6 August 2020. *Paul Robertson*

Nos 56091/103 work the empty 1351 Boston Sleaford Sidings-Carlisle Kingmoor VQ past Muston on 22 May 2019. *Bill Atkinson*

No. 60046 *William Wilberforce* hauls a rake of new JNA wagons past Great Hale Drove on 25 June 2020. *Bill Atkinson*

DB Cargo

Contact details

Website: https://uk.dbcargo.com
Twitter: @DBCargoUK

Key personnel

Chief Executive: Andrea Rossi
Chief Operating Officer: Dr Dirk Nolte

Overview

DB Cargo is the country's largest Railfreight operator, but from being the dominant player 25 years ago (as EWS) it has slowly seen its traffic levels reduced as other companies have taken work from it. Even the 280 new locos it ordered in 1996 have been trimmed to about 170.

However, with a fleet of overhauled 20-odd Class 60s, 160 Class 66s and a handful of active Class 67/90/92s, DB Cargo is still a big player on the UK Railfreight scene.

For the future, the company has publicly stated its intention to use more electric traction, which could see some of its long-withdrawn Class 90/92s returned to traffic.

The company also offers maintenance and repainting facilities for other operators at its main Toton base.

Left: In silver Drax livery, 60066 passes Attenborough on 25 March 2019 with an oil train from Humberside. *Paul Robertson*

Below: DB Cargo is slowly repainting its locos into its red livery. No. 66100 *Armistice 100* arrives at Onllwyn with empty HTAs forming the 0847 from Margam on 21 July 2020. The train would be loaded with coal for Immingham briquetting works. *Paul Shannon*

Class 60

EWS inherited the full ex-BR fleet of 100 Class 60s in 1996 and started withdrawing them from 2004. In recent times it has sold several locos to Colas, GBRf and DC Rail, while some have been sold for preservation and one, 60006, has now been scrapped, leaving it with 78 locos of which typically only 20 are in traffic at any one time. Any loco in the WQBA/WQCA/WQDA is unlikely to run again without major expenditure.

Those locos in traffic are used on any remaining heavy trainload flows in the DBC portfolio. No. 60074 *Luke* has recently been repainted into Puma Energy grey livery.

60001	WCAT	DBC	DBC	TO	
60003	WQDA	EWS	DBC	TY (U)	*Freight Transport Association*
60005	WQDA	EWS	DBC	TY (U)	
60007	WCBT	DBC	DBC	TO	*The Spirit of Tom Kendall*
60009	WQBA	EWS	DBC	C (U)	
60010	WCBT	DBC	DBC	TO	
60011	WCAT	DBC	DBC	TO	
60012	WQBA	EWS	DBC	TC (U)	
60013	WQDA	TEW	DBC	TC (U)	*Robert Boyle*
60015	WCBT	DBU	DBC	TO	
60017	WCBT	DBC	DBC	TO	
60018	WQDA	EWS	DBC	TY (U)	
60019	WCAT	DBC	DBC	TO	*Port of Grimsby & Immingham*
60020	WCBT	DBC	DBC	TO	*The Willows*
60022	WQDA	EWS	DBC	TO (U)	
60023	WQDA	EWS	DBC	TY (U)	
60024	WCAT	DBC	DBC	TO	*Clitheroe Castle*
60025	WQDA	EWS	DBC	TY (U)	
60027	WQDA	EWS	DBC	TY (U)	
60030	WQDA	EWS	DBC	TO (U)	
60031	WQDA	EWS	DBC	TY (U)	
60032	WQDA	TRN	DBC	TY (U)	
60033	WQCA	COR	DBC	TC (U)	*Tees Steel Express*
60034	WQBA	TEW	DBC	TO (U)	*Carnedd Llewelyn*
60035	WQBA	EWS	DBC	TO (U)	
60036	WQBA	EWS	DBC	TO (U)	*GEFCO*
60037	WQDA	EWS	DBC	TY (U)	
60038	WQCA	EWS	DBC	TO (U)	
60039	WCAT	DBC	DBC	TO	*Dove Holes*
60040	WCAT	DBC	DBC	TO	*The Territorial Army Centenary*
60041	WQCA	EWS	DBC	TC (U)	
60042	WQDA	EWS	DBC	TY (U)	
60043	WQBA	EWS	DBC	TO (U)	
60044	WCAT	DBC	DBC	TO	*Dowlow*
60045	WQBA	EWS	DBC	TC (U)	*The Permanent Way Institution*
60048	WQCA	EWS	DBC	TO (U)	
60049	WQBA	EWS	DBC	TO (U)	
60051	WQDA	EWS	DBC	TO (U)	
60052	WQDA	EWS	DBC	TO (U)	*Glofa Tŵr The last deep mine in Wales Tower Colliery*
60053	WQBA	EWS	DBC	TY (U)	

60054		WCBT	DBC	DBC	TO	
60057		WQBA	TEW	DBC	TO (U)	*Adam Smith*
60058		WQBA	EWS	DBC	TO (U)	
60059		WCBT	DBC	DBC	TO	*Swinden Dalesman*
60061		WQCA	TRN	DBC	TC (U)	
60062		WCAT	DBC	DBC	TO	*Stainless Pioneer*
60063		WCAT	DBC	DBC	TO	
60064		WQBA	TEW	DBC	TO (U)	*Back Tor*
60065		WCAT	EWS	DBC	TO	*Spirit Of Jaguar*
60066		WCAT	DRA	DBC	TO	
60067		WQBA	TEW	DBC	TY (U)	
60068		WQBA	TEW	DBC	TO (U)	
60069		WQBA	EWS	DBC	TC (U)	*Slioch*
60070		WQBA	TLH	DBC	TO (U)	
60071		WQBA	EWS	DBC	TO (U)	*Ribblehead Viaduct*
60072		WQBA	TEW	DBC	TC (U)	
60073		WQBA	TEW	DBC	TO (U)	*Cairn Gorm*
60074		WCAT	PUM	DBC	TO	*Luke*
60075		WQBA	EWS	DBC	TC (U)	
60077		WQBA	TEW	DBC	TC (U)	
60078		WQBA	MEW	DBC	TY (U)	
60079		WQBA	DBC	DBC	TO (U)	
60080		WQBA	EWS	DBC	TO (U)	
60082		WQBA	TEW	DBC	CE (U)	
60083		WQBA	EWS	DBC	TY (U)	
60084		WQBA	TEW	DBC	TC (U)	
60088		WQBA	TEW	DBC	TY (U)	
60089		WQBA	EWS	DBC	TY (U)	
60090		WQBA	TEW	DBC	TC (U)	
60091		WCBT	DBC	DBC	TO	*Barry Needham*
60092		WCBT	DBC	DBC	TO	
60093		WQBA	EWS	DBC	TY (U)	
60094		WQCA	EWS	DBC	TY (U)	*Rugby Flyer*
60097		WQBA	EWS	DBC	TY (U)	
60098		WQBA	EWS	DBC	TO (U)	
60099		WQBA	TAS	DBC	TO (U)	
60100		WCAT	DBC	DBC	TO	*Midland Railway - Butterley*
60500	60016	WQBA	EWS	DBC	TO (U)	

Two Class 67s are in Pullman umber and cream colours to match the VSOE coaches. No. 67021 stands at Salisbury with a Bath-bound Belmond Pullman on 6 December 2017. *Mark Pike*

Class 66

The first Class 66s are now over 20 years old. Of the 250 locos ordered by EWS and now passed over to DB Cargo, ten have been sold to GBRf and 75 have been redeployed with Euro Cargo Rail in France or DB Polska in Poland (see page 348). Five locos are now on long-term lease to DRS (and listed on page 283).

66001	WBAE	DBS	DBC	TO	
66002	WBAE	EWS	DBC	TO	
66003	WBAE	EWS	DBC	TO	
66004	WBAR	EWS	DBC	TO	
66005	WBAE	MRD	DBC	TO	*Maritime Intermodal One*
66006	WBAR	EWS	DBC	TO	
66007	WBAR	EWS	DBC	TO	
66009	WBAE	DBC	DBC	TO	
66011	WBAE	EWS	DBC	TO	
66012	WBAE	EWS	DBC	TO	
66013	WBAE	EWS	DBC	TO	
66014	WBAR	EWS	DBC	TO	
66015	WBAR	EWS	DBC	TO	
66017	WBAR	DBS	DBC	TO	
66018	WBAE	DBC	DBC	TO	
66019	WBAR	EWS	DBC	TO	
66020	WBAE	DBC	DBC	TO	
66021	WBAR	DBC	DBC	TO	
66023	WBAT	EWS	DBC	TO	
66024	WBAE	EWS	DBC	TO	
66025	WBAR	EWS	DBC	TO	
66027	WBAE	DBC	DBC	TO	
66030	WBAR	EWS	DBC	TO	
66034	WBAE	DBC	DBC	TO	
66035	WBAE	DBC	DBC	TO	*Resourceful*
66037	WBAR	EWS	DBC	TO	
66039	WBAE	EWS	DBC	TO	
66040	WBAR	EWS	DBC	TO	
66041	WBAR	DBC	DBC	TO	
66043	WQBA	EWS	DBC	TO (U)	
66044	WBAE	DBC	DBC	TO	
66047	WBAE	MRD	DBC	TO	*Maritime Intermodal Two*
66050	WBAE	EWS	DBC	TO	*EWS Energy*
66051	WBAR	MRD	DBC	TO	*Maritime Intermodal Four*
66053	WBAE	EWS	DBC	TO	
66054	WBAR	EWS	DBC	TO	
66055	WBLT	DBC	DBC	TO	*Alain Thauvette*
66056	WBLE	EWS	DBC	TO	
66057	WBLE	EWS	DBC	TO	
66059	WBLE	EWS	DBC	TO	
66060	WBAR	EWS	DBC	TO	
66061	WBAE	EWS	DBC	TO	
66063	WBAE	EWS	DBC	TO	

66065	WBAR	DBC	DBC	TO	
66066	WBAR	DBC	DBC	TO	*Geoff Spencer*
66067	WBAR	EWS	DBC	TO	
66068	WBAR	EWS	DBC	TO	
66069	WBAR	EWS	DBC	TO	
66070	WBAT	DBC	DBC	TO	
66074	WBAE	DBC	DBC	TO	
66075	WBAE	EWS	DBC	TO	
66076	WBAE	EWS	DBC	TO	
66077	WBAR	DBC	DBC	TO	*Benjamin Gimbert G.C.*
66078	WBAE	DBC	DBC	TO	
66079	WBAR	EWS	DBC	TO	*James Nightall G.C.*
66080	WBAE	EWS	DBC	TO	
66082	WBAE	DBC	DBC	TO	
66083	WBAR	EWS	DBC	TO	
66084	WBAR	EWS	DBC	TO	
66085	WBAR	DBC	DBC	TO	
66086	WBAE	EWS	DBC	TO	
66087	WBAE	EWS	DBC	TO	
66088	WBAE	EWS	DBC	TO	
66089	WBAR	EWS	DBC	TO	
66090	WBAE	MRD	DBC	TO	*Maritime Intermodal Six*
66092	WBAE	EWS	DBC	TO	
66093	WBAE	EWS	DBC	TO	
66094	WBAE	DBC	DBC	TO	
66095	WBAE	EWS	DBC	TO	
66096	WBAR	EWS	DBC	TO	
66097	WBAE	DBS	DBC	TO	
66098	WBAE	EWS	DBC	TO	
66099	WBBE	EWS	DBC	TO	
66100	WBBE	DBC	DBC	TO	*Armistice 100*
66101	WBBE	DBS	DBC	TO	
66102	WBBE	EWS	DBC	TO	
66103	WBBE	EWS	DBC	TO	
66104	WBBT	DBC	DBC	TO	
66105	WBAR	DBC	DBC	TO	
66106	WBBE	EWS	DBC	TO	
66107	WBBT	DBC	DBC	TO	
66109	WBAR	PDP	DBC	TO	*Teesport Express*
66110	WBBE	EWS	DBC	TO	
66111	WBBE	EWS	DBC	TO	
66112	WBBE	EWS	DBC	TO	
66113	WBBE	DBC	DBC	TO	
66114	WBBT	DBS	DBC	TO	
66115	WBAE	EWS	DBC	TO	
66116	WBAE	EWS	DBC	TO	
66117	WBAE	DBC	DBC	TO	
66118	WBAE	DBS	DBC	TO	
66119	WBAE	EWS	DBC	TO	

66120	WBAE	EWS	DBC	TO	
66121	WBAE	EWS	DBC	TO	
66124	WBAR	DBC	DBC	TO	
66125	WBAE	EWS	DBC	TO	
66127	WBAT	EWS	DBC	TO	
66128	WBAE	DBC	DBC	TO	
66129	WBAR	EWS	DBC	TO	
66130	WBAR	DBC	DBC	TO	
66131	WBAE	DBC	DBC	TO	
66133	WBAE	EWS	DBC	TO	
66134	WBAE	DBC	DBC	TO	
66135	WBAE	DBC	DBC	TO	
66136	WBAE	DBC	DBC	TO	
66137	WBRT	EWS	DBC	TO	
66138	WQBA	EWS	DBC	TO (U)	
66139	WBAE	EWS	DBC	TO	
66140	WBAE	EWS	DBC	TO	
66142	WBAR	MRD	DBC	TO	*Maritime Intermodal Three*
66143	WBRT	EWS	DBC	TO	
66144	WBAR	EWS	DBC	TO	
66145	WQBA	EWS	DBC	TO (U)	
66147	WBAE	EWS	DBC	TO	
66148	WBAE	MRD	DBC	TO	*Maritime Intermodal Seven*
66149	WBAE	DBC	DBC	TO	
66150	WBAE	DBC	DBC	TO	
66151	WBAE	EWS	DBC	TO	
66152	WBAE	DBS	DBC	TO	*Derek Holmes Railway Operator*
66154	WBAE	EWS	DBC	TO	
66155	WBAE	EWS	DBC	TO	
66156	WBAE	EWS	DBC	TO	
66158	WBAE	EWS	DBC	TO	
66160	WBAE	EWS	DBC	TO	
66161	WBAE	EWS	DBC	TO	
66162	WBAR	MRD	DBC	TO	*Maritime Intermodal Five*
66164	WBAE	EWS	DBC	TO	
66165	WBAR	DBC	DBC	TO	
66167	WBAE	DBC	DBC	TO	
66168	WBAR	EWS	DBC	TO	
66169	WBAR	EWS	DBC	TO	
66170	WBAE	EWS	DBC	TO	
66171	WBAR	EWS	DBC	TO	
66172	WBAE	EWS	DBC	TO	*Paul Mellany*
66174	WBAE	EWS	DBC	TO	
66175	WBAE	DBC	DBC	TO	*Rail Riders*
66176	WBAR	EWS	DBC	TO	
66177	WBAT	EWS	DBC	TO	
66181	WBAR	EWS	DBC	TO	
66182	WQAB	DBC	DBC	TO (U)	
66183	WBAE	EWS	DBC	TO	

66185	WBRT	DBS	DBC	TO	*DP World London Gateway*
66186	WBAE	EWS	DBC	TO	
66187	WBAE	EWS	DBC	TO	
66188	WBAR	EWS	DBC	TO	
66192	WBAR	DBC	DBC	TO	
66194	WBAR	EWS	DBC	TO	
66197	WBAE	EWS	DBC	TO	
66198	WBAR	EWS	DBC	TO	
66199	WBAE	EWS	DBC	TO	
66200	WBAE	EWS	DBC	TO	
66206	WBAR	DBC	DBC	TO	
66207	WBAE	EWS	DBC	TO	
66221	WBAR	EWS	DBC	TO	
66230	WQBA	DBC	DBC	TO (U)	

Class 67

Of the 30 Class 67s delivered in 1999/00, two have been sold to Colas Rail (now owned by Beacon Rail).

Several locos are now withdrawn from service following loss of contracts or introduction of new rolling stock. However, four locos are due to be used on long-term hire by Transport for Wales with 67008/014/017/025, now in TfW livery.

67001	WAAC	ARV	DBC	CE	
67002	WAAC	ARV	DBC	CE	
67003	WQBA	ARV	DBC	CE (U)	
67004	WQAB	DBC	DBC	CE (S)	
67005	WAAC	RTO	DBC	CE	*Queen's Messenger*
67006	WAAC	RTO	DBC	CE	*Royal Sovereign*
67007	WAAC	EWS	DBC	CE	
67008	WACC	TFW	DBC	CE	
67009	WQBA	EWS	DBC	CE (U)	
67010	WAAC	DBC	DBC	CE	
67011	WQBA	EWS	DBC	CE (U)	
67012	WAAC	CRS	DBC	CE	
67013	WAAC	DBC	DBC	CE	
67014	WACC	TFW	DBC	CE	
67015	WAAC	CRS	DBC	CE	
67016	WAAC	EWS	DBC	CE	
67017	WACC	TFW	DBC	CE	
67018	WQBA	DBS	DBC	CE (S)	*Keith Heller*
67019	WQBA	EWS	DBC	TO (U)	
67020	WAAC	EWS	DBC	CE	
67021	WAAC	PUL	DBC	CE	
67022	WQBA	EWS	DBC	CE (S)	
67024	WAAC	PUL	DBC	CE	
67025	WACC	TFW	DBC	CE	
67026	WQBA	JUB	DBC	CE (U)	*Diamond Jubilee*
67028	WAAC	DBC	DBC	CE	
67029	WQAB	DMS	DBC	CE (S)	*Royal Diamond*
67030	WQBA	EWS	DBC	CE (U)	

Class 90

EWS in inherited 25 Class 90s at privatisation but there is very limited work for them. A recent development was to have been the hiring of five locos for Grand Central for its Blackpool-Euston service and while the first there locos were prepared at Crewe EMD, the plan for the new operation has now been shelved.

A few other locos are used on WCML modal trains, although the company has stated publicly it wants to look at using more electric traction, which could see some more locos reinstated. Some, however, have been withdrawn for over 15 years now and could only return following major expenditure.

This locos in the WQAA pool, however, can be reactivated relatively quickly if required.

90017		WQBA	EWS	DBC	CE (U)	
90018		WQAB	DBS	DBC	CE (U)	*Pride of Bellshill*
90019		WEDC	DBC	DBC	CE	*Multimodal*
90020		WEDC	GCR	DBC	CE	
90021		WQAA	FIR	DBC	CE (U)	
90022	90222	WQBA	REW	DBC	CE (U)	*Freightconnection*
90023	90223	WQBA	RFE	DBC	CE (U)	
90024	90224	WEAC	MAA	DBC	CE	
90025	90125, 90225	WQBA	RFD	DBC	CE (U)	
90026	90126	WEDC	GCR	DBC	CE	
90027	90127, 90227	WQBA	RFD	DBC	CE (U)	*Allerton T&RS Depot*
90028	90128	WEDC	DBC	DBC	CE	*Sir William McAlpine*
90029	90129	WEDC	GCR	DBC	CE	
90030	90130	WQBA	EWS	DBC	CE (U)	
90031	90131	WQBA	EWS	DBC	CE (U)	*The Railway Children Partnership: Working for Street Children Worldwide*
90032	90132	WQBA	EWS	DBC	CE (U)	
90033	90133, 90233	WQBA	RFE	DBC	CE (U)	
90034	90134	WEDC	DRU	DBC	CE	
90035	90135	WEAC	DBC	DBC	CE	
90036	90136	WEDC	DBC	DBC	CE	*Driver Jack Mills*
90037	90137	WEAC	DBC	DBC	CE	*Christine*
90038	90138, 90238	WQBA	RFE	DBC	CE (U)	
90039	90139, 90239	WEDC	DBC	DBC	CE	
90040	90140	WQAA	DBC	DBC	CE(S)	
90050	90150	DHLT	TTG	ARV	CB (U)	

A few Class 90s are still in traffic with DB Cargo; 90018 heads south at Wandel, between Carstairs and Abington, on 9 July 2018 with the 1739 Mossend-Dagenham Dock empty car train. *Robin Ralston*

Class 92

A fleet that is now over 25 years old, the Class 92s have been woefully underused since day one. EWS inherited 30 locos and while it has redeployed some in Romania and Bulgaria – some of which have since been sold – it is still left with 18 locos for its Channel Tunnel operations, of which it is lucky to ever need more than five at any one time.

Locos in the WQAB and WQBA are unlikely to run again in the UK for DB Cargo any time soon.

92004	WQBA	EUE	DBC	CE (U)	*Jane Austen*
92007	WQBA	EUK	DBC	CE (U)	*Schubert*
92008	WQBA	EUE	DBC	CE (U)	*Jules Verne*
92009	WQBA	DBC	DBC	CE (U)	*Elgar*
92011	WFBC	EUE	DBC	CE	*Handel*
92013	WQBA	EUE	DBC	CE (U)	*Puccini*
92015	WFBC	DBC	DBC	CE	
92016	WQBA	DBC	DBC	CE (U)	
92017	WQBA	STO	DBC	CE (U)	*Bart the Engine*
92019	WFBC	EUE	DBC	CE	*Wagner*
92029	WQAB	EUE	DBC	CE (U)	*Dante*
92031	WQBA	DBC	DBC	CE (U)	*The Institute of Logistics & Transport*
92035	WQBA	EUK	DBC	CE (U)	*Mendelssohn*
92036	WFBC	EUE	DBC	CE	*Bertolt Brecht*
92037	WQBA	EUE	DBC	CE (U)	*Sullivan*
92041	WFBC	EUE	DBC	CE	*Vaughan Williams*
92042	WFBC	DBC	DBC	CE	

Left: Only a handful of DB Cargos 30 Class 92s remain with the company in the UK; 92042 arrives at Stafford with a test run from Crewe on 4 February 2016. *Mark Pike*

Below: DB Cargo operates a handful of mail trains using the Royal Mail's own Class 325 freight EMUs. Nos 325004/007 pass Wandel on the 1749 Shieldmuir-Warrington on 21 May 2019. *Robin Ralston*

Class 325

Four-car electric multiple units based on the Class 365 Networker units were acquired by Royal Mail – which still owns them – and are used for some WCML mail trains, running usually as 12-car sets. They are maintained and operated by DB Cargo. All are in the PPMB pool.

				DTPMV	MPMV	TPMV	DTPMV	
325001	ROM	ROM	CE	68300	68340	68360	68301	
325002	ROM	ROM	CE	68302	68341	68361	68303	
325003	ROM	ROM	CE	68304	68342	68362	68305	
325004	ROM	ROM	CE	68306	68343	68363	68307	
325005	ROM	ROM	CE	68308	68344	68364	68309	
325006	ROM	ROM	CE	68310	68345	68365	68311	
325007	ROM	ROM	CE	68312	68346	68366	68313	
325008	ROM	ROM	CE	68314	68347	68367	68315	*Peter Howarth CBE*
325009	ROM	ROM	CE	68316	68348	68368	68317	
325011	ROM	ROM	CE	68320	68350	68370	68321	
325012	ROM	ROM	CE	68322	68351	68371	68323	
325013	ROM	ROM	CE	68324	68352	68372	68325	
325014	ROM	ROM	CE	68326	68353	68373	68327	
325015	ROM	ROM	CE	68328	68354	68374	68329	
325016	ROM	ROM	CE	68330	68355	68375	68331	

DB Cargo Managers' train

This short train features a Driving Van Trailer and three Mk 3 coaches offering conference facilities and catering, and is used to take staff, customers and stakeholders to events and rail installations.

It runs with a Class 67 in push-pull mode. No. 67029 was the nominated loco and painted in the same silver to match the DVT – the coaches are maroon – but any push-pull fitted Class 67 can be used.

10211	DBM	DBC	TO	Mk 3 RFM
10546	DBM	DBC	TO	Mk 3 SLEP
11039	DBM	DBC	TO	Mk 3 FO
82146	DMS	DBC	TO	Driving van trailer

On 29 March 2019, 67029 *Royal Diamond* works the 1420 Wakefield Europorte-Peterborough DBC Company Train and passes Cromwell. *Bill Atkinson*

Direct Rail Services

Contact details

Website: www.directrailservices.com
Twitter: @DRSgovuk

Key personnel

Managing Director: Chris Connelly
Engineering Director: Alistair Brown

Overview

DRS was set up in 1995 to haul nuclear flask traffic, which it still operates today. It has diversified into freight with Intermodal, Network Services, infrastructure, passenger hire and charter operations added to its portfolio.

The majority of the firm's flows are operated using Class 66, 68 and 88 locos but the firm also retain a fleet of Class 37s and 57s, both with and without train supply.

It supplies Class 68s to both Chiltern Railways (68008-015) and Transpennine Express (68019-034) for passenger operations. It also supplies four Class 57/3s (57304/307-309) to Avanti West Coast for Thunderbird duties on the WCML.

It recently took five Class 66s from DB Cargo on long-term hire with an option for five more that has yet to be taken up. The last of its Class 20s were retired from front-line service in January 2020 and will be disposed of shortly.

The firm issued a tender for ten new locomotives some time ago, but as yet no orders have been placed.

No. 37402 *Stephen Middlemore* works the 0857 York Holgate-Stowmarket RHTT move past Sleaford North Junction on 3 September 2019. *Bill Atkinson*

Class 20

The locos that started the DRS operation, a handful of the elderly Type 1s had been retained for RHTT operations until autumn 2019. The remaining locos are all in store and are to be sold.

20301	20047	XHHP	DRC	DRS	BH (U)	
20302	20084	XHHP	DRC	DRS	BKR (S)	
20303	20127	XHHP	DRC	DRS	YK (U)	*Max Joule 1958-1999*
20304	20120	XHHP	DRC	DRS	BH (U)	
20305	20095	XHHP	DRC	DRS	BKR (S)	
20308	20187	XHHP	DRC	DRS	BH (U)	
20309	20075	XHHP	DRC	DRS	BH (U)	
20312	20042	XHHP	DRC	DRS	BH (U)	

Class 37

DRS bought its first Class 37s in 1997 and has slowly been building up its fleet. That said, withdrawals are now happening although some will be retained for charters, IM trains and other duties.

Class 37/0

Original locos with main generators. All have modified cabs.

37038		XHNC	DRN	DRS	KM
37059		XHNC	DRN	DRS	KM
37069		XHNC	DRN	DRS	KM
37218		XHNC	DRN	DRS	KM
37259	37380	XHSS	DRC	DRS	KM (S)

Class 37/4

Refurbished locos fitted with electric train supply. These locos are used for saloon, charter, RHTT, snowplough and IM work, plus any passenger hire contracts. No. 37423 has a modified cab,

37401	37268	XHAC	BLL	DRS	KM	*Mary Queen of Scots*
37402	37274	XHAC	BLL	DRS	KM	*Stephen Middlemore 23.12.1954 – 8.6.2013*
37405	37282	XMAC	DRC	DRS	KM	
37407	37305	XHAC	BLL	DRS	KM	*Blackpool Tower*
37409	37270	XHSS	BLL	DRS	KM (S)	*Lord Hinton*
37419	37291	XHAC	ICM	DRS	KM	*Carl Haviland 1954-2012*
37422	37266	XHAC	DRU	DRS	KM	
37423	37296	XHAC	DRX	DRS	KM	*Spirit of the Lakes*
37424	37279	XHAC	BLL	DRS	KM	*Avro Vulcan XH558*
37425	37292	XHAC	REG	DRS	KM	*Sir Robert McAlpine/Concrete Bob*

Class 37/6

Locos converted initially for use by Eurostar but all sold to DRS, although some have since been sold to other operators. They were originally fitted with through ETS wiring, but this has been removed. Nos 37602/605/0609/609 have modified cabs.

37602	37082, 37502	XHHP	DRC	DRS	ZG (U)
37603	37039, 37604	XHHP	DRC	DRS	LT (U)
37604	37007, 37506	XHHP	DRC	DRS	LT (U)
37605	37036, 37507	XHHP	DRC	DRS	DF (U)
37606	37090, 37508	XHHP	DRC	DRS	CB (U)
37609	37115, 37514	XHHP	DRN	DRS	LT (U)

Class 37/7

Refurbished loco fitted with ballast weights and no train heating.

37716	37094	XHNC	DRN	DRS	KM

Class 57

Re-engineered Class 47s fitted with General Motors engines.

Class 57/0

Original ex-Freightliner locos without train heating.

57002	47322	XHCK	DRN	DRS	KM	*Rail Express*
57003	47317	XHCK	DRN	DRS	KM	
57004	47347	XHHP	DRC	DRS	LT (S)	
57007	47332	XHSS	DRN	DRS	KM (S)	*John Scott 12.5.45-22.5.12*
57008	47060	XHHP	DRC	DRS	LT (S)	
57009	47079	XHHP	DRC	DRS	LT (S)	
57010	47231	XHHP	DRN	DRS	LT (S)	
57011	47329	XHPP	DRC	DRS	LT (U)	
57012	47204	XHHP	DRC	DRS	LT (S)	

Class 57/3

ETH locos originally built for Virgin West Coast to act as Thunderbird rescue locos, and all modified to have retractable Dellner couplers fitted. Those locos in the XHVT pool remain as WCML standby locos. No. 57306 is often spot-hired to FGW while 57301/305/310/312 are sub-leased to Rail Operations Group (see page 305).

57302	47251, 47589, 47827	XHSS	DRC	DRS	ZG (S)	*Chad Varah*
57303	47554, 47705	XHSS	DRN	POR	KM (U)	*Pride of Carlisle*
57304	47055, 47652, 47807	XHVT	DRN	DRS	KM	*Pride of Cheshire*
57306	47242, 47659, 47814	XHAC	DRN	POR	KM	*Her Majesty's Railway Inspectorate 175*
57307	47225	XHVT	DRN	DRS	KM	*Lady Penelope*
57308	47091, 47647, 47846	XHVT	DRN	DRS	KM	*James Ferguson*
57309	47254, 47651, 47806	XHVT	DRN	DRS	KM	*Pride of Crewe*
57311	47032, 47662, 47817	XHSS	DRC	DRS	BO (S)	*Thunderbird*

No. 68004 *Rapid* stabled at Derby on 11 February 2016. *Mark Pike*

Class 66

DRS ordered three batches of ten Class 66s before returning its first ten locos and ordering four more to give it a fleet of 24. Since then 66411-420 have been returned to their ROSCOs but the five ex-Fastline Freight Class 66/3s were taken on by the company to give it its current fleet of 19 locos, now supplemented by five 66/0s on long-term hire from DB Cargo and in the process of being repainted, although they are not being renumbered.

Class 66/0

Locos on long-term hire from DB Cargo. Those in EWS colours will be repainted soon.

66031	XHIM	EWS	DBC	KM
66091	XHIM	DRX	DBC	KM
66108	XHIM	EWS	DBC	KM
66122	XHIM	EWS	DBC	KM
66126	XHIM	EWS	DBC	KM

Class 66/3

Former Fastline Freight locos. Fitted with RETB.

66301	XHIM	DRX	BEA	KM	*Kingmoor TMD*
66302	XHIM	DRX	BEA	KM	*Endeavour*
66303	XHIM	DRX	BEA	KM	
66304	XHIM	DRX	BEA	KM	
66305	XHIM	DRX	BEA	KM	

DRS

Class 66/4

The original third and fourth batches of Class 66s ordered by DRS in 2007 and 2008 respectively.

66421	XHIM	DRX	MAQ	KM	*Gresty Bridge TMD*
66422	XHIM	DRX	MAQ	KM	
66423	XHIM	DRX	MAQ	KM	
66424	XHIM	DRX	MAQ	KM	
66425	XHIM	DRX	MAQ	KM	
66426	XHIM	DRX	MAQ	KM	
66427	XHIM	DRX	MAQ	KM	
66428	XHIM	DRX	MAQ	KM	*Carlisle Eden Mind*
66429	XHIM	DRX	MAQ	KM	
66430	XHIM	DRX	MAQ	KM	
66431	XHIM	DRX	MAQ	KM	
66432	XHIM	DRX	MAQ	KM	
66433	XHIM	DRX	MAQ	KM	
66434	XHIM	DRX	MAQ	KM	

No. 57304 *Pride of Cheshire* approaches Basingstoke with an Eastleigh to Willesden wagon move on 23 December 2015. *Mark Pike*

Showing off the latest, plain, DRS blue livery, 66431 passes Ilkeston on 7 May 2020. *Paul Robertson*

Class 68

The first 15 of these Caterpillar-engined, Vossloh-designed Bo-Bo locos were built in Spain but the remaining 19 locos were built by Stadler (which acquired Vossloh). Fitted with electric train supply. Nos 68008-015 are dedicated for use by Chiltern Railways and 68019-034 likewise for Transpennine Express, and all have push-pull capability. When not in use with these TOCs, they may appear on general DRS duties.

68001	XHVE	DRN	BEA	CR	*Evolution*
68002	XHVE	DRN	BEA	CR	*Intrepid*
68003	XHVE	DRN	BEA	CR	*Astute*
68004	XHVE	DRN	BEA	CR	*Rapid*
68005	XHVE	DRN	BEA	CR	*Defiant*
68006	XHVE	DRX	BEA	CR	*Daring*
68007	XHVE	DRX	BEA	CR	*Valiant*
68008	XHVE	DRN	BEA	CR	*Avenger*
68009	XHVE	DRN	BEA	CR	*Titan*
68010	XHCE	CRS	BEA	CR	*Oxford Flyer*
68011	XHCE	CRS	BEA	CR	
68012	XHCE	CRS	BEA	CR	
68013	XHCE	CRS	BEA	CR	
68014	XHCE	CRS	BEA	CR	
68015	XHCE	CRS	BEA	CR	
68016	XHVE	DRN	BEA	CR	*Fearless*
68017	XHVE	DRN	BEA	CR	*Hornet*
68018	XHVE	DRN	BEA	CR	*Vigilant*
68019	TPEX	TPE	BEA	CR	*Brutus*
68020	TPEX	TPE	BEA	CR	*Reliance*
68021	TPEX	TPE	BEA	CR	*Tireless*
68022	TPEX	TPE	BEA	CR	*Resolution*
68023	TPEX	TPE	BEA	CR	*Achilles*
68024	TPEX	TPE	BEA	CR	*Centaur*
68025	TPEX	TPE	BEA	CR	*Superb*
68026	TPEX	TPE	BEA	CR	*Enterprise*
68027	TPEX	TPE	BEA	CR	*Splendid*
68028	TPEX	TPE	BEA	CR	*Lord President*
68029	TPEX	TPE	BEA	CR	*Courageous*
68030	TPEX	TPE	BEA	CR	*Black Douglas*
68031	TPEX	TPE	BEA	CR	*Felix*
68032	TPEX	TPE	BEA	CR	*Destroyer*
68033	XHVE	DRN	DRS	CR	
68034	XHVE	DRN	DRS	CR	

Electro-diesel 88007 *Electra* works the 0624 Daventry-Mossend past Beckfoot on 25 June 2020. *Anthony Hicks*

Class 88

Electro diesel versions of the Stadler Class 68 fitted with electric train supply and used mostly for intermodal traffic on the WCML.

88001	XHVE	DRE	BEA	CR	*Revolution*	88006	XHVE	DRE	BEA	CR	*Juno*
88002	XHVE	DRE	BEA	CR	*Prometheus*	88007	XHVE	DRE	BEA	CR	*Electra*
88003	XHVE	DRE	BEA	CR	*Genesis*	88008	XHVE	DRE	BEA	CR	*Ariadne*
88004	XHVE	DRE	BEA	CR	*Pandora*	88009	XHVE	DRE	BEA	CR	*Diana*
88005	XHVE	DRE	BEA	CR	*Minerva*	88010	XHVE	DRE	BEA	CR	*Aurora*

Coaches

DRS has several Mk 2 coaches but following the end of their passenger contracts with ScotRail, Greater Anglia and Northern, these are all currently in warm store.

It also owns four Mk 2 coaches used as escort vehicles for some nuclear trains. Four coaches were briefly on hire to Loram and reliveried in its colours.

No	Livery	Type			
5810	Loram	Mk 2 TSO	6173	DRS Blue	Mk 2 TSO
5919	Loram	Mk 2 TSO	6177	ScotRail Saltire	Mk 2 TSO
5937	DRS Blue	Mk 2 TSO	6183	ScotRail Saltire	Mk 2 TSO
5945	ScotRail Saltire	Mk 2 TSO	9419	DRS Blue	Mk 2 Escort coach
5955	ScotRail Saltire	Mk 2 TSO	9428	DRS Blue	Mk 2 Escort coach
5965	ScotRail Saltire	Mk 2 TSO	9488	ScotRail Saltire	Mk 2 BSO
5971	DRS Blue	Mk 2 TSO	9506	DRS Blue	Mk 2 Escort coach
5976	ScotRail Saltire	Mk 2 TSO	9508	DRS Blue	Mk 2 Escort coach
5987	ScotRail Saltire	Mk 2 TSO	9521	DRS Blue	Mk 2 BSO
5995	DRS Blue	Mk 2 TSO	9525	Loram	Mk 2 BSO
6001	DRS Blue	Mk 2 TSO	9527	ScotRail Saltire	Mk 2 BSO
6008	DRS Blue	Mk 2 TSO	9539	ScotRail Saltire	Mk 2 BSO
6027	ScotRail Saltire	Mk 2 TSO	9704	DRS Blue	Mk 2 DBSO
6046	Loram	Mk 2 TSO	9705	DRS Blue	Mk 2 DBSO
6064	DRS Blue	Mk 2 TSO	9707	DRS Blue	Mk 2 DBSO
6117	DRS Blue	Mk 2 TSO	9709	DRS Blue	Mk 2 DBSO
6122	DRS Blue	Mk 2 TSO	9710	DRS Blue	Mk 2 DBSO
6137	ScotRail Saltire	Mk 2 TSO	9713	Anglia Railways	Mk 2 DBSO

Freightliner

Contact details

Website: www.freightliner.co.uk
Twitter: @RailFreight

Key personnel

Managing Director: Neil McNicholas
Engineering & Operations Services Director: Tim Shakerley

Overview

One of the original six former British Rail freight operations sold in the mid-1990s, Freightliner was a management buyout and the only FOC not bought by WCTC. Initially just an intermodal operator, it has diversified and expanded and now operates bulk trainloads in many markets.

It initially relied on a fleet of Class 66s, which at one time reached 130 locos, but several have since been redeployed in Poland or returned to their ROSCOs. It acquired 20 Class 70s, of which only 19 were delivered successfully, and recently has acquired 14 Class 59s having won the contract for haulage of the Mendip stone trains. It owns one Class 47 used for route learning.

Until recently, its electric fleet was a mix of elderly Class 86s dating from 1965 and ten newer Class 90s dating from 1990. In the last year it has acquired 13 former Greater Anglia Class 90s, which will replace Class 86s, although some of these older locos will be retained while the 90s are overhauled and could be kept in reserve to boost traffic growth.

Class 08

Several Class 08s are retained for depot and terminal shunting.

08530	DDIN	FLR	POR	SM	
08531	DDIN	FPH	POR	FX	
08575	DHLT	FLR	POR	LH (U)	
08585	DDIN	FLR	POR	SM	*Vicky*
08624	DDIN	FPH	POR	FX	*Rambo Paul Ramsey*
08691	DDIN	FLG	FLI	LH	*Terri*
08785	DDIN	FLR	POR	TP	
08891	DHLT	FLR	POR	ZG (U)	

Class 47

Freightliner's once-sizeable Class 47 fleet is now reduced to a single loco used mostly for route learning.

47830	47061, 47649	DFLH	GYP	FLI	CB	*Beeching's Legacy*

Class 59

The Class 59/0s were originally ordered by Foster Yeoman and operated by BR and then EWS/DB Cargo. No. 59003 was moved to Germany but bought by GBRf in 2014.

The 59/1s were originally Amey Roadstone locos later absorbed into Aggregates Industries fleet along with the other 59s.

The 59/2s were ordered by National Power and delivered in 1995 but sold to EWS in 1998. All 14 locos are now in the DFHG pool.

Class 59/0

Former Foster Yeoman locos, 59003 is owned by GBRf.

59001	AGI	FHH	MD	*Yeoman Endeavour*
59002	AGI	FHH	MD	*Alan J Day*
59004	AGI	FHH	MD	*Paul A Hammond*
59005	AGI	FHH	MD	*Kenneth J Painter*

Class 59/1

Former ARC locos

59101	HAN	FHH	MD	*Village of Whatley*
59102	HAN	FHH	MD	*Village of Chantry*
59103	HAN	FHH	MD	*Village of Mells*
59104	HAN	FHH	MD	*Village of Great Elm*

Class 59/2

Former National Power/EWS locos

59201	DBC	FHH	MD	
59202	DBC	FHH	MD	*Alan Meadows Taylor MD Mendip Rail Limited*
59203	GWD	FHH	MD	
59204	DBC	FHH	MD	
59205	DBC	FHH	MD	
59206	GWD	FHH	MD	*John F Yeoman Rail Pioneer*

Class 66

The Class 66/5 and 66/6s were the original Freightliner orders, while the 66/4s are former DRS locos taken on when they became available. The 66/6s are regeared for heavy freight.

Class 66/4

Former DRS locos, three of which have been redeployed in Poland.

66413	DFIN	GWO	MAQ	LD	*Lest We Forget*
66414	DFIN	FPH	MAQ	LD	
66415	DFIN	GWD	MAQ	LD	*You Are Never Alone*
66416	DFIN	FPH	MAQ	LD	
66418	DFIN	FPH	MAQ	LD	*Patriot – In Memory Of Fallen Railway Employees*
66419	DFIN	GWD	MAQ	LD	
66420	DFIN	FPH	MAQ	LD	

No. 66587 *As One We Can* has been painted in a striking pink customer livery for ONE. On 28 August 2019 it passes Stanton Gate. *Paul Robertson*

Heavy Haul 66615 works the 0659 Tunstead-Peterborough aggregates past Uffington (Lincolnshire) on 31 August 2018. *Bill Atkinson*

Class 66/5

Freightliner's standard locos were ordered in multiple batches from 1999 to 2008 and several have since been redeployed in Poland.

66501	DFIM	FLR	POR	LD	*Japan 2001*
66502	DFIM	FLR	POR	LD	*Basford Hall Centenary 2001*
66503	DFIM	GWD	POR	LD	*The Railway Magazine*
66504	DFIM	FPH	POR	LD	
66505	DFIM	FLR	POR	LD	
66506	DFIM	FLR	EVS	LD	*Crewe Regeneration*
66507	DFIM	FLR	EVS	LD	
66508	DFIM	FLR	EVS	LD	
66509	DFIM	FLR	EVS	LD	
66510	DFIM	FLR	EVS	LD	
66511	DFIM	FLR	EVS	LD	
66512	DFIM	FLR	EVS	LD	
66513	DFIM	FLR	EVS	LD	
66514	DFIM	FLR	EVS	LD	
66515	DFIM	FLR	EVS	LD	
66516	DFIM	FLR	EVS	LD	
66517	DFIM	FLR	EVS	LD	
66518	DFIM	FLR	EVS	LD	
66519	DFIM	FLR	EVS	LD	
66520	DFIM	FLR	EVS	LD	
66522	DFIM	FLR	EVS	LD	
66523	DFIM	FLR	EVS	LD	
66524	DFIM	FLR	EVS	LD	
66525	DFIM	FLR	EVS	LD	
66526	DFIM	FLR	EVS	LD	*Driver Steve Dunn (George)*
66528	DFIM	FPH	POR	LD	*Madge Elliot MBE Borders Railway Opening 2015*
66529	DFIM	FLR	POR	LD	
66531	DFIM	FLR	POR	LD	
66532	DFIM	FLR	POR	LD	*P&O Nedlloyd Atlas*
66533	DFIM	FLR	POR	LD	*Hanjin Express/Senator Express*
66534	DFIM	FLR	POR	LD	*OOCL Express*
66536	DFIM	FLR	POR	LD	
66537	DFIM	FLR	POR	LD	
66538	DFIM	FLR	EVS	LD	
66539	DFIM	FLR	EVS	LD	
66540	DFIM	FLR	EVS	LD	*Ruby*
66541	DFIM	FLR	EVS	LD	
66542	DFIM	FLR	EVS	LD	
66543	DFIM	FLR	EVS	LD	
66544	DFIM	FLR	EVS	LD	
66545	DFIM	FLR	POR	LD	
66546	DFIM	FLR	POR	LD	
66547	DFIM	FLR	POR	LD	
66548	DFIM	FLR	POR	LD	
66549	DFIM	FLR	POR	LD	

66550	DFIM	FLR	POR	LD	
66551	DFIM	FLR	POR	LD	
66552	DFIM	FLR	POR	LD	*Maltby Raider*
66553	DFIM	FLR	POR	LD	
66554	DFIM	FLR	EVS	LD	
66555	DFIM	FLR	EVS	LD	
66556	DFIM	FLR	EVS	LD	
66557	DFIM	FLR	EVS	LD	
66558	DFIM	FLR	EVS	LD	
66559	DFIM	FLR	EVS	LD	
66560	DFIM	FLR	EVS	LD	
66561	DFIM	FLR	EVS	LD	
66562	DFIM	FLR	EVS	LD	
66563	DFIM	FLR	EVS	LD	
66564	DFIM	FLR	EVS	LD	
66565	DFIM	FLR	EVS	LD	
66566	DFIM	FLR	EVS	LD	
66567	DFIM	FLR	EVS	LD	
66568	DFIM	FLR	EVS	LD	
66569	DFIM	FLR	EVS	LD	
66570	DFIM	FLR	EVS	LD	
66571	DFIM	FLR	EVS	LD	
66572	DFIM	FLR	EVS	LD	
66585	DFIN	FLR	MAQ	LD	
66587	DFIN	ONE	MAQ	LD	*AS ONE, WE CAN*
66588	DFIN	FLR	MAQ	LD	
66589	DFIN	FLR	MAQ	LD	
66590	DFIN	FLR	MAQ	LD	
66591	DFIN	FLR	MAQ	LD	
66592	DFIN	FLR	MAQ	LD	*Johnson Stevens Agencies*
66593	DFIN	FLR	MAQ	LD	*3MG MERSEY MULTIMODAL GATEWAY*
66594	DFIN	FLR	MAQ	LD	*NYK Spirit of Kyoto*
66596	DFIN	FLR	BEA	LD	
66597	DFIN	FLR	BEA	LD	*Viridor*
66598	DFIN	FLR	BEA	LD	
66599	DFIN	FLR	BEA	LD	

No. 70020 passes Shipley Gate on the Erewash Valley on 3 December 2019. *Paul Robertson*

Class 66/6

Regeared locos for heavy trainload haulage. Some have been redeployed in Poland.

66601	DFHH	FLR	POR	LD	*The Hope Valley*
66602	DFHH	FLR	POR	LD	
66603	DFHH	FLR	POR	LD	
66604	DFHH	FLR	POR	LD	
66605	DFHH	FLR	POR	LD	
66606	DFHH	FLR	POR	LD	
66607	DFHH	FLR	POR	LD	
66610	DFHH	FLR	POR	LD	
66613	DFHH	FLR	EVS	LD	
66614	DFHH	FLR	EVS	LD	*1916 Poppy 2016*
66615	DFHH	FLR	EVS	LD	
66616	DFHH	FLR	EVS	LD	
66617	DFHH	FLR	EVS	LD	
66618	DFHH	FLR	EVS	LD	*Railways Illustrated Annual Photographic Awards Alan Barnes*
66619	DFHH	FLR	EVS	LD	*Derek W. Johnson MBE*
66620	DFHH	FLR	EVS	LD	
66621	DFHH	FLR	EVS	LD	
66622	DFHH	FLR	EVS	LD	
66623	DFHH	GWD	MAQ	LD	

Freightliner has taken 13 ex-Greater Anglia 90s into its fleet and they are entering traffic. No. 90014 was the first to be repainted and was named *Over the Rainbow*. *Freightliner*

Class 70

General Electric heavy freight locos built in Pennsylvania. Originally an option for ten more was included in the original deal, but not exercised after poor initial reliability. No. 70012 never made it to the Freightliner fleet after the loco was dropped during unloading at Newport Docks, severely damaging it. It was returned to the United Sates and is now used as a test bed loco. Many locos are stored.

70001	DFGI	FPH	MAQ	LD	*PowerHaul*
70002	DFGI	FPH	MAQ	LD	
70003	DFGI	FPH	MAQ	LD	
70004	DHLT	FPH	MAQ	CB (U)	*The Coal Industry Society*
70005	DFGI	FPH	MAQ	LD	
70006	DFGI	FPH	MAQ	LD	
70007	DFGI	FPH	MAQ	LD	
70008	DFGI	FPH	MAQ	LD	
70009	DHLT	FPH	MAQ	LD	
70010	DFGI	FPH	MAQ	LD	
70011	DHLT	FPH	MAQ	LD (U)	
70013	DHLT	FPH	MAQ	LD (U)	
70014	DHLT	FPH	MAQ	CB (S)	
70015	DFGI	FPH	MAQ	LD	
70016	DFGI	FPH	MAQ	LD	
70017	DFGI	FPH	MAQ	LD	
70018	DHLT	FPH	MAQ	LD (U)	
70019	DHLT	FPH	MAQ	LD	
70020	DFGI	FPH	MAQ	LD (S)	

Class 86

Ex-BR 25kV AC electric locos that have been the mainstay of the Freightliner intermodal operations under the wires for 25 years. Now being replaced by Class 90s and retired from traffic. No. 86251 is a source of spares only and has never run for the company.

86251		VIR	EPEX	FLI	CB (U)
86604	86004, 86404	FLH	DFNC	FLI	CB
86605	86005, 86405	FLH	DHLT	FLI	CB (U)
86607	86007, 86407	FLH	DFNC	FLI	CB
86608	86008, 86408, 86501	FLH	DFNC	FLI	CB
86609	86009, 86409	FLH	DFNC	FLI	CB
86610	86010, 86410	FLH	DHLT	FLI	CB (U)
86612	86012, 86312, 86412	FLH	DHLT	FLI	CB (U)
86613	86013, 86313, 86413	FLH	DFNC	FLI	CB
86614	86014, 86314, 86414	FLH	DHLT	FLI	CB (U)
86622	86022, 86322, 86422	FPH	DFNC	FLI	CB
86627	86027, 86327, 86427	FLH	DHLT	FLI	CB (U)
86628	86028, 86328, 86428	FLH	DHLT	FLI	CB (U)
86632	86032, 86432	FLH	DFNC	FLI	CB
86637	86037, 86437	FPH	DFNC	FLI	CB
86638	86038, 86438	FLH	DFNC	FLI	CB
86639	86039, 86439	FLH	DFNC	FLI	CB

Class 90

Given there were not enough 90s to go round at privatisation, Freightliner has had to wait for 25 years for a fleet of ex-Virgin / Anglia locos to become available to supplement its original ten-strong fleet. No. 90016 was a direct replacement for 90050 in 2004.

90003		DFLC	AGA	POR	CB	
90004		DFLC	AGA	POR	CB	*City of Chelmsford*
90005		DFLC	AGA	POR	CB	*Vice-Admiral Lord Nelson*
90006		DFLC	AGA	POR	CB	*Roger Ford/Modern Railways Magazine*
90007		DFLC	AGA	POR	CB	*Sir John Betjeman*
90008		DFLC	AGA	POR	CB	*The East Anglian*
90009		DFLC	AGA	POR	CB	
90010		DFLC	AGA	POR	CB	
90011		DFLC	AGA	POR	CB	*East Anglian Daily Times Suffolk & Proud*
90012		DFLC	AGA	POR	CB	*Royal Anglian Regiment*
90013		DFLC	AGA	POR	CB	
90014		DFLC	GWD	POR	CB	*Over The Rainbow*
90015		DFLC	AGA	POR	CB	*Colchester Castle*
90016		DFLC	FLR	POR	CB	
90041	90141	DFLC	FLR	POR	CB	
90042	90142	DFLC	FPH	POR	CB	
90043	90143	DFLC	FPH	POR	CB	
90044	90144	DFLC	GWD	POR	CB	
90045	90145	DFLC	FPH	POR	CB	
90046	90146	DFLC	FLR	POR	CB	
90047	90147	DFLC	GWD	POR	CB	
90048	90148	DFLC	FLG	POR	CB	
90049	90149	DFLC	FPH	POR	CB	

Class 86s are being phased out; 86613/628 head south at Wandel on the 1814 Coatbridge-Crewe container train on 9 July 2018. *Robin Ralston*

GB Railfreight

Contact details

Website: www.gbrailfreight.com
Twitter: @GBRailfreight

Key personnel

Managing Director: John Smith
Engineering Director: Bob Tiller

Overview

Although still regarded as a 'newcomer' to the scene, the reality is GBRf has been operating for over 20 years now and had grown rapidly due to shrewd management, a 'can do' attitude and innovative management.

It has grown from a fleet of just seven new Class 66s to a fleet of over 150 locos of various types. Staff levels are now over 600.

GB Railfreight is now the third largest railfreight operator in the UK, with a turnover in excess of £200m. It is one of the fastest-growing companies in the railway sector and transports goods for a wide range of customers.

The company operates freight trains in many markets across the country, especially in the intermodal, infrastructure, aggregates and coal sectors,

As well as operating freight, the company also has contracts to operate the Caledonian Sleeper passenger operation, supplying its own locos (Class 73/9s and 92s) to haul CS's CAF Mk 5 coaches. It also undertakes stock moves for ROSCOs and TOCs either using its own locos to haul the trains or to provide drivers to move the units under their own power.

It also has a nationwide charter licence and operates the Royal Scotsman luxury train each summer.

GBRf relies mostly on Class 66s for the majority of its operations, with Class 73s – both original and rebuilt 73/9s – for infrastructure and test train work.

It has a small fleet of three Class 47s for moving multiple units and coaching stock for ROSCOs and TOCs and a fleet of ten Class 60s for some of its heavier trains. A single 59/0 was also acquired for heavy trainload work.

The most exciting development within the GBRf fleet is the Class 69 project, where ex-BR Class 56s are being rebuilt with the same GM engines as used in Class 66s. Ten locos are authorised for conversion with the possibility of another six being sanctioned. For the project, GBRf acquired 18 redundant Class 56s from UK Rail Leasing and DC Rail.

The firm also continues to acquire Class 66s from other operators, with 13 so far sourced from mainland Europe (66747-751/790-797) and ten from DB Cargo (66780-789).

GBRf makes no secret of its desire to acquire new locos, especially any spare Class 66s, and will continue to consider buying or leasing any such spare examples.

More Class 73/9 conversions remain a possibility, but would only be forthcoming with a suitable business case to support the investment.

Class 08/09

GBRf owns for ex-BR standard shunters, which are used at Whitemoor and Trafford Park in Manchester. They are on the GBWM pool.

08925	GWS	GBR	WG
08934	GWS	GBR	BH (U)
09002	GWS	GBR	WG
09009	GWS	GBR	Trafford Park

Class 47

Three Class 47s were bought from Colas Rail in 2017 and are used to move rolling stock, for which they have Dellner couplers fitted. They are also occasionally used for charters. They are in the GBDF pool.

47727	47047, 47569	CAL	GBR	LR	*Edinburgh Castle/Caisteal Dhùn Èideann*
47739	47035, 47594	GBB	GBR	LR	
47749	47076, 47625	BRB	GBR	LR	*City Of Truro*

Class 56

GBRf has acquired 18 Class 56s, of which ten are to be converted to Class 69s (see page 301). Most were acquired in an unserviceable condition, but 56081/098/104/312 have seen occasional main-line use.

56009			BLE	GBR	ZW (U)
56032		GBGS	FER	GBR	ZW (U)
56077		UKRS	LHO	GBR	LR (U)
56081		GBGD	UKR	GBR	PK
56098		GBGD	RFO	GBR	LR (U)
56104		UKRL	UKR	GBR	CA
56106		UKRS	UKR	GBR	LR (U)
56312	56003	GBGD	DCR	GBR	LR (U)

GBRf has three Class 47s used mostly for Rail Services. No. 47727 *Edinburgh Castle/Caisteal Dhùn Èideann* hauls new Bombardier unit 720501 past Stanton Gate on 26 May 2020. *Paul Robertson*

Class 59

One of the original five Class 59/0s acquired by Foster Yeoman from 1986, 59003 was redeployed in Germany in 1997. GBRf bought the loco in 2014 and returned it to UK operation. It is in the GBYH pool.

59003	GBF	GBR	RR	*Yeoman Highlander*

Class 60

Ten Class 60s bought by Colas Rail Freight from DB Cargo in 2013 and then overhauled. In 2018 they were sold to GBRf, who then sold them to Beacon Rail and leases them back. Three locos have also been acquired directly from DBC for spares.

60002	GBTG	COL	BEA	RR	
60004	WQDA	EWS	DBC	TY (U)	
60008	WQDA	EWS	DBC	TC (U)	*Sir William McAlpine*
60014	WQDA	TEW	DBC	TY (U)	
60021	GBTG	GBF	BEA	RR	*PENYGHENT*
60026	GBTG	BEA	BEA	RR	*HELVELLYN*
60047	GBTG	COL	BEA	RR	
60056	GBTG	COL	BEA	RR	
60076	GBTG	COL	BEA	RR	
60085	GBTG	COL	BEA	RR	
60087	GBTG	COL	BEA	RR	
60095	GBTG	GBF	BEA	RR	
60096	GBTG	COL	BEA	RR	

A handful of Class 56s are used for ad hoc duties by GBRf; 56098 passes Trowell on 4 July 2019. *Paul Robertson*

Class 66

The mainstay of the GBRf traction fleet, the first seven locos were acquired in 2001 and since then the fleet has grown, initially to 32 locos then 14 locos were acquired from various ROSCOs having been used by DRS, Advenza Freight, Freightliner and Colas (66733-746). Thirteen locos have been sourced from mainland Europe (66747-751 / 790-797). Twenty-eight were ordered as new-build machines from Progress Rail in Muncie, Indiana, (66752-779) and ten locos were acquired from DB Cargo (66780-789).
No. 66751 has a Scharfenberg coupler fitted. The GBFM locos and 66738 have RETB fitted.

66701		GBBT	GBO	EVS	RR	
66702		GBBT	GBR	EVS	RR	*Blue Lightning*
66703		GBBT	GBR	EVS	RR	*Doncaster PSB 1981-2002*
66704		GBBT	GBR	EVS	RR	*Colchester Power Signalbox*
66705		GBBT	GBR	EVS	RR	*Golden Jubilee*
66706		GBBT	GBR	EVS	RR	*Nene Valley*
66707		GBBT	GBR	EVS	RR	*Sir Sam Fay*
66708		GBBT	GBR	EVS	RR	*Jayne*
66709		GBBT	MSC	EVS	RR	*Sorrento*
66710		GBBT	GBR	EVS	RR	*Phil Packer BRIT*
66711		GBBT	AGI	EVS	RR	*Sence*
66712		GBBT	GBR	EVS	RR	*Peterborough Power Signalbox*
66713		GBBT	GBR	EVS	RR	*Forest City*
66714		GBBT	GBR	EVS	RR	*Cromer Lifeboats*
66715		GBBT	GBR	EVS	RR	*Valour*
66716		GBBT	GBR	EVS	RR	*Locomotive & Carriage Institution Centenary 1911-2011*
66717		GBBT	GBR	EVS	RR	*Good Old Boy*
66718		GBLT	LUB	EVS	RR	*Sir Peter Hendy CBE*
66719		GBLT	GBR	EVS	RR	*Metro-Land*
66720		GBLT	EMY	EVS	RR	
66721		GBLT	LUW	EVS	RR	*Harry Beck*
66722		GBLT	GBR	EVS	RR	*Sir Edward Watkin*
66723		GBLT	GBZ	EVS	RR	*Chinook*
66724		GBLT	GBF	EVS	RR	*Drax Power Station*
66725		GBLT	GBZ	EVS	RR	*Sunderland*
66726		GBLT	GBF	EVS	RR	*Sheffield Wednesday*
66727		GBLT	MRT	EVS	RR	*Maritime One*
66728		GBLT	GBF	EVS	RR	*Institution Of Railway Operators*
66729		GBLT	GBF	EVS	RR	*Derby County*
66730		GBLT	GBF	EVS	RR	*Whitemoor*
66731		GBLT	GBF	EVS	RR	*Capt. Tom Moore A True British Inspiration*
66732		GBLT	GBF	EVS	RR	*GBRf The First Decade 1999-2009 John Smith MD*
66733	66401	GBFM	GBR	POR	RR	*Cambridge PSB*
66735	66403	GBBT	GBR	POR	RR	*Peterborough United*
66736	66404	GBFM	GBR	POR	RR	*Wolverhampton Wanderers*
66737	66405	GBFM	GBR	POR	RR	*Lesia*
66738	66578	GBBT	GBR	BEA	RR	*Huddersfield Town*
66739	66579	GBFM	GBR	BEA	RR	*Bluebell Railway*
66740	66580	GBFM	GBR	BEA	RR	*Sarah*
66741	66581	GBBT	GBR	BEA	RR	*Swanage Railway*
66742	66406, 66841	GBBT	GBR	BEA	RR	*ABP Port Of Immingham Centenary 1912-2012*
66743	66407, 66842	GBFM	ROY	BEA	RR	
66744	66408, 66843	GBBT	GBR	BEA	RR	*Crossrail*
66745	66409, 66844	GBRT	GBR	BEA	RR	*Modern Railways The First 50 Years*
66746	66410, 66845	GBFM	ROY	BEA	RR	

66747		GBEB	GBF	GBR	RR	*Made In Sheffield*
66748		GBEB	GBF	GBR	RR	*West Burton 50*
66749		GBEB	GBF	GBR	RR	*Christopher Hopcroft MBE 60 Years Railway Service*
66750		GBEB	GBF	BEA	RR	*Bristol Panel Signal Box*
66751		GBEB	GBF	BEA	RR	*Inspirational Delivered Hitachi Rail Europe*
66752		GBEL	GBF	GBR	RR	*The Hoosier State*
66753		GBEL	GBF	GBR	RR	*EMD Roberts Road*
66754		GBEL	GBF	GBR	RR	*Northampton Saints*
66755		GBEL	GBF	GBR	RR	*Tony Berkeley OBE RFG Chairman 1997-2018*
66756		GBEL	GBF	GBR	RR	*Royal Corps Of Signals*
66757		GBEL	GBF	GBR	RR	*West Somerset Railway*
66758		GBEL	GBF	GBR	RR	*The Pavior*
66759		GBEL	GBF	GBR	RR	*Chippy*
66760		GBEL	GBF	GBR	RR	*David Gordon Harris*
66761		GBEL	GBF	GBR	RR	*Wensleydale Railway Association 25 Years 1990-2015*
66762		GBEL	GBF	GBR	RR	
66763		GBEL	GBF	GBR	RR	*Severn Valley Railway*
66764		GBEL	GBF	GBR	RR	
66765		GBEL	GBF	GBR	RR	
66766		GBEL	GBF	GBR	RR	
66767		GBEL	GBF	GBR	RR	
66768		GBEL	GBF	GBR	RR	
66769		GBEL	GBF	GBR	RR	
66770		GBEL	GBF	GBR	RR	
66771		GBEL	GBF	GBR	RR	*Amanda*
66772		GBEL	GBF	GBR	RR	*Marie*
66773		GBNB	GBP	GBR	RR	*Pride Of GB Railfreight*
66774		GBNB	GBF	GBR	RR	
66775		GBNB	GBZ	GBR	RR	*HMS Argyll*
66776		GBNB	GBF	GBR	RR	*Joanne*
66777		GBNB	GBF	GBR	RR	*Annette*
66778		GBNB	GBF	GBR	RR	*Cambois Depot 25 Years*
66779		GBEL	GYP	GBR	RR	*Evening Star*
66780	66008	GBOB	CMX	GBR	RR	*The Cemex Express*
66781	66016	GBOB	GBF	GBR	RR	
66782	66046	GBOB	GBZ	GBR	RR	
66783	66058	GBOB	BIF	GBR	RR	*The Flying Dustman*
66784	66081	GBOB	GBF	GBR	RR	*Keighley & Worth Valley Railway 50th Anniversary 1968-2018*
66785	66132	GBOB	GBF	GBR	RR	
66786	66141	GBOB	GBF	GBR	RR	
66787	66184	GBOB	GBF	GBR	RR	
66788	66238	GBOB	GBF	GBR	RR	*Locomotion 15*
66789	66250	GBOB	BLL	GBR	RR	*British Rail 1948-1997*
66790	CD66403	MBDL	GBF	BEA	RR	
66791	CD66404	MBDL	BEA	BEA	RR	*Neil Bennett*
66792	CD66405	MBDL	GBF	BEA	RR	
66793	29004	MBDL		BEA	RR (U)	*Dave Meehan*
66794	29005	MBDL		BEA	RR (U)	*Ted Gaffney*
66795	29006	MBDL		BEA		
66796	29007	MBDL		BEA		
66797	513-09	MBDL		BEA		

Note: 66795-797 due in UK in early 2021

Left: The only Class 59 in the GBRf fleet is 59003 *Yeoman Highlander*. It was at Westbury on 26 February 2019. *Mark Pike*

Below: GBRf bought ten Class 60s from Colas, and they are slowly being reliveried. No. 60021 *Penyghent* works a Lynemouth-Tyne Dock train. *GBRf*

Below: Class 66s are the main traction for GBRf. On 15 July 2020, 66738 *Huddersfield Town* heads south from Spalding with the 1558 Rotherham Masborough-London Gateway container train. *Pip Dunn*

Class 69

This new class of locos uses Class 56 donor bodies and bogies, but the same GM engines as used in the Class 66s. The first locos are undergoing construction at Longport and the initial example is expected to be in traffic in early 2021. The donor locos 'running order' is subject to change.

69001	56031	UND	BEA	LT (Z)
69002	56057, 56311	UND	BEA	LT (Z)
69003	56018	UND	BEA	LT (Z)
69004	56069	UND	BEA	LT (Z)
69005	56007		BEA	LT (Z)
69006	56128		BEA	LT (Z)
69007	56037		BEA	LT (Z)
69008	56038		BEA	LT (Z)
69009	56065		BEA	LT (Z)
69010	56060		BEA	LT (Z)

Class 73

Class 73s have been part of the GBRf fleet since 2004 and the number of locos has steadily increased. Most were put back into traffic in their original condition, but in 2013 a contract to have five rebuilt with MTU engines by Brush was agreed. This was then increased by six more locos when GBRf won the contract to haul the Caledonian Sleeper trains.

GBRf retain several 'original' 73s and has four donor locos that are held in reserve should more 73/9s overhauls be sanctioned.

Class 73/1

These are original locos with EE diesel engines. Nos 73201/212/213 are ex-Gatwick Express locos. Nos 73107/136 remain dual braked. GBRf retains 73101/110/134/139 in strategic reserve as donor bodies should more 73/9s be authorised subject to a business case and funding.

73101	73801	GBSD	PUL	GBR	ZG (U)	
73107		GBED	GBF	GBR	SE	*Tracy*
73109		GBED	GBZ	GBR	SE	*Battle of Britain – 80th Anniversary*
73110		GBBR	EBY	GBR	ZG (U)	
73119		GBED	GBR	GBR	SE	*Borough of Eastleigh*
73128		GBED	GBR	GBR	SE	*OVS BULLEID CBE*
73134		GBBR	ICO	GBR	BL (U)	
73136		GBED	GBF	GBR	SE	*Mhairi*
73139		GBSD	UND	GBR	ZG (U)	
73141		GBED	GBF	GBR	SE	*Charlotte*
73201	73142	GBED	BRB	GBR	SE	*Broadlands*
73212	73102	GBED	GBF	GBR	SE	*Fiona*
73213	73112	GBED	GBF	GBR	SE	*Rhodalyn*

Class 73/9

It is impossible to think of the 73/9s as anything other than new locomotives, with just the bodies and the bogies retained from the donor locos they were rebuilt from. Even the bodies have had a high level of work on them.

The first five locos are generally used for Network Rail work, either Infrastructure Monitoring or infrastructure support duties.

The six Caledonian Sleeper locos are different in many ways from their NR classmates and are used solely on sleeper trains north of Edinburgh to Inverness, Aberdeen and Fort William. For this they have Dellner couplers and snowploughs, and their third-rail capability is isolated.

73961	73120, 73209	GBNR	GBF	GBR	SE	*Alison*
73962	73125, 73204	GBNR	GBF	GBR	SE	*Dick Mabbutt*
73963	73123, 73206	GBNR	GBF	GBR	SE	*Janice*
73964	73124, 73205	GBNR	GBF	GBR	SE	*Jeanette*
73965	73121, 73208	GBNR	GBF	GBR	SE	
73966	73005	GBCS	CAL	GBR	EC	
73967	73006, 73906	GBCS	CAL	GBR	EC	
73968	73117	GBCS	CAL	GBR	EC	
73969	73105	GBCS	CAL	GBR	EC	
73970	73103	GBCS	CAL	GBR	EC	
73971	73122, 73207	GBCS	CAL	GBR	EC	

Class 92

GBRf has 16 Class 92s, the locos originally owned by Eurostar and SNCF. Twelve have been refurbished and returned to use, while four remain at Brush Loughborough as spare/donor locos and are unlikely to be revived.

The locos are used on Caledonian sleeper work between Euston-Glasgow Central/Edinburgh, which calls on at least five locos a day. Others are used on freight work.

Nos 92021/040/045/046 are unlikely to be returned to traffic.

92006	GBSL	CAL	GBR	WB	
92010	GBST	CAL	GBR	WB	
92014	GBSL	CAL	GBR	WB	
92018	GBST	CAL	GBR	WB	
92020	GBET	GBF	GBR	WB	
92021	GBSD	EUK	GBR	BL (U)	*Purcell*
92023	GBSL	CAL	GBR	WB	
92028	GBST	GBF	GBR	WB	
92032	GBST	GBF	GBR	WB	*IMechE Railway Division*
92033	GBSL	CAL	GBR	WB	
92038	GBST	CAL	GBR	WB	
92040	GBSD	EUK	GBR	BL (U)	*Goethe*
92043	GBST	GBF	GBR	WB	
92044	GBST	EUK	GBR	WB	*Couperin*
92045	GBSD	EUK	GBR	BL (U)	*Chaucer*
92046	GBSD	EUK	GBR	BL (U)	*Sweelinck*

Many GBRf Class 66s are painted in customer liveries, such as Biffa Waste 66783 *The Flying Dustman*, which was working the 1224 Middleton Towers-Goole Glassworks sand train; it approaches March on 13 June 2018. *Bill Atkinson*

Class 73s are a big part of the GBRf fleet; re-engineered 73963 *Janice* and 73962 *Dick Mabbutt* work the 1230 Derby RTC-Tonbridge West Yard IM train past Barrow-on-Soar on 1 July 2015. *Bill Atkinson*

Rail Operations Group

Contact details

Website: www.railopsgroup.co.uk
Twitter: @railoperationsgroup

Key personnel

Managing Director: Karl Watts

Overview

Rail Operations Group is a small but growing specialist TOC with an expertise in moving passenger rolling stock. It regularly moves new stock after construction or delivery to the UK, or between storage sites. It also moved multiple units transferring to or from maintenance facilities before or after overhaul.

Some moves are done by using ROG staff to drive the units but most are carried out using its locomotives, either its own or those on long-term lease from Europhoenix or DRS.

ROG has fitted Dellner couples to some of its Class 37s and 47s to allow it to haul units without the need for barrier wagons.

It also offers initial shakedown testing for new trains, such as the Class 397 CAF units built for Transpennine Express.

A new venture by the company has been its Orion service, which will use Class 319s converted to freight use. ROG also occasionally hires Class 20s from HNRC and Michael Owen.

Class 37

These locos are owned by Europhoenix but currently on exclusive use to ROG. They have Dellner couplers fitted and are used mostly for EMU moves. The company is seeking the more Class 37s. All are in the GROG pool.

37510	37112	EPX	EPX	LR	*Orion*
37601	37005, 37501	EPX	EPX	LR	*Perseus*
37608	37022, 37512	EPX	EPX	LR	*Andromeda*
37611	37171, 37690	EPX	EPX	LR	*Pegasus*
37800	37143	EPX	EPX	LR	*Cassiopeia*
37884	37183	EPX	EPX	LR	*Cepheus*

No. 37611 hauled new Crossrail 345056 from store for delivery as the 1518 Old Dalby to Old Oak Depot past Ashwell on 19 September 2019. *Bill Atkinson*

Class 43

Four Class 43s have been bought by DATS but are being operated by ROG. They are in the MBDL pool.

43052	EMB	DATS	RJ
43054	EMB	DATS	RJ
43066	EMB	DATS	RJ
43076	EMB	DATS	RJ

Class 47

These ex-Riviera Trains Class 47s are used mostly for stock moves. Nos 47843/847 are spares donors only.

47812	47239, 47657	GROG	ROG	ROG	LR	
47813	47129, 47658	GROG	ROG	ROG	LR	*Jack Frost*
47815	47155, 47660	GROG	ROG	ROG	LR	*Lost Boys 68-88*
47843	47090, 47623	SROG	OXB	ROG	LR (U)	
47847	47179, 47577	SROG	LLB	ROG	LR (U)	
47848	47068, 47632	GROG	OXB	ROG	LR	

Class 57/3

These locos are sub-leased from DRS and are used mostly for stock moves.

57301	47069, 47638, 47845	GROG	DRC	POR	LR	*Goliath*
57305	47164, 47571, 47822	GROG	ROG	POR	LR	*Northern Princess*
57310	47037, 47563, 47831	GROG	DRU	POR	LR	*Pride of Cumbria*
57312	47330	GROG	ROG	POR	LR	

Class 91

Two Class 91s have been leased from Eversholt for use on the Data Acquisition and Testing Services (DATS) train.

91122	91022	EROG	VEC	EVS	LR
91128	91028	EROG	VEC	EVS	LR

ROG sub-leases some Class 57/3s from DRS; 57303 *Pride of Carlisle*, with 47813 *Jack Frost* on the rear, top-and-tail two translator vehicles as the 1316 Old Dalby to Leicester LIP, passing Copleys Brook, Melton Mowbray, on 14 May 2019. *Bill Atkinson*

Class 319

Ex-Thameslink Class 319s are being modified to haul freight in roll-cages and on pallets. The first unit to be prepared is 319373, which will remain a standard Class 319 (apart from its internal arrangement), while 319009/010 are to be converted to Class 769 bi-mode units.

				DMC	MS	TS	DMS
319009	TLW	POR	LM (U)	77307	62899	71780	77306
319010	TLW	POR	ZG (U)	77309	62900	71781	77308
319373	ORO	POR	ZG	77483	63055	71941	77482

Mk 3 coaches

ROG has secured many of the former Arriva Trains Wales Mk 3 coaches, previously used on the Holyhead-Cardiff route but replaced by Mk 4s.

They have been bought speculatively for business growth in either the passenger or non-passenger sectors.

10249	ARV	Mk 3 RBF
12176	ARV	SO
12177	ARV	SO
12178	ARV	SO
12179	ARV	SO
12180	ARV	SO
12181	ARV	SO
12182	ARV	SO
12183	ARV	SO
12184	ARV	SO
12185	ARV	SO

Driving Van Trailers

82306	ARV	DVT
82308	ARV	DVT

ROG undertakes many moves of rolling stock for store, scrap or overhaul. No. 47815 *Lost Boys 68-88* passes Badgeworth on the approach to Cheltenham with ex-GWR Mk 3 coaches from Laira depot to store at Ely. The date is 15 May 2019. *Jack Boskett*

An interesting train operated by ROG is the DATS OHLE test train, which uses ex-EMR power cars 43054/066 with ex-LNER 91122 and 91128. The 1256 Doncaster to Peterborough passes Creeton, south of Grantham, on 6 August 2020. *Bill Atkinson*

The companies that supply maintenance and spot hire to the railways have an overlap, and hence are included together in this one section. Some of these firms provide just one aspect, be it spot hire or maintenance, while others provide both. Some have loco fleets, some don't.

Small companies that support these two markets are not included.

Alstom West Coast Traincare

Contact details

Website: www.alstom.com/alstom-uk-and-ireland

Key personnel

Managing Director: Peter Broadley

Overview

The move to franchises meant a different way trains were procured and maintained. Trains were leased as the franchises were too short to allow any TOC to order their own rolling stock, because the time to have the fleets constructed, accepted, tested and finally introduced was way too long.

Given that trains would be passed to whoever was the next franchise operator, maintenance was often also best done by third-party contractors.

This led to – initially – Bombardier and Alstom offering maintenance as part of the package for many new train orders. For Alstom, it created its West Coast Traincare operation, which took over the former InterCity depots at Polmadie, Manchester Longsight, Edge Hill, Oxley and Wembley. It also has a site at Widnes Technology Centre.

It uses these sites to maintain the Pendolino fleet, initially with Virgin and now with Avanti. It also undertakes running repairs and minor exams on other AVC stock plus is available for third-party contract work; for example, at Polmadie the Caledonian Sleeper coaching stock is maintained. AWC has ten Class 08s based at its various depots.

Alstom also runs the depot at Chester for Transport for Wales Class 175 units and also has a site at Crofton in West Yorkshire.

Class 08

Depot shunters at AWCT sites.

08451	ATZZ	BRW	ALS	LO	*MA SMITH*
08454	ATLO	BRW	ALS	WD	
08611	ATLO	BRW	ALS	WB	
08617	ATLO	BRW	ALS	OX	*Steve Purser*
08696	ATLO	BRW	ALS	WB	
08721	ATLO	BRW	ALS	WD	*Longsight TMD*
08764	ATLO	BRW	ALS	PO	
08790	ATLO	BRW	ALS	EG	
08887	ATZZ	BRW	ALS	PO	

Arlington Fleet Services

Contact details

Website: www.arlington-fleet.com
Twitter: @ArlingtonFleet

Key personnel

Managing Director: Barry Stephens
Systems Director: John Campbell

Overview

AFS holds a long-term lease on the former BREL / Alstom Eastleigh Works. Nine acres is undercover, rail connected workshops. There are two 50t, eight 30t and two 16t gantry cranes. There are three paint booths and a wheelshop plus shotblasting shops and welding / fabrication shops.

AFS can work on most locomotive types with work ranging from 'G-exams' to simple servicing. The bulk of the heavy work has been for GBRf, DRS and Rail Operations Group with Classes 08, 37, 43, 47, 57, 59, 66 and 73 receiving heavy exams, bogie overhauls, collision repairs and exams and modifications.

The key clients for ago repairs are Touax, GBRf, Freightliner, Network Rail, STVA, Transport for London and VTG. Repairs and maintenance for hauled coaching stock for the charter market for Riviera Trains and LSL is also undertaken.

The site is carrying out body repairs, repaints and conversions on Class 319s for Rail Operations Group and Porterbrook. AFS also owns two Class 442s that will be converted for alternative uses.

The company also owns two shunters, both based at Eastleigh; one Class 07 and one Class 08.

Arlington Fleet Services has 07007 based at its Eastleigh works for shunting vehicles inside the works. It was in use on 20 March 2019. *Pip Dunn*

Class 07

This shunter was inherited as part of the takeover of Eastleigh Works.

07007	MBDL	BRW	AFS	ZG

Class 08

Shunter bought from EWS.

08567	MBDL	EWS	AFS	ZG

Class 47

Bought from DRS.

47818	47240, 47663	MBDL	DRU	ZG (U)

Class 489

EMU translator vans.

68501	61281
68504	61286

Boden Rail Engineering

Contact details

E-mail: Neil.boden@bodenrailengineering.co.uk

Key personnel

Managing Director: Neil Boden

Overview

Previously based at the old Metro Cammell works at Washwood Heath, when this site was sold for redevelopment, BRE moved to the former East Midlands Trains depot at Nottingham Eastcroft.

BRE undertakes most of the day-to-day maintenance and running of the Colas Rail Class 37 and 56 fleets. BRE also owns 37240 and 50050 *Fearless*, which are both passed for main-line running and are occasionally used for spot hire work, mostly collecting Colas locomotives. Both locos are in the COFS pool.

Class 37

37240	TRN	BOD	NM

Class 50

50050	BRB	BOD	NM	*Fearless*

Brodie Engineering

Contact details

Website: www.brodie-engineering.co.uk

Key personnel

Managing Director: Gerry Hilferty

Overview

Founded in 1996, Brodie Engineering offers refurbishment, maintenance, overhaul and repair services to TOCs and FOCs.

It operates from a depot in Kilmarnock that has indoor capacity for up to 14 vehicles, stabling capacity for a further 11 vehicles, pits for underframe maintenance including an underframe wash area, 28-metre paint booth, jacks for vehicle lifts, fabrication facilities and a water test facility.

The company also owns 156478. This two-car unit was written off by Angel Trains after suffering severe flood damage and sold to Brodie Engineering. It subsequently rebuilt the unit and it has returned to ScotRail, leased directly.

Carnforth Railway Restoration and Engineering Services

Contact details

Website: https://westcoastrailways.co.uk/crres

Overview

In 1990, businessman David Smith bought enough shares to take control of the operation at Carnforth from Bill McAlpine This deal included the Carnforth Railway Restoration and Engineering Services division – part of Steamtown since 1984.

CRESS is the specialist locomotive and coach restoration arm that operates alongside West Coast Railways, and offers full or partial overhaul of steam and diesel locomotives and rolling stock as well as vehicle restoration, maintenance and repainting services.

Chrysalis Rail

Contact details

Website: chrysalisrail.com

Key personnel

Managing Director: Chris Steele

Overview

Chrysalis Rail is a UK-based rolling stock service supplier specialising in refurbishment, vehicle enhancement, modification and heavy maintenance projects designed to enhance passenger rolling stock.

Chrysalis has a site at the former GWR depot at Landore in Swansea, South Wales. It closed in 2018 but reopened in August 2019 for its new user.

Chrysalis Rail is undertaking a full interior and exterior refurbishment of the Northern Class 333s at Holbeck. It has also undertaken work for Transport for Wales on its Class 153s and for ScotRail on its Class 156s.

Chrysalis undertook an interior refresh and exterior surface corrosion repair project for Siemens on 127 Class 450s and 45 Class 444s, a total of 733 vehicles, for South Western Railway.

The company has preserved 08663 on hire, via Rail Support Services.

Class 20189 Ltd

Contact details

E-mail: Owen-michael@btinternet.com

Key personnel

Managing Director: Michael Owen

Overview

A small spot hire umbrella organisation comprising the three Class 20s owned by Michael Owen and two locos owned by the Class 20 Locomotive Society preservation group.

All five locos are main-line registered and have been hired in the past to GBRf, DB Schenker and WCR. They have also been used by the London Underground and two locos are in Metropolitan Railway maroon livery.

More recently 20227 has been on hire to the North Norfolk Railway – which operates to Cromer on the national network – while the other locos have been hired by the likes of Vintage Trains, DC Rail, ROG and Loram.

The company is in negotiations to buy another Class 20 from a preservation group.

Michael Owen owns a handful of Class 20s, which have been hired to several TOCs from time to time. On 5 May 2018, 20189/205 were at Victoria having arrived on a charter from Dungeness. *Pip Dunn*

Class 20

One loco, 20227, is on long-term hire to the North Norfolk Railway, the remainder are used for spot hire.

20007	MOLO	GYP	MOW	SK	
20142	MOLO	MRM	MOW	SK	*Sir John Betjeman*
20189	MOLO	BRB	MOW	SK	
20205	MOLO	BRB	CTL	SK	
20227	MOLO	MRM	CTL	SK	*Sherlock Holmes*

Europhoenix

Contact details

Website: https://europhoenix.co.uk

Key personnel

Managing Director: Glenn Edwards

Overview

Europhoenix has been successful at selling and redeploying locos abroad; mostly Class 56s, 87s and 87s in Hungary and 87s in Bulgaria. It currently has two Class 91s – 91117/120 – ready to export to Hungary as trial locos for freight but their move has been held up by the Covid-19 crisis.

At home it has a fleet of nine Class 37s, six of which are in traffic and midway through a five-year hire deal to Rail Operations Group. It is looking to acquire further Class 37s if they become available on the market.

Between 2008 and 2012, Europhoenix exported Class 87s to Bulmarket in Bulgaria; followed by three Class 56s and eight Class 86s to Floyd in Hungary and a further 86 to Bulgaria.

Class 37

Most Europhoenix Class 37s are on long-term hire to Rail Operations Group (see page 304). These locos listed here are stored. No. 37901 is likely to return to traffic, while 37207 is in reserve. No. 37146 is unlikely to be resurrected.

37146		EPUK	CCE	EPX	LR (U)	
37207		MBDL	BRB	EPX	LR (U)	
37901	37150	EPUK	EPX	EPX	LR (U)	*Mirrlees Pioneer*

Class 91

Following its success selling Class 86s and 87s into mainland Europe, Class 91s are the next locos that Europhoenix is likely to redeploy abroad. Two locos have been acquired as demonstrators, but the project has stalled due to the Covid-19 pandemic.

91117	91017	EPEX	EPX	EPX	ZF (S)
91120	91020	EPEX	EPX	EPX	ZF (S)

On 17 July 2019, Europhoenix 37601 heads south through Natton near Ashchurch working a positioning move from Leicester to Portbury Dock to collect a rake of new TPE stock to transport north to Crewe the following day. *Jack Boskett*

Gemini Rail Services

Contact details

Website: www.geminirailgroup.co.uk

Key personnel

Chief Executive Officer: Tim Jenkins

Overview

Gemini Rail offers a wide range of services from UK centres, including full overhauls for passenger rolling stock, and has a dedicated wheelshop facilities offering light, medium and heavy wheelset overhauls. It main operations are undertaken at Wolverton Work.

Hanson & Hall Rail Services

Contact details

Website: www.hansonhallrail.co.uk
Twitter: @HallRail

Key personnel

Managing Director: Garcia Hanson

Overview

Hanson & Hall Rail Services Solutions was founded in 2018 by Garcia Hanson, who owns 50008 *Thunderer*, which is used for occasional stock moves and freight wagon transfers. It also arranges the transfer of DMUs and EMUs. It worked with DC Rail or DB Cargo to provide drivers.

Class 50

50008	DCRO	LAB	GAR	LR (U)	*Thunderer*

Hanson Traction owns one loco that is main-line registered; 50008 *Thunderer*. On 19 July 2018 it was top-and-tailing with the Class 50 Alliance's 50007 *Hercules* on a Stoneblower mileage accumulation run, seen passing Cossington. *Bill Atkinson*

Harry Needle Railroad Company

Contact details

Website: www.harry-needle.co.uk

Key personnel

Managing Director: Harry Needle

Overview

Harry Needle Railroad Company (HNRC) specialises in locomotive spot hire, maintenance/repair and stock storage. It recently took over the 15-acre former wagon repair depot at Worksop, which is now its main base for storing vehicles. It also has a maintenance facility at Barrow Hill.

The company owns six main-line registered Class 20s, which are available for spot hire. It also has 43 Class 08/09s and several industrial shunters both on contracts or available for hire, three Class 37s for main-line spot hire – often used by Colas – and four Class 47s, although these are not presently main-line registered. It also owns examples of Classes 20, 25 and 27, which are not currently available for hire.

The firm has invested £6m in the development of Worksop, and it can take 20 vehicles a week for repair, refurbishment and maintenance.

HNRC has main-line registered Class 20s and 37s for hire, as well as a fleet of Class 08 shunters, of which only about ten are in use. On 20 May 2020, on hire to ROG, 20118 *Saltburn-by-the-Sea* and 20132 *Barrow Hill Depot* head west through Ley Crossing with a rake of ex-GWR Mk 3 stock bound for Newport docks for scrapping. *Jack Boskett*

Class 08

HNRC has a large fleet of Class 08/09 shunters, although many are held in reserve.

08389		HNRS	EWS	HNR	Cardiff Tidal	
08428		HNRL	EWS	HNR	Barrow Hill (U)	
08500		HNRL	EWS	HNR	Burton (U)	
08502		HNRL	NOR	HNR	East Kent Railway	
08503		HNRL	BLU	HNR	Barry Island Railway	
08527		HNRL	TTG	HNR	Rossington	
08578		HNRS	EWS	HNR	Long Marston (U)	
08623			DBS	HNR	Hope Cement Works (U)	
08630		HNRL	CEL	HNR	Cardiff Tidal	*Celsa Endeavour*
08653		HNRS	EWS	HNR	Long Marston (U)	
08676		HNRL	EWS	HNR	East Kent Railway	
08685		HNRS	EWS	HNR	East Kent Railway	
08700		HNRS	BRW	HNR	Ilford	
08701		HNRS	RES	HNR	Long Marston (U)	
08706			EWS	HNR	Wishaw (U)	
08711		HNRS	RES	HNR	Burton (U)	
08714		MBDL	EWS	HNR	Hope Cement Works (U)	
08742		HNRL	RES	HNR	Barrow Hill (U)	
08765		HNRS	HNO	HNR	Barrow Hill (U)	
08782		HNRL	COR	HNR	Barrow Hill (U)	
08786		HNRS	DEP	HNR	Barrow Hill (U)	
08798			EWS	HNR	Barrow Hill (U)	
08799			EWS	HNR	East Kent Railway	
08802		HNRS	EWS	HNR	Wishaw (U)	
08804		WQDA	EWS	HNR	East Kent Railway	
08818		HNRL	GBR	HNR	Worksop	*Molly*
08824		HNRL	BLK	HNR	Barrow Hill (U)	
08834		HNRL	HNR	HNR	Allerton	
08865		HNRL	EWS	HNR	Central Rivers	
08877		HNRS	DEP	HNR	Cardiff Tidal	
08879		HNRL	EWS	HNR	Hope Cement Works	
08892		HNRL	DRS	HNR	Old Dalby	
08904		HNRL	EWS	HNR	Worksop	
08905		HNRS	EWS	HNR	Hope Cement Works (U)	
08918		HNRS	DEP	HNR	Burton (U)	
08924		HNRS	GBR	HNR	Barrow Hill	
08943		HNRL	HNR	HNR	Barrow Hill	
08944			BLK	HNR	Bury (U)	
08954		HNRL	BRW	HNR	Longsight	
08994	08462	HNRS	EWS	HNR	Burton (U)	

Class 09

Like the Class 08s, many locos are held in reserve.

09006		HNRS	EWS	HNR	Burton (U)
09014		HNRS	DEP	HNR	Burton (U)
09106	08759	HNRL	HNR	HNR	Cardiff Tidal
09201	08421	HNRL	DEP	HNR	Hope Cement Works (U)

Class 20

The end of a hire contract with GBRf for Class 20s has seen two main-line registered locos sold to LSL, leaving six locos for spot hire – with Loram, ROG and DC Rail all using the locos from time to time.

HNRC also has Class 20s based at Hope Cement Works, and until recently had vehicles at Scunthorpe Steelworks. Currently, of the firm's 20 locos, six remain main-line registered, while two are in industrial use. Some are in a condition where they could be reactivated and others are essentially for spare parts only.

20056		HNRL	COY	HNR	Scunthorpe Steelworks (U)	
20066			TAT	HNR	Hope Cement Works (U)	
20069			BRB	HNR	Worksop (S)	
20087		MBDL	BRB	HNR	Worksop (U)	
20110			GYP	HNR	Worksop (S)	
20118		GBEE	RSR	HNR	Barrow Hill	*Saltburn-by-the-Sea*
20121		HNRS	HNO	HNR	Barrow Hill (U)	
20132		GBEE	RSR	HNR	Barrow Hill	*Barrow Hill Depot*
20166		HNRL	HNO	HNR	Leeming Bar	
20168			HOP	HNR	Hope Cement Works	*Sir George Earle*
20311	20102	HNRL	HNO	HNR	Barrow Hill	
20314	20117	HNRL	HNO	HNR	Barrow Hill	
20901	20101	GBEE	GBR	HNR	Worksop	
20903	20083	HNRS	DRU	HNR	Burton (U)	
20904	20041	HNRS	DRU	HNR	Burton (U)	
20905	20225	GBEE	GBR	HNR	Worksop	
20906	20219		HOP	HNR	Hope Cement Works	

Class 25

The three Class 25s in the HNRC fleet were all recently acquired from preservation groups. A return to the main line for one or two has been mooted but has been put on hold.

25057			BRB	HNR	Worksop (U)
25283	25904	MBDL	GYP	HNR	Reid Freight Longport (U)
25313			BRB	HNR	Leeming Bar (U)

Class 27

Like the Class 25s, an acquisition from a preservation group, the sole HNRC Class 27 is part of its heritage fleet.

27066	27103, 27212	BRB	HNRL	HNR	Barrow Hill (U)

Class 37

HNRC had dabbled with Class 37s several years ago but sold the locos to DRS and all have since been scrapped. In recent times it bought three Class 37/6s from DRS and has hired them, mostly for IM work. They remain main-line registered and available for hire.

37607	37103, 37511	COTS	DRU	HNR	BH
37610	37181, 37687	MBDL	BLU	HNR	BH
37612	37179, 37691	COTS	DRU	HNR	BH

Class 47

HNRC has four Class 47s, three of which are in use as train supply locos at Wabtec Doncaster, Old Dalby and HNRC's own Worksop site. A fourth loco is stored at Barrow Hill.

47703	47514	HNRS	UND	HNR	ZF (I)	
47714	47511	HNRL	ANG	HNR	AH (I)	
47715	47502	MBDL	NSD	HNR	WK (I)	*Haymarket*
47769	47491	HNRS	VIR	HNR	BH (U)	*Resolve*

Hunslet Engine Co.

Contact details

Website: www.wabtec.com/business-units/hunslet-engine

Overview

Founded in 1864, Hunslet Engine Company is a designer and manufacturer of shunting, industrial, tunnelling and specialised locomotives and provides a bespoke design and manufacturing service for the UK and export markets.

It also has a spot hire business for its fleet of Class 08 and other industrial locomotives.

Class 08

08401		GRE	HUN	LHGS Barton-under-Needwood	
08445		MAL	HUN	Daventry	
08615	RFSH	HUN	HUN	Shotton	*Uncle Dai*
08823	KDSD	HUN	HUN	Shotton	*Kelva*
08873	DDIN	RES	HUN	LHGS Barton-under-Needwood	

Loram

Contact details

Website: www.loram.co.uk
Twitter: @LoramUK

Key personnel

Managing Director: Richard Kelly
International Business Development Director: Andrew Watson

Overview

Loram bought the Derby-based company Rail Vehicle Engineering Ltd (RVEL) in 2016 and now looks after the Network Rail Class 73 and Infrastructure Monitoring vehicle fleets, and, since January 2020, the maintenance of the New Measurement Trains.

It also offers a range of maintenance to other third-party companies, including heavy 'F-' and 'G-exam' overhauls, vehicle life extensions, modifications and routine maintenance. Recent work has been 'F-exams' on DRS Class 37s and 57s and on NR's four Class 97/3s.

The company also owns C2101, a production Rail Grinder, which is contracted for five years to Network Rail. It is also currently involved in major re-power programmes for alternative propulsion for ROSCOs, TOCs and technology OEMs.

Loram – which is an American-owned company – has a freight train operating licence that it uses for moving and operating infrastructure equipment. It has recently hired Class 20s from Michael Owen and Class 37s from DRS, along with four DRS Mk 2s that were used to put its operating licence and control function to the test. The coaches were temporarily reliveried into Loram colours.

The company has its own drivers and staff, but works closely with FOCs for drivers on routes or traction it is not familiar with. It has no aspirations to operate passenger or freight trains.

Nemesis Rail

Contact details

Website: www.nemesisrail.com

Key personnel

Managing Director: Martin Sargent

Overview

Based at the old DB Schenker depot at Burton on Trent, Nemesis Rail rose out of the collapse of FM Rail in 2007.

It offers vehicle maintenance and overhaul services to several companies, and does work for Riviera Trains and West Coast Railways among others.

It also has many locos stored at its site, including some shunters and Class 20s from HNRC. The management team also owns a collection of ex-BR locos, which are at Burton or the Battlefield Line, and has just 31128 still main-line registered and occasionally used by WCR.

It also owns several locos that are essentially preserved – such as 33019, 47640 and 73114 – and these are listed in the preserved section.

Class 08

The company's sole 08 is used for shunting at Burton. It is vacuum braked only.

08168	GRW	NEM	BU

Nemesis Rail has main-line registered 31128 *Charybdis* and it occasionally sees use. It pauses at Cardiff Central with a 0900 Burton-on-Trent-Canton coach move on 18 September 2019. *Glen Batten*

Class 25

The two Class 25s are stored at Burton.

25067	GYP	NEM	BU (U)
25265	BRB	NEM	BU (U)

Class 26

Neither Class 26 has worked for nigh on two decades now.

26004	TLC	NEM	BU (U)
26011	BRB	NEM	BU (U)

Class 31

The only main-line registered loco in the Nemesis fleet is 31128, which is occasionally used by West Coast Railways. No. 31461 has not worked for over 25 years.

31128		NRLO	BRB	NEM	BU	*Charybdis*
31461	31129	NRLO	CCE	NEM	BU (U)	

Class 37

Once based at the Great Central Railway, the sole Class 37 moved to Burton in 2011 has not worked since.

37255	NRLS	CCE	NEM	BU (U)

Class 45

For a period 45112 was the only main-line registered Peak but has not worked on the national network since 2007. It has occasionally been used for shunting at Burton.

45112	BRB	NEM	BU (U)	*Royal Army Ordnance Corps*

Class 47

The only operational 47 in the fleet is 47375 on long-term hire in Hungary (see page 346). The proposal to send three others to follow it did not materialise. No. 47640 is at the Battlefield line but it too has not worked for some time (see page 391).

47488		NRLS	GYP	NEM	BU (U)	
47701	47493	NRLO	TWO	NEM	BU (U)	*Waverley*
47744	*47250, 47600*	NRLS	EWS	NEM	BU (U)	

Pullman Rail

Contact details

Website: www.pullmanrail.co.uk
Tel: 029 2036 8850

Overview

Pullman Rail is part of the Colas Rail group and is based at the former EWS depot at Cardiff Canton. It has been serving the rail industry for the last two decades, providing technical expertise and quality workmanship.

It offers complete overhaul projects to repair and maintenance. It can also undertake bogie and wheelset overhaul to accident damage repair and overhaul of passenger vehicles.

Class 08

Cardiff Canton depot shunter

08499	BLE	PUL	Cardiff Canton	*Redlight*

Rail Support Services

Contact details

Website: www.railwaysupportservices.co.uk

Key personnel

Managing Director: Andrew Goodman
Operations Manager: Paul Fuller

Overview

Railway Support Services specialises in the spot hire of shunting locomotives and has a fleet of over 20 Class 08s available for short- or long-term hire to customers.

The company also assists rerailing activities and has several sets of portable MFD hydraulic lifting gear with a total capacity of over 500 tons that is used for the rerailing of all types of railway vehicles. These jacks are also ideal for maintenance, such as lifting locos for bogie swaps or lifting wagons.

RSS also specialises in moving railway vehicles, rails, sleepers and other permanent way materials around the UK, Europe and the world for maintenance and repairs.

Three of these locos are owned by Vulcan Rail (see page 331), a small spot company that hires to RSS, which then places them in industry as required. No. 08536 is being refurbished at Wishaw, 08784 is on hire to Progress Rail at Longport and 08922 is on hire to Hitachi at Newton Aycliffe.

Rail Support Services has a large fleet of Class 08s that are hired to several users. No. 08460 was at Eastleigh on 20 May 2019 shunting in the yard. *Antony Christie*

Class 08

RSS spot hire fleet.

08405	MBDL	EWS	DBC	Neville Hill	
08411	MBDL	BRW	RSS	Wishaw	
08441	MBDL	RSS	RSS	Bounds Green	
08460	MBDL	RSS	RSS	Eastleigh	*Spirit Of The Oak*
08480	MBDL	RSS	RSS	Bristol Barton Hill	
08484	MBDL	RSS	RSS	Norwich Crown Point	*Captain Nathaniel Darell*
08511	MBDL	RSS	RSS	Eastleigh	
08580	MBDL	EWS	RSS	Bounds green	
08593	MBDL	RSS	RSS	Wishaw (U)	
08632	MBDL	LOR	RSS	Derby Loram	
08670	MBDL	RSS	RSS	Bescot	
08683	MBDL	EWS	RSS	Norwich Crown Point	
08703	MBDL	EWS	RSS	Wigan Springs Branch	
08709	MBDL	EWS	RSS	Wishaw	
08738	MBDL	RSS	RSS	Felixstowe	
08752	MBDL	GEM	RSS	Wolverton Works	
08757	WQBA	RES	RSS	Telford Steam Railway	
08921		EWS	RSS	Wishaw (U)	
08939	MBDL	RSS	RSS	Chasewater Railway	

RMS Locotec

Contact details

Website: www.rmslocotec.com

Key personnel

Managing Director: Bill Warriner
Fleet Director: Brian Lark

Overview

Rail Management Services, trading as RMS Locotec and known for its Class 08 hire business, has recently been acquired by Proviso Holdings and so avoided going into administration. Proviso Holdings also owns rolling stock leasing and maintenance company Eastern Rail Services.

RMS Locotec has an extensive fleet of Class 08s, many on hire to businesses across the UK.

Class 08

Spot hire fleet.

08308	MRSO	FSR	RMS	Wolsingham
08375	MBDL	BLK	RMS	Boston Docks
08423		RMS	RMS	PD Ports Middlesbrough
08523	MRSO	RMS	RMS	Wolsingham
08573	MRSO	BLK	RMS	Wolsingham
08588	MRSO	RMS	RMS	Loram Derby
08613		RMS	RMS	Wolsingham
08622		BLK	RMS	Ketton
08648	MRSO	RMB	RMS	ScotRail Inverness
08754	RMSX	RMS	RMS	Wolsingham
08756	MRSO	DEP	RMS	Wolsingham
08762	MRSO	BLK	RMS	Yarmouth
08788	MRSO	RMS	RMS	PD Ports Middlesbrough
08809	MRSO	RMS	RMS	Ketton
08847	MBDL	COT	RMS	PD Ports Middlesbrough
08871	MBDL	COT	RMS	Ilford
08874	MBDL	SIL	RMS	Wolsingham
08885		RMS	RMS	Wolsingham
08913		MAL	RMS	EMR Kingsbury
08936	MBDL	RMS	RMS	Wolsingham

St Leonards Rail Engineering

Contact details

Website: www.hastingsdiesels.co.uk
E-mail: 2020@hastingsdiesels.co.uk

Key personnel

Managing Director: John White
Operations Manager: Andy Armitage

Overview

Based in the original depot used to maintain the Hastings DEMUs, St Leonards Railway Engineering has expanded beyond its original remit of maintaining its preserved stock and undertake maintenance for TOCs.

It services Class 73s used by GBRf and Govia as well as undertaking routine servicing on the Class 171s used by Govia on its Marshlink Ashford-Hastings operations.

It also looks after Hastings Diesels' Class 201 main-line registered but preserved Class 201 DEMU (see page 360). It also has an ex-Southern Region Class 07 diesel shunter based at the site.

Class 07

Depot shunter.

07011	GWS	SLE	St Leonards

Transmart Trains

Transmart owns a single Class 73 that is based at Eastleigh Works. The loco is in the MBED pool.

Class 73

73133	TMT	TMT	Eastleigh Works

Transmart Trains' 73133 in the Eastleigh Arlington works complex on 4 January 2019. *Mark Pike*

UK Rail Leasing

Contact details

Website: www.ukrl.co.uk

Key personnel

Chairman: Mark Winter
Managing Director: Kristian Mengel

Overview

UKRL is a rail vehicle engineering, fleet management and traction provider to the UK rail industry. It owns and works out of the former DB Cargo depot at Leicester, where it carries out maintenance for many types of traction.

It repairs locos and wagons and looks after the Europhoenix, ROG and Hanson Traction fleets.

It once had a sizeable fleet of Class 56s but sold them to GB Railfreight for conversion to Class 69s. It has retained one loco, 56303, but this is damaged following an altercation at Wembley Yard, and also two Class 37/9s that were previously preserved.

Class 37/9

Both Class 37/9s were bought from preservation groups. Main-line returns have been mooted but these seem unlikely to happen any time soon.

37905	UKRM	UKR	GYP	LR (S)
37906	UKRM	UKR	RFO	BAT (S)

Class 56

Having sold all its Class 56s to GBRf, one loco was not included in the deal due to collision damage it sustained in Wembley Yard.

56303	56125	HTLX	DCG	UKR	WN (U)

Wabtec

Contact details

Website: www.wabtec.com

Overview

Wabtec recently merged with GE Transportation and is a huge global company with plenty of operations in the UK.

Its main facility is at the former Doncaster Works, which covers 22 acres of the former British Rail Engineering Limited (BREL) Works, with the former Crimpsall shops operated by Bombardier and the old carriage works, which was once operated by RFS in the 1990s, also now part of the Wabtec empire.

It has other sites in the UK, including the former Andrew Barclay Works at Kilmarnock and Brush Traction at Loughborough. It also owns well-known railway companies such as Brecknell Willis, Faiveley, LH Group Services, Hunslet Engine, Napier and Vapor Stone Rail systems.

Wabtec also owns Axiom Rail, which was previously part of the DB Schenker operation.

One of Wabtec's fleet of Class 08 shunters, some of which are used within the maintenance business while others are hired out, 08853 stands in the Wabtec complex at Doncaster on 12 February 2019. *Mark Pike*

Class 08

Spot hire fleet.

08472	RFSH	BLK	WAB	EC	
08571	HBSH	BLK	WAB	Daventry	
08596	HBSH	BLK	WAB	EC	
08669	RFSH	BLK	WAB	Hams Hall	*Bob Machin*
08724	HBSH	BLK	WAB	ZF	
08853	RFSH	BLK	WAB	ZF	

Artemis Intelligent Power

Contact details

Website: www.artemisip.com

Former InterCity West Coast, Virgin Trains and Chiltern Railways' Driving Van Trailer 82113, previously owned by Porterbrook, has been covered at the Bo'ness & Kinneil Railway in Scotland to a self-propelled vehicle that combines hydrostatic transmission with regenerative braking to reduce emissions.

It has been renumbered 19001 and is regarded as a Class 19, although the vehicle is not on TOPS and is not passed for main-line use.

The project is funded by the Rail Safety and Standards Board (RSSB) in conjunction with Artemis Intelligent Power, a company specialising in hydraulic machines. The vehicle is being developed so it can store braking energy, which could then be released during acceleration.

It uses JCB diesel engines that drive hydraulic pumps and in turn they drive hydraulic motors mounted on the axles.

No. 82113 moved to Bo'ness in July 2017 for the conversion and the 'locomotive' undertook some trials on the five-mile heritage line from August 2018.

BCRRE Class 799

Contact details

Website: www.birmingham.ac.uk/research/railway/index.aspx

The Class 799 is a four-car, hydrogen-powered HydroFlex test train rebuilt from a redundant Thameslink Class 319 unit, 319001. It retains its 25kV AC and 750V DC capabilities.

The plain white unit was unveiled in June 2019 at the *RAIL* live event at Long Marston, where it was demonstrated on a short section of track.

The project is being financed by Porterbrook in conjunction with the University of Birmingham's Centre for Railway Research and Education (BCRRE). In September 2020 it undertook the first of its main line tests on the National network.

799001	319001	WHI	POR	LM	77291	62891	71772	77290

Hydrogen emission-free trains

Contact details

Website: www.arcolaenergy.com

There are several projects planned to create hydrogen-powered trains and the concept is seen as offering an emission-free alternative to diesel trains on remote lines where electrification is not viable.

Hydrogen and fuel cell specialist Arcola Energy is working with Brodie Rail Engineering at Kilmarnock to convert a redundant ex-ScotRail EMU, 314209 (vehicles 64599, 71458 and 64600), to run emission-free using hydrogen. The project is being delivered with input from the University of St Andrews.

Arcola Energy is also working with VivaRail to offer emission-free Class 230s. The concept train will consist of two-cars, one housing two battery modules and one with the fuel cell and tanks, all of which will be underneath the train.

In May 2018 plans were announced to convert some Eversholt Rail Class 321 units to HMUs – hydrogen multiple unit – using Alstom hydrogen cells. The conversion was called the Breeze and designated Class 600.

The £1m project to develop Breeze trains involves reengineering BREL-built Class 321s, many of which should come off lease from Greater Anglia in 2021 when replaced by new-build trains.

Alstom says the investment could allow the HMUs to be ready by 2024, supporting the government's aims to eliminate diesel-only trains from the main-line network by 2040.

The Class 600 will be converted at Alstom's Widnes Transport Technology Centre and when the project is in series production, it could create more than 200 engineering jobs.

Hydrogen trains emit no emissions besides water, and Eversholt and Alstom say they are most suited to regional services on routes that are not currently electrified.

Alstom will build on the development of the Coradia iLint in Germany, the first hydrogen-powered train to operate regular passenger services in the world.

Brush/FLEX Bi-mode MUs

In among this myriad of new types are the FLEX trains, which are former Thameslink Class 319 dual-voltage units that have been converted into bi-mode or tri-mode units.

Following their replacement by Class 700s, the fleet of 86 dual-voltage four-car EMUs were spare. Some were taken by TOCs, such as Northern (on a short-term basis, pending new trains), and London Midland, with just 319004 being scrapped.

These are all four-car sets – as per their original build – and are five 769/0s and four 769/4s for TfW, eight 769/4s for Northern, 19 769/9s for GWR and two other units for freight use for Rail Operations Group. These are being converted in 2020/21 and the first sets have been on test or are being used for staff training.

EMU conversions rebuilt from Class 319s

Northern	769424/426/431/434/442/450/456/458
Transport for Wales	769002/003/006-008, 769445/452
GWR	769922/923/925/927/928/930/932/935-940/943/944/946/947/949/959
ROG	319009/010

Meteor Power Class 08

Contact details

Website: www.meteorpower.com

Two locos listed as in industrial use (page 331) are 08629/649, which were formerly based at Wolverton Works but have since been replaced and duly acquired by Meteor Rail. No. 08629 has gone to the nearby Princes & Risborough Railway but 08649, which was in poor condition and had a broken crank, is now being re-engineered at MR's Silverstone, where it is being fitted with a low-emission hybrid traction package based on automotive technology.

The grant-funded work is being undertaken as part of a research programme backed by the Department for Transport. In February 2020 08649 had its EE engine and generator removed and replaced by a new generator and battery pack. It has been fitted with a Euro 3a 6.8-litre John Deere PowerTech 6068HFU82 diesel engine rated at 285hp. This will be modified to meet Euro 5 standards.

The engine drives a generator that trickle-charges a battery pack assembled using four modules recycled from Tesla Model 3 cars, giving a combined storage capacity of 300kWh. Each of the four batteries can be recharged by the diesel engine in less than an hour. The batteries can also capture and store regenerative braking energy.

No. 08649 retains its original traction motors, but has been fitted with a new control system for the compressors and vacuum pumps. The cab desk is unchanged but the control system voltage has been reduced from 400V to 24V DC to improve safety.

The loco will be tested for a month at the Chinnor & Princes Risborough Railway but the planned trials set for April were inevitably delayed due to the Covid-19 restrictions and they were due to move in October. After these tests the loco will go on hire to a TOC for further testing.

A second loco, unlikely to be 08649, will then be acquired and rebuilt and fitted with a similar brand-new powertrain. The 08s are being modified to offer a low-emission, lower-cost 'new' shunting loco but with the grandfather rights of a 08.

In the future, Meteor Power is planning to rebuild a Class 37 with similar technology to offer a low-cost 'new Type 3'.

Industrial Locos

In the 1960s hundreds of surplus BR diesel shunters were sold for industrial use for use at collieries, steelworks, quarries and other railheads. They were sold exceptionally cheaply and replaced steam. Initially it was mostly Class 02/03/04/05/10/11s, followed later by Class 07/08/14s from the 1970s. These sales also affected many specialist builders of industrial diesel locos at the time, including Hunslet, Fowler, Ruston et al.

Demand for industrial locos has diminished dramatically due to the major reduction of heavy industry in the UK. However, some sites still require a shunting loco and several former BR/EWS Class 08/09s remain in what is best described as 'industrial use'.

Even what constitutes an 'industrial' loco is a grey area. Some sites prefer to hire locos from the likes of Rail Support Services, RMS Locotec and Harry Needle Railroad Company (see pages 315-318), while others prefer to own the locos outright.

This list details those locos in use, or owned by, industrial sites. They change over at short notice, or indeed may not work very often. It is a very fluid area, and subject to change.

This section, therefore, rounds up those locos that 'don't really fit anywhere else'.

Class 08

08296	Blue	Aggregates Industries	Whatley Quarry (U)	
08410	AV Dawson red	AV Dawson	Middlesbrough	
08442	LNWR grey	Arriva	Eastleigh (U)	
08447	Purple	John Russell	Deanside Transit	
08516	LNWR grey	Arriva	Bristol Barton Hill	*Rory*
08568	RCG	Knorr Bremse	Wishaw	*St Rollox*
08598	Potter Group yellow	AV Dawson	Middlesbrough	
08600	AV Dawson red	AV Dawson	Middlesbrough	
08602	Blue	Bombardier	Derby Litchurch Lane	
08629	Knorr Bremse blue/green	Meteor Power	Chinnor	
08643	Green	Aggregates Industries	Merehead Quarry	
08649	Knorr Bremse blue/green	Meteor Power	Silverstone	
08650	Blue	Aggregates Industries	Wishaw	
08652	Blue	Aggregates Industries	Wishaw	
08663	BR Blue	Hanson & Hall traction	Landore	
08682	Multi coloured	Bombardier	Derby Litchurch Lane	*Lionheart*
08730	ABP Ports blue	ABB Ports	Chasewater Railway	
08735	Arriva	Arriva	Eastleigh	
08743	Blue	ICI	Wilton	*Bryan Turner*
08774	AV Dawson red	AV Dawson	Middlesbrough	*Arthur Vernon Dawson*
08783	EWS red/gold	EMR	Kingsbury (U)	
08810	LNWR grey	Arriva	Eastleigh	*Richard J. Wenham Eastleigh Depot*
08846	Blue	Bombardier	Neville Hill	
08868	Arriva	Arriva	Crewe LNWR	
08872	EWS red/gold	EMR	Attercliffe	
08903	Blue	ICI	Wilton	*John W Antill*
08912	BR Blue	AV Dawson	Middlesbrough (U)	
08922	Departmental grey	Vulcan Rail	Newton Aycliffe	
08927	BR green		Bescot	
08933	Blue	Aggregates Industries	Whatley Quarry	
08947	Blue	Aggregates Industries	Whatley Quarry	
08956	BR Blue/Serco branding	Serco	Wishaw	
08536	Departmental grey	Vulcan Rail	Newton Aycliffe	
08784	Departmental grey	Vulcan Rail	Longport	

Class 09

09022	Blue	Victoria Ports	Boston Docks
09023	EWS red/gold	EMR	Attercliffe (U)
09204	Arriva	Arriva	Crewe LNWR

Off Lease Rolling Stock

The mass of new trains being introduced at the moment, plus changing legislation forcing many older vehicles off the rails, means there are several locomotives, multiple units and coaches now 'off lease'.

These are vehicles owned by the Rolling Stock Leasing companies that currently do not have a user. Some will go for scrap, others may be redeployed with other TOCs, some will be sold for reuse or preservation and some will be held in reserve pending possible reuse elsewhere.

Any vehicle or unit listed here may be sent for scrap, sold moved or redeployed at short notice.

Eversholt

The following Class 91s are in the SAXL pool and stored at either Doncaster Royal Mail Terminal, Bounds Green or Doncaster Works. Some are expected to move to Europhoenix (joining 91117/120) for redeployment in Europe, although the global Covid-19 pandemic has at least delayed this move.

Class 91

91102	91002	VEC	EVS	DB (S)
91103	91003	VEC	EVS	ZF (U)
91104	91004	VEC	EVS	DB (S)
91108	91008	VEC	EVS	ZF (U)
91112	91012	VEC	EVS	DB (S)
91113	91013	VEC	EVS	DB (S)
91115	91015	VEC	EVS	DB (S)
91116	91016	VEC	EVS	DB (S)
91118	91018	VEC	EVS	DB (S)
91121	91021	VEC	EVS	DB (S)
91125	91025	VEC	EVS	DB (S)
91126	91026	VEC	EVS	DB (S)
91129	91029	VEC	EVS	DB (S)
91131	91031	VEC	EVS	DB (S)
91132	91023	VEC	EVS	DB (S)

Mk 4 coaches

10300-305/307/308/311/315/318/320/321/323/324/326/330-332, 11201/219/277/278/280-283/287/289/298/299, 11301-307/310/311/314/316/318-322/327/329/330, 11401-405/407/409-411/414/416/418/430, 11998/999, 12200-204/207/209-211/213-216/222/224/225/229-232, 12300-302/304/305/307/308/310/312/315-317/321/323/324/326/327/329, 12401/402/405/410/411/414/415/417/419-421/423/425/428/433/434/436-440/443/445/448-450/452/453/458/459/461-463/467/468/471/477478/480/483/484/486/488/489, 12513/514/518/520/522/526/533/534, 82200-207/209/215/218/219-222/227/228/231

Class 315

Ex-LOROL units

315801	LOR	EVS	WB (S)	64461	71281	71389	64462
315809	LOR	EVS	NN (S)	64477	71289	71397	64478
315815	LOR	EVS	WB (S)	64489	71295	71403	64490
315833	LOR	EVS	IL	64525	71313	71421	64526

Service vehicles

6352	13465, 19465		EVS	Mk 2	Mk 4 barrier
6353	13478, 19478		EVS	Mk 2	Mk 4 barrier
975864	3489	BLU	EVS	Mk 1	EMU translator
975867	1006	BLU	EVS	Mk 1	EMU translator
975875	34643	BLU	EVS	Mk 1	EMU translator
977087	34971	BLU	EVS	Mk 1	EMU translator

Porterbrook

A number of former East Midlands Railway and Great Western Railway Class 43 HST Power cars are in the SBXL pool.

HST power cars

43043	EMB	POR	LM (S)
43044	EMB	POR	NL (U)
43045	EMB	POR	LM (S)
43053	FGB	POR	LM (S)
43056	FGB	POR	LM (S)
43061	EMB	POR	LM (S)
43063	FGB	POR	LA (U)
43064	EMB	POR	LM (S)
43069	FGB	POR	LM (S)
43070	FGB	POR	LM (S)
43071	FGB	POR	LM (S)
43075	EMB	POR	LM (S)
43078	FGB	POR	LM (S)
43079	FGB	POR	LM (S)
43081	EMB	POR	LM (S)
43082	EMB	POR	LM (S)
43086	FGB	POR	LA (U)
43087	FGB	POR	LM (S)
43091	FGB	POR	LA (S)
43159	FGB	POR	LM (S)
43161	FGB	POR	LA (S)
43180	FGB	POR	LA (S)
43193	FGB	POR	LM (S)
43196	FGB	POR	LA (S)
43197	FGB	POR	LM (S)
43277	VEC	POR	BH (U)
43290	VEC	POR	BH (U)
43300	VEC	POR	NL (U)

Mk 3 coaches

10413-415/417, 10522/526/527/531/542/544/551/553/561, 10605/680/689, 10706, 11018/048/066-070/072/073/075-078/080-082/085/087/088/090-096/098/099, 11100/101, 12005/009/012/013/015/016/021/024/026/027/030-032/034/035/037/040-042/046/051/056/057/060-062/064/066/073/079/081/082/084/089/090/093/097/099/100, 42103/105/107-110/114-116/118/120/122/125/126/129/130/132/133/137-139/141-143/146-148/150/151/153/154/159/161/164/166/167/170

HST trailers

40101/102/104/107/109/112-114/119, 40701/702/708/740, 40805/807/810/811, 41062/068/083/095, 41151/152/183, 42092, 42109/110/115/117/123/125/128/130/159/160/163/166/178/182/186/190/194, 42205/210/225/227-229/232/233/237/247/286/294, 42303/305-309/320-322/326/330-335/340/364/381-383, 44027/050/057/073/075/080/100, 46008/017

DVT

82101-103/105/107/112/118/121/132/133/136/143/152

Class 319

				DMC	MS	TS	DMS
319011	TLW	POR	LM (S)	77311	62901	71782	77310
319362	NOR	POR	LM (S)	77461	63044	71930	77460
319363	NOR	POR	LM (S)	77463	63045	71931	77462
319364	NOR	POR	LM (S)	77465	63046	71932	77464
319365	NOR	POR	LM (S)	77467	63047	71933	77466
319371	NOR	POR	LM (S)	77479	63053	71939	77478
319374	NOR	POR	LM (S)	77485	63056	71942	77484
319376	NOR	POR	LM (S)	77489	63058	71944	77488
319377	NOR	POR	LM (S)	77491	63059	71945	77490
319380	NOR	POR	LM (S)	77497	63062	71948	77496
319382	NOR	POR	LM (S)	77975	63094	71980	77976
319451	FIR	POR	LM (S)	77439	62965	71870	77438
319453	FIR	POR	LM (S)	77443	62967	71872	77442
319454	PBK	POR	LM (S)	77445	62968	71873	77444
319455	FIR	POR	LM (S)	77447	63969	71874	77446

Service vehicles

6376	1021, 975973	POR	Mk 1	EMU translator
6377	1042, 975975	POR	Mk 1	EMU translator
6378	1054, 975971	POR	Mk 1	EMU translator
6379	1059, 975972	POR	Mk 1	EMU translator
6393	81609, 92196	POR	Mk 1	HST barrier
6394	80878, 92906	POR	Mk 1	HST barrier

Angel

Eight ex-GWR Power Cars remain off lease in the SCEL pool, of which 43018 is a spares donor for ScotRail while the other seven remain stored at Ely.

43017	FGB	ANG	EY (U)
43020	FGB	ANG	LA (S)
43023	FGB	ANG	LM (S)
43024	FGB	ANG	EY (U)
43025	FGB	ANG	EY (U)
43165	FGB	ANG	EY (U)
43174	FGB	ANG	EY (U)
43185	ICS	ANG	HA (U)
43190	FGB	ANG	EY (U)
43191	FGB	ANG	LA (U)
43206	BRG	ANG	GW (U)
43311	VEC	ANG	GW (U)
43312	BRG	ANG	GW (U)
43313	VEC	ANG	LA (U)
43315	VEC	ANG	EY (U)
43367	VEC	ANG	EY (U)

HST trailers

40704/706/713/715/720/734/742, 41087/088/091/092, 41118/170, 42024/026, 42104/106/122/134/158/161/171/172/179-181/188, 42215/219/226/235/241-244, 42323/340/347/355/357/363, 42504/506/554/569, 44001/007/010/011/015/018/031-034/038/039/056/058/059/093/098

Class 142

Former Northern and Transport for Wales railbuses.

				DMS	DMSL
142003	NOR	ANG	NH (S)	55543	55593
142007	NOR	ANG	NH (S)	55548	55598
142014	NOR	ANG	NH (S)	55555	55605
142018	NOR	ANG	NH (S)	55559	55609
142023	NOR	ANG	NH (S)	55564	55614
142032	NOR	ANG	NH (S)	55573	55623
142035	NOR	ANG	NH (S)	55576	55626
142041	NOR	ANG	NH (S)	55582	55632
142043	NOR	ANG	NH (S)	55584	55634
142045	NOR	ANG	NH (S)	55586	55636
142047	NOR	ANG	NH (S)	55588	55638
142056	NOR	ANG	NH (S)	55706	55752
142070	NOR	ANG	NH (S)	55720	55766
142086	ARV	ANG	CF (S)	55736	55782
142095	NOR	ANG	NH (S)	55745	55791

Class 153s

Former East Midlands Trains units.

				DMSL
153302	EMT	ANG	EY (S)	52308
153318	EMT	ANG	EY (S)	52318
153368	EMT	ANG	EY (S)	57368
153372	EMT	ANG	EY (S)	57372
153374	EMT	ANG	EY (S)	57374
153382	EMT	ANG	EY (S)	57382

Class 317/6

Former Greater Anglia units

				DTC	MS	TC	DTS
317655	AGA	ANG	PQ (S)	77206	62852	71740	77226
317656	AGA	ANG	PQ (S)	77207	62853	71741	77227
317657	AGA	ANG	EY (S)	77208	62854	71742	77228
317659	AGA	ANG	EY (S)	77210	62856	71744	77230
317660	AGA	ANG	EY (S)	77211	62857	71745	77231
317661	AGA	ANG	PQ (S)	77212	62858	71746	77232
317662	AGA	ANG	EY (S)	77213	62859	71747	77233
317663	AGA	ANG	EY (S)	77214	62860	71748	77234
317664	AGA	ANG	PQ (S)	77215	62861	71749	77235
317665	AGA	ANG	IL (U)	77216	62862	71750	77236
317667	AGA	ANG	IL (U)	77218	62864	71752	77238
317668	AGA	ANG	EY (S)	77219	62865	71753	77239
317669	AGA	ANG	EY (S)	77280	62886	71762	77284
317671	AGA	ANG	EY (S)	77282	62888	71764	77286
317672	AGA	ANG	EY (S)	77283	62889	71765	77287

Class 317/7

Former London Overground units.

				DTS	MS	TS/TC	DTS
317708	LOR	ANG	NN (S)	77007	62668	71584	77055
317709	LOR	ANG	NN (S)	77008	62668	71585	77056
317710	LOR	ANG	NN (S)	77009	62670	71586	77057
317714	LOR	ANG	IL	77013	62674	71590	77061
317719	LOR	ANG	NN (S)	77018	62679	71595	77066
317722	LOR	ANG	PQ (S)	77021	62682	71598	77069
317723	LOR	ANG	IL	77022	62683	71599	77070
317729	LOR	ANG	IL	77028	62689	71605	77076
317732	LOR	ANG	IL	77031	62692	71608	77079

Class 317/8

Former London Overground units.

317887	LOR	ANG	XX (S)	77043	62704	71606	77077	
317888	LOR	ANG	EY (S)	77030	62691	71607	77078	
317889	LOR	ANG	XX (S)	77032	62693	71609	77080	
317890	LOR	ANG	WY (S)	77033	62694	71610	77081	
317891	LOR	ANG	EY (S)	77034	62695	71611	77082	
317892	LOR	ANG	EY (S)	77035	62696	71612	77083	*Ilford Depot*

Service vehicles

Current No.	Old Nos.	Livery	Owner	Type	Role
6330	14084, 975629	FIR	ANG	Mk 2	HST barrier
6336	81591, 92185	FIR	ANG	Mk 1	HST barrier
6338	81581, 92180	FIR	ANG	Mk 1	HST barrier
6340	21251, 975678	BLU	ANG	Mk 1	HST barrier
6344	81263, 92080	BLU	ANG	Mk 1	HST barrier
6346	9422	BLU	ANG	Mk 2	HST barrier
6348	81233, 92963	FIR	ANG	Mk 1	HST barrier
64664			ANG	Class 508	EMU translator
64707			ANG	Class 508	EMU translator
975974	1030	BLU	ANG	Mk 1	EMU translator
975978	1025	BLU	ANG	Mk 1	EMU translator

Department for Transport

These ex-Great Northern Class 365 25kV AC EMUs are now owned by the Department for Transport and available for short-term lease by TOCs. Some were used but ScotRail pending the deliveries of the Class 385s, but they have all been returned now. They are in store at Crewe.

				DMC	TS	PTS	DMC
365501	TLW	DFT	CB (S)	65894	72241	72240	65935
365503	TLW	DFT	CB (S)	65896	72245	72244	65937
365505	TLW	DFT	CB (S)	65898	72249	72248	65939
365507	TLW	DFT	CB (S)	65900	72253	72252	65941
365509	TLW	DFT	CB (S)	65902	72257	72256	65943
365513	TLW	DFT	CB (S)	65906	72265	72264	65947
365515	TLW	DFT	CB (S)	65908	72269	72268	65949
365517	TLW	DFT	CB (S)	65910	72273	72272	65951
365519	TLW	DFT	CB (S)	65912	72277	72276	65953
365521	TLW	DFT	CB (S)	65914	72281	72280	65955
365523	TLW	DFT	CB (S)	65916	72285	72284	65957
365525	TLW	DFT	CB (S)	65918	72289	72288	65959
365527	TLW	DFT	CB (S)	65920	72293	72292	65961
365529	TLW	DFT	CB (S)	65922	72297	72296	65963
365531	TLW	DFT	CB (S)	65924	72301	72300	65965
365533	TLW	DFT	CB (S)	65926	72305	72304	65967
365535	TLW	DFT	CB (S)	65928	72309	72308	65969
365537	TLW	DFT	CB (S)	65930	72313	72312	65971
365541	TLW	DFT	CB (S)	65934	72321	72320	65975

Arriva

Arriva Trains has sold most of its redundant Mk 3 stock to ROG but retains one Mk 3 DVT.

Mk 3 DVT

82307

Network Rail

After an ill-fated public flotation of the national infrastructure as Railtrack in the mid-1990s, following a series of tragic high-profile accidents, some caused by inadequate maintenance, in 2002 the network was renationalised as Network Rail.

Network Rail owns, operates and develops Britain's railway infrastructure of 20,000 miles of track, 30,000 bridges, tunnels and viaducts and the thousands of signals, signal boxes, level crossings and stations.

It also manages 20 of the largest stations, namely Birmingham New Street, Bristol Temple Meads, Clapham Junction, Edinburgh Waverley, Glasgow Central, Guildford, Leeds, Liverpool Lime Street, Manchester Piccadilly, Reading and most major London termini including London Bridge, Cannon Street, Charing Cross, Euston, King's Cross, Liverpool Street, Paddington, St Pancras International, Victoria and Waterloo. The other stations – of which there are over 2,500 – are managed by the train operating companies.

Network Rail has created 14 new routes, which are supported by five regions, each led by a Managing Director. The regions are Eastern, North West & Central, Scotland's Railway, Southern and Wales & Western. They were formed in June 2019 and have the budget and capability to take on more responsibility from other parts of the business.

The routes are responsible for operations, maintenance and minor renewals, including the day-to-day delivery of train performance and the relationship with their local train operating companies.

Phase two of the programme started in November 2019 and is designed to strengthen NR's new regions and further build Network Services and Route Services. This new structure sets NR up for more devolution and to be more responsive to the needs of train operators, passengers and freight users by bringing its people closer to those it serves.

Network Rail Regions and Routes

- **Eastern Region**: Routes: Anglia, East Midlands, North and East and East Coast
- **North West and Central Region**: Routes: North West, Central, West Coast Mainline South
- **Scotland's Railway**
- **Southern Region**: Routes: Kent, Sussex, Wessex Route, Network Rail High Speed
- **Wales & Western Region**: Routes: Wales Route, Western

Train operation

Network Rail is not allowed to operate its own trains, and accordingly all its movements – Infrastructure Monitoring (IM), infrastructure support (ballast and material trains – the old BR Departmental sector) and track machine moves – have to be undertaken by third-party TOCs and FOCs.

However, NR does own a few locomotives, It has a Class 08 based at Derby RTC (albeit currently stored), four Class 37 (reclassified as Class 97/3s) used for ERTMS workings west of Shrewsbury, three HST power cars for the New Measurement Train and three Class 73s for working IM trains – one standard loco and two trial re-engineered Cummins-powered Class 73/9s. It also owns a Class 150 DMU and Class 313 EMU and several coaches for use for IM trains.

NR has seven operations bases and five delivery depots for materials. Its IM trains are based at the former Derby RTC and maintained by Loram and operated by Colas. There are 24 seasonal treatment fleet bases, from Scotland to the south-east, where Multi-Purpose Vehicles (MPVs) – two-car 'freight multiple units' – are based for weed killing and other maintenance roles. The company also has six SITT snow-clearing trains based in the south-east.

The IM fleet

Infrastructure monitoring allows NR to monitor the condition of the track and pre-plan any maintenance in a proactive manner rather than a reactive 'wait for it to fail, then repair it' manner.

The New Measurement Train (NMT) monitors and records track condition information at speeds up to 125mph. It helps locate and identify faults before they become a safety issue or affect performance.

The NMT uses two HST power cars and a rake of Mk 3 trailers, and is a unique, hi-tech machine introduced 15 years ago. It is equipped with the newest, hi-tech measurement systems, track scanners and a high-resolution camera to measure the condition of the track, especially on the busiest and fast main lines.

The NMT covers 115,000 miles in a year and captures around 10TB of image data every 440 miles. Because it can run at up to 125mph, it identifies faults faster and more accurately than ever before so engineers can then make repairs or plan maintenance to prevent serious incidents such as derailments.

A laser sensor gives information about the profile of the rail head, measuring shape and movement optically. At the same time, transducers and accelerometers mechanically measure the up and down movement of the train as it travels along the rails. This data provides information on track geometry – the shape and profile of the rail head and the twist of the track.

NR also has a plain line pattern recognition (PLPR) system that uses a series of lasers and cameras to detect faulty track components as the train passes over them. Image analysis software uses an algorithm to compare what the cameras see with an image of how the track should look. For example, it can identify missing Pandrol clips, which secure rails to the sleepers, allowing teams on the ground to replace them quickly.

Infrastructure wagons

NR also has a High Output Ballast Cleaning (HOBC) train, and it owns around 1,000 wagons to carry aggregates such as ballast and remove waste from work sites. Among this fleet are box wagons to remove waste; autoballaster wagons with 'trap doors' at the base that release ballast directly beneath, on to the track; and tilting wagons to position switches and crossings during track renewal work.

It has a rail delivery train that can carries 108m section of rails from the British Steel plant in Scunthorpe to be welded into 216m lengths at NR's long welded rail depot in Eastleigh, Hampshire. Some are welded into place at the worksites.

The ballast cleaning system (BCS) and track renewal system (TRS) trains operate in a conveyor process, renewing the track as they move along it. Both the BCS and TRS are supported by tamper/dynamic track stabiliser machines that accurately position the track and consolidate ballast after renewal.

It also owns rail grinders – a grinding train that maintains the track and helps to increase the lifespan of the rail by removing small layers of metal from the railhead, helping to keep the track in good condition.

Stoneblowers restore the line and level of the track by correcting its vertical (height) and lateral (left or right) profile. They measure the track to work out where it needs to be lifted to bring it level, and how much it needs to be moved side to side to ensure correct alignment.

Tampers are track maintenance machines that make sure the track is correctly aligned and has a smooth level along the rail. They help to prevent the risk of trains derailing, and ensure smooth, comfortable journeys for passengers and freight trains. Tamping machines insert large tools called tines into the ballast – the stones beneath the track – and then force the tines together to move ballast under the sleepers. The tamping machine moves additional ballast under the sleepers to raise the height of the track and can move the track sideways if required.

Specialist machines help NR's engineers to keep the railway open all year round and bearing in mind the effects of weather are a challenge for the railway, and weather conditions can severely impact the day-to-day running of services, they provide a vital service.

Rain can result in flooding and damage infrastructure such as bridges, lineside equipment and the track, or lead to landslips – while rails can buckle and overhead lines sag in extreme summer heat. Autumn leaf fall causes operational problems for the signalling system and reduces railhead condition, which can make trains slide on the track even when braking, and so run past signals at danger or merely not stop in a platform as the driver intends.

Track clearance

Poor railhead condition restricts the ability of a train to start from a station, accelerate and climb hills, which means it can lose time, delay passengers and affect the timetable.

As a result each autumn, NR contracts the running of hundreds of RHTTs – Railhead Treatment trains – which are operated by the FOCs and use either its 32 MPVs or 29 sets of top-and-tailed loco-hauled wagons with RHTT tanks and equipment. These cover sections of track well known for suffering poor rail head conditions.

The snow and ice treatment trains (SITTs) help clear snow from the conductor rails and prevent ice freezing to them again. Both MPVs and SITTs scrape ice off the conductor railhead and spray the rails with hot liquid anti-icer that prevents ice sticking to the conductor rail head.

There are 24 MPVs used on the third-rail routes of Kent, Sussex, Wessex and Mersey Rail, while ten locomotive-hauled SITTs are deployed in Kent and Sussex.

The third type of winter de-icing train, the winter development vehicle (WDV), is built to blow hot air around the running rails – specifically around points and crossings – to melt snow and ice that is stopping the points from working. The WDV is also equipped with steam lances to melt the more built-up stubborn ice deposits.

Also in NR's arsenal to clear snow are patrols using locos fitted with three-piece miniature snowploughs (MSPs), which are hired and operated by GBRf, DRS, WCR, ROG and others. MSPs work effectively in snow depths of up to 18in. For heavier drifts, Beilhack V or independent snowploughs propelled by locomotives are used.

Network Rail also has two now blowers in Scotland, which are fitted with propellers that cut through and blow away snow drifts. A special hydraulic turntable within the machine makes it possible for the snow blower to turn around on its own if needed.

Eight of NR's MPVs are equipped to spray herbicides to control plant growth on the tracks. This maintains safe walking routes for workers, allows drivers to see signals, prevents damage to trains caused by vegetation and maintains the stability of our structures.

No. 97302 works the 0900 Doncaster West Yard-Derby RTC IM train, past the site of Blotoft signal box on 10 February 2016. *Bill Atkinson*

NR fleet

Class 08

NR owns one Class 08, 08417, based at Derby for shunting test train vehicles. It is in the QADD pool.

08417 NRY NET ZA (U)

Class 37

NR owns one Class 37, which was bought as a spare loco for possible conversion to a Class 97/3s. While it was not needed, it went on loan to the Great Central Railway but was damaged in a shunting incident. Although it has been repaired, the loco has been used as a spares donor for the Class 97/3 fleet.

37198 NRY NET ZA (U)

Class 43

There are presently three MTU-powered HST power cars, leased from Porterbrook, which are used for the NMT. Nos 43013/014 have buffers fitted. NR is understood to be taking three more power cars, with 43053/056/071 mooted, as short-term cover while, these locos are upgraded with ECTS. All are in QCAR pool.

43013	NRY	POR	ZA	*Mark Carne CBE*
43014	NRY	POR	ZA	*The Railway Observer*
43062	NRY	POR	ZA	*John Armitt*

Hired-in 37612, with 37219 *Jonty Jarvis* on the rear, work the 0937 Derby RTC-Skegness IM train, passing Bottesford on 31 October 2019. *Bill Atkinson*

Class 73/1

NR still owns one standard Class 73, previously preserved 73138. Its other locos, 73141/212/213, were sold to GBRf. No. 73138 is occasionally used for hauling IM trains and is in the QADD pool.

73138	NET	NRY	ZA

Class 73/9s

Two Class 73s were rebuilt by RVEL (later taken over by Loram) at Derby and fitted with two Cummins engines in place of their EE engine. Heavy delayed and problematic when first put into traffic, they are now performing well and are used for hauling IM trains. They have recently been modified to run off bio-LPG as well as diesel. Both are in the QADD pool.

73951	73104	NRY	NET	ZA	*Malcolm Brinded*
73952	73113, 73211	NRY	NET	ZA	*Janis Kong*

Class 97/3

When ERTMS was implemented on the Cambrian lines, NR needed some locos to pilot to work any trains along these lines that would otherwise use locos not fitted with ERTMS.

Accordingly, four Class 37/0s were acquired from HNRC and overhauled and fitted with ERTMS. The system on 97301 is different to that on 97302-304. WCR's 37668/669 also have the same ERTMS system as used on 97301 and these can also work on these lines.

They work charter trains, infrastructure support and monitoring trains, saloon visits and other traffic should it be needed, such as freight, Royal trains or special workings. All are in the QETS pool.

97301	37100	NRY	NET	ZA	
97302	37170	NRY	NET	ZA	*Ffestiniog and Welsh Highland Railways/ Eheilffrdd Ffestiniog Ac Eryri*
97303	37178	NRY	NET	ZA	
97304	37217	NRY	NET	ZA	*John Tiley*

Class 950

This purpose-built IM test train, based on a two-car Class 150/1 Sprinter DMU, was built in 1987 and initially a Class 180, before being added to the Departmental fleet.

				DMSL	DMS
950001	NRY	NET	ZA	999600	999601

Class 313

This former Silverlink unit is used for ERTMS testing.

				DMS	TS	BDMS
313121	NRY	BEA	ZG	62549	71233	62613

Above: The Network Rail New Measurement Train, with 43062 *John Armitt* leading, travels south past Tredington Crossing near Cheltenham bound for Reading on 7 July 2020. *Jack Boskett*

Right: One of two re-engineered Class 73/9s, 73951 *Malcolm Brinded* passes Barrow upon Trent on 24 September 2018. *Paul Robertson*

Below: Inspection saloon 975025 *Caroline*, hauled by 37409 *Lord Hinton*, passes Loughborough on 3 April 2019. *Antony Christie*

Test Coaches

Network Rail currently has an extensive fleet of test train coaches. They are usually ex-BR coaches such as Mk 1 and 2 vehicles, although some are former multiple units and the New Measurement Train uses HST Mk 3 trailer vehicles.

Those vehicles listed as Class 488s were initially Mk 2 coaches later converted to Gatwick Express stock and reclassified as multiple units.

Current No.	Old Nos.	Livery	Owner	Type	Role
1256	3296	NRY	NRY	Mk 2	Plain line pattern recognition coach
5981		NRY	NRY	Mk 2	Plain line pattern recognition coach
6260	81450, 92116	NRY	NRY	Mk 1	Generator van
6261	81284, 92988	NRY	NRY	Mk 1	Generator van
6262	81064, 92928	NRY	NRY	Mk 1	Generator van
6263	81231, 92961	NRY	NRY	Mk 1	Generator van
6264	80971, 92923	NRY	NRY	Mk 1	Generator van
9481		NRY	NRY	Mk 2	Staff coach
9516		NRY	NRY	Mk 2	Test train brake force runner
9523		NRY	NRY	Mk 2	Test train brake force runner
9701	9528	NRY	NRY	Mk 2	Driving Brake
9702	9510	NRY	NRY	Mk 2	Driving Brake
9703	9517	NRY	NRY	Mk 2	Driving Brake
9708	9530	NRY	NRY	Mk 2	Driving Brake
9714	9536	NRY	NRY	Mk 2	Driving Brake
9801	5760	FIR	ERS	Mk 2	Test train brake coach
9803	5799	FIR	ERS	Mk 2	Test train brake coach
9806	5840	FIR	ERS	Mk 2	Test train brake coach
9808	5871	FIR	ERS	Mk 2	Test train brake coach
9810	5892	FIR	ERS	Mk 2	Test train brake coach
62287		NRY	NRY	Class 421	Ultrasonic test coach
62384		NRY	NRY	Class 421	Ultrasonic test coach

Led by 37219, the Plain Line Pattern Recognition trains passes Spalding on 15 October 2016. *Pip Dunn*

72612	6156	NRY	NRY	Class 488/3	Test train brake force runner	
72616	6007	NRY	NRY	Class 488/3	Test train brake force runner	
72630	6094	NRY	NRY	Class 488/3	Structure gauging train coach	
72631	6096	NRY	NRY	Class 488/3	Plain line pattern recognition coach	
72639	6070	NRY	NRY	Class 488/3	Plain line pattern recognition coach	
82111		NRY	NRY	Mk 3	Driving van trailer	
82124		NRY	NRY	Mk 3	Driving van trailer	
82129		NRY	NRY	Mk 3	Driving van trailer	
82145		NRY	NRY	Mk 3	Driving van trailer	
99666	3250	NRY	NRY	Mk 2	Structure gauging train coach	
975025	60755	GRE	NRY	Class 202	Inspection saloon	
975091	34615	NRY	NRY	Mk 1	Overhead line equipment test coach	*Mentor*
975814	11000, 41000	NRY	NRY	HST Mk 3	New Measurement Train	
975984	10000, 40000	NRY	NRY	HST Mk 3	New Measurement Train	
977868	5846	NRY	NRY	Mk 2	Radio survey coach	
977969	14112, 2906	NRY	NRY	Mk 2	Staff coach	
977974	5854	NRY	NRY	Mk 2	Track inspection train coach	
977983	3407, 72503	NRY	NRY	Mk 2	Electrification measurement coach	
977984	40501	NRY	NRY	HST Mk 3	New Measurement Train	
977985	6019, 72715	NRY	NRY	Class 488/3	Structure gauging train coach	
977986	3189, 99664	NRY	NRY	Mk 2	Structure gauging train coach	
977993	44053	NRY	NRY	HST Mk 3	New Measurement Train	
977994	44087	NRY	NRY	HST Mk 3	New Measurement Train	
977995	40719, 40619	NRY	NRY	HST Mk 3	New Measurement Train	
977997	72613, 6126	NRY	NRY	Class 488/3	Radio survey coach	
999550		NRY	NRY	Mk 2	Track recording coach	
999602	62483	NRY	NRY	Class 421	Ultrasonic test coach	
999605	62482	NRY	NRY	Class 421	Ultrasonic test coach	
999606	62356	NRY	NRY	Class 432	Ultrasonic test coach	
977869	5858	NRY	NRY	Mk 2	Infrastructure maintenance coach	

Network Rail's Class 150-derived IM unit 950001 on display at Long Marston during the Rail Live event on 20 June 2019. *Jack Boskett*

Ex-UK Locos Abroad

Several locos of different classes have been sold, reallocated or leased for use abroad. This is especially true since privatisation.

When DB Schenker took over EWS, it started to redeploy surplus Class 66s in France and Poland and Class 92s in Bulgaria and Romania. It has since sold some of the latter.

It also did hire deals for Class 37s in Spain, France and Italy – deals that have all long since finished – while several 56s and 58s were also hired for infrastructure projects in France that have also been concluded.

Several Class 58s were also moved to Spain, some of which were then sold to Transfesa and subsequently scrapped.

Freightliner has also moved several spare Class 66s to Poland, while Class 56s, 86s and 87s redundant in the UK have been sold abroad to Hungary and Bulgaria by Europhoenix. Class 91s could follow.

A single Class 47 has been sent to Hungary by Nemesis Rail.

Pre-privatisation exports

Many shunters of Class 03, 04, 06, 07, 08 and 14 were sold to Italy, Spain, Belgium, France and Liberia in the 1960s and '70s. Also, all seven Class 77s DC electric locos were sold to the Netherlands in 1968.

Most have been scrapped now, although a handful have been repatriated for preservation. The following three locos are thought to still be intact abroad, although the Class 08s in Liberia may well have been scrapped now, having not been used for decades.

Class 03

D2156	03156	ITY	BLU

Class 08

D3047	13047	LAM	LAM
D3092	13092	LAM	LAM

Note: Both these locos may have been scrapped.

Post-Privatisation exports

Class 47

A single Class 47, 47375, was leased by Nemesis Rail to Hungarian operator Continental Rail solutions in 2015. The deal could have seen three other locos follow it (47488/701/744) but this never happened. The loco has since been spot-hired to a couple of different operators, and most recently has been used to haul coal trains to the Romanian border. The loco is still on TOPS in the NRLO pool.

92 70 00 47375-5	47375	CSM	CON	HUN	*Falcon*

Class 56

Thirty Class 56s were hired by EWS to Fertis between 2004 and 2007 and all returned to EWS and were then sold.

Two of those locos, along with a third that had previously been sold for preservation, were then sold by Europhoenix to Hungarian operator Floyd. One loco is used for spares only, while the other two are used for freight trains in the country.

92 55 0659 001-5	56101	FLY	FLY	HUN
92 55 0659 002-3	56115	FLY	FLY	HUN
92 55 0659 003-1	56117	FER	FLY	HUN (U)

Class 58

Class 58s were hired by EWS to ACTS in the Netherlands, Seco Rail and Fertis in France and GIF and Continental Rail in Spain. Nine of the Spanish locos were later sold to Transfesa, of which eight were then scrapped – 58015/020/024/029-031/043/041 in late 2019 and early 2020.

Of 28 locos left in Europe, 24 remain stored in France and four in Spain. The French locos are owned by DB Cargo.

	58001	WQCA	DBC	ETF	AZ (U)
	58004	WQCA	DBC	TSO	AZ (U)
	58005	WQCA	DBC	ETF	AZ (U)
	58006	WQCA	DBC	ETF	AZ (U)
	58007	WQCA	DBC	TSO	AZ (U)
	58009	WQCA	DBC	TSO	AZ (U)
	58010	WQCA	DBC	TSO	AZ (U)
	58011	WQCA	DBC	TSO	AZ (U)
	58013	WQCA	DBC	ETF	AZ (U)
	58018	WQCA	DBC	TSO	AZ (U)
	58021	WQCA	DBC	ETF	AZ (U)
	58025	WQCA	DBC	CON	AB (U)
	58026	WQCA	DBC	TSO	AZ (U)
L52	58027	WQCA	DBC	CON	AB (U)
	58032	WQCA	DBC	ETF	AZ (U)
	58033	WQCA	DBC	TSO	AZ (U)
	58034	WQCA	DBC	TSO	AZ (U)
	58035	WQCA	DBC	TSO	AZ (U)
	58036	WQCA	DBC	ETF	AZ (U)
5814	58038	WCQA	TFA	ETF	AZ (U)
5811	58039	WQCA	DBC	ETF	AZ (U)
	58040	WQCA	DBC	TSO	AZ (U)
L36	58041		TFA	CON	AB (U)
	58042	WQCA	DBC	ETF	AZ (U)
5812	58044	WQCA	DBC	ETF	WP (U)
	58046	WQCA	DBC	TSO	AZ (U)
	58049	WQCA	DBC	ETF	AZ (U)
L53	58050	WQCA	DBC	CON	AB (U)

Class 66

Surplus traction in the UK saw both EWS (now DB Cargo) and then Freightliner redeploying Class 66s. Sixty-four went to France with the former, while 15 EWS locos and 18 Freightliner locos have moved to Poland.

The DBC locos occasionally return to the UK for heavy maintenance, although such transfers are rare these days.

The Freightliner Poland locos have been renumbered in the 660xx series for Class 66/5s and 6660x series for Class 66/6s. FPL also owns seven 'Class 66s' numbered 66001-007, which were new-build locos and did not work in the UK.

DB Cargo's Euro Cargo Rail subsidiary also operates 60 'Class 66s', numbered 77001-060, which were also new-build and did not work here. All WGEP locos have their swinghead couplers removed, while WGEA locos retain them.

92 70 0 066010-4	66010	WGEA	EWS	DBC	AZ
92 70 0 066022-9	66022	WGEA	EWS	DBC	AZ
92 70 0 066026-0	66026	WGEA	EWS	DBC	AZ
92 70 0 066028-6	66028	WGEA	EWS	DBC	AZ
92 70 0 066029-4	66029	WGEA	EWS	DBC	AZ
92 70 0 066032-8	66032	WGEA	EWS	DBC	AZ
92 70 0 066033-6	66033	WGEA	EWS	DBC	AZ
92 70 0 066036-9	66036	WGEA	EWS	DBC	AZ
92 70 0 066038-5	66038	WGEA	EWS	DBC	AZ
92 70 0 066042-7	66042	WGEA	EWS	DBC	AZ
92 70 0 066045-0	66045	WGEA	EWS	DBC	AZ
92 70 0 066049-2	66049	WGEA	EWS	DBC	AZ
92 70 0 066052-6	66052	WGEA	EWS	DBC	AZ
92 70 0 066062-5	66062	WGEA	EWS	DBC	AZ
92 70 0 066064-1	66064	WGEA	EWS	DBC	AZ
92 70 0 066071-6	66071	WGEA	EWS	DBC	AZ
92 70 0 066072-4	66072	WGEA	EWS	DBC	AZ
92 70 0 066073-2	66073	WGEA	EWS	DBC	AZ
92 70 0 066123-5	66123	WGEA	EWS	DBC	AZ
92 70 0 066146-6	66146	WGEP	EWS	DBC	PN
92 70 0 066153-2	66153	WGEP	EWS	DBC	PN
92 70 0 066157-3	66157	WGEP	EWS	DBC	PN
92 70 0 066159-9	66159	WGEP	EWS	DBC	PN
92 70 0 066163-1	66163	WGEP	DBR	DBC	PN
92 70 0 066166-4	66166	WGEP	EWS	DBC	PN
92 70 0 066173-0	66173	WGEP	EWS	DBC	PN
92 70 0 066178-9	66178	WGEP	DBR	DBC	PN
92 70 0 066179-7	66179	WGEA	EWS	DBC	AZ
92 70 0 066180-5	66180	WGEP	EWS	DBC	PN
92 70 0 066189-6	66189	WGEP	DBR	DBC	PN
92 70 0 066190-4	66190	WGEA	EWS	DBC	AZ
92 70 0 066191-2	66191	WGEA	EWS	DBC	AZ
92 70 0 066193-8	66193	WGEA	EWS	DBC	AZ
92 70 0 066195-3	66195	WGEA	EWS	DBC	AZ
92 70 0 066196-1	66196	WGEP	EWS	DBC	PN
92 70 0 066201-9	66201	WGEA	EWS	DBC	AZ
92 70 0 066202-7	66202	WGEA	EWS	DBC	AZ
92 70 0 066203-5	66203	WGEA	EWS	DBC	AZ
92 70 0 066204-3	66204	WGEA	EWS	DBC	AZ
92 70 0 066205-1	66205	WGEA	EWS	DBC	AZ
92 70 0 066208-4	66208	WGEA	EWS	DBC	AZ

92 70 0 066209-2	66209	WGEA	EWS	DBC	AZ
92 70 0 066210-0	66210	WGEA	EWS	DBC	AZ
92 70 0 066211-8	66211	WGEA	EWS	DBC	AZ
92 70 0 066212-6	66212	WGEA	EWS	DBC	AZ
92 70 0 066213-4	66213	WGEA	EWS	DBC	AZ
92 70 0 066214-2	66214	WGEA	EWS	DBC	AZ
92 70 0 066215-9	66215	WGEA	EWS	DBC	AZ
92 70 0 066216-7	66216	WGEA	EWS	DBC	AZ
92 70 0 066217-5	66217	WGEA	EWS	DBC	AZ
92 70 0 066218-3	66218	WGEA	EWS	DBC	AZ
92 70 0 066219-1	66219	WGEA	EWS	DBC	AZ
92 70 0 066220-9	66220	WGEP	DBR	DBC	PN
92 70 0 066222-5	66222	WGEA	EWS	DBC	AZ
92 70 0 066223-3	66223	WGEA	EWS	DBC	AZ
92 70 0 066224-1	66224	WGEA	EWS	DBC	AZ
92 70 0 066225-8	66225	WGEA	EWS	DBC	AZ
92 70 0 066226-6	66226	WGEA	EWS	DBC	AZ
92 70 0 066227-4	66227	WGEP	DBR	DBC	PN
92 70 0 066228-2	66228	WGEA	EWS	DBC	AZ
92 70 0 066229-0	66229	WGEA	EWS	DBC	AZ
92 70 0 066231-6	66231	WGEA	EWS	DBC	AZ
92 70 0 066232-4	66232	WGEA	EWS	DBC	AZ
92 70 0 066233-2	66233	WGEA	EWS	DBC	AZ
92 70 0 066234-0	66234	WGEA	EWS	DBC	AZ
92 70 0 066235-7	66235	WGEA	EWS	DBC	AZ
92 70 0 066236-5	66236	WGEA	EWS	DBC	AZ
92 70 0 066237-3	66237	WGEP	EWS	DBC	PN
92 70 0 066239-9	66239	WGEA	EWS	DBC	AZ
92 70 0 066240-7	66240	WGEA	EWS	DBC	AZ
92 70 0 066241-5	66241	WGEA	EWS	DBC	AZ
92 70 0 066242-3	66242	WGEA	EWS	DBC	AZ
92 70 0 066243-1	66243	WGEA	EWS	DBC	AZ
92 70 0 066244-9	66244	WGEA	EWS	DBC	AZ
92 70 0 066245-6	66245	WGEA	EWS	DBC	AZ
92 70 0 066246-4	66246	WGEA	EWS	DBC	AZ
92 70 0 066247-2	66247	WGEA	EWS	DBC	AZ
92 70 0 066248-9	66248	WGEP	DBR	DBC	PN
92 70 0 066249-8	66249	WGEA	EWS	DBC	AZ
66013	66411	DHLT	FPH	MAQ	FP
66015	66412	DHLT	FPH	MAQ	FP
66014	66417	DHLT	FPH	MAQ	FP
66016	66527	DHLT	FLR	EVS	FP
66017	66530	DHLT	FLR	POR	FP
66018	66535	DHLT	FLR	POR	FP
66009	66582	DHLT	FLR	EVS	FP
66010	66583	DHLT	FLR	EVS	FP
66011	66584	DHLT	FLR	EVS	FP
66008	66586	DHLT	FLR	MAQ	FP
	66595	DHLT	FLR	BEA	FP
66603	66608	DHLT	FLR	POR	FP
66605	66609	DHLT	FLR	POR	FP
66604	66611	DHLT	FLR	POR	FP
66606	66612	DHLT	FLR	POR	FP
66602	66624	DHLT	FLR	MAQ	FP
66601	66625	DHLT	FLR	MAQ	FP
	66954	DHLT	FLR	BEA	FP

Class 86

Several Class 86s made redundant by Virgin, Anglia Railways and Network Rail have been exported to Bulgaria and Hungary.

Floyd in Hungary has nine locos, all of which have been returned to traffic including 86424, which was originally earmarked as just being a source of spares.

Bulmarket in Bulgaria has a mixed Class 86 / 87 fleet. Of the former, it has six operational locos and one spares donor, 86233. All locos were exported via Europhoenix.

New No.	BR Nos.	Livery	Operator	Country	Name
91 52 00 85003-2	86213	BMT	BMT	BUL	*Lancashire Witch*
91 55 0450 005-6	86215	FLY	FLY	HUN	
91 55 0450 006-6	86217, 86504	FLY	FLY	HUN	
91 55 0450 004-1	86218	FLY	FLY	HUN	
91 55 0450 007-4	86228	FLY	FLY	HUN	
9152 00 85005-2	86231	BMT	BMT	BUL	*Lady of the Lake*
91 55 0450 003-3	86232	FLY	FLY	HUN	
	86233, 86506	EBY	BMT	BUL (U)	
9152 00 85006-2	86234	BMT	BMT	BUL	
9152 00 85004-7	86235	BMT	BMT	BUL	*Novelty*
91 55 0450 008-2	86242	FLY	FLY	HUN	
91 55 0450 001-7	86248	FLY	FLY	HUN	
91 55 0450 002-5	86250	FLY	FLY	HUN	
91 55 0450 009-0	86424, 86324, 86024	FLY	FLY	HUN	
91 52 00 85001-6	86701, 86503, 86205	BMT	BMT	BUL	*Orion*
91 52 00 85002-4	86702, 86260, 86048	BMT	BMT	BUL	*Cassiopeia*

The only Class 47 to be moved abroad is Nemesis Rail's 47375, which is now based in Hungary with Continental Rail Solutions. On 9 June 2018, the loco was on a charter train that took it into Austria, seen at Wiener Neustadt. *Anthony Sayer*

Class 87

Redundant former Virgin West Coast Class 87s were the first locos Europhoenix sold abroad, with 17 sent to Bulgarian rail operator BZK, although not all were returned to traffic and some have since been withdraw from use.

Bulmarket, also in Bulgaria, has taken four locos, which are in traffic.

New No.	BR No.	Livery	Operator	Country	Name
91 52 00 87003-7	87003	BZK	BZK	BUL	
91 52 00 87004-5	87004	BRZ	BZK	BUL	*Britannia*
91 52 00 87006-0	87006	DGB	BZK	BUL (U)	
91 52 00 87007-8	87007	COT	BZK	BUL	
87008-9	87008	COT	BZK	BUL (U)	
91 52 00 87009-4	87009	BMT	BMT	BUL	
91 52 00 87010-2	87010	BZK	BZK	BUL	
91 52 00 87012-8	87012	NSE	BZK	BUL	
91 52 00 87013-6	87013	BZK	BZK	BUL (U)	
87014-7	87014	BZK	BZK	BUL (U)	
91 52 00 87017-7	87017	EPX	BMT	BUL	*Iron Duke*
91 52 00 87019-3	87019	LNR	BZK	BUL	
91 52 00 87020-1	87020	BZK	BZK	BUL	
91 52 00 87022-7	87022	DGB	BZK	BUL (U)	
91 52 00 87023-5	87023	EPX	BMT	BUL	*Velocity*
91 52 00 87025-0	87025	BMT	BMT	BUL	
91 52 00 87026-8	87026	BZK	BZK	BUL	
91 52 00 87028-4	87028	DRS	BZK	BUL	
91 52 00 87029-2	87029	BZK	BZK	BUL	
91 52 00 87033-4	87033	BZK	BZK	BUL	
91 52 00 87034-2	87034	BZK	BZK	BUL	

Several Class 87s have been exported to Bulgaria via Europhoenix and one, 87004, was exported in BR blue with its *Britannia* name. On 21 June 2019, the loco was at Razdelna. *Anthony Sayer*

Class 92

The story of Class 92s abroad is slightly different. When DB took over the EWS operation it inherited 30 Class 92s, of which only a fraction could be employed in the UK. Accordingly, in May 2013 it started to move surplus locos to Romania and Bulgaria.

Some of these have now been sold to Russian company LocoTech for use by Transagent Spedicija in Croatia and have been repainted into Transagent black or red. All remain in the WGEE pool.

New No.	BR No.	Livery	Owner	Country	Name
91 53 0 472 002-1	92001	DBR	TAR	CRO	*Mircea Eliade*
91 53 0 472 003-9	92002	DBZ	DBC	CRO	
	92003	EUE	TRA	CRO	*Beethoven*
91 53 0 472 005-4	92005	CRO	TAB	CRO	
91 53 0 472 001-3	92012	TRA	TRA	CRO	
88002	92022	EUE	DBC	ROM (U)	*Charles Dickens*
91 53 0 472 004-7	92024	TRA	TAR	CRO	
91 70 00 92025-1	92025	EUE	DBC	ROM	*Oscar Wilde*
	92026	EUE	TRA	CRO	*Britten*
91 70 00 92027-7	92027	EUE	DBC	ROM	*George Eliot*
91 52 16 88030-1	92030	EUE	DBC	ROM	*Ashford*
91 70 00 92034-3	92034	EUE	DBC	ROM	*Kipling*
91 53 0 472 006-2	92039	DBR	TRA	CRO	*Eugen Ionescu*

Left: Bulmarket in Bulgaria took a handful of Class 86s and 87s. The former 86260/86702 has now been renumbered as 85002 and was seen at Obraztsov Chiflik in northern Bulgaria near the Romanian border on 19 June 2019. *Anthony Sayer*

Below: The whole Class 92 story is one of missed potential and complicated locos that have been overtaken and left behind in terms of their technological ability. The former 92024, now numbered 472004-7 and painted in DB Red, stands at Filiasi in Romania on 22 May 2018. *Anthony Sayer*

Floyd in Hungary took nine Class 86s and three Class 56s from the UK. No. 450007-4 – once 86228 – stands at Budapest Keleti in Hungary on 8 June 2019. *Anthony Sayer*

There were suggestions circulating in 2020 that the Class 92s in Bulgaria might be withdrawn during 2021 as they are becoming too expensive to maintain. No. 88027 – the former 92027 and still named *George Eliot* – was at Pirdop on 17 June 2019. It still sports its BR double arrow and Crewe Electric cast plaques! *Anthony Sayer*

Main-line Preservation Groups

There are several established preservation groups that have returned their locomotives to main-line registration. Some are used mostly for charters, while others have enjoyed long-term hire contracts with TOCs and FOCs.

Individuals who own locos that are main-line registered are included in the TOC/FOC that uses them.

Class 20 Locomotive Society

Contact details

Website: https://class20locosociety.co.uk

Overview

Although in partnership with Michael Owen, the CTLS owns three Class 20s, two of which are main-line registered; 20205/227. The former is on a long-term hire agreement to Owen, while 20227 is currently on hire to the North Norfolk Railway and is used for those dining services that the NNR runs through to Cromer on the national network, top-and-tailing with steam. It has had spells on hire to GBRf and DB Cargo (see page 311).

Class 40 Preservation Society

Contact details

Website: www.cfps.co.uk

Overview

The CFPS owns three Class 40s, one of which is main-line registered; 40145. It has recently returned to traffic after having new wheelsets fitted. It has been used solely for charter trains and loco-positioning moves, usually operated by West Coast Railways, although it has been used by EWS. In August 2020, the loco went on a six-month hire to LSL.

40145	CFSL	BRB	CFP	BQ

Class 50 Alliance

Contact details

Website: www.fiftyfund.org.uk

Overview

The C50A has six Class 50s under its care, of which three are main-line registered. No. 50044 *Exeter* has only just returned to use having failed on a charter in July 2012. It is possible it could return to the national network in 2021.

However, 50007 *Hercules* and 50049 *Defiance* are used for the majority of the C50A's main-line activities. As well as working charters, the locos are available to hire for other companies, most notably GB Railfreight, whose livery they currently carry. They have been used for occasional ad hoc stock and freight work for GBRf but have also been used for route learning with CrossCountry Trains. They are also able to be operated by Vintage Trains, WCR and DBC's safety cases.

The group also owns 50031 *Hood*, 50035 *Ark Royal* and has a long-term arrangement to look after 50033 *Glorious*. Of these, 50031 was once main-line registered but has not run as such since 2007. The C50A has previously had hire contacts with Valley Lines and Arriva Trains Wales.

The Class 50 Alliance has had 23 years of main-line running to its name. Two of its locos are on semi-occasional hire to GB Railfreight; 50007 *Hercules* and 50049 *Defiance* work the 1043 Leicester-Burton Wetmore on 7 August 2020 to collect a Class 769 unit for GWR. *Anthony Hicks*

50007	CFOL	GBR	CFA	KR	*Hercules*
50044	CFOL	BRB	CFA	KR	*Exeter*
50049	CFOL	GBR	CFA	KR	*Defiance*

Class 56 Group

Contact details

Website: www.class56group.co.uk

Overview

The C56LG owns two Class 56s: preserved 56006 based at the East Lancashire Railway and main-line registered 56301, which has been used by UK Rail leasing for spot hire. After recent wheelset and traction motor repairs, the loco is once again available for hire.

56301	56045	UKRL	JFU	CFS	LR

The Deltic Preservation Society's 55009 Alycidon is main-line registered but has been out of action since March 2019 after suffering a major failure. On 18 June 2018, it was back at King's Cross on a charter from Linlithgow. *Pip Dunn*

Deltic Preservation Society

Contact details

Website: http://thedps.co.uk

Overview

The DPS owns three Class 55s, one of which is main-line registered; 55009 *Alycidon*. Unfortunately the loco suffered a serious failure in March 2019 and is currently undergoing repairs at Barrow Hill.

Of its other locos, 55019 *Royal Highland Fusilier* was previously main-line registered but does not have OTMR. No. 55015 *Tulyar* in undergoing a protracted full rebuild and is being returned to main-line standard, but whether it has the necessary equipment fitted to allow it to operate as such is yet to be decided.

55009	DBLX	BRB	DPS	BH (U)	*Alycidon*

D05 Preservation Group

Contact details

Website: www.facebook.com/D05pres

Overview

The group owns 37688 *Great Rocks*, 47712 *Lady Diana Spencer* and 47828, which are all on long-term hire to Locomotive Services (see page 224).

The D05 Preservation Group owns three locos that are main-line registered. On 17 April 2019, 47828 leads WCR's 57001 and Nemesis Rail's 31128 past Morecambe South Junction on a light engine move from Burton to Carnforth. *Rob France*

Diesel Traction Group

Contact details

Website: www.westernchampion.co.uk

Overview

One of the pioneer diesel preservation groups set up in the late 1970s, it owns a fascinating collection of former BR diesels, namely the only surviving Class 17 Clayton D8568, Class 35 Hymek D7029, Class 42 Warship D821 *Greyhound* and Class 52 Western D1015 *Western Champion*.

The latter is main-line compliant and the only Class 52 passed to haul trains on Network Rail. It has been out of use for a few years now but has returned to operation at its home, the Severn Valley. It was fully expected the loco could have returned to action in 2020 – the first BR blue Western on the main line since February 1977 following a recent repaint – but the pandemic has put paid to that. Hopefully it should return to use in 2021.

D1015 MBDL BYP DTG KR *Western Champion*

Les Ross

Contact details

Website: www.86259lesross.com

Overview

Former radio DJ Les Ross owns 86259 *Peter Pan*, which is often used by WCR, especially from Euston to Preston on 'Cumbrian Mountain Express' charters. Despite WCR now acquiring 86401 *Mons Meg*, it is expected that 86259 will continue to find use on these trains.

86259 86045 MBEL EBY LES WN *Les Ross/Peter Pan*

National Railway Museum

Contact details

Website: www.railwaymuseum.org.uk

Overview

The NRM at York has two locos that are main-line registered: 47798 *Prince William* and 55002 *The King's Own Yorkshire Light Infantry*. However, following a change of policy both are now on display only and not expected to see any use as such. The Class 55 is also currently only able to run on one engine, so would be precluded from hauling charter trains as such.

Class 09

This loco is regarded as the museum's shunter rather than a restored exhibit. It is passed to run on the national network such as at York station.

09017 NRM NRM YK

Class 47

The ex-Royal Train loco has been used on the main line. It retains main-line registration and is occasionally used on the national network.

47798	47072, 47609, 47834	MBDL	RTP	NRM	YK	*Prince William*

Class 55

The loco was returned to main-line registration, but sadly only worked one train before suffering an engine failure. Restricted to one engine, it was still able to work occasional loco moves, but was not allowed to run charters. Following the reorganisation of the NRM, it is now regarded as a static exhibit.

55002	DBLX	GYP	NRM	YK (S)	*The King's Own Yorkshire Light Infantry*

North Yorkshire Moors Railway

Contact details

Website: www.nymr.co.uk

Overview

The NYMR operates 'main-line' trains on the Network Rail line between Battersby and Whitby. Most such trains are actually only operated between Grosmont and Whitby and use steam, but Class 25 D7628 (25278) is also approved for running on the Battersby to Middlesbrough section of the Esk Valley Line.

It is possible one of the line's two Class 24s may also be upgraded for running on this line but presently both are undergoing overhaul (see page 385).

25278	MBDL	NYM	GYP	GO	*Sybilla*

Scottish Class 37 Group

Contact details

Website: https://37025.tumblr.com

Overview

The S37G owns 37025 *Inverness TMD*, currently on long-term hire to Colas Rail Freight. It has worked a handful of charter trains operated by GB Railfreight. It is based at the Bo'ness & Kinneil Railway when not in use with Colas.

The loco has an operational steam heat boiler, the only main-line diesel to have this feature, and has also been modified to have through ETS wiring. The S37G also owns 37261, which is being restored, and parts donor 37214 (see page 389).

No. 37403 *Isle of Mull* is owned by the SRPS and has spent four years on hire to DRS; on 3 August 2017 it was on an inspection saloon duty at Chippenham. The loco is now off hire. *Mark Pike*

Scottish Railway Preservation Society

Contact details

Website: www.srps.org.uk

Overview

The SRPS owns 37403 *Isle of Mull*, which spent 2016-20 on hire to DRS. It was returned to its home at Bo'ness in July 2020. It retains full main-line registration and is likely to haul some SRPS charters trains, possibly with 37025, in 2021, operated most likely by either GBRf or WCR.

37403	37307	RAJV	BLL	SRP	BO	*Isle of Mull*

Stratford Class 47 Group

Contact details

Website: www.stratford47group.co.uk

Overview

The S47G owns three Class 47s: preserved 47367 / 596 at the Mid Norfolk Railway and main-line 47580 *County of Essex*. The latter has enjoyed several years available for spot hire, the vast majority of its work being with WCR where its dual-brake capability has been incredibly useful to the TOC.

Currently the loco is out of traffic at Carnforth undergoing repairs, which have stalled due to the pandemic (see page 234).

71A Locomotive Group

Contact details

Website: www.71alocogroup.co.uk

Overview

The Swanage Railway-based group owns Class 33 D6515 *Lt Jenny Smith RN*. The loco is used mostly for occasional charters operated by either GBRf or WCR.

33012	MBDL	GYP	SOA	SR	*Lt Jenny Lewis RN*

Hastings Diesels

Contact details

Website: www.hastingsdiesels.co.uk

Overview

One of the few groups to have a main-line registered heritage multiple unit, this group owns and operates a six-car 'Hastings' Class 201 DEMU.

Only five of its seven cars are Class 201 vehicles, as the TRSB and TSL 70262 are former EMU vehicles.

The unit is used regularly on charters across the country, although usually in the south of England, with GBRf the usual train operator it uses.

			DMBS	TSL	TSL	TRSB	TSL	DMBS	
201001	GRE	SE	60116	60529	70262	69337	60501	60118	*Mountfield/Tunbridge Wells*
Spare			60000						*Hastings*

D6515 *Lt Jenny Lewis RN* (33012) is the only main-line registered preserved Class 33. It arrives at Eastleigh light from Swanage on 24 July 2019. *Mark Pike*

Works, Depots and Maintenance Facilities

The old locomotive works of Swindon, Doncaster, Glasgow et al have changed dramatically over recent years. Many of the famous establishments have been closed, rationalised or changed function but some still survive, albeit much changed.

The Freightliner depot at Crewe on 14 June 2018 sees redundant Class 86s outside donating parts to keep other locos in traffic. *Pip Dunn*

Depot	Code	Operators	Services
Aberdeen Clayhills	AC	ScotRail, LNER	Servicing, stabling
Allerton Liverpool	AN	Northern	Maintenance
Ashford	AD	Hitachi	Maintenance
Aylesbury	AY	Chiltern Railways	Maintenance
Barrow Hill	BH	Barrow Hill Engine Shed Society	Maintenance
Barton-Under-Needwood	CZ	LH Group Services (Wabtec)	Maintenance
Bedford Cauldwell Walk	BF	Thameslink	Maintenance
Bescot	BS	DB Cargo	FOC
Birkenhead North	BD	Stadler (Merseyrail)	Maintenance
Bletchley	BY	West Midlands Railway	Stabling
Bo'ness	BO	Scottish Railway Preservation Society	Stabling
Botanic Gardens Hull	BG	Northern	Stabling
Bournemouth West	BM	South Western Railway	Maintenance
Bounds Green	BN	Hitachi (LNER)	Maintenance
Brighton Lovers Walk	BI	Govia Thameslink	Maintenance
Bristol Barton Hill	BK	Arriva Traincare	FOC
Bristol St. Philip's Marsh	PM	Great Western Railway	Maintenance
Burton Central Rivers	CZ	Bombardier (Cross Country Trains)	Maintenance
Burton-on-Trent	BU	Nemesis Rail	Maintenance
Barrow-in-Furness		Northern	Stabling

Cambridge	CA	CrossCountry Trains	Stabling
Carnforth Steamtown	CS	West Coast Railway	Maintenance
Cardiff Canton	CF	Transport for Wales, Pullman Rail	Maintenance
Carlisle Kingmoor	KD	Direct Rail services	FOC
Chester	CH	Alston (Transport for Wales)	Maintenance
Clacton		Greater Anglia	Stabling
Colchester		Greater Anglia	Stabling
Corkerhill	CK	ScotRail	Maintenance
Craigentinny Edinburgh	EC	ScotRail, LNER	Maintenance
Crewe Basford Hall	CB	Freightliner	FOC
Crewe Carriage Shed	CP	Arriva	Stabling
Crewe DMD	CD	Locomotive Services Ltd	Maintenance
Crewe International	CE	DB Cargo	Maintenance
Crewe Gresty Bridge	CR	Direct Rail Services	FOC
Crewe LNWR	CL	LNWR Heritage Centre	Maintenance
Crewe Works	ZC	Bombardier	Works
Crofton	XW	Bombardier	Maintenance
Derby RTC	ZA	Loram	Maintenance
Derby Litchurch Lane	ZD	Bombardier	Manufacturing
Derby Etches Park	DY	East Midlands Railway	Maintenance
Doncaster Works	ZF	Wabtec	Works
Doncaster Belmont Yard	DB	DB Cargo	FOC
Doncaster Carr	DR	Hitachi	Maintenance
Doncaster RMT	DM	DB Cargo	Stabling
Doncaster Roberts Road	DN	Progress Rail	FOC
Eastfield Glasgow	ED	ScotRail	Servicing, stabling
East Ham	ME	c2c	Maintenance
Eastleigh	EH	DB Cargo	FOC
Eastleigh Works	ZG	Arlington Fleet Group	Works
Edinburgh Haymarket	HA	ScotRail	Maintenance
Exeter	EX	Great Western Railway	Maintenance
Fort William	FW	West Coast Railways, GB Railfreight	Stabling
Fratton (Portsmouth)	FR	South Western Railway	Stabling

No. 56009, which may be converted to a Class 69, the remains of the shell of collision write-off 66048 and recently imported and modified 66790 stand at the Progress Rail site at Longport on 9 June 2019.
Antony Christie

Gillingham	GI	Southeastern	Stabling
Great Yarmouth	GY	Eastern Rail Services	Stabling
Glasgow Springburn	ZH	Knorr Bremse	Works
Hornsey	HE	Thameslink	Maintenance
Holyhead	HD	Transport for Wales	Stabling
Ilford	IL	Greater Anglia	Maintenance
Ilford Level 5 Works	ZI	Bombardier	Works
Immingham	IM	DB Cargo	Stabling
Inverness	IS	ScotRail	Maintenance
Kidderminster	KR	Class 50 Alliance	Maintenance
Kilmarnock	ZK	Wabtec	Works
Kilmarnock	ZM	Brodie Rail Engineering	Works
Knottingley	KY	DB Cargo	FOC
Leeds Midland Road	LD	Freightliner	FOC
Leicester	LR	UK Rail Leasing, Europhoenix	Maintenance
Liverpool Edge Hill	EG	Alstom	Maintenance
Loughborough	LB	Brush Traction (Wabtec)	Works
Longport (Stoke-On-Trent)	LT	Progress Rail	Works
Machynlleth	MH	Transport for Wales	Stabling
Margam	MG	DB Cargo	FOC
Merehead	MD	Aggregates Industries	FOC
Motherwell	ML	Direct Rail Services	Servicing, stabling
Manchester Ardwick	AK	Siemens (Transpennine Express)	Maintenance
Manchester Longsight Electric	LG	Northern	Maintenance
Manchester International Traincare	MA	Alstom	Maintenance
Manchester Newton Heath	NH	Northern	Maintenance
Neville Hill Leeds	NL	East Midlands Railway, LNER, Northern	Maintenance
Newcastle Heaton	HT	Northern, LNER, Grand Central	Maintenance
Newton Aycliffe		Hitachi	Manufacturing
Newport		CAF	Manufacturing
Northampton King's Heath	NN	Siemens	Maintenance
Northam Southampton	NT	South Western Railway	Maintenance
North Pole	NP	Hitachi (Great Western Railway)	Maintenance

The main engineering base for DB Cargo is at Toton depot near Nottingham. On 22 February 2019, Class 60s, 66s and 67s can be seen, albeit many of them withdrawn. *Antony Christie*

Norwich Crown Point	NC	Greater Anglia	Maintenance
Nottingham Eastcroft	NE	East Midlands Railway	Maintenance
Nottingham Eastcroft	NE	Boden Rail Engineering	Maintenance
Old Dalby	OD		Test track/storage
Old Oak Common	OH	Heathrow Express	Maintenance
Old Oak Common	OC	Crossrail	Maintenance
Oxley	OX	Alstom	Maintenance
Oxford	OF	Great Western Railway	Stabling
Peterborough	PG	GBRf	FOC
Peterborough	PB	DB Cargo	FOC
Plymouth Laira	LA	Great Western Railway	Maintenance
Polmadie	PO	Alstom	Maintenance
Penzance Long Rock	PZ	Great Western Railway	Maintenance
Ramsgate	RM	Hitachi	Maintenance
Reading	RG	Great Western Railway	Maintenance
Redhill	RD		Servicing, stabling
Rugby	RU	Colas	Stabling
Ryde	RY	South Western Railway	Maintenance
Salisbury	SA	South Western Railway	Maintenance
Selhurst	SU	Southern	Maintenance
Shields Road Glasgow	GW	ScotRail	Maintenance
Slade Green	SG	Southeastern	Maintenance
Soho	SI	West Midlands Trains	Maintenance
Southall	SH	West Coast Railways/LSL	Stabling
St Blazey	BZ	DB Cargo	Stabling
St Leonards	SE		Maintenance
Stewarts Lane	SL	VSOE	Maintenance
Stourbridge Junction	SJ	Chiltern Railways	Stabling
Southampton Maritime	SM	Freightliner	FOC
Swansea Landore	LE	Chrysalis Rail	Maintenance
Temple Mills	TM	Eurostar	Maintenance
Three Bridges	TB		Maintenance
Tyne Yard	TY	LNER	Servicing, stabling
Tonbridge	TN	GB Railfreight	FOC
Toton	TO	DB Cargo	FOC
Tyseley	TS	West Midlands Railway	Maintenance
Tyseley Locomotive Works	TM	Vintage Trains	Maintenance
Warrington Arpley	WA	DB Cargo	FOC
Wembley Traincare	WB	Alstom	Maintenance
Westbury	WY	DB Cargo	FOC
Wigan Springs Branch	SP	Northern	Servicing, stabling
Willesden	WN	London Overground	Maintenance
Wolsingham	WO	RMS Locotec	Maintenance
Wolverton Works	ZN	Gemini	Works
Worcester	WS	West Midlands Trains	Stabling
Worksop	WK	HNRC	Stabling
Yoker	YO	ScotRail	Stabling
York	YK	Transpennine Express	Stabling

The British Rail used to lead the field in manufacture of locomotives and rolling stock and virtually all of the British Rail fleet was manufactured at home.

Today, the story is very much changed with rolling stock coming from Japan, Switzerland, Germany and Spain among others.

Some assembly of rolling stock is undertaken in the UK, including Canadian company Bombardier at Derby Litchurch Lane, Japan's Hitachi at Newton Aycliffe and Spain's CAF at Newport, with Spanish company Talgo looking to start operations at Longannet in Fife.

Bombardier has recently been subject to an acquisition by French company Alstom. This has been approved in principle by the EU and was pending approval by Alstom shareholders, expected in late 2020.

Alstom has assembled trains in the UK, at the now closed Washwood Heath site in Birmingham, including the Class 390 Pendolinos, although the bodyshells for these were imported from Italy.

Alstom

Alstom had an initial flurry of orders in the mid-1990s but delays in deliveries, followed by further reliability issues, did not help the firm, leading many TOCs to look elsewhere, at Siemens and Hitachi in particular.

While the company has had no successes in winning business in the recent tranche of new train orders, its recent plans to acquire Bombardier will no doubt see it back in the running.

Class	Ordering TOC	Type	Unit numbers	Formations	Buying ROSCO	Delivered	Type	Subsequent redeployment
175/0	First North Western	Coradia	175001-011	11x2-car (22)	Angel	1999-2000	DMU	Now with Transport for Wales
175/1	First North Western	Coradia	175101-116	16x3-car (48)	Angel	1999-2001	DMU	Now with Transport for Wales
180	First Great Western	Adelante	180101-114	14x5-car (70)	Angel	2000-01	DMU	180101/105/107/112/114 now with Grand Central. 180109-111/113 now with East Midlands Railway
334	ScotRail	Juniper	334001-040	40x3-car (120)	HSBC	1999-2001	ACEMU	
390/0	Virgin West Coast	Pendolino	390001-053	53x9-car (477)	Angel	2001-05	ACEMU	390001-034 delivered as 8-cars, increased to 9-car in 2004/05. Some sets now increased to 11-cars.
390/1	Virgin West Coast	Pendolino	390154-157	4x11-car (44)	Angel	2010-12	ACEMU	
390/1	Virgin West Coast	Pendolino		31x2-car (66)	Angel	2010-12	ACEMU	Additional two cars inserted into 9-car Class 390s
458	South West Trains	Juniper	458001-030	30x4-car (120)	Porterbrook	1998-2000	DCEMU	Sets reformed as 5-car using vehicles from Class 460s, along with 6 additional 5-car
460	Gatwick Express	Juniper	460001-008	8x8-car (64)	Porterbrook	1998-99	DCEMU	Now disbanded and converted to Class 458/5s for South Western Railway

Bombardier

Bombardier UK's headquarters are at Derby Litchurch Lane works. The company has consistently assembled new trains for the UK market since the mid-1990s.

More recently it has been producing the Aventra commuter trains, and 2,660 vehicles have been ordered for the Crossrail Elizabeth line (Class 345), London Overground (Class 710), Greater Anglia (Class 720), South Western Railway (Class 701), West Midlands Trains (Class 730) and c2c (Class 720/6) franchises. These units were designed and built in Britain and are still in production, with the SWR and AGA trains rolling off the production line in late 2020.

Bombardier built the 557 vehicles for the Class 168/170-172 Turbostar two-, three- and four-car DMU ranges, and the 2,786 vehicles for the Class 357/375-379/387 Electrostar EMU ranges, which come in 25kV AC, 750V DC and dual-voltage variants and three-, four- and five- car configurations.

Bombardier is also responsible for the Class 220, 221 and 222 Voyager/Meridian family of DEMUs that were built for Virgin CrossCountry (Later Arriva's Cross Country Trains) and Midland Mainline (later East Midlands Railways). MML also took on the 222/1s originally ordered by Open Access operator Hull Trains. In total 495 vehicles were built and delivered, or altered, to run in four-, five-, seven- and nine-car formations.

Away from Heavy rail, Bombardier has recently built 1,751 cars for the London Underground for its Circle, District, Hammersmith & City, Victoria and Metropolitan lines and 162 Flexity light rail vehicles for Manchester Metrolink, Croydon Tramlink and Blackpool Transport.

Class	Ordering TOC	Type	Unit numbers	Formations	Buying ROSCO	Delivered	Type	Subsequent redeployment
168/0	Chiltern Railways	Clubman	168001-005	5x4-car (20)	Porterbrook	1997/98	DMU	
168/1	Chiltern Railways	Turbostar	168106-110	2x4-car, 3x3-car (17)	Porterbrook	2000-02	DMU	
168/1	Chiltern Railways	Turbostar	168111-113	3x3 car (9)	HSBC	2000-02	DMU	
168/2	Chiltern Railways	Turbostar	168214-219	3x3-car, 3x4-car (21)	Porterbrook	2003-06	DMU	
170/1	Midland Mainline	Turbostar	170101-117	17x2-car (34)	Porterbrook	1998-99	DMU	CrossCountry Trains
170/1	Midland Mainline	Turbostar	Centre cars for 170101-110	10x1-car (10)	Porterbrook	2001	DMU	CrossCountry Trains
170/2	Anglia Railways	Turbostar	170201-208	8x3-car (24)	Porterbrook	1999	DMU	Transport For Wales
170/2	Anglia Railways	Turbostar	170270-273	4x2-car (8)	Porterbrook	2002	DMU	Transport For Wales
170/3	South West Trains	Turbostar	170301-309	9x2-car (18)	Porterbrook	2000-01	DMU	Chiltern as 168321-329 170309 was previously 170399 and spent 11/07-05/15 with Transpennine Express
170/3	Central Trains	Turbostar	170397-398	2x3-car (6)	Porterbrook	2002	DMU	CrossCountry Trains
170/3	Hull Trains	Turbostar	170393-396	4x3-car (12)	Porterbrook	2004	DMU	ScotRail
170/4	ScotRail	Turbostar	170401-415	15x3-car (45)	Porterbrook	1999-2001	DMU	
170/4	ScotRail	Turbostar	170416-424	9x3-car (27)	HSBC	1999-2001	DMU	170416-420 with East Midlands Railway 170421/423 with Southern as 171201/202 (2-car) with their centre cars and those six vehicles from 170422/424 now with Southern as 171401/402 (4-car)

170/4	ScotRail	Turbostar	170425-434	10x3-car (30)	Porterbrook	2003-05	DMU	
170/4	ScotRail	Turbostar	170450-461	12x3-car (36)	Porterbrook	2004-05	DMU	170453-461 Northern
170/4	ScotRail	Turbostar	170470-478	9x3-car (27)	Porterbrook	2001-05	DMU	170472-478 Northern
170/5	Central Trains	Turbostar	170501-523	23x2-car (46)	Porterbrook	1999-2000	DMU	170501-517 West Midlands Trains 170518-523 CrossCountry Trains
170/6	Central Trains	Turbostar	170630-639	10x3-car (30)	Porterbrook	1999-2000	DMU	170630-635 West Midlands Trains 170636-639 CrossCountry Trains
171/7	Southern	Turbostar	171721-730	10x2-car (20)	Porterbrook	2003-05	DMU	
171/8	Southern	Turbostar	171801-806	6x4-car (24)	Porterbrook	2004	DMU	
172/0	LOROL	Turbostar	172001-008	8x2-car (16)	Angel	2009-10	DMU	West Midlands Trains
172/1	Chiltern Railways	Turbostar	172101-104	4x2-car (8)	Angel	2009-10	DMU	
172	London Midland	Turbostar	172211-222	12x2-car (24)	Porterbrook	2010-11	DMU	West Midlands Trains
172	London Midland	Turbostar	172331-345	15x3-car (45)	Porterbrook	2010-11	DMU	West Midlands Trains
220	Virgin CrossCountry	Voyager	220001-034	34x4-car (136)	HBOS	2000-01	DEMU	CrossCountry Trains
221	Virgin CrossCountry	Super Voyager	221101-144	40x5-car 4x4-car (216)	HBOS	2001-02	DEMU	221101-118/142/143 Avanti West Coast 221119-141 CrossCountry Trains 221144 disbanded. All 5-car sets now apart from 221141
222/0	Midland Mainline	Meridian	222001-023	7x9-car 16x4-car (127)	HSBC	2003-05	DEMU	East Midland Railways reformed as 6x7-car and 17x5-car
222/1	Hull Trains		222101-104	4x4-car (16)	HSBC	2005	DEMU	East Midland Railways
357/0	LTS Rail	Electrostar	357001-046	46x4-car (184)	Porterbrook	1999-2001	ACEMU	c2c
357/2	LTS Rail	Electrostar	357201-228	28x4-car (112)	Angel	2001/02	ACEMU	c2c 357212-228 now numbered 357322-328
375/3	Connex SouthEastern	Electrostar	375301-310	10x3-car (30)	HSBC	2001-02	ACEMU	Southeastern Trains
375/6	Connex SouthEastern	Electrostar	375601-630	30x4-car (120)	HSBC	1999-2001	ACEMU	Southeastern Trains
375/7	Connex SouthEastern	Electrostar	375701-715	15x4-car (60)	HSBC	2001-02	ACEMU	Southeastern Trains
375/8	Connex SouthEastern	Electrostar	375801-830	30x4-car (120)	HSBC	2004	ACEMU	Southeastern Trains
375/9	Connex SouthEastern	Electrostar	375901-927	27x4-car (108)	HSBC	2003-04	ACEMU	Southeastern Trains
376	Southeastern Trains	Electrostar	376001-036	36x5-car (180)	HSBC	2004-05	ACEMU	
377/1	Connex South Central	Electrostar	377101-164	64x4-car (256)	Porterbrook	2002-03	ACEMU	Southern
377/2	Connex South Central	Electrostar	377201-215	15x4-car (60)	Porterbrook	2003-04	ACEMU	Southern
377/3	Connex South Central	Electrostar	377301-328	28x3-car (84)	Porterbrook	2001-02	ACEMU	Southern Originally numbered 375311-338
377/4	Connex South Central	Electrostar	377401-475	75x4-car (300)	Porterbrook	2004-05	ACEMU	Southern

Train Builders

377/5	Southern	Electrostar	377501-523	23x4-car (92)	Porterbrook	2008-09	ACEMU	
377/6	Southern	Electrostar	377601-626	26x5-car (130)	Porterbrook	2012-13	ACEMU	
378/1	LOROL	Capitalstar	377501-523	57x5-car (285)	QW rail	2009-15	ACEMU	New as 3-cars, extended to 4-cars and now 5-cars
379	Greater Anglia	Electrostar	379001-030	30x4-car (120)	MQ	2010-11	ACEMU	
345	Crossrail	Bombardier Aventra	345001-070	70x9-car (630)	345 Rail Leasing	2016-18	ACEMU	Option for 17x9-car
377/7	Southern	Electrostar	377701-708	8x5-car (40)	Porterbrook	2013-14	DVEMU	
378	LOROL	Capitalstar	38401-457	57x1-car (57)	QW Rail	2014-15	EMUMC	Additional cars
387/1	Thameslink	Electrostar	387101-129	29x4-car (116)	Porterbrook	2014-15	DVEMU	
387/1	GWR	Electrostar	387130-174	45x4-car (180)	Porterbrook	2016-17	DVEMU	
387/2	Southern (Gatwick Express)	Electrostar	387201-227	27x4-car (108)	Porterbrook	2015-16	DVEMU	
387/3	c2c	Electrostar	387301-306	6x4-car (24)	Porterbrook	2016	DVEMU	
710/1	LOROL	Aventra	710101-130	30x4-car (120)	TfL	2019	ACEMU	
710/2	LOROL	Aventra	710256-273	18x4-car (72)	TfL	2019	DVEMU	
710/2	LOROL	Aventra	710274-279	6x5-car (30)	TfL	2020	DVEMU	
720/1	Greater Anglia	Aventra	720101-122	22x10-car (220)	Angel	2020	ACEMU	This order has been cancelled and changed to 44 5-car 720/5
720/5	Greater Anglia	Aventra	720501-589	133x5-car (665)	Angel	2020	ACEMU	
701/1	MTR South West	Aventra	701001-060	60x10-car (600)	Rock Rail/SL	2020	DCEMU	
701/5	MTR South West	Aventra	701501-530	30x5-car (150)	Rock Rail/SL	2020	DCEMU	
730/0	West Midlands Trains	Aventra	730001-036	36x3-car (108)	Corelink Rail	2020-21	ACEMU	
730/1	West Midlands Trains	Aventra	730101-129	29x5-car (145)	Corelink Rail	2020-21	ACEMU	
730/2	West Midlands Trains	Aventra	730201-216	16x5-car (80)	Corelink Rail	2020-21	ACEMU	
720/6	c2c	Aventra	720501-610	10x6-car (60)	Porterbrook	2021	ACEMU	

Train Builders

CAF

Spanish builder CAF (Construcciones y Auxiliar de Ferrocarriles, which translates as Construction and other railway services) had its first dabble into the UK market with the Heathrow Express Class 332s, a joint venture with Siemens that was delivered in 1997-98. A similar venture was the Class 333s for Arriva Trains Northern, delivered in 2001-03.

However, it is the last five years where CAF has really 'come to the table' for delivering new trains for the UK, and has even set up a plant in Newport South Wales that is now assembling Class 196s for West Midlands Trains and Class 197 for Transport for Wales, having built some Class 195/331s for Northern.

CAF has also built Class 397s for Transpennine Express and some Mk 5 loco-hauled coaches for both TPE and Caledonian Sleeper. It is perfectly poised to win more orders, should any be forthcoming.

Class	Ordering TOC	Type	Unit numbers	Formations	Buying ROSCO	Delivered	Type	Subsequent redeployment
332	Heathrow Express		332001-014	14x4-car (56)	HEx	1997-98	ACEMU	
332	Heathrow Express			5x1-car (5)	HEx	2002	ACEMU	Additional centre cars added to 332005-009
333	Northern Spirit		333001-016	16x4-car (64)	Angel	2001-03	ACEMU	Delivered as 16x3-car, upgraded to 4-car in 2002/03. Now with Northern
195/0	Northern	Civity UK	195001-025	25x2-car (50)	Eversholt	2017-18	DMU	
195/1	Northern	Civity UK	195101-133	33x3-car (99)	Eversholt	2017-18	DMU	
331/0	Northern	Civity UK	331001-031	31x3-car (93)	Eversholt	2017-19	ACEMU	
331/1	Northern	Civity UK	331101-112	12x4-car (48)	Eversholt	2017-19	ACEMU	
397	TPE	Civity UK	397001-012	12x5-car (60)	Eversholt	2019	ACEMU	
Mk 5	Caledonian Sleeper		15001-011	11x1-car (11)	Lombard Finance	2018	LHCS	
Mk 5	Caledonian Sleeper		15101-110	10x1-car (10)	Lombard Finance	2018	LHCS	
Mk 5	Caledonian Sleeper		15201-214	14x1-car (14)	Lombard Finance	2018	LHCS	
Mk 5	Caledonian Sleeper		15301-340	40x1-car (40)	Lombard Finance	2018	LHCS	
Mk 5a	TPE		11501-513	13x1-car (13)	Beacon Rail	2018	LHCS	
Mk 5a	TPE		12701-739	39x1-car (39)	Beacon Rail	2018	LHCS	
Mk 5a	TPE		12801-814	14x1-car (14)	Beacon Rail	2018	LHCS	
Mk 5a	TPE		11801-813	13x1-car (13)	Beacon Rail	2018	DVT	
196/0	West Midlands Trains	Civity UK	196001-012	12x2-car (24)	Corelink Rail	2020	DMU	
196/1	West Midlands Trains	Civity UK	196101-114	14x4-car (56)	Corelink Rail	2020	DMU	
197/0	TfW (Wales & Borders)	Civity UK	197001-051	51x2-car (102)			DMU	
197/1	TfW (Wales & Borders)	Civity UK	197101-126	26x3-car (78)			DMU	

Train Builders

Hitachi

Hitachi delivered its first UK trains in 2006-09 for Southeastern for the HS1 operations out of St Pancras International to Kent. A fleet of 29 six-car Class 395 Javelin units, and a new depot at Ashford to maintain them, were delivered.

The company's biggest success has been its AT300 platform, which uses similar bodyshells as the 395s and forms the InterCity Express Programme – the trains to replace the HSTs and Class 91s on the East Coast and Great Western franchises.

Between LNER and GWR, 1,237 vehicles have been ordered in a mix of electric and bi-mode units of five-, six- and nine-car formation of Classes 800, 801 and 802.

The success of these trains, which have been built in Kasado in Japan but mostly assembled at Newton Aycliffe in Country Durham, has led to orders with five other operators. Transpennine Express took 19 five-car Class 802/2s, Hull Trains has five five-car Class 802/3s in traffic, while Avanti West Coast (Class 805/807), East Midlands Railways (Class 810) and new Open Access operator East Coast Trains (Class 803) have orders being delivered presently.

As well as the A300s, Hitachi also offers the AT200 series of commuter and outer suburban EMUs, which has so far only yielded one order; with ScotRail taking 234 vehicles in a mix of three- and four-car sets. All are now in traffic.

Class	Ordering TOC	Type	Unit numbers	Formations	Buying ROSCO	Delivered	Type	Subsequent redeployment
395	Southeastern	Javelin	395001-029	29x6-car (174)	Angel	2006-09	ACEMU	
385/0	ScotRail	AT200	385001-046	46x3-car (138)	Caledonian Rail Leasing Ltd^^	2017-19	ACEMU	Being delivered; option for 10x3-car sets
385/1	ScotRail	AT200	385101-124	24x4-car (96)	Caledonian Rail Leasing Ltd^^	2017-19	ACEMU	
800/0	GWR	AT300	800001-036	36x6-car (216)	Eversholt	2013-18	BMMU	
800/1	VTEC	AT300	800101-113	13x9-car (117)	Agility Trains	2013-18	BMMU	
800/2	VTEC	AT300	800201-210	10x5-car (50)	Agility Trains	2016-18	BMMU	
801/3	GWR	AT300	800301-321	32x9-car (288)	Eversholt	2016-18	BMMU	
801/1	VTEC	AT300	801101-112	12x5-car (60)	Agility Trains	2016-18	BMMU	
801/2	VTEC	AT300	801201-230	30x9-car (270)	Agility Trains	2016-18	BMMU	
802/0	GWR	AT300	802001-022	22x5-car (110)	Eversholt	2018	BMMU	
802/1	GWR	AT300	802101-114	14x9-car (126)	Eversholt	2018	BMMU	
802/0	TPE	AT300	802201-219	19x5-car (95)	Angel	2018	BMMU	
802/3	Hull Trains	AT300	802301-205	5x5-car (25)	Angel	2019	BMMU	
803	East Coast Trains	AT300	803001-005	5x5-car (25)	Beacon	2021	BMMU	
805	Avanti West Coast	AT300	805001-013	13x5-car (65)	Rock Rail	2022	BMEMU	Order placed
807	Avanti West Coast	AT300	807001-010	10x7-car (70)	Rock Rail	2022	ACEMU	Order placed
810	East Midlands Railway	AT300 Aurora	810001-033	33x5-car (165)	Rock Rail	2023	BMMU	Order placed

Train Builders

Progress Rail

American company Progress Rail, part of the Caterpillar Group, built the last Class 66s for the UK market, but emission legislation changes means this production line has now ceased.

However, the company not only supports Class 66s in the UK, it is also building the new Class 69s for GBRf using redundant Class 56s as donor bodies and fitting General Motors engines that are these same as those used in Class 66s.

Siemens

While the initial glut of post-privatisation orders were in the main snapped up by Bombardier and Alstom, Siemens broke into the market – in no part small due to late deliveries from others – in 2002 with a fleet of 21 four-car Class 360 Desiro 25kV AC units for First Great Eastern. An order for five five-car Class 360/2s for Heathrow Connect soon followed.

However, it was the massive order from South West Trains to replace Mk 1 slam-door trains that really saw the German manufacturer get a foothold in the UK market. This consisted of 45 five-car Class 444s and 110, later increased to 127, four-car Class 450 Desiro 750V DC units.

The company won its only order for DMUs with Transpennine Express and delivered 51 three-car Class 185 units to the franchise. Some of these are due for replacement soon and will be redeployed.

The Class 350 25kV AC version of the Desiro UK has been a popular unit and is the mainstay of the current West Midlands Trains fleet, which has been bolstered by the ten Class 350/4s order by TPE but since replaced by Class 397 units.

It has since secured orders with ScotRail for 130 Class 380 vehicles in a mix of three- and four-car formations but its biggest order to date has been the 1,140 Class 70 vehicles for the Thameslink franchise. These eight- and 12-car trains are all now in service. They have been joined by 150 similar metro-style Class 717s for the Great Northern operation and 150 Class 707 vehicles ordered by SWT but 'rejected' by SWR when it took over this franchise. They are due to move to Southeastern.

Siemens also won a major coup with its Velaro high-speed train design, of which 272 vehicles are in use with Eurostar as Class 374s.

Class	Ordering TOC	Type	Unit numbers	Formations	Buying ROSCO	Delivered	Type	Subsequent redeployment
185	Transpennine	Desiro UK	185101-151	51x3-car (153)	HSBC	2005-06	DMU	
350/1	London Midland	Desiro UK	350101-130	30x4-car (120)	Angel	2004-05	ACEMU	Ordered by the SRA; West Midlands Trains
350/2	London Midland	Desiro UK	350231-267	37x4-car (148)	Porterbrook	2008-09	ACEMU	West Midlands Trains
360	First Great Eastern	Desiro UK	360101-121	21x4-car (84)	Angel	2002-03	ACEMU	Due to move to East Midlands Railway
360/2	Heathrow Connect	Desiro UK	360201-205	5x5-car (25)	HEx	2002-06	ACEMU	Crossrail
380/0	ScotRail	Desiro UK	380001-022	22x3-car (66)	Eversholt	2009-10	ACEMU	
380/1	ScotRail	Desiro UK	380101-116	16x4-car (64)	Eversholt	2009-10	ACEMU	
444	South West Trains	Desiro UK	444001-045	45x5-car (225)	Angel	2003-04	DCEMU	South Western Railway
450	South West Trains	Desiro UK	450001-127	127x4-car (508)	Angel	2002-06	DCEMU	South Western Railway
350/3	London Midland	Desiro UK	350368-377	10x4-car (40)	Angel	2014	ACEMU	West Midlands Trains

350/4	TPE	Desiro UK	350401-410	10x4-car (40)	Angel	2013-14	ACEMU	West Midlands Trains
374	Eurostar	Velaro e320	374001-034	34x8-car (272)	Eurostar (UK)	2012-17	ACEMU	
700/0	Thameslink	Desiro City	700001-060	60x8-car (480)	Cross London Trains	2014-18	DVEMU	
700/1	Thameslink	Desiro City	700101-155	55x12-car (660)	Cross London Trains	2013-18	DVEMU	
707	SWT	Desiro City	707001-030	30x5-car (150)	Angel	2015-17	DVEMU	South Western Railway
717	Great Northern	Desiro City	717001-025	25x6-car (150)	Rock Rail	2018-19	DVEMU	

Stadler

Swiss manufacturer Stadler is another newcomer to supplying trains for the UK market and has won big orders for fleet replacement with Merseyrail and Greater Anglia.

Its Class 745/755s are being delivered for the latter, while the first Class 777s for Merseyrail are now undergoing UK testing and units are rolling off the production line and being shipped by rail from Switzerland via the Channel Tunnel.

Looking ahead, Stadler also has orders with Transport for Wales for 11 four-car Class 231 metro units and 89 vehicles – seven three-car and 21 four-car Class 756s – and 36 three-car Class 398 metro EMUs.

Stadler also acquired Vossloh, which designed and started the construction of the DRS Class 68s, but later 68s and the Class 88s were all built as Stadler locomotives.

Class	Ordering TOC	Type	Unit numbers	Formations	Buying ROSCO	Delivered	Type	Subsequent redeployment
777	Merseyrail		777001-052	52x4-car (208)	Merseytravel	2018	DCEMU	
755/3	Greater Anglia	Flirt	755325-338	14x3-car (42)	Rock Rail	2019	BMMU	
755/4	Greater Anglia	Flirt	755401-424	24x4-car (96)	Rock Rail	2019	BMMU	
745/0	Greater Anglia	Flirt	745001-010	10x12-car (120)	Rock Rail	2019	ACEMU	
745/1	Greater Anglia	Flirt	745101-110	10x12-car (120)	Rock Rail	2019	ACEMU	
231	TfW (Metro)	Flirt	tbc	11x4-car (44)			DEMU	
756/0	TfW (Central Metro)	Flirt	756001-007	7x3-car (21)			TMMU	
756/1	TfW (Central Metro)	Flirt	756101-117	17x4-car-car (68)			TMMU	
398	TfW (Central Metro)	Citylink		36x3-car (108)			Metro	

Talgo

Spanish builder Talgo currently has no orders for UK operators but is looking at creating a factory at Longannet in Fife to build for both the UK and other international markets.

It has outline planning permission for 80,000 sq m of factory space, which will be rail-connected.

It is bidding for the contract to supply trains for HS2 – and it expected that successful bidder for that contract could be advised by the end of year.

VivaRail

VivaRail doesn't build trains as such but converts former London Underground units into both DMUs and EMUs.

Its first two units were three-car test trains, while three two-car units have been delivered to London Midland – now West Midlands Trains – for use on the Bedford-Bletchley Marston Vale line.

Subsequent orders have been five three-car sets for Transport for Wales for the Wrexham to Birkenhead line, while the first EMUs will be the five two-car Class 484 sets for the Isle of Wight to replace the aging 80-plus-year-old Class 483 units.

Class	TOC	Numbers	Formations	Owner	Delivered	Type
230	London Midland (trial)	230001	1x3-car (3)	VivaRail	Rebuilt 2015	DMU
230	London Midland (trial)	230002	1x2-car (3)	VivaRail	Rebuilt 2015	BEMU
230	TfW (Wales & Borders)	230006-010	5x3-car (15)	VivaRail	Rebuilt 2015	DMU
230	London Midland	230003-005	3x2-car (6)	VivaRail	Rebuilt 2015	DMU
484	SWR	484001-005	5x2-car (10)	Lombard	Rebuilt 2020	DCEMU

Parry People Movers

The Parry People Mover is a novel single-car railbus, of which two were ordered by London Midland as the Class 139. They work exclusively on the ¾-mile Stourbridge Town to Stourbridge Junction branch for West Midlands Trains.

Another PPM single car has been at the Severn Valley Railway for testing but has yet to be placed with a customer.

Class	Ordered by	Numbers	Formations	ROSCOs	Delivered	Type	Notes
139	London Midland	139001/002	2x1-car (2)	Porterbrook	2007/08	DMU	Now with West Midlands Railway

Train Builders

New Trains on Order

Since privatisation there have been two main tranches of new train orders. First, there was the initial burst when many of the new franchises were won on bids that included new trains.

This offered rich pickings for Alstom and Bombardier especially but other companies such as CAF did get in on the act. Then Siemens did well out of the Mk 1 replacement programme.

More recently there has been another wave of new train orders with Bombardier, CAF, Siemens, Hitachi and Stadler.

In the last five years we have seen new trains for Northern, Crossrail, ScotRail, GWR, Southern, c2c, Thameslink. South West Trains (now South Western Railway), London Overground, Greater Anglia, Transpennine express and LNER. Open Access operator Hull Trains has also renewed its fleet.

In the next five years some of these fleets will be delivered alongside new trains for Merseyrail, Transport for Wales, West Midlands Trains and new Open Access operator East Coast trains (a First Group company) and Avanti West Coast.

CAF has set up an assembly plant at Newport; Northern's 195025 was in the final stages of its build on 21 February 2020. *Antony Christie*

Japanese manufacturer Hitachi has been assembling its AT200 and AT300 trains at Newton Aycliffe. On 5 May 2013, ScotRail's 385007 was being prepared for delivery. *Rob France*

Class	TOC	Builder/model	Numbers	Quantity	Owner	Type
196/0	West Midlands Trains	CAF Civity	196001-012	12x2-car (24)	Corelink Rail	DMU
196/1	West Midlands Trains	CAF Civity	196101-114	14x4-car (56)	Corelink Rail	DMU
197/0	TfW (Wales & Borders)	CAF Civity	197001-051	51x2-car (102)		DMU
197/1	TfW (Wales & Borders)	CAF Civity	197101-126	26x3-car (78)		DMU
230	TfW (Wales & Borders)	VivaRail	230006-010	5x3-car (15)	VivaRail	DMU
231	TfW (South Wales Metro)	Stadler Flirt	tbc	11x4-car (44)		DEMU
398	TfW (Central Metro)	Stadler Citylink		36x3-car (108)		Metro
484	SWR	VivaRail	484001-005	5x2-car (10)	Lombard	DCEMU
701/0	MTR South West	Bombardier Aventra	701001-060	60x10-car (600)	Rock Rail/SL	DCEMU
701/5	MTR South West	Bombardier Aventra	701501-530	30x5-car (150)	Rock Rail/SL	DCEMU
720/1	Greater Anglia	Bombardier Aventra	720101-122	22x10-car (220)	Angel	ACEMU
720/5	Greater Anglia	Bombardier Aventra	720501-589	89x5-car (445)	Angel	ACEMU
720/6	c2c	Bombardier Aventra	720601-606	10x6-car (60)	Porterbrook	ACEMU
730/0	West Midlands Trains	Bombardier Aventra	730001-036	36x3-car (108)	Corelink Rail	ACEMU
730/1	West Midlands Trains	Bombardier Aventra	730101-129	29x5-car (145)	Corelink Rail	ACEMU
730/2	West Midlands Trains	Bombardier Aventra	730201-216	16x5-car (80)	Corelink Rail	ACEMU
756/0	TfW (Central Metro)	Stadler Flirt	756001-007	7x3-car (21)		TMMU
756/1	TfW (Central Metro)	Stadler Flirt	756101-117	17x4-car (68)		TMMU
777	Merseyrail	Stadler	777001-052	52x4-car (208)	Merseytravel	DCEMU
769	Northern	BREL/Brush FLEX	769424/426/431/434/442/450/456/458	8x4-car (32)	Porterbrook	BMEMU
769	Transport for Wales	BREL/Brush FLEX	769002/003/006-008	9x4-car (36)	Porterbrook	BMEMU
769	GWR	BREL/Brush FLEX	769922/923/925/927/928/930/932/935-940/943/945/947/949/952/959	19x4-car (76)	Porterbrook	BMEMU
769	ROG	BREL/Brush FLEX	319009/010	2x4-car (8)	Porterbrook	BMEMU
799	Demo unit	BREL/Brush FLEX	799001	1x4-car (8)	Porterbrook	BMEMU
803	East Coast Trains (FirstGroup)	Hitachi AT300	803001-005	5x5-car (25)	Beacon Rail	BMMU
803	East Coast Trains	Hitachi AT300	803001-005	5x5-car (25)	Beacon	BMMU
805	Avanti West Coast	Hitachi AT300	805001-013	13x5-car (65)	Rock Rail	BMEMU
807	Avanti West Coast	Hitachi AT300	807001-010	10x7-car (70)	Rock Rail	ACEMU
810	East Midlands Railway	Hitachi AT300	810001-033	33x5-car (165)	Rock Rail	BMMU

Note: some of these fleets are now being delivered and are undergoing testing

New Trains on Order

Type	
DMU	Diesel Multiple Unit
ACEMU	25kV AC Electric Multiple Unit
DVEMU	Dual voltage 25kV AC Electric Multiple Unit; 750V DC third rail and 25kV AC
EMUMC	Electric Multiple Unit motored centre car
BMMU	Electro-Diesel Bi-mode Multiple unit; 25kV AC and diesel engine(s)
DCEMU	750V DC Electric Multiple Unit

Beyond 2025

It would be a brave man who predicts wheat the order books for new trains will look like after this lasts tranche of orders is delivered.

There will still be some old trains like Class 150s, 156s and 158s that will be ripe for replacement as well as Class 165/166, 365/465/466 units from the last knockings of BR.

A host of new trains for ScotRail and GWR are in the sidings at Newton Aycliffe pending delivery on 5 May 2018. Alongside shunter 08484 are 385107, 385031, 800307 and 800308. *Rob France*

Right: The bodyshell for a Class 196 for West Midlands Railway is being fitted out at CAF's Newport site on 21 February 2020. *Jack Boskett*

Below: Siemens has built its trains for the UK in Europe; Class 700 bodyshells are being fabricated at Krefeld in Germany in July 2016. *Paul Bigland*

Below: New Bombardier Aventra units destined for Greater Anglia, 720540 and 720539 pass Stafford on a Rugby to Wolverton, via Crewe, test run on 11 August 2020. *Brad Joyce*

Heritage Lines

If there is one rail sector that has been truly devastated by the Covid-19 pandemic, then it is the heritage railways. Essentially tourist attractions run by dedicated volunteers, they lost the whole summer and when they were able to reopen it was subject to strict social distancing regimes that seriously restricted the number of passengers they could carry. That was combined with an apprehension from their clientele on whether to travel or not.

At the height of lockdown, volunteers were not even able to at least make progress in restoration projects while the railways were otherwise closed.

Most will, hopefully, 'bounce back' in 2021 but many have written off 2020 as 'null and void' so to speak.

There are many heritage railways across the country that, through the hard work of volunteers and donations from the public, strive to recreate the past glories of the railway. This is Arley station on the Severn Valley Railway, which has been lovingly restored to a typical country station from the last century. D9551 calls with the 1118 Bridgnorth-Kidderminster on 20 May 2017. *Pip Dunn*

Standard gauge heritage railways

Railway	Phone	Website
Appleby Frodingham RPS	07889 297271	www.afrps.co.uk
Aln Valley	0300 030 3311	www.alnvalleyrailway.co.uk
Avon Valley	0117 932 7296	www.avonvalleyrailway.co.uk
Ayrshire RPS	n/a	www.scottishindustrialrailwaycentre.org.uk
Barrow Hill Roundhouse	01246 472450	www.barrowhill.org.uk
Barry Island	01446 748816	http://barrytouristrailway.co.uk
Battlefield Line	01827 880754	www.battlefield-line-railway.co.uk
Beamish Museum & Tramway	0191 370 4000	www.beamish.org.uk
Bluebell	01825 720800	www.bluebell-railway.co.uk
Bodmin & Wenford	01208 73666	www.bodminandwenfordrailway.co.uk
Bo'ness & Kinneil	01506 822298	www.srps.org.uk/railway
Border Union	n/a	https://wrha.org.uk/border-union-railway
Bowes	0191 416 1847	www.bowesrailway.co.uk
Bristol Harbour	0117 352 6600	https://bristolharbourrailway.co.uk
Caledonian	01561 377760	www.caledonianrailway.com
Chasewater	01543 452623	www.chasewaterrailway.co.uk
Chinnor & Princes Risborough	01844 354117	www.cprra.co.uk
Cambrian Railways Trust	01691 831569	www.cambrianrailways.com
Cholsey & Wallingford	01491 835067	www.cholsey-wallingford-railway.com
Churnet Valley	01538 360522	www.churnet-valley-railway.co.uk
Colne Valley	01787 461174	www.colnevalleyrailway.co.uk
Dartmoor	01837 55367	www.dartmoor-railway-sa.org
Dean Forest	01594 845840	www.deanforestrailway.co.uk
Derwent Valley	01904 489966	https://dvlr.org.uk
East Anglian Railway Museum	01206 242524	www.earm.co.uk
East Kent	01304 832042	https://eastkentrailway.co.uk
East Lancashire	0161 764 6360	www.east-lancs-rly.co.uk
East Somerset	01749 880417	www.eastsomersetrailway.com
Ecclesbourne Valley	01629 823076	www.e-v-r.com
Eden Valley	017683 42309	www.evr-cumbria.org.uk
Elsecar Heritage	01226 746746	www.elsecarheritagerailway.co.uk
Embsay & Bolton Abbey	01756 710614	www.embsayboltonabbeyrailway.org.uk
Epping and Ongar	01277 365200	www.eorailway.co.uk
Fife Heritage	n/a	www.fifeheritagerailway.co.uk
Foxfield	01782 396210	www.foxfieldrailway.co.uk
Gloucestershire Warwickshire	01242 621405	www.gwsr.com
Great Central	01509 230726	www.gcrailway.co.uk
Great Central Nottingham	0115 940 5705	www.gcrn.co.uk
Gwili	01267 230666	www.gwili-railway.co.uk
Helston	07901 977597	www.helstonrailway.co.uk
Invergarry & Fort Augustus Museum	n/a	www.invergarrystation.org.uk
Isle of Wight Steam	01983 882204	www.iwsteamrailway.co.uk
Keighley & Worth Valley	01535 645214	www.kwvr.co.uk
Keith & Dufftown	01340 821181	https://keith-dufftown-railway.co.uk
Kent & East Sussex	01580 762943	www.kesr.org.uk
Lakeside & Haverthwaite Railway	01539 531594	www.lakesiderailway.co.uk
Lathalmond Museum	07379 914801	https://www.shed47.org
Lavender Line	01825 750515	www.lavender-line.co.uk

Lincolnshire Wolds	01507 363881	www.lincolnshirewoldsrailway.co.uk
Llanelli & Mynydd Mawr	n/a	www.llanellirailway.co.uk
Llangollen	01978 860979	www.llangollen-railway.co.uk
Mangapps Railway Museum	01621 784898	www.mangapps.co.uk
Mid Hants	01962 733810	www.watercressline.co.uk
Middleton	0113 271 0320	www.middletonrailway.org.uk
Mid Norfolk	01362 690633	www.mnr.org.uk
Midland Railway Butterley	01773 570140	www.midlandrailway-butterley.co.uk
National Railway Museum	0800 047 8124	www.railwaymuseum.org.uk
Nene Valley	01780 784444	www.nvr.org.uk
Northamptonshire Ironstone	01604 702031	www.nir.org.uk
Northampton and Lamport	01604 820327	www.nlr.org.uk
North Norfolk	01263 820801	www.nnrail.co.uk
North Yorkshire Moors	01751 472508	www.nymr.co.uk
North Tyneside	0191 200 7146	www.ntsra.org.uk
Pontypool & Blaenavon	01495 792263	http://pontypool-and-blaenavon.co.uk
Paignton & Dartmouth	01803 555872	www.dartmouthrailriver.co.uk
Peak Rail	01629 580381	www.peakrail.co.uk
Poulton & Wyre	n/a	www.pwrs.org
Radstock to Frome Railway Trust	n/a	www.radstocktofromerailwaytrust.co.uk
Ribble Steam	01772 728800	https://ribblesteam.org.uk
Rocks by Rail	07873 721941	www.rocks-by-rail.org
Royal Deeside	01330 844416	www.deeside-railway.co.uk
Rushden Transport Museum	01933 213066	https://rhts.co.uk
Severn Valley	01299 403816	www.svr.co.uk
Spa Valley	01892 537715	www.spavalleyrailway.co.uk
Somerset & Dorset	01761 411221	https://sdjr.co.uk
South Devon	01364 642338	www.southdevonrailway.org
Stainmore	07584 429481	www.kirkbystepheneast.co.uk
Strathspey	01479 810725	www.strathspeyrailway.co.uk
Swanage	01929 425800	https://swanagerailway.co.uk
Swindon & Cricklade	01793 771615	www.swindon-cricklade-railway.org
Tanfield Steam	0191 388 7545	www.tanfield-railway.co.uk
Telford Steam	07765 858348	www.telfordsteamrailway.co.uk
Tyseley Locomotive Works	0121 708 4960	www.vintagetrains.co.uk
Weardale	01388 529566	www.weardale-railway.org.uk
Wensleydale	0845 450 5474	https://wensleydale-railway.co.uk
West Somerset	01643 704996	www.west-somerset-railway.co.uk
Whitwell & Reepham	01603 871694	https://whitwellstation.com

Preserved Locos

How a loco is classed as 'preserved' is a grey area but for the purpose of this book, they are those vehicles that are at heritage railways, owned by heritage groups and regardless if they have been restored or not.

This includes some locos that may never have run, or realistically are unlikely to ever run again. It does not include locos located at heritage sites that are owned by FOCs or spot-hire companies that are listed under their relevant owners, unless those owners do not regard them as assets for the business, for example the locomotives owned by Jeremy Hosking that are either at, or due to move, to Margate for static display.

This list includes those locos that are owned by preservation groups for the supply of spare parts – such as 37214 and 47761 – and unlikely to ever be restored unless sold to another group/individual.

Those locos owned by preservation groups but are main-line registered and either on long-term hire to FOCs/TOCs or used for charter work or spot hire are included on page 354.

Names are listed even if the plates are not presently fitted because the loco is partway through overhaul. Locos are listed at their home railway unless on a long-term loam, but locos do move about and visit other railways or sites. The number the vehicle normally/currently carries is in bold. Locos that carry identities of other classmates are not listed as such.

One of the few Class 05 diesel hunters in preservation, D2587 stands at Rowsley on Peak Rail on 20 August 2019. *Antony Christie*

Class 01

D2953	11503	GWS	PKR
D2956	11506	BLK	ELR

Class 02

02003	D2853	GWS	BH
	D2854	GWS	PKR
	D2858	GWS	MRB
	D2860	GWS	NRM
	D2866	BRW	PKR
	D2867	IND	BAT
	D2868	GWS	PKR

Class 03

03018	D2018	BRW	MRM	
03020	D2020	BRW	MRM	
03022	**D2022**	BRB	SCR	
	D2023	GWS	KES	
	D2024	IND	KES	
03027	D2027	BRW	PKR	
03037	D2037	BLK	RDR	
	D2041	BLK	CVR	
	D2046	IND	PVR	
	D2051	GNY	NNR	
03059	**D2059**	GWS	IWR	
03062	**D2062**	GWS	ELR	
03063	**D2063**	BRW	NNR	
03066	D2066	BRW	BH	
03069	**D2069**	GWS	VBR	
03072	**D2072**	GWS	LHR	
03073	D2073	BRW	RAC	
03078	**D2078**	BLK	NTR	
03079	**D2079**	BRW	DVR	
03081	D2081	BRW	MRM	
03089	D2089	GWS	MRM	
03090	**D2090**	GNY	NRS	
03094	**D2094**	GWS	RDR	
03099	D2099	BRW	PKR	
03112	**D2112**	GWS	RVR	
03113	D2113	BRW	PKR	
	D2117	MAR	LHR	
03118	D2118	BRW	GCN	
03119	D2119	BRW	EOR	
03120	**D2120**	GNY	FHR	
	D2133	GWS	WSR	
03134	**D2134**	IND	RDR	
	D2138	GWS	MRB	
	D2139	GNY	PKR	
03141	**D2141**	IND	PBR	
03144	D2144	BRW	WR	
03145	D2145	BRW	MOL	
	D2148	GWS	RSR	
03152	**D2152**	GRE	SCR	
03158	**D2158**	GWS	MRM	*Margaret-Ann*
03162	D2162	BRW	LLR	
03170	**D2170**	GWS	EOR	
	D2178	GWS	GIR	
03179	D2179	UND	RHR	
03180	D2180	BRW	PKR	
	D2182	GRN	GWR	
	D2184	BLK	CVR	
03189	D2189	BRW	RSR	
	D2192	BLK	PDR	*Titan*
03197	D2197	BRW	MNR	
	D2199	GWS	PKR	
03371	D2371	BRW	PDR	
03399	D2399	BRW	MRM	
03901	D2128, 03128	BLK	PKR	

Class 04

	D2203	GNY	EBR
	D2205	GSW	PKR
	D2207	GWS	NYM
	D2229	GRE	PKR
	D2245	GWS	DVR
	D2246	GWS	SDR
	D2271	GNY	SDR
	D2272	GRE	PKR
	D2279	BLK	PKR
	D2280	BLK	NNR
	D2284	GWS	PKR
	D2289	IND	PKR
	D2298	GNY	BRC
	D2302	GWS	MOL
04110	D2310	BRW	BAT
	D2324	IND	BU
	D2325	GWS	MRM
	D2334	GWS	MNR
	D2337	GWS	PKR

Class 05

05001	**D2554**, 97803	GWS	IWR
	D2578	GWS	MOL
	D2587	GWS	PKR
	D2595	GWS	RSR

Class 06

06003	**D2420**, 97804	GWS	PKR

Class 07

07001	D2985	BRW	PKR	
07005	D2989	IND	GCR	
07010	D2994	BRW	AVR	
07012	D2996	BRW	BH	
07013	D2997	BRW	ELR	

Class 08

	D3000	GNY	WK	
	D3002	BLK	PVR	
	D3014	GWS	PDR	*Samson*
08011	**D3018**	GWS	CPR	*Haversham*
	D3019	UND	CRT	
08015	**D3022**	GWS	SVR	
08016	D3023	BRW	PKR	
08022	D3030	IND	CWR	*Lion*
08032	D3044	BRW	MHR	*Mendip*
08046	D3059	BRW	CAL	*Brechin City*
08054	D3067	BRB	EBR	
08060	**D3074**	IND	CWR	*Unicorn*
08064	**D3079**	BLK	NRS	
	D3101	BLK	GCR	
08102	**D3167**	GWS	LWR	
08108	**D3174**	BLK	KES	*Dover Castle*
08114	**D3180**	GRE	GCN	
08123	**D3190**	GRE	CWR	
08133	**D3201**	GWS	SVR	
08164	D3232	BRW	ELR	*Prudence*
	D3255	UND	MAL	
	D3261	GWS	SCR	
08195	**D3265**	BLK	LLR	
08202	D3272	BRW	AVR	
08220	D3290	BRW	GCN	
08238	D3308	BRW	DFR	*Charlie*
08266	D3336	DEP	KWV	
08288	D3358	UND	MHR	
08331	D3401	BLK	MRB	
08359	**D3429**	GWS	TSR	
08377	**D3462**	GWS	WSR	
08436	**D3551**	LSW	SWR	
08443	**D3558**	GWS	BKR	
08444	D3559	GWS	BWR	
08471	**D3586**	GWS	SVR	
08473	D3588	BRW	DFR	
08476	**D3591**	BLK	SWR	
08479	D3594	BRW	ELR	
08490	**D3605**	BLK	STR	
08495	D3610	BRW	NYM	
08528	**D3690**	GWS	DVR	
08556	D3723	GWS	NYM	
08590	D3757	BRW	MRB	
08604	D3771	BRW	DRC	*Phantom*
08605	D3772	DBS	EVR	*G R Walker*
08633	D3800	EWS	CHV	
08635	D3802	BRW	SVR	
08663	D3830	BRW	LE	
08694	D3861	EWS	GCN	
08700	**D3871**	OXB	EVR	
08767	**D3935**	GWS	NNR	
08769	**D3937**	GWS	DFR	*Gladys*
08772	**D3940**	GWS	NNR	
08773	D3941	BRW	EBR	
08795	D3963	BLK	LMR	
08830	D3998	BLK	PKR	
08850	D4018	BRB	NYM	
08881	**D4095**	GWS	SHL	
08888	**D4118**	GWS	KES	
08896	D4126	EWS	SVR	
08907	**D4137**	GWS	GCR	
08911	D4141	NRM	NRM	*Matey*
08915	D4145	BRW	NTR	
08937	D4167	GWS	DAR	*Bluebell Mel*
08993	D3759, 08592	EWS	KWV	*Ashburnham*
08995	D3854, 08687	EWS	WI	
97808	D3993, 08825	NSO	CPR	

Class 09

09001	D3665	EWS	PKR	
09004	D3668	BRW	SCR	
09010	**D3721**	GWS	SDR	
09012	**D4100**	GWS	SVR	*Dick Hardy*
09015	D4103	EWS	AUR	
09017	D4105	NRM	NRM	
09018	**D4106**	GWS	BLU	
09019	**D4107**	GWS	WSR	
09024	D4112	DEP	ELR	
09025	**D4113**	GWS	EKR	
09026	**D4114**	GWS	SPA	*Cedric Wares*
09107	D4013, 08845	BRW	SVR	

Class 10

	D3452	BLK	BWR	
	D3489	BLK	SPA	*Colonel Tomline*
10119	D4067	BRW	GCR	*Margaret Ethel – Thomas Alfred Naylor*
	D4092	GWS	BH	

Class 11

	12052	BLK	CAL
	12077	GWS	MRB
12049	12082	GWS	MHR
	12083	BLE	BAT
	12088	GWS	ALN
	12093	GWS	CAL
	12099	BLK	SVR
	12131	BLK	NNR

Class 12

15224	GWS	SPA

Unclassified locos

D2511	GWS	KWV
D2767	GWS	BKR
D2774	GWS	STR
18000	GWR	DRC

PWM/Class 97

97650	PWM650	BRW	PKR
97651	**PWM651**	GWS	SCR
97654	PWM654	BWS	PKR

Class 14

	D9500	GWS	PKR
	D9502	GWS	ELR
	D9504	GWS	KES
	D9513	NCB	EBR
	D9516	GWS	DRC
	D9518	NCB	WSR
	D9520	GWS	NVR
	D9521	BRW	DFR
	D9523	MWS	WEN
14901	D9524	BLU	PKR
	D9525	GWS	PKR
	D9526	GWS	WSR
14029	D9529	BRB	NVR
	D9531	GWS	ELR
	D9537	BLK	EVR
	D9539	GWS	RSR
	D9551	GOP	SVR
	D9553	GWS	WI
	D9555	GWS	DFR

Class 15

DB968000	**D8233**	GYP	ELR

Class 17

D8568	BRB	SVR

Class 20

20001	**D8001**	GFY	EOR	20057	**D8057**	GYP	CHV	20137	**D8137**	GFY	GWR
20016	**D8016**	BRB	CAL	20059	**D8059**	GYP	MHR	20154	**D8154**	BRB	GCN
20020	D8020	BRB	BKR	20063	D8063	CFD	BAT	20169	**D8169**	UND	WEN
20031	D8031	TLC	KWV	**20081**	**D8081**	BRB	CAL	20188	**D8188**	GYP	MRB
20048	D8048	BRB	MRB	**20088**	**D8088**	RFS	CAL	**20214**	D8314	GYP	LHR
20050	**D8000**	GNY	NRM	20098	**D8098**	GNY	GCR	**20228**	D8128	BRB	BIR

Class 23

D5910	UND	BH

Class 24

24032	**D5032**	GYP	NYM	
24054	**D5054**, TDB968008	GNY	ELR	*Phil Southern*
24061	**D5061**, RDB968007, 97201	GNY	NYM	
24081	**D5081**	BRB	GWR	

The sole surviving Class 17 Clayton Type 1, D8568 leaves Highley with the 1518 from Bridgnorth-Kidderminster on 20 May 2017. *Glen Batten*

Class 20s D8188 and D8059 work a goods train away from Thame Junction Loop for Chinnor on 10 May 2017. *Bill Atkinson*

Class 25

25035	**D5185**	GYP	GCR	
25059	D5209	BRB	KWV	
25067	**D5217**	GYP	BU	
25072	**D5222**	GRE	CAL	
25083	D5233	BRB	CAL	
25173	**D7523**	GYP	BAT	
25185	**D7535**	BRB	SDR	*Mercury*
25191	D7541	GYP	SDR	
25235	D7585	BRB	BKR	
25244	**D7594**	UND	KES	
25262	**D7612**, 25901	GYP	SDR	
25265	D7615	BRB	BU	
25279	**D7629**	GYP	ELR	
25309	**D7659**, 25909	GYP	PKR	
25321	**D7671**	GYP	MRB	
25322	D7672, 25912	BRU	CHV	*Tamworth Castle*

Class 26

26001	**D5301**	GNY	CAL	
26002	**D5302**	GNY	STR	
26004	D5304	TLC	BU	
26007	D5300	RSR	BH	
26010	**D5310**	GFY	LLR	
26011	D5311	BRB	BU	
26014	**D5314**	GNY	CAL	
26024	D5324	BRB	BKR	
26025	**D5325**	GNY	STR	
26035	D5335	BRB	CAL	
26038	D5338	BRB	BKR	*Tom Clift 1954-2012*
26040	D5340	BRB	WAV	
26043	**D5343**	BRB	GWR	

Class 27

27001	D5347	BRB	BKR
27005	D5351	BRB	BKR
27007	**D5353**	UND	CAL
27024	D5370, ADB968028	GYP	CAL
27050	**D5394**, 27106	GNY	STR
27056	D5401, 27112	UND	GCR
27059	D5410, 27123, 27205	UND	LR
27066	D5386, 27103, 27212	BRB	BH

Class 28

D5705	ADB968006, S15705	GYP	ELR

Class 31

31018	D5500	BRB	NRM	
31101	D5518	BRB	AVR	
31105	D5523	NRY	MRM	
31106	D5524	BRB	WR	*Spalding Town*
31108	D5526	RFO	MRB	
31119	D5537	BRB	EBR	
31130	D5548	RFO	AVR	
31162	D5580	BRB	MRB	
31190	D5613	GOP	WR	
31203	**D5627**	GNY	PBR	*Steve Ogden GM*
31206	D5630	CCE	RHR	
31207	**D5631**	GNY	NNR	
31210	D5634	RFO	DFR	
31233	D5553	NRY	MRM	
31235	D5662	BRB	DFR	
31255	D5683	EWS	MNR	
31270	D5800	REG	BU	*Athena*
31271	D5801	TLA	LLR	*Stratford 1840-2001*
31285	D5817	NRY	WR	
31289	D5821	EBP	RHR	*Phœnix*
31327	**D5862**	GYP	STR	
31418	D5522	BRB	MRB	
31430	D5695, 31265, **31530**	BRB	SPA	*Sister Dora*
31435	**D5600**, 31179	GYE	EBR	
31438	D5557, 31139, 31538	BRB	EOR	
31454	D5654, 31228, 31554	ICM	WEN	
31459	D5684, 31256	BRB	WR	
31463	**D5380**, 31297, 31563	GOP	GCN	
31465	D5637, 31213, 31565	NRY	WR	
31466	D5533, 31115	EWS	DFR	
31514	D5814, 31414	DCE	MRB	
31601	D5609, 31186	DCR	EVR	*Devon Diesel Society*
97205	D5581, 31163	RTC	CPR	

Class 25 D7535 is now based at the South Devon Railway. It stands at Buckfastleigh on 27 April 2019 with a train for Totnes Littlehempston. *Antony Christie*

Class 33

33002	D6501	DEP	SDR	
33008	**D6508**	GYP	BAT	*Eastleigh*
33018	D6530	BRB	MRM	
33019	D6534	DCE	BAT	*Griffon*
33021	D6539	POR	CHV	*Eastleigh*
33035	D6553	BRB	WR	
33046	D6564	SWT	ELR	
33048	**D6566**	GYP	WSR	
33052	**D6570**	GNY	KES	*Ashford*
33053	D6571	BRB	CPR	
33057	**D6575**	GYP	WSR	
33063	D6583	TMF	SPA	*RJ Mitchell – Designer Of The Spitfire*
33065	D6585	BRB	SPA	*Sealion*
33102	D6513	BRB	CHV	*Sophie*
33103	D6514	DEP	EVR	*Swordfish*
33108	D6521	BRB	SVR	
33109	D6525	DEP	ELR	*Captain Bill Smith RNR*
33110	D6527	DEP	MRM	
33111	D6528	BRB	SWR	
33116	D6535	BRB	GCR	
33117	D6536	BRB	ELR	
33201	D6586	BRB	BAT	
33202	D6587	BRB	MNR	*Dennis G. Robinson*
33208	**D6593**	GYP	BAT	

Class 35

	D7017	GYP	WSR
	D7018	GYP	WSR
	D7029	BRB	SVR
	D7076	BRB	ELR

Class 26 D5310 is based at the Llangollen Railway but visited the Gloucestershire Warwickshire Railway in 2019 for repairs. It stands in the yard at Toddington. *Jack Boskett*

Class 37

37003	D6703	BRB	LR	
37009	D6709, 37340	BRB	GCN	
37023	D6723	UND	PBR	
37029	**D6729**	GYP	EOR	
37032	**D6732**, 37353	GYP	NNR	
37037	**D6737**, 37321	BRB	SDR	
37042	D6742	EWS	EDR	
37075	D6775	TTG	KWV	
37097	D6797	BRB	CAL	*Old Fettercairn*
37108	D6808, 37325	BLL	RAC	
37109	D6809	BRB	ELR	
37142	D6842	BRB	BWR	
37214	D6914	WCR	BKR	
37215	D6915	BRB	GWR	
37216	**D6916**	GYP	PBR	
37227	D6927	TLM	CPR	
37248	**D6948**	GYP	GWR	
37250	D6950	DCE	WEN	
37261	D6961	DRU	BKR	
37263	D6963	DEP	TSR	
37264	D6964	LLB	NYM	
37275	**D6975**	BRB	PDR	
37294	D6994	BRB	EBR	
37308	D6608, 37274	UND	SVR	
37310	D6852, 37152	BRB	PKR	*British Steel Ravenscraig*
37350	**D6700**, 37119	GYP	NRM	
37503	D6717, 37017	EWS	WEN	
37674	D6869, 37169	RSR	WEN	
37679	D6823, 37123	TTG	ELR	
37703	D6767, **37067**	DRU	BKR	
37714	D6724, 37024	TLM	GCR	*Cardiff Canton*

Class 40

40012	**D212**, 97407	BRB	MRB	*Aureol*
40106	D306	GFY	SVR	*Atlantic Conveyor*
40118	D318, 97408	BRB	TRM	
40122	**D200**	GNY	NRM	
40135	**D335**, 97406	BRB	ELR	

Class 41

41001	43000, ADB975812	BRP	DY

Class 42

	D821	MYP	SVR	*Greyhound*
	D832	BRB	ELR	*Onslaught*

Class 43

43002		HST	NRM	*Sir Kenneth Grange*
43018		FGB	RAC	
43048		EMB	LR	
43089		EMB	LR	

Class 44

44004	**D4**	BRB	MRB	*Great Gable*
44008	**D8**	GYP	PKR	*Penyghent*

Class 45

45015	D14	BRB	BAT	
45041	D53	BRB	MRB	*Royal Tank Regiment*
45060	D100	BRB	BH	*Sherwood Forester*
45105	D86	BRB	BH	
45108	D120	BRB	ELR	
45112	D61	BRB	BU	*Royal Army Ordnance Corps*
45125	**D123**	GYP	GCR	*Leicestershire And Derbyshire Yeomanry*
45132	D22	BRB	EOR	
45133	D40	BRB	MRB	
45135	D99	BRB	ELR	*3rd Carabinier*
45149	D135	BRB	GWR	

One of four surviving Class 35 Hymeks, in 2019 D7018 returned to traffic after a 25-year overhaul. It calls at Blue Anchor with the 1203 Minehead-Bishops Lydeard. *Antony Christie*

Class 46

46010	D147	BRB	GCN
46035	D172, 97403	BRB	PKR
46045	**D182**, 97404	BYP	MRB

Class 47

47004	D1524	GYP	EBR	
47077	D1661, 47613, 47840	BRB	WSR	*North Star*
47105	D1693	BRB	GWR	
47117	**D1705**	BRB	GCR	*Sparrowhawk*
47192	D1842	GFY	RAC	
47205	D1855, 47395	RFD	NLR	
47292	D1994	BLL	GCN	
47306	D1787	RFE	BWR	*The Sapper*
47367	D1886	BRB	MNR	*Kenny Cockbird*
47376	D1895	FTT	GWR	*Freightliner 1995*
47401	D1500	BRB	MRB	*North Eastern*
47402	D1501	GYP	ELR	
47417	**D1516**	GYP	MRB	
47449	**D1566**	BRB	LLR	
47484	D1662	GWR	WI	*Isambard Kingdom Brunel*
47579	D1778, 47183, 47793	BRE	MHR	*James Nightall GC*
47596	D1933, 47255	GYP	MNR	
47635	D1606, 47029	LLB	EOR	*Jimmy Milne*
47640	D1921, 47244	LLB	BAT	*University of Strathclyde*
47643	D1970, 47269	IOS	BKR	
47761	D1619, 47038, 47564	RES	MRB	
47765	D1643, 47059, 47631	SCR	ELR	
47771	D1946, 47503	RES	ZG	
47785	D1909, 47232, 47665, 47820	EWS	WEN	
47799	D1654, 47070, 47620, 47835	ROY	EDR	*Prince Henry*
47841	D1726, 47134, 47622	ICS	MAR	*The Institution of Mechanical Engineers*

Class 50

50002	**D402**	BRB	SDR	*Superb*
50015	D415	LLB	ELR	*Valiant*
50017	D417	NSO	GCR	*Royal Oak*
50019	D419	LLB	MNR	*Ramillies*
50021	D421	LLB	ZG	*Rodney*
50026	D426	NSD	ZG	*Indomitable*
50027	D427	NSR	MHR	*Lion*
50029	D429	LLB	PKR	*Renown*
50030	D430	LLB	PKR	*Repulse*
50031	D431	ICS	SVR	*Hood*
50033	D433	LLB	SVR	*Glorious*
50035	D435	BRB	SVR	*Ark Royal*
50042	D442	LLB	BWR	*Triumph*

Class 52

	D1010	MYP	WSR	*Western Campaigner*
	D1013	BRB	SVR	*Western Ranger*
	D1023	BRB	NRM	*Western Fusilier*
	D1041	UND	ELR	*Western Prince*
	D1048	BRB	MRB	*Western Lady*
	D1062	BRB	SVR	*Western Courier*

Class 55

55015	**D9015**	GYP	BH	*Tulyar*
55016	**D9016**	GYP	MAR	*Gordon Highlander*
55019	D9019	BRB	BH	*Royal Highland Fusilier*

Class 56

56006		BRB	ELR
56097		TLC	GCN

Class 58

58012		TMF	BAT
58016		FER	LR
58022		TMF	EVR
58023		MLB	LR
58048		EWS	BAT

Class 42 Warship D821 *Greyhound* arrives at Quorn & Woodhouse with the 1400 Loughborough-Leicester North on 7 September 2019. Only two of these diesel hydraulics survive. *Pip Dunn*

Class 60

60050		EWS	WEN	
60081		GWR	MAR	
60086		TEW	WEN	

Class 71

71001	**E5001**	GYP	NRS	

Class 73

73002	E6002	LLB	ZG	
73003	**E6003**	GYP	SCR	*Sir Herbert Walker*
73114	E6020	LLB	BAT	
73118	E6024	EUS	BIR	
73129	**E6036**	EBP	GWR	
73130	E6037	EUS	FIN	
73140	E6047	NSR	SPA	
73210	E6022, 73116	IGX	EVR	*Selhurst*

Class 76

76020	**E26020**	BLK	NRM	

Class 77

1502	**E27000**	BLK	MRB	*Electra*
1505	**E27001**	DNS	MSIM	*Ariadne*
1501	E27003	DNS	TIL	*Diana*

Class 81

81002	E3003	BRB	BH	

Class 82

82008	E3054	ICO	BH	

Class 83

83012	**E3035**	EBY	BH	

Class 84

84001	E3036	BRB	BKR	

Class 85

85006	E3061, 85101	BRB	BH	

Class 87

87001		BRB	NRM	*Stephenson*
87035		BRB	RAC	*Robert Burns*

Class 89

89001		ICS	SI	*Avocet*

Prototype Type 5 diesel-electric Co-Co

DP1		POW	NRS	*Deltic*

Prototype 500hp diesel-electric 0-6-0

D226	D0226	GRE	KWV	

Pilot Scheme Class 44 Peak D8 *Penyghent* works the 0852 Holt-Sheringham, between Weybourne and Sheringham on 9 June 2017. *Bill Atkinson*

Main-line Steam

There are currently four train operating companies that can run main-line, steam-hauled trains on the National Network; DB Cargo (page 270), West Coast Railways (page 231), Locomotive Services Limited (page 224) and Vintage Trains (page 239).

Of those, WCR is the current leader in the field having won much business from initially EWS (now DBC) and then FM Rail (which went bust in 2007).

While LSL, WCR and VT all own some of their own steam locos, many locos are owned by private groups and individuals but are main-line registered and used by some or all of the TOCs that can operate steam. Many steam locos come with their own support coaches for their crew.

There are some timetabled steam operations, most notably the Fort William to Mallaig 'Jacobite' that even appears in the GB timetable. WCR also runs from York (Holgate Sidings) to Scarborough on its 'Scarborough Spas Express, – these trains originate in Lancashire diesel-hauled – and its 'Dalesman' from Hellifield to Carnforth. There are also a number of repeat itinerary charter trains such as the 'Torbay Express' from Bristol TM to Kingswear and the 'Cumbrian Mountain Express'.

Registered locos

All steam locos registered for main-line operation must meet NR's standards by having TPWS, OTMR and GSMR, although locos restricted for the Battersby to Whitby line do not. Locos do not need to be dual braked, although several steam locos are now upgraded as such for ease of operation. WCR and Vintage Trains both operate vacuum-braked trains, while LSL and DB Cargo presently do not.

Other steam locos are registered to be hauled on the national network, and may be assigned TOPS numbers, but these are not included here.

As a rule, locos have a boiler examination that, if approved, gives them a ten-year ticket to run on the network, although these may be reduced in length, or indeed extended. Once a ticket has expired, however, the loco is usually either stopped for overhaul or retired for heritage line use only.

LNER 'K1' 62005 passes Achnasheen on the Kyle of Lochalsh line on 2 May 2017 with the 'Great Britain X' trip.
Jack Boskett

Loco	Type	Wheels	Name	Owner	TOPS No.	Brakes	Notes/restrictions
4936	GWR 49xx	4-6-0	*Kinlet Hall*	VT	98536	V	Limited to 60mph
4953	GWR 49xx	4-6-0	*Pitchford Hall*	VT	98553	V	Limited to 60mph
4965	GWR 49xx	4-6-0	*Rood Ashton Hall*	VT	98565	V	Limited to 60mph
5029	GWR 4073	4-6-0	*Nunney Castle*	VT	98728	X	
5043	GWR 4073	4-6-0	*Earl of Mount Edgcumbe*	VT	98743	V	
6024	GWR 60xx	4-6-0	*King Edward I*	Private	98824	X	
702	GWR 4073	4-6-0	*Clun Castle*	VT	98729	V	
7752	GWR 57xx	0-6-0T		Private	98452	V	Limited to 35mph
9466	GWR 94xx	0-6-0T		Private	98466	V	Limited to 45mph
9600	GWR 8750	0-6-0T		Private	98457	V	Limited to 45mph
30777	SR N15	4-6-0	*Sir Lamiel*	Private	98577	V	
30825	SR S15	4-6-0		Private	98625	V	Limited to 45mph
30926	SR Schools	4-4-0	*Repton*	Private	98726	V	For use between Battersby and Whitby only, limited to 45mph
31806	SR U	2-6-0		Private	98406	V	Limited to 60mph
34046	SR West Country (rebuilt)	4-6-2	*Braunton*	LSL	98746	X	
34067	SR Battle of Britain	4-6-2	*Tangmere*	WCR	98767	X	
35018	SR Merchant Navy (rebuilt)	4-6-2	*British India Line*	WCR	98818	V	
35028	SR Merchant Navy (rebuilt)	4-6-2	*Clan Line*	Private	98828	X	
44767	LMS 5MT	4-6-0		Private	98567	V	Limited to 45mph
44871	LMS 5MT	4-6-0		WCR	98571	X	Limited to 60mph
44932	LMS 5MT	4-6-0		WCR	98532	V	Limited to 60mph
45212	LMS 5MT	4-6-0		Private	98512	V	Limited to 60mph
45231	LMS 5MT	4-6-0	*The Sherwood Forester*	Private	98531	X	Limited to 60mph

West Coast Railways' 'Merchant Navy' 35018 *British India Line* stands at the Yeovil Railway Centre after arriving with a main-line charter on 9 July 2019. *Mark Pike*

45305	LMS 5MT	4-6-0	*Alderman A E Draper*	Private	98505	V	Limited to 60mph
45407	LMS 5MT	4-6-0	*The Lancashire Fusilier*	Private	98507	X	Limited to 60mph
45428	LMS 5MT	4-6-0		Private	98528	V	For use between Battersby and Whitby only, limited to 45mph
45596	LMS 5XP	4-6-0	*Bahamas*	Private	98696	V	
45690	LMS 5XP	4-6-0	*Leander*	Private	98690	V	
45699	LMS 5XP	4-6-0	*Galatea*	WCR	98699	V	
46100	LMS 7P	4-6-0	*Royal Scot*	LSL	98702	X	
46115	LMS 7P	4-6-0	*Scots Guardsman*	WCR	98715	V	
46201	LMS 8P	4-6-2	*Princess Elizabeth*	Private	98801	X	
46233	LMS 8P	4-6-2	*Duchess of Sutherland*	Private	98834	X	
48151	LMS 8F	2-8-0		Private	98851	V	Limited to 50mph
60007	LNER A4	4-6-2	*Sir Nigel Gresley*	Private	98898	X	
60019	LNER A4	4-6-2	*Bittern*	Private	98819	X	
60103	LNER A3	4-6-2	*Flying Scotsman*	NRM	98872	X	
60163	LNER A1	4-6-2	*Tornado*	A1SLT	98863	X	
61264	LNER B1	4-6-0		Private	98564	V	
61306	LNER B1	4-6-0	*Mayflower*	Private	98506	V	
62005	LNER K1	2-6-0		Private	98605	V	Limited to 50mph
70000	BR 7MT	4-6-2	*Britannia*	LSL	98700	X	
70013	BR 7MT	4-6-2	*Oliver Cromwell*	Private	98713	V	
71000	BR 8P	4-6-2	*Duke of Gloucester*	Private	98802	X	
75029	BR 4MT	4-6-0		Private	98429	V	For use between Battersby and Whitby only, limited to 45mph
76079	BR 4MT	2-6-0		Private	98476	X	For use between Battersby and Whitby only, limited to 60mph
76084	BR 4MT	2-6-0		Private	98484	V	Limited to 60mph

Right: GWR 'Castle' Class 7029 *Clun Castle* storms up Brimscombe bank in the Stroud Valley with a Vintage Trains excursion on 18 May 2019. *Jack Boskett*

Overleaf: BR '7MT' 70000, running as 70022 *Tornado*, leaves Bristol Temple Meads on 2 August 2020 with a Kingswear train. *Jack Boskett*

70022

Charter Promoters

There are several established charter promoters who run trains throughout the year. As a rule they buy in train operation and coach hire and merely hire the train, sell tickets and make their profit that way.

There are several types of charter trains;

Day excursions: These usually head to cities or towns of interest for sightseeing, sometimes with off train options to local attractions.

Landcruises: Typically three or four days and often to Scotland, the emphasis is on scenery, at seat fine dining, quality hotels and off train options.

Multi-traction tours: Lots of different – usually freight – locos hauling short legs of the trip.

Heritage traction: Preserved or old ex-BR locos likes 20s, 37s, 40145, D1015, Class 50s and the like working high-mileage long says, often taking locos to their former stamping grounds.

Freight line tours: Trips to routes, branch line, curves, spurs, loops and yards that do not normally have passenger trains. Sometimes may use rare traction.

Steam tours: Day excursion trains hauled in part or totally by steam traction.

Branch Line Society

Tel: 07785 112044

Website: www.branchline.org.uk

The BLS specialises in covering rare track using a variety of TOCs, including loco-hauled trains and multiple units. It also raises thousands of pounds each year for good causes.

The Branch Line Society runs trains to cover unusual track and raises money for charity in the process. On 20 July 2019, 37521 stands at Hull with the 'Luca Pezzulo Express', which visited Drax Power station and Stocksbridge steelworks. *Pip Dunn*

Nenta Traintours

Tel: 01692 406152
Website: www.nentatraintours.co.uk
Nenta runs typically three or four loco-hauled trains from East Anglia to the likes of Carlisle, Plymouth or Scarborough. It tends to use Riviera Trains as its rolling stock provider and DRS as its train operator with top-and-tail Class 68s its usual traction. It has previously operated with EWS, WCR and FMR.

Pathfinder Tours

Tel: 01453 835414
Website: www.pathfindertours.co.uk
One of the busiest promoters, Pathfinder typically runs between 30 and 35 trains a year with a mix of day excursions, enthusiast railtours, land cruises and steam-hauled trains.

It was started by Peter Watts as F&W Railtours in 1973 and has run over 1,000 excursions in the following 47 years. It uses Riviera Trains with DRS, GBRf and DB Cargo as its main TOCs.

Pathfinder Tours, and its previous incarnation as F&W Railtours, has been operating trains for 47 years now. It uses a mix of traction and TOCs and on 13 June 2014 DRS 37423 and 37402 power through Northway, north of Ashchurch, heading a charter to Swanage. *Jack Boskett*

Railway Touring Company

Tel: 01553 661500
Website: www.railwaytouring.co.uk
King's Lynn-based promoter set up by Nigel Dobbing, who sadly passed away in early 2019, RTC runs mostly steam-hauled trains across the country. It also runs rail trips abroad.

It exclusively uses West Coast Railways for train operation. Each year its runs its nine-day 'Great Britain' trip, which covers all four corners of the country behind steam.

It likes to recreate days of old, taking steam locos back to their old haunts, but also enjoys delivering 'firsts'; taking a steam loco to a route or destination they never visited in their first main-line careers.

Railway Touring Company specialises in steam-hauled charters. LMS '8P' 6233 *Duchess of Sutherland* passes Crawford on 4 May 2017 with the Day 6 Glasgow Central-Oxenholme leg of the 'Great Britain X' tour. *Jack Boskett*

Retro Railtours

Tel: 0161 3309055
Website: www.retrorailtours.co.uk

The brainchild of James Palmer, who ran his first train when just 18 and since then has run typically two trains a year for local clientele in the Huddersfield and Manchester areas.

Day trips, ideally with exotic heritage traction, to an interesting destination is his usual recipe and by running infrequently, he's gained a loyal customer base.

Retro also ran a bespoke football train taking Huddersfield Town fans to their victorious play-off final win at Wembley on 2017.

Retro Railtours typically runs one or two trains each year using DRS as TOC and Riviera Trains for coaches. No. 68016 *Fearless* passes Colton South Junction with one of its charters, from Chesterfield to Edinburgh on 28 August 2017. *Anthony Hicks*

Rail Charter services, the promotion arm of LSL, runs day trips across the country. No. 47712 *Lady Diana Spencer* emerges from Blea Moor tunnel on 20 August 2020 with the 0835 Skipton-Appleby 'Staycation Express'. *Anthony Hicks*

Saphos Trains/Rail Charter Services

Tel: 0800 038 5320
Website: https://saphostrains.com
New to the market, running its first trains in 2018, Saphos is the charter promotion arm of Locomotive Services, it promotes mostly steam-hauled trains.

Also part of the same business is Rail Charter Services, which uses more modern rolling stock and modern traction for day trips. It ran the 'Staycation Express', a series of Skipton to Appleby day trips in the summer of 2020, some of the first socially distanced charters to run during the Covid pandemic.

Scottish Railway Preservation Society

Tel: 01698 263814
Website: www.srps.org.uk
The SRPS is one of the few promoters that owns its own coaches and has a rake of Mk 1s based at Bo'ness.

Once a big EWS customer, it moved a lot of its business to WCR in the mid-00s, although now uses a mix of WCR, GBRf and DB Cargo to run its trains. It runs a few steam-hauled trains each summer using mostly WCR as its TOC.

It also runs typically as many as seven or eight diesel-hauled charters a year mainly to Mallaig, Kyle of Lochalsh and Oban, but also runs some trains to popular English destinations like York, Chester or Keighley. Trains start from a mix of locations as far south as Carlisle, but typically from the central belt.

It also owns main-line registered 37403 *Isle of Mull* and has access to 37025 *Inverness TMD*, and plans to run trains using these 37s and its coaches.

Statesman Rail

Tel: 0845 310 2458
Website: www.statesmanrail.com
Statesman Rail now operates with LSL and runs a series of day excursions using mostly diesel-hauled trains, but steam sometimes features.

Steam Dreams

Tel: 01483 209888
Website: www.steamdreams.com
As its names suggest, Steam Dreams is essentially a steam charter promoter. It uses WCR as its sole train operator, covers predominately the south of England and likes repeat itinerary trains.

UK Railtours

Tel: 01438 715050
Website: www.ukrailtours.com
UKR is one of the best known names in the UK charter market and has been in business since 1975, starting as the Lea Valley Railway Club, then Hertfordshire Railtours and now UK Railtours.

The year 2020 has been a bad one for the company, with the coronavirus and the sad passing of its founder and driving force John Farrow.

However, John's daughter Liz now runs the business and will be looking to take it forward in 2021. It specialises in day excursions to destinations of interest, land cruises and freight line enthusiasts' tours.

UK Railtours has been running trains for over four decades now and always liked to achieve the unusual, such as taking Class 73s to Paignton! Nos. 73128 *OVS Bulleid* and 73107 *Tracy* pass Torre on 16 July 2016 with an excursion from Basingstoke. 73962/963 are on the other end. *Antony Christie*

Vintage Trains

Tel: 0121 708 4960
Website: www.vintagetrains.co.uk
Vintage Trains started as a promoter specialising on steam-hauled trains from its base in Tyseley in Birmingham. It had an emphasis on GWR steam. It also ran a few diesel-hauled trains, mostly worked by WCR.

In 2018 it opted to gain its own train operating licence and it can now operate its own trains, plus for third parties (see page 239).

It still runs several in house steam-hauled charters mostly from the West Midlands, It initially is restricting its operations to a few preferred routes such as the Welsh Marches, Stratford on Avon and Oxford.

It has also run some third-party trains for the likes of the Branch Line Society and Polar Express.

West Coast Railways

Tel: 0844 850 4685
Website: www.westcoastrailways.co.uk
As well as being a nationwide train operator in its own right (see page 231), WCR promotes many trains itself, including repeat itinerary steam-hauled trains such as the Jacobite, Scarborough Spas Express and Dalesman.

It also runs its Spirit of the Lakes programme and other day excursions, hauled by both steam and diesel traction, and occasionally electric.

West Coast Railways runs many of its own charters and also now owns the Northern Belle. No. 57314 arrives Birmingham International with the ECS for a day excursion on 5 August 2018. *Pip Dunn*

Scrapyards

There are several scrapyards heavily involved with the disposal of old railway assets, locomotives, coaches, multiple, units and wagons.

Currently few locos are being scrapped – by August no locos had been broken up in 2020 – but scrapyards have been busy dealing with disposals as a result of the massive changes to passenger fleets that has seen several redundant DMU, EMU and coaches being sent for scrap.

Those vehicles have not had the necessary modifications to make them compliant for the railway in 2020 and are deemed too old to be worth investing in, leaving scrap as the only alternative.

The main breakers involved at the present time are CF Booth at Rotherham, Sims Metals at Newport, and European Metal Recycling at Kingsbury.

Ron Hull Jnr in Rotherham and Raxstar in Cardiff are also used for scrapping vehicles, the latter tending to do so 'on site' at the location of the condemned vehicle.

Please be aware that visits to these sites, if at all, are on a pre-controlled basis and by appointment only.

CF Booth

Website: www.cfbooth.com

CF Booth in Rotherham is one of the most active scrapyards when it comes to disposal of redundant railway assets. Recently it has been breaking up redundant LNER Mk 4 coaches and FGW Mk 3 HST trailers.

Hours of business: Monday-Friday 0800-1700, Saturday 0800-1200.

Older rolling stock that has no useful life left is being disposed of in various scrapyards. On 7 December 2019, Pacer railbus 142005 is broken up at CF Booth's Rotherham site. *Rob France (taken with permission)*

Ron Hull

Website: www.ronhull.co.uk
Another Rotherham-based scrap dealer, in recent years it has scrapped examples of Classes 08, 31, 37, 47, 56, 73 and 86 but has not disposed of too much railway rolling stock in recent times.

European Metal Recycling

Website: www.emrgroup.com
EMR has several sites across the UK, but the one that undertakes the most disposal of railway stock is at Kingsbury, next to the Birmingham to Tamworth main line.

It recent years it has scrapped examples of 08, 09, 11, 20, 31, 33, 37, 47, 56, 58, 86 and 87, not to mention the Class 373 Eurostar sets.

It still has four Class 08/09 shunters – two at Kingsbury and two at its Attercliffe site in Sheffield – pending disposal or sale. They are 08783/913 at the former and 08872 and 09023 at the latter.

Raxstar

E-mail: info@raxstarltd.co.uk
Raxstar, not to be confused with a Luton rapper, was once a prolific breaker in the early 2000s, disposing of examples of Class 08, 33, 37, 47, 50, 56 and 58. The company is much reduced in its railway activities of late, especially regarding locomotives.

However, it has recently disposed of Mk 3 coaches, Class 442 units, track machines and wagons at its permanent base at Eastleigh.

Sims Metal Management

Website: www.simsmm.co.uk
This company has been busy scrapping many redundant coaches and multiple units at its Newport site. Recently passing through for disposal have been Class 142 DMUs and Class 313, 314, 315 and 508 EMUs, as well as ex LNER and FGW Mk 3 and 4 coaches.

HS2

HS2 – High Speed 2 – is the new proposed High Speed line from London to Birmingham (phase 1). The aspiration is to then extend to Manchester and Leeds (phase 2). HS1 is the 67-mile line from London St Pancras to the Channel Tunnel.

The project has been controversial from day one, especially over its ballooning cost predictions that have risen from £16bn to £33bn (just for phase 1) and £36bn to £89bn for Phase 1 and 2. Other estimates suggest it could cost as much as £106bn. However, the initial cost/benefit ratios was said to be 2.3:1 over 60 years, so for every pound spent, £2.30 is generated, although other models suggest it is more like 1.3:1 or 1.5:1. However, both scenarios still suggest it will, in the grand scheme of things, be an investment that is ultimately worthwhile. It will also give a huge boost to the construction industry.

Initial poor publicity by the pro-HS2 bodies did not help, mainly going on time savings rather than HS2's biggest benefit, which is creating capacity and allowing fast trains to be taken off the existing Birmingham NS-Euston WCML and thus releasing that route for local and freight trains.

HS2 will use a new station in Birmingham built on the site of the old Curzon Street station and new platforms at London Euston. It will serve Old Oak Common in west London and Birmingham Interchange, near Solihull. It is expected it will take just 49 minutes to cover the 100 miles from Euston to Curzon Street.

Much of Phase 1 is due to be in tunnels – which ramp up the costs – with eight miles in London underground and another ten miles in the Chiltern Hills.

On phase 2, if approved, stations at Long Eaton and Manchester Interchange will link with other transport networks. It will also connect with other trains at Crewe.

HS2 will connect with the existing network at various stages and some trains will run directly from HS2 on to the existing network. This means the trains cannot be built to a bigger loading gauge but it does offer operational flexibility, especially in offering through services and so opening up the accessibility of HS2 to other parts of the network. As such there are no current plans to extend the high-speed network north of Leeds or Manchester to either Newcastle or Liverpool, and high-speed rail to Scotland via the west or east coast routes remains unlikely any time soon.

Once opened, HS2 plans to offer capacity of up to nine trains an hour from its opening in 2026 but that should rise to 18 trains an hour to and from London from 2033 when Phase 2 opens. Initially, services on HS2 are part of the Avanti West Coast franchise and it will be responsible for running all aspects of the service including ticketing, trains and the maintenance of the infrastructure.

A rolling stock depot will be built in Washwood Heath, Birmingham. The Phase 1 infrastructure maintenance depot will be north of Aylesbury in Buckinghamshire, between Steeple Claydon and Calvert. Staveley in Derbyshire and Stone, in Staffordshire, are identified as similar sites for Phase 2.

Livery codes

ADV Advertising / promotional livery
ADZ Advenza Freight blue
AGG Greater Anglia grey
AGI Aggregates industries turquoise and silver
ANG Anglia Railways turquoise
ARB Arriva blue
ARV Arriva Trains Wales turquoise, unbranded
AVD AV Dawson red
AWC Avanti West Coast dark green
BAF Bardon Aggregates blue with Freightliner branding
BBM Battle of Britain Memorial Flight graphics
BDB Boston Docks blue
BEA Beacon Rail blue
BIF Biffa red bodyside, orange cabs (GBRf)
BLE Unspecified plain blue
BLK British Railways black
BLL British Rail 'large logo' blue with yellow cabs
BLU British Rail blue yellow cabsides
BMT Bulmarket red
BRB British Rail blue with full yellow ends
BRE British Rail blue with large numbers and emblems
BRF British Rail blue with Union flags
BRG British Rail blue and grey
BRL British Rail blue large logo blue with black roof
BRP British Rail blue grey prototype HST
BRW British Rail blue with wasp stripes
BRY British Railways blue with Foster Yeoman branding
BRZ BZK BR blue
BYP British Rail blue with small yellow panels
BZK BZK (БЪлгарска ЖеиезолЪтна Компания) green and yellow
C2C c2c white
CAC Carmine & Cream
CAL Caledonian Sleeper dark turquoise
CAP Cappagh blue
CAS Castle Cement light grey
CCE Civil engineers' grey / yellow 'Dutch'
CCT Civil engineers' grey / yellow 'Dutch' with Transrail logos
CEL Celsa black with orange cab
CEM Cemex white and blue
CFD Chemins de fer Départméntaux orange
CMX Cemex white (GBRf)
COL Colas Rail Freight orange, yellow and black
CON Continental rail blue
COR Corus silver
COT BZK Cotswold Rail silver
COU Colas Rail Freight orange, yellow and black unbranded
COY Corus yellow
CRO Original Chiltern Railways with blue band along the windows / upper body and red line along the lower bodyside
CRS Chiltern Railways silver / grey
CRW new Chiltern Railways by Arriva livery with blue band bordered by upper light blue and lower grey band.
CSM Continental Railway Solution maroon
DBC DB Cargo red
DBM DB Cargo Manager's Train silver
DBR Deutsche Bahn all over red
DBS DB Schenker red
DBU DB red unbranded
DCG Devon & Cornwall Railways green
DCN DC Rail revised light grey
DCR DC Rail grey
DEP Departmental grey
DGB BZK DRS blue with orange cab
DMS DB Cargo manager's train silver
DNS Nederlandse Spoorwegen grey / yellow
DRA Drax silver
DRC DRS blue with Compass logos
DRE DRS blue with new Compass logos (Class 88)
DRN DRS blue with new Compass logos
DRS DRS blue original
DRU DRS blue, unbranded

DRX DRS blue with smaller Compass logos
DST Deanside Transit lilac
EBY Electric blue yellow panels
ECR Euro Cargo Rail light grey
EMB East Midlands Trains plain blue
EMP East Midlands Railway all over purple
EMR East Midlands Railway purple / white
EMT East Midlands Trains blue / red / orange
EMU East Midland Trains unbranded
EMW East Midlands Railway white
EMY GBRf with Emily Woodman graphics
EPX Europhoenix silver
ESB Eurostar blue / grey / yellow
ESO Eurostar original grey
ETF Eurovia Travaux Ferroviaires yellow
EUE Eurostar grey with EWS logos
EUT Eurotunnel grey
EUY Eurotunnel grey / yellow
EWS EWS maroon and gold
EWR EWS maroon and gold with RSS logos
FEC First East Coast
FER Fertis grey
FEU Fertis grey unbranded
FGA First Great Western blue with advertising wrap
FGB First Great Western blue
FGO Fragonset black unbranded
FGU First Great Western blue unbranded
FGS First Great Western 'special' graphics
FIR First Group plain blue
FLG Freightliner two-tone grey
FLR Freightliner green with yellow cabs
FLS Freightliner green with Shanks advertising
FLY Floyd black
FPG Freightliner green unbranded
FPH Freightliner 'Powerhaul' green, yellow and grey
FRG Fragonset black
FSR First ScotRail blue
FTF Fall the Fallen graphics
GAW Greater Anglia white
GBB GB Railfreight blue with orange numbers
GBF GB Railfreight blue and orange
GBP GB Railfreight with pride rainbows
GBR GB Railfreight blue and orange Europorte style
GBO GB Railfreight blue and orange original style
GBZ GB Railfreight blue and orange with minor variations
GCR Grand Central black / orange
GEX Gatwick Express red
GFY British Railways green full yellow ends
GLA Glaxo chemicals blue and dark grey
GOP Golden Ochre with yellow panels
GNY British Railways green no yellow ends
GRE Unspecified plain green
GRW British Railways green with wasp stripes
GWD Genesee & Wyoming darker orange and black
GWE Great Western Railway (pre-BR) green
GWO Genesee & Wyoming lighter orange and black
GWS British Rail green with wasp stripes
GWR Great Western Trains all over green
GYP British Railways green with yellow panels
HAN Hanson aggregates blue and silver
HAR 'Harry Patch' black graphics
HEC Heathrow Express Connect
HEX Heathrow Express silver
HNO Harry Needle Railroad Company orange
HOP Hope Construction white with purple solebar
HST Original blue, grey, yellow HST
HUL Hull Trains blue
HUN Hunslet green
ICM BR InterCity 'Mainline'
ICO BR InterCity original style
ICS BR InterCity Swallow style
IGX BR InterCity Gatwick Express
IOS BR InterCity original with ScotRail branding
IND Industrial livery
ISL Island Line red
JUB DB Cargo Diamond Jubilee silver
JFU Jarvis Fastline unbranded grey
KBR Knorr Bremse green, white and blue

KER	Kernow black
LAB	'Laira' blue with grey roof
LAM	Lamco orange
LEM	LNER red with EMR branding
LHO	Loadhaul original
LMR	London Midland Railway dark green / black / white
LNE	LNER white / red
LNR	BZK LNWR blackberry black
LNW	LNWR dark green / grey
LOR	London Overground
LSW	LSWR black
LUB	GBRf London Transport Museum black with graphics
LUW	GBRf London Transport Museum white with graphics
LZY	LZY green, white purple (Eurostar)
MAA	DB Cargo with WH Malcolm graphics
MAL	WH Malcolm, green, yellow and blue
MAR	Lakeside & Haverthwaite Railway lined maroon
MER	Merseyrail grey / yellow
MEW	Mainline Freight blue with EWS logos
MFY	Maroon with full yellow ends
MID	Midland Railway maroon
MLB	Mainline Freight blue
MRD	DB Cargo Maritime blue
MRM	Metropolitan Railway maroon
MRT	GBRf Maritime blue
MSC	GBRf with Medite Sorrento graphics
MWS	Maroon with wasp stripes
MYP	Maroon with yellow panels
NBL	Northern plain blue
NBU	Northern Belle umber and cream unbranded
NCB	National Coal Board blue
NEX	National Express
NOB	Northern Belle umber and cream
NOR	Northern purple
NRA	National Railway Museum advertising wrap
NRB	National Railway Museum light blue
NRM	National Railway Museum maroon
NRY	Network Rail yellow
NSD	Network SouthEast revised darker blue
NSE	BZK Network SouthEast red white and blue
NSO	Network SouthEast original with white window frames
NSR	Network SouthEast revised with blue window frames
ONE	Ocean Network Express magenta
OXB	Oxford blue
PAT	Harry Patch graphics
PDP	PD Ports blue
POW	Powder blue
PRI	Pride vinyl
PUM	Puma Energy dark grey
PUL	Pullman umber and cream
RCA	Railcare red white and blue
RCG	Railcare grey and white
RED	Unspecified plain red
REG	Regional Railways blue and grey
RES	Rail Express systems red and dark grey
REW	Railfreight Distribution 'European' two-tone grey with EWS logos
RFD	Railfreight Distribution two-tone grey with RfD logos
RFE	Railfreight Distribution 'European' two-tone grey with RfD logos
RFO	Railfreight Original grey
RFS	RFS grey
RMB	RMS Locotec black
RMS	RMS Locotec blue
ROG	Rail Operations Group blue
ROM	Royal Mail postal red
ROY	Royal Scotsman plum
RSR	Railfreight Red stripe
RTC	Railway Technical Centre red and blue
RTO	Royal Train plum
RTP	Royal Train Res style
SCO	British Rail ScotRail
SCR	ScotRail Saltire blue
SCT	ScotRail Seven Cities
SEB	Southeastern blue
SEW	Southeastern white
SIL	Silverlink green, purple and white
SOU	Southern green and white
SPE	Bombardier special purple, green, blue and red
STO	Stobart Rail advertising

SWA	South West Trains advertising/promotional
SWB	South West Trains blue
SWM	South West Trains Metro red
SWO	South Western Railway (initial trial livery)
SWP	South Western Railway Pride
SWR	South Western Railway
SWU	South West Trains blue unbranded
SWW	South West Trains white
TAB	Tata Blue
TAS	Tata Silver
TFL	Transport for London
TEW	Trainload grey with EWS logos
TFW	Transport for Wales
TKB	Thameslink Blue
TLA	Trainload grey with Aggregates logos
TLC	Trainload grey with Coal logos
TLH	Trainload grey with Loadhaul logos
TLK	Thameslink white
TLM	Trainload grey with Metals logos
TMF	Trainload grey with Mainline Freight logo
TMT	Transmart Trains green
TPE	Transpennine Express silver/blue/purple
TTG	Two-tone unbranded Railfreight grey
TRN	Transrail grey
TSO	TSO yellow
UKR	UK Rail Leasing grey with yellow cabs
UND	Undercoat/unpainted/primer
VEA	Virgin Trains red with advertising branding
VEC	Virgin Trains East Coast With LNER branding
VEM	Virgen red with EMR branding
VFS	Virgin Trains Flying Scotsman
VIR	Virgin Trains red
WCR	West Coast Railways maroon with yellow panels
WHI	plain unbranded white
WMG	West Midlands Trains gold/purple
XCT	CrossCountry Trains
XRL	Crossrail

Pool codes

ATLO	Alstom Traincare Locomotives
ATZZ	Alstom Traincare Locomotives For Disposal
AWCA	West Coast Railway Operational Diesel Locomotives
AWCX	West Coast Railway Stored Diesel Locomotives
BREL	Boden Rail Engineering
CDJD	Central Services/Serco Railtest Ex Serco Shunters
CFOL	Class 50 Operations Ltd
CFSL	Class 40 Stored Locos
COFS	Colas Rail Freight
COLO	Colas Rail Freight Hire Locomotives
COLS	Colas Rail Freight Stored Locomotives
COTS	Colas Rail Freight Locomotives For Refurbishing
DBLX	Deltic Preservation Society
DCRO	DCR Class 50/56
DCRS	DCR Class 60
DDIN	Freightliner Shunter Fleet
DFGH	Freightliner Heavy Haul
DFGI	Freightliner Intermodal
DFHG	Freightliner Heavy Haul
DFHH	Freightliner Heavy Haul
DFHJ	Freightliner Heavy Haul RHTT/Limited Use
DFIM	Freightliner Intermodal Modified
DFIN	Freightliner Intermodal Low Emission
DFLC	Freightliner Intermodal
DFLH	Freightliner Heavy Haul
DFNC	Freightliner Awaiting Maintenance
DHLT	Freightliner Stored/Not In Main Line Use Locomotives
EFOO	First Great Western FGW Class 57/6
EFPC	First Great Western FGW Class 43
EFSH	First Great Western FGW Shunters
EHPC	Arriva CrossCountry HST Power Cars
EJLO	London Midland Shunters
ELRD	East Lancashire Railway Operational Locomotives
EMPC	East Midlands Trains HST Power Cars
EMSL	East Midlands Trains Shunters
EPEX	Europhoenix For Scrap/Export
EPUK	Europhoenix UK Locomotives

GBBR GBRf Class 73/9 - Brush Repowered
GBBT GBRf UK Cab - Long Range Fuel Tanks
GBCH GBRf Caledonian Sleeper
GBCS GBRf Re-Engineered
GBEB GBRf Euro Cab - Long Range Fuel Tanks
GBED GBRf Electro Diesel Locos For Hire
GBEE GBRf On Hire Class 20
GBEL GBRf Euro Cab -Standard Fuel Tanks
GBET GBRf Stored Locos
GBFM GBRf RETB Fitted Locomotives
GBGD GBRf Class 56 operational
GBGS GBRf Class 56 stored
GBHN GBRf Long Term Hire Locomotives
GBLT GBRf UK Cab - Standard Fuel Tanks
GBNB GBRf New Build Locos
GBNR GBRf For Network Rail Use
GBRT GBRf Restricted Locos
GBSD GBRf Stored Locos
GBSL GBRf Caledonian Sleepers
GBST GBRf Caledonian Sleepers/Channel Tunnel
GBWM GBRf Shunting Duties
GBYH GBRf General Pool
GCHP Grand Central HST Power Cars
GPSS Eurostar UK Operate From TI (DBC Maintained)
GROG Rail Operations Group Operational Locos
HAPC ScotRail Class 43
HBSH Virgin Trains East Coast On Hire To VTEC
HISE Rail Vehicle Engineering East Midlands Trains Shunters
HTLX Hanson Traction Operational Locomotives
HYWD South West Trains Thunderbird Locos
IANA Greater Anglia Loco Fleet
IECA Virgin Trains East Coast Operational Locomotives
IECP Virgin Trains East Coast HST power cars
KDSD Bombardier Doncaster
LSLO Locomotive Services Limited, operational locos
LSLS Locomotive Services Limited, stored locos
MBDL Non TOC Private Owner - Diesel locos
MBED Non TOC Private Owner - Class 73
MBEL Non TOC Private Owner - Electric locos
MOLO RT Rail Limited Hired Fleet Shunter locos
MRLO RMS Locotec Ex-FM Rail Operational Locos
MRLS RMS Locotec Ex-FM Rail Stored locos
MRSO RMS Locotec Ex-FM Rail Operational Shunters
NRLO Nemesis Rail Locomotives On Hire
NRLS Nemesis Rail Ex-FM Rail Stored locos
QACL Network Rail Load Bank
QADD Network Rail Diesel Locos
QCAR Network Rail HST Power Cars
QETS Network Rail European Signalling
RCZH Knorr Bremse Rail Systems Springburn Works Shunters
RCZN Knorr Bremse Rail Systems Wolverton Works Shunters
RFSH Wabtec Rail Locomotives
RMSX RMS Locotec Locomotives
RTSO Riviera Trains Operational Shunters
RVLO Railway Vehicle Engineering Derby Operational Locomotives
SAXL Eversholt Rail Off Lease Locos
SBXL Porterbrook Leasing Off Lease Locos
SCEL Angel Train Contracts Off Lease Locos
TTLS Traditional Traction/Railway Support Services
UKRL UK Rail Leasing On Lease
UMRM UK Rail Leasing Not Main Line
UKRS UK Rail Leasing Stored
WAAC DB Cargo UK
WABC DB Cargo UK RETB Fitted
WAWC DB Cargo UK Arriva Wales Hire
WBAE DB Cargo UK Fitted With Stop/Start Technology
WBAR DB Cargo UK Remote Condition Monitoring Equipment
WBAT DB Cargo UK General
WBBE DB Cargo UK RETB & Stop/Start Technology Fitted
WBBT DB Cargo UK RETB Fitted
WBLE DB Cargo UK Lickey Bankers With Stop/Start Technology

WBLT	DB Cargo UK
WBTT	DB Cargo UK RHTT - Tripcock Fitted
WCAT	DB Cargo UK Standard Fuel Range
WCBT	DB Cargo UK Extended Fuel Rail
WDAM	DB Cargo UK
WEAC	DB Cargo UK
WFBC	DB Cargo UK HS1 Equipped
WGEA	DB Cargo UK Euro Cargo Rail
WGEE	DB Cargo UK Eastern Europe
WGEP	DB Cargo UK Poland
WQAA	DB Cargo UK Locomotives Stopped Serviceable - Group 1A
WQAB	DB Cargo UK Stored Locomotives Group 1B
WQBA	DB Cargo UK Stored Locomotives Stored Serviceable - Group 2
WQCA	DB Cargo UK Stored Locos For Component Recovery - Group 3
WQDA	DB Cargo UK Stored Locomotives Surplus - Group 4
XHAC	Direct Rail Services Operational Locos - ETS Equipped
XHCC	Direct Rail Services Operational Locos - Northern (Cumbrian Coast Workings)
XHCE	Direct Rail Services Hire To Chiltern Railways
XHCK	Direct Rail Services Operational Locos
XHIM	Direct Rail Services Intermodal Locos
XHNC	Direct Rail Services Nuclear Traffic
XHSS	Direct Rail Services Stored Locos
XHTP	Direct Rail Services Locos For Transpennine Express
XHVE	Direct Rail Services Vossloh Locos
XHVT	Direct Rail Services West Coast Thunderbird Locos
XYPA	Mendip Rail Operational Locomotives
XYPO	Mendip Rail Operational Locomotives

Owner codes

ACL	AC Locomotive Group
AGI	Agility Trains
AGO	Andrew Goodman
ALS	Alstom
ANG	Angel Trains
ARV	Arriva Group
BEA	Beacon Rail
BEV	Beaver Sports
BEN	Steve Beniston
BOD	Neil Boden
BRO	Brodie Rail Engineering
CAP	Cappagh Group (DC Rail)
CFA	Class 50 Alliance
CFP	Class 40 Preservation Society
CFS	Class 56 Group
CLT	Cross London Trains
COL	Colas Rail Freight
CRL	Caledonian Rail Leasing
CTL	Class 20 Locomotive Society
DBC	DB Cargo
DCR	DC Rail
DfT	Department for Transport
DPS	Deltic Preservation Society
DRS	Direct Rail Services
DTG	Diesel Traction Group
EEG	English Electric Group
EMT	East Midlands Trains
EPX	Europhoenix
EUK	Eurostar
EVS	Eversholt Leasing
FIR	First Group
FLI	Freightliner
GAR	Garcia Hanson
GBR	GB Railfreight
GWR	Great Western Railway
HAN	Hanson Aggregates
HJE	Howard Johnston
HNR	Harry Needle Railroad Company
LES	Les Ross
LOL	London Overground
LOM	Lombard Finance
LON	London Midland
LSL	Locomotive Services Limited
MAQ	Macquarie Group

MET	MerseyTravel
MOW	Michael Owen
NEM	Nemesis Rail
NET	Network Rail
NRM	National Railway Museum
POR	Porterbrook
ROC	Rock Rail
ROG	Rail Operations Group
SFG	Stratford Class 47 Group
SOA	71A Locomotives
SRP	Scottish Railway Preservation Society
STG	Scottish Class 37 Group
SWR	South Western Railway
UKR	UK Rail Leasing
VIN	Vintage Trains
WCR	West Coast Railways
XRLL	Crossrail

Spot hire/industrial owners

AFS	Arlington Fleet Services
AVD	AV Dawson
BOM	Bombardier
BMT	Bulmarket (Bulgaria)
BZK	BZK (БЪлгарска ЖеиезолЪтна Компания - Bulgaria)
CON	Continental Rail Solutions (Hungary)
CRB	Chris Beet
EMD	Electromotive Diesels
EMR	European Metal Recycling
FLY	Floyd (Hungary)
ITY	Private owner in Italy
KBR	Knorr Bremse
LAM	Lamco Mining
LOR	Loram
NYM	North Yorkshire Moors Railway
RSS	Railway Support Services (Traditional Traction)
SEC	Serco
SLE	St Leonards Engineering
TFA	Transfesa
TMT	Transmart Trains
TLW	Tyseley Locomotive Works
VIC	Victoria Group (Boston Docks)
WAB	Wabtec

Heritage railway locations

ALL	Allely's yard, Studley
ALN	Aln Valley Railway
AVR	Avon Valley Railway
BAT	Battlefield Line
BH	Barrow Hill Roundhouse
BKR	Bo'ness & Kinneil Railway
BIR	Barry Island Railway
BLU	Bluebell Railway
BRC	Buckingham Railway Centre
BWR	Bodmin & Wenford Railway
BU	Burton on Trent
CAL	Caledonian Railway
CHR	Chasewater Railway
CHV	Churnet Valley Railway
CPR	Chinnor & Princes Risborough Railway
CRT	Cambrian Railways Trust
CWR	Cholsey & Wallingford Railway
CVR	Colne Valley Railway
DFR	Dean Forest Railway
DAR	Dartmoor Railway
DRC	Didcot Railway Centre
DVR	Derwent Valley Light Railway
EBR	Embsay Steam Railway
EDR	Eden Valley Railway
EKR	East Kent Railway
ELR	East Lancashire Railway
EOR	Epping and Ongar Railway
ESR	East Somerset Railway
EVR	Ecclesbourne Valley Railway
FHR	Fawley Hill Railway
GWR	Gloucestershire Warwickshire Railway
GCR	Great Central Railway
GCN	Great Central Railway Nottingham
GIR	Gwili Railway
IWR	Isle of Wight Steam Railway
KWV	Keighley & Worth Valley Railway
KES	Kent & East Sussex Railway
LHR	Lakeside & Haverthwaite Railway
LMR	Llanelli & Mynydd Mawr Railway
LLR	Llangollen Railway
LWR	Lincolnshire Wolds Railway
MAL	Private site Malton
MHR	Mid Hants Railway
MNR	Mid Norfolk Railway

MOL	Moreton-on-Lugg	RVR	Rother Valley Railway
MRB	Midland Railway - Butterley	SCR	Swindon & Cricklade Railway
MRM	Mangapps Railway Museum	SDR	South Devon Railway
NRM	National Railway Museum York	SPA	Spa Valley Railway
NRS	National Railway Museum Shildon	STM	Stainmoor Railway
NLR	Northampton and Lamport Railway	STR	Strathspey Railway
NNR	North Norfolk Railway	SWR	Swanage Railway
NVR	Nene Valley Railway	SVR	Severn Valley Railway
NYM	North Yorkshire Moors Railway	TBR	Trawsfynydd & Blaenau Railway
NTR	North Tyneside Railway	TIT	Titley Junction
PBR	Pontypool & Blaenavon Railway	TSR	Telford Steam Railway
PDR	Paignton & Dartmouth Railway	VBR	Vale of Berkeley Railway
PKR	Peak Rail	WH	Washwood Heath
PVR	Plym Valley Railway	WI	Wishaw
RAC	Railway Age Crewe	WEN	Weardale Railway
RDR	Royal Deeside Railway	WEA	Wensleydale Railway
RHR	Rushden Heritage Railway	WSR	West Somerset Railway
RSR	Ribble Steam Railway		

Vehicle check list

This list is the locos and multiple units (by unit number) that remain either in the UK or abroad. Their TOPS numbers are listed regardless of what identity they carry. Eurotunnel/Eurostar trains are also listed, while preserved locos are given at the end.

Also included in red are new trains that are on order. These are not included in the main body of the text if they do not have individual vehicle numbers known at the time of going to press. Also, these set numbers could change, and those listed are based on the information previously released by the ordering TOCs.

Two locos included here but not in the main body of text are the remains of collision write-offs 66048 and 70012. Their damaged bodies remain intact at Longport and Erie (Pennsylvania) respectively but the vehicles are not owned by a FOC, TOC or ROSCO.

03084	08423	08511	08598	08648	08706	08774	08824	08899	08947
03196	08428	08516	08600	08649	08709	08780	08834	08903	08950
D2381	08441	08523	08602	08650	08711	08782	08836	08904	08954
	08442	08525	08611	08652	08714	08783	08846	08905	08956
07007	08445	08527	08613	08653	08721	08784	08847	08908	08994
07011	08447	08530	08615	08663	08724	08785	08853	08912	D3047
	08451	08531	08616	08669	08730	08786	08865	08913	D3092
08021	08454	08536	08617	08670	08735	08788	08868	08918	
08168	08460	08567	08622	08676	08737	08790	08870	08921	09002
08296	08472	08568	08623	08678	08738	08798	08871	08922	09006
08308	08480	08571	08624	08682	08742	08799	08872	08924	09007
08375	08483	08573	08629	08683	08743	08802	08873	08925	09009
08389	08484	08575	08630	08685	08752	08804	08874	08927	09014
08401	08485	08578	08631	08690	08754	08805	08877	08933	09017
08405	08499	08580	08632	08691	08756	08809	08879	08934	09022
08410	08500	08585	08641	08696	08757	08810	08885	08936	09023
08411	08502	08588	08643	08700	08762	08818	08887	08939	09106
08417	08503	08593	08644	08701	08764	08822	08891	08943	09201
08418	08507	08596	08645	08703	08765	08823	08892	08944	09204

20007
20056
20066
20069
20087
20096
20107
20110
20118
20121
20142
20166
20189
20205
20227
20301
20302
20303
20304
20305
20308
20309
20311
20312
20314
20901
20903
20904
20905
20906

25057
25278
25283
25313

31128
31452
31461

33012
33025
33029
33030
33207

37025
37038
37057
37059
37069
37099
37116
37146
37165
37175
37190
37198
37207
37218
37219
37240
37254
37259
37401
37402
37403
37405
37407
37409
37418
37419
37421
37422
37423
37424
37425
37510
37516
37517
37518
37521
37601
37602
37603
37604
37605
37606
37607
37608
37609
37610
37611
37612
37667
37668
37669
37676
37685
37688
37706
37710
37712
37716
37800
37884
37901
37905
37906

40013
40145

43003
43004
43005
43009
43010
43012
43013
43014
43015
43016
43017
43020
43021
43022
43023
43024
43025
43026
43027
43028
43029
43030
43031
43032
43033
43034
43035
43036
43037
43040
43041
43042
43043
43044
43045
43046
43047
43048
43049
43050
43052
43053
43054
43055
43056
43058
43059
43060
43061
43062
43063
43064
43066
43069
43070
43071
43073
43075
43076
43078
43079
43081
43082
43083
43086
43087
43088
43089
43091
43092
43093
43094
43097
43098
43122
43124
43125
43126
43127
43128
43129
43130
43131
43132
43133
43134
43135
43136
43137
43138
43139
43140
43141
43142
43143
43144
43145
43146
43147
43148
43149
43150
43151
43152
43153
43154
43155
43156
43158
43159
43160
43161
43162
43163
43164
43165
43168
43169
43170
43171
43172
43174
43175
43176
43177
43179
43180
43181
43182
43183
43185
43186
43187
43188
43189
43190
43191
43192
43193
43194
43195
43196
43197
43198
43206
43207
43208
43238
43239
43251
43257
43272
43274
43277
43285
43290
43295
43296
43299
43300
43301
43302
43303
43304
43305
43306
43307
43308
43309
43310
43311
43312
43313
43314
43315
43316
43317
43318
43319
43320
43321
43357
43366
43367
43378
43384
43423
43465
43467
43468
43480
43484

45118

47194
47237
47245
47270
47355
47368
47375
47488
47492
47501
47526
47580
47593
47701
47703
47712
47714
47715
47727
47739
47744
47746
47749
47760
47768
47769
47772
47773
47776
47786
47787
47798
47802
47804
47805
47810
47811
47812
47813
47815
47816
47818
47826
47828
47830
47832
47843
47847
47848
47851
47853
47854

50007
50008
50044
50049
50050

D1015

55002
55009
55022

56009
56032
56049
56051
56077
56078
56081
56087
56090
56091
56094
56096
56098
56101
56103
56104
56105
56106
56113
56115
56117
56301
56302
56303
56312

57001
57002
57003
57004
57005
57006
57007
57008
57009
57010
57011
57012
57301
57302
57303
57304
57305
57306
57307
57308
57309
57310
57311
57312
57313
57314
57315
57316
57601
57602
57603
57604
57605

58001
58004
58005
58006
58007
58009
58010
58011
58013
58018
58021
58025
58026
58027
58032
58033
58034
58035
58036
58038
58039
58040
58041
58042
58044
58046
58049
58050

59001
59002
59003
59004
59005
59101
59102
59103
59104
59201
59202
59203
59204
59205
59206

60001
60002
60003
60004
60005
60007
60008
60009
60010
60011
60012
60013
60014
60015
60017
60018
60019
60020
60021
60022
60023
60024
60025
60026
60027
60028
60029
60030
60031
60032
60033
60034
60035
60036
60037
60038
60039
60040
60041
60042
60043
60044
60045
60046
60047
60048
60049
60051
60052
60053
60054
60055
60056
60057
60058
60059
60060
60061
60062
60063
60064
60065
60066
60067
60068
60069
60070
60071
60072
60073
60074
60075
60076
60077
60078
60079
60080
60082
60083
60084
60085
60087
60088
60089
60090
60091
60092
60093
60094
60095
60096
60097
60098
60099
60100
60500

66001
66002
66003
66004
66005
66006
66007
66009
66010
66011
66012
66013
66014
66015

66017	66078	66139	66200	66416	66542	66611	66746	66953	68023
66018	66079	66140	66201	66417	66543	66612	66747	66954	68024
66019	66080	66142	66202	66418	66544	66613	66748	66955	68025
66020	66082	66143	66203	66419	66545	66614	66749	66956	68026
66021	66083	66144	66204	66420	66546	66615	66750	66957	68027
66022	66084	66145	66205	66421	66547	66616	66751		68028
66023	66085	66146	66206	66422	66548	66617	66752	67001	68029
66024	66086	66147	66207	66423	66549	66618	66753	67002	68030
66025	66087	66148	66208	66424	66550	66619	66754	67003	68031
66026	66088	66149	66209	66425	66551	66620	66755	67004	68032
66027	66089	66150	66210	66426	66552	66621	66756	67005	68033
66028	66090	66151	66211	66427	66553	66622	66757	67006	68034
66029	66091	66152	66212	66428	66554	66623	66758	67007	
66030	66092	66153	66213	66429	66555	66624	66759	67008	69001
66031	66093	66154	66214	66430	66556	66625	66760	67009	69002
66032	66094	66155	66215	66431	66557	66701	66761	67010	69003
66033	66095	66156	66216	66432	66558	66702	66762	67011	69004
66034	66096	66157	66217	66433	66559	66703	66763	67012	69005
66035	66097	66158	66218	66434	66560	66704	66764	67013	69006
66036	66098	66159	66219	66501	66561	66705	66765	67014	69007
66037	66099	66160	66220	66502	66562	66706	66766	67015	69008
66038	66100	66161	66221	66503	66563	66707	66767	67016	69009
66039	66101	66162	66222	66504	66564	66708	66768	67017	69010
66040	66102	66163	66223	66505	66565	66709	66769	67018	
66041	66103	66164	66224	66506	66566	66710	66770	67019	70001
66042	66104	66165	66225	66507	66567	66711	66771	67020	70002
66043	66105	66166	66226	66508	66568	66712	66772	67021	70003
66044	66106	66167	66227	66509	66569	66713	66773	67022	70004
66045	66107	66168	66228	66510	66570	66714	66774	67023	70005
66047	66108	66169	66229	66511	66571	66715	66775	67024	70006
66048	66109	66170	66230	66512	66572	66716	66776	67025	70007
66049	66110	66171	66231	66513	66582	66717	66777	67026	70008
66050	66111	66172	66232	66514	66583	66718	66778	67027	70009
66051	66112	66173	66233	66515	66584	66719	66779	67028	70010
66052	66113	66174	66234	66516	66585	66720	66780	67029	70011
66053	66114	66175	66235	66517	66586	66721	66781	67030	70012
66054	66115	66176	66236	66518	66587	66722	66782		70013
66055	66116	66177	66237	66519	66588	66723	66783	68001	70014
66056	66117	66178	66239	66520	66589	66724	66784	68002	70015
66057	66118	66179	66240	66522	66590	66725	66785	68003	70016
66059	66119	66180	66241	66523	66591	66726	66786	68004	70017
66060	66120	66181	66242	66524	66592	66727	66787	68005	70018
66061	66121	66182	66243	66525	66593	66728	66788	68006	70019
66062	66122	66183	66244	66526	66594	66729	66789	68007	70020
66063	66123	66185	66245	66527	66595	66730	66790	68008	70801
66064	66124	66186	66246	66528	66596	66731	66791	68009	70802
66065	66125	66187	66247	66529	66597	66732	66792	68010	70803
66066	66126	66188	66248	66530	66598	66733	66793	68011	70804
66067	66127	66189	66249	66531	66599	66735	66794	68012	70805
66068	66128	66190	66301	66532	66601	66736	66795	68013	70806
66069	66129	66191	66302	66533	66602	66737	66796	68014	70807
66070	66130	66192	66303	66534	66603	66738	66797	68015	70808
66071	66131	66193	66304	66535	66604	66739	66846	68016	70809
66072	66133	66194	66305	66536	66605	66740	66847	68017	70810
66073	66134	66195	66411	66537	66606	66741	66848	68018	70811
66074	66135	66196	66412	66538	66607	66742	66849	68019	70812
66075	66136	66197	66413	66539	66608	66743	66850	68020	70813
66076	66137	66198	66414	66540	66609	66744	66951	68021	70814
66077	66138	66199	66415	66541	66610	66745	66952	68022	70815

70816	86612	90012	91119	92046	143608	150124	150233	153306	153380
70817	86613	90013	91120		143609	150125	150234	153307	153381
	86614	90014	91121	97301	143610	150126	150235	153308	153382
73001	86622	90015	91122	97302	143611	150127	150236	153309	153383
73101	86627	90016	91124	97303	143612	150128	150237	153310	153384
73107	86628	90017	91125	97304	143614	150129	150238	153311	153385
73109	86632	90018	91126		143616	150130	150239	153312	
73110	86637	90019	91127	139001	143617	150131	150240	153313	155341
73119	86638	90020	91128	139002	143618	150132	150241	153314	155342
73128	86639	90021	91129		143619	150133	150242	153315	155343
73133	86701	90022	91130	142002	143620	150134	150243	153316	155344
73134	86702	90023	91131	142003	143621	150135	150244	153317	155345
73136		90024	91132	142004	143622	150136	150245	153318	155346
73138		90025		142006	143623	150137	150246	153319	155347
73139	87002	90026	92001	142007	143624	150138	150247	153320	
73141	87003	90027	92002	142010	143625	150139	150248	153321	156401
73201	87004	90028	92003	142012		150140	150249	153322	156403
73202	87006	90029	92004	142014	144001	150141	150250	153323	156404
73212	87007	90030	92005	142018	144002	150142	150251	153324	156405
73213	87008	90031	92006	142023	144005	150143	150252	153325	156406
73235	87009	90032	92007	142032	144008	150144	150253	153326	156408
73951	87010	90033	92008	142035	144009	150145	150254	153327	156410
73952	87012	90034	92009	142041	144012	150146	150255	153328	156411
73961	87013	90035	92010	142043	144014	150147	150256	153329	156413
73962	87014	90036	92011	142045	144015	150148	150257	153330	156414
73963	87017	90037	92012	142047	144016	150149	150258	153331	156415
73964	87019	90038	92013	142056	144018	150150	150259	153332	156420
73965	87020	90039	92014	142058	144019		150260	153333	156421
73966	87022	90040	92015	142061	144020	150201	150261	153334	156423
73967	87023	90041	92016	142065	144021	150202	150262	153335	156424
73968	87025	90042	92017	142068	144022	150203	150263	153351	156425
73969	87026	90043	92018	142069	144023	150204	150264	153352	156426
73970	87028	90044	92019	142070		150205	150265	153353	156427
73971	87029	90045	92020	142071	150001	150206	150266	153354	156428
	87033	90046	92021	142072	150002	150207	150267	153355	156429
86101	87034	90047	92022	142073		150208	150268	153356	156430
86213		90048	92023	142074	150101	150209	150269	153357	156431
86215	88001	90049	92024	142075	150102	150210	150270	153358	156432
86217	88002	90050	92025	142076	150103	150211	150271	153359	156433
86218	88003		92026	142079	150104	150213	150272	153360	156434
86228	88004		92027	142077	150105	150214	150273	153361	156435
86231	88005	91101	92028	142078	150106	150215	150274	153362	156436
86232	88006	91102	92029	142080	150107	150216	150275	153363	156437
86233	88007	91103	92030	142081	150108	150217	150276	153364	156438
86234	88008	91104	92031	142082	150109	150218	150277	153365	156439
86235	88009	91105	92032	142083	150110	150219	150278	153366	156440
86242	88010	91106	92033	142085	150111	150220	150279	153367	156441
86248		91107	92034	142086	150112	150221	150280	153368	156442
86250	90001	91108	92035	142087	150113	150222	150281	153369	156443
86251	90002	91109	92036	142090	150114	150223	150282	153370	156444
86259	90003	91110	92037	142095	150115	150224	150283	153371	156445
86401	90004	91111	92038		150116	150225	150284	153372	156446
86424	90005	91112	92039	143601	150117	150226	150285	153373	156447
86604	90006	91113	92040	143602	150118	150227		153374	156448
86605	90007	91114	92041	143603	150119	150228	153301	153375	156449
86607	90008	91115	92042	143604	150120	150229	153302	153376	156450
86608	90009	91116	92043	143605	150121	150230	153303	153377	156451
86609	90010	91117	92044	143606	150122	150231	153304	153378	156452
86610	90011	91118	92045	143607	150123	150232	153305	153379	156453

156454
156455
156456
156457
156458
156459
156460
156461
156462
156463
156464
156465
156466
156467
156468
156469
156470
156471
156472
156473
156474
156475
156476
156477
156478
156479
156480
156481
156482
156483
156484
156485
156486
156487
156488
156489
156490
156491
156492
156493
156494
156495
156496
156497
156498
156499
156501
156502
156503
156504
156505
156506
156507
156508
156509
156510
156511
156512
156513
156514
156902
156907
156909
156912
156916
156917
156918
156919
156922

158701
158702
158703
158704
158705
158706
158707
158708
158709
158710
158711
158712
158713
158714
158715
158716
158717
158718
158719
158720
158721
158722
158723
158724
158725
158726
158727
158728
158729
158730
158731
158732
158733
158734
158735
158736
158737
158738
158739
158730
158741
158745
158747
158749
158750
158752
158753
158754
158755
158756
158757
158758
158759
158760
158762
158763
158765
158766
158767
158769
158770
158773
158774
158777
158780
158782
158783
158784
158785
158786
158787
158788
158789
158790
158791
158792
158793
158794
158795
158796
158797
158798
158799
158806
158810
158812
158813
158815
158816
158817
158818
158819
158820
158821
158822
158823
158824
158825
158826
158827
158828
158829
158830
158831
158832
158833
158834
158835
158836
158837
158838
158839
158840
158841
158842
158843
158844
158845
158846
158847
158848
158849
158850
158851
158852
158853
158854
158855
158856
158857
158858
158859
158860
158861
158862
158863
158864
158865
158866
158867
158868
158869
158870
158871
158872
158880
158881
158882
158883
158884
158885
158886
158887
158888
158889
158890
158901
158902
158903
158904
158905
158906
158907
158908
158909
158910
158950
158951
158956
158957
158958
158959

159001
159002
159003
159004
159005
159006
159007
159008
159009
159010
159011
159012
159013
159014
159015
159016
159017
159018
159019
159020
159021
159022
159101
159102
159103
159104
159105
159106
159107
159108

165001
165002
165003
165004
165005
165006
165007
165008
165009
165010
165011
165012
165013
165014
165015
165016
165017
165018
165019
165020
165021
165022
165023
165024
165025
165026
165027
165028
165029
165030
165031
165032
165033
165034
165035
165036
165037
165038
165039
165101
165102
165103
165104
165105
165106
165107
165108
165109
165110
165111
165112
165113
165114
165116
165117
165118
165119
165120
165121
165122
165123
165124
165125
165126
165127
165128
165129
165130
165131
165132
165133
165134
165135
165136
165137

166201
166202
166203
166204
166205
166206
166207
166208
166209
166210
166211
166212
166213
166214
166215
166216
166217
166218
166219
166220
166221

168001
168002
168003
168004
168005
168106
168107
168108
168109
168110
168111
168112
168113
168214
168215
168216
168217
168218
168219
168321
168322
168323
168324
168325
168326
168327
168328
168329

170101
170102
170103
170104
170105
170106
170107
170108
170109
170110
170111
170112
170113
170114
170115
170116
170117
170201
170202
170203
170204
170205
170206
170207
170208
170270
170271
170272
170273
170393
170394
170395
170396
170397
170398
170401
170402
170403
170404
170405
170406
170407
170408
170409
170410
170411
170412
170413
170414
170415
170416
170417
170418
170419
170420
170425
170426
170427
170428
170429
170430
170431
170432
170433
170434
170450
170451
170452
170453
170454
170455
170456
170457
170458
170459
170460
170461
170470
170471
170472
170473
170474
170475
170476
170477
170478
170501
170502
170503
170504
170505
170506
170507
170508
170509
170510
170511
170512
170513
170514
170515
170516
170517
170518
170519
170520
170521
170522
170523
170630
170631
170632
170633
170634
170635
170636
170637
170638
170639

171201
171202
171401
171402
171721
171722
171723
171724
171725
171726
171727
171728
171729
171730
171801
171802
171803
171804
171805
171806

172001
172002
172003
172004
172005
172006
172007
172008
172101
172102
172103
172104
172211
172212
172213
172214
172215
172216
172217
172218
172219
172220
172221
172222
172331
172332
172333
172334
172335
172336
172337
172338
172339
172340
172341
172342
172343
172344
172345

175001
175002
175003
175004
175005
175006
175007
175008

175009
175010
175011
175101
175102
175103
175104
175105
175106
175107
175108
175109
175110
175111
175112
175113
175114
175115
175116

180101
180102
180103
180104
180105
180106
180107
180108
180109
180110
180111
180112
180113
180114

185101
185102
185103
185104
185105
185106
185107
185108
185109
185110
185111
185112
185113
185114
185115
185116
185117
185118
185119
185120
185121
185122
185123
185124
185125
185126
185127
185128
185129
185130
185131
185132
185133
185134
185135
185136
185137
185138
185139
185140
185141
185142
185143
185144
185145
185146
185147
185148
185149
185150
185151

195001
195002
195003
195004
195005
195006
195007
195008
195009
195010
195011
195012
195013
195014
195015
195016
195017
195018
195019
195020
195021
195022
195023
195024
195025
195101
195102
195103
195104
195105
195106
195107
195108
195109
195110
195111
195112
195113
195114
195115
195116
195117
195118
195119
195120
195121
195122
195123
195124
195125
195126
195127
195128
195129
195130
195131
195132
195133

196001
196002
196003
196004
196005
196006
196007
196008
196009
196010
196011
196012
196101
196102
196103
196104
196105
196106
196107
196108
196109
196110
196111
196112
196113
196114

197001
197002
197003
197004
197005
197006
197007
197008
197009
197010
197011
197012
197013
197014
197015
197016
197017
197018
197019
197020
197021
197022
197023
197024
197025
197026
197027
197028
197029
197030
197031
197032
197033
197034
197035
197036
197037
197038
197039
197040
197041
197042
197043
197044
197045
197046
197047
197048
197049
197050
197051

197101
197102
197103
197104
197105
197106
197107
197108
197109
197110
197111
197112
197113
197114
197115
197116
197117
197118
197119
197120
197121
197122
197123
197124
197125
197126

201001

220001
220002
220003
220004
220005
220006
220007
220008
220009
220010
220011
220012
220013
220014
220015
220016
220017
220018
220019
220020
220021
220022
220023
220024
220025
220026
220027
220028
220029
220030
220031
220032
220033
220034

221101
221102
221103
221104
221105
221106
221107
221108
221109
221110
221111
221112
221113
221114
221115
221116
221117
221118
221119
221120
221121
221122
221123
221124
221125
221126
221127
221128
221129
221130
221131
221132
221133
221134
221135
221136
221137
221138
221139
221140
221141
221142
221143
221144

222001
222002
222003
222004
222005
222006
222007
222008
222009
222010
222011
222012
222013
222014
222015
222016
222017
222018
222019
222020
222021
222022
222023
222101
222102
222103
222104

230001
230002
230003
230004
230005
230006
230007
230008
230009
230010

231001
231002
231003
231004
231005
231006
231007
231008
231009
231010
231011

313121
313201
313202
313203
313204
313205
313206
313207
313208
313209
313210
313211
313212
313213
313214
313215
313216
313217
313219
313220

315801
315805
315809
315811
315815
315818
315819
315820
315824
315826
315829
315830
315833
315834
315837
315838
315839
315843
315844
315847
315848
315849
315851
315852
315853
315854
315856
315857

317337
317338
317339
317340
317341
317342
317343
317344
317345
317346
317347
317348
317501
317502
317503
317504
317505
317506
317507
317508
317509
317510
317511
317512
317513
317514
317515
317649
317650
317651
317652
317653
317654
317655
317656
317657
317658
317659
317660
317661
317662
317663
317668
317664
317665
317666
317667
317669
317670
317671
317672
317708
317709
317710
317714
317719
317722
317723
317729
317732
317881
317882
317883
317884
317885
317886
317887
317888
317889
317890
317891
317892

318250
318251
318252
318253
318254
318255
318256
318257
318258
318259
318260
318261
318262
318263
318264
318265
318266
318267
318268
318269
318270

319005
319009
319010
319011
319012
319013
319214
319215
319216
319217
319218
319219
319220
319361
319362
319363
319364
319365
319366
319367
319368
319369
319370
319371
319372
319373
319374
319375
319376
319377
319378
319379
319380
319381
319382
319383
319384
319385
319386
319429
319433
319441
319451
319453
319454
319455
319457
319460

320301
320302
320303
320304
320305
320306
320307
320308
320309
320310
320311

320312
320313
320314
320315
320316
320317
320318
320319
320320
320321
320322

320401
320403
320404
320411
320412
320413
320414
320415
320416
320417
320418
320420

321301
321302
321303
321304
321305
321306
321307
321308
321309
321310
321311
321312
321313
321314
321315
321316
321317
321318
321319
321320
321321
321322
321323
321324
321325
321326
321327
321328
321329
321330
321331
321332
321333
321334
321335
321336
321337
321338
321339
321340
321341
321342
321343
321344
321345
321346
321347
321348
321349
321350
321351
321352
321353
321354
321355
321356
321357
321358
321359
321360
321361
321362
321363
321364
321365
321366
321402
321405
321406
321407
321408
321409
321410
321419
321421
321422
321423
321424
321425
321426
321427
321428
321429
321430
321431
321432
321433
321434
321435
321436
321437
321438
321439
321440
321441
321442
321443
321444
321445
321446
321447
321448
321901
321902
321903

322481
322482
322483
322484
322485

323201
323202
323203
323204
323205
323206
323207
323208
323209
323210
323211
323212
323213
323214
323215
323216
323217
323218
323219
323220
323221
323222
323223
323224
323225
323226
323227
323228
323229
323230
323231
323232
323233
323234
323235
323236
323237
323238
323239
323240
323241
323242
323243

325001
325002
325003
325004
325005
325006
325007
325008
325009
325011
325012
325013
325014
325015
325016

331001
331002
331003
331004
331005
331006
331007
331008
331009
331010
331011
331012
331013
331014
331015
331016
331017
331018
331019
331020
331021
331022
331023
331024
331025
331026
331027
331028
331029
331030
331031
331101
331102
331103
331104
331105
331106
331107
331108
331109
331110
331111
331112

332001
332002
332003
332004
332005
332006
332007
332008
332009
332010
332011
332012
332013
332014

333001
333002
333003
333004
333005
333006
333007
333008
333009
333010
333011
333012
333013
333014
333015
333016

334001
334002
334003
334004
334005
334006
334007
334008
334009
334010
334011
334012
334013
334014
334015
334016
334017
334018
334019
334020
334021
334022
334023
334024
334025
334026
334027
334028
334029
334030
334031
334032
334033
334034
334035
334036
334037
334038
334039
334040

345001
345002
345003
345004
345005
345006
345007
345008
345009
345010
345011
345012
345013
345014
345015
345016
345017
345018
345019
345020
345021
345022
345023
345024
345025
345026
345027
345028
345029
345030
345031
345032
345033
345034
345035
345036
345037
345038
345039
345040
345041
345042
345043
345044
345045
345046
345047
345048
345049
345050
345051
345052
345053
345054
345055
345056
345057
345058
345059
345060
345061
345062
345063
345064
345065
345066
345067
345068
345069
345070

350101
350102
350103
350104
350105
350106
350107
350108
350109
350110
350111
350112
350113
350114
350115
350116
350117
350118
350119
350120
350121
350122
350123
350124
350125
350126
350127
350128
350129
350130
350231
350232
350233
350234
350235
350236
350237
350238
350239
350240
350241
350242
350243
350244
350245
350246
350247
350248
350249
350250
350251
350252
350253
350254
350255
350256
350257
350258
350259
350260
350261
350262
350263
350264
350265
350266
350267
350368
350369
350370
350371
350372
350373
350374
350375
350376
350377
350401
350402
350403
350404
350405
350406
350407
350408
350409
350410

357001
357002
357003
357004
357005
357006
357007
357008
357009
357010
357011
357012
357013
357014
357015
357016
357017
357018
357019
357020
357021
357022
357023
357024
357025
357026
357027
357028
357029
357030
357031
357032
357033
357034
357035
357036
357037
357038
357039
357040
357041
357042
357043
357044
357045
357046
357201
357202
357203
357204
357205
357206
357207
357208
357209
357210
357211
357312
357313
357314
357315
357316
357317
357318
357319
357320
357321
357322
357323
357324
357325
357326
357327
357328

360101
360102
360103
360104
360105
360106
360107
360108
360109
360110
360111
360112
360113
360114
360115
360116
360117
360118
360119
360120
360121
360201
360202
360203
360204
360205

365502
365504
365506
365508
365510
365511
365512
365514
365516
365518
365520
365522
365524
365528
365530

365532	375624	375908	377102	377161	377411	377471	377706	378256	380104
365534	375625	375909	377103	377162	377412	377472	377707	378257	380105
365536	375626	375910	377104	377163	377413	377473	377708		380106
365538	375627	375911	377105	377164	377414	377474		379001	380107
365539	375628	375912	377106	377201	377415	377475	378135	379002	380108
365540	375629	375913	377107	377202	377416	377501	378136	379003	380109
365501	375630	375914	377108	377203	377417	377502	378137	379004	380110
365503	375701	375915	377109	377204	377418	377503	378138	379005	380111
365505	375702	375916	377110	377205	377419	377504	378139	379006	380112
365507	375703	375917	377111	377206	377420	377505	378140	379007	380113
365509	375704	375918	377112	377207	377421	377506	378141	379008	380114
365513	375705	375919	377113	377208	377422	377507	378142	379009	380115
365515	375706	375920	377114	377209	377423	377508	378143	379010	380116
365517	375707	375921	377115	377210	377424	377509	378144	379011	
365519	375708	375922	377116	377211	377425	377510	378145	379012	385001
365521	375709	375923	377117	377212	377426	377511	378146	379013	385002
365523	375710	375924	377118	377213	377427	377512	378147	379014	385003
365525	375711	375925	377119	377214	377428	377513	378148	379015	385004
365527	375712	375926	377120	377215	377429	377514	378149	379016	385005
365529	375713	375927	377121		377430	377515	378150	379017	385006
365531	375714		377122	377301	377431	377516	378151	379018	385007
365533	375715	376001	377123	377302	377432	377517	378152	379019	385008
365535	375801	376002	377124	377303	377433	377518	378153	379020	385009
365537	375802	376003	377125	377304	377434	377519	378154	379021	385010
365541	375803	376004	377126	377305	377435	377520	378201	379022	385011
	375804	376005	377127	377306	377436	377521	378202	379023	385012
375301	375805	376006	377128	377307	377437	377522	378203	379024	385013
375302	375806	376007	377129	377308	377438	377523	378204	379025	385014
375303	375807	376008	377130	377309	377439	377601	378205	379026	385015
375304	375808	376009	377131	377310	377440	377602	378206	379027	385016
375305	375809	376010	377132	377311	377441	377603	378207	379028	385017
375306	375810	376011	377133	377312	377443	377604	378208	379029	385018
375307	375811	376012	377134	377313	377444	377605	378209	379030	385019
375308	375812	376013	377135	377314	377445	377606	378210		385020
375309	375813	376014	377136	377315	377446	377607	378211	380001	385021
375310	375814	376015	377137	377316	377447	377608	378212	380002	385022
375601	375815	376016	377138	377317	377448	377609	378213	380003	385023
375602	375816	376017	377139	377318	377449	377610	378214	380004	385024
375603	375817	376018	377140	377319	377450	377611	378215	380005	385025
375604	375818	376019	377141	377320	377451	377612	378216	380006	385026
375605	375819	376020	377142	377321	377452	377613	378217	380007	385027
375606	375820	376021	377143	377322	377453	377614	378218	380008	385028
375607	375821	376022	377144	377323	377454	377615	378219	380009	385029
375608	375822	376023	377145	377324	377455	377616	378220	380010	385030
375609	375823	376024	377146	377325	377456	377617	378221	380011	385031
375610	375824	376025	377147	377326	377457	377618	378222	380012	385032
375611	375825	376026	377148	377327	377458	377619	378223	380013	385033
375612	375826	376027	377149	377328	377459	377620	378224	380014	385034
375613	375827	376028	377150	377342	377460	377621	378225	380015	385035
375614	375828	376029	377151	377401	377461	377622	378226	380016	385036
375615	375829	376030	377152	377402	377462	377623	378227	380017	385037
375616	375830	376031	377153	377403	377463	377624	378228	380018	385038
375617	375901	376032	377154	377404	377464	377625	378229	380019	385039
375618	375902	376033	377155	377405	377465	377626	378230	380020	385040
375619	375903	376034	377156	377406	377466	377701	378231	380021	385041
375620	375904	376035	377157	377407	377467	377702	378232	380022	385042
375621	375905	376036	377158	377408	377468	377703	378233	380101	385043
375622	375906		377159	377409	377469	377704	378234	380102	385044
375623	375907	377101	377160	377410	377470	377705	378255	380103	385045

385046
385101
385101
385102
385103
385104
385105
385106
385107
385108
385109
385110
385111
385112
385113
385114
385115
385116
385117
385118
385119
385120
385121
385122
385123
385124

387101
387102
387103
387104
387105
387106
387107
387108
387109
387110
387111
387112
387113
387114
387115
387116
387117
387118
387119
387120
387121
387122
387123
387124
387125
387126
387127
387128
387129
387130
387131
387132
387133
387134
387135
387136
387137
387138
387139
387140
387141
387142
387143
387144
387145
387146
387147
387148
387149
387150
387151
387152
387153
387154
387155
387156
387157
387158
387159
387160
387161
387162
387163
387164
387165
387166
387167
387168
387169
387170
387171
387172
387173
387174
387201
387202
387203
387204
387205
387206
387207
387208
387209
387210
387211
387212
387213
387214
387215
387216
387217
387218
387219
387220
387221
387222
387223
387224
387225
387226
387227
387301
387302
387303
387304
387305
387306

390001
390002
390005
390006
390008
390009
390010
390011
390013
390016
390020
390039
390040
390042
390043
390044
390045
390046
390047
390049
390050
390103
390104
390107
390112
390114
390115
390117
390118
390119
390121
390122
390123
390124
390125
390126
390127
390128
390129
390130
390131
390132
390134
390135
390136
390137
390138
390141
390148
390151
390152
390153
390154
390155
390156
390157

395001
395002
395003
395004
395005
395006
395007
395008
395009
395010
395011
395012
395013
395014
395015
395016
395017
395018
395019
395020
395021
395022
395023
395024
395025
395026
395027
395028
395029

397001
397002
397003
397004
397005
397006
397007
397008
397009
397010
397011
397012

398001
398002
398003
398004
398005
398006
398007
398008
398009
398010
398011
398012
398013
398014
398015
398016
398017
398018
398019
398020
398021
398022
398023
398024
398025
398026
398027
398028
398029
398030
398031
398032
398033
398034
398035
398036

442402
442403
442404
442406
442408
442409
442410
442411
442413
442414
442415
442416
442417
442418
442419
442420
442422
442423

444001
444002
444003
444004
444005
444006
444007
444008
444009
444010
444011
444012
444013
444014
444015
444016
444017
444018
444019
444020
444021
444022
444023
444024
444025
444026
444027
444028
444029
444030
444031
444032
444033
444034
444035
444036
444037
444038
444039
444040
444041
444042
444043
444044
444045

450001
450002
450003
450004
450005
450006
450007
450008
450009
450010
450011
450012
450013
450014
450015
450016
450017
450018
450019
450020
450021
450022
450023
450024
450025
450026
450027
450028
450029
450030
450031
450032
450033
450034
450035
450036
450037
450038
450039
450040
450041
450042
450043
450044
450045
450046
450047
450048
450049
450050
450051
450052
450053
450054
450055
450056
450057
450058
450059
450060
450061
450062
450063
450064
450065
450066
450067
450068
450069
450070
450071
450072
450073
450074
450075
450076
450077
450078
450079
450080
450081
450082
450083
450084
450085
450086
450087
450088
450089
450090
450091
450092
450093
450094
450095
450096
450097
450098
450099
450100
450101
450102
450103
450104
450105
450106
450107
450108
450109
450110
450111
450112
450113
450114
450115
450116
450117
450118
450119
450120
450121
450122
450123
450124
450125
450126
450127

5701
5702
5703
5704
5705
5706
5707
5708
5709
5710
5711
5712
5713
5714
5715
5716
5717
5718
5719
5720
5721
5722
5723
5724
5725
5726
5727
5728
5729
5730
5731
5732
5733
5734
5735
5736
5737
5738
5739
5740
5741
5742
5750
455801
455802
455803
455804
455805
455806
455807
455808
455809
455810
455811
455812
455813
455814
455815
455816
455817
455818
455819
455820
455821
455822
455823
455824
455825
455826
455827
455828
455829
455830
455831
455832
455833
455834
455835
455836
455837
455838
455839
455840
455841
455842
455843
455844
455845
455846
5847
5848
5849
5850
5851
5852
5853
5854
5855
5856
5857
5858
5859
5860
5861
5862
5863
5864
5865
5866
5867
5868
5869
5870
5871
5872
5873
5874
5901
5902
5903
5904
5905
5906
5907
5908

5909
5910
5911
5912
5913
5914
5915
5916
5917
5918
5919
5920

456001
456002
456003
456004
456005
456006
456007
456008
456009
456010
456011
456012
456013
456014
456015
456016
456017
456018
456019
456020
456021
456022
456023
456024

458501
458502
458503
458504
458505
458506
458507
458508
458509
458510
458511
458512
458513
458514
458515
458516
458517
458518
458519
458520
458521
458522
458523
458524
458525
458526
458527
458528
458529
458530
458531
458532
458533
458534
458535
458536

465001
465002
465003
465004
465005
465006
465007
465008
465009
465010
465011
465012
465013
465014
465015
465016
465017
465018
465019
465020
465021
465022
465023
465024
465025
465026
465027
465028
465029
465030
465031
465032
465033
465034
465035
465036
465037
465038
465039
465040
465041
465042
465043
465044
465045
465046
465047
465048
465049
465050
465151
465152
465153
465154
465155
465156
465157
465158
465159
465160
465161
465162
465163
465164
465165
465166
465167
465168
465169
465170
465171
465172
465173
465174
465175
465176
465177
465178
465179
465180
465181
465182
465183
465184
465185
465186
465187
465188
465189
465190
465191
465192
465193
465194
465195
465196
465197
465235
465236
465237
465238
465239
465240
465241
465242
465243
465244
465245
465246
465247
465248
465249
465250
465901
465902
465903
465904
465905
465906
465907
465908
465909
465910
465911
465912
465913
465914
465915
465916
465917
465918
465919
465920
465921
465922
465923
465924
465925
465926
465927
465928
465929
465930
465931
465932
465933
465934

466001
466002
466003
466004
466005
466006
466007
466008
466009
466010
466011
466012
466013
466014
466015
466016
466017
466018
466019
466020
466021
466022
466023
466024
466025
466026
466027
466028
466029
466030
466031
466032
466033
466034
466035
466036
466037
466038
466039
466040
466041
466042
466043

483002
483004
483006
483007
483008
483009

484001
484002
484003
484004
484005

507001
507002
507003
507004
507005
507006
507007
507008
507009
507010
507011
507012
507013
507014
507015
507016
507017
507018
507019
507020
507021
507023
507024
507025
507026
507027
507028
507029
507030
507031
507032
507033

508103
508104
508108
508111
508112
508114
508115
508117
508120
508122
508123
508124
508125
508126
508127
508128
508130
508131
508136
508137
508138
508139
508140
508141
508143

700001
700002
700003
700004
700005
700006
700007
700008
700009
700010
700011
700012
700013
700014
700015
700016
700017
700018
700019
700020
700021
700022
700023
700024
700025
700026
700027
700028
700029
700030
700031
700032
700033
700034
700035
700036
700037
700038
700039
700040
700041
700042
700043
700044
700045
700046
700047
700048
700049
700050
700051
700052
700053
700054
700055
700056
700057
700058
700059
700060
700101
700102
700103
700104
700105
700106
700107
700108
700109
700110
700111
700112
700113
700114
700115
700116
700117
700118
700119
700120
700121
700122
700123
700124
700125
700126
700127
700128
700129
700130
700131
700132
700133
700134
700135
700136
700137
700138
700139
700140
700141
700142
700143
700144
700145
700146
700147
700148
700149
700150
700151
700152
700153
700154
700155

701001
701002
701003
701004
701005
701006
701007
701008
701009
701010
701011
701012
701013
701014
701015
701016
701017
701018
701019
701020
701021
701022
701023
701024
701025
701026
701027
701028
701029
701030
701031
701032
701033
701034
701035
701036
701037
701038
701039
701040
701041
701042
701043
701044
701045
701046
701047
701048
701049
701050
701051
701052
701053
701054
701055
701056
701057
701058
701059
701060
701501
701502
701503
701504
701505
701506
701507
701508
701509
701510
701511
701512
701513
701514
701515
701516
701517
701518
701519
701520
701521
701522
701523
701524
701525
701526
701527
701528
701529
701530

707001
707002
707003
707004
707005
707006
707007
707008
707009
707010
707011
707012
707013
707014
707015
707016
707017
707018
707019
707020
707021
707022
707023
707024
707025
707026
707027
707028
707029
707030

710101
710102
710103
710104
710105
710106
710107
710108
710109
710110
710111
710112
710113

710114
710115
710116
710117
710118
710119
710120
710121
710122
710123
710124
710125
710126
710127
710128
710129
710130
710256
710257
710258
710259
710260
710261
710262
710263
710264
710265
710266
710267
710268
710269
710270
710271
710272
710273
710274
710275
710276
710277
710278
710279

717001
717002
717003
717004
717005
717006
717007
717008
717009
717010
717011
717012
717013
717014
717015
717016
717017
717018
717019
717020
717021
717022
717023
717024
717025

720101
720102
720103
720104
720105
720106
720107
720108
720109
720110
720111
720112
720113
720114
720115
720116
720117
720118
720119
720120
720121
720122
720123
720124
720125
720126
720127
720128
720129
720130
720131
720132
720133
720134
720135
720136
720137
720138
720139
720140
720141
720142
720143
720144

720501
720502
720503
720504
720505
720506
720507
720508
720509
720510
720511
720512
720513
720514
720515
720516
720517
720518
720519
720520
720521
720522
720523
720524
720525
720526
720527
720528
720529
720530
720531
720532
720533
720534
720535
720536
720537
720538
720539
720540
720541
720542
720543
720544
720545
720546
720547
720548
720549
720550
720551
720552
720553
720554
720555
720556
720557
720558
720559
720560
720561
720562
720563
720564
720565
720566
720567
720568
720569
720570
720571
720572
720573
720574
720575
720576
720577
720578
720579
720580
720581
720582
720583
720584
720585
720586
720587
720588
720589

720601
720602
720603
720604
720605
720606
720607
720608
720609
720610

730001
730002
730003
730004
730005
730006
730007
730008
730009
730010
730011
730012
730013
730014
730015
730016
730017
730018
730019
730020
730021
730022
730023
730024
730025
730026
730027
730028
730029
730030
730031
730032
730033
730034
730035
730036
730101
730102
730103
730104
730105
730106
730107
730108
730109
730110
730111
730112
730113
730114
730115
730116
730117
730118
730119
730120
730121
730122
730123
730124
730125
730126
730127
730128
730129
730201
730202
730203
730204
730205
730206
730207
730208
730209
730210
730211
730212
730213
730214
730215
730216

745001
745002
745003
745004
745005
745006
745007
745008
745009
745010

745101
745102
745103
745104
745105
745106
745107
745108
745109
745110

755325
755326
755327
755328
755329
755330
755331
755332
755333
755334
755335
755336
755337
755338

755401
755402
755403
755404
755405
755406
755407
755408
755409
755410
755411
755412
755413
755414
755415
755416
755417
755418
755419
755420
755421
755422
755423
755424

756001
756002
756003
756004
756005
756006
756007

756101
756102
756103
756104
756105
756106
756107
756108
756109
756110
756111
756112
756113
756114
756115
756116
756117

769002
769003
769006
769007
769008
769421
769424
769426
769431
769434
769442
769445
769448
769450
769452
769456
769458
769922
769923
769925
769927
769928
769930
769932
769935
769936
769937
769938
769939
769940
769943
769944
769946
769947
769949
769959

777001
777002
777003
777004
777005
777006
777007
777008
777009
777010
777011
777012
777013
777014
777015
777016
777017
777018
777019
777020
777021
777022
777023
777024
777025
777026
777027
777028
777029
777030
777031
777032
777033
777034
777035
777036
777037
777038
777039
777040
777041
777042
777043
777044
777045
777046
777047
777048
777049
777050
777051
777052

799001

800001
800002
800003
800004
800005
800006
800007
800008
800009
800010
800011
800012
800013
800014
800015
800016
800017
800018
800019
800020
800021
800022
800023
800024
800025
800026
800027
800028
800029
800030
800031
800032
800033
800034
800035
800036
800101
800102
800103
800104
800105
800106
800107
800108
800109
800110
800111
800112
800113
800201
800202
800203
800204
800205
800206
800207
800208
800209
800210
800301
800302
800303
800304
800305
800306
800307
800308
800309
800310
800311
800312
800313
800314
800315
800316
800317
800318
800319
800320
800321

801101
801102
801103
801104
801105
801106
801107
801108
801109
801110
801111
801112
801201
801202
801203
801204
801205
801206
801207
801208
801209
801210
801211
801212
801213
801214
801215
801216
801217
801218
801219
801220
801221

801222
801223
801224
801225
801226
801227
801228
801229
801230

802001
802002
802003
802004
802005
802006
802007
802008
802009
802010
802011
802012
802013
802014
802015
802016
802017
802018
802019
802020
802021
802022
802101
802102
802103
802104
802105
802106
802107
802108
802109
802110
802111
802112
802113
802114
802201
802202
802203
802204
802205
802206
802207
802208
802209
802210
802211
802212
802213
802214
802215
802216
802217
802218
802219
802301
802302
802303
802304
802305

803001
803002
803003
803004
803005

805001
805002
805003
805004
805005
805006
805007
805008
805009
805010
805011
805012
805013

807001
807002
807003
807004
807005
807006
807007
807008
807009
807010

810001
810002
810003
810004
810005
810006
810007
810008
810009
810010
810011
810012
810013
810014
810015
810016
810017
810018
810019
810020
810021
810022
810023
810024
810025
810026
810027
810028
810029
810030
810031
810032
810033

950001

Channel tunnel
3007
3008
3015
3016
3205
3206
3209
3210
3211
3212
3213
3214
3215
3216
3217
3218
3219
3220
3221
3222
3223
3224
3229
3230
9999

4001
4002
4003
4004
4005
4006
4007
4008
4009
4010
4011
4012
4013
4014
4015
4016
4017
4018
4019
4020
4021
4022
4023
4024
4025
4026
4027
4028
4029
4030
4031
4032
4033
4034

9005
9007
9011
9013
9015
9018
9022
9024
9026
9029
9033
9036
9037

9701
9702
9703
9704
9705
9706
9707
9708
9709
9710
9711
9712
9713
9714
9715
9716
9717
9718
9719
9720
9721
9722
9723

9801
9802
9803
9804
9806
9808
9809
9810
9812
9814
9816
9819
9820
9821
9823
9825
9827
9828
9831
9832
9834
9835
9838
9840

0001
0002
0003
0004
0005

0006
0007
0008
0009
0010

0031
0032
0033
0034
0035
0036
0037
0038
0039
0040
0041
0042

Preserved locos
D2953
D2956

D2853
D2854
D2858
D2860
D2866
D2867
D2868

03018
03020
03022
D2023
D2024
03027
03037
D2041
D2046
D2051
03059
03062
03063
03066
03069
03072
03073
03078
03079
03081
03089
03090
03094
03099
03112
03113
D2117
03118
03119
03120
D2133
03134
D2138
D2139
03141
03144
03145
D2148
03152
03158
03162
03170
D2178
03179
03180
D2182
D2184
03189
D2192
03197
D2199
03371
03399
03901

D2203
D2205
D2207
D2229
D2245
D2246
D2271
D2272
D2279
D2280
D2284
D2289
D2298
D2302
D2310
D2324
D2325
D2334
D2337

D2511
D2554
D2578
D2587
D2595

D2767
D2774

06003

07001
07005
07010
07012
07013

D3000
D3002
D3014
08011
D3019
08015
08016
08022
08032
08046
08054
08060
08064
D3101
08102
08108
08114
08123
08133
08164
D3255
D3261
08195
08202
08220
08238
08266
08288
08331
08359
08377
08436
08443
08444
08471
08473
08476
08479
08490
08495
08528
08556
08590
08604
08605
08633
08635
08663
08694
08700
08767
08769
08772
08773
08795
08830
08850
08881
08888
08896
08907
08911
08915
08937
08993
08995
97808

09001
09004
09010
09012
09015
09017
09018
09019
09024
09025
09026
09107

D3452
D3489
D4067
D4092

12052
12077
12082
12083
12088
12093
12099
12131

15224

18000

97650
97651
97654

D9500
D9502
D9504
D9513
D9516
D9518
D9520
D9521
D9523
D9524
D9525
D9526
D9529
D9531
D9537
D9539
D9551
D9553
D9555

D8233

D8568

20001
20016
20020
20031
20048
20050
20057
20059
20063
20081
20088
20098
20137
20154
20169
20188
20214
20228

D5910

24032
24054
24061
24081

25035
25059
25067
25072
25083
25173
25185
25191
25235
25244
25262
25265
25279
25309
25321
25322

26001
26002
26004
26007
26010
26011
26014
26024
26025
26035
26038
26040
26043

27001
27005
27007
27024
27050
27056
27059
27066

D5705

	31435	33102	37075	37714	45112	47449	50033	60050	
31018	31438	33103	37097		45125	47484	50035	60081	83012
31101	31454	33108	37108	40012	45132	47579	50042	60086	
31105	31459	33109	37109	40106	45133	47596			84001
31106	31463	33110	37142	40118	45135	47635	D1010	71001	
31108	31465	33111	37214	40122	45149	47640	D1013		85101
31119	31466	33116	37215	40135		47643	D1023	73002	
31130	31514	33117	37216		46010	47761	D1041	73003	87001
31162	31601	33201	37227	41001	46035	47765	D1048	73114	87035
31190	97205	33202	37248		46045	47771	D1062	73118	
31203		33208	37250	D821		47785		73129	89001
31206	33002		37255	D832	47004	47799	55015	73130	
31207	33008	D7017	37261		47077	47841	55016	73140	
31210	33018	D7018	37263	43002	47105		55019	73210	
31233	33019	D7029	37264	43018	47117	50002			
31235	33021	D7076	37275		47192	50015	56006	76020	
31255	33035		37294	44004	47205	50017	56097		
31270	33046	37003	37308	44008	47292	50019		1502	
31271	33048	37009	37310		47306	50021	58012	1505	
31285	33052	37023	37350	45015	47367	50026	58016	1501	
31289	33053	37029	37503	45041	47376	50027	58022		
31327	33057	37032	37674	45060	47401	50029	58023	81002	
31418	33063	37037	37679	45105	47402	50030	58048		
31430	33065	37042	37703	45108	47417	50031		82008	

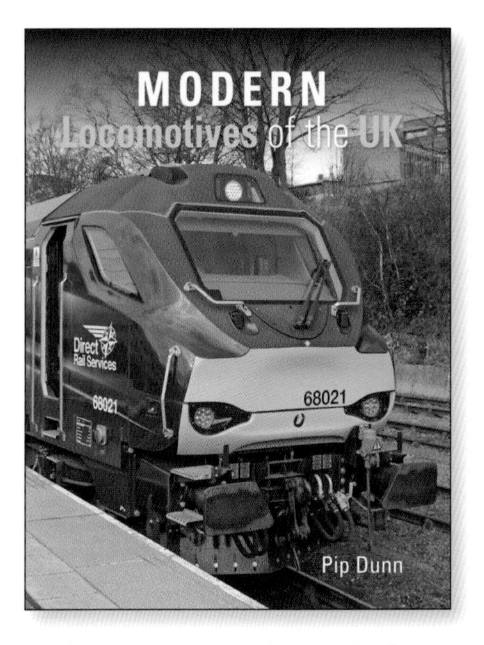

Modern Locomotives of the UK

Pip Dunn

Post privatisation locomotive hauled passenger trains have become ever more a rarity today with most additions to the passenger fleet having been in the form of diesel and electric multiple units. Even so, some new locomotive types have now been introduced for freight and specialist passenger use and *Modern Locomotives of the UK* provides their story from conception, to ordering, construction, testing, delivery and entry into traffic.

This book includes chapters on each of the new Classes: 66, 67, 68, 70 and 88 and examines areas such as teething troubles, regular operations, liveries and names. It also features the Class 59s; the first privately owned locos on the network in 1986 and the forerunner to the Class 66.

Author Pip Dunn also covers the major rebuilds of ex-BR classes such as the 57s, both types of 73/9 and the GBRf Class 56 project. Included is a section on rebuilding projects and new loco orders that were mooted but never happened such as re-engineering the Class 60s, Caterpillar engines for Class 37s and the 'Green Goat' Class 20.

Modern Locomotives of the UK is a comprehensive and authoritative survey of the locomotives of the post–privatisation era and a must have for all those interested in the current railway scene in Britain.

ISBN: 9780860936961
256 pages
£25.00

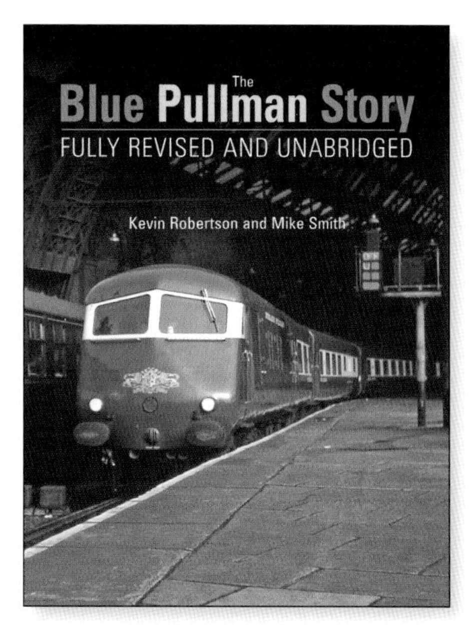

The Blue Pullman Story

Fully Revised and Unabridged

Kevin Robertson and Mike Smith

This is a completely revised and updated edition of the definitive history of the Blue Pullman, spanning from their inception in the 1955 Modernisation Plan, through to their final demise in the scrap yards of South Wales two decades later.

The development of the Blue Pullmans involved political and management decisions, the trials and tribulations of the actual design and the sometimes difficult involvement of outside design consultants, before their eventual entry into service on the London Midland and Western Regions.

It was never a completely settled service. Staffing and labour relations issues, mechanical problems and an eventual concentration of all the sets on the Western Region put too many special trains in one place. At the same time, the Pullman brand and the willingness of the travelling public to pay supplementary fares to travel on them was finding less favour.

A considerable amount of new material sine the original publication has been unearthed, both from official and private sources including plans and photographs, many seen here for the very first time. *The Blue Pullman Story* leaves no stone left unturned in the quest to tell their full story, one of ambition, hope and eventual despair, and sadly one without a happy ending.

ISBN: 9780860936886
400 pages
£40.00

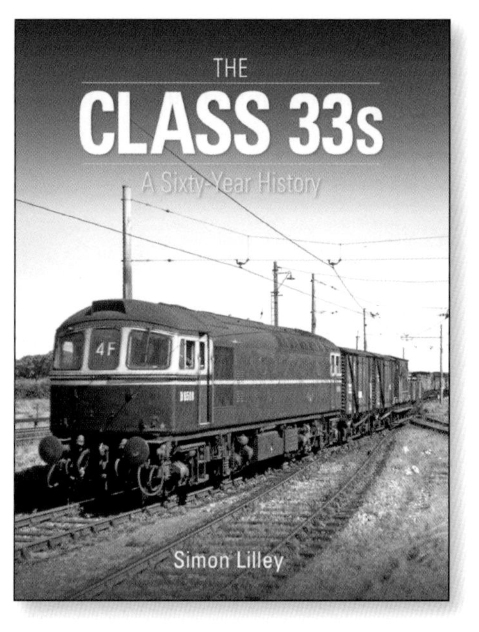

The Class 33s

Simon Lilley

1960 saw the first BRCW Ltd Type 3s, later TOPS Class 33, enter service on the Southern Region. The 98 locomotives were ordered as part of the Kent coast modernisation scheme. The final 12 locos had bodies 7 inches less wide than the rest of the class to allow them to work through the narrow tunnels between Tunbridge Wells and Hastings. For many years they were the mainstay of the Southern Region's locomotive fleet and were widely used across the south and west of England and beyond.

The Class 33s is the first detailed history of the class for 30 years, telling the story of these popular and successful locomotives from inception, through their design and operations to withdrawal from service. It draws on original source material from a number of archives and sheds new light on many aspects of these locomotives over their 60 years of service. This book is illustrated throughout with many photographs, almost all of which are published for the first time.

This is a welcome reappraisal of a long lived and respected class which will be of interest to modern traction enthusiasts and those modelling the post steam era on BR.

ISBN: 9781910809662
224 pages
£25.00

Rail Atlas of Great Britain and Ireland
15th Edition
Stuart Baker

Now in its 15th edition, *Rail Atlas of Great Britain and Ireland* is one of the most successful and sought after railway titles ever published. It provides the most accurate and reliable guide to the current railway network in the British Isles. Preserved lines, freight terminals, LRT schemes, passenger stations, lines under construction and proposed lines from Network Rail to High Speed 1 are all detailed and lines open to all traffic are differentiated from the single tracks used by freight only.

The mapping on each page overlaps with that on adjoining pages to make it easier to follow a long distance route and, where appropriate, additional detailed inset maps show the complex railway developments in metropolitan areas such as Nottingham and Manchester, and an enlarged detail section on Greater London.

This fully updated new edition retains the convenient format established in previous editions making *Rail Atlas of Great Britain and Ireland* the essential work of reference for both railway enthusiasts and those working in the rail industry.

ISBN: 9780860936817
152 pages
£20.00

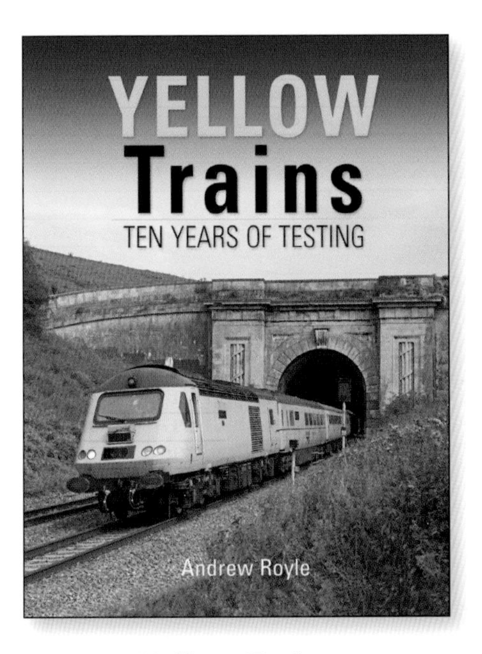

Yellow Trains

Andrew Royle

Operated by Network Rail, Yellow Trains are a regular sight to commuters and passengers on all parts of the railway system. These distinctive trains are designed to check, assess and monitor the track, bridges and tunnels on both passenger and freight only lines.

In the past these checks were done principally by staff on foot, so naturally today's high-speed railway demands something different and as such, the various test trains have evolved. Filled to the roof with the most sophisticated equipment found anywhere and speeding along the lines at up to 125mph, they will check the alignment of the track and distance to structures, as well as locating defects that require attention.

Author Andrew Royle has spent many years engaged as a computer technician on a variety of the different test trains and in the course of his travels has covered much of the network. *Yellow Trains* is his story, both technical and personal- from the purpose of the equipment and how it operates to the trials and tribulations of using it.

ISBN: 9781910809587
160 pages
£25.00